People of the Promise

People of the Promise

Sunday Sermons for Weekday Christians

Robert Campbell

Westminster United Church
Winnipeg, Canada

Westminster United Church
745 Westminster Avenue
Winnipeg, Manitoba
R3G 1A5 Canada

The poem on page 89 is from *The Scarlet Pimpernel* by Baroness Orczy, adapted by Beverley Cross (London: Samuel French, 1988), page 24.

The poem "To David" on page 152 is reprinted with the permission of the author, Robert P. Thompson.

Cover design: Doowah Design
Interior design: Sharon Caseburg

This book was printed and bound in Canada by Friesens for Westminster United Church.

National Library of Canada Cataloguing in Publication Data

Campbell, Robert, 1953-
People of the promise

Includes bibliographical references.
ISBN 0-9681384-0-3

1. United Church of Canada—Sermons. 2. Sermons, Canadian (English)* I. Westminster United Church (Winnipeg, Man.) II. Title.
BX9882.C37 2002 252'.0792 C2001-911614-4

For

Mom and Dad,
who made sure the church would be part of my life,

and Linda and James,
who now share with me the life of the church.

Contents

Preface

Some years ago, the congregation of Westminster United Church in Winnipeg, Manitoba, which I have been privileged to serve since 1989, raised a sum of money to enable the publication of a book of my sermons. They wanted worshippers at Westminster to have an opportunity to spend more time with some of the messages that they had heard on Sunday mornings and they wanted the messages themselves to have the opportunity to reach a wider audience. This launched me on a project of selecting a suitable collection and adapting it to make what was intended for the ear suitable for the eye.

The book that has resulted does not centre around a particular theme, but I hope that these sermons all demonstrate the conviction that is stated in the title of the last sermon, which has also become the title of the book: *People of the Promise*. I believe that Christians are called to live their daily lives in light of the promises of God. These promises are revealed in Jesus Christ and need to be reclaimed afresh by every generation as it engages with the biblical witness and testimony to Jesus.

All the sermons in this book have been preached to the people of Westminster Church, but not all began their life in this congregation. Some were given first to the folk of the United Churches of Holland and Cypress River, two villages in south-central Manitoba where I first ministered, while one was preached to the congregation of Knox Church in the town of Roblin, where I grew up and experienced the call to ministry. Moving to a new parish gave me an opportunity to take messages that had been well received in the country and adapt and rework them for an urban group of listeners. The fact that many of these messages have been helpful to both rural congregations and to a city-wide, downtown congregation makes me hope that they will be attractive to a diverse readership.

I have generally selected sermons that are not tied too specifically to a certain time or occasion in the life of a congregation. But even those that are occasional in nature are ones that I trust readers will easily be able to adapt to their own congregational, community, or personal situation.

I want to express my appreciation to Robert Thompson, a graduate of the University of Toronto, for the permission he has given to use his poem "To David" which appears in the sermon "Why Should We Care?" I became aware of the poem when it appeared in the bulletin of a Remembrance Day service I attended at the university's Soldiers' Tower in 1977 while I was studying for my divinity degree. Mr. Thompson tells me that the David in question died in his nation's service at the age of 20 or 21. He came from a well-to-do Toronto family of which he was the only son.

Many thank yous are due to those who have helped make the publication of this book possible. The people of Westminster Church gave generous moral and financial support to the project and, as the years elapsed, gently encouraged and prodded their minister to get it done. Alan Sweatman first proposed the idea of a sermon book, marshalled the support of the board and congregation for the initiative, and made the necessary contacts to get the project moving. My colleagues on staff at Westminster, particularly Rose Ferries, picked up the slack when I needed to be closeted away and working on the book to the neglect of other duties. Invaluable advice in the selection of sermons to be included was given by Dawne McCance, Professor of Religion at the University of Manitoba, Marilyn Morton, the book's editor, and the Revs. John and Michelle Hogman, colleagues and friends in ministry. Marilyn proved a wonderful editor to work with, always competent and helpful, ever patient. Sharon Caseburg made herself available at short notice to attend to the design of the book's interior, as did Doowah Design for its cover. Finally, but most importantly, Linda and James were very good about letting their husband and father consume a great deal of family time in the effort to bring the book to publication.

Robert Campbell

Baptism

The Fairness of Grace

Matthew 20:1-16

"... 'These last worked only one hour, and you have made them equal to us who have borne the burden of the day and the scorching heat.'"

—Matthew 20:12

One of the things we often do in our congregation's worship is gather at the font for baptism. This sacrament of baptism, the rite by which we are received into membership in Christ's church, is surrounded by and suffused with the language of grace. It is often said that, in baptism, the action is from God's side and thus it is a demonstration of God's outgoing love. Those being baptized are passive, symbolizing that this is something done for them, not by them; that they are not being baptized because they have earned it, but because God has chosen it. No merit needs to be demonstrated by the one being baptized; no worth needs to be proved. We are not received into the church because we have somehow qualified for membership, but because God elects to receive us as we are, whoever we may be.

It therefore seems appropriate to baptize not just adults but infants, for this demonstrates physically what we say about grace.

A young child is a receiver, not a giver. A baby has manifestly not merited or earned anything in its young life. It also seems appropriate to baptize with few conditions, and not only the children of parents who have been active in the church all their lives, but also the children of those who have only recently responded to the gospel and have no credentials to prove that they belong here. Belonging is a determination made by God, not us.

Though I know of no congregation that has ever been in complete agreement about the meaning and method of baptism, by and large the words we say about this sacrament and the way we practise it are accepted by this congregation. Members do not seem to be greatly troubled that something so vital to the life of the church is performed so readily, with so few qualifications. Is this because we have understood the message of grace and taken it to heart? Or is this because the message of grace is submerged by the trappings of baptism? Is it possible that we are so enamoured with the beautiful babies and the sentiment of the occasion that we have not really heard the message of the sacrament?

Baptism is about grace. We are comfortable with baptism. But are we really comfortable with the gospel of grace? If grace were proclaimed in different circumstances, would we be as accepting as we are when the little children are brought to the font? Jesus once told a parable to illustrate God's unmerited grace, and the response of some of the characters to grace was quite the opposite of our response to baptism.

It happened this way. Simon Peter, conscious of how much he had given up to be a disciple of Christ, and speculating as to whether he might be rewarded for this at the end of the day, approached Jesus and said, "Look, we have left everything and followed you. What then will we have?" (Matthew 19:27). Jesus assured him that his reward in heaven would be great, as indeed would be the reward of all who had made sacrifices to follow him. "But," cautioned Jesus, "many who are first will be last, and the last will be first" (19:30).

To illustrate this cryptic comment, Jesus told the story of

the kingdom of heaven being like a landowner who goes out one morning to hire labourers to work in his vineyard. After settling with them how much they will be paid for the day, he sends them to it. Then, at periodic intervals throughout the morning and into the late afternoon, he returns to the market-place. Each time finding labourers who are idle because no one has yet hired them, he sends them all into his vineyard, the last group going in at five o'clock, the last hour of the working day.

There is nothing particularly startling in the story so far, but at the end of the day, when it is time to settle with the labourers, he tells the manager to pay the last ones first. Now, you can guess there is going to be trouble. The people who have worked all day long are made to stand in line, tapping their feet, shifting impatiently from one side to the other, exchanging looks of exasperation, while those who have put in a bare hour step up to receive their wages. But there is a pleasant surprise. The eleventh-hour workers receive twelve hours of pay. This is good news. "If the owner can afford to pay them a full day's wage, what kind of bonus are we going to get?" think the others to themselves. "What a piece of luck to be hired by this generous owner."

But then, the owner gives just a day's pay to those that came at three o'clock, and just a day's pay to those that came at noon, and just a day's pay to those that came at nine, and not a penny more than a day's pay to those who went out into the vineyard at six. "The cheapskate. The miserable, rotten skinflint. Doesn't he know how hard we worked? Doesn't he know how hot it was? Doesn't he know what it's like to bend over those vines all day? He should try it himself before pulling a stunt like this, paying them as much as us, when they didn't even get their hands dirty. And the way he did it. Deliberately raising our hopes and then insulting us. Rubbing our noses in it. What a mean trick!" Or so these labourers must think.

Well, friends, you and I know that the landowner, the God figure in this parable, having arranged this demonstration to make a point, and knowing full well that he has caused offence, is not about to give in to this grumbling. "Come on, fellows," he says, in effect, "I've been fair with you. I paid you exactly what you bargained for. If I want to give those who worked one hour the same amount, what is it to you? It's my money. Can I not do what I choose with it? Or are you envious because I am generous?"

This parable and baptism are both about grace—the unmerited, unearned, undeserved favour of God. I have never known people not to respond warmly to the proclamation of God's grace in a service of baptism—or at least we respond warmly to the babies. Do we respond so warmly to its proclamation in this story, in the equal payment of all the workers? I daresay we do not. Oh, we know that the ones who went into the field at dawn received a wage that was, strictly speaking, just. But it seems so unjust when compared with the wage given those who worked a twelfth of the time. Put us in the position of those who sweated through the heat of the day, and no doubt we, too, would have felt abused, mocked, taken advantage of. We, too, would have grumbled with resentment.

When we talk about grace at the font, perhaps it does not get beyond being a concept, an idea. But here, in the vineyard, grace becomes all too visible and real. That is because, in the parable, the part of grace is played by money, and money is a very big reality to us. When money enters the picture we pay attention. What money does affects us directly. Money and our self-interest go hand in hand.

The language of grace is easy to take when our self-interest is not at stake, but when self-interest is affected we can become quite suspicious about grace. And here in this story, with money cast in the role of grace, strange things happen. Money is doled out in a way that offends our fundamental values about its use. It is distributed arbitrarily and not according to effort or accomplishment or worthiness. It is not used to encourage performance but in a way that discourages those who have worked hard. It gets into the wrong hands. It is wasted. The owner is profligate with it. We are sure that a business could not function the way this vineyard does. And we are right. If the kingdom of heaven were a business operating on money according to the values of this world, it would have been placed in receivership long ago. But the kingdom of heaven runs on grace; the kingdom seems to have an exhaustless supply of the capital of grace, and when the capital is unlimited, the owner can afford to be profligate.

Now, in our story, when money stops acting like money and starts acting like grace, people become resentful. Is it possible that they are not ready for grace? And we, if we are at all in sympathy with those who grumble, is it possible that we are not yet ready for grace? If we are bothered by eleventh-hour workers getting as much as those who laboured all day, how will we feel when we see eleventh-hour Christians go into the kingdom of heaven, some of them before us? We are the ones who have kept the church going, given money, attended faithfully, run programs, taught Sunday school, reached out to the community, performed service after service. How will we feel when those who have offered little by comparison are given a place beside us at the table in the kingdom? Will we still think grace such a good idea?

The parable of the labourers in the vineyard is told in order to leave us in no doubt about what grace is to God and about how key grace is to God's nature and God's plan. In the church, when we talk about grace, we generally speak in terms of being equal before God. This parable keeps such talk from deteriorating into sentimental mush. This parable tells us the truth about being equal: It is not that we start equal but that we finish equal, and not through our efforts but God's. This is grace, and yet this is precisely what offends the hard-working labourers. Remember their complaint? "These last worked only one hour, and you have made them equal to us who have borne the burden of the day and the scorching heat" (20:12).

Now, if we identify with those hired at the eleventh hour, we will no doubt be grateful that this is the way grace works. However, if we identify with those who worked the whole day—and most of us church people have earned the right to side with those workers—we may find ourselves resistant to grace. We have done a very good job of earning God's favour, of working our way into God's kingdom, but grace means that you cannot earn your way in. Grace means that no amount of effort will improve your standing in the eyes of God at the expense of someone else. Grace means that no one comes in except at God's behest, and God brings in some pretty undeserving types.

If, when we read this parable, the thought of God's acting graciously does not go over well with us, that is a normal reaction. After all, the values of the kingdom are so very different from the values of the world deeply ingrained in us. But will we rest content with our first reaction? Will we let our resistance have the last word? Having heard the parable, what are we going to do? Go away grumbling like the labourers hired first thing in the morning? That option is open to us.

Still, do you imagine that is what the first listener, Simon Peter, did? If there was anyone who had borne the "burden of the day and the scorching heat" in the service of the kingdom, it was Peter. If there was anyone who, hearing this story, had the right to be disappointed, it was Peter. Somehow, though, I do not think that is how the man responded. I believe he went away rejoicing at God's grace, rejoicing at those brought in at the eleventh hour. I believe Peter was able to come to see things as the vineyard owner saw them.

Friends, you can see how God's grace really works, how it makes the first last and the last first, and you can go away grumbling or you can go away rejoicing. Today, I give you two reasons to go away rejoicing. The first is that God himself has earned the right to be gracious. Not that God needed to. God, being God, could simply have done as he pleased. As the landowner in the parable says, "Am I not allowed to do what I choose with what belongs to me?" (20:15). But God does not proceed that way. Instead, God, through his Son, himself comes to bear the burden of the day and the scorching heat. Jesus Christ laboured in the vineyard from dawn till dusk. The full payment to those with just an hour's work behind them comes not from the hand of one who is removed from the struggle, someone without sympathy for those who worked long and hard. The payment comes from one whose Son shared the burden every step of the way, a Son who finally carried the cross on his shoulders. Jesus Christ rejoices at the full payment of those latecomers to the vineyard. Can we do anything less?

Second, those who were hired early were not, if they would only stop to think about it, placed at some disadvantage by getting no more pay than those who came late. They, in fact, had a double benefit. They not only got the wage, but they had an opportunity to work in the master's vineyard. If the kingdom of heaven is like this vineyard, is it not better to be in the vineyard now than to have to stand out in the marketplace until the last minute?

Think of it again in terms of baptism. Do we really believe that the children to whom grace is shown at the font, and who are taken into the kingdom's service by baptism, are at some disadvantage to those children who will not be baptized, who may not find the kingdom until late in life, perhaps not even until the end of life? Do we really believe that God's grace is not fair to those whom we baptize as infants?

A friend in ministry told me of a time when she was leading a study group in her congregation. In the first session, as an introduction exercise, all the participants were asked to give their name and earliest memory of church. They went about the circle telling their stories, and finally came to one person who said, "My earliest memory of church is from when I was 30 years old. And for me there is a certain sadness in hearing these accounts of learning the stories of Jesus and being taught to pray and love God as a child. I never had that. There is a gentle magic in having been given faith as a child that I'll never be able to recover as an adult."

Brothers and sisters, those who are baptized as infants do receive a full measure of grace. For others, grace means that the full wage will be given, even though they were not around to learn what the wage was about. But for the little ones received here at this font, grace means that they will not only get the full wage but will get to spend the whole day in the vineyard.

What a blessing: to be called by God at the beginning of the day; to share in that for which God's Son lived and gave his life. What grace: to be called now into the kingdom that has no end.

Communion

A Place at the Table

Luke 16:19-31

"He said to him, 'If they do not listen to Moses and the prophets, neither will they be convinced even if someone rises from the dead.'"

—Luke 16:31

ARE YOU DISTURBED BY THE PARABLE OF THE RICH MAN AND Lazarus? Does it upset you to hear of the treatment of the poor beggar Lazarus: unable to fend for himself, hungry, desiring but a few crumbs from a rich man's table, and unable to compete for those scraps with the dogs who pester him and lick his sores? And the rich man: though he deserves to take a fall, are you not distressed by his torment in Hades, with not a drop of water to cool his parched tongue, and no help to be had from any quarter?

This is a story of such suffering and punishment that the shine is taken off everything in it that should be good and satisfying. The rich man's wealth, which should be a positive thing, is merely grotesque, marred by the unsightly man lying at the gate. Lazarus' blessedness in the afterlife is overshadowed by the rich man's torment—and the threat that the man's brothers will soon join him in the place of anguish. There is little hope in this parable, and much despair.

If you find this story unsettling, you are not alone. I want to tell you of someone else who is bothered by it—God. For God, this story is profoundly dissatisfying. God objects that such a huge gulf has grown up in this life between the well-heeled man and Lazarus, and that there is no contact between them. God objects that such a huge chasm exists between them in the afterlife, and that there is now no possibility that there will ever be contact between them.

God would have been satisfied only if things had turned out differently: had there been some provision for Lazarus from the rich man's table, had both been able to share a place at Abraham's right hand at the table in the kingdom of God. This story gives no pleasure to God. God does not want the role of avenger of Lazarus and punisher of the rich man. God does not want to see any of this come to pass.

So how is it, then, if the Almighty desired a different outcome, that things were allowed to drift to such a sorry state? The first sign that something is going wrong is found in the relationship—or, precisely, the lack of it—between these two characters. You have Lazarus who, for some reason—bad luck (he might have had an accident that prevented him from doing his job), laziness (he might have been that kind of person who just cannot hold a job), social circumstances (an economic downturn or technological changes might have led to his job disappearing); we are never told—finds himself destitute, ill, incapacitated, starving, his survival in question. He gets himself to a place where he reasons help might be forthcoming.

You would think he has chosen well, for the person to whose gate he crawls is exceedingly rich. But nothing happens—at least not for Lazarus. The rich man spends profusely on himself—dressing luxuriously, feasting sumptuously—but when the scraps are thrown out for the dogs, no provision is made for the man at the gate.

It does not appear that the problem with the rich man is that he is rich. Jesus has just finished telling another parable in which a rich man was the good character, generous, merciful. Wealth is not the issue. The problem appears to be the man's failure to use his wealth as a means of blessing for another human being in need. It is not that the rich man has done bad things but that he has done nothing. He had the means but he chose not to act.

He may not even have known that Lazarus existed, his servants judging him to be the kind of person who would not want to be told what was going on outside the gate. And if he did know about Lazarus, he certainly did not want to think about the man's plight. For he thought he could not enjoy his wealth if he allowed himself to be confronted by those dying of a lack of this world's goods.

The rich man did not have anything against Lazarus. He wished him no ill. He just did not want to have anything to do with the poor beggar. And he got his way. He successfully avoided Lazarus until his dying day. And when he got to the next life, he found that he was not going to have to be bothered with Lazarus there either. For now a great chasm had been fixed between them and neither could cross to the other side.

Of course, by now the roles had been completely reversed. Before, the rich man had sat at table while Lazarus pined at the gate. Now Lazarus sat at table, while the rich man dwelt in misery. Before, Lazarus had perished for want of a crumb; now, his counterpart perished for want of a drop of water. Before, Lazarus had to contend with the pestering dogs; now, the rich man had to abide the pestering flames. The tables had been turned. Only one thing had remained constant: the lack of contact between the two.

But why should the rich man complain about his fate? He did not want to share a table with Lazarus before. Why would he want to share one now? The only thing motivating a change of his heart is his discovery that the other side of splendid isolation is miserable isolation.

Now that it is too late, he begins to say the things people always say when it's too late: "Had I only known, I would have done things differently." "Please warn my brothers; you didn't warn me." But of course God had warned him. God had sent Moses to give the law detailing his obligations to his fellow humans. God had sent the prophets to keep reminding him of his obligations under the law.

The clear message of the law and the prophets to this man was that his fate and his destiny were bound up with the fate and destiny of the neighbour at his gate. The clear message of the law and the prophets was that, though his wealth was a blessing from God, it could become a curse if it was mishandled and not used to bless others. The clear message of the law and the prophets was that it was not the riches he amassed but the people he cared for that determined his destiny. And the rich man's problem is that he did not believe this, and his plight is that he will be forced to spend eternity witnessing the truth of what he did not believe.

What a parable of despair. God would have preferred a story with a different ending, one in which the rich man and Lazarus feasted together at the great banquet in his kingdom. But for the story to have had a different ending, it would have required a different beginning. God wanted to bring both these men to his table, but he needed some hint that the rich man was prepared for this, some glimmer that he regarded Lazarus as a person fit to be at table with. God never got that glimmer.

God wanted nothing more than to save the rich man, but he could not save him in isolation from Lazarus. And since the rich man wanted nothing to do with Lazarus, well, what more could God do? It is not that God set up the chasm. The rich man fixed the chasm all by himself.

For the sake of vivid storytelling, Jesus draws in this parable some pretty stark contrasts between the characters and between their conditions. Nor does he hesitate to fix our attention on what is crude and distasteful in life. And so we find this passage upsetting. And we are uneasy, I suspect, not just because the parable is about the dark side of life but because we begin to feel the story drawing us in.

It is not that the characters typify us by their circumstances. It is the rare person in any circle in which we move whose wealth is as great as the rich man's or whose poverty is as extreme as that of Lazarus. No, we are drawn into the story because we begin to realize the issue is not really luxurious clothes and sumptuous feasting, in which case most of us would be let off the hook. The real issue is *unconcern:* being so wrapped up in self and so attentive to the wants and needs of self that we do not notice or do not care to notice Lazarus. We are drawn into this parable whenever life gives us means and then places in our way people who can be helped only if we use our means, and then in our unconcern we do nothing—and let them lie at the gate.

This parable does not come to us as *social commentary*, and so this sermon should not be full of social commentary. You will note that Jesus does not make any comments about how horrible it is that Lazarus gets attention from no one but the dogs. There is no speculation as to what could have gone wrong with society to produce this situation, no suggestion of social programs to alleviate it. That is not Jesus' agenda here. The parable contains no *moralizing*, so this sermon should not be full of moralizing. Jesus does not go on at great length about how heartless the rich man is, how he ought to have done something. Why bother moralizing when basic decency should have made it obvious to this wealthy fellow that he was obliged to do something?

What this parable really is is a *warning*. And my obligation in this sermon is to warn you that there is an afterlife, and how we treat our fellow humans in this life will have a great effect on how we fare in the next. If the parable has about it an ominous quality, that is precisely what Jesus intended.

Some may protest, "If the way we treat the Lazaruses in our lives now will affect our eternal destiny, why does God not give us clearer guidance to keep us from going astray and missing the mark? Why did God not tell the rich man to do something about Lazarus in order to save his own soul?" But God did. God gave him Moses and the prophets to lay out a law of compassion and mercy, hospitality being one of the larger themes of the Old Testament.

That law is still there for us. Moreover, God has spoken to us in a more personal manner by giving us his Son to illustrate the way of compassion and mercy. And Christ himself has spoken more dramatically still by making a centrepiece of his church a table—a table around which all are invited to gather to feast with him.

The table is a place for *fellowship*, where we are to have fellowship not only with Christ but with one another. It is a preview of that great banquet in the kingdom where the redeemed will have fellowship not only with God but with one another. It is no accident that Jesus chooses as the place of communion a public place where the invitation to gather is widely extended.

But this table is also a place of *warning*. When we come to it, its message to us is to be sure that what we do here is a reflection of what is going on in the rest of our lives. This table begs us to consider: Is there anyone lying at the gate in our lives? Do we have any Lazaruses who have not yet been fed from our table? The message of today's parable is that Lazarus must be got from the gate and brought to the table before it is too late, for him and for us.

We will get no other warnings than this one that we receive by coming to a table that says we are not in communion with Christ if we are not in community with Lazarus. If we will not listen to its message, then nothing else is likely to persuade us. If we evade this word, spoken to us with absolute clarity, what more can we expect God to do?

The best thing that can be said about the story of the rich man and Lazarus is that it need not come true—for anyone. God does not want it to come true. God invites all to his great banquet hall—the rich man, Lazarus, ourselves. We can exclude ourselves only by excluding others. For we cannot have God without having Lazarus.

The good news is, we are still in the time of grace. We are still in the time when we can respond to God and the invitation that goes out. We are still in the time when people can be cared for, compassion demonstrated, when we may bring to the table those lying at the gate.

It is not yet too late. The chasm is not fixed in place. In fact, God hopes to be able to remove it. Will God get his way?

Sabbath

Sunday Best

Mark 2:23-3:6

Then he said to them, "The sabbath was made for humankind, and not humankind for the sabbath; so the Son of Man is lord even of the sabbath."

—Mark 2:27-28

WHAT DID OUR DEVOUT MOTHERS AND GRANDMOTHERS THINK when, on a Sunday morning, they went to church and listened to lessons of scripture such as this morning's reading from the Gospel of Mark? Do you suppose they felt in any way challenged by Jesus' ringing declaration that "the sabbath was made for humankind, and not humankind for the sabbath"?

Did Christ's pronouncement serve to soften the determination of these devout women that games of cards would never, ever, ever be played in their homes on a Sunday? Or did it never occur to them that card games on the sabbath might not have made Jesus' top ten list of deadly sins?

Hearing that Jesus' disciples actually did something worldly on the sabbath—picked cobs of corn—might they have loosened up to the point of allowing the singing of popular songs on the sacred day? Or, the disciples' behaviour notwithstanding, did they hold to the unalterable conviction that only hymns were suitable for a Sunday?

Do you suppose the healing by Jesus—on the sabbath, and in church—of a man with a withered hand might have freed up our devout foremothers to countenance the polishing of a shoe or the pressing of a shirt on Sunday morning? Or were they, in fact, impervious to the gospel to the point of considering a shoe shined on Sunday to be an affront to God?

Many of us are old enough to have some remembrance of the rigid and austere treatment of Sunday by previous generations. Throughout the nineteenth century and the first half of the twentieth, the list of activities forbidden or frowned upon on Sunday rivalled the Pharisees' list of don'ts for the sabbath in the time of Christ. And, of course, in the old days nearly everybody attended church—in the morning and again in the afternoon or evening. There was scarcely anything else to do.

Our devout ancestors certainly attempted to do the right thing by the sabbath day. On the surface it appears that the Pharisees were trying to do the right thing as well. Part of remembering the sabbath day to keep it holy was, in their minds, to refrain from doing work on it. And they had drawn up a very long list of what constituted work. One of the items on the list was plucking heads of grain, or corn, even if only to satisfy one's hunger. And so the Pharisees administered a stern rebuke to Jesus when they saw his friends doing precisely that.

Jesus rebuked his detractors in return. He might have done otherwise. He might have drawn his followers aside and told them to respect the sensibilities of these devout men. He might have said to the disciples, "If you want to pluck grain on the sabbath, be more discreet; do it away from the public roads. Don't give these people an opportunity to make an issue of it." But no, if the Pharisees would make an issue of it, so would he. He defended his followers for working to satisfy their hunger. He reminded his opponents that no less a person than King David had technically broken the religious laws by eating holy bread reserved for priests at a time when he was famished and there was no other food available to meet his need.[1]

If the Pharisees would make an issue of work on the sabbath, so would he by healing a man with a withered hand on that day, in full view of the worshipping community. He could have put off the healing for a day; the crippled man had lived with his affliction for a long time, and surely one more day would not have mattered. However, Jesus had a point to make and proceeded to make it at a great deal of risk to his own safety.

"Humankind [was not made] for the sabbath," he announced. The sabbath was not more important than people. And so he would not be prevented, merely by the fact that it was a particular day of the week, from performing an act of mercy for someone in need.

To be fair to our devout mothers and grandmothers, most of them certainly did not share the spirit of the Pharisees: an exclusive spirit, more concerned to use the sabbath day as a tool to separate good people from bad people than to receive and honour it as a gift from God; a vengeful and vindictive spirit, more concerned with judging others' alleged misuse of the sabbath than with finding positive ways to spend the day. Our devout mothers and grandmothers had much nobler motivations, but the fact is, their rigidity rivalled that of the Pharisees. And if they were unmoved by Jesus' recasting of the sabbath day, we may be glad that, in our time, we have not remained similarly unmoved. The sabbath is no longer our tyrant. We have rid ourselves of those shackles; and, given the words and actions of Jesus, we have done so quite rightly.

However, while the sabbath is no longer our tyrant, there is a growing awareness that it is no longer our servant either. In our time, the sabbath, far from being a weight on our shoulders, threatens to disappear into thin air. We are not here referring to

---

1. 1 Samuel 21:1-6.

the fact that a considerable amount of necessary work is done on Sundays. Such work, typified by what goes on in hospitals, care homes, and police stations, would certainly seem justified if the incidents in today's gospel lesson are any measure of truth. However, the myriad of activities taking place on Sunday has long since gone beyond the range of what is necessary for the functioning of our common life as a society. These days, most Sunday work is mandated for the convenience of the consumer. By no stretch of the imagination can it be called necessary. Moreover, the pressure is on for Sunday to become more and more a wide-open day like any other in the week.

Not only commerce, but recreation, contributes to this trend. Traditionally, Sunday has been a day for recreation, and rightly so. But recreation is increasingly becoming organized recreation. When this happens, people are frequently required to give up their sabbath to serve someone else's pleasure, whether this be working at a booth at some tournament on a Sunday because one has to take one's turn for the community organization of which one is a part or whether this be getting one's child to a game on Sunday because this is the family's responsibility to the team and, not only that, because being there is the price of staying on the team.

Routinely, today, people are giving up the sabbath. Some Christians are letting go of their sabbath reluctantly, others willingly. While our devout mothers and grandmothers may have needed to hear and to take to heart Jesus' words "Humankind [was not made] for the sabbath," we may need to hear and to take to heart his words "The sabbath was made for humankind."

The sabbath was, in fact, made. It is a part of God's creation. It was made after human beings were made. It was made for their sake. It is, in God's mind, such a valuable gift that its status is enshrined in one of the Ten Commandments of the law: "Remember the sabbath day, and keep it holy" (Exodus 20:8).

The sabbath day signifies two things. It signifies a mandated rest from work. According to the Book of Exodus,[2] after the

---

2. Exodus 20:11.

work of creation God rested. The commandment to honour the sabbath is therefore a declaration that what is good for God is good for us. We are blessed with a sabbath rest. Secondly, it signifies a release from bondage. According to the Book of Deuteronomy,[3] the sabbath celebrates God's rescue of the people of Israel from slavery at the hands of their harsh Egyptian taskmasters. Later on, Christians, grateful for their release from the bondage of sin through the work of Jesus Christ, essentially moved the sabbath from Saturday to Sunday, the Lord's Day, the Day of Resurrection. This move was completely within the spirit of the original law about the sabbath as recorded in the Book of Deuteronomy.

So, the sabbath is God's gift to God's people. Christians have for themselves changed the day of sabbath observance, but they have never imagined that God did not make the sabbath, or that the sabbath was unimportant, until now.

What ought to be done about this state of affairs?

Well, we could begin by remembering and praying for those folk in our congregation who have no choice but to earn their living on Sunday, who would like to be in church with the faithful but who cannot, who would like this to be their day of rest and cannot take it as such. As we remember them and think of their situation, those of us who do not have to work on Sunday might do well to ask ourselves if any of the freedoms and choices we exercise on this day are contributing to their loss of a sabbath. How does our membership in the body of Christ and our responsibility for the health of all the members of the body guide the way we use our Sunday?

Many Christians are business people who employ workers, and if they are in the retail field their workers are likely to be working this day. What ought we to be asking business people who are members of the body of Christ? Well, in a competitive marketplace in a changed world, asking them to stay closed on Sunday seems to me to be asking them to make our sacrifices for us. And that is not fair, especially when so many

---

3. Deuteronomy 5:15.

professing Christians are going out and shopping on their sabbath. Moreover, it is not just Christians whom our businesses serve, but people of other faiths with different sabbaths and secular people who do not live with a religious command to keep a sabbath day.

Yet, I do think it would be fair and right to ask Christian employers to do what they can to arrange work schedules in such a way that those who desire a sabbath are able to have it, if not on a Sunday, on another day when it is possible for them to make a sabbath with their families. Christian business people who will do this for their employees will be doing their part to honour the sabbath day to keep it holy.

One thing that ought not to be done is for the church to go on a campaign to close down Sunday and make it the day of quiet it was in years gone by. Such a campaign would not work in today's society, and even if the church were a powerful enough institution to make it happen, which it is not, imposition of a sabbath is not the answer. The sabbath is God's gift to humanity. It is commanded by God, but it cannot be imposed by us. It can only be accepted in freedom. Otherwise, it is a tyrant and not a servant.

We might also ask ourselves the reasons why people give up the sabbath. One may be a reaction against the dour, solemn, and lifeless sabbath formerly practised by the church. If that is the case, there is no worry. A more creative approach by the church to the sabbath will lead to a more positive reaction. A more likely reason that people give up the sabbath is that they have given up the faith. The cure for this is not a multitude of Sunday laws. Rather, it is a better evangelism by the church. For when faith in God begins to flourish, it will surely be accompanied by an appreciation of God's benefits and gifts, and a desire to make the most of them. And one of these gifts is the sabbath.

Those of us who come to church fairly regularly on Sundays are the ones in our society who do take the sabbath seriously. In a time when we have lost confidence in the hard-and-fast rules of our devout mothers and grandmothers, but also have no confidence in secular society's replacements for our Christian traditions, we may well be wondering where we should look to find guidance for the use of the sabbath. Quite simply, we look to Jesus. He did say, "The Son of Man is lord even of the sabbath." If he is the lord of the sabbath, then he is the one who defines its character and use. And he does this freely. In two short incidents he demolishes a legalistic approach to the sabbath, practised by the Pharisees and, subsequently, by far too many branches of Christianity.

In place of regulations and legalisms, Jesus merely asks us to consider whether our use of the sabbath meets human need—our own and others'. When he asserts that the sabbath was made for people, he is not giving us licence to do as we please but is instead recognizing that the sabbath was God's gift for human need. So, Jesus specifically allows necessary work and encourages deeds of mercy and kindness on the sabbath. By this, human need is addressed.

The sabbath also provides an opportunity for meeting another basic human need, the need for worship and renewal. Where does the healing of the crippled man take place? In the synagogue. On the sabbath day, if you wanted to find Jesus, you found him in the synagogue. There was simply no question about this. If Jesus did not question the need for public worship, why are his followers questioning it today?

People have often been heard to remark, "For us, Sunday is a day for family." It should be. It should be a day to strengthen the bonds and deepen the ties within our natural families. It should also be a day to do the very same thing within our church family. The sabbath offers us an opportunity to assemble as God's people to share and celebrate the faith and the mission that give our lives meaning.

Our devout forbears may have got hung up on inconsequentials in forbidding that pack of cards to come out or demanding that nothing but hymns be sung on a Sunday. But in other matters, such as attending church as regularly as they could, they were true to Jesus' interpretation of the sabbath. May we value the gift of the sabbath as much as they did and may we always strive for the mind of Jesus to find ways to use it creatively.

Advent

Being Ready

Matthew 24:29-44

"Therefore you also must be ready, for the Son of Man is coming at an unexpected hour."

—Matthew 24:44

THE SECULAR CALENDAR BEGINS WITH JANUARY 1, BUT THE church's calendar begins with the First Sunday of Advent, which falls in either late November or early December. It is an appropriate place for our year to begin. For Advent means "coming," and this is, therefore, the season of preparation for God's coming into the world.

Or, is it really? For most of us, is it not instead a preparation for Christmas? Surely Advent has come to mean the rehearsing, the re-enacting, the reliving of a past event—the birth of Jesus at Bethlehem. It is less a preparation to meet the God who is coming than a preparation to celebrate the God who came. It is not a time for looking ahead. It is a time for looking back.

Now, there is nothing wrong with looking back, particularly to something as important to the faith as the coming of Christ into the world. But the people who created the church year, and with it the season of Advent, wanted us to be looking ahead as well. And so, on the first Sunday in Advent, just as our minds are beginning to fill once again with images of shepherds and angels, a manger in a stable, kings and camels and a star, they ask us to read passages of scripture that talk not about how Jesus came but about the fact that he will come again.

The people who gave us the church year wanted to forge a strong connection between the birth of Christ at Bethlehem and his coming again at the end of time. For them, the purpose of looking back to what God had done in the birth of his Son was to fortify hope in what God would yet do. The point of recalling the story of the Incarnation was to draw from it confidence that the God who had thus penetrated human history would do so again.

How well did the framers of the church year succeed? Not very well, I fear. Every year, on the First Sunday of Advent, the gospel lesson is about the second coming. But the second coming is not high on the list of expectations of most church people, much less the general public. Christ's return is not a hope we seem to hold dearly or to pray for earnestly. Instead we seem to be content to review once a year the time he did come and to make a big event of that.

Why have we, as a Christian people, lost interest in what is one of the central themes of the New Testament? Why have we so willingly neglected something that is talked about in the gospels, in the letters of Paul, in the letters of Peter, and in the Book of Revelation? I can think of two possible reasons why we have played down talk of Christ's second coming.

The first would be that, unlike the writers of the New Testament, we believe that Christ accomplished everything that needed accomplishing in his first coming; that in his ministry he fulfilled all the hopes and dreams that the prophets had articulated on behalf of God's people; that he did everything the Messiah was expected to do. It could be that we believe he brought the *peace* of which Isaiah dreamed when he said:

they shall beat their swords into plowshares,
and their spears into pruning hooks;
nation shall not lift up sword against nation,
neither shall they learn war any more.
(Isaiah 2:4)

It could be that we believe he brought the *justice* of which Isaiah dreamed when he said:

with righteousness he shall judge the poor,
and decide with equity for the meek of the earth;
he shall strike the earth with the rod of his mouth,
and with the breath of his lips he shall kill the wicked.
(Isaiah 11:4)

It could be that we believe he brought the *healing* of which Isaiah dreamed when he said:

Then the eyes of the blind shall be opened,
and the ears of the deaf unstopped;
then the lame shall leap like a deer,
and the tongue of the speechless sing for joy.
(Isaiah 35:5-6)

Perhaps we are satisfied that life is now as God finally wants it to be, and we do not feel there is a need for Christ to come again.

If that is the case, then we are easily satisfied. But I do not believe for a moment that this is the case, that this is the real reason we have given up talking about and hoping for the second coming.

I believe the real reason is that his coming has been so long delayed that it now seems like too much to hope for. Two thousand years is a long time. Two thousand years of unfulfilled hopes. Two thousand years, and the prophecies of the triumph of God's kingdom are still not translated into reality. And so, regardless of what the Bible says and what the doctrines of the church say about Christ's second coming, many of us, perhaps most of us, have given up expecting that God will act to bring to pass the dreams of his prophets.

And though in church the preacher may talk urgently about holding fast to the hope of his coming, we go away thinking it is really not going to happen; or if indeed the kingdom is going to come we will just have to make it happen ourselves; or perhaps the best thing to do is not to worry about it at all and just get on with life.

That is the problem, is it not? *Expectation has dried up.* Friends, my word to you today is this: It was just when expectation had dried up that the Son of God was born. Jesus did not come to a world waiting for his arrival with bated breath. He came to a people who had virtually given up on his coming and consequently took next to no notice of his arrival.

Look at the story in Luke's gospel. Half the country had come to Bethlehem for the census. The inns were packed. The crowds who could have welcomed him were there. And the angels tried to get out the message that a saviour had been born. But nobody came except a few simple shepherds—the only ones not so weighed down by the cares and interests of the world that they could actually see and take note when something new was going on.

Look at the story in Matthew. A star in the sky. A sign. And you would think that some of the chief priests and scribes would have said to themselves, "Could this be it? Could it really be happening? Is this just possibly a sign of the Messiah's coming after all these centuries?" But no, it was only foreigners who were interested in the star. The leaders of Israel had lost their expectation.

So he came and so his coming was missed; and it was only many, many years later, after a certain vocal and growing group had become persuaded that this Jesus had been raised from the dead, that people began to ponder the implications of his coming and to realize that the Messiah had been among them.

How could he have come and been missed when Israel had

such a heritage of faith and hope, when its prophets had seen such visions and dreamed such dreams? It happened in the same way it happens among us. People read their scriptures and went to the synagogue to hear their rabbis teach and preach. And they sang their version of "O Come, O Come Emmanuel." But they went home saying to each other, "The rabbis keep telling us the Messiah is coming, but they've been telling us this for a long time; the prophets they quote have been dead for hundreds of years and their predictions haven't come true yet. We know better. We know it's not likely to happen. What sense in putting our eggs in that basket? We have to get on with life and leave the dreaming to the rabbis." So they lost the expectation and missed his coming. Will we, having also lost the expectation, be likewise unprepared?

Friends, it should not surprise us that Jesus, in talking about the coming of the Son of Man to establish God's rule, harboured no illusions about the level of expectation around this promise. Unacknowledged for who he was by virtually the entire nation of Israel, which had been diligently prepared for his coming, Jesus did not delude himself that people would wait for the second coming with vigilance.

That is why he finds it necessary to exhort, "You also must be ready, for the Son of Man is coming at an unexpected hour." That is why his images of the coming of the Son of Man are so frighteningly stark: a flood, a kidnapping, a thief in the night. It is as if Jesus is saying, "Do not allow yourselves to be overtaken by events."

When the Son of Man comes and our world is shaken up, turned upside down—for so it will need to be for those visions of the prophets to find fulfilment—will we be ready? When the Son of Man comes and we find out just how transitory are all those efforts and labours and projects in which we have invested ourselves, will we be ready?

Friends, it is going to happen. If we believe that Christ did come as promised, why would we doubt the announcement of his return? Why would we give up hope because the night is long?

We must be ready, for it will happen when we least expect it. Our readiness is not the readiness of people who know when it will happen. If we knew the hour, we could put on white robes and go and meet him on the mountaintop. But we do not know. The fact that we do not know is really our permission to go on living life in an ordinary fashion—making our plans, raising our families, developing our interests, preparing for our retirements. But we need to live that life with a certain detachment, recognizing how provisional and impermanent all those things are.

If readiness for Christ's coming does not mean stopping everything, as some fanatics have done over the years, it does mean not being taken by surprise when it happens. But how can we be ready when life itself demands that we give our attention to the here and now and makes us preoccupied with our plans, our interests, our jobs, our families—when life itself will not let us invest much energy in the hope of his long-awaited coming?

I believe there is no better way of maintaining readiness than the frequent gathering with Christ's people for worship and the fellowship of the Lord's Supper. It is the tradition in our church always to celebrate Communion the Sunday before Christmas, the message of this table and the meal we share around it being one way to keep alive the message of Advent.

When you think of it, what a blessedly impractical act this Sacrament is. How little it has to do with all the supposedly important things in life. And yet, this Sacrament will never let us forget, never let us drift too far from the one supremely important fact. For what is this meal but, as St. Paul calls it, a proclaiming of the Lord's death until he comes? Jesus says, "You also must be ready, for the Son of Man is coming at an unexpected hour." It is when we come to this table that we are made ready by being shown once again that what is truly important to us, and what we must hold onto at all costs, is that

the Christ who died
is the Christ who is risen
and also the Christ who will come again.

Christmas

The Joy That Is for All People

Luke 2:1-20

But the angel said to them, "Do not be afraid; for see—I am bringing you good news of great joy for all the people: to you is born this day in the city of David a Savior, who is the Messiah, the Lord."

—Luke 2:10-11

One of the authentic words of Christmas is "joy." The prophets stir up hope in the coming of the Messiah whom we praise as the "joy of every longing heart."[1] The angel appears in the hills announcing "good news of great joy." Joy is a hallmark of both our Advent and Christmas carols. Joy is what we want to experience during this holy season. We would surround Christmas with gladness and delight.

I had always assumed that joy belonged to the religious side of Christmas until one year I heard the word used in a different context. The Hudson's Bay Company ran a series of commercials on television showing off many of the wonderful Christmas presents that could be purchased in its stores. At the close

1. From Charles Wesley's hymn "Come, Thou Long-Expected Jesus."

of each message a voice would confide to viewers, "We think you'll find joy at the Bay."

So I went to the Bay, and what did I find? JOY—printed in bold letters on shopping bags, in displays, on balloons hanging from the ceiling. Did I find the reality those letters represent? Well, that is a more difficult question.

This shopping giant's promotional venture reminds us that the church does not own the word "joy." Others feel free to use it and put their own spin on it. And, in reality, all of us look for joy in many different ways and places at Christmastime. We have made many things of this season. Christians are often heard to complain about the loss of the true meaning of Christmas—the excessive commercialism, the plethora of secular carols, the myriad of social activities, the invitation to overindulgence, the focus on Santa Claus—and to lament that the religious aspect of the festival has lost its prominence and the birth of Jesus has receded into the background.

But Christians need to remember that the church did not invent Christmas out of nothing, but itself took over a pagan festival full of long-standing traditions, and recast it to focus attention on the Incarnation. The church made what it wanted out of an existing season, so we can hardly carp if people make what they want out of the Christmas season. And if many of the things we do or lift up at this time of year that are not particularly religious in fact create joy, we ought to celebrate rather than complain.

Still, there is one question we must ask: Do our Christmas customs bring joy for all the people? You see, in this text the angel not only brings news of great joy, but a joy that is for *all* the people. And so, we are led to ask, Where do we find this joy that is for all?

Do we find it, for example, in our Christmas custom of buying and gift giving? Do we find it at the Bay? There is much to be said for this. I still have memories of childhood Christmases, of hours poring over the Eaton's catalogue, and months of eager anticipation of expected gifts, and many dreams coming true on the big day. Not all of those presents brought long-lasting pleasure, but many did. Even as an adult, I find that it is still a wonderful moment to open those packages that for weeks have piqued my curiosity from under the tree. And I have had the joy of seeing others appreciate and value gifts I have given, and, with this, the joy of feeling appreciated and valued myself.

Yet, this is not a joy that is for all people. The very fact that our church has a White Gift Service every year to collect items for Christmas hampers tells us that. Many in our society do not have the resources to participate in this culture of buying and giving. So many children do not get to crawl under the tree and shake and poke presents and ache with excitement at what might be under the wrapping. So many parents must be sick with worry about how they will ever provide a good Christmas for their children. The Cheer Board might bring a hamper, but no hamper will cure feelings of inadequacy born of the fact that others are providing while they cannot.

The Christmas that revolves around things, presents, material goods, does provide joy for some, but it just brings pain into the lives of others. No season more clearly separates the haves from the have-nots. So this is not the joy that is for all people.

Is the joy that is for all found in the experience of children? So often we say that "Christmas is for children," that, through their innocent eyes, something really special can be made of this ancient holiday. There is much to this. In church, I have observed the faces of parents as they watched their children performing a nativity pageant. The young members of the congregation come forward to be Mary and Joseph, and shepherds and angels, and an even younger member is brought in to be Jesus. And what I have seen in the faces of these parents is happiness, a real glow.

I have watched the faces of the same parents in school gyms and community centres on the night of the school Christmas concert. The kindergarten children come out in their star costumes, each with a letter on the front, and if they line up correctly, they spell MERRY CHRISTMAS, and if they don't, well, that's the fun of a Christmas concert. The older children put on a play about the latest crisis at the North Pole, and my, who would have thought that such talent was growing up in our classrooms? And at the end of the evening the whole group stands on the risers at the front to sing "Silent Night" and "We Wish You a Merry Christmas," and just as the last verse gets started, the eyes of the younger ones begin to bulge and bodies begin to quiver as you-know-who ho ho hos his way into the back of the room. Oh, I have seen the faces of parents beam on those occasions.

Now I am having my own turn as my son works his way through those years when Christmas is a magical experience. I have seen his face light up as each present comes into the house, and I've watched him tear the wrapping off a gift and exclaim, "Oh wow, Daddy!" and rush over to show his new treasure.

There certainly is joy in watching children at Christmas and seeing the world through their eyes. But this is not a joy that is for all people. For not all people get to have children and grandchildren. There was a time during our long, long wait to adopt a child when I spent my Christmases wondering if I'd ever get to take a picture of my son dressed up as a shepherd or to help my daughter hang up her stocking on the fireplace. Our prayer was answered, but it is not so for all. If Christmas is for children and about children, then the joy of it is not for all.

Now, also, we look for joy in the festivities of Christmastime, and are they not especially appreciated here in the frozen North—a precious antidote to the cold and dark of winter? The seasonal parties and gatherings enable us to see a different side of people, to socialize with those to whom we might normally do no more than say hello, to break down the barriers that office hierarchies, social status, ethnic groupings, and financial ability often erect between us. With the coming of the festive season we have something in common, and we are given permission to put work aside without guilt and enjoy one another, permission to strike up great conversations with strangers, permission to do something different.

And there are always the special touches. The party that unexpectedly ends up in carolling around the piano. The person who turns up at the front door to drop off a gift of Christmas baking and becomes a guest for the evening. The young friends in my home town who have found that the best way to be with one another on Christmas Eve is to attend one another's church services—a church crawl, something that would have scandalized their parents a generation ago.

There is joy in the Christmas festivities, but even this is not a joy that is for all people. If you are afflicted by loneliness or depression, what you see going on around you might not lift you out of it but drive you in deeper. And of course, sometime in the next couple of weeks, there will be the annual story on the newscast of how suicides are always at their peak at this time of year.

If self-control is not your strong suit, the word you remember from Christmas may not be "joy" but "hangover" or, worse still, "breathalyser," and your family's memories may be of a father who never arrived home on Christmas Eve in any shape to help put up the stockings. Things are pretty well shut down at this church between Christmas and New Year's, as our tenants and groups take a break, but one group that never cancels a meeting is the Adult Children of Alcoholics. Its leaders tell us that for it, and groups like it around the city, the meetings at Christmastime are absolutely indispensable. So the joy of Christmas festivities is not a joy that is experienced by all.

Is there joy for all in the custom of going home for Christmas? Getting together with family is one of the great joys for me. I get a lump in my throat at the beginning of December when they play "I'll Be Home for Christmas" on the radio. And as the day approaches I listen anxiously to the weather forecasts, hoping to hear nothing about a storm moving in from Colorado or Montana, praying that travel will be possible on the twenty-fifth. At airports, people put up with the most terrible conditions—wall-to-wall travellers, never-ending lineups, long delays—to get home at just this time of year, to have the joy of spending this special season with family.

Yet, this is not a joy for all the people. I can think of many a Christmas Eve during the years in my first charge when, after services, at about 9:30, we would start the 3½-hour drive for my home town and the waiting family. By midnight, you would have expected to be alone on the highway; but no, every three or four minutes there would be another transport truck, just like clockwork, an endless stream. And you'd wonder, Does our economy really require that they be out on the road alone on Christmas Eve? Maybe some of the men driving those trucks would make it home for Christmas. I'm sure many would not, but would spend Christmas on the road hundreds, even thousands, of miles from their loved ones.

And what of those who have no home? What about the homeless at Christmas? What of those who have a home but no family—or whose family is divided, or broken? For them, homecoming is often about anxiety and stress, not joy. So the joy of a family reunion for Christmas is not a joy that is for all people.

So, is there such a joy? The angel, speaking to the shepherds, said, "I am bringing you good news of great joy for *all* the people" (italics mine). What is this joy that is for all, this joy that does not separate those of us who have it made from those of us who cannot make it?

It is a joy that comes from God. Unlike the other joys of which I've spoken, which arise out of things that we do, and out of what we make of the season, this one arises out of what God does, and out of what God makes of the season. Other joys we must, to some extent, manufacture, or at least create the setting for. And some are able to do this and some are not able. With the joy that is for all, God acts, and we believe and receive.

What is this joy? "To you is born this day in the city of David a Savior." God is with us. God is here. God has come down to earth from heaven. That is our joy. And what a different joy it is. The joys of our Christmas customs require a departure from our normal routine and everyday circumstances. They require us to set aside for a time our cares and concerns and duties. That is why they can never be more than a joy for some. The joy that is for all comes into our lives where life is really lived; it comes to us in those places from which we cannot manufacture any escape. God does not create a special time or a special situation. God invests ordinary time with a special person.

The joy of Christ's coming is a joy that is for all because, unlike other joys, it is available even to those who have no power to command the course of life. In the story in Luke, it is those least able to make something special of a season—shepherds—to whom the angel speaks. They belong in this story precisely because they are people who do not belong. To the religious authorities, they are simply the unclean. To the comfortable, they are simply the poor and marginal. And let us resist the temptation to romanticize them, for, as one preacher notes, "Even today, the shepherds are the scruffiest and earthiest of all the people in that part of the world."[2] So it is not to the included but the excluded that the angel comes. Moreover, it is not during some festivities to which they have been invited, but at work, doing their ordinary duties, that these men are brought into the story. And where are they sent

2. Roger Lovette of Baptist Church of the Covenant, Birmingham, Alabama, "Waiting for the Birth," *Covenant Word*, December 24, 1994.

to but Bethlehem, where the bureaucrats are conducting the census and people are paying their taxes? There is no break in this story from the stuff of everyday, no precious holiday season. Yet, still the joy comes.

And what is the sign of this joy? It is the birth of a babe, but not the kind of birth to make the news. In Roman Empire days, poets and orators would herald the birth of one born to be emperor. That would cause a general rejoicing in society—just as there was in our own time when Princess Diana emerged from the hospital with Prince William in her arms. But no such hoopla surrounds this birth. This is a babe born to poor parents and having his first sleep in a feeding trough in a stable in a backwater town, unnoticed by those who crowd the nearby inn. Let us resist the urge to romanticize this scene as well—the temptation to bring the angels from the hillsides right up to the barn door, and to gather animals around the Holy Family to watch the child in silent worship, and, above all, "to run next door to Matthew and borrow his royal visitors with their gold, frankincense, and myrrh (Matthew 2:1-12)."[3] Let us not soften or sentimentalize the scene by pushing the rough-hewn participants to the background and replacing them with more acceptable figures.

For that would be to obscure the joy, which is this: When people cannot rise to the heights, God stoops to the depths. God is there not just for those with means to create their joy but for those who have no means. For those who must do without, God does without. God comes to those who feel the least deserving, who feel they have the least claim on him because they have so little claim on anything else. And hope begins to be born in a God who cares, a God who shares their poverty that one day they might share God's riches.

But there is yet another reason why the joy of Christ's coming is a joy that is for all. In his coming, God addresses the

---

3. Fred B. Craddock, *Luke—Interpretation: A Bible Commentary for Teaching and Preaching* (Louisville: John Knox Press, 1990), p. 35.

anxiety of us all—not only of the poor but of the rich, not only of the struggling but of the successful, not only of the outsiders but of the insiders—the anxiety that, ironically, we try to block out with our multiplicity of Christmas customs, and that the pagans before us attempted to combat with their celebrations of the winter solstice, the anxiety that beyond us there is nothing but a void—darkness. God addresses the need of us all, the need to know that beyond us there is not a void but God—a God to whom we may come because he has taken the initiative to come to us.

This birth in Bethlehem tells us that we are not alone, that God is with us. And, if Luke is right, God is with us no matter how close we feel to the joys of the season or how far we feel removed from them. We do not have to make this Christmas season. God has made it for us. God has brought a joy that is for all the people.

Epiphany

Confessing Christ in a Pluralistic World

John 1:19-34

The next day he saw Jesus coming toward him and declared, "Here is the Lamb of God who takes away the sin of the world!"

— John 1:29

It is commonly observed that Canadian society is becoming steadily more pluralistic. Our nation is home to many racial, ethnic, and religious groupings. Not only are we no longer an *exclusively* Christian society but, year by year, we are becoming less of an *essentially* Christian society. My brother lives in a relatively new suburb in Calgary. The first house of worship to go up in that development was a Moslem mosque. You can see the minaret from my brother's backyard. To go to a United Church, he and his family have to drive to a neighbouring suburb. A sign of the times—our nation's changing identity.

People are sometimes accommodating to religious pluralism. In December, when politicians send out cards and calendars to their constituents, they no longer contain Christmas greetings, but all-purpose season's greetings. Legislative assemblies are now more likely to begin their sessions with a generic prayer than a Christian prayer. Similarly, public schools, so as not to cause offence to non-Christians, have gradually been eliminating Christian religious exercises from the school day. These days, the school concert in December is seldom called a "Christmas" concert, and even if it still retains that title, it rarely focusses on the birth of Christ. There are many signs around us of accommodation to the new religious pluralism.

Yet, there are also signs of resistance. Whether it is a Moslem girl who wishes to wear the chador in a public school in Montreal, or whether it is a Sikh who wishes to wear the turban rather than the traditional RCMP headgear, you can be sure that religious practices that are different from what we are used to in Canada will generate controversy, get plenty of media coverage and, occasionally, become the focus of battles in the courts. Whenever we debate immigration policy in this country, religious and racial matters are not far below the surface. It is not always easy for people of different religious and cultural backgrounds to live together harmoniously.

Pluralism affects not just the larger society but also the church. Pluralism suddenly transforms passages such as today's lesson from the Gospel of John into difficult reading. I used to serve in a small town in southern Manitoba. There, where Christianity was the only faith represented, I could easily preach this passage simply as instruction about who Christ is. But here, in the city, where I may well be sharing my bus seat with a Moslem, where I drive past a Hindu centre on my way to work, where I serve a congregation in which many members have long-standing friendships with people from the Jewish community—here I find that the hard edges of the passage come into stark relief. In a few compact verses, Jesus is uncompromisingly presented as the Son of God, the vehicle of God's Holy Spirit, the pre-existent one, and the Lamb of God who takes away the sin of the whole world. Against the background of pluralism it is possible to see this passage less as innocent instruction and more as an assault on the claims of other faiths. The implication for the reader is straightforward: if this gospel is right, then many are wrong.

In our increasingly multi-faith society, what are we to do

with such an exclusivist witness to Jesus? Does holding fast to such universalistic statements about Christ deny the truth in other expressions of faith? Does it foster attitudes that lead to hostility between religious groups? And does pluralism demand that we somehow begin to see passages such as today's gospel with different eyes?

There is no doubt that many factors are pushing us towards a reinterpretation of the gospel. The prevailing mood in the church is one of tolerance and compromise, of acceptance and mutual recognition. We want to avoid the appearance that we alone have the right answers, particularly in something as personally important as faith. We know that people who hold other beliefs or profess no belief can be as sincere, earnest, and good as any Christian. So we do not want to say that they cannot find fulfilment without following the way of Jesus.

Moreover, we have long since left behind the days when we ignorantly dismissed other world religions as heathen faiths. We know now that these faiths have long and noble histories, substantial accomplishments, and learned theologies. We know that they are not primitive but highly developed. We would find it hard these days to sing Rudyard Kipling's words about "lesser breeds without the law."[1] Many in the church have come to the view that the claims of Christ must be modified and other religions acknowledged as equally true for their own adherents.

A colleague of mine once stated the issue this way in an article in *The United Church Observer:* "Can we who are Christians be both loyal to Jesus Christ and at the same time open to the religious experience of people who name other saviors?"[2] His answer is yes, and he says in defence of his argument that the kind of "one and only" talk about Jesus that we find in today's lesson is really "love talk"—language that the early Christians

---

1. From the hymn "God of Our Fathers, Known of Old."

2. Peter Wyatt, "Jesus the good, but not only, shepherd," *The United Church Observer,* August 1986, p. 41. At this point in the article, Rev. Wyatt is referring to Paul F. Knitter's book, *No Other Name? A Critical Survey of Christian Attitudes toward the World Religions* (Maryknoll, N.Y.: Orbis Books, 1985).

used to express their feelings about Jesus, and which was never intended to exclude people of other faiths who could not make such a confession about Jesus. He argues that we should adopt the same approach and avoid making any claims about Jesus' superiority over other religious figures, saviours, prophets, and thinkers.

Such a reinterpretation of the thrust of the gospel accommodates us well to the pluralism of our age. But there is a big problem with it. It seems to be based on the notion that a pluralistic environment is a new factor for Christians and was not present when the gospels were written. This is simply not true. In fact, the writer who chose to include in his gospel these statements of John the Baptist was living not only in a pluralistic world but one in which Christianity was locked in a decisive struggle with a rival faith. And his words were penned against a backdrop of controversy and contention.

The fourth gospel was written for a community that experienced the sharp pull of the church on the one hand and the synagogue on the other. It was not a situation in which, with everybody being essentially like-minded, the writer felt that he could witness to Christ in the highest terms without causing any controversy or upset. Rather it was a situation in which, because people were *not* like-minded, he felt compelled to render this witness to Christ. For him good relations were less important than holding up Christ in all his fullness to the world. Therefore, to interpret this passage as if what is said in it is true only for Christians and is not meant to be heard or to cause offence beyond the boundaries of the church would be thoroughly to pervert the intention of the gospel writer.

He took pluralism as a mandate not for softening but for sharpening the Christian witness to the world. What would cause this writer to be so unaccommodating? Simply this: he believed that God had made a choice. It started with the choice of Israel to be God's people amongst all the peoples of the world. This patronage was not capriciously given or extended because God is a God who has favourites. The choice was arbitrary, it is true, but it was made for a purpose. To Israel God said, "I will give you as a light to the nations, that my salvation may reach to the end of the earth" (Isaiah 49:6). So the choice of Israel was made to accomplish a plan by which God intended to benefit all humankind.

The gospel writer believed that, when the time was right, God had further chosen one from Israel, in whom he would dwell fully, on whom his Spirit would descend and remain, in whom would finally be fulfilled the mission given to the chosen race. God chooses first a people, then a person, to be the instrument of his purpose with the creation.

Because God has made a choice, because his salvation resides in Christ and not in another, or others, the potential is there for those who are outside the immediate circle of this Christ to take offence. If the Christian gospel has the potential to offend, it ought to be at this point and no other. And we, to whom this gospel is entrusted, ought to do nothing, for the sake of quick and superficial harmony, to remove this offence. For the exclusiveness is not ours but God's. God has chosen to manifest his love for the world in a particular person and to begin the healing of the world through a particular means. If we believe this to be true—if we believe he has chosen to dwell in Christ and to save the world through Christ—how could we let the demands of pluralism silence us on this point? John the Baptist did not. John the gospel writer did not. We must not. For what good would we be if we were to give up the witness that called us into being as the church in the first place? Just as in the gospel writer's world, the growing pluralism in our world mandates a sharing rather than a subduing of what we believe about Christ.

If we take this point of view and act accordingly, does it mean that there are no accommodations to be made to the folk of other faiths with whom we share this country? Certainly not. There is a great deal of accommodating to do to manifest our good will for those seekers who do not see things our way.

Consider this: While John's gospel was conceived and brought forth in a society that, like ours, was pluralistic, there is one significant difference between our world and his that would demand change on our part if our relationship to other faiths were to parallel that of the early church's to the non-Christian world.

In those days the bearers of the witness to Christ were relatively powerless in society. Today, they are powerful. In the last two or three centuries, during which the church has experienced great expansion and Christianity has become a world religion—indeed, the biggest world religion—its witnesses and missionaries and evangelists have spoken out of a position of strength and dominance. One has to wonder whether it is the witness to Christ that has triumphed or the commercial and technical superiority of Western culture. And in our own nation, now considered pluralistic, Christianity is nevertheless still the majority and a most influential faith.

What a contrast this is with the world of John the Baptist. John spoke not from within the elite of the nation but from a position of relative insignificance. He was an itinerant preacher, a travelling prophet, functioning well outside the circles of power. His witness to Jesus was uncompromising and exalted, but he had nothing in himself with which to enforce people's acceptance of it. Those who were looking for the Christ, the Messiah, the Son of God, might be directed to Jesus by the force of the Baptist's preaching and the clarity of his message. But those who were not looking were free to pay no attention. And they didn't, for John the Baptist was a nobody.

What a contrast also with the world of John the evangelist. He wrote and addressed his gospel to a society in which the Jewish synagogue was far more powerful than the Christian church. People were free to regard his work as pretentious nonsense from an unknown hack. And most did, except some who were searching, yearning.

And the one witnessed to, Jesus of Nazareth, had no power to compel. He came from such an obscure background that John twice says of him, "I myself did not know him" (John 1:31, 33). John did not know who he really was until he saw the Spirit descend upon him as a dove from heaven.

Everything about the setting of today's gospel lesson bespeaks minority and powerlessness. Reflect on this: John's gospel was not written until at least the first Christian generation had passed away. Surely, in that time, someone more influential than John the Baptist would have come forth to give testimony to Jesus Christ, someone who could compel attention, someone whose witness the evangelist would have been glad to highlight in his gospel. I'm sure that, after the first generation, there was such testimony to be had. But as if to say "The success of my gospel will depend not on the testimony of those with money, power, influence, worldly advantages, but on the strength of the witness itself," John the writer includes only the testimony of the first witness, John the Baptist, the one who had no power but the power of the word he preached, and nothing by which to compel except the compelling nature of the one to whom he pointed.

If there is guidance for us in the fact that this stirring witness to Christ is set in such modest surroundings, it is surely this: While we must not accommodate other faiths by softening our witness to Christ as God's chosen instrument of salvation, we must be prepared to accommodate other faiths on perhaps every other point. We must learn to give up that which is not essential to our witness. We must learn not to depend in any way on the strength of our numbers, our position in society, the vitality of our civilization, the power of our technology—on anything that is inessential to our proclamation.

If we can learn to do what the early Christians had no choice but to do—to testify from powerlessness rather than authority, to offer a witness cloaked in humility rather than hegemony—then, if there is any offence given in our proclamation, it will be not because the strong have dominated the weak but because God's choice of Christ and God's resolve to work through the Lamb will have cut to the heart of the hearer.

If we do not make accommodations in terms of influence and power in our pluralistic world, then any victories we win will not be for our Lord but for us, and will rest on the wrong foundation. However, if we shed those trappings—and no one shed them more completely than John the Baptist—then if we are successful it will only be because, through our witness, people have seen in Jesus of Nazareth the Lamb of God. We will have pointed to him, but it will be the Holy Spirit who has persuaded the people who he is.

In our pluralistic world, there are many things that we can give up for the sake of treating people of other faiths with dignity and respect, for surely, in the end, our interest is not in a Christianity triumphant over other religions. There is one thing we ought not to give up: this witness borne by the Baptist to Christ, for our one great interest is that everyone be granted an opportunity to come to know the one whom we are trying to come to know—the Lamb of God who takes away the sin of the world.

Transfiguration

The Glory of God in the Face of Christ

2 Corinthians 4:1-6; Matthew 17:1-9

And he was transfigured before them, and his face shone like the sun, and his clothes became dazzling white.
—Matthew 17:2

There is an uncompromising statement at the beginning of John's gospel that "No one has ever seen God" (John 1:18). Well, that seems to go without saying. Such a thing would be impossible. But I would like you to imagine for a moment that the impossible is possible. If someday you were to lay eyes upon the deity, if you were actually to see God, what would you do—aside from cowering or fleeing? What would you do after the encounter was over and you had managed to survive it? I'd speculate that you might do one of two things. You might keep it all to yourself and not breathe a word to anybody. After all, as no one else has ever seen God, people would most likely not believe that you had. The safest thing would be to say nothing. At least, that way, nobody would think you were delusional. On the other hand, you might proclaim your experience to everybody. You might just find it impossible to stop talking about something so marvellous and wonderful. Those would be your options. You might see God and keep quiet, or you might see God and become loquacious.

Today's gospel lesson features three followers of Jesus—Peter, James, and John—who came as close as anyone ever has to seeing God. Jesus drew them apart from the other disciples and the crowds, and together they climbed a high mountain. And while they were on the mountaintop, Jesus was transfigured; that is, his appearance was completely changed. The only way they could describe this strange happening was to say that his face shone like the sun and his clothes became dazzling white, as white as light. The three disciples knew, in that moment, that God was with Jesus, was doing this to Jesus, was somehow in Jesus. They knew that when they saw the face of Jesus shining like the sun, they were seeing the face of God.

When it was all over—and really, it was over in a moment—these three disciples did neither of the two things that I suggested you or I might do. They did not keep quiet about what had happened, at least not for long. After Jesus' crucifixion and resurrection, when they went about preaching in his name and calling on people to believe in him, they included this event in their stories of him. Peter once wrote about the transfiguration in a letter to some Christians,[1] and this occurrence became well enough known in the early church that Matthew, Mark, and Luke, when they came to write their gospels, all decided to incorporate it.

One would think that the disciples and gospel-writers would have kept quiet about it—this strange event that did not fit easily into the ministry that Jesus had conducted, this weird incident that many people might doubt had really happened and, doubting it, might doubt the truth of the whole gospel. They could well have kept quiet about it, for when they proclaimed Jesus it was "Jesus crucified and risen," not "Jesus transfigured." Believing in Jesus meant believing in his resurrection, not his transfiguration. So they might well have suppressed this

1. 2 Peter 1:16-18.

event. Why not keep it to themselves as their own private and personal experience? After all, Jesus had taken them aside from the others. He had deliberately not shown himself this way to anyone else. And besides, the story does not flatter the disciples. They clearly have difficulty figuring out what this all means. Peter starts to make a suggestion only to be cut off by the voice of God. And our picture of them is of three men lying flat on their faces in fear.

Yet, despite all the incentives to the contrary, these men did not believe they had a right to keep silent about the transfiguration. They came to see it as an event that had something to say about the faith, and so they felt compelled to talk about it after Jesus was raised from the dead.

But neither did they do the other thing I said we might do. They did not go on and on about their mountaintop experience. They recounted the event sparingly and gave few details. This seems strange. If they were going to talk about it, why not build it up and make something of it? Why not give a full analysis of the sound of God's voice? Why not give us descriptions of Moses and Elijah? Why not tell us what was going through their own minds as they witnessed the dazzling light?

When they went out to proclaim Christ, why did they not make the miraculous transfiguration the centrepiece of their preaching? That they did not do this is clear, for when Matthew sat down to record the witness of the disciples to Jesus, he gave the central place to the cross and a lesser place to the transfiguration. Moreover, there is not one word in his gospel about how Peter, James, and John felt, about what this experience did for them or to them. In fact, there is not one word about what the transfiguration means, neither here nor in any of the books of the New Testament—though there is plenty of discussion about the meaning of the cross.

One would expect Matthew to give prominence to this event on the mountaintop, this spectacle that reveals Jesus not just as a person close to God but a person from God. One would expect Matthew to construct his gospel so that it builds to the transfiguration as a marvellous climax. But, oddly, he does not do this. Rather, it is the crucifixion towards which his story moves. No doubt Matthew was just being true to the apostolic witness. If Peter, James, and John were reticent about this event and would speak only sparingly of it, that is what he would have to do. And sparing he is. The transfiguration is barely a blip in his gospel, unaccounted for, unexplained; it is just there.

Seeing God in the shining face of Christ is something, therefore, that requires mentioning, but demands not to be blown out of proportion. It is a story that must be told, for it has something to teach us, but it must be told in a low-key way so that we will not mistake it for the high point of the gospel. The gospel does not culminate in the transfiguration but in that event upon which the transfiguration is a commentary, namely, the crucifixion. For like every other incident in the gospels, the transfiguration is there to tell us something about the cross.

In an encounter that immediately precedes the transfiguration in Matthew's gospel, Peter makes a confession of faith in Jesus. He sums up everything he has experienced in this person he has chosen to follow, and he says, "You are the Messiah, the Son of the living God" (Matthew 16:16). Jesus responds by indicating that the Messiah must go to Jerusalem and suffer at the hands of the religious leaders and be killed. Peter is scandalized: "God forbid it, Lord! This must never happen to you" (16:22).

Peter's alarm demonstrates admirable loyalty but also a fundamental misperception of the Messiah's mission. To show where God stands on this matter, Jesus takes Peter and the other members of the inner circle up the mountain, and there the glory of God shines from him. And what does he discuss with them as they descend afterwards to the plain? Does he discuss what it felt like to be transformed into a blaze of glory? No. What he discusses is his impending death. And no sooner do they rejoin the other disciples than Jesus is at it again, talking of how he is to be delivered into the hands of men who will kill him. So the transfiguration is surrounded by predictions of his passion.

Now, Peter could not understand a saviour who would suffer. He could not see how the Messiah—God's anointed one—could allow himself to be so treated. But here, on the mountain, God puts God's seal on the saviour who is to suffer. God's glory shines in the face of Jesus at the very moment the end of Jesus is being made clear. What Peter learns from this, and what Matthew must intend us to see, is that a suffering saviour is not foreign to God but within the plan of God, that this is not an accident but a design and, moreover, that in some sense God is the one who comes down from the mountain and sets his face towards Jerusalem—that, indeed, it is in some sense God who winds up on the cross.

On the mountaintop, the glory of God shone in the face of Christ and in his garments. But these garments—are they not the same ones Jesus removed to wash the feet of his disciples? Is the glory of God not to be found in this act of servanthood? And are they not the very garments over which the soldiers gambled at the foot of the cross? Is the glory of God not present at that horrific moment?

And this face that shone like the sun—is this not the same face that was kissed by Judas when he betrayed Jesus and avoided by Peter when he denied him? Is this not the face that was spat upon and struck and slapped during the mock hearing in front of the scribes and elders, the face that was jeered at by the crowd who shouted, "Let him be crucified!" (Matthew 27:22)? Is this not the face that was streaked with blood drawn by a crown of thorns, the face derided by those who snapped, "If you are the Son of God, come down from the cross" (Matthew 27:40)? Is it not the face that was smothered with a vinegar-filled sponge? Is it not the same face that we see disfigured in pain, abandonment, and death?

The glory of God shines not just in the *transfigured* face of Christ, but in the *disfigured* face of Christ—the face that bore the pain and anguish and sin and woe of the world. For the face that shone on the mountain is the face we see on the cross. And the God who was there on the mountain is the God who was there on the cross.

This is not a God who stands aside from the trouble and cruelty of the world, a God who is absent while a crescendo of rejection builds against his Christ, who lifts not a finger while the anointed one is scandalously and unjustly put to death, and who, at some later point, rides to the rescue in the resurrection. This is the God who was there all along: the God who was on the mountaintop, but came down from the mountain, and walked the road to the cross, and advanced to the pain and sacrifice.

This is a hard thing both to comprehend and to accept. Certainly, Jesus did not expect immediate understanding and acceptance from his disciples, for as Matthew tells it, he commanded them, "Tell no one about the vision until after the Son of Man has been raised from the dead" (Matthew 17:9). You can see why. If Peter could not understand that the Christ must suffer, that would be even harder for him to accept after he had seen Christ transfigured with God's glory. Perhaps only from beyond the cross, from the perspective of the resurrection, would he be able to accept that the transfiguration by itself was not important. Its importance lay in the fact that the one who was transfigured bore the disfigurement of the cross.

The challenge here is not only for the disciples who were witnesses that day—and who gave every sign of wanting to stay up on the mountain—but for us, who have so often persuaded ourselves that where God is really to be found is in the sublime experience of the mountaintop, away from the press and pain of life; that God is found in those special moments when we are able to rise above everything and the light shines with dazzling brightness; that God is found when we can escape from the world that wearies us and wears us down.

The challenging truth is that we do not need to go up the mountain to find God. God comes down the mountain to find us, to find us through Jesus Christ, the one who meets us in our needs, who strengthens us against our weakness, who binds our brokenness, who comforts our sorrows, who shares our grief, who heals our diseases, and who, in the end, dies for our sin.

Peter, James, and John have gone up the mountain for us, and what they have to report is that the glory of God is only rarely on the mountain; it is regularly down amongst us. They are not anxious that we share their experience of the shining face and dazzling garments, of the bright cloud, and of the voice of God. But they are insistent that we need to come to terms, as they did, with the cross. For the person they proclaim to us is not the Christ of the mount but the Christ of the cross.

On the mountain of transfiguration, these apostles glimpsed the glory of God; they saw in whom the glory resided. But only at the mountain of Calvary did they see God's glory in its fullness, in the ultimate of love and sacrifice. It is there that they saw, and we may truly see, the glory of God in the face of Jesus Christ.

Lent

The Fox and the Hen

Luke 13:31-35

"Jerusalem, Jerusalem, the city that kills the prophets and stones those who are sent to it! How often have I desired to gather your children together as a hen gathers her brood under her wings, and you were not willing!"

—Luke 13:34

I IMAGINE THERE CANNOT BE MANY THINGS MORE DISTRESSING THAN receiving a death threat, particularly when the threat is related to something very major in your life such as your vocation or a cause for which you are standing. There cannot be many things more alarming and upsetting than being put in danger for speaking the truth as you see it, for standing up for what you believe is right, for fulfilling some mission to which you feel called.

The author Salman Rushdie recently gave a television interview in connection with a just-published book. Seeing him brought back for me vivid memories of the time he received a death threat, the time he was placed under a sentence of death by the Ayatollah Khomeini of Iran for writing his book *The Satanic Verses*. Imagine what it must have been like for Mr. Rushdie when that blow fell. The phone in his apartment rings. It is the author's publisher on the line: "Salman, have you heard any news broadcasts this morning? No? Well, I'm afraid I've got some very distressing news. The Ayatollah Khomeini has pronounced a fatwa against you. The claim is that *The Satanic Verses* blasphemes Islam. There are also threats against us if we don't remove all copies from circulation. Salman, I don't think it would be wise to shrug this off. We'll need to be in touch with the police and the Home Office right away." Can you imagine the rest of Mr. Rushdie's day? Reaching a trembling hand to the radio, turning it on to find that the phone call just concluded was not a dream, hearing the execution order pronounced against him, hearing the amount of the bounty on his head rising with each successive broadcast, and then listening to reports of assassination squads on their way from Iran to England to perform the bloody task.

Rushdie had little choice but to go into hiding. For years he was required to live in secret, a virtual prisoner of the security forces assigned to protect him. Even now, with Khomeini long gone, the sentence of death withdrawn by the Iranian authorities, and the ability to travel in public restored, he must wonder if someday he will encounter a fanatic determined belatedly to carry out the order. Life will really never be normal for him again. I would not have blamed Rushdie had he asked himself whether his book, as important as it was to him, and as true as he believed it to be, was really worth dying for. To carry on year after year under the threat of death without recanting is to display an impressive level of commitment. I do not know that I could have done it.

As you cast your mind over world affairs, you may be able to think of some who have carried on in dangerous circumstances. Martin Luther King, Jr., springs to my mind. Battling against great resistance in the cause of civil rights for African Americans; knowing that many of the powerful people ranged against him were murderous, wanting to see him dead; living under the constant threat of the assassin's bullet; but never giving up the struggle. Surely, for such a person as King, if dwelling daily with danger could not make him abandon his cause, then nothing could. For what could be worse than the threat of death?

I can think of something. What could be worse is the threat of death coupled with the failure of the mission you are dying for. What could be worse is risking life only to be rejected by the people you set out to help. If King had not been able to generate a groundswell of support and enthusiasm among the black community for the cause of civil rights, then could you imagine him laying his life on the line for the cause? What would have been the point? No, it was the tremendous vigour and breadth of the movement he led that made the risk worth taking.

Similarly, for Mr. Rushdie, I do not know whether he will feel able ever again to write a critique of the way Islam has sometimes been practised. But I could not imagine him continuing to take risks unless he felt that there is an ear open to him at least somewhere in the Islamic world. For a while a person can live with the threat of death; for a while a person can live with the pain of rejection; but surely a person cannot live with both. Surely not.

Not unless that person is Jesus of Nazareth. As St. Luke tells us, Jesus endured—at the same time—the danger of death at the hands of his enemies and the anguish of rejection by those for whom he took this risk.

At the beginning of our story, Jesus is being advised to get out of Galilee because King Herod wants to kill him. Herod governed that province, and every time some public figure got too prominent and popular, Herod got nervous. He feared an undermining of his power. And so, like a crafty and destructive fox, he would strike. Murder was no concern. He had already arranged the death of John the Baptist. Now it was getting to be time to put Jesus out of the way.

Jesus has a reaction to Herod's threat: "Go and tell that fox for me, 'Listen, I am casting out demons and performing cures today and tomorrow, and on the third day I finish my work'" (13:32). In other words, "Herod, I'm not afraid of you. I'm going to complete the work I have set for myself in Galilee."

But Jesus goes on to say, "Yet today, tomorrow, and the next day I must be on my way, because it is impossible for a prophet to be killed outside of Jerusalem" (13:33). In other words, "Herod, I take your threat seriously enough to be careful, not because I fear dying at your hands, but because, if I must die, it must be as a prophet, and the place for a prophet to die is at Jerusalem."

Jesus saw himself as one of a long line of prophets sent by God to his chosen people of Israel. Because Jerusalem was the centre of Israel's religious life, when a prophet was ready to make his appeal he did it in Jerusalem. So, if Jesus gave Herod a wide berth, it was not out of fear for himself but out of concern that he live long enough to fulfil his mission.

Now, it is when Jesus turns his thoughts to Jerusalem that the real weight of the burden upon him becomes apparent. For he does not anticipate a warm welcome in that city. He expects that his offer of God's grace will not be accepted. He remembers what happened to the prophets who went before him: they were resisted, opposed, harassed, and many of them were killed. He thinks back to the reaction his own ministry has aroused thus far: opposition in his home town, conflict with the Pharisees, the enmity of Herod. And he does not expect to fare any better in Jerusalem.

That raises the question "Why carry on?" If he had felt that, despite the danger, there was an opportunity for Jerusalem to be a triumph, you could see him taking such a course. But he anticipates rejection at Jerusalem. Why stick with such a dangerous mission when success does not seem to be in the cards? Is this not the time for Jesus to cut his losses and go back to the carpenter's shop? Why go on?

I believe it is love that impelled Jesus forward. Jesus, the Son of God, is the revealer of God, and here he is revealing God as the energetic, untiring lover and wooer of his beloved. This is the God who, even though his prophets have been killed and his messengers have been stoned, never stops loving his people.

It is the prophet Hosea who heard God say,

> When Israel was a child, I loved him, and out of Egypt I called my son. The more I called them, the more they went from me; they kept sacrificing to the Baals, and offering incense to idols. Yet it was I who taught Ephraim to walk, I took them up in my arms; but they did not know that I healed them. I led them with cords of human kindness, with bands of love. I was to them like those who lift infants to their cheeks. I bent down to them and fed them.... How can I give you up, Ephraim? How can I hand you over, O Israel? (Hosea 11:1-4, 8)

This God has reached out in love so many times, has tried to reach his people in so many ways, has suffered rejection so often. Yet, he must try once again, through his Son.

In our story, Jesus reacts to Herod's threat with some indignation, but Herod is not really able to get under his skin. At worst, he is an irritant. But Jesus' reaction to the refusal of his people is something else again—something we were not prepared for. It is a woeful lament, a wail of grief: "Jerusalem, Jerusalem ...! How often have I desired to gather your children together as a hen gathers her brood under her wings ...!" (13:34). What kind of song is this? This is a love song—God's love song, Jesus' love song to his people. But the love is scorned, spurned: "How often have I desired to gather your children ... and you were not willing!" When the love is spurned, what can a love song become but a lament?

How vulnerable God makes himself. Nobody should be that exposed. Quite unlike Herod, the fox, who can resort to violence, to abusive power, Jesus, the hen, can operate only by the appeal of love. And when the love is rejected, what can it lead to except a broken heart that pours out its pain in lament?

If you and I were to reach out to someone in love and then find ourselves rebuffed, what would we do? We would find it so easy to draw back, pull in our horns, resolve that we are never going to risk like that again. But what does God do? He keeps sending one prophet after another, one messenger after another, finally his own Son. He keeps reaching out his arms to those who shun his embrace. Oh the pain. Oh the pain in the heart of God.

I find there is one question I must ask myself about this lament. You may want to ask it of yourselves. Where do I stand in relation to it? Am I a singer of this song, with Jesus, or am I one for whom this lament is sung? Do I share with Jesus in his grief over those who continue to rebuff him and, with him, the offer of God's grace? Or am I one of those who have caused Jesus this anguish?

Popular Christian thought invites me to think of myself as a singer of this song, one who shares Jesus' grief over wayward Jerusalem. After all, I am a Christian. I have not killed any prophets or stoned anyone sent with a message from God. I am on Jesus' side. This was vividly illustrated for me a few years back when Linda and I had an opportunity to attend the Black Hills Passion Play in Spearfish, South Dakota. The Passion Play is, of course, the story of the last week of Jesus' life which is played out in and around Jerusalem. If you are ever in the Black Hills, you really must see the passion as it is performed by the people of Spearfish. It is a great spectacle, and I could tell that for many in the audience it was a moving spiritual experience.

But I had this concern: The way the play was staged, the audience was more or less given the role of judge and jury over the people of Jerusalem. We weren't allowed to overlook the selfishness of the priests and the shortsightedness of the crowds. The playwright's objective was clearly to bring the audience to the point where, by the time Jesus was led away to Calvary, we would be thinking, "You stupid people. How could you do this to this man? O Jerusalem, Jerusalem, killing the prophets and stoning those who are sent to you!" The playwright wanted to make us singers of the lament.

I went away wondering if the passion might have been done differently, if the playwright might have invited us up onto the stage to take our place among the people of Jerusalem. I wondered if, instead of giving us caricatures of the high priests, he might have shown us men of integrity trying to preserve the historic faith of Israel against this man who was turning everything upside down. I wondered if he might have allowed the crowd to appear a little more intelligent. In the play as we saw it, when it came time for Pilate to ask the crowd whether Jesus or Barabbas should be released to them, Jesus stood regally beside the Roman governor, clad in an impeccable white robe, every hair in place, perfectly composed, while Barabbas, half man, half beast, with a hairpiece that looked like a floor mop, cowered in the corner. And the crowd chose Barabbas. It was unbelievable.

What the playwright should have shown us is what really must have happened. We should have seen a roughed-up Jesus, bowed and beaten from a night of scourging, his robe ripped almost to shreds, his legs barely able to hold him up. We should have seen a Rambo-like Barabbas, strutting before the crowd, flexing his muscles and sneering insolently at his guards. After all, Barabbas was in prison for committing murder during an insurrection, and nobody had yet laid a finger on him. We should have seen Jesus as the bloodied, helpless hen and Barabbas as the predatory fox. And perhaps, then, we would have understood why the people of Jerusalem might have reasoned that a fox could do more for them than a hen, that a fox like Barabbas could offer a real challenge to foxes like Herod and Pilate. And perhaps we might have imagined that the crowd was right in its assessment of Jesus, and that we might have scorned him, too. And so, we would have become ones for whom the lament is sung.

"Jerusalem, Jerusalem, the city that kills the prophets and stones those who are sent to it! How often have I desired to gather your children together as a hen gathers her brood under her wings, and you were not willing!"

As a Christian believer who struggles to accept Christ and his way, I want to think of myself as a singer of this love song, this lament over Jerusalem. I want to believe that it is others who have rebuffed Christ and caused him great sorrow. I want to locate myself with those children who are nestled under the wings of the hen.

But, every once in a while, something happens to shake my confidence that this is the way things are. I well remember the day that Salman Rushdie's life was threatened. I was sitting at my kitchen table, having my first cup of coffee of the day, when I heard the radio report that the Ayatollah had sentenced Rushdie to death. And when I heard that, I just banged my fist on the table and shouted to the empty room, "Why doesn't somebody kill that Khomeini?"

I guess that reaction tells me I'm still much more likely to run with the foxes than to seek shelter under the hen's wing. And so the lament continues to be sung for me—maybe sometimes for you. But, I draw comfort from this: So long as the lament is still being sung, it means that God is still reaching out in his love and through his pain—to me and to you.

Palm Sunday

Demonstrating Disciples and Singing Stones

Luke 19:29-40

As he was now approaching the path down from the Mount of Olives, the whole multitude of the disciples began to praise God joyfully with a loud voice for all the deeds of power that they had seen, saying, "Blessed is the king who comes in the name of the Lord! Peace in heaven, and glory in the highest heaven!" Some of the Pharisees in the crowd said to him, "Teacher, order your disciples to stop." He answered, "I tell you, if these were silent, the stones would shout out."

—Luke 19:37-40

It is Palm Sunday. On this day Christians seek to capture in their worship something of the excitement, enthusiasm, and electricity that marked Jesus of Nazareth's attention-grabbing entrance into Jerusalem that first Palm Sunday commencing the most turbulent and fateful week of his life. To that end, our church, like many others, begins the service with a procession. The choir tours the sanctuary singing festive hymns, and the children follow, enthusiastically waving their palm branches.

Palm Sunday provides a ready-made opportunity for children to participate physically in the church's worship. It gives them permission to move about and make some noise when so often they are required to keep still and be quiet. Our Palm Sunday hymns mandate the children's involvement. Listen to some of their lines:

> All glory, laud and honour to you, Redeemer, King,
> to whom the lips of children made sweet hosannas ring.
> ("All Glory, Laud, and Honour")

> Into the city I'd follow the children's band,
> waving a branch of the palm tree high in my hand;
> one of his heralds, yes, I would sing
> loudest hosannas! Jesus is king!
> ("Tell Me the Stories of Jesus")

> Hosanna, loud hosanna the happy children sang;
> through pillared court and temple the joyful anthem rang;
> . . . the Lord of earth and heaven rode on in lowly state,
> content that little children should on his bidding wait.
> ("Hosanna, Loud Hosanna")

> The glory of our king was seen
> when he came riding by,
> and all the children waved and sang,
> "Hosanna, King most high!"
> ("The Glory of Our King")

I think these hymns have got it partly right. Children would certainly have been part of this great event. They had been special to Jesus during his ministry. Parents had often brought their children to him for a blessing. And it is only natural to assume that those who had come with their families to Jerusalem for the Passover would bring their young ones out to see Jesus' colourful arrival at the city gates. Certainly, the children wouldn't have settled for anything less. They wouldn't have stood quietly by and missed a parade.

When I imagine myself in Jerusalem that day, the first picture that develops is of my son tugging at my sleeve and imploring me, "Daddy, Daddy, let's go see what's happening." The next picture I get is of him insisting that I cut down a palm branch so he can have one of his own to wave. And the final picture is of him picking up the chant that is filling the air: "Blessed is the king who comes . . . blessed is the king who comes . . . blessed is the king who comes." Children pick up things so quickly.

So I think the Palm Sunday hymns have got it partly right. But a number of them have also got it partly wrong. These are the ones that leave adults out of the picture. And, just so, perhaps we are getting it partly wrong in church when we don't ask you adults to come out of the pews and join the liturgical procession and we don't give you your own palm branches to wave. If we rely solely on our hymns to paint the picture of this day, what we are likely to see is Jesus riding into the city surrounded by a band of exuberant, carefree children who are making a lot of noise and creating quite a commotion. But, if we take a look at any of the four gospel accounts, we get a different picture.

Today, we are reading Luke's version. In it, we find that it is Jesus' own disciples who spread their garments on the road in front of him. We find that it is a larger group of followers—again presumably adults, for they, too, are called disciples—who raise their voices in those chants and acclamations that we have come to associate with Jesus' triumphal entry. Yes, children would have joined in, but how could they have been initiators? Whose child would have been advanced enough in the study of the scriptures to select from the psalms and the prophets appropriate texts to shout as Jesus passes? "Blessed is the king who comes in the name of the Lord! Peace in heaven, and glory in the highest heaven!" Whose child would have come up with this?

Really, the evidence of scripture is that the first Palm Sunday, at least, was very much an adult affair. You can take this even deeper. What we have in this Palm Sunday procession is not a spontaneous gathering of a crowd around Jesus—in which case it might be possible to see children in a primary role. What we have here is a well-orchestrated demonstration. Jesus has no plans to walk quietly into the city. He intends to announce his coming. With a mind to how the Old Testament prophecies image the coming of the king, he has already made prior arrangements for the use of the colt of an ass. The disciples are ready to do their part to enhance the royal imagery by laying down their garments in front of the beast. The large group of supporters is primed with the chants they will use. And, like any demonstration, this one has the potential for growth. As the crowd milling about becomes aware of the approaching commotion, many of its number will join in and lend their "hosannas" to those of Jesus' supporters.

These are the dynamics of this event. Unquestionably, some of what happens is spontaneous—people getting caught up in the passion of the moment. But any spontaneity is made possible by what is planned; it is the servant of what has already been orchestrated. What is taking place at the beginning of this fateful week is something that is quite purposeful and something that you and I are clearly meant to take note of and to be involved in.

It is Jesus who has put together this demonstration. To what purpose? One answer that has traditionally been given, and is certainly correct as far as it goes, is that it is to make a public statement about who he is. It is to proclaim his kingship, and to make clear the nature of his kingship. Thus, we see Jesus choosing to ride into Jerusalem on a donkey rather than on a stallion, signifying to those who know their scriptures that he comes as a king of peace and not a warrior king. Palm Sunday is thus the occasion on which Jesus finally declares who he is.

If we leave things there, we might well conclude that Jesus has arranged this happening primarily for his own sake and that the disciples and other followers are merely bit players acting out their parts. But there is more going on here. And that is hinted at in a fascinating verse in which Jesus implies that his followers are more than a supporting cast.

Remember how the Pharisees become indignant when Jesus is acclaimed the king who comes in the name of the Lord. How dare Jesus allow himself to be spoken of in such terms, to be so closely identified with God! The language of "glory in the highest" is to be reserved for Almighty God and not bandied about for some itinerant preacher come to town.

So the Pharisees tell Jesus to rebuke his disciples, to make them shut up. And he responds, "I tell you, if these were silent, the stones would shout out." "If there were no demonstration today," Jesus is saying, "if my followers did not lift these cries to heaven, then the very stones on the ground and in the city wall and in the temple gate would raise the chorus. The stones would sing out because you cannot suppress the truth. My kingship does not depend on the demonstration of my disciples. Silence them, and the sound will still go out; the very creation will bear witness to me."

Whatever else is meant by this talk of the singing stones, Jesus is certainly indicating that *this Palm Sunday demonstration is not taking place because he needs it.* His kingship does not rest on the ability of his followers to sway the multitudes. That is why it is so pointless for the Pharisees to try to silence them. So what is happening? Since we do not have here a "political convention" kind of demonstration with the placard wavers trying to garner support for their candidate, since this demonstration is not to secure kingship but to proclaim it, and since Jesus would in no way have been any less a king had his disciples been mute and all the witnessing been left to the stones, why do it in the first place? Why demonstrate at all?

One possible answer is that *Jesus is doing this not for himself but for the sake of his disciples.* He is staging this demonstration not to persuade the general public but to give those already persuaded a chance to show their loyalty. Jesus encourages this adulation because he knows that every time his followers are asked to demonstrate their loyalty, it will be a test of that loyalty and an occasion for it to be deepened and strengthened. Jesus also knows what his followers need to learn—that the proclamation of his kingship is not something that can be done without consequences. They will encounter antagonism and resistance from the Pharisees today, but the sooner they learn to cope with antagonism and resistance the better, for there is worse to come.

I do not believe that Jesus harboured any great expectation that his disciples would stick by him in the toughest hours. Good Friday shows they did not. But he would have wanted his disciples to be able to remember a time when they encountered hostility and did stand behind him. Palm Sunday became such a time. When Easter came, they had to look back at Good Friday in shame. But they were able to look back at Palm Sunday with pride and think, "At least then we got it right." And this made them more determined than ever to keep getting it right.

So the disciples demonstrated on Palm Sunday. That word "demonstration" has a hard edge about it, not quite in keeping with what the church has generally made of this day. Perhaps we have grown accustomed to the image of a joyful procession that leaves everyone in a good humour. Or maybe we have been living with a picture of a happy parade with the crowds cheering as Jesus passes by. But, more than a procession and more than a parade, this was a demonstration, and, while there was cheering, the event was flavoured with the kind of controversy that is caused by any demonstration today.

Should we have expected otherwise? Jesus was always the subject of controversy. Why should this day have been any different?

When we begin to see that first Palm Sunday as a controversial and divisive rather than a harmonious and unifying experience, when we begin to imagine Jesus' entry into Jerusalem as a kind of first-century peace march, we might also begin to think about where to place ourselves in the picture. Would we position ourselves, perhaps, with the Pharisees? Do we find ourselves wishing that Jesus would ask his followers to pipe down? If only they would be quiet, we wouldn't have any conflict. The last thing we want to have among church people is conflict. Doesn't Jesus realize that letting his disciples go on shouting these slogans is going to stir things up and make life in this city pretty uncomfortable for the lot of us?

Or, would we position ourselves with the demonstrators? That is a hard thing to do. Most of us have never walked in a demonstration and waved a placard and chanted for the television cameras. We think most of the people who do are certainly not moderate individuals. We find it much more natural to shun the limelight and lead quiet lives, even if we feel strongly about an issue and admire those who are demonstrating for a cause. To demonstrate is to step out into exposed territory. It is to become marked. It is to be set apart. There could be repercussions for career, business, relationships, standing in the community. Most of us would make poor demonstrators, as we have long since learned to avoid standing out from the crowd.

Where do we position ourselves on Palm Sunday as Jesus rides into the city surrounded by his cheering band of supporters? Do we perhaps number ourselves among the spectators—sympathetic to Jesus, no doubt, yet wanting to keep a safe distance from him, not wanting to put ourselves on the line for him and his cause?

Perhaps we step back from those who wave the palms because we know what Jesus knows and they do not. We know how this is going to end. Do we reason that, if we join in the shouts of "Hail to the king" now, we will feel worse at the cries of "Crucify him" later? If we don't commit ourselves now, then there will be no danger of betraying him a few days hence.

Do we stand back from those who shout "Hosanna," thinking we can wait until Easter Sunday to declare our loyalty? But what does Easter do except say "yes" to the demonstration of Palm Sunday? What does it do but say "amen" to those who proclaimed his kingship on the first day of the week?

Palm Sunday tests where we stand in relation to Christ. *Do we want to "shout out" or "shut up"?* When I ask that, I am not referring to what happens here in church, where the atmosphere is supportive and there is no cost to praising Jesus. Of course, here, we will "shout out." But what about out in the world, where some are for him, and some are against him, and many are indifferent? Will you demonstrate out in the world, where there may be a cost? Will you affirm his lordship and seek to live under it out in the world where it may bring you into conflict with some and give offence to others?

Most Christians I know, myself included, would recoil at the thought of giving offence to others in matters of belief and faith. It is strange we should be so reluctant. Jesus was not. His Palm Sunday demonstration gave powerful offence—offence to people who mattered. But it mattered more to Jesus that his followers be empowered to speak the truth about him and to point to him as the one in whose way lay the fulfilment of God's promises.

For many years now, the church has succumbed to the temptation to turn Palm Sunday into a colourful but essentially harmless day for children. A more faithful use of the day would be to give *both* young and old palm branches to wave. Palm Sunday is a day for adults, too. It is a day on which Jesus calls us, as he called his first followers, to put things on the line. He does not want our private good will—which might melt away like snow in the spring at the first sign of trouble. He wants our public loyalty. He knows that every time we demonstrate our loyalty to him, we are deepening our commitment to him. And our commitment needs to be deep in order to weather the storms that will batter and erode it and to withstand the compromises and allurements that will make us want to forget it.

The call of Palm Sunday is to go into the world with a voice and a life that say, "Blessed is the king who comes in the name of the Lord! Peace in heaven, and glory in the highest heaven!" Now, if we are silent, if we will not demonstrate our loyalty to the Lord, all is not lost; the stones will still shout out. And this church's walls contain an impressive collection of them. But would it not be sad if only they were left to tell the truth about Christ?

EASTER

The Difference Easter Makes

Revelation 1:4-8

Grace to you and peace ... from Jesus Christ, the faithful witness, the firstborn of the dead, and the ruler of the kings of the earth.

—Revelation 1:4-5

EVERY YEAR AT THIS TIME WE OBSERVE THE EASTER SEASON, SEVEN Sundays of the church year to hear and reflect on the gospel accounts of the resurrection and the appearances and commands of the risen Christ. Does what we do in this season make any difference? In ourselves? In the world around us?

If these questions were the subject of a debate, I think I would find it easier to argue the negative than the affirmative. Surely, the great problem and disappointment with the resurrection is not so much that there are those who do not believe it but that, for so many of those who do believe it, it does not change anything. If this is what things have come to, if the resurrection is just history recalled to mind every March or April, if Easter is merely an anniversary duly observed, then the events of Easter might as well not have happened, at least for us.

If this is what things have come to, then we modern Christians are occupying very different territory from the first

Christians. For them, Easter made all the difference in the world. It never settled into being merely a liturgical observance or an official doctrine. It was the great event in the light of which they lived their whole lives. It spoke to them of the promises of God; it interpreted for them the meaning of life; it demanded of them a new way of living.

Today's text from the Book of Revelation is evidence of this reality. It was written many years after the first flush of the resurrection, after the apostles had got over their initial astonishment and wonder and disbelief, after the early church had had a chance to reflect on the remarkable events of Christ's rising and his appearances to his followers, and to ponder their meaning. Today's text represents the changes the people of God found in their lives, their world, and their way of seeing things after a generation of being Easter people. It represents the difference Easter made for them, and should make for us.

This text gives us three titles for Jesus. Each title is given in light of his resurrection. Each title implies something that has changed for Christians because of Easter.

The first title for Jesus is that of *faithful witness*. The resurrection is God's vindication of Jesus, God's confirmation that Jesus is the witness on whom we can rely. Jesus himself claimed to be a witness for God. After speaking of the nature of God and the demands of God, he claimed to be speaking of what he had known and bearing witness to what he had seen. When brought before Pilate he said, "For this I came into the world, to testify to the truth" (John 18:37). But how do we know that Jesus is to be accepted as a witness for God? How do we know he had first-hand knowledge of God and of God's will? Anyone could claim that.

For a time the matter was open to doubt. Even Jesus' disciples were not sure that he was God's faithful witness after he had been taken in hand by the authorities and placed on trial before Pilate. They abandoned him, and they do not strike me as the kind of people who would have abandoned someone they were persuaded was a faithful witness for God. Still, every indication was that the fishermen were going back to their boats, and the tax collector was going back to his office. It was the resurrection that changed that. The resurrection—God's great "yes" to the work of Christ—made them realize that Christ was indeed the faithful witness. And that, in turn, transformed them into faithful witnesses for Christ, witnesses who were so sure of God's confirmation of Christ's ministry that they themselves became willing to lay down their lives for him.

The resurrection does indeed make a difference as you look back on the ministry of Jesus, for it confirms in the most powerful way that what he said is true. The words of comfort are true:

> "Come to me, all you that are weary and are carrying heavy burdens, and I will give you rest" (Matthew 11:28);
> "Whoever comes to me will never be hungry, and whoever believes in me will never be thirsty" (John 6:35);
> "Ask, and it will be given you; search, and you will find; knock, and the door will be opened for you" (Matthew 7:7).

It is true. If Christ is indeed raised from the dead, there is absolutely no reason to hold back your life from him any longer, and there is every reason to turn to him and abide in him, and to receive the comfort and strength he offers.

The words of challenge are true:

> "If anyone forces you to go one mile, go also the second mile" (Matthew 5:41);
> "Love your enemies and pray for those who persecute you" (Matthew 5:44);
> "Do not store up for yourselves treasures on earth . . . but store up for yourselves treasures in heaven. . . . You cannot serve God and wealth" (Matthew 6:19-20, 24);
> "If any want to become my followers, let them deny themselves and take up their cross and follow me. For

> those who want to save their life will lose it, and those who lose their life for my sake, and for the sake of the gospel, will save it" (Mark 8:34-35).

Words that challenge conventional wisdom, words not easy to accept much less put into practice, but words that are true. It is not optional any longer to go the second mile or love your enemies or take up your cross. These are not suggestions that we are allowed to take or leave as we choose. For these words come to us not from just any teacher but from the one whom God raised from the dead and thereby vindicated as the faithful witness. That is the difference Easter makes.

The second title of Christ in this verse from Revelation is a more familiar one. He is *the firstborn of the dead.* The word "firstborn" implies that the resurrection of Christ is not the one and only resurrection but the first of many. In this title is contained the promise that, as Christ has been raised, so we will be raised.

In the time of Christ, the resurrection of the dead was a hope held by some, but by no means all, Jews. Jesus encouraged all who followed him to trust in that hope. The phrases that seem so familiar to us today were so startlingly new to his followers:

> "I go to prepare a place for you" (John 14:2);
> "Because I live, you also will live" (John 14:19);
> "Everyone who believes in him may not perish but may have eternal life" (John 3:16);
> "I am the resurrection and the life. Those who believe in me, even though they die, will live" (John 11:25).

Whether his followers really believed in this hope during his earthly ministry, they had no doubt of it after Christ's resurrection. His resurrection became a promise to them of their own.

The resurrection went on to become the unanimous claim of the New Testament. It permeates the letters of Peter and Paul. And it is vividly imaged in the Book of Revelation. St.

Paul points out quite candidly that this means that the Christian life is focussed as much on the next life as this one. He says this in a letter to fellow believers: "If for this life only we have hoped in Christ, we are of all people most to be pitied" (1 Corinthians 15:19). In other words, our hope in Christ is also a hope for the next life. The resurrection of Christ is, for us, God's great "yes," a "yes" that overcomes the times when the world says "no." It is an affirmation that all the doubts and difficulties, all the struggles and trials, all the pains and hurts this world can inflict upon us are not just capped off by death but overcome in victory.

Surely then the resurrection changes things. It changes the way we look at life. It frees us from attachment to or oppression by the world. The world of turmoil, the world that wearies us and wears us down, no longer has the final say. Any bad thing the world can do is undone by the great "yes" of the resurrection. Any pain or trial we must bear will not be the last thing we bear. The last, and eternal, thing we bear will be the easy yoke and light burden of Jesus Christ.

The resurrection of the dead frees us from the terrible tyranny that tells us that this world provides the only chance we will ever have to make it, to prove ourselves, to find peace and happiness. The resurrection of the dead frees us from conformity to the world so we can conform to Christ. There is a captivating phrase later in the Book of Revelation about those who have conquered evil on this earth and have taken their places with Christ in heaven. It says of them, "They did not cling to life even in the face of death" (12:11). Even the thought of persecution and martyrdom could not drive them away from faithfulness to Christ, for the promise of the resurrection meant they could safely put Christ ahead of the world. They did not cling to their earthly lives because they knew they already possessed an eternal life.

If the resurrection of Christ, the firstborn of the dead, and thereby the guarantor of our resurrection, cannot take the pressure off our lives, then nothing can. But if we truly believe, then the resurrection cannot fail to change things for us and to help us overcome the world. That is another difference Easter makes.

The third title for Christ we encounter today is *the ruler of the kings of the earth*. Now, our initial reaction to this may be "Well, it's not really working out that way, is it?" But wait. If Christ is raised, then all the power relationships of this world are changed. If Christ is raised, then the power that raised him is vaster than that which any earthly authority can command. If Christ is raised from the dead, then his reign will endure long past that of earthly rulers, whose power dies with them and sometimes does not even endure to their deaths.

If Christ is raised from the dead, there is no doubt where our loyalties must be. The religious authorities had power. Pontius Pilate had power. Between them, they used their power to put Jesus to death. An impressive demonstration. A reminder to us all of the way the world works. The disciples took the hint and scattered to the winds. But then came the resurrection, an even more impressive demonstration. It tells us there is no longer any excuse to scatter. Ultimate power is in the hands of God and he has bestowed it upon Jesus Christ. Christ is the ruler of the kings on earth.

Now, kings, queens, princes, potentates, dictators, ayatollahs, presidents, and prime ministers do not always recognize who is ruler over them. They do not always act as though one day they will have to account to Jesus Christ for the way they have exercised their power. Those in authority—not just political but any kind of authority over others—have often made the kind of absolute claims over those under them that can rightfully be made only by Christ. Christians need to be alert for this, for their faith tells them that no earthly authority is absolute—only the authority of Christ, the one authority that is unfailingly exercised in love. The kings on earth may not now recognize Christ as their ruler. One day they will have no choice. The resurrection tells us that for sure.

Christians, who have seen how the resurrection has changed all relationships, will not be so blind as the kings on earth. They will recognize Christ as ruler and give him unswerving loyalty. Or will they? Will we? Is such a commitment to Christ a cornerstone of our lives, or is something holding us back from making it? If we are reluctant, perhaps it is because we do not believe the resurrection all that deeply. Perhaps, when all is said and done, we still take the state, or the market, or the world of high technology, a hundred times more seriously than we take God. The authority of earthly rulers and powers is a hundred times more real to us than the authority of the risen Christ.

If that is the case, we are brought back to where we started. An Easter season that merely observes an event in the distant past is one thing. That kind of Easter does not change a thing. It has no effect on the nightly newscast or Saturday paper. But Easter as a proclamation and reception of Christ as the faithful witness, the firstborn of the dead, and the ruler of the kings of the earth is quite another thing. That kind of Easter makes a difference.

Are we prepared to let Easter make a difference? To do that we must go beyond giving a casual nod of belief at the resurrection and get right down to hearing its implications for our lives and our world. We need to begin believing in the resurrection with all our hearts, as an event that can transform our lives today.

If you want to believe with all your heart, begin by asking Jesus Christ to come into your heart. After all, he is the risen Lord. Through the Holy Spirit, he can do this. But before you take the step, remember that it is a risky, unsettling business. It will change everything for you.

For indeed, if Christ is raised from the dead, how can things ever be the same again?

Easter Season

When Love Doubts

John 20:19-28

Then he said to Thomas, "Put your finger here and see my hands. Reach out your hand and put it in my side. Do not doubt but believe." Thomas answered him, "My Lord and my God!"

—John 20:27-28

Last Sunday, as our Easter service concluded and the congregation began to stream out of the sanctuary, the mood in the lobby was decidedly upbeat. I was greeted with warm handshakes, big smiles, and many wishes of "Happy Easter." One worshipper even carried the liturgy out of the sanctuary with him, taking my hand and greeting me with the words I had proclaimed at the beginning of the service: "Christ is risen!" I was glad to reply to him as the congregation had earlier responded to me: "He is risen, indeed!" It was thrilling for me to be able to share with other Christians in the joy of our Lord's resurrection.

A noted American minister, William Willimon, who preaches at the chapel of Duke University, reports a different kind of experience after one Easter Sunday service. Most of his congregation that day had manifested the positive spirit that grasped our own last week, but he says,

> there was this young man, surely a student, who filed through the door, shaking my hand, saying only, "I don't know. I just don't know."
>
> As we all danced forth into the warm glow of Easter, the certainty of our faith having been renewed by the music, and the message, and the crowd, and the chapel, as I remember, he was able only to stumble. To our assured "Christ the Lord is risen today, Alleluia!" he alone said, "I don't know. I just don't know."[1]

Now, the young man didn't identify himself to Dr. Willimon but I think I know his name. You know it, too. His name is Thomas. And I hope that Thomas, who is finding it so hard to believe, found his way back to the chapel the following Sunday. For the first Sunday after Easter is the Sunday for him, just as the first Sunday after Easter was the Sunday for Thomas in the Gospel of John. Thomas was the one who, you will recall, was not there when Jesus appeared to the other disciples in the locked room on the evening of the resurrection. He is the one who, upon hearing their report that they had seen the Lord, told them, in effect, that they were "seeing things." He just could not believe it and would not believe it unless he could see for himself the mark of the nails in Jesus' hands, and put his finger in them just to be sure he was not seeing a ghost.

Thomas is, of course, the doubter—Doubting Thomas—and he speaks for all those who, though they may never speak up, leave the church on an Easter Sunday, or on any Sunday when we proclaim the faith that God is alive and God is working and God's promises are true and God may be trusted and the kingdom of God will come—who leave the church saying to themselves, "I don't know. I just don't know." If you are Thomas, either outspoken about your doubt or holding it deep

---

1. William H. Willimon, "The Fear of Easter," *Pulpit Resource* 22, no. 2 (April-June 1994): p. 6.

down inside of you to hide it from others, perhaps even from yourself, today's message about your namesake is for you. But even if you are not Thomas, this sermon is for you, for Thomas may be your son or daughter. Thomas may be your husband or wife. Thomas may be a friend for whom you want only the best and about whom you are deeply concerned. And, as one who has found and has been found by the risen Christ, you need to know what to do with and what to do for the Thomas in your life.

Now the problem with being Thomas, at least in the Christian culture I grew up in, and probably the culture Christians have grown up in for the last 20 centuries, is that it is not acceptable to be Thomas. The words "Doubting Thomas" are never spoken as a compliment; they are usually spat out as an insult. Thomas the recalcitrant one. Thomas the one who won't get on board. Thomas whose faith is so suspect. How often have sermons on today's lesson begun by dumping on this disciple who demanded cold, hard evidence, and finished by saying wonderful things about the faith of those who are willing to believe without such evidence? Thomas has become a wonderful straw man for preachers to knock down. Small wonder that his soulmates who occupy our pews from time to time are apt to keep their doubts to themselves, that only rarely will somebody shake the minister's hand and say, "I don't know. I just don't know."

Well, friends, I don't think we have been fair to Thomas over the years. Rather than allow him an honourable place in the church, we have turned him into an object lesson on unfaith. We have certainly not taken time to get to know him, to find out where he is coming from, why it is so hard for him simply to accept the word of the others, why he can't settle for anything less than to touch the flesh of the risen Lord. So, the first thing we owe to Thomas is to try, for a bit, to get into his shoes.

Here we have to exercise our imaginations, for the Gospel of John doesn't do psychological studies of its characters. And, moreover, there are only three references to Thomas in the whole book. But perhaps enough is written to allow us to say something.

The first time we see Thomas—chapter 11—he is with Jesus and the other disciples somewhere across the Jordan River where John had been doing his baptizing. One day word comes that Lazarus, a friend of Jesus, is ill. Lazarus lives at Bethany, on the Mount of Olives, just a couple of miles to the east of Jerusalem. Thomas probably imagines that Jesus will want to go to be with his friend, and the thought must fill him with foreboding. For Jerusalem spells trouble. Every time Jesus has gone up to the city there has been nothing but conflict, controversy, heated debate with people who have access to the levers of power. Thomas can see where this is leading. If Jesus will not be content to remain in the countryside where he is popular, if he persists in taking his message and mission to Jerusalem where he has made enemies with dangerous people, well, it's bound to lead to violent confrontation, to a battle that Jesus cannot win.

Yet, how can Jesus not go to visit his sick friend? But he doesn't. He bides his time for a couple of days. Then out of some interior knowledge—for no other message has come—he announces to the disciples, "Lazarus is dead," and says that now the time has come to go to Judea, to Bethany. Thomas must be dumbfounded. If Jesus didn't go while Lazarus was alive, what possible point is there to going into the lion's den now that nothing more can be done for him? I suspect that Thomas is impatient with his Lord. He thinks this is a foolhardy move. But I want you to hear his final word. He throws up his arms and in effect says to his fellow disciples, "If he insists on going, let us also go, that we may die with him." Thomas thinks this is what will happen. Jesus will not survive another trip to the holy city. But he is not about to abandon his Lord. Thomas may be pessimistic. He may fear what's coming. But he is not cowardly. Whatever happens, he will be there.

The second time we see Thomas—chapter 14—it is the night before Good Friday. The world is closing in on Jesus, and Jesus knows it. The conviction amongst the elite that something must be done about him has now been translated into action. Plots to capture and try him are now being played out. He gathers his disciples together for one last meal and to sum up for them what his ministry has been about and to prepare them for the time when he will no longer be with them. He says things like "Do not let your hearts be troubled," which probably goes over the heads of some of them who do not realize how desperate circumstances have become. But I suspect it does not go over Thomas's head. He will be well aware of the danger.

Then Jesus is saying, "In my Father's house there are many dwelling places.... I go to prepare a place for you" (14:2). I can't imagine Thomas wants to hear this. How can Jesus leave them now? How can he take the best three years of their lives and then suddenly leave? Then Jesus is saying, "You know the way to the place where I am going" (14:4). Thomas's heart is screaming, "The only place I want to go is out of town fast. We can still do it. The streets are dark. We can avoid the soldiers and sentries. In God's name, why are we still sitting here talking?" So Thomas blurts it out; he can't hold it in any longer: "Lord, we do not know where you are going. How can we know the way?" (14:5). His voice betrays the alarm that recognizes that the precipice is near and the desperation that senses there is but little time to change course. Perhaps he is clinging to a hope that, at the last minute, Jesus will come up with an answer that means life, not death; that Jesus will find a way to keep his ministry going in the face of all the threats. "How can we know the way?" he says, for how is a loyal disciple to follow a rabbi who is no longer there?

Then comes the reply: "I am the way, and the truth, and the life" (14:6). That ends the exchange. Thomas has no more questions. As one preacher has said, "In response to the serenity and the majesty of those words, there can be only silence."[2] And in that silence, Thomas has to accept that Jesus is resolved on his great confrontation, that he will not be turned aside, that he

---

2. Herbert O'Driscoll, *A Year of the Lord: Reflections of Christian faith from the advent of the Christ Child to the reign of Christ as King* (Toronto: Anglican Book Centre, 1986), p. 100.

really is going to leave them. The man he has loved so much that he set aside his career and livelihood to follow him, that he sacrificed his worldly prospects to be with him, the man who has filled his heart with wonderful dreams of a world that truly could be different, who has given him a taste of abundant life, is now really going to leave him. And Thomas says no more. It is other disciples who carry the conversation forward. Thomas says no more. He does not have to wait for the cross to pierce his heart. It is already broken.

The next time we should see Thomas, he is not there. That is with the other disciples in the room on Easter night, the time of the first appearance. John doesn't give the reason for his absence, so again we have to speculate. Maybe he is missing because, while like the others he has experienced fear and disillusionment and fatigue and despair in these last few days, he has also experienced something more: anger and hurt. Maybe he is angry and hurt because he believes he has been abandoned. And so he can't bring himself to sit in the same room as the other disciples, who are just sad and despairing, because he knows he will wind up saying bitter things about Jesus, and he loves Jesus so much that he will just not let them hear him talk that way. He finds a private place to nurse his own special grief.

It is a while before he can rejoin their company. When he does, he is told their wondrous story. But he cannot seem to believe it. It is not that he distrusts these men. It is not that he thinks they would talk idly about something so momentous. It is that he believes he has been abandoned, and when you have been abandoned the assurances of others don't seem to carry much weight. When your heart has been broken, you have reason to doubt. So Thomas needs more than the story, or even the proof, of a great miracle. If that were all he needed, he would be prepared to trust these friends.

But what he really needs is the proof of a great love. He wants to know whether he can trust this risen one. He is like a child who, once abandoned, will never let his parents out the door again. He is like a wife who, once forsaken, wonders whether she will ever be able to trust her husband again. That is why, for Thomas, just hearing the good news is not enough; he needs to encounter Jesus again and find out where he stands. That is why, when the encounter happens, he does not turn to the others and say, "Well, I guess you were right. It sure does look like Jesus." Rather, he speaks directly to the one who went away from him. And his words are the words of one who has loved, and loves again: "My Lord and my God!" He becomes the first in the scriptures to confess the divinity of Christ. Now he knows what he did not know before. Jesus' death was not his abandonment. It was his redemption. And now he can go on. Now his doubt has been answered.

As I said earlier, the problem with being Thomas is that it has never been acceptable in the church to be Thomas. But when we flesh out the story and consider the relationship of this disciple and his Lord, can we imagine Thomas in any other place than the church? You see, Thomas is a doubter, not a sceptic. The sceptic makes sure to stand at quite a safe distance from Jesus Christ, from the church, from the faith, from the way of discipleship. The sceptic makes sure to keep the quarrel with the faith in the head and not let it get too close to the heart. The sceptic never loses anything because the sceptic never risks anything, never gives anything of himself or herself to God. You tend not to find sceptics in the church.

But you do find Thomas. For Thomas is someone who has once believed, who has once made a commitment, who has once dedicated his life, who has once made himself vulnerable before God and others, who has once declared his love for Christ for everyone to hear, and who has somewhere been disappointed after all that. Thomas is everyone who has counted upon God and felt that God has let him down. Thomas is everyone who has felt abandoned by God, by the church, left with nothing to hold onto in the midst of all the pains and sufferings in life.

Yes, Thomas is a doubter, but Thomas is not a quitter. I'm sure you noticed how a week after the crucifixion, he is not to be found back in Galilee taking up whatever he did before. He is still with the other disciples in Jerusalem. You see, Thomas may not believe right now. But he's no sceptic. He wants to believe.

If you are Thomas, if you are walking in those shoes today, what can I say to you out of the Gospel of John? What I have to say to you at the very least is that it is all right to be Thomas. It is all right to have been disappointed with the faith. It wouldn't have been faith if it couldn't be disappointed. It wouldn't have been love if it couldn't be wounded. It wouldn't have been loyalty if it couldn't feel like betrayal and abandonment. It's all right to be Thomas. And the place for you, Thomas, is inside the room, with the other disciples, with the other members of the community of faith, for it is inside the room, in their company, that he will appear to you and present his hands so that you can put your finger into the mark of the nails and recover what you thought you had lost.

If you are not Thomas—if you are the women who ran from the tomb in amazement, frightened, but not doubting that he had risen; if you are the men who supped with him at Emmaus and knew him in the breaking of the bread, and have felt his presence ever since when you have gathered at his table; if you are among those who live because he lives—you need to know that it is all right for your brother or sister to be Thomas and that there needs to be a place in the church for Thomas. You need to make sure that Thomas is welcome. If Thomas is hard to get along with, you need to remember that Thomas is struggling, filled with conflict at the deepest level of his being. If Thomas does hurtful things, you need to remember that Thomas is hurting. Above all you need to remember that you have a responsibility never to let Thomas go. For, really, Thomas doesn't want to go. Thomas doesn't want to give up on the faith, on the church, on Jesus Christ. Thomas believed once and Thomas wants nothing more than to believe again.

But you cannot persuade Thomas to believe, and I cannot persuade Thomas to believe. Thomas needs to put his own hands into those rich wounds. Thomas has to touch and feel for himself and come to know that he has not been abandoned. Thomas has to encounter the risen Christ, and that is up to the risen Christ working through the Holy Spirit. We can be helpers. Thomas may have had that encounter already and doesn't know it yet. So we may get to be interpreters for him. Or we can be thought-provokers, faith-instillers, Spirit-supporters. Our task is to keep Thomas connected with the faith until he encounters the one who will restore his faith.

If you are Thomas, it would be presumptuous of me to say how this story will end for you. You will write the ending. But let me tell you how the story of the first Thomas ended. The tradition of the church is that he is the one who travelled to India and evangelized a group of Syrian Christians who, to this day, form a worshipping community in and around the city of Madras. There he suffered martyrdom as did so many of the first generation of apostles. So Thomas followed his Lord to death, not in Bethany, but in a far-off place in search of a far-off kingdom. He would not abandon his Lord who indeed had not abandoned him. And today, because Thomas wrestled with his doubt, the community of believers is larger and more vigorous than it would otherwise have been.

So Thomas, my friend, wrestle with your doubt, and who knows what through your wrestling might yet be done for your own faith and for the faith of others.

Pentecost

The Elusive, Effective Spirit

John 15:26-27; 16:4b-15

"When the Spirit of truth comes, he will guide you into all the truth; for he will not speak on his own, but will speak whatever he hears, and he will declare to you the things that are to come."

—John 16:13

THE FRENCH REVOLUTION WAS NOT A POETIC TIME, BUT IT LEFT us with at least one well-known verse:

> We seek him here, we seek him there,
> Those Frenchies seek him everywhere,
> Is he in Heaven—is he in Hell?
> That damned elusive Pimpernel?[1]

So went the little ditty about the Scarlet Pimpernel, the legendary English aristocrat who saved many a French aristocrat from the guillotine during that blood-stained period. The Pimpernel could never be found: a shadow of a man, perhaps he

---

1. From *The Scarlet Pimpernel*, a play by Baroness Orczy, adapted by Beverley Cross (London: Samuel French, 1988), p. 24.

was imaginary. But no, his work was evident every time a jail door creaked open to reveal an empty cell, every time a condemned enemy of the people turned up in England.

Like the Pimpernel, the Spirit of God is elusive, and cannot be found. "We seek him here, we seek him there." Where is this person? Yet, many will testify that this elusive Spirit is real. They will acknowledge the activity of this Counsellor, this Comforter, this heavenly Dove, this Fire and Wind of God. Some will even go so far as to say that there is a church of Jesus Christ today only because of the work of the Holy Spirit.

Life in the Spirit is both the glory and the frustration of Christian people. It is our glory because it means that our faith is the faith of free people. It must be chosen. It cannot be forced upon us. An invisible Spirit cannot coerce us the way some visible tyrant might.

However, such a life is our frustration because we sometimes feel unsure of the Spirit. In moments of panic we ask ourselves, Is it all real? We tend to associate knowledge and certainty with what we can see, touch, and feel; and the Spirit certainly does not fit into any of those categories. The Spirit can be confused with our own human vanities and desires. How often do we say that we did something because the Spirit moved us? But is it the Spirit of Christ who is doing the moving or our own spirit?

Surely Christ's first disciples have us twenty-first-century disciples at a disadvantage. They had Jesus in the flesh. He was a physical person to them. They could watch him in action. They could ask a question directly and get a direct answer. "Explain to us the parable of the sower and the seed. Explain to us the meaning of that miracle you did." And Jesus was there to explain.

We think we are at a disadvantage to the first disciples, but the fact is, that is not true. The apostles, who knew Christ in the flesh, were slow to understand who he really was. At the end of Jesus' ministry—not the beginning, mind you, but the end—we have Philip saying to Jesus, "Show us the Father, and we will be satisfied," and receiving the consternated reply, "Have I been with you all this time, Philip, and you still do not know me?" (John 14:8-9). Nor did the crowds who witnessed his miraculous signs and heard his awesome preaching evidence any faith in Jesus as the Son of God.

Faith in Jesus began when he was no longer physically present, when he was no longer visible, when, like the Father, he was unseen. The Gospel of John begins with the words "No one has ever seen God" (John 1:18) and ends with the affirmation "Blessed are those who have not seen and yet have come to believe" (John 20:29). So, those who have seen Christ have no advantage over us.

This is made clear by the first verse of today's gospel lesson. Jesus tells the disciples, "I still have many things to say to you, but you cannot bear them now" (John 16:12). His physical presence could not give them the complete picture. A more complete explanation of his purpose and truth would have done no good at that time. It is almost as if, when he was present with them physically, there would be more danger of their misinterpreting him than later, when he was present with them spiritually.

Therefore, when Christ prepared to depart from this world, he did not do what leaders, religious and otherwise, normally do to ensure their continued influence. He gave no special body of teaching to his followers. He left them no strategy for mission. He gave them no structure for the church. What he left, instead, was a promise of the Spirit. Jesus could not handle every situation for his disciples before it happened, but he promised to be with them in every situation, as it happened, and with what they needed. So, the very first Christians had to live life in the Spirit. No other way would do. The same is true for us.

By life in the Spirit, we mean life in Christ. The Holy Spirit is the Spirit of Christ and not a separate being. We know this because Jesus used the title "the Spirit of truth" for the one who will guide his followers into all the truth; and, in the Gospel of John, Jesus and the truth are one and the same thing. The

Spirit's functions are to lead us into the truth—that is, into the presence of Christ—and to declare the things that are to come—that is, to help Christians to understand the significance of what Jesus has said and done as it relates to the life they must live, the challenges they must face, and the questions they must answer.

How does the Spirit do this work within us? The answer is, the Spirit works elusively, invisibly. If I could explain how, it would mean either that the Spirit is no longer invisible or that I could know more about the third person of the Trinity than any other human being has ever known. We have to tread humbly in this area, keeping in mind the words of Jesus to Nicodemus: "The wind blows where it chooses, and you hear the sound of it, but you do not know where it comes from or where it goes. So it is with everyone who is born of the Spirit" (John 3:8).

I cannot explain the miracle of life and how it is that a seed may grow into a plant when it is placed in a garden, but I can speak of what must be done to a garden plot to accommodate a seed in such a way that it will grow. It is in this way that I can speak confidently about the Spirit. Three things must happen before God's Comforter can draw near and appear within our hearts.

First, we must hold fast to the church and remain within the Christian fellowship. Jesus' promises of the Spirit are always made to a group as a group—whether to the disciples or to crowds of listeners. In Matthew's gospel, we hear him saying that when two or three are gathered in his name, he is there in the midst of them (Matthew 18:20). This is his way of saying that the Spirit works in individuals when the individuals are in community.

Sometimes we hear people say, "I do not need to be a part of the fellowship. I do not have to go to church to be a Christian." But this is an attitude that refuses the greatest gift Christ has to offer, the gift of his presence. Let us allow the apostle Paul to be our example in this area. When the Spirit of Christ confronted him and he had his great conversion experience on the road to

Damascus, he was by himself. He was not in church or with the church. However, the first thing he did was to seek out Christian believers and join in Christian fellowship (Acts 9). This is remarkable for a man who had so recently persecuted the church; and we know that the church remained a crucial part of his life ever after. He realized that the only way for him to grow in the Spirit was to do so in the company of other believers.

Second, we have to be prepared to work with the Spirit if we expect the Spirit to work in us. A young preacher decided that he was going to live by the Spirit. He determined not to give a thought through the week to the sermon he was going to preach on Sunday, lest he interfere with the creative flow of the Spirit within him. When the day came, he walked into the pulpit without a note but confident of God's guidance. He silently said a fervent prayer that the Spirit would lay upon his heart what he was to say. And the Spirit answered, "Next week, start preparing earlier."

If the Spirit is to work in us, we must work with the Spirit. And our work as Christians is to abide in the word of Christ. Christ's promise is that those who continue in his word will know the truth. The Spirit cannot fulfil Christ's promise to show us the truth unless we remain in Christ's word. Now, the reason we are to be prepared to devote ourselves to the study of Christ's word is that the Spirit is not teaching new truth but, rather, the same truth as Christ taught. Jesus says of the Counsellor, "He will take what is mine and declare it to you" (John 16:14). The Spirit does not speak on the Spirit's own authority but rather what the Spirit hears from the ascended Christ. Therefore, if we are unfamiliar with the word of Christ, the Spirit will have nothing to work with in speaking to our hearts.

Again, let us follow the lead of the apostle Paul. He did not presume, once he had had his conversion experience, that he was a competent Christian. He did not set out forthwith to convert the Gentiles. That was not to come for years. Paul's first need was to learn more of the story of Jesus from those who had known him, and the evidence is that Peter, the leader of the infant church, was helpful to him in this (Galatians 1:18-19).[2] He spent a considerable length of time in reflection on the things Jesus did and taught, and focussed his great mind in particular upon the events of that last fateful week that culminated in the crucifixion and resurrection (1 Corinthians 11:23ff. and 15:3ff.). He expected, when he ultimately started his mission, that the Spirit would lay on his heart what to do and say, but only because he had disciplined himself in the gospel of Jesus first, and had given the Spirit something to interpret.

The Spirit's function is to help us interpret the word of Christ for the particular situation in which we find ourselves. But before that can happen, there must be a word of Christ in us to interpret.

Third, if the Spirit is to work in us, we must be willing to be guided. Jesus did not say that the Spirit would explain the truth, or would show the truth, or would clear up all mysteries about the truth, but rather that the Spirit would guide us into the truth. This implies that the discovery of the things of Christ is a journey, in fact a lifelong journey, in which we are led by another. Are we willing to embark upon such a course? Since the truth is not a discovery we make, or a conclusion we draw, but a gift we receive from God, we must have a guide if we are to find it. To have a guide means we are to be dependent. Are we willing to be dependent?

Years ago, I noticed in the newspaper one day the obituary of the Sherpa guide who assisted Edmund Hillary on the first successful climb to the top of Mount Everest. Until reading the obituary, I had not given a thought to anyone but Hillary in the whole enterprise. But, when you think about it, it is clear that the great adventurer would never have made it to the top without the help of this man who told him where to go and how to get there. He could not have done it without a guide.

---

2. The name or title given by Jesus to his chief disciple is usually rendered "Peter"—from the Greek for "rock," *petros*—but in this and a few other passages in the New Testament it is rendered "Cephas"—from the Aramaic for "rock," *kepha*.

When the Americans come up to take advantage of the sporting areas in the Canadian Shield, they do not go into the bush without local guides who know the area. They rely on guides to get them to the places where the fish are to be caught or the game is to be stalked, and then to get them back out of the bush again.

You entrust yourself to a guide. You go where you are told and do as you are asked by this person—or you do not achieve your destination or your goal. Jesus says we can arrive at his truth only if we are guided by his Spirit. Are we prepared to be guided? There are people around who want to handle life on their own terms; they scarcely expect guidance and would not know how to recognize it or accept it if it were offered to them. Are we such people, or are we ones whom the Spirit can indeed lead to Christ?

To speak of what is necessary for the Spirit to do the Spirit's work is not, of course, to speak of how this work is done. How the Counsellor works remains a mystery, for the Breath of God is elusive. You cannot get a handle on the Spirit; you cannot contain this mighty, rushing wind; you cannot get hold of the flames that light on every sainted head; you cannot pin down the heavenly Dove. But the elusive Spirit is the effective Spirit. Though nobody can speak with certainty about this one who proceeds from the Father and the Son, the interesting thing is that, when the Spirit is working, people find themselves more certain than ever about Jesus Christ.

MINISTRY

Role Models or Faith Models?

Hebrews 13:1-8

Remember your leaders, those who spoke the word of God to you; consider the outcome of their way of life, and imitate their faith. Jesus Christ is the same yesterday and today and forever.

—Hebrews 13:7-8

CHARLES BARKLEY IS A RATHER WELL KNOWN BASKETBALL STAR. Though I don't follow the game, I've read enough of the sports pages to know that, right up to his retirement, he was considered one of the premier players in the National Basketball Association. It is not the skill he demonstrated on the court that I want to lift up, but something he once said to reporters. Apparently, he had been involved in a couple of late-night altercations in places where you wouldn't take your mother. When the media asked him how he squared this type of behaviour with his function as a role model for youth, Barkley shot back that he didn't consider himself a role model and that, moreover, people shouldn't look to professional athletes to be role models. He was prepared to have his athletic prowess and abilities subjected to scrutiny, but he said, in effect, "Don't ask me to be a role model for your boy." I wonder if a generation of American parents who encouraged their sons to "run like O.J." would feel that there is some wisdom in Mr. Barkley's remark.

Yet, even though many of our role models continually fail us, we keep demanding to have them. In this, the church is no different from any sector of society. In 1988, the United Church of Canada experienced the most tumultuous year of its history. That year, there culminated a great debate over homosexuality and how it ought to affect a person's eligibility to be considered for the ministry. During that debate we found out what many church people are looking for in their ministers. Over and over again, I heard the assertion that ministers ought to be role models for their people. Congregational statements directed to the General Council repeatedly made the same point.

Yet, many ministers echo Charles Barkley. They do not want to be perceived that way. They do not want to be put on a pedestal, or have any special status, or have a standard of conduct applied to them that is not applied to everybody.

I find that I, too, have resisted the role model idea and have had to ask myself why. Is it a fear of being scrutinized? The idea of having the whole of one's life open to public evaluation is fairly daunting. Is it a feeling of inadequacy? A sense that there are wiser, deeper, maturer Christians around than I, and that the faithful would be better off modelling themselves after them? Is it because there is so much disagreement over what being a good role model means that one fears being caught in a crossfire of competing expectations?

Whatever the reasons, despite the resistance, the demand is insistent. Therefore, it is important that we spend time with today's lesson from the Letter to the Hebrews, a passage that sheds light on this issue. Obviously, it is a text about modelling. Phrases such as "remember your leaders," "consider the outcome of their way of life," and "imitate their faith" allow no other conclusion. The expectation of this writer is that leaders of the church will be models for the faithful and that the faithful will make every effort to model themselves after their leaders.

This text supports a number of things I think people are

looking for when they say pastors should be role models. First, it affirms the desire to have examples for Christian living. It recognizes that we are not self-sufficient as Christians—that we need the influence and patterning of other Christians to help us grow in the faith.

I am not aware of any part of the New Testament that speaks of Christian living as an individual attainment, that suggests Christian character is best worked at on one's own. Everywhere, the Christian life is thought of as a community activity. So, for example, the writer to the Hebrews exhorts his readers to continue in mutual love, to keep meeting together, always to be considering how to stir up one another to love and good works.

Now, if Christianity is to be a shared thing, we are entitled to look for examples of Christian growth and maturity, and the author of this letter points us to the church's leaders. Those who preach and teach the word of God have the right to expect that what they say will be attended to seriously. But they need to know that they are expected to offer to the church more than their preaching. They are to offer a manner of living worthy of being remembered, an outcome of life worthy of being considered, a faith worthy of being imitated. To be a leader in the church is to be an example. There is no getting around that.

Second, this text affirms the desire for high moral standards, something very much on people's minds when they talk about role models. It is easy to see why there is such a desire these days. We have lived through a generation in which the social consensus over moral questions has fallen apart, in which people have been robbed of the stability, the security, the safety of clearly defined standards of and expectations about behaviour in their personal, family, and working lives. Personal choice has been exalted, but many find themselves wondering what the right choices are. They look for help and guidance but find that the church, which speaks out so forcefully in matters of public policy, is strangely vague and inarticulate in addressing matters of personal morality.

Christians who are concerned about moral questions will find that the writer to the Hebrews keeps company with them. In his mind, Christians are not to live any way they please, but are to be prepared to accept both responsibilities and restraints. So he presents to the Christian community three moral imperatives.

First, he calls us to practise *hospitality*. He reminds us that we are responsible for the well-being of other Christians, both those we know and those who may be strangers to us. Christian fellowship is not to be disdained but taken up and worked at.

Second, he calls us to *fidelity*. We are admonished to hold marriage in honour. It is this kind of attitude that will encourage sexual responsibility and protect individuals at the level of their deepest intimacy and vulnerability.

Third, he calls us to *simplicity*. We are to avoid the love of money and to be content with the goods we have, knowing that God will not fail those who put their trust in him.

Hospitality. Fidelity. Simplicity. Here we have an ethic that our culture desperately needs. For what a terrible social harvest we have reaped from the decline in hospitality, from the loss of a sense of community and, with it, the loss of the belief that we are responsible in this society not just for ourselves but for one another. And what drastic consequences have flowed from the abandonment of the imperative of fidelity and the corresponding loss of sexual restraint. And what damage has been done to the earth's ecology and what an unsustainable economy has been created through our unbridled lust for material goods, through the insatiable demand for more and more things.

The virtues of hospitality, fidelity, and simplicity have gone out of fashion, and society, families, and individuals are paying a price. The need for change is urgent, and the church might find no better vocation at this time than to model these virtues for a world that has lost them.

And what of the church's leaders? Must these standards not also be their standards? Of course. How else will they be in a position to prepare the church to exercise its vocation? And how could the church commend these standards to society if they are not held by those who, by office, are representative of the church?

When people ask for high standards in the personal lives of their pastors, they are asking nothing more than St. Paul did when he said that one who aspires to leadership must be "hospitable, a lover of goodness, prudent, upright, devout, and self-controlled" (Titus 1:8). We must be able to rely on our leaders both to proclaim and to embody these virtues.

Much of what people are asking for when they say ministers need to be role models is supported by the letters of the New Testament in general and this passage from Hebrews in particular. However, there is an interesting twist in this text which suggests we cannot stop here but must look at the issue more deeply.

After giving his list of moral imperatives to his readers, the writer does not go on to say what you would have expected: "Imitate the morality of your leaders." Rather, he tells them to imitate the faith of their leaders. There is no doubt that the writer would have expected ministers to set a moral tone. But it is their faith, he says, that needs to be imitated. Is it possible that, if he were advising us today, rather than insist that ministers be *role models* he would insist that they be *faith models?*

You may wonder, Is there really a difference between the two, or is this just splitting hairs? Well, what is a role model? Is this not one who maintains and puts into practice a commonly accepted set of standards as both an example and an inspiration for others? And what is a faith model? Is this not one who places trust in an external power and orders life in obedience to that power and who, in so doing, becomes an example and inspiration for others? In the end, a role model points to self, while a faith model points beyond self to something greater, to someone else. And who is that someone else? The very next verse of our lesson tells us: "Jesus Christ is the same yesterday and today and forever." I believe the writer to the Hebrews is telling us that ministers are to be models. Their lives are to be models of faith in Christ for the sake of the faith of the members of the church.

It is when we begin to compare the concept of role model with that of a model of faith in Christ that we can begin to perceive the dark side of the demand for role models.

Yes, there is a dark side as well as a good side. The demand for a role model can actually take Jesus Christ right out of the picture. The lowest point of my life in the church came in the aftermath of the great debate in 1988 over sexuality and eligibility for ministry. I had occasion to attend a raucous meeting in a suburban church, during which, at one point, a woman rose to assert that the only persons fit to be ministers were those who were married and had children, for only such persons could be role models for her and her family. The more vehement she became, the lower into my chair I sank. For, while I was married, I had no children and, stuck at the time on a long adoption waiting list, had no great expectations that I would ever have children. I began to wonder how many people would consider that I was unfit for ministry on account of not having a "complete" family. Now, you may think the woman's comments were wildly out of line, but nobody in the congregation rose to challenge her. In fact, I sensed that she had a great deal of support in the room.

Friends, do you see what is happening? Suddenly, Jesus Christ is no longer the cornerstone of the church. The family is—the nuclear, two-parent, two-child family at that. There is a dark side to the demand for role models. It frequently has nothing to do with the gospel.

Moreover, what are we to make of the fact that some of the greatest faith models in the church's history, acting by faith in Christ and accomplishing great things that changed the lives of countless people, would never have been acceptable as role models?

There was a Reformation, which delivered the church from a clerical captivity and gave the Bible directly to the people through translation into their native languages, largely because of the faith and drive of Martin Luther. But anything I have read about Luther tells me that his judgement was greatly clouded by deep and erratic emotions. These days he wouldn't pass the personality and psychiatric tests necessary to get into the ministry. And besides, he was crude and earthy: "No, Johnny, you cannot belch at the dinner table just because Uncle Martin does." "No, Johnny, just because Uncle Martin talks about his sex life at family reunions doesn't mean Mommy and Daddy are going to." Friends, Martin Luther was not a good role model.

There is a Presbyterian Church, from which this congregation descends, because of the fearlessness and determination of Scotland's John Knox. But what I have read of Knox indicates that he was bigoted, narrow-minded, rude, hostile to women, and generally contrary—not a good role model.

One of the great faith models of our time was Martin Luther King, minister and civil rights activist. By faith he dreamed dreams, moved mountains, and changed America forever. But Martin Luther King was, at times, unfaithful in his marriage—not a good role model.

What if these people, and many like them, had been disqualified from ministry because they were not good role models? Can you imagine what would have been lost? Fortunately they were not disqualified even though we must candidly be critical of some of their behaviour. They remain heroes of the church. And though their behaviour may not always have been worthy of imitation, their faith is.

In the end, isn't the biggest problem with the demand for role models that it leaves you stuck in what is essentially the religion of law and requirement and performance—the religion of the Pharisees? And isn't that the religion from which Jesus came to free us? The problem in being a role model is that one can never play the role well enough. And the problem with constructing a religion on role models is that it has no way of dealing with the fact observed by St. Paul that "all have sinned and fall short of the glory of God" (Romans 3:23). In the end, does it leave any room for forgiveness, for the realization that our place in God's family comes not from our virtue but from God's grace?

Would it not be better to move into the realm of grace where the task of Christian leaders is to be models of faith? Faith models point people not to themselves but to Christ, for only he is absolutely constant, dependable, reliable. He is the one who was never in danger of falling out of a role because he never had to play a role in the first place.

Faith models do not trust in their own goodness but in the goodness of Christ. They do not believe that, in the end, people would be saved by imitating them. But they know people will be saved by imitating their faith in the one who has power to save.

The one thing that Christians are instructed to imitate is their leaders' faith. Now, there may be many other things worth imitating in many of the church's ministers. That is well and good. But the one thing commanded is to imitate faith. And that means ministers must be sure they have a faith to imitate. That will no doubt make their lives harder rather than easier.

A role is scripted; a life of faith is not.

A role can be acted; faith can only be acted upon.

Role models will spend much time figuring out the expectations of people who look to them. Faith models will spend much time figuring out the expectations of Jesus Christ.

A role model's first concern will be to maintain human standards. A faith model's first concern will be to maintain obedience to Christ, even in conflict with human standards, and to show in daily living how a life of obedience to Christ is possible.

A role model will settle for human approval. A faith model will seek approval from God.

It is understandable in these days of rapid change and fluid values that people are asking for role models. But what they really need to be asking for is faith models. For it is by faith that we come closer to the one true model: "Jesus Christ [who] is the same yesterday and today and forever."

DISCIPLESHIP

Blessing or Burden?

Matthew 5:1-16

> *"You are the light of the world. A city built on a hill cannot be hid."*
>
> —Matthew 5:14

IT HAPPENS TOO OFTEN IN CHRISTIAN PREACHING AND TEACHING that passages in the Bible that ought to give a blessing to people instead lay a burden upon them. Words first uttered to uplift folk, to restore their souls, and to revitalize their lives are somehow transformed into a heavy load to be borne along with all the other loads life lays on the back. And so it often seems, both to its practitioners and to its detractors, that Christianity is a burdensome thing.

The words read today from Matthew's gospel about Jesus' followers being the salt of the earth and the light of the world have suffered this fate. I strongly suspect they were spoken as blessing. They are recorded right after the beatitudes, which are a veritable manifesto of blessing. "Blessed are the poor in spirit. ... Blessed are those who mourn.... Blessed are the meek.... Blessed are the merciful.... Blessed are the pure in heart.... Blessed are the peacemakers," says Jesus, and on it goes. Surely, the words that follow are intended as blessing. And yet, any sermon I can recall on the subject of salt and light has managed to turn Jesus' pronouncement into a burden.

It happens this way: Before a preacher is too far into the message, the words of the text have been subtly altered so that Jesus is no longer saying "You are the salt of the earth.... You are the light of the world" but rather "You ought to be the salt of the earth." That dastardly word, "ought," has intruded where Jesus gave it no place, and when "ought" becomes part of the text, then *blessing* gives way to *burden.*

When "ought" becomes part of the text, then Christians are led to believe that the salt and light that the world so desperately needs are something they have to produce in themselves by dint of great trial and effort. "Ought" makes you think you have to transform yourself from what you are to a completely different person before you are allowed out of the saltshaker. "Ought" makes you climb a mountain to that height where you are fit to be the world's light. "Ought" makes being the world's salt and light a terrible worry, for what if you should fall short, what if you do not measure up, when so much depends on you?

Friends, how do you respond? When I hear the words "You ought to be the salt of the earth; you ought to be the light of the world," I want to say, "I'm not ready for this, and I'm not sure I want to endure the hard work and suffering of getting ready."

Yet, some people have been happy to accept these words of Jesus as a burden. The classic example would be the Puritans, those early settlers of North America who strove to make New England a godly and holy society. A favourite text for them was "A city built on a hill cannot be hid." That city on the hill they understood to be themselves, and they determined to spare no effort to make themselves pure and perfect, people of piety and good character. "Ought" was a word they took to readily, and just as readily imposed on others.

The Puritans no longer exist as a distinct group, but their spirit is very much alive in a great deal of the preaching on this passage which exhorts us to reach higher and higher to be fit for this great calling God has given us. It is sometimes said that being the world's salt and light demands from us a noticeably higher standard of morality than from non-Christians. Our task ought to be the defeat of vice and the encouragement of propriety through the setting of a good example. Every generation of Christians has been given a list of things from which Christians ought to refrain in order to set a high moral standard.

It is sometimes said that being the world's salt and light demands of us a noticeably keener sense of justice than is evident among non-Christians. So we are missing the mark if we are not on the front lines of the combat against racism, sexism, poverty, or any other evil.

Well, no doubt, a high morality is right and good. And a keen sense of justice is right and good. You could add to these virtues a generous charity, and a deep regard for human worth, and a great respect for life's sanctity. But when these things are put to us in terms of "ought," when we are told that only continuous striving and struggling on these fronts will make us fit to be the earth's salt and the world's light, then a great burden is laid upon us, a burden of performance. And is it a wonder that, in these terms, many find Christianity too exhausting and its price too high?

But let us suppose, for a moment, that Jesus intended these words not as a burden but as a blessing. This is not such a wild idea as it might first seem, for elsewhere in the gospels Jesus expresses considerable anger at the laying of burdens upon people. He once denounced the scribes and Pharisees in these terms: "They tie up heavy burdens, hard to bear, and lay them on the shoulders of others" (Matthew 23:4). And as for the burden he himself offered, he said, "Take my yoke upon you, and learn from me; for I am gentle and humble in heart, and you will find rest for your souls. For my yoke is easy, and my burden is light" (Matthew 11:29-30). So, let us assume that when Jesus preached the Sermon on the Mount it was not the laying of a burden but the gift of a blessing he had in mind.

That means we need to hear his words not as they have been

revised by many centuries of tradition but as he spoke them. Jesus' words to his disciples then and to you, his disciples today, are these: "You *are* the salt of the earth. . . . You *are* the light of the world" (italics mine). This is what you are now—not what you ought to be, not what you need to get ready to be, not what you must strive for, not what you must shape up to become. You are the salt of the earth, just as you are. You are the light of the world, just as you are. This is God's blessing through Christ to you. This is your blessing to the world.

Now, you may ask, "How is it possible for us to have this blessing? We don't deserve it." True, you have not deserved it. You may ask, "How can we be the salt of the earth, the light of the world? We haven't earned it." Again true. You have not earned it. You may say, "How can Jesus use this kind of language about us when we are anything but perfect?" This is true. You are anything but perfect. "How can we be a city built on a hill? We are not ready for it." This is *not* true. God thinks you are ready.

You see, God never intended that the city built on a hill should be a society of perfect Christians demonstrating to the world how to be a perfect world. If that were the case, how could we ever be ready? God intended that the city built on the hill should be composed of people who shared every imperfection and the same sinful condition as all the people on the surrounding plain. God blesses us—the city built on the hill—as the light of the world not because we are better or potentially better than others and have something to offer on that account, but because our problems—the same as theirs—are being attended to and we have something to offer on that account.

The light that God wants the world to see in us is not the light of perfection but the light of redemption. What God expects men and women to see when they look at Christians is not people who are morally and piously superior but people who have learned to admit freely their shortcomings and failings and have learned to live by trust in the grace of Christ and to open their lives to the healing touch of Christ's Spirit. The light of Christians is that, in them, both the need of the human race and the means of meeting that need are clearly shown. The light of Christians, in the end, illuminates not themselves but the one true light, Jesus Christ.

So, what do people see when they see us? Do they see in us a people who show that we know we have been redeemed? Or do they see a people who would rather hide the need for redemption? The great irony, friends, is that no sooner does Christ declare us the light of the world on the basis of blessing than we decide we would rather become the light of the world on the basis of burden. You can see why this might be. We have attached ourselves to a Lord who commands attention, and therefore to be a Christian is to be on display. Being so visible as Christians, there is something in us that inclines us to display ourselves as righteous saints rather than redeemed sinners.

We start focussing on what we ought to be rather than what we are. We start thinking of perfection rather than grace. We begin to have a certain exalted vision of ourselves. We lay this burden upon ourselves, but do we ever live up to the vision? How can we live up to a vision of perfection? Do we seriously think we can create a perfect society? The Christian church has been hard at work on this for 20 centuries, but if we in the church can see that it is nowhere close to happening, surely the world can see it as well. Do we seriously think the church could be a model of perfection for society? If we can look around the church and see mirrored in its members every sin and shortcoming that is evident in the wider society, surely the world can, too. If we follow this course, if we try to be the light of the world by dint of our own effort, in the end there will be no light to a world in darkness.

But what if we were to lay down the burden of perfection and accept the blessing of redemption? What if we were prepared to be a part of that city on the hill that is a city of fallen, broken, wounded, imperfect people who know their condition, who know their need of a saviour, and are not ashamed that the world should see their condition and need? What if we were prepared to be a part of that city on the hill that has a cross standing beside it, that has found its saviour and is not ashamed that the world should know it owes everything to Christ? Would such a city be worth watching? Would such a city have anything to offer the world? Would a light stream from it?

It is because, deep down, we know the answer to this question that we must accept that, in the end, the gift the church offers to the world is not perfection but humility. Letting our light shine means being honest about ourselves, so people might see that what is special about the citizens of the city on the hill is not their character but their redeemer and healer. The Lord knows, there are enough struggling people out there who, if they knew this, would be glad to be part of that city.

Prayer

What to Pray For

Luke 11:1-13

> *"If you then … know how to give good gifts to your children, how much more will the heavenly Father give the Holy Spirit to those who ask him!"*
>
> —Luke 11:13

When was the last time you pounded on a neighbour's door at midnight—a neighbour, by the way, who always has the lights out at 10 o'clock—begging for some loaves of bread to feed company who had just arrived? I know I haven't done it recently. So, when I read Jesus' story of a man who does just that, it sounded a bit far-fetched. Biblical scholars insist, however, that this is not the case. They tell us that, in the world of Palestine in the time of Christ, it would not be surprising for guests to arrive so late. In a dusty countryside with a hot climate, when people moved about on foot and not in air-conditioned cars, travel was often deferred until the evening. And as for troubling the neighbour, well, to have no food available when visitors arrived was a major failure in hospitality, so, failing 7-Eleven, you really had no choice but to go and knock on your neighbour's door and hope a.) that his cupboard wasn't as bare as yours, and b.) that this was not the beginning of the end of your friendship.

Granted then that the story Jesus tells is a plausible one, the theme of it appears to be pretty obvious: persistence pays. The man, needing bread, keeps pounding on his friend's door until the friend eventually gets up and gives him what he wants to keep him from waking the household and the whole neighbourhood. But, on closer examination, I'm not really sure that the gospel writer is mainly concerned about persistence. If that were the case, his story would not ring entirely true.

We all know from experience that persistence does not always pay. I remember once being in a carload of people who had travelled from my home town of Roblin to a meeting in Winnipeg. After it was over, we were just starting the five-hour trip back home quite late on a Saturday night when our driver informed us that he would not bother getting gas in the city. Rather, he would fill up at Minnedosa, where a station on the highway remained open all night. Now, maybe I'm just a pessimist by nature, but this seemed to me like tempting fate, and I spent the first leg of our journey in deep foreboding. When we got to Minnedosa around two a.m. and found the gas station in question closed up tight, my foreboding was transformed into serious anxiety. No problem, said our driver, there's always Shoal Lake. But Shoal Lake, as we drove by, was a picture of peaceful repose. We pushed on and just barely made it to Russell around four a.m. Our driver told us not to worry. He knew a garage owner who lived right next to his business. Jonesy, he called him. He would ask Jonesy to get up and give us some fuel. Well, he pounded on Jonesy's door for 10 minutes before getting an answer, to the effect that Jonesy had no intention of coming out and filling our car at that hour. I suppose he did not want to set a precedent. Our driver pleaded with him for a further 10 minutes, to no avail. So he got back in the car, and we drove a mile further, conked out, and had to sit at the roadside until business hours, while our driver ruminated that Jonesy wasn't such a Good Samaritan after all. Making me realize that we were stuck in the wrong parable.

Well, remembering that persistence does not always yield dividends, I looked at the biblical story again to see whether the writer might be trying to make a different point. This passage is set in the context of prayer, coming right after the occasion on which Jesus gives a model prayer to his disciples. But the main point of these words is not persistence in prayer. God is not being compared to an unwilling householder, the idea being that if we continually batter God with our prayers, God will give in and answer us. Rather, God is being contrasted with the reluctant householder. Whereas people often have to be badgered to be generous with one another—and sometimes don't respond even then—God wants to give us good gifts. And the source of God's generosity is his own graciousness, not our persistence.

So what we really have here is an assurance that prayer will be answered. Jesus' statement to this effect is absolute and unqualified. There is no hemming or hawing, no ifs, ands, or buts: "Ask, and it will be given you; search, and you will find; knock, and the door will be opened for you. For everyone who asks receives, and everyone who searches finds, and for everyone who knocks, the door will be opened" (Luke 11:9-10).

If we accept this assurance that God does answer prayer, then our persistence is not the hassling of an unwilling God but the drawing near to a generous one. And if there is a problem around praying to such a God, it is not a question of how hard to bang on the door, it is knowing what to ask of the one inside. The problem is knowing "What do I really need?" "What does the person for whom I'm praying really need?" "Do my needs about which I pray conflict with the needs of others?" "Is it right to pray about my particular concerns?" These are often difficult questions to answer, questions that can cause us anxiety if we are in a situation where prayer seems to be required but what is needed is unclear.

I remember one time this happened in my family. My grandmother, in her late 80s, suffered a severe and debilitating stroke. This was a woman who had been robust all her life, who had delivered nine children at home, and who had been in the hospital only once—to have a toe operated on. Now, she lay in great pain, could hardly talk and could not eat because her throat was paralyzed, and could not even open her eyes to see her family. It seemed fairly certain she would not live, that it was just a matter of time for her. So, for what should we have prayed? Should we have prayed for her to survive, expecting that if she did, she would be virtually helpless, a condition to which we knew her fiercely independent personality was singularly ill-suited? Should we have prayed for her to die quickly to be spared any more suffering? It didn't seem right to want her to die, but considering the pain she was experiencing and the fact that she herself wanted to go, it did not seem right to pray for her to live. In short, it was a real dilemma for us because we honestly did not know what was best. It is the kind of dilemma that so often faces those confronted by terminal illness, either their own or that of someone close to them.

Well, in our case, in retrospect, it turns out that there was much we did not know. For, surprisingly, Grandma pulled through the crisis and went on to make more of a recovery than anyone thought possible. She lived for two or three more years, and while her quality of life was not what she or her family would have hoped for, she nevertheless had some good moments and got to see a few more great-grandchildren into the world. The experience of being in a situation in which one had to pray, and did not know what to pray for, and then found out that there were totally unexpected possibilities present, has suggested something to me. That is, the best thing to do is to take our concerns to God without a dogmatic sense of what the outcome needs to be, but rather recognizing that God knows best, and trusting that God cares enough to do the best thing for us.

Isn't the best prayer one that accepts that we do not need to be in control as long as we know that God's purpose for us and for our world is being worked out? I think we all know this instinctively, though I do not pretend that acceptance of it is always easy. Our lip service to God's greater wisdom can easily lapse into doubt if things do not work out the way our hearts are demanding. It is tempting to start distrusting God or to feel that God is paying no attention to us when things do not turn out as we had hoped. It requires no small discipline to discern God's greater purpose if the sick are not always healed, if troubled marriages are not always held together, if drought-stricken lands do not always receive rain, if war-torn societies are not always given peace, and if the oppressed do not always receive justice. I don't think trust comes easily, even—or especially—trust in God.

But trust is, finally, the crucial thing. Jesus knows this to be the case. And he tacitly acknowledges it when, after boldly asserting that all who ask receive, all who search find, and all who knock have doors opened, he goes on to say something about the nature of the one who does the giving, revealing, and opening. He makes his point by analogy: "Is there anyone among you who, if your child asks for a fish, will give a snake instead of a fish? Or if the child asks for an egg, will give a scorpion? If you then, who are evil, know how to give good gifts to your children, how much more will the heavenly Father give the Holy Spirit to those who ask him!" (Luke 11:11-13). If we can be trusted to offer the best that we have to our children, can we not trust God to offer the best that he has to us, his children? Of course, God's best is the Holy Spirit. When Jesus says that God will give the Holy Spirit to those who ask, he means that what God is prepared to give is God's very self. God is always present for us. God wants nothing more than to draw closer to us and to draw us closer to him.

Reading these words of Jesus, I begin to think that I should be able to pray to God the way my eight-year-old son talks to me. His language contains the implicit trust of one who knows I am always there for him. And so, everything comes out in an unguarded and unfiltered way. When he's unhappy with me, he will let me know in no uncertain terms, but the next minute he'll be trying to make me laugh at a new joke that he has just read in a book. His requests—and they are many—come surrounded by a steady stream of conversation about what is going well or badly in his day, what happened in school or in the school ground, what he liked on television, what he learned on the Internet, what upcoming event he is looking forward to. Everything that is important to him, I get to know. He doesn't hold back anything that he is thinking or feeling.

To his "Daddy, can I do this?" or "Daddy, can I have that?" my answer has to be no as often as yes. And though he may not like it when I say no, he can come to accept it because deep down he senses that, even if I do not give him everything he wants, I am giving myself to him. His "Daddy, I love you" comes as often after a no as it does after a yes. That is the language of trust. Can we not go to God in the same way, trusting that he loves us even more than we love our children, that he is prepared to hear whatever may be on our hearts, that he will unfailingly give us what we need, which is mainly himself?

In his model prayer, Jesus told us to pray each day for our daily bread. Well, the generosity of God is such that, even if we do not ask, he will still provide what we need in the way of material goods and spiritual resources for each day's living. That is what parents do for their children. A father and mother can give their children the things they need, even though they never ask for them or even know their need. But they cannot give themselves and their love except to those who are ready and eager to receive them. It is the same with God. All the good gifts of the Father are summed up and find their fulfilment in the gift he most wants to give us—himself. This is the one gift that he cannot give without our asking. And it is the gift that goes to the root of life.

So when we pray, what should we pray for? For what we believe we need? Yes. For God to give others what we believe they need? Certainly. For God to do what is best when we cannot know what is best? Definitely. But, above all, let us pray for the Holy Spirit. For to live life in the presence of the God who is always there for us is to have all things.

Mercy

Finding Your Neighbour, Finding Yourself

Luke 10:25-37

"Which of these three, do you think, was a neighbor to the man who fell into the hands of the robbers?" He said, "The one who showed him mercy." Jesus said to him, "Go and do likewise."

—Luke 10:36-37

THE PARABLE OF THE GOOD SAMARITAN IS ONE OF THE BEST known and most frequently told Bible stories. Just about anyone who has had any church connection at all has been involved in acting it out at one time or another. When I was a boy and we did it in my Tyro Group, I was given the part of one of the thieves. My task was to deliver a fake punch to the victim in order to bring him to his knees. Alas, my fake punch was not aimed very well, and it landed square on the victim's chin. Fortunately, this accident did not affect the flow of the skit, as the victim collapsed just as he was supposed to.

This parable has a prominent place in every Sunday school curriculum. We all grew up with it. We know it well. Or do we?

Sometimes I wonder, especially when I hear the way people use the term "Good Samaritan." In our culture and in our community, one of the great compliments we pay to a person is to say that he or she is a Good Samaritan. And as you listen to what is said about those who are so labelled, you normally get a picture of people who just make it a part of their lives to be helpful and who are always doing things for others—neighbourly people. Rightfully, these Good Samaritans are admired in the community.

Now, I hope you will understand that it is no criticism of those whom we thus hold in high esteem to say that they have little in common with the Samaritan in Jesus' parable. None of the people in the church or the wider society whom I have heard called a Good Samaritan is an *outsider.* Yet, that is what Samaritan really means: a person from the wrong background, the wrong class, unchurched, unwashed, unacceptable.

The word "good" does not appear in Jesus' story, yet the narrative has come down through the years with the unofficial title of the "Parable of the Good Samaritan." Perhaps that is because the people to whom Jesus first told it were surprised to hear that there could be such a person as a "good" Samaritan.

In our circle, people get labelled "Good Samaritans" because they are busy doing things for their friends and next-door neighbours. But, in the parable, it was a stranger in distress who was given aid by the man from Samaria—a stranger, one in whom he had no personal interest.

We so misuse the label "Good Samaritan" that I wonder if we have really heard the story. We seem to have reduced it to an entertaining little morality play on the virtues of being helpful, when it is really about finding our neighbour and, so, finding ourselves. I suggest that we need to live with the parable a little while longer and let it speak to us afresh.

Of course, we cannot begin with the parable, for it does not stand on its own. It is a story that might never have been told were it not for the fact that a certain man—who was having a great deal of difficulty figuring out the way life works—came to Jesus with a question: "Teacher, what must I do to inherit eternal life?" (Luke 10:25).

This gentleman is a lawyer, you can just tell—a man who

likes to be organized, everything in its place, all his responsibilities clarified, all his obligations listed. "Teacher, eternal life is my objective. Please give me a program of action to follow in order to achieve this goal."

Now, Jesus can see that he is dealing here with the type of person who does not ask a question unless he also has the answer. Still, that's all right. If he has had a good upbringing and proper religious education, he ought to know the answer anyway. So our Lord's reply to the man goes something like this: "You tell me. What is written in the law? What do you read there? Surely you've learned this in Sunday school. You can recite it back to me."

And the man has learned something in Sunday school. He has studied the Book of Deuteronomy, where it says, "You shall love the Lord your God with all your heart, and with all your soul, and with all your might" (6:5). And he has studied the Book of Leviticus, where it says, "You shall love your neighbor as yourself" (19:18). So he quotes these scriptures to Jesus.

Jesus commends his response: "You have given the right answer; do this, and you will live" (10:28). End of conversation. Or is it? By now the lawyer is probably feeling a tad silly for having put a question with so obvious an answer, an answer memorized from his boyhood. He needs to get back on top of the conversation. "Not so quickly, Rabbi," he says. "That's not fair. Surely you can offer me more than what I've already read in the scriptures. You're not going to make me be satisfied with that, are you? Tell me, just who is my neighbour that I'm supposed to love as myself?"

Again Jesus will not conform to the man's expectations. The first question, he turned back. This one he answers, not with information, not with a legalistic definition, but instead with a story. An anecdote, if you please. A parable, and this for a lawyer who is used to telling people, "Just answer yes or no."

Now, it is not as if Jesus could not have given a simple, one-sentence answer. Anyone who hears this parable can sum it up in one sentence: "Whoever needs you is your neighbour." And

Jesus might have said just that to this disputatious man. But, of course, the man would have replied, "Just what do you mean by need?" And on and on it would have gone, and they would not really have got anywhere. Jesus knows that what this fellow really needs is not an answer but a change in the way he looks at life. That's why the lawyer gets a story instead of an answer, for stories are told to help us see life in a different way.

The trouble with our lawyer friend is that he wants eternal life on terms that he can control and at minimal cost. "What must I do? Just give me a set of instructions. I can handle that." "Who is my neighbour? Let me just narrow down the range of people who might fit into that category." The fellow speaks as if some folk might actually be excluded. At bottom, he is dealing with life questions at the mundane level of law, duty, and obligation. "Whom ought I to be prepared to love as myself? And just what does that involve?"

Jesus will not play this fellow's game. He sees that the man needs not an answer to his question but a whole new understanding of life, and perhaps that will happen if he can get into a story that will show him a different way of looking at things. Let us listen to the story with him.

We find ourselves on a dusty Palestinian road. "A man was going down from Jerusalem to Jericho, and fell into the hands of robbers, who stripped him, beat him, and went away, leaving him half dead" (Luke 10:30). So the scene is set. Given the context of the discussion that has preceded the telling of this story, I think it is pretty clear that Jesus intends the man in trouble to be thought of as "neighbour."

"Now by chance a priest was going down that road" (10:31). By chance—do you really think so? I think Jesus intends that it should be a priest who arrives on the scene first, for, like a lawyer, he will be a member of one of the established families of the upper class—part of the bedrock of society. Jesus, I suspect, wants the lawyer to see himself in the character of the priest.

So, what happens? The priest sees the man lying half dead

and in desperate need on the road and immediately begins arguing with himself about what to do with this victim of a lawless society, this neighbour thrown into his path by misadventure.

"Good grief, the poor fellow!" he may well be saying to himself. "Lucky it didn't happen to me. I should stop and help him. But his robbers might still be lurking nearby, just waiting to get their hands on another victim. I'd better get out of here. On the other hand"—here, conscience, bolstered by his religious training, starts arguing with his fear—"it would be cowardly not to help. After all, God has put this poor fellow in my way. I'm a priest: I can't be faint-hearted in such situations. I'd be denying God and failing to show compassion."

It looks as if the priest is going to do something, but just as he reaches for a cloth to bind up the man's wounds, it occurs to him: "Who is my neighbour, really? This fellow whom I don't know at all? This stranger, who may well be a criminal himself, a decoy for robbers behind the rocks? I have to think of other people—my family, my parishioners: my real neighbours. If I had only myself to think about, I'd take the risk, but I have others who depend on me. Besides, I have all the collection money from the temple in my pocket; it would be foolish to hang around here a second longer and risk having it fall into the hands of those thieves. Anyway, it's a well-travelled road. Someone else is bound to come along in a few minutes to help this poor chap." So on and on the priest goes, calling up various reasons to justify his inaction and salving his conscience with the idea that his duty to help this man is superseded by other, even more important duties.

And he persuades himself sufficiently that he does nothing, and passes by. However, he does not really believe his reasons—any more than we believe them when we reason that way to ourselves—for he passes by "on the other side" (10:31). He takes a long detour around the victim in order not to have to see him clearly, for he knows the sight of the man would accuse him and knock down his flimsily built house of reasons. He makes the detour and tries to put the man out of his mind, but

I doubt that he will quickly rid his thoughts of the image of that beaten fellow.

The next person down the road is a Levite. What a coincidence: another member of our lawyer's social circle. Imagine his reaction to the crime scene: "Oh no," he says to himself, "what a tragedy; the roads are so poorly policed these days. I must stop and see what I can do." Coming a little closer he gasps, "Good grief, this fellow is in pretty bad shape. What if he's already dead from his injuries? If I touch him I will be unclean for seven days. I won't be able to perform my duties at the temple, and I'm expected there this very afternoon. People are counting on me. I can't take the chance. I sure hope somebody who can afford to touch him will come along soon." So he, too, passes by—"on the other side." Of course, he is not convinced by his own logic. But it will have to do.

Perhaps by now the lawyer is getting the point. It is not enough to ask "Who is my neighbour?" and to hear Jesus answer "Anyone who needs you is your neighbour." Because, if you are so inclined, you will always be able to rationalize that the person who needs you does not really need you at all, or needs someone else more than you, or is not as much of a neighbour as others who have a more pressing claim upon you.

The trouble with your rationalizations is that, while they may prevent you from doing what is needed, they will never satisfy you. In fact, they will cost you. When you pass by on the other side, you may save your skin, but you do so at the cost of losing your soul. In passing by on the other side, you not only deny your neighbour, you deny yourself; for the truth is, you need that person lying on the road as much as he needs you. You need to help and heal him: his need for mercy is matched by your need to be merciful. It is not just for his sake that you come to the rescue. It is also for your sake. Neither of you can be really human, really alive, without the other. And every time you pass by and leave him to his own misery, you both suffer for it.

The story is not yet done. The lawyer has to hear about one

more person travelling down the road. This fellow is not from his social circle. When the Samaritan sees the victim, he binds up his wounds, sets him on his own beast, and takes care of him. And his reward is to go down in history as the "Good Samaritan," which does not seem to be quite the right title, because it implies that the priest and the Levite were bad. And I don't think they were bad people, no worse than you or I have been on many occasions. They were not *bad* so much as *blind*—either wilfully or ignorantly—to the reality of life. The Good Samaritan was not *good* so much as he was *perceptive* to life's reality—which is that many people who might surprise us turn out to be our neighbours. It often happens by accident and we do not get much choice in the matter. And when it stares us in the face who our neighbour is, the real question is not "Is this person my neighbour?" but "What am I going to do about this person whom life has made my neighbour?" And what we do, friends, really determines how rich our own lives will be.

Now, what the Samaritan did for the man was good, but it was good as much for himself as for the victim. Of the three men who chanced on that unfortunate scene, he was the one who would sleep that night. For he was the one who accepted life and human relationships as God has made them.

Do you suppose the lawyer learned anything from the story? Do you suppose he learned enough to stop asking pointless questions like "Who is my neighbour?" Do you suppose he learned to ask what needs to be asked: "How can I be a neighbour? How can I find my neighbour and, in finding my neighbour, find my own humanity?"

FORGIVENESS

Judgement Is Reserved

John 7:53-8:11

Jesus ... said to her, "Woman, where are they? Has no one condemned you?" She said, "No one, sir." And Jesus said, "Neither do I condemn you. Go your way, and from now on do not sin again."

—John 8:10-11

I WENT TO THE TEMPLE THIS MORNING. ACTUALLY, LATELY I'VE been going every day. You see, Jesus of Nazareth is in town, and he's been teaching there, and I simply don't want to miss hearing anything he says. I have never heard anyone speak about God and faith and life with such power and clarity. And he's so refreshing. He expounds the law and the prophets to us, but he makes them seem so new. Our scriptures come alive in his hands. I'm learning so much.

But, I have to be honest. I'm not going just for the great teaching. The fact is, any time Jesus teaches there is bound to be controversy, because the scribes and the Pharisees always come along and start arguing with him. He really gets their goat. And, well, I don't mind seeing the sparks fly.

But today, I think the Pharisees went too far. They weren't

satisfied just to argue. No, they had to create a scene. They dragged right into the Temple courtyard a woman who they claimed had been caught in the act of adultery. Then they asked Jesus what should be done with her. And they so much as told him the answer. They said the law commands that she be stoned for her sin. Well, technically, that's true. I looked it up. The Book of Leviticus specifies death for adultery (20:10), and the Book of Deuteronomy indicates that it is to be death by stoning (22:22-24).

Well, I don't mind telling you that I was pretty uncomfortable with the whole business. I don't condone what this woman did, but to be humiliated in front of a crowd of people—there must have been at least a hundred of us. And to have her life threatened! One old rabbi told me afterwards he had never seen the like in all his 80 years. He couldn't remember when the law had ever been applied that way. For the longest time, these adultery matters have been settled by divorce. He wasn't sure whether the Pharisees really wanted to go back to taking the ancient laws literally or whether they were just trying to create a difficult situation for Jesus. I suspect it was the latter. The only reason we were exposed to this spectacle was that the Pharisees wanted to embarrass Jesus in front of his supporters. After all, if they'd really wanted to take the scripture literally, both of the guilty people would have been hauled before Jesus, because both offenders are to die. But I didn't see any sign of the man she was supposed to have been sleeping with. They didn't seem to be too interested in exposing his sin and applying capital punishment to him.

You could see what they were really up to. They were just trying to trap Jesus. If he were to say "Don't punish the woman," he would be contradicting the law, and then they would have an excuse to bring a charge against him. And if he were to say "Go ahead and punish her," then he would look as mean and nasty as they were, and that wouldn't have gone over very well with the crowd.

It was disgusting what they were trying to do. But I have to admit that I was fascinated and curious to see how Jesus would handle the challenge. I couldn't imagine him opposing the law, but then again, I couldn't see him willingly parting with the reputation for concern and caring and compassion that he had worked so hard to gain.

Well, what a treat to see Jesus' performance. It was masterful. The whole crowd was tense, silent, holding its breath, waiting for his answer. But he didn't give it right away. He bent down and traced on the ground for a while. What was he doing? Playing for time? Or letting the suspense deepen for effect? It seemed like an eternity. I guess it was really only a few seconds. Then he lifted his head to speak. What would he say? "Let the poor woman go," or "Go ahead and stone her"?

When he finally spoke, it stunned us all. "Go ahead and inflict the punishment," he seemed to be saying, "but let the one who is sinless be the first to cast a stone." What a brilliant stroke! He didn't go against the law, so the Pharisees had nothing to pin on him. But he didn't allow any harm to come to the woman. So the Pharisees came off as mean and snarly, and Jesus came out of it smelling like a rose. The man is so smart and smooth that, if I were King Herod, I'd start paying attention.

I couldn't help but think back to the time—maybe you were there—when they tried to lay another trap. They asked him if it is lawful to pay taxes to Caesar or not. So, if he says yes, then he disappoints all the patriotic Israelites who would like the Romans to go to you-know-where. And if he says no, then they can report him to the Romans as an agitator, subverting the rule of the Empire. So, what does he say: "Yes, pay your taxes," or "No, do not"? He does neither, if you please. He comes back at them in a flash: "Give ... to the emperor the things that are the emperor's, and to God the things that are God's" (Matthew 22:21). Now, what does that mean? Boy, were they consternated. You'll wait a long time before you see our religious leaders put one over on Jesus of Nazareth.

Well, it was quite a day, and I had a lot to think about on the way home. And it was as I was walking home, and running the day's events over in my mind, that I began to get the impression that more had taken place in this little drama at the Temple than I had at first realized. What I thought I had seen was Jesus work his way out of a tight spot, and get the woman off the hook, and embarrass the Pharisees. But maybe what I had really been witnessing was him ministering both to that woman and to those men.

What made me start to think along these lines was the feelings I began to have towards the woman after the confrontation was over. When the Pharisees dragged her in, I really felt for her. She was such a pitiful sight, head bowed down, shoulders drooping. Her eyes never left the ground in front of her; she never looked at any of us. Well, how could she? The shame of being exposed like that. And the fear of what was to come next: those men really appeared to mean business.

Well, I felt for her at that point. I did not think of what she'd done; I could only think of how miserable she must feel at being put on display and branded as an immoral woman in front of a bunch of strangers.

So, I was glad Jesus protected her. But afterwards, when her accusers had gone, I began to feel differently. She was no longer a woman in danger, just a person who had committed an immoral act. Now, her business is none of my business, but I thought Jesus might have given her a bit of a talking to, that he might have at least tried to impress upon her that what she'd done was really wrong, that this was not a good way to live her life. Instead, what does he do? Gives her a gentle tap on the wrist and essentially says, "Has no one condemned you? I don't condemn you either; now go and don't do it again."

Well, does he really think she's going to pay any attention to that? I was a bit disappointed, I don't mind telling you. Now, don't get me wrong. I'm a moderate man. I don't want to go back to the old days of capital punishment for sins of the flesh. That's a little on the barbaric side. We've come a long way from that. We're more enlightened now. By the same token, I wonder if we've become too enlightened. I was offended at the thought of stoning the woman, but I was a little indignant when Jesus didn't point out to her the seriousness of her transgression and the destructiveness of her behaviour.

Well, I was indignant until it suddenly hit me what had actually taken place. I guess I wasn't listening carefully enough at the time, because now I realized that Jesus really had made it clear that what the woman had done was a very bad thing and that she was a very great sinner. I thought of the things that Jesus hadn't said. He hadn't said, "Let the woman go. We don't regard adultery as seriously these days as they did in Moses' day." He hadn't said, "This is one commandment that needs to be updated." He hadn't said, "Who this woman is sleeping with is a private matter and not for us to talk about in the Temple." No, what he said was, in effect: "We know what the law is. We know she is guilty of breaking it. The punishment prescribed is great because the crime she committed is great. Go ahead and stone her. Death is what sinners deserve. It is what they have earned. Of course, the one who throws the first stone had better be sinless— had better be sure he has the moral authority to enforce the law. Otherwise, enforcing the law will only make a mockery of it."

When you stop to think about it, Jesus was not letting the law down at all. He was upholding it. He wasn't soft on adultery. He clearly indicated that the law was right and the woman was in the wrong.

But he let the woman go with an encouragement to do right in the future. That taught me something about how he believes the law should be used. To him, the laws we have in the Books of Moses, in all their awful severity, are not there to help some holier-than-thou types to terrorize someone like this woman, even if she has behaved badly. They are there to expose to such a person the depth of her sin and to show her how much she needs to be rescued by God. The law is not there to drag her down, but to raise her up by demonstrating her need and showing where it can be met. I hope she got the message. I hope she didn't go home with the attitude "Well, that's that. I can do whatever I want and get away with it." For, if she goes back to her old ways, she will die. Her spirit will die. She will cease to know what love is, for how can you know love when you do not practise commitment and trust and fidelity?

I hope that doesn't happen. I hope she got the message. And I think she may have, for in Jesus she got a good glimpse at what righteousness combined with love looks like. Now that she has seen such beauty, now that something beautiful has been done in her life, it may well be that she will want more of it.

Also, it's becoming clear to me that Jesus was ministering to the Pharisees, too. I didn't see it at first. I was too full of his victory over them. It was only on the walk home that I realized Jesus hadn't been trying to win a victory at all. Do you know that he didn't speak one word of criticism to them, though their behaviour had been pretty disgraceful? They had used this woman as a pawn in their offensive. Well, that is just as bad as the adultery they condemned. I have always been taught that the sin in sexual immorality is the sin of not treating people seriously, of using them for personal gratification, of failing to develop proper relationships, of treating people as objects. But this is precisely what this woman was to them: an object to be used in a cat-and-mouse game with Jesus. They didn't care if she was repentant or not, if she could be changed or not, if the relationship with her husband could be repaired or not. She was just an object to them.

And who were they anyway to complain about her adultery? Jesus once said that lusting after someone in your heart was as much adultery as committing the physical act (Matthew 5:27-28). Did they really expect us to believe that they'd never lusted?

And their self-righteousness was nauseating. More than that, it was distressing. I would never have imagined it to be so easy to dress up a sin in a cloak of righteousness. There is nothing you can do with adultery to make it look right and good. But their mean-spiritedness was impeccably tailored, and all the more dangerous because it could be made to look religious and carry an air of respectability.

Yet, for all this, Jesus did not utter one word of criticism nor of condemnation to those Pharisees. He didn't wag his finger at them. Instead, he used it to write on the ground—I'd like to know what, probably their sins—so that they would realize that he knew the dirt on them. Maybe they began to worry that he would expose and humiliate them just as they had done the woman.

But he didn't. There was no lecture, no exposing, no condemnation. Just a simple request that they look at themselves before doing anything. He asked them to examine their own hearts. I think he was saying to them in a very quiet way that they should not look at this woman's wrongdoing as permission to launch a program of self-righteous enforcement of the law. Rather, her problems should make them look inward to discern the sin that is common to all of us.

Now, if Jesus had given these men a verbal blast—which they richly deserved—I doubt that it would have done much more than harden the lines between them. Instead, he delivered a more subtle rebuke. I am sure it stung, nevertheless: to be embarrassed in front of the crowd that was supposed to witness Jesus' embarrassment. But perhaps some of them, if they aren't too far gone in their hatred of Jesus—the perceptive ones—when they look back on this incident, will realize that he was resisting the urge to do battle and was trying to help. He was going as easy as he could on them. Perhaps some of them who can still recognize truth will take Jesus' gentle rebuke to heart. Maybe they will begin to look more carefully at themselves and see what their self-righteousness has made of them. Maybe there is hope for them, too.

There is one more thing that struck me on the way home. That is the remarkable fact that the one who could have cast the stone at the woman—and at the Pharisees—did not. Jesus said, "Let anyone among you who is without sin be the first to throw a stone at her" (8:7). If any of us in that crowd was without sin, it was surely he. If any of us was fit to pass judgement, it was Jesus himself. But the interesting thing is, the one who could have passed judgement, reserved judgement.

His judgement is so keen, but he doesn't want to be a judge. Afterwards he said to us, "You judge by human standards; I judge no one" (8:15). He doesn't want to be a judge, but I wonder: some are saying he is the Messiah, the one who is to come. If that is so, one day he will have to judge us.

But he certainly doesn't want to do it now. He seems to want us to judge ourselves and to see for ourselves how much we need him to show the way. If it is true that he is the Messiah, then he is a very kind one, because he obviously wants us to be ready for the judgement when he passes it.

I feel so lucky to have been at the Temple today. I got to be a spectator at an event I think people are going to be talking about for a long time. I'm glad I was just a spectator and not one of the participants. But I wonder, will I always be so lucky? What if one day I were to find myself and all my sins exposed for the world to see? It happened to that woman this morning. It could happen to me. Where would I turn then? Would there be someone like Jesus there for me?

Or, what if I were on the other side? What if someday I were to be given a position in the community that required me to uphold morality and maintain the standards of the law? That's really what we've asked of the Pharisees. If I were in their position, what would I do? Would I do as they did, or would I be able to be like Jesus for someone in trouble?

Community

The Table of Healing

Matthew 9:9-13

When the Pharisees saw this, they said to his disciples, "Why does your teacher eat with tax collectors and sinners?" But when he heard this, he said, "Those who are well have no need of a physician, but those who are sick."
—Matthew 9:11-12

GOING OUT FOR LUNCH IS SOMETHING I NORMALLY LOOK FORWARD to. Whether it's strictly for pleasure or to mix business with pleasure, it is nice to be able to share a pleasant setting with friends and to enjoy good food capably served up. But there was a time when going out for lunch was a source of anxiety in my life. That was at the beginning of my work in my first church in the small town of Holland, Manitoba.

Picture the new minister, only recently arrived in the village, going into the local restaurant at lunchtime. The customers know who he is. The new person in town tends to be fairly noticeable. But he does not yet know who they are, or, at best, has only a vague idea. And so he is anxious. There is one vacant table in the corner, but he does not want to go to it for fear of being thought stuck-up or unsociable. Yet, he is reluctant to ask for an empty space at one of the occupied tables. He does not want to barge in uninvited or impose himself on people who might be uncomfortable with his presence. Truly, this is an awkward situation—or at least in his mind it is. You can imagine his relief when one of the diners waves a hand and says, "There's a seat here. Care to join us?"

Immediately his problem is solved. He has a place. He has been accepted. He belongs. It will be a good lunch after all.

A table is more than just a place for eating. The food on top of it is often less important than the people around it. The table is a place for being included, being affirmed, being cared for.

At least, this is what the table meant for Jesus. During his public years, it became a focal point of his ministry. It figured prominently in his parables about the kingdom of heaven. "The kingdom of heaven may be compared to a king who gave a wedding banquet for his son. . . . [and] the wedding hall was filled with guests," went one such story (Matthew 22:1-14). Remember who was invited to sit at table that night? The table was also the place where he made many of his most pointed public statements (Luke 7:36-50, 14:1-14, 19:1-10). Finally, it was the place where he gathered his disciples for that meal that we still share today (Matthew 26:20-29).

In today's lesson from Matthew, we find Jesus at table "in the house"; whose house, we are not quite sure. But the way things are described, the situation is more reminiscent of a small-town restaurant than it is of a private home. Eating appears to have been a fairly public business in Israel. And so, in our story, a group of people simply walks in and joins Jesus and his disciples at table. And the Pharisees are hanging around, watching what's going on, waiting to see what's going to happen. It is a public event.

Now, when you mention Jesus and the Pharisees in the same paragraph, you can be reasonably sure you are headed for controversy. And this time is no exception. The Pharisees corner some of Jesus' disciples and ask them why their teacher eats with tax collectors and sinners. Now, the question is not posed to elicit information, as if they are prepared to hear some good reason why Jesus is doing this. Rather, it is intended as a pronouncement of judgement, as if to say, "Your friend keeps some pretty questionable company."

That is probably true. The company was questionable. The tax collectors were people who made their living by raising revenue from their fellow Jews for the hated Roman masters. They were people who had sold out their countryfolk—though maybe it was the only work they could find. In any event, tax collectors were to their fellow Jews what replacement workers are today to strikers on the picket line—scabs. And the sinners? Well, there were probably two kinds. Some were folk who were careless about obeying the details of the religious law, the kind of people who really do not make a good contribution to the tone of the community. Others were folk who were guilty of serious moral lapses—some of them probably not far from jail.

So it is not surprising that the Pharisees should go on the offensive: "Why does your teacher eat with tax collectors and sinners?" (9:11). Jesus is quick to defend his action. "Those who are well," he says, "have no need of a physician, but those who are sick" (9:12). I always used to think of this as a figure of speech. Jesus is *like* a physician. The Pharisees are *like* those who are well. The tax collectors and sinners are *like* those who are sick. But Matthew does not interpret the remark as a figure of speech. He takes it literally. I understood this when I read the passage in its context in the whole of the ninth chapter of Matthew's gospel. It is full of healings. Jesus heals a paralyzed man; he raises a young girl from a mortal illness; he cures a hemorrhaging woman; he gives sight to two blind men; he gives the ability to speak to a dumb man possessed by a demon. And in the middle of all this activity, he eats with tax collectors and sinners.

So, in a chapter that is all about healings, when Jesus speaks about eating with tax collectors and sinners in terms of a physician tending to those who are ill, we are clearly meant to interpret his remark literally. These people *are* ill. They *are* sick.

In what sense are they ill? Well, these people are *out of circulation*, they are *outcasts*. And in the mind of Jesus this is an illness. In a sense, that was the problem experienced by the other sick people in this chapter. Due to their physical ailments, they were out of circulation, they had no real place in the community, and that may well have been the worst part of their illness. They needed to have their physical powers restored in order to reclaim a valued place in society. The tax collectors and sinners may have been well, physically, but they experienced the same kind of isolation, and the healing they needed was *acceptance, inclusion, fellowship*. And Jesus gave it to them by having them at his table. For him the table was a place of healing. And the sinners who sat with him there experienced healing as surely as the paralyzed man who was told to take up his bed and walk. He returned to the community, and they found themselves in community.

Why were the Pharisees so bothered by this healing ministry of Jesus? I suppose there were two reasons. First, they feared a *loss of standards*. Having someone to your table, or being seen in public at table with someone, registers a kind of social acceptance. The Pharisees no doubt believed that in accepting tax collectors and sinners at his table, Jesus was making light of their sins and problems. In fact, this was not the case. In welcoming these people, Jesus did not accept their condition as a healthy one. He did not sentimentalize about them or pretend that everything was all right with them. He was not suggesting that, in their own coarse way, they were as good as, possibly even better people than, the Pharisees. They were not. Jesus admitted that straight out. The Pharisees were well. The people he had at his table were ill. And if it is a loss of standards to be with someone who is ill, so be it.

Secondly, the Pharisees feared *contamination*. If you got too close to the tax collectors and sinners, what was wrong with them might well rub off on you. Or at the very least, in the eyes of other people, you would now be connected with their sins and problems. Well, for Jesus, if there was a risk of contamination in being with someone who was ill, so be it. For Jesus was a healer, a doctor, one who lives with such a risk in order to fulfil his calling.

When the Pharisees put their question, "Why does your teacher eat with tax collectors and sinners?" (9:11), they were making an implied criticism. Jesus' reply was an implied rebuke: "Go and learn what this means, 'I desire mercy, not sacrifice'" (9:13). That's a quote from the Old Testament prophet Hosea (Hosea 6:6). Hosea was proclaiming God's judgement on religious people who were good at performing their churchly duties but not good at performing the duty of caring for others. The prophet was saying to them that their sacrifices, their rituals, if not accompanied by mercy, by compassion for others, were not pleasing to God, but an offence. Their religious vows needed to be acted upon.

When Jesus told the Pharisees to learn about mercy, I think he was saying to them that they, too, needed to be acting on their religious vows. They, too, could, and should, be performing this ministry of healing. Jesus did not see eating with sinners as something only he should be doing. There was nothing preventing the Pharisees from having sinners at their tables; there was only mercy appealing to them to show hospitality to those less favoured.

"Go and learn what this means, 'I desire mercy, not sacrifice.'" It is at this point, with this statement, that we are taken into today's lesson and told that we have a healing ministry to perform. We may well ask, "When would we ever get the opportunity?" We do not think of inviting people for dinner or sitting down across from someone in a café as ministry. And most of the time it is not. Most of the time the people with whom we sit at table are well. They are in circulation, included. They do not lack for acceptance or community. What we offer them at table is nothing more significant than good food and pleasant conversation. More than this they do not need.

But even in our congregation and the circle of those whom we know, there are people who are not in circulation, not included, not accepted, who do lack for community—the tax collectors and sinners of our day. They are people who are cast out—outcasts. Sometimes it is their own fault; sometimes they are victims of circumstance. Such people are around us. The fellowship of the table is something we can provide for them and something that will help.

From time to time, the opportunity to participate in the healing ministry of the table has come my way. I can remember an occasion many years ago when a novice teacher I knew was let go from his position for incompetence. I do not know whether that was really the problem or whether he was simply not yet ready to teach. In any event, he was soon to be gone from job and community. The school division wasn't going to waste any more time on him. Linda and I had had some involvement with him but did not know him well enough that we felt obligated to have him over for supper before he left. And certainly the counsel of society is always "Don't get involved with losers, with people who can't do anything for you." Besides, it would be awkward; what kind of conversation do you have at supper with somebody who has just lost his job? Yet, the feeling kept coming back: "We ought to have him over."

So, we did. We invited him for supper. And, in the end, we were glad we did. Sitting at table with him was not a way of saying "We think the superintendent was stupid for letting you go." For all we knew, the decision was a correct one. The message we were trying to communicate was simply "We know you are having problems. We really don't care at this point who's right and who's wrong. But we do care about you, and we are concerned about the stress and the pain and the worry that are oppressing you right now." Perhaps at that moment that young man needed the healing community of the table more than he needed the knowledge that there would soon be another job for him. In any event, the table was the place to say "We care."

Another case: I have a friend who got into trouble; some serious allegations were levelled at him and his life began to be led under a cloud. He had been a socially active person with many friends, a frequent visitor in many homes. But, when his difficulty came upon him, he said it was as if a wall had been built around him. His contacts dried up; it was as if people willed him no longer to exist. To put it in the language of Matthew 9, he did not experience the same welcome when he was ill that he did when he was well.

Imagine what it would be like for such a person to go to a local restaurant such as I described at the beginning—to see vacant chairs beside people he knows, and yet to realize that all he can do is go over and sit at the empty table in the corner, that there really is no other place for him.

Now, friends, it is not easy to sit at table with someone in trouble, someone disreputable, someone labelled a "sinner." It can be awkward. You do not know what to talk about or not to talk about. It is even tougher, as I experienced, to sit at table in public with such a person under the gaze of interested people in the community who have already made up their minds about him. It's tough. But Jesus never said the healing ministry of the table would be easy. He merely said, "I desire mercy, not sacrifice."

Having a coffee with a person with a problem may not solve the problem. It is, however, a first step in that it says, "I accept you as a person." Without that, nothing can happen. Jesus knew that if you kept the tax collectors and sinners isolated and excluded, they would always be tax collectors and sinners. But if you included them, if you accepted them, they might one day amount to something more.

Friends, we know that the Pharisees never accepted Jesus' call to the healing ministry of the table. Will we do better and heed his desire for mercy? I think a powerful incentive for us is the remembrance that when Jesus receives us at his table here in this church, he does not do so on the basis of our worthiness. One communion prayer states our position quite frankly: "We do not presume to come to this thy Table, O merciful Lord, trusting in our own righteousness, but in thy manifold and great mercies. We are not worthy so much as to gather up the crumbs under thy Table."[1] If we receive a welcome and healing when we come, it is because Jesus, in his great love, does not hesitate to dine with us.

If we can be healed at the Lord's table, may others not be healed at ours?

---

1. "Prayer of Humble Access," in *Service Book of the United Church of Canada* (Toronto: Ryerson Press, 1969), p. 27.

JUSTICE

Refugees: Divine and Human

Matthew 2:13-23

> *Then Joseph got up, took the child and his mother by night, and went to Egypt, and remained there until the death of Herod.*
>
> —Matthew 2:14-15

YOU PEOPLE OF WESTMINSTER CHURCH ARE NOW PREPARING TO do again what you have ably done in the past, which is to host a family seeking refuge in Canada and to help them settle into a new, safe, stable, and productive life in this city. As we look forward to the hoped-for arrival of the Saric family, now in Serbia and late of Bosnia, those of you who have been around this congregation for some time may be remembering your experience with the Conchas, a family who sought refuge on account of the threat posed by the Pinochet regime in Chile and who, through your efforts, are now an established part of the Winnipeg community. It is folk such as the Conchas who help put a human face on a great scourge of the twentieth century, the forced uprooting of people.

When I was ministering in the town of Holland, I received a card on Christmas Eve one year from a family who had come there as refugees from Vietnam and after a few years had moved on to Winnipeg. In somewhat tentative English the message on the card expressed eloquently what it means to people in a refugee camp to find that, halfway around the world, there are those who are prepared to take them in. The note went like this: "My dear people. Please take my great opportunity to thank all the people of Holland.... Holland is my birth place in new life and the people in Holland are my parents. My family missed you very much. Have a Merry Christmas and a Happy New Year, from Hom, Lee, and boys."

Receiving this card right in the middle of our nativity celebrations reminded me of a particular part of the Christmas story and of the fact that our Lord Jesus himself was born in a humble stable only to become a refugee. For as Matthew reports, "An angel of the Lord appeared to Joseph in a dream and said, 'Get up, take the child and his mother, and flee to Egypt, and remain there until I tell you; for Herod is about to search for the child, to destroy him'" (2:13).

Joseph's flight to Egypt was actually the culmination of a long tradition. Egypt was the classic land of refuge for those fleeing from tyranny and danger in Palestine. When King Solomon's regime became oppressive with heavy taxes and forced labour, one man who stood against him was Jeroboam. Solomon saw the danger posed to him by this potential rival and sought to kill him, but Jeroboam fled and took refuge in Egypt (1 Kings 11:40). Another time, a prophet named Uriah spoke up against a particularly corrupt king named Jehoiakim. Things became so dangerous for him that he had to flee to Egypt for safety (Jeremiah 26:21). David, when King Saul was out for his blood, took refuge in the south (1 Samuel 21-30). Of course, it worked the other way around as well. For we remember the story of Moses, a refugee from Egypt, waiting for God's call to take a whole nation out as refugees (Exodus 2-3).

So many people who play a significant part in the Bible story had to flee for their lives at one time or another. Consequently, any reading of the Bible prepares us well to hear the sad story of refugees in many parts of the world today. In the late 1970s, when Canada and other countries were taking in the Vietnamese boat people, it was commonly said that there were 10 million refugees throughout the world. On the eve of the millennium, the number has skyrocketed to an estimated 45 million refugees, most of them women and children, uprooted from their homes by war, human rights violations, or environmental disaster.

Their situations and their stories may vary, but they all have one thing in common. According to a document put out by the United Nations High Commission for Refugees it is this: "Refugees are human beings who have had to take one of the most difficult decisions ever: to cut their roots. Move. Sometimes out of blind fear because their lives were in danger, on other occasions because they simply could not breathe intellectually."[1] The document goes on to say, "We do not have to list the scores of reasons people have had and will have for reaching this decision. Newspapers, radio, and television have illustrated them for decades and there will be new, sad stories in the future. Because people are what they are. The world creates refugee problems."

Yes, indeed it does, and as we look back at the story of the flight into Egypt, we find that the world has not, and people have not, changed very much in 2,000 years. The dilemma so many millions face today is the same as that faced by Jesus' parents.

Today's passage from Matthew is divided into three sections. Each one sheds some light on the plight and problem of refugees.

In the first section an angel comes to Joseph and instructs him to flee to Egypt, for Herod wishes to find the baby Jesus and kill him. While it is not mentioned directly, there is an

1. United Nations High Commission for Refugees, Geneva, *The refugee problem isn't hopeless. Unless you think so,* 1975, p. 3.

important point in this: Is it not a good thing that there was an Egypt to flee to? What if the borders had been blocked? What if Egyptian tradesmen had said, "Our economy will never support another carpenter"? What if government administrators had protested, "This is bound to swell the social assistance rolls"? What if pollsters had found people in the street objecting, "The Israelite culture will never mix with our own. Soon they will be swamping us"?

These are the very kinds of objections that are often raised when people seek refuge in our country. Their culture or faith won't mix with ours; they will bring their old enmities with them; they will be an economic burden; there aren't enough jobs for those who already live here; our social and health-care systems are already overtaxed. These people aren't our problem. We have enough problems of our own. And though you can statistically prove that refugees normally go very quickly from being burdens upon us to being contributors to our economy, it seems very hard to change attitudes.

Now, I don't dismiss concerns about refugees and I do not pretend that it is easy to help people whose culture and language and faith are new to us to find a home here. But whenever I am tempted to wash my hands and say it is more than we can handle, that these people are not our problem, I have to remind myself that my wife's ancestors were economic refugees from Scotland, shoved off the land when the landowners found raising sheep for wool to be more profitable than collecting rents from the tenants who had always done the farming. Her ancestors found refuge and a new life here at the Selkirk Settlement. And I have to remind myself that my ancestors were political refugees from the United States after the War of Independence, people who had everything taken from them because they wouldn't renounce their loyalty to the British Crown. They found a new life in Upper Canada and subsequently on these Prairies. How many people in this congregation do not have refugees somewhere in their family histories?

When I'm tempted to say these people aren't our problem, I

sometimes make the mistake of reading the Bible and coming across verses such as Exodus 22:21, where it says, "You shall not wrong or oppress a resident alien, for you were aliens in the land of Egypt." The Bible repeatedly and unfailingly urges and enjoins hospitality towards the stranger in the land, the outcast, and the refugee. Jesus adds his name alongside those of all other refugees when he says, in effect, "I was a stranger and you welcomed me. The way you treat those considered unimportant by the world is the way you treat me" (Matthew 25:31-46). Those who are inclined to refuse hospitality should ask themselves, What would have been the result had the Egyptians refused entry to Joseph, Mary, and the Babe? What would have happened if they had said, "These people aren't our problem; we have enough problems of our own"?

The second part of this passage depicts the violence against the innocent of this world. Herod, in his determination to be rid of the perceived threat to his throne, orders the murder of all the young boys in and around Bethlehem. So 20 or 30 or 200 or 300 children pay the price of an evil man's folly. It is hard to imagine how anyone could be so wicked. But to people who say "This couldn't have happened," I say, "The evidence is all around us to this very day."

The death of Pol Pot in 1998 brought back to my mind the slaughterhouse that was Cambodia after the Khmer Rouge took over in the mid-1970s. One of the things this new government did was to take youngsters, put them on trial, and find them guilty of being children of the intellectual class. These same children were then chained together in bomb craters and buried alive.

Then there is Bosnia. The details of that country's civil war are starting to get hazy in my mind, but one memory that will always stay crystal clear is reading that a very high percentage of victims felled by snipers during the siege of Sarajevo were children. This was not a case of little ones being in the wrong place at the wrong time when mortar shells exploded. No, it was a case of somebody lining them up in his sights, knowing exactly whom he was killing, and doing it without mercy because, after all, there is no better way to kill your adversary's future than to kill his children. Just another little item in the news that reminds us that Herod is still with us.

Now, it is not the main point of these verses from Matthew, but I think it is important to note that when people flee, the motivation is not that opportunity is better elsewhere but rather that life has become impossible where they now are. Only rarely is flight a self-serving act. Much more often it is an act of desperation. It is what you must do because a great danger stalks your homeland and threatens your family. Joseph did not flee to Egypt because he disliked Herod or thought he was a bad king. He fled because he thought Herod presented an imminent threat to his son, and because Herod was the kind of tyrant, as the slaughter of the innocents proves, who would stop at nothing to achieve his objectives.

The boat people did not leave Indochina because they were disenchanted with Communism. You don't float around in a dilapidated craft in the South China Sea exposing yourself to the threat of pirates and typhoons because you don't like your government. You do it because the government has deprived you of your possessions and now threatens to deprive you of your life.

Those who now are trying to get out of the Balkans aren't doing it simply because life is better elsewhere, though of course they cannot help but know that life is better elsewhere. No, they are fleeing because as long as people like Slobodan Milosevic and Radovan Karadic are calling the shots in that part of the world, there will be no end to the cycle of violence, killing, and displacement that has put a new euphemism into our language—"ethnic cleansing."

When people are oppressed and frightened to the point where they fear for their lives and those of their children, they have no choice but to flee. And there must be a place to flee to. It is our ability and responsibility to provide a place of refuge. As Christians, it is our calling to recognize the basic dignity owed to people as members of God's creation. When that dignity is robbed and they seek refuge with more fortunate folk, it is a mark of civilization to take them in. To put it simply, to refuse a refugee is basically to refuse our Lord and our faith.

This is not to say that there are no legitimate points of disagreement over refugee policy and procedure. I do not think there is a specifically Christian point of view on whether or not there should be a landing fee or how big a landing fee should be. People of good will might legitimately disagree on such a matter. I do not think there is a specifically Christian point of view on how many refugees our country can properly accommodate every year. Currently, Canada settles about 10,000 refugees annually, 3,000 of them assisted by church groups. But we receive an additional 30,000 requests every year from people to whom our borders remain closed. What is a manageable and just figure? People of good will might disagree about this, but surely people of good will can insist that discussion of this issue remain high on our nation's political agenda. People of good will might well disagree on what kind of procedures and how much bureaucracy and what kind of time lines should be in place to screen out criminals and false claimants. I do not think there is a specifically Christian position on that issue and on many other technical ones.

But there is a specifically Christian attitude that must govern our approach to these issues, and that is *openness to the refugee.* For Jesus and his ancestors, hospitality was a hallmark of the reign of God. And today, as uprooted people arrive empty-handed on another doorstep, often after a death-defying journey, their hope lies in the hospitality of others. That is why I am so proud of this congregation's history of welcoming refugees and of its determination to do it again now that both need and opportunity have presented themselves.

Now, in the third part of today's story from Matthew, Herod having died, Joseph obeys an angel's command to return to Israel with the child. This reminds us, of course, that salvation for Israel was possible only when Jesus could return home. Something similar can be said of our world today. The refugee problem will not be solved by our taking in refugees, though that is our responsibility. It will be solved only when refugees are free to return and rebuild their lives in their homeland—indeed, when there is no need to tear up roots at all.

Of course, to any realist that seems like a distant dream, for there is never any end to those evil conditions that lead to people being on the run in the first place. It seems that every time one Herod dies, another appears on the scene to take his place. But a second specifically Christian attitude is *hope*. And hope is manifested when free people tell their governments loudly and clearly that they do not want it to be business as usual with tyrants throughout the world who abuse and oppress their citizens or segments of their citizenry. Hope is manifested when free people tell their governments loudly and clearly that they are prepared to make sacrifices to help out the oppressed in strife-torn countries. Hope is manifested when free people tell their governments loudly and clearly that extending the rule of law in this world is even more important than securing good trade deals.

Successes don't necessarily come easily or frequently to those who live and act in hope. But we hold onto hope, and we are prepared to act, not because we expect everything to change tomorrow but because we trust God's promise that his kingdom will come and his will will be done, and we want our actions to be in tune with his rule.

We know that God would not have come down and been born at night among the beasts if he hadn't really cared about the trials and tribulations of every human being. We know that God would not have endured danger, and fear, and flight, if he had not taken to his own heart the suffering of all who endure danger and fear and flight. And so, because God has cast in his lot with the stranger and the refugee, we cast in our lot as well. And until the day when all the Herods of this world lie vanquished, and people need no longer live in fear, we pray that God will sustain the refugees and oppressed people everywhere with the knowledge that his own Son has shared their plight.

Postscript:

This sermon was given in January 1999, when the people of Westminster Church were beginning to raise the funds necessary to sponsor a refugee family from Bosnia then living in a refugee camp in Serbia. The money was raised quickly, but the outbreak of hostilities between NATO *and Serbia over the future of Kosovo delayed refugee proceedings and raised fears that the family might remain trapped in the former Yugoslavia. On September 21 of that year, the prayers of both the congregation and the family were answered as Zeljko and Lela Saric and their three daughters, Violeta, Iovana, and Danijela, arrived in Winnipeg, their new home.*

Remembrance

Why Should We Care?

They shall not grow old,
as we that are left grow old;
Age shall not weary them,
nor the years condemn.
At the going down of the sun
and in the morning,
We will remember them.[1]

A MAN WHO HAD BEEN A STUDENT AT THE UNIVERSITY OF TORONTO, had enlisted during the Second World War, and had served overseas, returns after the war to take up his studies again. One day he reads the list of the university's war dead on the wall of Soldiers' Tower in the centre of the campus and comes upon the name of a student he had known. And it moves him to write this poem:

---

1. "The Tryst," commonly spoken at Remembrance Day services in the British Commonwealth.

To David

They wrote me you'd been killed
Somewhere in France, that fall of '44.
It had moved me some,
But we were not close friends
And that was a time of many dyings.

When we first met
I had not liked you,
But through friends our lives touched many times,
And in the end, although I never sought you out,
I found pleasure in your company.

The last time but one we met
We stood not far from here
And talked of freshman things.
Our lives touched just once more
And by the greatest chance.

It was in some far place;
I raised my head as we were marching by
And met your eyes.
We smiled a greeting so oddly met
And then you were gone.

We talked of you on our return:
But to me it always seemed that you were just away,
Until this moment when I stopped to read this wall;
Then I am sudden sick, and shocked to find
I really care that you are dead.[2]

---

2. The poem is by Dr. Robert P. Thompson, who received a Ph.D. in zoology from the University of Toronto in 1963.

I have entitled this sermon "Why Should We Care?" For the older generation, this poem perhaps says as much as needs to be said in answer to that question. The names on the honour rolls, plaques, tablets, monuments, and cenotaphs are the names of people that you knew and valued. Their presence strengthened you. Their death has diminished you.

The younger generation can read this poem, and ones like it, and can imagine what the experience is like, but it is not their experience. And they may well ask, "Why should we care? Why should we keep up Remembrance Day? We are reading the names of people we never knew—gone before we were even born. Why should we care?"

The young as well as old should care, first, because these men and women who served their country in their youth and who gave their lives in their prime *remind us through their blood of the true cost of war*. It is a reminder that is more necessary than ever today. All people under 30 and many under 40 have no recollection of the Vietnam War, much less the two world wars and the Korean War. While some may know of these conflicts through study, and have some general understanding of war, most of our youth and young adults now think of war in terms of what we have recently experienced—the war in the Persian Gulf or the NATO bombing campaign in Serbia. And while there may be great relief that these wars were over so quickly and so decisively, there is a danger that those who have no other experiences with which to compare them may be lulled into the belief that, so long as you are powerful and have great technology, war is something you can pursue without terrible danger or great cost—at least, great cost to yourself. And yet, how rare are such wars, wars so one-sided that virtually everyone from this side who went came back.

The men and women who died serving this country in the two world wars serve us today by telling a different story. A member of Westminster Church who grew up on Dorchester Avenue between Harrow and Guelph Streets told me about the four young men from that short block who went off to fight against the Axis powers. The one from next door, who had just been married, didn't come back. Her brother's best friend, from two doors down, didn't come back. The one at the end of the street didn't come back. The one from across the street didn't come back. None of them came back. They tell us a different story.

The names of the men and women on the plaques in this church tell us a different story—so many of these names with red crosses beside them.[3] In the Gulf War, if my memory serves me correctly, Canada lost nobody. The Americans, the major coalition partner, lost only a few more people than Westminster Church lost in the two great wars. Had it not been for a Scud missile unluckily falling on a barracks in Dahrain, there would be fewer crosses on the American tablets commemorating that war than on the tablets in this one church.

The tablets in this church tell the real truth about war, a truth that we must care enough to hear. The lists of our dead, the cards that have gone out into the congregation today,[4] are a reminder that even wars you win can devastate you. We must care enough to allow these dead to speak to us and particularly to our young, so that no one will be fooled by recent experience into thinking that war can be a quick fix to recalcitrant problems, and deceived into believing that war does not cause as many troubles as it relieves.

Today, the older generation of our congregation does not need any help to hear the voices of our dead. Two minutes of silence are all that it takes for the voices to come flooding back. But for the younger generation the voices of our dead need help. They need the help of parents and grandparents who will teach the young ones the history of our nation on the battle-

---

3. The honour rolls in Westminster Church contain the names of 796 men and women connected with the congregation who served in the armed forces during the two world wars. Of these, 70 from the First World War and 34 from the Second World War did not return.

4. A custom in the Remembrance Sunday service at Westminster Church is to give younger worshippers a card bearing the name of one of the 104 from

field. To our youth, who may have received the subtle message from television that war is something from which we can be insulated, and something that affects only those who live in places like Baghdad and Belgrade, you need to be able to talk about what happened to Canadians at Vimy and Passchendaele and Dieppe and Hong Kong. You need to show them pictures of mud-filled and rat-infested trenches, pictures of men after they have been scorched by mustard gas, and pictures of cemeteries filled with endless rows of crosses.

You need to show them picture books like one I saw recently with photo after photo of lovely beaches, prosperous towns, and idyllic country scenes in Europe, all accompanied by black-and-white photos of the same locations shot during wartime—the beaches littered not with bathers but with bodies, the streets of the towns filled with rubble from the bombed-out buildings, the country roads filled with straggling columns of prisoners and wounded.[5] These pictures will give you something to talk about that our young people need to know.

Do not let them grow up without reading about the Holocaust and seeing the videos of the death camps. Do not let them reach adulthood without encountering footage of Hitler's Nuremberg rallies. Care enough to show them what was seen by the men and women whose names are listed on our church's roll of honour, and what took so many of them before their time. Our war dead serve us still by telling us the truth about the cost of war. And people who know that truth might just avoid a similar suffering.

Second, we should care because *we have inherited a country for which these folk made a sacrifice.* Their blood was shed in a way that has meaning beyond their own generation. As a Christian people, we know that the shedding of blood sometimes

---

the church who died in the services during the two world wars. The purpose of this is to ensure that, during the two minutes of silence, those too young to have lost someone in these conflicts will have a name to think of and those who made the supreme sacrifice will have their names remembered.

5. Ken Bell, *The Way We Were* (Toronto: University of Toronto Press, 1988).

has great significance and makes a great claim upon us. We follow a Lord of whom it is said in the Letter to the Ephesians that his self-offering on the cross broke down the dividing wall of hostility between those who were enemies, that he brought those who were far off near, and that he made peace through the shedding of his blood (2:13-17). As followers of Jesus, we know that the shedding of blood may not only be tragic or monstrous or criminal—as it was in his case—but that it may also be redemptive and life-giving—as it was in his case.

Now, we must be careful and clear in saying this because not all shedding of blood has a redemptive quality. Sometimes life is stolen. It was stolen from six million Jews. It was stolen often from prisoners and from citizens of occupied communities. It was stolen from countless millions of civilians and non-combatants. We do not find anything redemptive in these deaths. But we speak of Christ's dying, finally, in a positive and not a negative way, as a triumph rather than a disaster, because he offered up his life and, in so doing, offered people peace and a new life.

And so with these men and women who speak to us from these tablets and honour rolls today. They offered up their lives voluntarily, with some nobility, for a cause that they believed to be just, and in answer to their country's declared need. This was their sacrifice, and, surely, it has made a claim upon us. Surely the flower of our youth was not asked to shed its blood on our nation's behalf on distant battlefields so that we might be complacent about the fate of the country that asked of them this service. Put quite simply, our command is to honour the blood shed under the flag of this nation by devoting ourselves to its well-being.

Do we care enough to cherish and make reverent and serious use of the freedom people died to preserve? I hesitate to imagine what our lot would have been had the Nazis prevailed. It would certainly have been even worse than the fate of the nations of eastern Europe who, at the end of the war, were not liberated by the armies of the West but occupied by the forces of the Soviet Union—nations that had to live for 40 years under repression, intimidation, and brutality; nations where the state sought to override the individual, the family, and the faith; nations where the wrong sentiment expressed within the hearing of the wrong set of ears could quickly lead to imprisonment or worse; nations where the state wielded tools of terror and the people lived, at worst, in fear and, at best, without hope.

Let us remember that our rights as a free people were on the line in the Second World War. The right to assemble with others and to discuss matters of common concern without fear of censorship or retribution. The right to watch a news program or read a paper and to expect that what we are seeing and reading constitutes the free exchange of ideas and perspectives and not just the propaganda of the state. The right to practise our faith freely and not to become second-class citizens thereby. The right to fair treatment before the law, to live in a land where the words "police" and "state" do not go side by side. The right to vote in free, fair, and democratic elections, to choose our representatives and leaders, those who will govern us. These rights were saved for us by the sacrifice of many.

Our freedoms have been handed to us. Unlike the people of Poland and Hungary and South Africa and Chile and East Timor and Serbia and Kosovo and so many other places, we have not had to struggle desperately over the last half-century, to endure great hardships, and to make huge sacrifices to attain them. That struggle was waged for us by those we remember today. Do we care? Do we care enough to use responsibly and wisely the freedoms we have been given and to guard them for the future?

Do we care enough to employ our freedom not just for private gain or personal satisfaction but in the cause of building this nation in whose service those we remember perished? I know that, in these times, nationalism and patriotism are viewed by many with unease, or even suspicion. And that is understandable, for the major wars our country has fought were caused, in part, by a certain exclusive and corrosive kind of nationalism.

And it is understandable in that, as we look to the future in our rapidly changing world, we are told that we will be citizens of a global village where national entities will be less and less important. But, for all the horrors of the past and the adjustments of the present, I believe that there are still going to be nations and that there is, in our nation, something to be commended to the global village of nations.

As you reflect upon the great clashes of the twentieth century, you realize that our national experiment is just the opposite of the national experiments of our adversaries. World War I arose out of narrow nationalisms that set one ethnic group against another in a struggle that made individuals mere fodder for realizing the claims of their nations. World War II became inevitable because of the aspirations of a national vision, founded upon the values of blood and soil and folk, whose adherents sought to establish the superiority of one part of humanity over others. Theirs was a national experiment that would have consigned all those considered inferior—Jews, Slavs, Gypsies, homosexuals, the physically or mentally disabled, indeed any who were different—to the status of slaves or to extinction.

Our nation has conducted a different experiment. It began with a different kind of nationalism, one that put two nations together, one that has evolved into a nationalism that seeks to find a respected and valued place for people from dozens of cultures and ethnic groupings and a variety of religions. Our experiment has not been without its mistakes, some of them grave, some of them denied for a long time and redressed only after a great deal of soul-searching. We might think of the use of immigrant minorities as cheap labour during the building of the national infrastructure, the internment of particular ethnic groups in wartime, the failure to make our nation serve the interests of its aboriginal peoples as well as it has served the interests of its many waves of newcomers. But these failures have arisen not out of adherence to but departure from the fundamental premises of the nation. From the national experiment upon which we have embarked, goodness can come.

From the national experiment vanquished by the people we honour today, the only possible end was disaster, destruction, and death.

Do we care enough to work hard on our fragile national experiment? It needs to be nurtured with great dedication and devotion. For the nation that is Canada is not a political necessity. Its emergence was not obvious. Its continued existence is not inevitable. Our nation is the product of a covenant, a conscious decision. It is a covenant that has been achieved from the beginning by accommodation, negotiation, and compromise. It is a covenant that understands that our unity may never be taken for granted, for there will always be forces that attempt to drive our people apart and disrupt our national harmony. That is the nature of the land we have inherited. It is a covenant that understands that tensions and grievances in our national life will always need to be moderated by people of good will. But, while we are not an automatic nation, we are a model nation for a world seeking a new and better kind of nationalism, a world that needs to see there is a way forward that does not involve retreat into the old ethnic and religious nationalisms, a world that at the peril of its survival must never again descend into the abyss of tribe against tribe, of us against them.

Today, we remember people who had the grace to die for our country. Surely we can find the grace to live energetically for it. They sacrificed themselves for the privilege of its freedom and for the legacy of its diverse and inclusive approach to nationhood. Do we care enough to keep faith with those who were asked by their country to dash over the top of the trenches into no-man's-land, or to wade ashore at Dieppe into the teeth of cannon and machine guns? Remembrance Day tells us that things more important than the grievances and contentions of our own time have gone on in this country, things that obligate us, things that require from us the best that we have to give.

Those who laid down their lives in our great wars have given us our marching orders. These are to preserve and build this nation as a model for the world. So, whatever baggage we may carry to the great questions of our national life, let us be sure to carry the burden of remembrance. And let us never forget the plea that comes to us from those who have made the final sacrifice:

> If ye break faith with us who die
> We shall not sleep, though poppies grow
>   In Flanders fields.[6]

---

6. John McCrae's "In Flanders Fields" first appeared in *Punch* in the issue of December 8, 1915.

Note on Final Two Sermons

Winnipeg's Westminster Presbyterian Church was established in 1892. Within a generation, the congregation had outgrown its first building, and a new church was dedicated in 1912. Church Union of Presbyterians, Methodists, and Congregationalists was then still 13 years from fulfilment, but the people of Westminster expected that they would be a part of the new denomination when it was formed. Evidence of this is that each of the three largest windows in the sanctuary contains the symbol of one of the uniting denominations. A rose window in the balcony features an open Bible, the symbol of the Congregational Church. One nave window represents the Holy Spirit with a descending dove, the symbol of the Methodist Church. The nave window opposite displays a burning bush, the symbol of the Presbyterian Church.

On each of the nave windows, surrounding the symbol, is an unrolled scroll containing a biblical text. The verse on the Methodist window is Psalm 42:8: "Yet the Lord will command his lovingkindness in the daytime, and in the night his song shall be with me..." (KJV). It captures the Methodist emphasis on the immanence and approachability of God and the importance of the personal experience of God in the believer's life of faith. The verse on the Presbyterian window is Revelation 11:15:

"The kingdoms of this world are become the kingdoms of our Lord, and of his Christ; and he shall reign for ever and ever" (KJV). It captures the Presbyterian emphasis on the transcendence and sovereignty of God and the conviction that God's purpose and plan for the believer and for the world may be trusted without fail.

The two sermons that follow were preached on these texts on the occasions of the 99th and 100th Anniversary services of Westminster Church. Because Westminster normally invites a guest preacher to give the sermon on Anniversary Sunday, I was doubly honoured as the congregation's minister to be asked to preach at the services that would open and close our centennial year. The choice of texts was obvious, given that these verses were so important to the folk who had begun the congregation and nurtured it through the first 20 years of its life. They are verses that testify to a faith worthy of being passed from one generation to the next.

Hope

The God of My Life

Psalm 42

Yet the Lord will command his lovingkindness in the daytime, and in the night his song shall be with me, and my prayer unto the God of my life.

—Psalm 42:8 (KJV)

THE FIRST TIME I SET FOOT IN THE SANCTUARY OF WESTMINSTER Church, I was immediately drawn to the two main windows in the nave that so clearly make the statement "We want the light of God's creation to stream into this place." And of course, I noticed that on each window is a scroll, and on each scroll is a verse. The verse on the south window, "The kingdoms of this world are become the kingdoms of our Lord, and of his Christ; and he shall reign for ever and ever" (Revelation 11:15, KJV), I recognized right away. Anyone who knows Handel's "Hallelujah Chorus" knows these words. And I could understand why such a powerful affirmation might be chosen for a place to which the eye is naturally drawn. But the verse on the north window, which I have taken as the text for this sermon, was not familiar. I was not sure that I had ever heard it or read it before. Looking it up, I was surprised to find that it was from a psalm that I did know, a psalm frequently set to hymns and anthems, often used in worship, with verses that you and I would recognize instantly. Yet, this verse I had not remembered; it had made no impression on me.

I wondered, Why did the leaders of this church choose this verse, of all verses, when there are so many celebrated texts around? I think they not only wanted to say, as they have said with the south window, that God is ruler of nations and lord of history and sovereign over all creation, but that God is also one who is deeply concerned for you, that God is the God of your life.

Now for most of us, and for much of our lives, this may not really be an issue. We manage to fill our days so full of important and pressing activities that we do not really notice whether the Lord is commanding his loving-kindness. And even after dark there is so much on our minds and on our plates that we do not hear the song of God that may be with us. We manage quite well most of the time without the assurance that God is the God of our lives.

Yet, I believe the minister and elders of the congregation showed wisdom in placing this verse on the nave window and, in so doing, making the statement "This is important. You need to pay attention to this." For every worship service brings into this sanctuary someone in great need. There may be people in this church today who, this very hour, need to have the assurance that is proclaimed on this window. And those of us who do not need to know the truth of this verse today will need to know it someday. There comes a time in every life when, if these words are true, they are the difference between life and death. There comes a time in every life when the only thing of any importance is to know that God is the God of our life—that we are not abandoned, that we are not alone.

This is the verse our forbears want you to learn now so that, when life turns against you, you will be equipped for the struggle. This is a text that must be true for you when tragedy intrudes into your life: when disaster or theft or accident or ruin or suicide comes upon you. This is a text that must be true for you when your job disappears or your business fails and you have nowhere to turn. This is a text that must be true for you when life does not realize its promise and you cannot seem to find success. This is a text that must be true for you when love is lost, when a marriage breaks down, when partner or friend or mother or father or daughter or son fails you. This is a text that must be true for you when death knocks at the door or chronic illness lands at the front step. This is a text that must be true for you when you are fighting a lonely and desperate struggle against some compulsion or obsession. This is a text that must be true for you when you feel that no one else is there for you and you wonder, Is God there? Is God the God of my life?

If you should ever find yourself down and discouraged, lost and alone, then suddenly it will matter whether or not these words are true. There are times in life when a person of faith needs to know that God is near, needs to be able to say with assurance, "Yet the Lord will command his lovingkindness in the daytime, and in the night his song shall be with me."

It was in just such circumstances that the psalmist wrote these words, a time of despair and deprivation in his own life. The verse on its own sounds rather comfortable and middle-class, but when you see it in its context you realize that it has struggled to be born in a pretty impoverished environment. Indeed, had all been going well in the life of the psalmist there would have been no poem, no affirmation. If he had not been so cast down, if his soul were not so disquieted, he would not have been spending much time thinking of how important God was to him. But as it is, he is consumed with everything he has lost.

Who is this person? He is one of the sons of Korah, members of the tribe of Levi, who held the office of keepers of the door of the temple in Jerusalem and who, under King David, the musician king, had been given expanded duties as musicians in the temple. But now David's rule has been challenged by his son Absalom, and the king has been forced to flee the city.[1] The psalmist has fled with him, possibly never to return to Jerusalem, perhaps sentenced to spend the rest of his days hunted and hiding in the Judean hills.

As he thinks of what he has lost—his job, his vocation, the major source of his happiness and fulfilment—he is reduced to tears. All he has left are memories of how he "went with the throng, and led them in procession to the house of God, with glad shouts and songs of thanksgiving" (Psalm 42:4). Well, such songs are his no more. He feels that God has meted out to him some great punishment: "All your waves and your billows have gone over me" (42:7). He feels he is sinking fast. He has lost everything. And the greatest affront of all, as one who has served God all his life, is to be scorned by the scoffers who suggest he has been deserted by the very one he served: "Where is your God?" (42:3). Every taunt is another twist of the knife. And maybe the taunters are right, especially the ones that have taken up residence inside his own soul: "When shall I come and behold the face of God?" (42:2). Yes, even God appears lost to him.

But it is at this point that the psalmist begins to win his battle. However abandoned he may feel, he will not abandon hope. He talks to himself. He keeps telling himself to hope in God; he keeps instructing himself to have faith. And in doing so, he creates an opening for God. He realizes after all that he is not alone. He finds he is able to say, "The Lord will command his lovingkindness in the daytime, and in the night his song shall be with me."

What does this mean? "The Lord will command his lovingkindness," or loving mercy, or steadfast love. Note how the sentence starts. "The Lord will command." What would you expect to hear after that? The Lord will command his troops, armies, forces, power, mighty deeds. This is the way you would expect the sentence to be completed. And certainly, at that moment, this son of Korah would have welcomed a reinforcing army sent at the Lord's command. Yet the writer perceives that

---

1. 2 Samuel 15-16.

it is not raw power but loving-kindness that is commanded. In his strength, God is conveying concern and compassion for this beleaguered servant. How much better a gift. In the daytime, in the face of constant trial and torment, the psalmist knows that God will not abandon him but will send out mercy to him to help with every test.

"And in the night his song shall be with me." The struggle of the day is over, but the struggle of the night begins. The struggle to stay alive until sundown has been won, but now it is time for him to lie in the open air, under the vast night sky, fully conscious of his smallness and insignificance, and to rehearse and relive his woes, all the troubles of the day—churning them over and over in his mind. Last night, all he could hear was the sound of the little waterfalls of the Judean hills, and in his dispirited condition they seemed to him like great cataracts, billows and waves of God, that were gradually overwhelming him.

But now, he hears something else: a song, a song from God. You would have expected the psalmist to attempt a song to God, but now, a remarkable thing: one comes from the other direction. What kind of song? When the earth is quiet and the birds are hushed. What kind of song? I think it must have been a song of solace and comfort, unravelling the care of the day, soothing the strain of the struggle. Above all, it must have been the kind of song our mothers sang to us to help us go to sleep—to put aside our fears of the night and of the dark and to drift away into slumber. The words of such a song do not matter. It could be a song without words. It need only be a song that says "Safety, my child. There is nothing to fear. I will take care of you." "In the night his song shall be with me."

"And my prayer unto the God of my life." God sings. The soul sings back. God sings. The soul knows it has someone to pray to. God sings. The soul knows that when it matters, when the chips are down, God really is "the God of my life."

How can such an extraordinary statement of faith come from someone in such extraordinary distress? This would seem to be the creed of good times, not bad. But for this statement to be true, it must be true in the bad times. And it must be true in the depths, not only for the psalmist but for us.

Now, when we ask how we can get for ourselves this assurance that the psalmist had, we must remember that he never had any comfortable assurance. Not only did his affirmation have to be won out of hard struggle, it had to be won again and again and again. No sooner does he triumph than he falls back into despair: "I say to God, my rock, 'Why have you forgotten me?'" (42:9). Are these the words of the man who had just finished praying a prayer to "the God of my life"? They certainly are. What we see in this psalm is not the assurance of faith but rather the struggle for faith. No sooner has the psalmist affirmed his faith than it must face a new challenge. Faith is never a settled matter. God is never a possession. This poet had to tell himself before to hope in God. He will have to tell himself the same thing again. It is rough.

Yet, I am glad he does not hide from us the struggle, and the frequent lapses back into despair. I have always been suspicious of talk about God that seems to come too easily, and of those who chatter glibly about having God in their lives. I find like this psalmist that God has to be struggled for. I find that the language of my soul, like his, is so often the language of complaint and self-pity, not the language of satisfied self-assurance. That is why I trust this poet, and that is why I am so excited that, in the midst of his distress, he could write these lines about God's nearness and that he could let those lines stand for posterity.

But are his words true? This is what we really want to know. And yet, how in the realm of faith can we say anything for sure? Instead, we must search for what the heart may trust, and find in that the confirmation the heart needs. The psalmist searched his memory and held in remembrance the worship of the people of God in the temple. We Christians may search our memories and lift out of our remembrance the example of our Lord Jesus. Christ himself could have been author of the words "The Lord will command his lovingkindness in the daytime, and in the night his song shall be with me, and my prayer unto the

God of my life." They are a perfect summary of his life, and yet he had to make them true through the most bitter experience imaginable, the experience of his last day.

We know the cruel way he was treated: the unjust arrest and show trial designed to reduce him to a common criminal; the connivance of the civil and religious authorities in destroying his name and everything for which he had worked; the humiliation by soldiers who interspersed their taunts and mockery with beatings and scourging. Yet, this was not the worst.

We know the sheer physical suffering of the cross: how he was forced to carry it himself to the place of his execution, stumbling under its heavy load; how he hung upon it under a blazing sun, thirsting, gasping, struggling for each breath until he could breathe no more and suffocation took him. Yet, even this was not the worst.

The worst was his sense that he was walking this last mile alone. Abandoned by the people who clamoured for another's release and were content to shout "Let him be crucified!" (Matthew 27:22) when asked their will about their recent hero. Abandoned by his disciples: by Judas who sold him out, by Peter who denied he even knew him, by them all, in the end—for it was the women and other friends, and not any of the Twelve, who were left to claim the body and get it to the tomb. Abandoned, it seemed, even by God. At his baptism, the Spirit had descended upon him and a voice had spoken from heaven: "This is my Son, the Beloved, with whom I am well pleased" (Matthew 3:17). But, now, no words came. Not in the Garden of Gethsemane, when he poured out his soul to his Father, nor on the Mount of Calvary during the long hours of torment.

He felt very much alone, and could well have cried, "I say to God, my rock, 'Why have you forgotten me?'" Indeed, similar words did escape his lips—an anguished cry of dereliction, a stark realization of what had happened to him. And if the words "My God, my God, why have you forsaken me?" (Matthew 27:46) had been the last ones he uttered, we would not have thought any less of him nor expected something more from him.

But they were not his last words. In that bitter cry, he overcame his bitterness, and in that lonely plea, he grasped a presence. He found that he did not face the end alone. Exhaustion forced him to give up the fight, but it could not make him give up the argument with himself to keep hoping in God. And his hope was rewarded. In his hour of trial and from depths no human being can imagine, he found the loving-kindness that was commanded from above; and in the darkness of the ninth hour—the darkness of the earth's blackest nighttime—he heard the song that spoke of safety and banished fear. And thus he was given strength to lift up different words to heaven: "Father, into your hands I commend my spirit" (Luke 23:46). This was his prayer to the God of his life.

And so, friends, it is not just the psalmist who has put these words on the window of our church. It is also Jesus who has put them there: Jesus whose very life and death are a demonstration of the nearness of God.

As a preacher I would like to offer arguments in favour of this verse, and why we should accept it, and why we know it to be true. But the poem does not offer arguments; instead it shows us the psalmist's argument with himself, his own spiritual struggle. "Hope in God," he keeps repeating to himself. He is like an early version of John Wesley, who said, "Live by faith until you have faith." We, like the psalmist, must be willing to argue with ourselves, and, as Wesley has instructed, we must be prepared to live by faith until we have faith.

Faith

People of the Promise

Hebrews 11:1-3, 8-16

> *The kingdoms of this world are become the kingdoms of our Lord, and of his Christ; and he shall reign for ever and ever.*
>
> —Revelation 11:15 (KJV)

THE TWO GREAT NAVE WINDOWS IN THIS SANCTUARY DECLARE THE faith of the founders of this congregation and the builders of this church. For on each window is a scroll, and on each scroll is a key verse of scripture. I took as the text of my sermon on our 99th Anniversary the words on the north window: "Yet the Lord will command his lovingkindness in the daytime, and in the night his song shall be with me" (Psalm 42:8, KJV). This verse speaks so intimately about God. It says to everyone who reads it, "God is personally concerned for you. God is the God of your life." It expresses the faith that you and I are indeed children of a loving God.

The verse on the south window I have saved for today: "The kingdoms of this world are become the kingdoms of our Lord, and of his Christ; and he shall reign for ever and ever." Here the language of intimacy gives way to the language of majesty. The faith expressed here is that the God who cares for us individually, who names each of us, who receives us one at a time through the waters of baptism, is also ruler of nations, and lord of history, and sovereign over all creation. Not just you and I, but the whole world—past, present, and future—is in the divine hands.

The psalmist, by his own example, draws us to the God who provides help for today. The visionary of the Book of Revelation, by his bold proclamation, anchors us in the God who determines the outcome of all things.

The words on the south window convey the confidence that abounded in 1912, the year this church was dedicated. We see in them the enthusiasm of a vibrant young congregation, outgrowing its first home in a mere 20 years, attaining such significance and influence that the Governor General himself would come to lay the cornerstone of the new building.

We see in them also the triumphalism of a world Christianity then at the zenith of its optimism. The nineteenth century had been the great missionary century. The church had seen a remarkable expansion throughout the world. The faith was on the march in tandem with steady advances in education, medicine, science, and technology. Christians had come to feel that they were living on the eve of a wondrous new age. They sensed that the kingdoms of this world were indeed becoming the kingdoms of our Lord and of his Christ. To those who first sat in the pews under these windows, the kingdom was a great Christian agenda, and that agenda was nearing completion.

But you all know what happened. Just two years after attending the first service in this sanctuary, the young men of Westminster began to shed their blood in the fields of Flanders in the madness of the Great War. The cost in lives to this church is clearly indicated in the memorial tablets on the sanctuary walls. But what was the cost to the self-confidence of Christians, both here and throughout the world? When it was all over, did the people who sat under these words about God's kingdom really believe them anymore? Or did they conclude in their hearts, even if they did not say it aloud, that the stained glass represented wishful thinking and perhaps mistaken judgement on the part of those who had chosen the text? And even if their confidence in the kingdom managed to survive the First World War, could it possibly have outlasted the ravages of the Depression and the even greater bloodiness of the Second War with its genocidal holocausts and legacy of nuclear terror?

So much of the world's history since the happy days when this window was installed seems to deny its claim. How do we read it today? What does this generation make of God as ruler of nations and lord of history? To my knowledge, nobody has ever suggested replacing the window. And every Easter Sunday the choir still sings the "Hallelujah Chorus," rejoicing in those very words. But are they true? Can these words continue to be the rock on which Westminster takes its stand? Can they still be the hope by which we commend ourselves to the world?

They cannot if we understand the kingdom of God to be a program. The kingdom of God as a program prospered through the 1800s, and no doubt inspired many during the early years of this congregation's life. But the kingdom of God as a program failed, and failed forever, with the guns of August in 1914.

But to the visionary who gave us the Book of Revelation, the kingdom was never a program. In his book the words "The kingdoms of this world are become the kingdoms of our Lord, and of his Christ" are spoken as the announcement in heaven of a God-given reality not yet seen on earth. They are spoken as a promise. And it is as a promise that we are called to receive them today. A program is something we would effect—and in this case the Christian church failed to effect it—but a promise is something upon which we wait. While it may and while it should govern how we act, while it may and while it should determine what we do, it is something that, finally, we must receive by faith.

And so before I ask you whether or not you believe these words to be true, and before I ask you whether or not they are words that can anchor the life of Westminster in the century to come, I must ask you whether or not you are prepared to live by faith.

Now at first this might seem like an easy question. Faith is an honoured word in the Christian vocabulary. People commonly wish they had more faith than they do. You never seem to hear of people who have faith but wish they did not. So when I say "Are you prepared to live by faith?" your instinctive response might be "Yes, of course." But upon reflection, do you not find that faith frequently causes you pain and trouble, that it complicates rather than simplifies life, that it makes things harder rather than easier?

This was certainly the case for many of our spiritual ancestors, among them the people of faith listed in the eleventh chapter of Hebrews; and you have to wonder if, on many occasions, they might have wished to live by something else. Consider Abraham, whose adventure with God has led ultimately to our own. Abraham was a person of great faith. But see how faith disrupted his life.

We are told, "By faith Abraham obeyed when he was called" (Hebrews 11:8). That in itself should raise our eyebrows. How often do we connect faith with obedience, with submitting to the will of another?

"By faith [he] obeyed when he was called to set out." To set out from where? From the land of Ur, one of the great centres of economic development and civilization in the ancient world. We who are only a generation or two removed from the European settlement of the Prairies can understand that there are good reasons why people sometimes pull up their roots and leave their homeland to go to a new place. Our forbears who came here did so to gain political or religious freedom or economic opportunities denied them where they lived. But Abraham possessed none of those good reasons. In Ur, he and Sarah had it all. Their life was made. They did not need to move. Yet, faith made them do it. By faith, Abraham obeyed the call to give up his home and go to a new place.

Now, the positive side is that this new place was to be his: "He was to receive [it] as an inheritance." But where was it? He didn't know. He wasn't told. "He set out, not knowing where he was going." All he could reasonably assume was that, wherever he was being called, it was to an economic backwater.

When he finally got there, he found his inheritance wasn't

yet his. "By faith he stayed for a time"—did not settle down, but stayed for a time—"in the land he had been promised, as in a foreign land." For the rest of his life he was never more than a sojourner, a stranger, a foreigner in Canaan "living in tents, as did Isaac and Jacob, who were heirs with him of the same promise." I wonder what tenting was like after gracious living in his home back in Ur. How did it seem to him, not being able to buy land or to build a home in his land of promise? The only land he ever owned in Canaan was the grave he purchased for himself and his wife.

We read that, in the end, Abraham "died in faith without having received the promises" (11:13). To go all that time, to do all those things and then to have to die in faith—not in fulfilment, but with his faith unrewarded. How do you put a positive gloss on such an outcome?

If Abraham's experience of faith is in any way typical, do we really want to live by it? What kind of commendation of faith is the writer giving here, when it does not solve problems but creates them, when it does not make life easier but harder, when it leads not to satisfaction but to dissatisfaction, not to comfort but to discomfort, not to security but to peril?

Yet, the eleventh chapter of Hebrews is offered up to readers as an argument for faith, as an exhortation to hold fast to it. Could it be perhaps that, in praising a faith that does not make things fall into place but out of place, the writer is using the word differently than we do when we wish we had more of it?

Generally, the reason we want faith is that we think of it as the glue that holds things together. We treat it as a condition of our hearts and minds that gives us greater certainty about God and a greater ability to accept what comes our way in life. But this is not what the writer to the Hebrews is talking about. We place faith in the realm of feelings and attitudes. But Hebrews never once talks about how Abraham felt. For Abraham, faith was not about feelings but about actions and commitments. It meant investing all that he was, and all that he had, in a promise made by God. It meant acting upon that promise, being driven by it night and day. We do not know anything for sure about the state of Abraham's emotions, but we know he was given a promise, that it was important to him above all things, that he trusted it, and that he unswervingly travelled toward it. This was his faith, and the faith of his family.

What is the promise of God that creates such faith? In the language of the Letter to the Hebrews, it is the promise of a place of inheritance, a city with foundations, a homeland, a better country. That sort of language is sprinkled throughout the Bible right up to the end of the Book of Revelation with its vision of the new Jerusalem coming down out of heaven from God.

But other language is also used. The promise was recast by Christ in his teaching and through Christ on the cross. It is a promise that God's kingdom will come, that his will shall be done on earth as in heaven; a promise that Christ who has conquered sin and death will reign over the living whom he has redeemed. It is a promise that "the kingdoms of this world are [to] become the kingdoms of our Lord, and of his Christ; and he shall reign for ever and ever."

God has promised a day when human sin and suffering will be no more. Only God's righteousness will remain.

God has promised a day when the blots on our conscience will be removed. Only the purity of Christ will remain.

God has promised a day when the darkness of ignorance will be banished by the perfect light of God's truth.

God has promised a day when the hatred and enmity that scar the earth with war and oppression will cease. And all that remains will be the love that was poured out on the cross.

God has promised a day when our anxieties will disappear, and the peace which passes understanding will be ours eternally.

This is the promise, made first to Abraham, renewed and expanded for us by Christ.

If, like Abraham, we believe the promise, if it is to us more important than anything else, we will need the faith he had. For faith is simply the act of forsaking all else to live by and for God's promise. And it is faith that is needed, for with a promise, you are dealing with something that is out of your hands, always in the future, dependent for its fruition on the one who has promised.

So I ask you again, and perhaps now it is not so simple: Are you prepared to live by faith? Surely that depends on what you think of the promise. Do you think enough of it to count yourselves as Abraham did, strangers and exiles on this earth, dissatisfied with the current state of affairs, renouncing the idea that worldly things have any ultimate value? Do you desire a better country? Do you look forward to the city that has foundations, whose architect and builder is God?

If not, you do not need faith. Instead, you can accommodate yourselves to life as it is and make your way in the world as best you can. Just about anything else in the world—besides what is promised—can be had by hard work, or perseverance, or cunning, or good luck. That is true in our individual lives and it is certainly true in our life as a church. You do not need to have faith to build a church that is successful in worldly terms. No, it is just with the promise that faith is the only recourse. Faith admits having to wait on God, having to attune our lives to what is not yet, and holding on patiently until God makes it so.

I am sure there are days when we are all tempted to give it up—and either to run the church for its own sake, ministering to worldly values and needs, or to run away from this flawed, fractious, frayed organization of sinners called to be saints. But then we remember the promise and all that God has done for us since he first made it, and what God accomplished through those who first heard it. And, above all, we remember Jesus Christ, who gave himself up for us because he believed in the promise.

And, doing so, we find strangely that our faith does keep us going, particularly through days of struggle and trial. Westminster has had such days, and we know that there will be more of them. We have had to watch while our surroundings changed and our church ceased to be the centre of the life of the neighbourhood. We have had to watch as the attitudes of people changed, and an indifference settled upon society, and the great crowds no longer flocked in. When prestige wanes, and the earthly rewards are not there, and it is a struggle to carry on, you are saddened, perhaps dismayed, but you are not defeated. For your investment is not in this institution nor in this building but in the promise to which they have borne great witness for a century—a promise that does not change, though the world falls away, for the one who promised is faithful.

People of the promise do not crave worldly success in their personal lives or church lives. They crave fulfilment of the promise. Worldly success will not divert them from their one hope; lack of it will not cause them to abandon it.

People of the promise do not expect anything in their personal or church lives to be settled and permanent. The only thing that is permanent is the city with foundations whose builder and maker is God. The only thing that is settled is that the kingdoms of this world are to become the kingdoms of our Lord and of his Christ. And though this be beyond our reach, yet we journey towards it rather than settle for anything less.

One final time, friends: Are you prepared to live by faith? Do not ask for it if what you are looking for is something to make life tidier, easier, more comfortable. That's not what God means by faith. Ask for it only if you are looking for power for yourself and for this church community to live by the promise and hold fast to the promise. Ask for it only if the promise means so much to you that you are prepared to become travellers to that better country, and sojourners and exiles in this one. Ask for it only if you are prepared to die in faith, as many have before you, not having received what was promised but having greeted it from afar.

But do ask for faith. Do live by it. For the God who calls us to stake all on the promise we have received is the same God who has already suffered the shedding of his only Son's blood to make that promise, and who has staked his name on keeping it.

znajdziemy się na bruku, a wierz mi, kiepsko się szuka pra
cji. Jeżeli o mnie chodzi, przynajmniej do września nie mo
z miasta. Wyłożyłam za mieszkanie z góry i nie mam zam
forsy. Mikula płaci śmiesznie mało, jednak płaci.

– Myślę, że jakąś, niewielką, szansę mamy – pow
W każdym razie warto spróbować, nim nas wyleją.

Wielkie oczy Julii wędrowały od Leszka do K
na stół zawalony dokumentami, bo nie znała si
pożyczkach ani spisach dłużników. Dla niej n
siedziała wśród przyjaciół, którzy dopuścili
Czuła się wyróżniona, dowartościowana i w
też nie wyobrażała sobie życia bez pracy.
z nudów i rozpaczy pewnie tak. Dlatego ch
rolinie, nawet gdyby przyszło troszeczkę
szeczkę wystarczy.

– Słuchajcie! – zawołała w przypływ
nie wiecie nic, ja nie wiem nic, nikt z n
ment, żeby zawiązać spisek. Jest kw
stami i do dzieła. Tylko do jakiego?

– Idzisz ją! – ucieszył się Leszek
lodzietna mrówka! Nazwę nam w
że nic nie wie!

– Spokojna głowa! – Karolina przer
dre pytania są najważniejsze. Teraz wystarczy,
wych odpowiedzi.

Logiczny wywód przyjaciółki, poparty ojcowskim całusem Le
ostatecznie przekonał Julię, że znalazła się po właściwej stronie.

– Do kogo należą grunty? – spytała od niechcenia, w ramach zadawania mądrych pytań, o których napomknęła Karolina.

– Jakie grunty?

– Biurowiec, hale, magazyny stoją przecież na jakimś gruncie, prawda? – wyjaśniła niepewnie Julia. – Pytam, do kogo należy ta ziemia, bo... jeżeli do Mikulowej, to... a jeżeli nie do Mikulowej... to uregulowanie praw własności wymaga... – plątała się coraz bardziej, przekonana, że pytanie, ściągnięte od rodzonej matki, nie było najmądrzejsze. Leszek patrzył na nią uważnie, wreszcie zerwał się z fotela i zaczął krążyć po gabinecie.

– Mógłbyś usiąść – poprosiła Julia. – Takie dreptanie przypomina mi Chochlę.

– Fuj! – Usiadł posłusznie. – Myślę, że grunty możemy sobie darować. Nie ma sposobu, żeby ustalić, kto jest właścicielem.

– Oczywiście, że jest sposób! – wtrąciła Karolina. – Tylko czy jest sens?

– Nie ma! – przyznał skwapliwie i sięgnął po zieloną teczkę.

Co wynikało z materiałów, to wynikało, ale zamierzeń szefów nie dało się z nich wyczytać. Kto znał prawdę? Mikulowie, może jeszcze ktoś, na pewno Edyta. Należało dotrzeć przynajmniej do jednej z tych osób. Sekretarkę wykluczyli pierwszą. Łatwiej byłoby włamać się do bankowego systemu komputerowego niż wyciągnąć z Edyty tajemnicę, której nie zamierzała zdradzić. Leszek obiecał wykorzystać swój męski czar i pociągnąć za język Mikulową. Nie robił większych nadziei sobie ani koleżankom. Szefowa lubiła jego towarzystwo w firmie, natomiast wcale nie musiała mieć ochoty na spotkanie poza firmą. Nie była kobietą skomplikowaną wewnętrznie, lecz nie była też całkowicie pozbawiona rozumu.

– No dobra, spróbuję rozgryźć tę babkę wielojajeczną – mruknął.

– Kogo? – zainteresowały się dziewczyny, przyzwyczajone bardziej do owadów niż do nabiału.

– Nie zauważyłyście, że ona każde zdanie zaczyna od ja? Jaja i jaja!

– Powiedziałabym raczej, że to nioska – roześmiała się Karolina.

– Nigdy nie wyrażam się aż tak źle o kobietach! – zaprotestował Leszek.

Mikulę zarezerwowała dla siebie Karolina. Miała pewne doświadczenie w postępowaniu ze starym capem, jak uparcie tytułowała dyrektora. Pozostawał jeszcze człowiek o nazwisku Bujała. Najgorsze, że dla nich pozostawał wyłącznie nazwiskiem, do którego nie potrafili dokleić żadnego faceta – ani młodego, ani starego. Z całą pewnością był prezesem firmy ubezpieczeniowej Spokój. A prywatnie? Podobno dom, podobno jacht. Ze skąpych informacji Leszka wynikało, że Bujała był personą znaną nie tylko w poważnym biznesie. W mieście mówiło się o jego powiązaniach z półświatkiem i miejscową mafią. Fortunę zrobił na handlu alkoholem i być może czymś jeszcze, wykorzystał sprzyjający moment, wszedł w spółkę z kapitałem zagranicznym i otworzył legalną firmę ubezpieczeniową. Na oko i w opinii wielu osób firma działała sprawnie.

– Do Bujały musi dotrzeć nasza mała! – stwierdziła Karolina.

– Ona? – spytał Leszek. Był nie mniej zdziwiony niż Julia.

– A kto? Ty? Mam przeczucie, że to powinna być kobieta.

– Dlaczego akurat kobieta? A może on już jedną ma! A może woli chłopaków? Jestem przeciwny załatwianiu poważnych spraw przez jakieś tiu, tiu. Poza tym Julia nie jest w typie gangsterów! – zdenerwował się Leszek.

Karolina spojrzała z jawną kpiną.

– Chcesz nas przekonać, że sam nie jesteś gangsterem? – Mrugnęła porozumiewawczo i roześmiała się na widok speszonej miny przyjaciela. – Z Juleczki zrobimy taką laskę, że głowa mała. Biorę to na siebie. Jak wejdzie do gabinetu Bujały, facet orła wywinie i trzeba go będzie reanimować.

– Mówicie o mnie tak, jakby mnie przy tym nie było! – zdenerwowała się Julia. – Dotrzeć mogę, ale co dalej?

– Dalej zagrasz tak pięknie jak dzisiaj z Edytą albo jak kiedyś z Chochlą. Pamiętasz? Nawet się biedny poczwarek nie domyślił, że zrobiłyśmy go w kolosalne jajo!

Julia natychmiast rozjaśniła się i uśmiechnęła. Opinia Karoliny sprawiła jej wielką przyjemność. Historia z Chochlą była zaledwie wprawką, maleńką etiudką, a ona czuła się stworzona do wielkich ról, co nie znaczy, że gardziła etiudami.

To było dawno, zaraz na początku pracy w komórce organizacyjno-prawnej. Któregoś ranka kierownik zagalopował się i klepnął magister Cierniak po siedzeniu. Klepnął radośnie, z idiotycznym chichotem i jak najbardziej zamierzenie. Karolina wściekła się, warknęła, że następnym razem odda z nawiązką. Chochla nie znał umiaru i chyba słabo znał kobiety, bo nie tylko powtórzył klepnięcie, lecz wciąż z tym samym chichotem dodał, że to całkiem prywatne żarty. W ramach prywatnej odpowiedzi na prywatny żart dostał dwa razy w twarz. Roztropny mężczyzna powinien w takiej sytuacji wykazać się zbiorową mądrością swojej płci, przeprosić i wyjść. Kierownik nie popisał się po raz drugi. Nie dość, że sam sprowokował głupią awanturę, że oberwał na własne życzenie, to jeszcze pobiegł na skargę do dyrektora. Jedynym świadkiem zajścia była Julia. Dziewczyna nie zmarnowała swojej szansy. Prześlicznie odegrała monodram, który w ciągu paru minut przekonał Mikulę, że nikt nie został spoliczkowany. Nie było żadnych klepnięć w tyłek czy w policzek, natomiast z całą pewnością kierownik prosił o dokument, którego pani magister nie chciała dać. Karolina za nic nie mogła sobie przypomnieć, o co chodziło, więc dyrektor zyskał pewność, że kierownik próbował wpakować swój nos w sprawy ściśle poufne. Ostatni, bardzo burzliwy akt spektaklu rozegrał się w gabinecie. Chochla opuścił scenę blady, przerażony i całkiem ogłupiały.

– Wkopałyście gzika za niewinność? – oburzył się Leszek.

– Skądże znowu! – zaprotestowała Karolina. – Twój gzik wysyłał mnie po blankiet delegacji. On mnie, rozumiesz? I dla zachęty wymierzył mi klapsa. Należała mu się nauczka za brak szacunku dla kobiet. A że Mikula w życiu by tego nie zrozumiał, więc Julia uprawdopodobniła sytuację. Chwyciła w lot, co jest grane i za to ją polubiłam. Ten dzień zapoczątkował naszą przyjaźń, prawda Juluś? – Uśmiechnęła się do zarumienionej dziewczyny. – A teraz równie ślicznie zagrasz przed Bujałą rolę informatyczki, która szuka pracy. Słyszałaś, że firma jest wzorowa, chciałabyś pod światłym kierunkiem pana prezesa... No co, mała, mam cię uczyć aktorstwa?

Oczy Julii błyszczały niczym dwa jupitery. Nabrała szalonej ochoty na tę rolę i za nic nie mogła zrozumieć wątpliwości Leszka, który upierał się, że to zbyt niebezpieczne posunięcie.

– Co może być niebezpiecznego w szukaniu pracy? – spytała zdziwiona. – Czy ty wiesz, w ilu ja byłam zakładach, u ilu klamek wisiałam, zanim Mikula zgodził się mnie przyjąć?

– Mikulowa cię przyjęła, a to zupełnie zmienia postać rzeczy – denerwował się Leszek.

– Oj, chyba ci się pogorszyło! – prychnęła Julia. – Jak mówię, że Mikula, to chyba wiem, co mówię. Szefową pierwszy raz zobaczyłam dopiero w firmie.

Karolina zręcznie przerwała spór. Była autorką pomysłu i nie życzyła sobie żadnych zmian. Powoli przyzwyczajała się do roli przywódcy spisku. Przed wyjściem, gdy Julia na moment zniknęła w łazience, nachyliła się do ucha kolegi:

– Co jest, staruszku? Zamazałeś się, twoja sprawa, ale roboty nam nie psuj. Nie chcesz chyba – pogroziła żartobliwie palcem – żebym uświadomiła ci żonę!

– Czemu nie, pod warunkiem, że zdobędziesz jej nowy adres. Od października mieszkam sam.

Karolina spoważniała i delikatnie pogładziła ramię chłopaka.

– Przepraszam, nie wiedziałam!

– Wiem... Nie chwalę się przesadnie, bo nie ma czym. I nie tęsknię przesadnie, bo nie ma za kim – powiedział cicho.

Od zniknięcia Chochli minęło kilka dni. Policja milczała, pozostawiając pracownikom domysły. W firmie powoli zwyciężała koncepcja romantyczna: miłosne opętanie, ucieczka i tak dalej. Najciekawsze było to i tak dalej, czyli co Chochla mógł robić z kobietą. Był typowym gawędziarzem seksualnym, a wiadomo, że gawędziarze niewiele mają wspólnego z ludźmi czynu.

Z samego rana Julia znalazła na swoim biurku kartkę. Tekst pod dwoma krwistymi serduszkami głosił, że ktoś nie może przestać o niej myśleć. Kto? Niestety, to była walentynkowa kartka, więc bez podpisu nadawcy. Rozbawiona zajrzała do pokoju magistrów.

– Leszku, to twoja sprawka, prawda? – pomachała kartką.

Zamruczał, potarł ręką policzek.

– Hm... nie. Ja mianowicie wiem, że walentynki są w lutym – powiedział po chwili namysłu.

– A kto mianowicie nie wie?

– Mianowicie ktoś, komu dziewczyna podoba się dłużej niż jeden dzień.

– Znasz kogoś, kto obchodzi walentynki codziennie? – Julia nie dawała za wygraną.

– Musiałbym się zastanowić... A właściwie czemu ja? Przecież to twoja kartka, ty się zastanawiaj! – Roześmiał się i swoim zwyczajem zniknął za gazetą.

Wróciła do sekretariatu z miłym uczuciem ciepła na duszy. Wiedziała oczywiście, że Leszek darzył ją sympatią nieco większą niż inne biurowe koleżanki i nie miała nic przeciwko temu. Mógł się zachwycać kolorem jej oczu i włosów, mógł całować ją w czoło, bo magister Wydroń nie wyglądał na człowieka, który przekracza towarzyskie normy. Julia była absolutnie spokojna, że walentynkowe wyznanie to jeszcze jeden niewinny i ładny żart. Ech, szkoda, że ta kartka nie nadeszła prosto z planu filmowego!

Dyrektor wrócił z Bydgoszczy i wpadł do firmy na dwadzieścia minut. Na Julię łypnął nieprzychylnie, ale o zwolnieniu nie wspomniał. Koniecznie chciał rozmawiać z magister Cierniak.

– Wyszła do Państwowej Inspekcji Pracy – powiedziała oschłym tonem Edyta.

Nie zważając na zły humor szefa, weszła za nim do gabinetu. Spokojnie wysłuchała gorzkich uwag na temat samowolnego opuszczania stanowiska pracy. Głos dyrektora grzmiał jak dzwon. Sekretarka mówiła cicho. Tylko jedno zdanie w całości dotarło do uszu Julii i mocno ją zaskoczyło.

– Z przerażeniem patrzę, że już nie głowa tobą rządzi, tylko ta część ciała, w której próżno szukać rozumu – powiedziała Edyta.

Zaraz potem Mikula ponownie wyjechał.

– Kiedy szef znajdzie dla mnie wreszcie czas? – spytała przygnębiona dziewczyna.

– Nie mów, że się stęskniłaś! To bardzo niebezpieczny facet. Ma zazdrosną żonę, kochankę i kobiety za nim szaleją – powiedziała Edyta.

– Jego harem, jego biznes! Pani Edytko, mówię pani pod słowem honoru: jeżeli szef nie da mi pracy przy komputerach, odejdę z firmy.

– Na twoim miejscu nie liczyłabym na komputery. Dyrektor ma poglądy konserwatywne i nie zatrudnia kobiet w działach technicznych. Uważa, że ścisłe, logiczne myślenie jest domeną mężczyzn.

– Oszalał czy co? Kiedy na niego patrzę, nasuwa mi się całkiem inny wniosek! – wykrzyknęła Julia i przerażona zakryła usta dłonią.

Edyta pokręciła głową.

– W firmie obowiązują wnioski szefa, drogie dziecko. Im prędzej to zrozumiesz, tym dla ciebie lepiej.

W znacznie gorszej sytuacji był Konrad Orzechowicz. Jeszcze nie dostał angażu i zakresu obowiązków. Dział personalny nie mógł wydać dokumentów bez podpisu dyrektora, inżynier Kiciński oficjalnie wciąż był kierownikiem, więc Konradowi nie pozostawało nic innego, jak czekać. Jeśli chciał, potrafił być cierpliwy. Zresztą innego wyjścia nie miał. Codzienne urzędowanie zaczynał od wizyty w sekretariacie. Zwykle zastawał samą Julię, bo Edyta od rana biegała gdzieś z Mikulową.

– Jest dyrektor?

Uśmiechała się i rozkładała ręce, co znaczyło, że dyrektora wcięło. Miała wielką ochotę porozmawiać z Orzechowiczem o etacie, choćby tylko spytać, czy ma już kogoś na oku, niestety, ledwie otworzyła usta, odwaga ją opuszczała. Tłumaczyła sobie, że to przez te brwi i oczy, które czyniły go podobnym do filmowego Marka Winicjusza. Patrzyła na brwi, serce jej waliło i nie umiała sklecić rozsądnego zdania. Gdyby chociaż spytał ją o plany zawodowe! Ale nie, skądże. Jego interesował tylko dyrektor Mikula.

Dopiero w czwartek dyrektor pojawił się w firmie, za to od samego rana. Zabronił Edycie wpuszczać interesantów, nie pozwolił łączyć rozmów telefonicznych, czyli był, ale jakby go nie było. Konrad zjawił się kilka minut po siódmej.

– Zawiadomię pana, kiedy szef będzie wolny – obiecała Edyta i nim zdążyła cokolwiek dodać, Orzechowicz starannie zamykał drzwi od strony dyrektorskiego gabinetu.

Zerwała się, chciała za nim biec i stanęła jak wryta.

– Zachowuje się pan jak ostatni palant, jak harcerzyk w czasie podchodów – krzyczał Orzechowicz.

Mikula coś tłumaczył, gęsto padały słowa firma, wspólny interes, a Orzechowicz swoje: palant, harcerzyk!

– Edytko, wejdź tam, wywlecz tego samobójcę! – Karolina patrzyła błagalnie na sekretarkę.

– Którego? – Edyta odzyskała spokój i nawet zdobyła się na ironiczny uśmiech. – W niebezpieczeństwie jest Mikula. O ile się znam na ludziach, twój Orzechowicz ma już angaż w kieszeni.

– Dlaczego mój Orzechowicz?

– Chcesz powiedzieć, że nie zrezygnowałaś z Mikuli?

Karolina wzruszyła ramionami i zamilkła. Edyta, zajęta przeglądaniem papierów, wcale nie czekała na odpowiedź. Chciała delikatnie ugryźć panią magister, ugryzła i to jej w zupełności wystarczyło. Krzyki w gabinecie powoli ucichły, rozmowa przybrała cywilizowany charakter. Kilka minut później do naczelnego weszła personalna z plikiem dokumentów. Nie siedziała długo. Wybiegła wzburzona, z twarzą pokrytą czerwonymi plamami. Nawet Julia zrozumiała, że dyrektor musiał znaleźć kozła ofiarnego i padło na tę bidulkę. Edytka znowu miała rację, pomyślała z uznaniem. Tylko czemu ścięła się z Karoliną i o co? Bo chyba się ścięła? Spojrzała na jedną, potem na drugą. Sekretarka wyglądała jak uosobienie spokoju. Udawała, że rozmowa za drzwiami zupełnie jej nie interesuje. Karolina niczego nie udawała. Na kilometr widać było, że najchętniej wsadziłaby głowę do środka, żeby jeszcze lepiej słyszeć, co Orzechowicz miał do powiedzenia na temat komputerów najnowszej generacji. Wyszedł spokojny, po swojemu poważny i nikt by nie pomyślał, że kilkanaście minut wcześniej wyzywał naczelnego od palantów. Spojrzał na Julię, zawahał się przez ułamek sekundy, ale nie powiedział nic. Karolina wybiegła za nim.

Krótki moment wahania był dla Julii niczym wiadro zimnej wody. Poczucie zmarnowanej szansy miało słony smak łez, o czym przekonała się, czując niemiłe drapanie w gardle. Pytania posypały się same. Dlaczego nie porozmawiałam wcześniej z Orzechowiczem? Dlaczego nie byłam jeszcze u Mikuli? I dlaczego, u diabła, to nie ja gram Ligię?

Ostatnie, choć wydawało się najmniej poważne, bolało najbardziej.

Koło południa została w sekretariacie sama i żeby nie oszaleć nad instrukcją obsługi kombajnu budowlanego, wzięła się do sortowania korespondencji. Była to praca rutynowa. Pieczęć sekretariatu, kolejny numer, data, sprawa i tak dalej. Każdą przesyłkę trzeba było otworzyć, pismo przeczytać. Podważyła brzeg niestarannie zaklejonej koperty i na biurko wypadły dwa zdjęcia. Odruchowo zerknęła na adres. Pod imieniem i nazwiskiem Edyty widniał dopisek: *do rąk własnych*. Całkiem niechcący i trochę bezmyślnie otworzyła prywatną korespondencję. Rozejrzała się bezradnie w poszukiwaniu kleju lub kawałka taśmy, żeby naprawić błąd. Oczywiście nie byłaby kobietą, gdyby przy okazji nie zerknęła na fotki. Raz, potem drugi. Miała przed sobą gotowe, choć nieco przestarzałe załączniki do sprawy rozwodowej. Pijaniutka para w pozach erotycznie jednoznacznych, na fotelu i na dywanie, gdzieś, w jakimś gabinecie. Nad nimi wielki napis na ścianie: *Dobra robota, to obowią...*

– Ale jajo – szepnęła zaskoczona. Porno w stylu retro?

Na odwrocie czarno-białych fotek widniał rok 1983. Edyta miała wtedy około trzydziestki, włosy długie do ramion i chyba nieco ostrzejszy makijaż. Julia patrzyła i patrzyła. Otrzeźwiała dopiero na dźwięk telefonu.

– Pan dyrektor zajęty, przekażę, proszę, dziękuję – odpowiadała machinalnie. Przytrzymując ramieniem słuchawkę, błyskawicznie zakleiła kopertę i odłożyła na brzeg biurka.

Kto potrafi skupić się na nudnej pracy w momencie, gdy został dopuszczony, a raczej sam się dopuścił do wielkiej tajemnicy? Julia nawet nie próbowała udawać, że przegląda instrukcję. Z obrzydzeniem odsunęła papierzyska jak najdalej od siebie. W głowie i przed oczami miała tylko zdjęcia. Nędzne fotki tak bardzo nie pasowały do kobiety, którą podziwiała za opanowanie, takt, subtelność i w ogóle za całokształt, że czuła się niemal oszukana. Już raz w życiu doświadczyła podobnego uczucia. To było strasznie dawno, w pierwszej, może drugiej klasie, kiedy niejaka Asia, szkolna papużka od serca, opowiedziała jej, co tak naprawdę wyczyniają dorośli po nocach. Wiedza Asi pochodziła z podglądania rodziców i była rzetelna. „Moi na pewno nie robią takich świństw!" – oświadczyła Julia z całą powagą swoich siedmiu wiosen. Nie negowała faktu, nie zarzucała Asi kłamstwa, uznała, że wszyscy mogą, z wyjątkiem mamy i taty. Komu miała wykrzyczeć, że Edyta na pewno nie była zdolna do takich świństw? A jeżeli była?

Im dłużej myślała o tajemniczej przesyłce, tym bardziej skłonna była podejrzewać, że to głupi żart, fotomontaż albo coś w tym rodzaju. Edyta otworzy kopertę, parsknie krótkim śmieszkiem, wzruszy ramionami i starannie podrze falsyfikaty. Niestety, ten moment jej umknął za sprawą pani Heni i Karoliny. Jak zwykle wpadły do sekretariatu razem. Jedna na drugą patrzeć nie mogła, lecz tak się jakoś składało, że zawsze chodziły w parze. Tym razem pomoc gospodarcza usiłowała się dowiedzieć, czy pani Aleksandra, czyli szefowa, jest już w firmie.

– Nie zauważyłam – odpowiedziała Julia.

Pani Henia wyglądała na mocno zafrasowaną. Niechętnie zerknęła na Karolinę, lecz magister Cierniak nie zamierzała opuszczać sekretariatu. Siedziała na biurku Julii i bawiła się linijką.

– Powinna już być – ciągnęła pani Henia – bo kazała dyrektorowi na siebie zaczekać. Gdyby nie kazała, już dawno by pofrunął ten... – ugryzła się najwyraźniej w język i dokończyła już innym tonem: – Że też taka piękna kobieta wzięła sobie na głowę taką zgryzotę!

– Widocznie kocha męża – bąknęła Julia.

– Kocha, kocha... jak psy dziada w ciasnej ulicy. Za te wszystkie romanse, za te zdrady to jemu można tylko chrześcijańskie miłosierdzie okazać, nic więcej. Z nawyku jest mu wierna. Drugiej takiej cnotliwej kobiety ze świecą szukać. Nie wierzysz?

– Ależ wierzymy, pani Heniu, wierzymy – wtrąciła Karolina. – Babki z wypchanym biustem muszą być cnotliwe, choćby z konieczności. Edyta panią prosi!

– Była tu?

– Właśnie wyszła.

Chwilę trwało, zanim pani Henia przetrawiła niesprawiedliwe słowa o wpływie biustu na cnotę i zdecydowała się wycofać. Edyta była jedyną osobą w firmie, przed którą czuła odrobinę respektu. Julia zerknęła na biurko sekretarki. Koperty nie było.

Pani Henia ponownie zajrzała do sekretariatu.

– Julciu, na momencik!

Przy magister Cierniak nie chciała wyskakiwać z wieczornym zebraniem kobiet, a prawdę mówiąc, wpadła tylko po to, by Julię zaprosić. Umówiły się o osiemnastej przed blokiem na Zbiegniewskiej.

– No, stara, widziałam angaż Orzechowicza! – Karolina nie mogła się już doczekać powrotu przyjaciółki. – Powiem ci, że całkiem dobre warunki sobie wykrzyczał.

– A co z Kicińskim?

– Od pierwszego odchodzi do Anwilu. To jego decyzja. Raczej pomyśl, co z tobą, i pogadaj z Orzechowiczem. On nie gryzie, mogę ci zaręczyć.

– Skoro ręczysz, to chyba spróbuję.

– Błagam, nie rób min jak Edyta! – jęknęła Karolina. – Na dzisiaj mam dość.

Musiała mieć dość, bo nie chciała powiedzieć Julii nic więcej i udawała, że nie pamięta żadnej sprzeczki.

Orzechowicz wreszcie był z siebie zadowolony. Przygotował się na potężną awanturę, sądził, że przyjdzie mu walczyć o pieniądze, i nawet nie zdążył pokazać na co go stać. Wystarczyło, że odrobinę podniósł głos, a już stary zmiękł, załatwił wszystko od ręki i pod dyktando. Ta jedna rozmowa przekreśliła Mikulę w oczach Konrada. Lubił twardych facetów, sam się do takich zaliczał i jak każdy macho gardził mięczakami. Nie odmawiał dyrektorowi sprytu, lecz o jego umiejętnościach menedżerskich miał jak najgorsze zdanie. Przede wszystkim był rozczarowany bałaganem w firmie i wcale tego nie ukrywał. Liczył na gwałtowny protest, na zwykłe w takich wypadkach tłumaczenia i był zaskoczony, kiedy Mikula przyznał mu rację.

– Wiem, wiem! – powiedział. – Komputeryzacja, stworzenie odpowiedniego systemu, to wszystko ułatwi dostęp do dokumentów i właściwy ich przepływ. Kupimy sprzęt w drugiej połowie maja.

– Dlaczego nie wcześniej? Przecież szkoda czasu?

Rozmawiali już całkiem spokojnie, prawie po przyjacielsku.

– Czasu szkoda, ale pojawiły się kłopoty finansowe. Skurczybyki, zlecają roboty, a płacić nie chcą. Co to za czasy, w których najtrudniej jest odzyskać własne pieniądze!

– Jest kilka wypróbowanych sposobów na odzyskanie pieniędzy. Niech mi pan udostępni listę dłużników, może da się coś zrobić?

– Ba! Nie ma takiej listy. Zginęła – powiedział Mikula.

Konrad domyślnie pokiwał głową. Zrozumiał, że nie w porę wyrwał się z propozycją i nie nalegał dłużej. W każdym razie załatwił prawie wszystko, co chciał załatwić, może z wyjątkiem jednego: nie wspomniał dyrektorowi o tej małej informatyczce z sekretariatu. Dziewczyna widać zagustowała w myciu szklanek i parzeniu kawy, bo nigdy więcej nie wróciła do rozmowy, zapoczątkowanej kiedyś przez Karolinę. Nie chciał na siłę uszczęśliwiać śmiesznej myszki o roztargnionym spojrzeniu zakochanej kobiety.

Karolina wyszła z sekretariatu zaraz po nim. Wydawała się podekscytowana i przejęta. Jak na kogoś, kto nie był przy rozmowie, wiedziała bardzo dużo.

– Czy ty przypadkiem nie podsłuchiwałaś pod drzwiami? – roześmiał się Konrad.

– Oczywiście że tak! Potraktowałeś starego capa wyjątkowo elegancko i nie umiałam odmówić sobie tej przyjemności.

– Jesteś niesamowita! – przyznał Konrad.

– Dlatego, że nie kłamię?

– Dlatego, że zaprzeczasz i zgadzasz się w momentach najmniej oczekiwanych.

– Współczuję ci, ssaczku, musiałeś mieć do czynienia z wyjątkowo nudnymi kobietami! – westchnęła.

Chciała jeszcze coś dodać, ale zadzwonił telefon. Stanęła sobie przy oknie, żeby udowodnić, że nie ma zwyczaju podsłuchiwania wszystkich rozmów. Ta akurat nie była zbyt interesująca. Rozmówca tokował, Konrad słuchał, czasem wtrącił słówko tak, częściej nie, ze dwa razy przyznał, że czegoś nie wie. Zaintrygowała ją dopiero sama końcówka:

– Dobra, Grzesiu, zadzwonię do ciebie wieczorem, teraz nie mogę mówić – powiedział Konrad.

– Następnym razem daj mi znak i wyjdę! – zdenerwowała się Karolina. – Zaręczam ci, że się nie obrażę. Każdy ma prawo do tajemnic służbowych.

– To była prywatna rozmowa z nudnym facetem i nie miałem ochoty jej ciągnąć – wyjaśnił.

– Grześ Bujała wie, że nazywasz go nudnym facetem? – spytała od niechcenia. Patrzyła przy tym prosto w oczy Konrada.

– Skądże znowu! Chyba nie zechcesz mu tego powtórzyć?

– Przecież mówiłam ci, że go nie znam.

– Całe szczęście. To jest facet, który ma o sobie wyłącznie dobre zdanie. Tak przynajmniej myślę. A mój koleś nazywa się Grzegorz Majdziak i naprawdę jest nudny.

Patrząc sobie głęboko w oczy, skończyli tę rozmowę, z której nic nie wynikało.

– A ciebie znowu gdzie niesie?

Matka czujnie wychyliła się z kuchni.

– Widzisz, jak ty mnie słuchasz! – zawołała z wyrzutem Julia. – Przecież wczoraj mówiłam, że mam wizytę u dentysty!

W wielkim pośpiechu narzuciła kurtkę i starannie zamknęła za sobą drzwi. Po pięciu latach spędzonych w stolicy i w akademiku wciąż jeszcze nie umiała się przyzwyczaić do przesłuchań: gdzie, po co, z kim, na jak długo i czy w ogóle warto. Zdaniem matki nie było warto opuszczać domu, o czym starała się za wszelką cenę przekonać córkę. Emilia Blendowa była niezmordowana, Julia z kolei uważała, że jest dorosła i żeby nie popaść w kompleksy więźnia, wypracowała sobie niezawodny system przepustek. Dentysta, lekarz, mechanik samochodowy, to były słowa wytrychy, które otwierały jej drzwi do kilku godzin wolności.

Z wielką ulgą wyszła przed dom. Rzadko miała okazję robić właściwy użytek z nóg i spacerować po własnym osiedlu. Szła sobie nieśpiesznie, zdziwiona, że to już naprawdę wiosna. Zza szyb matiza jakoś nie dostrzegała napęczniałych pąków na drzewach ani krokusów w ogródkach. Bez trudu odnalazła właściwy wieżowiec na Zbiegniewskiej. Drzwi do drugiej klatki były sprytnie zabezpieczone, tak by nie trzeba było korzystać z domofonu. Przy windzie czekała okrąglutka siwa kobieta.

– Które piętro? – spytała i natychmiast poinformowała Julię, że ona jedzie na ostatnie.

– Ja też.

– Pani na sesję? – ucieszyła się tamta.

– Chyba tak – przyznała Julia i uśmiechnęła się na myśl, że ma uczestniczyć ni mniej, ni więcej tylko w sesji, na którą zaprosiła ją pomoc gospodarcza.

Kobieta była znacznie starsza od Julii, mogła mieć około pięćdziesięciu lat. Patrzyła na dziewczynę z wyraźną sympatią. Nim winda dojechała na górę, zdążyła wyjaśnić, że znikąd nie da się wynieść tyle mocy i energii, co z babskich sesji.

Niewielkie pomieszczenie blokowej suszarni zostało tego popołudnia zamienione na salę obrad. Kobiety siedziały na krzesłach przyniesionych z domu, na turystycznych fotelikach i zwykłych deskach położonych na taboretach. W przejściu ustawiły torby i siatki, jakby przybiegły na spotkanie prosto z zakupów. Julia przycupnęła na desce obok nowej znajomej. Rozejrzała się ciekawie. Brudne szyby nie przepuszczały dziennego światła, goła żarówka zniekształcała rysy i rzucała dziwne cienie na ściany. Uczestniczek było kilkanaście, wszystkie raczej w wieku dojrzałym, niezbyt zadbane. Nigdzie nie mogła dostrzec Heni. I nic dziwnego. W firmie Henia była pomocą gospodarczą w czerwonym fartuchu, na sesji występowała w charakterze guru: niebieska garsonka, włosy prosto spod lokówki i obfita biżuteria. To ona właśnie wystąpiła na środek i rozpoczęła przedziwne misterium.

– Drogie kobitki! – powiedziała. – Żeby nam się lepiej medytowało, pomódlmy się najpierw do Świętego Ducha słowami naszego hymnu. Poproszę na środek panią Pasieczko.

Znajoma z windy spojrzała porozumiewawczo na Julię i ochoczo stanęła obok guru. Wysokim, niezbyt melodyjnym głosem zaintonowała coś, co podchwyciły tylko nieliczne panie. Widać nie wszystkie znały tekst, bo mamrotały pod nosem jedynie refren: „O Duchu, przyjdź i daj nam moc, żebyśmy miały siłę!”. Hymn był cudownie grafomański i tak niespójny, że momentami nie było wiadomo, czy bardziej przypomina litanię czy magiczne zaklinanie do świętej jogi. Joga z całą pewnością była indyjską świętą – tak wynikało z hymnu autorstwa pani Pasieczko.

Julia z trudem utrzymywała powagę. Stała niby w grupie, ale nie czuła żadnej więzi z pozostałymi kobietami. Patrzyła na nie oczami osoby z zewnątrz. Widziała poruszające się usta, słyszała nierówne głosy opiewające dusze białe jak lelije, przeczyste nadzieje i siłę medytacji świętej jogi. Fantastyczna scena, myślała gorączkowo, fantastyczna i nie do podrobienia. Tego nie można wymyślić, to trzeba zobaczyć, usłyszeć i sfilmować!

Hymn był długi, na szczęście miał też koniec. Zaróżowiona z emocji autorka wróciła na miejsce obok Julii.

– A teraz, wzmocnione przez Ducha, przystąpmy do medytacji – zarządziła pani Henia. – Postarajcie się oderwać umysły od powszedniości, nie myślcie o dzieciakach, o chłopach, tylko o rzeczach wielkich, wzniosłych. Każda jedna kobieta jest stworzona do wielkich rzeczy i trzeba mocno chcieć, aby niemożliwe stało się możliwe. No, to medytujemy!

Uczestniczki sesji posłusznie złożyły ręce na piersi, pochyliły głowy, jednak nie bardzo umiały oderwać się od powszedniości. Wokół krzeseł biegały z radosnym piskiem dzieci, z którymi mamy czy babcie nie miały co zrobić. Jedno domagało się soku, inne przewróciło torbę z zakupami i narobiło sporo bałaganu. Zniecierpliwiona pani Henia zadała medytacje do odrobienia w domu i otworzyła najważniejszą część obrad, czyli rozmowy psychologiczne. Jak żyć, żeby nie zwariować? Trzeba pokochać siebie i powtarzać przed lustrem: jestem wspaniała, jestem silna, dam sobie radę! – brzmiała odpowiedź. Co zrobić, gdy mąż pije? Powiedzieć, że się go kocha. Mężczyźni często piją z braku miłości. A co zrobić, jak bije?

– Odkąd poczułam w sobie moc, chłop ani razu po pijaku mnie nie uderzył! – pochwaliła się kobieta w granatowym skafandrze.

– Mnie też! – ochoczo dołączyła inna. – Tylko że ja uciekam, zanim wróci – wyjaśniła już ciszej, nieco zawstydzona.

Julia nie słuchała zbyt uważnie. Była na siebie zła, że usiadła tak daleko od drzwi. Dzięki naukom pani Heni czuła się silna, podniesiona na duchu i wzmocniona, jednak nie na tyle, by solo przepychać się wśród zafrasowanych kobiet i ich siatek. Posłusznie wstały, gdy pani Henia zarządziła łańcuch energetyczny, połączony z przekazywaniem znaku pokoju.

– Chwyćcie się za ręce i pamiętajcie, że przez was płynie teraz kosmiczna energia. Te, które mają nadmiar, obdzielą pozostałe i wszystkie wyjdziecie wzmocnione! – Pani Henia przekrzykiwała te kobiety, które chciały dzielić się doświadczeniami i wciąż wracały do pijanych mężów i niesfornych dzieci.

Julia wyszła szczęśliwa, że to już koniec. W windzie znowu natknęła się na panią Pasieczko, a właściwie już nie panią, tylko Wandę. Uczestniczki sesji, bez względu na wiek, zwracały się do siebie po imieniu.

– Odprowadź mnie, Julio, to sobie porozmawiamy – zaproponowała Wanda.

I Julia zamiast w prawo skręciła w lewo. Przez chwilę szły w milczeniu.

– Czy pani... przepraszam, czy wierzysz w medytacje, w przekazywanie energii i w ten cały... w to wszystko?

– No tak! Czytałam w gazecie, że nawet bardzo mądre kobiety medytują.

– Też czytałam i wydaje mi się, że robią to trochę inaczej.

– Każdy medytuje, jak umie. Nasza Henia mówi, że kiedy już się skupi, doznaje kosmicznego olśnienia. Podobno w ten sposób nauczyła się kochać wszystkich ludzi. – Julia gwałtownie zakaszlała i Wanda spojrzała na nią zafrasowana. – Wiem, o czym myślisz: wszystkich pokochać nie można. Też tak uważam. Weź takich moich sąsiadów! Nie pokochasz, choler jednych, choćbyś medytowała ruski rok. Dlatego chodzę na sesje, żeby zgromadzić w sobie energię. Urzędów na nich nie ma, policji nie ma, to może chociaż pozytywna energia pomoże mi wysłać ich w kosmos.

Wanda, szczęśliwa, że poderwała słuchaczkę, zaczęła szczegółowo i kwieciście opowiadać o swoich kłopotach z sąsiadami. Julia kiwała głową ze zrozumieniem, a jej myśli błądziły po planie filmowym. Stała obok Marka, za moment mieli grać jej ulubioną scenę uczty... – Boska moja! Kochaj mnie – szeptał aktor.

– ...i wiem dokładnie, że ta biedna Pałubska w grobie się przewraca – mówiła Wanda.

Na dźwięk znajomego nazwiska Julia natychmiast oprzytomniała.
– Kto?
– Bronia Pałubska świętej pamięci! Cały czas o niej opowiadam! Dwa lata temu zmarła i skończył się mój spokój. Mogła jeszcze pożyć, nie była stara. Stwierdzili u niej niewydolność nerek, spuchła biedaczka jak balon. A po niej to już się wprowadził taki element, że sodomka gomorka i żyć się nie da. Dom publiczny pod bokiem mi zrobili, ty wiesz, co to znaczy?! – zaszeptała znacząco.

Julia domyślała się, co to znaczy, lecz opowiadanie Wandy przestało ją interesować. Bronisława Pałubska, do tego świętej pamięci, nie budziła w niej żadnych emocji, podobnie jak nowi lokatorzy. Odprowadziła kobietę do najbliższego rogu i zaczęła pośpiesznie się żegnać.

– Wpadłabyś do mnie kiedy na kawę! O, tu już widać mój blok. Pogadamy, zobaczysz, jak mieszkam, obejrzysz moje książki z psychologii – kusiła z natarczywością charakterystyczną dla ludzi samotnych i spragnionych towarzystwa. – Może akurat trafisz na sodomkę gomorkę i sama się przekonasz, jakie piekło muszę przeżywać.

Julia obiecała, że kiedyś wpadnie i nawet przez moment pomyślała, że mogłaby, czemu nie. Ledwie jednak pożegnała Wandę, wiedziała, że nie odwiedzi jej nigdy. Zawróciła i raźnym krokiem poszła w swoją stronę. Przed sklepem z akcesoriami łazienkowymi mignęła jej charakterystyczna sylwetka w paltociku, z rękami w kieszeniach. Na wszelki wypadek przyśpieszyła kroku. Był wieczór, ciemno, a sylwetka tak podobna do Chochli, że nie chciała mącić sobie snów.

Edyta wściekała się zawsze na sucho, bez łez. Jej łagodne rysy nabierały nieprzyjemnej ostrości, a kąciki ust nieznacznie opadały. To był niezawodny znak, że nosiła w duszy burzę z piorunami. W takich chwilach najbliżsi współpracownicy ostrzyli zęby na pyszną antystresową drożdżówkę. Przepis Edyty brzmiał mniej więcej tak: „Rozczyń ciasto drożdżowe według dowolnego przepisu; gdy wyrośnie, uformuj kulę, wyobraź sobie wredną gębę prywatnego wroga i wal tak długo, aż wyczerpiesz wszystkie epitety, łącznie z nieprzyzwoitymi. Kiedy ochłoniesz, ciasto będzie doskonale wyrobione, a ty wyluzowana. Bez cienia obawy możesz je upiec i zjeść w gronie przyjaciół".

W przedświąteczny piątek Edyta przyniosła do biura pięknie wyrośniętą drożdżówkę.

– Jasny gwint! – westchnął łakomie Leszek. – Piekłaś dla higieny psychicznej czy już na święta?

– A to nie wszystko jedno?

– Niby tak, choć lubię wiedzieć, na czyją intencję grzeszę obżarstwem.

– Jedz! Wyrobiłam solidnie, więc powinno być strawne.

Znów była spokojna i bardzo dystyngowana. Nic, ani jeden muskuł, ani jedna kurza łapka nie mówiły o emocjach dnia poprzedniego, z wyjątkiem drożdżówki. Swoją miną mogła wyprowadzić w pole Karolinę i Leszka, ale nie Julię. Prawdę mówiąc, Julia też nie była pewna do końca. Dręczył ją anonimowy nadawca przesyłki. Fotograf? Możliwe. Życzliwi bliźni? Tych nie da się wykluczyć. Partner z balangi? Facet wydawał się znajomy. Z całą pewnością widziała już gdzieś ten charakterystyczny zarys podbródka i te uszka sterczące jak kokardki. Niestety, z dwóch klocków nie dało się ułożyć całego chłopa, na dodatek postarzonego o kilkanaście lat. Edytę poznała bez trudu, jego nie mogła i to ją męczyło.

Piątek był normalnym dniem pracy. Dyrektor wyjechał i nikt, łącznie z Edytą, nie miał serca do papierków. W powietrzu czuło się przedświąteczną atmosferę. Siedzieli, gawędzili o wielkanocnych przysmakach i było bardzo swojsko. Julia dyskretnie wyszła z pokoju. Postanowiła, i to za cenę utraty szacunku dla samej siebie, że jednak porozmawia z Orzechowiczem. Jeżeli on się zgodzi, myślała logicznie, ułatwi mi rozmowę z Mikulą. Nieśmiało uchyliła drzwi pokoju i byłaby uciekła, gdyby Kiciński jej nie zauważył. Zachował się bardzo ładnie. Nazwał Julię koleżanką i przedstawił Orzechowiczowi jako młodą, ambitną siłę.

– Myślę, kolego, że dla takich pięknych oczu warto przełamać antyfeminizm dyrektora! – powiedział i uśmiechnął się do Julii.

Miał miły sposób żartowania i w ogóle był ujmującym starszym panem. Nawet Orzechowicz przy nim wyglądał mniej groźnie, choć spoglądał na Julię z ironią i wcale nie skakał z radości, że nowy narybek sam pcha mu się w ręce.

– Dość długo zwlekała pani z przyjściem do nas – zauważył chłodno. – Myślałem, że się pani wystraszyła.

– Kogo? – Podniosła na niego wielkie oczy, przekonana, że odgadł jej najtajniejsze myśli. – Pana?

– Aż tak zarozumiały nie jestem. Myślałem raczej o myszy. To jest, wie pani, takie urządzenie połączone ogonkiem z komputerem – parsknął śmiechem, zadowolony z żartu.

Julia rzeczywiście bała się tej rozmowy, jednak wobec niezbyt wyrafinowanego dowcipu Konrada poczuła przypływ odwagi. Tak to już z nią było, że mobilizowała się w chwilach trudnych, gdy nie miała innego wyjścia. Spojrzała chłodno na roześmianego inżyniera.

– Mogę pana uspokoić. Według chińskiego kalendarza urodziłam się w roku kota. To myszy się mnie boją, nie odwrotnie – powiedziała z powagą. Była pewna, że podobnie jak ona, nie miał zielonego pojęcia o chińskim kalendarzu.

Kiciński zaczął wypytywać o studia i przebieg pracy zawodowej. Niewiele miała do opowiadania. Dyplom politechniki, specjalizacja taka i taka, biegła znajomość angielskiego i niemieckiego, ciekawa praca w Warszawie i kłopoty we Włocławku. Kiedy przeszli do tematów fachowych, uspokoiła się całkiem. Wyszła podbudowana. Orzechowicz już więcej nie próbował żartować, obiecał wystąpić do dyrektora z oficjalnym wnioskiem o przeniesienie. Biegnąc do sekretariatu, czuła u ramion skrzydła, które niestety opadły dość szybko. Nikt nie zwrócił na nią uwagi, wszyscy skupili się wokół pani prezes, która nietaktownie zwracała się wyłącznie do Edyty.

– A Cholewa, pardon, Chochla nie znalazł się, co? Ciekawostka, swoją drogą, nie uważasz? Nic ci się o słuch nie obiło? Myślisz, że on jeszcze żyje? Bo ja mam wątpliwości.

– Jak go psy nie rozszarpały, to na pewno żyje! – Głos Edyty zabrzmiał dziwnie twardo.

– Ja myślałam raczej o porachunkach, o jakimś napadzie, przypadkowym, ma się rozumieć. Nasze miasto nie jest już zaściankiem. A to się biznesmeni postrzelają w klubie, a to klub się spali. Mamy trochę atrakcji, nieprawdaż? Mógł i Cholewa w coś się zaplątać, nie uważasz? Ja uważam, że mógł.

– Najpewniej w troki od kalesonów mruknął Leszek, czym rozbawił Karolinę i Julię. Z trudem zapanowały nad wesołością. Pani prezes śmiała się wyłącznie ze swoich dowcipów i nie wypadało z nią konkurować. Leszek kilkakrotnie i ostentacyjnie westchnął.

– A tobie co? – zdziwiła się Edyta.

– Serce mi z bólu pęka, że pani prezes nie ma apetytu.

– Ależ ja mam! – Mikulowa spojrzała na swój talerzyk, na którym spoczywał nietknięty kawałek drożdżówki i wybuchnęła śmiechem. – No tak, jak ktoś ma tyle do powiedzenia co ja, to nie ma czasu jeść.

– Sam nie wiem, czy wolę patrzeć, jak pani je, czy słuchać pani głosu – znalazł się szarmancko magister Wydroń.

– Oj, panie Leszku! Jeszcze moment, a uwierzę panu. Jak myślisz, Edytko, mam uwierzyć czy nie?

– Jemu się nie wierzy, jego się słucha – wyjaśniła spokojnie Edyta, nie podnosząc głowy znad papierów.

– Ale ja mam do pana Leszka słabość – mizdrzyła się Mikulowa. – Ja...

– Auu! – jęknęła Julia i wszyscy, nie wyłączając pani prezes, spojrzeli w jej stronę.

– Uważaj, na tych krzesłach są zadry – powiedziała Karolina, choć wcześniej to jej palec ugodził Julię pod żebro.

Mikulowa chichotała już tylko z Leszkiem i od czasu do czasu brała na świadka Edytę.

– Ojej, powiedz mu coś, Edytko, no powiedz, bo ja już ze śmiechu nie mogę...

Dla Julii i Karoliny było jasne, że magister Wydroń przystąpił do realizacji planu aprilistów. Siedziały poważne, bo nie wypadało wychodzić z pokoju, w którym królowała pani prezes. Nie wypadało też gadać.

Julia obserwowała Mikulową i stwierdziła, że szefowa wygląda bardzo efektownie i wiosennie. Świeżo ufarbowane włosy były żółtsze niż puch kurczaka, zielona spódniczka krótsza, niż nakazywała metryka, lecz uwagę zwracała przede wszystkim radosna, rozświetlona twarz. Takie twarze miewają zakochane kobiety. Julia pomyślała nawet, że dyrektor wreszcie się ustatkował i wrócił na łono rodziny.

W drodze do domu usiłowała porozmawiać na ten temat z dziwnie zamyśloną Karoliną.

– Wierzę, że ona się zabujała, ale żeby we własnym chłopie, to raczej mało prawdopodobne! – orzekła przyjaciółka. I dodała, zasępiona: – Tylko czekaj! Dla naszego spisku takie zakochanie Mikulowej tak czy tak źle wróży.

– Myślisz, że zechce nam zmienić dyrektora? – spytała Julia.

– Kto wie, co jej biega po tej żółtej głowie! Tylko nie licz, że facet będzie mądrzejszy od Mikuli. Żaden geniusz nie poleci na nią, chyba że stuknięty.

– Podobno każdy geniusz jest lekko stuknięty.

– Nie wiem, nie znam żadnego! Gadaj lepiej, co załatwiłaś z Konradem?

– Właściwie to chyba wszystko. Zastanawiam się, jaki on jest naprawdę.

– W łóżku fantastyczny!

– Idź, ty cyniczko! Chodzi o to, jaki jest w życiu.

– Skąd mam wiedzieć? Za krótko go znam. Ten facet wymaga oswojenia, rozumiesz?

– Ani w ząb! – przyznała Julia. – Idziesz do łóżka z nieoswojonym facetem?

– Jasne! Tylko taki może mnie zaskoczyć.

Julia doceniała szczerość, jednak czuła zakłopotanie, ilekroć przyjaciółka zachowywała się tak, jakby pojęcie intymności było jej całkowicie obce. Dla Karoliny nie istniały tematy tabu. Opowiadała o orgazmie lub wymyślnych pieszczotach i nie zmieniając tonu, z taką samą miną przechodziła do niedomagań wątroby lub sposobów ochrony organizmu przed zimnem. Julia, która była idealistką i romantyczką – tak przynajmniej o sobie myślała – w zetknięciu z naturalizmem Karoliny czuła zażenowanie i najchętniej zmieniała temat.

– Co robisz w święta? Może wpadniesz do mnie?

– Dzięki, że o mnie pomyślałaś. Wprawdzie nie zanosi się, żebym była sama, ale nigdy nic nie wiadomo.

– Nie musisz wpadać sama – uśmiechnęła się Julia. – Mam zamiar cię zaskoczyć. Jutro wybieram się na zakupy i w święta będę nie ta sama.

Karolina gwałtownie zaprotestowała. Nie po to od kilku dni obmyślała nowy styl dla przyjaciółki, by ta pobiegła do pierwszego lepszego sklepu i za wielkie pieniądze kupiła kolejny namiot dla skautów. Obowiązkowo bury i z ogonami. Karolina pragnęła opakować piękne ciało Julii po swojemu, zgrać kolory z fasonami, zastanowić się nad fakturą tkanin, nad włosami, nad makijażem i w ten sposób zrobić z małej ósmy cud świata. Ale na to potrzebny był czas. A w ostatnią przedświąteczną sobotę Karolina oczywiście czasu nie miała. Musiała ogarnąć mieszkanie, przetrzeć okna, kupić coś do jedzenia, żeby nie zagłodzić Konrada. Wielkie przemienienie należało odłożyć do wtorku. Julia kiwnęła głową na znak zgody, choć z góry wiedziała, że nie dotrzyma obietnicy. Szybko zapalała się do nowych pomysłów i jak każdy słomiany ogień była bardzo niecierpliwa. Nie miała zamiaru czekać do wtorku.

Wysadziła przyjaciółkę na Budowlanych i zawróciła na osiedle Południe.

W sobotę od rana matka miotała się po domu spocona, zmęczona i zła jak osa. Jej gniewne burczenie docierało do pokoju Julii.

– Kto to wymyślił święta? Żeby nie dziecko, palcem bym nie ruszyła. Zdzisiek, ty mnie słyszysz?!

Zawieszała głos, robiła efektowną pauzę w oczekiwaniu, że mąż lub córka zaofiarują swoją pomoc. Wcale nie chodziło o pomoc, tylko o wytknięcie domownikom, że do żadnej pracy się nie nadają. Jeżeli milczeli, zmieniała nieco tekst.

– Wszystko na mojej głowie! Więcej nie dam się wrobić w żadne święta!

Nikt jej nie wrabiał, działała z własnej nieprzymuszonej woli, choć z upodobaniem obnosiła minę cierpiętnicy. Znosiła do domu zakupy, piekła, gotowała, żeby córka zachowała piękne wspomnienia z dzieciństwa. Córka miała co prawda lat dwadzieścia z ogonkiem, ale w domu wciąż występowała jako dziecko, maleństwo, które musi dostać makowiec na Wigilię i mazurek na Wielkanoc.

Julia bardzo lubiła święta, dopóki żył dziadek. Mieszkali wtedy w niewielkim domu z ogrodem na peryferiach miasta. Dziadek dbał o to, co się nazywa kolorytem i atmosferą świąteczną. Przed Wielkanocą znosił do domu donice ze specjalnie pędzonymi hiacyntami. W święta cały dom pachniał nie tylko jedzeniem, lecz także kwiatami. Stół przybrany był gałązkami bukszpanu, na środku stała wielka misa kraszanek, gotowanych w łuskach cebuli. Była też obowiązkowo szynka z kością. Dziadek sam ją peklował, sam wędził na podwórku. Zapach wonnego dymu był pierwszą oznaką zbliżających się świąt.

Zmarł, gdy Julia chodziła jeszcze do podstawówki. Rodzice natychmiast sprzedali stary dom z ogrodem, żeby nie pakować pieniędzy w remonty i choć stać ich było na nowy, wygodny, wybrali mieszkanie w blokach. Nie za wielkie, dwa pokoje z kuchnią na osiedlu Południe. Skromne mieszkanie nie kłuje ludzi w oczy, nie kusi złodziei, tłumaczyli córce. Byli ludźmi zamożnymi, ale skrzętnie tę zamożność ukrywali. Oczywiście na jedzeniu oszczędzać nie musieli. Nikt im też do garnków nie zaglądał, bo życie wiedli mało towarzyskie. Święta spędzali przed telewizorem. Patrzyli w ekran, posilali się, drzemali. Tak było od wielu lat. Drewniane jajka wielokrotnego użytku równie pięknie zdobiły stół jak kiedyś dziadkowe kraszanki, sztuczne żonkile przy stroiku nie gubiły płatków jak żywe hiacynty. Czar prysnął. Julia protestowała przeciwko takim świętom i prawie nie wystawiała nosa ze swojego pokoju, choć całe zamieszanie było przecież z myślą o dziecku, to znaczy o niej.

Tym razem dziecko miało całkiem inne problemy. Kupiło w kiosku kilka kobiecych pism i szukało dla siebie natchnienia. Wamp czy słodka idiotka? Kobieta sukcesu czy wyrafinowany kopciuszek? Jeżeli chodzi o kopciuszka, Karolina wystarczająco obrzydziła Julii ten wizerunek. Im dłużej wertowała magazyny poświęcone modzie, tym bardziej utwierdzała się w przekonaniu, że kreatorzy wolą chyba z kobiet kpić, niż je ubierać. Żadna z propozycji nie przypadła jej do gustu. Poczuła nagły przypływ żalu, że nigdy nie będzie elegancką damą, jak choćby Edyta lub Karolina. Pierwsza preferowała styl klasyczny: szmizjerki, kostiumy i od czasu do czasu garnitury, druga odważnie zestawiała kolory, podkreślała biust i zgrabne nogi. A co miała podkreślać ona, Julia? Stanęła przed lustrem i spojrzała na siebie krytycznie, oczami bezstronnego obserwatora.

– Przypominam koszmarka zagubionego w lesie – mruknęła niechętnie. – Wszystkiego za dużo, a urody chyba za mało?

Gwałtownie zapragnęła być inna, energiczna i piękna jak Karolina, dystyngowana jak Edyta, marzycielska jak pewna nieznajoma dziewczyna, którą znała wyłącznie ze zdjęć w kolorowych tygodnikach. Muszę się zmienić radykalnie, za jednym zamachem, postanowiła. Włosy ufarbuję, piegi przykryję fluidem, co do ciuchów, to zobaczę w sklepach.

Był sobotni ranek, lecz Julia, kiedy już wbiła sobie coś do głowy, to skutecznie. Zebrała się do wyjścia i dla spokoju sumienia spytała, czy nie trzeba pomóc.

– Wy z ojcem akurat nadajecie się do pomocy! – wykrzyknęła matka. – Najpierw trzeba wam pokazać krok po kroku, a potem jeszcze poprawić. Nie mam czasu na takie zabawy! Tylko proszę: żadnych gości w święta. Chyba nikogo nie zapraszałaś, co?

– W drugi dzień odwiedzi mnie koleżanka. Posiedzimy u mnie.

– Jasne, na gotowe to każdy chętny! Ta koleżanka nie ma swojego domu, żeby tak w święta zwalać się komuś na kark?

– I oczywiście Serafin będzie – dopowiedziała Julia z dziką satysfakcją.

Dlatego z dziką, że Serafin w ogóle nie był w planie. Okłamała chłopaka, wymyśliła wyjazd z rodzicami, byle mieć go z głowy na całe dwa dni. Gdyby matka nie była taka niechętna wobec jej znajomych, gdyby nie wyzłośliwiała się w ciemno na każdego, o kim Julia ledwie wspominała, nie straszyłaby jej Serafinem. A tak nie mogła się oprzeć. Matka prychnęła gniewnie kilka razy.

– Ty wychodzisz? – spytała z niepokojem.

– Tylko do drogerii. Skończył mi się krem.

– To kup pastę do zębów. Ja w twoim wieku żadnych kremów jeszcze nie używałam!

Sobotnie przedpołudnie wbrew wszelkim obawom okazało się porą idealną na zakupy. Kobiety, zajęte ostatnimi przygotowaniami do świąt, krzątały się po domach. Wszędzie, gdzie wchodziła, była jedyną klientką. Starannie ominęła dwa sklepy, w których kupowała swoje zamaszyste spódnice i wielkie swetry. Jak się zmieniać, to się zmieniać, pomyślała. Na początek wstąpiła do Galerii, gdzie najczęściej bywała Karolina. Niewielki sklep na rogu Kilińskiego nastroił ją optymistycznie. Pojedyncze serie, prosta elegancja, wszystko chciałoby się mieć. Rozejrzała się bezradnie po wieszakach. W oczach miała tęczę, w duszy rozterkę. Umiejętność wyboru nigdy nie była jej mocną stroną.

– W czym mogę pomóc? – spytała rutynowo ekspedientka.

– Proszę mnie ubrać – odpowiedziała Julia bezradnie i natychmiast dodała, że szuka czegoś do pracy i czegoś na wyjście. Mówiąc o wyjściu, wskazała bardzo elegancką białą bluzkę.

– Niech pani to odłoży – skarciła ją ekspedientka. – Błękitna biel nie jest dla pani. Écru, w ostateczności kość słoniowa. Proszę przymierzyć to!

Julia w staniku i w majtkach stała za kotarą, a ekspedientka donosiła jej spódniczki, bluzki i suknie. Patrzyła przy tym krytycznym okiem.

– Tego pani nie sprzedam. Wisi jak na haku.

– Z przodu leży ładnie! – protestowała Julia.

– Oprócz przodu jest jeszcze tył – wyjaśniła ekspedientka. – Co pani myśli o tym garniturze? Tabaczkowy brąz idealnie pasuje do pani karnacji, marynarka ma ciekawy krój.

– Dopóki mężczyźni nie zaczną biegać w sukienkach, nie włożę garnituru – odpowiedziała ze śmiechem.

Powoli zaczynała się czuć w przymierzalni jak ryba w wodzie. Nie męczyło jej wciąganie i zapinanie, rozpinanie i zdejmowanie, bo wszystkie te piękne szmatki odmieniały ją w sposób niewiarygodny. Kolory! Do tej pory znała dwa: ładny i brzydki. Teraz, patrząc uważnie w lustro, przekonała się, że są co najmniej jeszcze dwa: twarzowy i nietwarzowy. Srebrzysta, połyskliwa bluzka, która przepięknie wyglądała na wieszaku, na Julii straciła całą swoją urodę.

– Jest taka śliczna – westchnęła dziewczyna.

– Dla pani śliczniejsze będzie stare złoto.

Julia gratulowała sobie, że zaparkowała samochód na tyłach budynku, bo wyszła obładowana jak wielbłąd. Unosiła w objęciach lekki wiosenny kostium, elegancką suknię, dwie bluzki sweterkowe, dwie z materiału, żakiet i spódnicę. Uwierzyła ekspedientce i swojemu odbiciu w lustrze, że najpiękniejsze dla niej kolory to mahoń, ugier jasny, rdza, oliwkowa zieleń i écru. Zostawiła w sklepie równowartość dwu swoich pensji i gdyby w porę nie przypomniała sobie o butach, zostawiłaby więcej. Wpadła w zakupowy amok. Buty, kosmetyki, fryzjer... buty, kosmetyki, powtarzała, wycofując samochód. Z Kilińskiego pojechała na plac Wolności. Szukała eleganckich pantofli, lecz wciąż patrzyła na ciężkie z wyglądu platformy. Przywykła do szerokich, wygodnych trepów i nie bardzo potrafiła z nich zrezygnować.

– Czy to jest skóra?

– Ekologiczna.

– Ale ja bym chciała bydlęcą!

– Pani wie, ile kosztuje prawdziwa skóra? – spytała wyniośle ekspedientka.

Julia nie wiedziała, domyśliła się jednak, że nie wygląda na klientkę wartą skóry bydlęcej i posmutniała. Zerkając nerwowo na zegarek, obiegła kilka sklepów. Jak pasował rozmiar, to nie było odpowiedniego koloru i tak w kółko. Czas naglił. W świąteczną sobotę sklepy otwarte były znacznie krócej. W biegu niemal zdecydowała się na pantofle – ładne, lecz niezbyt wygodne. Kiedyś je w końcu rozczłapię, pomyślała optymistycznie, pędząc do perfumerii. I znowu dostała oczopląsu. Wbiła już sobie na szczęście do głowy, że kosmetyki muszą być zgrane z typem urody, czyli w ciepłych kolorach jesieni. Na inne w ogóle nie patrzyła, od razu poprosiła o brązowy tusz do rzęs, podkład jak najbardziej zbliżony do karnacji oraz zieleń i nefryt na powieki.

Do fryzjera wpadła piętnaście minut przed zamknięciem.

– Obciąć proszę i nałożyć kolor – wysapała.

Na szczęście fryzjerka nie miała zamiaru spędzać Wielkiej Soboty w zakładzie. Zgodziła się ostrzyc Julię, lecz o kolorze nie chciała słyszeć. We wtorek obiecała ją ufarbować nawet na zielono. I nie spytała, po co dziewczynie kolor, skoro jej własne włosy były niepowtarzalne i prześliczne.

Podjechała pod dom zmęczona i bardzo szczęśliwa. Chwilowo jeszcze jej uroda spoczywała w licznych torbach i reklamówkach, od czego jednak bujna wyobraźnia! Julia oczami duszy widziała już swoje nowe wcielenie. Może rzeczywiście Bujała wywinie orła na mój widok, pomyślała.

Konrad doszedł do wniosku, że jest nienormalny. Patrzył na świeżą zieleń za oknem, na świat budzący się do życia i zamiast też się obudzić, jak te ptaszki i kwiatki, stał markotny w oknie. Uległ życzeniu pięknej kobiety, miał z nią spędzić święta i nie odczuwał najmniejszej radości. Mało tego! Nagle zaczął żałować, że ominie go śniadanie u Orskich. A przecież wystarczyłby jeden telefon, jedno krótkie wyjaśnienie, że przyjdzie z dziewczyną. Miód na uszy Grażyny. Oj, te baby, baby! – pomyślał z niechęcią. Miał wszystkie cechy prawdziwego faceta, od fizycznych poczynając, na charakterze kończąc, i tylko z babami nie potrafił dojść do ładu. Tylko z babami! Albo one z nim, bo jeszcze żadnej nie udało się zatrzymać Konrada Orzechowicza na dłużej niż kilka miesięcy.

Na wspomnienie Karoliny poczuł dziwne uczucie, którego nie umiał nazwać. Ni to fascynacja, ni lęk. Była jedyną istotą w firmie, oprócz Kicińskiego, która wykazywała żywe zainteresowanie jego sprawami. Z Kicińskim, mimo różnicy wieku, prawie się zaprzyjaźnił, wobec Karoliny zachowywał dystans i nie bardzo rozumiał dlaczego. Gdyby jeszcze była brzydka, gdyby mu się tak bardzo nie podobała, to co innego!

– Coś mi się zdaje, panie kolego, że ten uroczy dołek w brodzie już należy do pana – zażartował niedawno Kiciński. – Gratuluję panu, to wyjątkowo piękna i atrakcyjna kobieta.

– Piękna – przyznał posępnie. – Ma w sobie coś!

– Pipeczkę, a co? Jak każda! – roześmiał się Kiciński.

Konradowi nawet w połowie nie było tak wesoło. Jego wątpliwości w żadnym stopniu nie dotyczyły anatomii. Pod tym względem Karolina była bez zarzutu, o czym przekonała go już na pierwszej randce. Chodziło o całkiem inną sferę doznań. Ona pociągała go i jednocześnie odpychała. Przy niej robił się jeszcze poważniejszy niż zwykle. Celne riposty przychodziły mu do głowy dopiero wtedy, gdy za dziewczyną zamykały się drzwi. Zaczynał żałować, że odeszła, brakowało mu jej żartów i śmiechu. Ona jest jak tajfun, myślał, gapiąc się smętnie w okno. Szybka, gwałtowna i niebezpieczna. Dla mnie chyba zbyt szybka.

Święta u Karoliny w niczym nie przypominały tych dawnych, u ciotki Eweliny czy u Orskich. Dziewczyna wynajmowała niewielką kawalerkę w bloku, korzystała z cudzych mebli i naczyń. Nie dał poznać po sobie, że zaskoczyło go nakrycie stołu, a mówiąc dokładniej – ławy. Obrus w kratkę, każdy talerzyk z innego kompletu i gdyby nie bazie w wazonie, nic nie wskazywałoby na uroczysty charakter śniadania. Karolina za to wyglądała jak zjawisko. Czarowała dekoltem czerwonej, obcisłej bluzki, czarowała klipsami i wielką gracją, z jaką poruszała się w zatłoczonym wnętrzu. Była radosna jak poranek.

– Mam nadzieję, że na wielkie obżarstwo nie liczysz? – zawołała ze śmiechem, wskazując Konradowi krzesło.

– Na wielkie nie, coś bym jednak zjadł – przyznał.

Nie celebrowała uroczystości – nie było pisanek, koszyczka ze święconym ani życzeń. Posiłek składał się z jaj w majonezie, białej kiełbasy, wędlin, chrzanu i rzodkiewek. Z wdziękiem wyjaśniła, że jako dama czuje się świetnie tylko na salonach, nigdy w kuchni.

– Często bywasz na salonach?

– Rzadziej, niż na to zasługuję. Znasz przysłowie, co się odwlecze i tak dalej? Już niedługo będę miała własny dom, salon i osobistą kucharkę.

Mówiła tonem lekkim i bardzo pewnym. Konrad milczał. Oczywiście mógł spytać, co planuje: napad na bank czy bogate małżeństwo, uznał jednak, że to jej sprawa. Jeżeli nawet małżeństwo, to na pewno nie z nim. Poczuł ulgę i zaraz za moment ostrą igiełkę zazdrości. Czuł tę igiełkę, ilekroć dziewczyna wspominała o innych mężczyznach. Znali się krótko, nigdy nie myślał o niej jak o przyszłej żonie, więc skąd ukłucie zazdrości? Chyba że to nie była zazdrość?!

– A twoje plany? – spytała Karolina. – Mam na myśli najbliższą przyszłość.

Wyrwała go z zamyślenia. Spojrzał spod zsuniętych brwi i uśmiechnął się jednym kącikiem ust. To był taki charakterystyczny uśmiech, którym zwykle pokrywał niepewność. Czeka na wyznanie, pomyślał, ale ją rozczaruję.

– Moje plany? Te dalsze, to bogate małżeństwo, willa z ogrodnikiem, choć bez kucharki, bo lubię gotować, samochód młodszy od mojego forda i tuzin dzieciątek. Te najbliższe są równie ambitne. Chętnie pozmywam po śniadaniu, potem zaproszę piękną dziewczynę na spacer. Wieczorem, do poduszki, skończę czytać Lema.

– Pytałam poważnie.

– Tak to właśnie zrozumiałem. W przeciwieństwie do ciebie lubię gotować, nie uciekam z kuchni i spokojnie możesz mi powierzyć zmywanie naczyń.

Roześmiała się i zaprotestowała tylko dla przyzwoitości. Na czas zmywania sama również przeniosła się do kuchni i próbowała pomagać. Zagracone pomieszczenie okazało się zbyt ciasne dla dwu osób. Z konieczności wciąż na siebie wpadali, choć może nie z konieczności, może to raczej Karolina tak manewrowała, żeby musiał poczuć jej bliskość. Na spacer już nie starczyło im ochoty, zdołali dojść jedynie do tapczanu.

Mocno spóźniony obiad składał się z jaj w majonezie, białej kiełbasy, wędlin i chrzanu. Rzodkiewki skończyły się przy śniadaniu.

– Jutro spróbuję coś ugotować. – Karolina przeciągnęła się leniwie. – Lubisz zapiekany makaron z wędliną?

– To może raczej ja coś ugotuję. – Konrad spojrzał na dziewczynę i błyskawicznie zmienił zdanie. – Nie. Jutro zapraszam cię do Zajazdu, zgoda?

Od czasu pamiętnego napadu matka nie dopuszczała Julii do drzwi. Na dźwięk każdego dzwonka biegła osobiście do przedpokoju. W drugi dzień świąt też nie dała się wyprzedzić.

– Jacyś obcy – zamachała gwałtownie ręką. – Facet i babka. Pewnie z tych, co nawracają ludzi. Siedź cicho, to sobie pójdą!

Cały szkopuł polegał na tym, że wcale cicho nie mówiła. Jeżeli Julia słyszała wyraźnie, to ci za drzwiami także musieli słyszeć.

– To na pewno do mnie! – powiedziała.

Matka stała z okiem przy judaszu i nie zamierzała opuszczać zajętej pozycji. Z wielkim trudem udało się Julii dopchać najpierw do wizjera, potem do zasuwy. Wśród zamieszania i radosnych okrzyków Karoliny musiała jakoś dokonać prezentacji. Z przyjaciółką nie miała kłopotu, Konrada przedstawiła jako swojego przyszłego szefa, co pozytywnie podziałało na matkę. Szef to szef, wiadomo!

– To ja nakryję do stołu w salonie – powiedziała pani Emilia.

– Nie, nie – zaprotestowała Julia. – Posiedzimy u mnie, porozmawiamy. Nie przeszkadzajcie sobie z tatą.

– Właśnie wracamy z obiadu – dodała Karolina.

– Od rodziców? – spytała pani Blenda.

Dopiero w pokoju Karolina rzuciła się na przyjaciółkę i zaczęła ją oglądać, dokładnie, po kobiecemu. Wprawdzie Julia nie zmieniła się aż tak radykalnie, jak sobie zaplanowała, jednak i tak było na co popatrzeć. Nie czesała się już w harcapik owiązany rzemykiem, lecz skróciła włosy do ramion. Bluzka z dzianiny podkreślała biust, a mahoniowy brąz spódnicy zgrabnie opinał biodra. I jakby tego było mało, dziewczyna zdobyła się na delikatny makijaż. Piegów nie udało się przykryć, bo wyłaziły spod fluidu, zwabione wiosennym słońcem, natomiast rzęsy pociągnięte brązowym tuszem dodały głębi jej wielkim, dziecinnym oczom.

– Dla mnie bomba! – krzyknęła Karolina. – Dlaczego ja uważałam, że masz krzywe nogi?

– Krzywe? – zdziwiła się Julia.

– No nie, ale tak myślałam. Żadna normalna dziewczyna nie zakrywa zgrabnych nóg aż po kostki. O biust też cię nie podejrzewałam, a tu proszę, co najmniej mała trójeczka! – wołała ubawiona.

Szczere zachwyty cieszyły Julię i peszyły równocześnie. Gdyby były same, to co innego, lecz wesolutka Karolina mogła powiedzieć dużo różnych rzeczy, niekoniecznie przeznaczonych dla ucha mężczyzny. Bezradnie spojrzała na Konrada i jeszcze bardziej się zmieszała. Nie uczestniczył w rozmowie, ograniczył się do patrzenia. Wcześniej nie posądzał Julii o krzywe nogi ani o brak biustu, ponieważ nawet nie zauważył, że ona ma jakieś nogi i jakiś biust. Mężczyźni myślą wyłącznie o detalach tych kobiet, które im się podobają. Julia była myszką, sierotką, nikim więcej. I nagle zamiast sierotki zobaczył śliczną dziewczynę, którą Karolina oglądała ze wszystkich stron.

– Daj spokój! – wmieszał się do rozmowy. – Wystraszysz panią i gotowa się przebrać.

– Niech tylko spróbuje! Wykopię ją z sekretariatu na bruk, chyba że wcześniej ucieknie pod twoje skrzydła.

Posłała Konradowi przeciągłe spojrzenie spod rzęs, które ożywiłoby nawet zasuszonego śledzia.

Pokój Julii nie był duży i musiał pomieścić wszystko, co potrzebne do życia: rozkładany fotel, który w nocy zamieniał się w łóżko, biurko z komputerem, telewizor, wieżę i jeszcze maleńki, okrągły stolik. Z konieczności siedzieli bardzo blisko siebie, Karolina z Konradem aż za blisko, co nie umknęło uwagi mamy Blendowej. Wniosła do pokoju córki tacę zastawioną domowej roboty wypiekami. A jak już weszła, to przysiadła na fotelu i włączyła się do rozmowy. Mówiła o świętach, o swoim wielkim zmęczeniu i przez cały czas uważnie wpatrywała się w Konrada.

– Ojej, państwu chyba niewygodnie, co? Tam jest jedno krzesło czy dwa?

– Dwa, mamo – powiedziała chłodno Julia.

– Bo jak jedno, to ja zaraz doniosę drugie.

– Dwa – powtórzyła dobitnie córka. – Pomożesz mi zrobić coś do picia?

Sposób nie był zbyt wyrafinowany, a mama Blendowa nie zamierzała poddać się bez walki. Żeby dać córce po nosie, zaczęła mówić o jej nowych fatałaszkach i o braku umiaru.

– Całkiem zwariowała ta moja Julia. Najpierw nosiła wszystkiego za dużo, aż jej nie było widać spod szmatek. Teraz takie to wszystko kuse, że aż nieprzyzwoite. Ja tego nie rozumiem, ja całe życie noszę suknie do pół łydki, to najbezpieczniejsza długość.

– Czy ja wiem? – udała zastanowienie Karolina. – Nogi wyglądają wtedy jak ucięta butelka, choć to oczywiście zależy od nóg.

– Jasne! – przytaknęła pani Emilia, która nic złego nie dostrzegła w butelce. – Te krótkie to ani ładne, ani moralne, a jakie drogie! Pani by też całą pensję wydała na łachy? – zwróciła się do Karoliny.

– Z przyjemnością! – wykrzyknęła. – Oczywiście gdybym mogła sobie na to pozwolić.

– A ja nie. Mnie wpajano od dziecka, że szata nie zdobi człowieka.

– O, to zależy od okoliczności – wyjaśniła poważnie Karolina. – Kiedy ubieramy się, żeby innym babom oko zbielało, to zdobi, a kiedy rozbieramy się dla swojego mężczyzny, to ma pani rację, wtedy jest bez znaczenia.

– Uhu, wie pani, to już poglądy zbyt śmiałe... ja nie wiem... inaczej pojmuję moralność – plątała się mama Blendowa.

– Przecież rozmawiacie o szatach, nie o moralności – wtrąciła Julia.

Pora była najwyższa, by delikatnie wyprowadzić matkę. Fukała potem, hałasowała w kuchni, kręciła się po przedpokoju, ale nie wróciła. Dopiero po wyjściu gości weszła, by przekonać Julię, że otacza się niewłaściwymi koleżankami. Karolina, jak było do przewidzenia, nie zyskała aprobaty, została odsądzona od czci, inteligencji, kultury i wiedzy. Mama Blendowa nie zostawiła na dziewczynie suchej nitki i wcale nie słuchała wyjaśnień Julii. Córka była głupia, nie znała życia, a matka znała. Za to Konrad wzbudził pozytywne zainteresowanie. Został oceniony jako mężczyzna kulturalny, choć niezbyt stanowczy.

– Widać, że chłopak z dobrego domu! To włocławiak? Żonaty czy rozwiedziony? Co robią jego rodzice? Dlaczego on utyka, miał wypadek?

Na żadne z tych pytań Julia nie znała odpowiedzi.

– Zlituj się, mamo! Miałam go na progu odpytać z życiorysu?

– Po co zaraz na progu?! Nie mówię, żeby ordynarnie i wprost, tylko dyplomatycznie. Ja po godzinie rozmowy wiem o człowieku wszystko.

– Wszystko, co chce ci powiedzieć – westchnęła Julia.

– O, nie! Tobie można wmówić każdą głupotę, ale ja znam się na ludziach. Tę twoją, pożal się Boże, przyjaciółkę, od razu rozszyfrowałam. Nic dobrego, pospolita łowczyni męża.

Wieczorem Julia zauważyła, że Marek Winicjusz ma jakieś inne oczy. Stali wśród cyprysów w ogrodzie Linusa, trzymali się za ręce.

– Czy nic złego spotkać cię nie może, Marku, za to, że opuściłeś Ancjum bez wiedzy cezara?

– Nie, droga moja – odpowiedział.

Potem mówił o swojej wielkiej tęsknocie, o lęku o nią i patrzył. Oczy miał inne, głębiej osadzone i ciemniejsze. Konrad to piękne imię i takie romantyczne, zauważyła bez większego związku ze sceną, którą rozgrywała w myślach. Kiedyś, wcale nie tak dawno, bo jeszcze w ostatniej klasie liceum, kiedy była pewna, że zostanie aktorką, marzyła o repertuarze romantycznym. Tydzień przed wysłaniem papierów na studia ojciec kategorycznie zapowiedział, że nie pozwoli jedynej córce biegać z gołym biustem po ekranie i grosza nie da na takie bezeceństwa. Z konieczności wybrała więc informatykę i nigdy nie przestała żałować, że świat nie obejrzy jej w roli Balladyny czy Marii Kalergis. Całkiem niedawno doszła do wniosku, że romantyczny repertuar wyraźnie faworyzuje mężczyzn. – Zupełnie jak Mikula – mruknęła w poduszkę. Na szczęście nie było to odkrycie naukowe, tylko takie na granicy zasypiania.

Utarło się, że pierwszy dzień po świętach zwykle upływa na narzekaniach. Z wyjątkiem pracoholików wszyscy inni ludzie wolą siadać przy zastawionych stołach niż przy zawalonych papierami biurkach i na to nie ma rady. Inżynier Orzechowicz pracoholikiem wprawdzie nie był, lecz z przyjemnością wracał do codziennych zajęć. Ranek był ciepły, nastrajał do rozważań. Próbował zebrać myśli i uporządkować fakty. Święta spędzone z Karoliną przewróciły do góry nogami jego spokojne życie. Wystarczyło, że parę razy złapał się na tęsknocie za własną rodziną, taką prawdziwą, z żoną, z dziećmi, i już wpadł w popłoch, że się roztkliwia jak stara panna. Był samotnikiem nie tyle z wyboru, ile ze strachu, tak przynajmniej twierdziła Grażyna Orska. Denerwował się na to gadanie, bo samo posądzenie o strach czy tchórzostwo było mu niemiłe, jednak w duchu przyznawał jej rację. Lubił swoją samotność i nie lubił. Przykre były zwłaszcza powroty do pustego mieszkania. Nikt nie czekał, nikt nie pytał, jak minął dzień, jak załatwił tę czy inną ważną sprawę.

– Czemu się tak zamyślasz? – pytała Karolina, ilekroć uciekał w te swoje rojenia o domu i żonie. Odpowiadał różnie, jak mu tam przyszła fantazja. Raz nawet zażartował:

– Próbuję ci udowodnić, że różnię się od czworonogów.

– Myślisz, że sama bym na to nie wpadła? Podrap mnie lepiej po plecach, ssaczku, przynajmniej będzie jakiś pożytek z twojej zadumy.

Rozciągnęła się wygodnie na wersalce. Wodził opuszkami palców po nagich plecach, a dziewczyna pomrukiwała z wdziękiem zadowolonej kotki. Wcale nie miał jej za złe, że ubierała się tylko wówczas, gdy wychodzili z domu. W jej negliżu, właściwie w nagości, nie było nic bezwstydnego. Natura obdarzyła ją tak hojnie, że nie uważała za stosowne chować pod łaszkami tych darów. Zachowywała się z prostotą człowieka pierwotnego i jednocześnie z wyrafinowaniem godnym salonów.

– Byłeś kiedyś żonaty? – spytała.

– A co, tak dobrze drapię, jakbym był?

Uniosła głowę, potem usiadła na podkulonych nogach.

– Nie musisz stosować uników, nie musisz odpowiadać, jeżeli nie chcesz. Spytałam tak sobie. Dobrze mi z tobą, ale nie chciałabym, żebyś miał jakieś złudzenia. Z nas nie będzie pary.

– Więc dlaczego jesteśmy razem?

– Dlaczego nie, jeżeli sprawia to nam przyjemność?

Nie odpowiedział, skinął tylko głową na znak potwierdzenia, że pary z nich nie będzie i niemal natychmiast poczuł zazdrość. Wcale nie chciał, by inni mężczyźni bezkarnie oglądali jej piękne ciało, te wszystkie cudowne wypukłości i wklęśnięcia.

– Wiesz co – powiedział powoli – z czterech działań arytmetycznych najmniej lubię dzielenie. A już z całą pewnością nie wyobrażam sobie dzielenia się z kimkolwiek szczotką do zębów i kobietą.

– Wiem. Wyglądasz na faceta zachłannego. Co do zębów, twoja sprawa, co do kobiety, powiem ci coś: w moim życiu zawsze jest tylko jeden mężczyzna. Jeżeli zainteresuję się drugim, po prostu odchodzę. Teraz jesteś ty i chcę być wobec ciebie uczciwa. Mam swoje plany, w których stały związek jest na ostatnim miejscu... lub na pierwszym, wszystko będzie zależało od okoliczności. Mam nadzieję, że nie czujesz się zgorszony ani kopnięty w ambicję?

Cały kłopot polegał na tym, że sam nie wiedział, jak się czuł, w każdym razie na pewno nie był zadowolony. Karolina miała niesamowity dar uszczęśliwiania mężczyzny i jednocześnie odzierania ze złudzeń. Zamierzał wstać i wyjść. Na zamierzeniu się skończyło. Wyszli, owszem, ale razem – najpierw na obiad do Zajazdu, potem do Julii. Nie miał ochoty na świąteczne wizyty, wystarczyło jednak, że ona miała.

Kiedy wieczorem zasypiał w swoim mieszkaniu i w swoim łóżku, wydawało mu się, że ktoś jest w pokoju. Pomyślał: Karolina, a nie wiadomo czemu zobaczył wielkie, nieco przestraszone oczy Julii. Całkiem fajna ta mała, pomyślał. Przewrócił się na drugi bok. O mamuśce już tego powiedzieć nie można, dodał, i była to ostatnia myśl przed zaśnięciem. Chociaż nie, mignęła mu chyba jeszcze raz twarz Julii.

Inna fryzura, inna sukienka i właściwie całkiem inna kobieta. Julia nie miała pojęcia, że będzie to zmiana tak widoczna. Poruszała się inaczej, chodziła inaczej i każde spojrzenie w lustro czy w szybę utwierdzało ją w przekonaniu, że wygląda o wiele lepiej. Co tam lepiej! Wyglądała bardzo dobrze, a to dodało jej pewności siebie. Ledwie pojawiła się w firmie, natychmiast wywołała maleńkie zamieszanie. Kierowca Czarek w ogóle jej nie poznał, natomiast Leszek Wydroń z wrażenia rymsnął na kolana.

– Droga pani inżynier! Jak to cudownie, że wreszcie wiem, gdzie się pani zaczyna, a gdzie kończy! – wykrzyknął zachwycony.

Długo potem udowadniał, że zbyt obszerne stroje są tym dla kobiety, czym worek dla kota. Zerkał przy tym z upodobaniem na Julię.

– Tylko się nie zakochaj, mój drogi, bo takiej zdrady nie przeżyję – uśmiechnęła się Edyta.

– O żadnej zdradzie nie ma mowy! – zaprzeczył gwałtownie. – Też dostaniesz swoją porcję komplementów, bo sam już nie wiem, czy wiosna na was podziałała czy co, że tak wypiękniałyście?

– Jeżeli o mnie chodzi, wyglądam na swoje trzydzieści pięć lat i nie musisz się wysilać – zapewniła sekretarka.

– Ostatnio już miałaś czterdzieści – przypomniał Leszek.

– Kobietą jestem i nic co babskie nie jest mi obce, nawet lata – odparła spokojnie. – Jeżeli czułam się na czterdzieści, to musiał mi podpaść ktoś niestrawny. Dziś mam trzydzieści pięć i ani miesiąca więcej.

Był to znany sposób Edyty na podporządkowanie sobie czasu. Zegar biologiczny cykał, a ona chwaliła się codziennie innym wiekiem, dbając jedynie o to, by przy żonglowaniu czasem nie przekroczyć granicy śmieszności i nie dać sobie lat osiemnastu. Miewała już siedemdziesiąt, szczególnie po naradach u szefa, lecz osiemnastu nigdy.

Julia śmiała się razem z nimi do momentu, gdy Orzechowicz przeszedł przez sekretariat i zniknął w gabinecie dyrektora. Potem już nikt nie potrafił jej rozruszać. W zastępstwie pani Heni zrobiła Edycie i Leszkowi herbatę, jednak do żadnej pracy umysłowej nie była zdolna.

Orzechowicz, wychodząc z gabinetu, zatrzymał się na moment przy jej biurku.

– Głowa do góry, pani Julio! – powiedział. – Przy najbliższej okazji porozmawiam jeszcze raz z dyrektorem.

– To znaczy, że się nie zgodził? – szepnęła.

– Głowa do góry! – powtórzył.

Nie po raz pierwszy Julia miała ochotę zapłakać szczerze i po babsku. Na szczęście przypomniała sobie o makijażu i bohatersko zapanowała nad łzami. Nie tylko ja mam kłopoty, pocieszyła się, wspominając Leszka i Karolinę. Pomogło. Całkiem spokojnie doczekała chwili, gdy zostały z Edytą same.

– Jak pani myśli, dlaczego dyrektor się nie zgodził? Jakie on ma wobec mnie zamiary?

– Jakie zamiary? – Sekretarka uniosła głowę i spojrzała bardzo poważnie. – Powiem ci jakie, dla mnie to nie jest tajemnicą. Mikula przyjął cię, bo zamierza mnie zwolnić. Ty zostaniesz jego sekretarką czy tam asystentką, jeszcze się waha, dlatego wciąż czekasz na zakres obowiązków.

– Myślałam, że rozmawiamy poważnie – westchnęła Julia.

– Bardzo poważnie.

– Wciąż pani powtarza, że Mikula durniem nie jest. Żaden mądry szef nie zwolni najlepszego w dziale fachowca, żeby go zastąpić niefachowcem. Równie dobrze mógłby za tym biurkiem usadzić Chochlę... gdyby się przypadkiem znalazł. Wiem, że nietrudno jest być lepszą od Chochli i nie o to mi chodzi.

– O kompetencje też nie chodzi, droga Julio. Łatwiej jest wychować sobie zupełnie zielonego pracownika niż podporządkować doświadczonego, z dobrą pamięcią. – Spojrzała na Julię i natychmiast zmieniła ton. – No, no, Julka, tylko bez fontanny. Nie życzę sobie, żebyś zaryczaną mordką psuła wspaniały image firmy. Jeszcze tu jestem i coś wspólnie wymyślimy. Widzisz, do czego doprowadziłaś? Po raz pierwszy od bardzo dawna poczułam się jak kobieta pięćdziesięcioletnia. To straszne!

Dziewczyna uśmiechnęła się blado. Poranne zadowolenie wyparowało z niej bez reszty i nie pomogła nawet zaskoczona mina pani prezes. Mikulowa wpadła do sekretariatu wypachniona i świeżutka. Jej wprawne oko natychmiast dojrzało Julię. Podfałszowane ołówkiem brewki powędrowały na środek czoła, wróciły na swoje miejsce, a pani prezes z ulgą potrząsnęła żółtymi lokami. Była przekonana, że w firmie pojawiła się nowa twarz i to bez jej wiedzy.

– Koniecznie powinnaś zmienić kolor włosów – stwierdziła. – O wiele lepiej będzie ci w czarnych... nie, chyba raczej w blond! Nie, jednak w czarnych, z całą pewnością. Mam rację?

Julia uśmiechnęła się z wyższością kobiety eleganckiej i pokręciła głową na znak, że koloru włosów nie zmieni. Mikulowa prychnęła obrażona i przestała zajmować się cudzymi włosami. Przeszła z Edytą do pustego gabinetu dyrektora i wiadomo było, że zabawią tam jakiś czas.

Julia bez większego zapału wzięła się do porządkowania korespondencji. Próbowała wrócić na plan filmowy, ale nawet to jej nie wychodziło. Już prawie była Ligią, już nawet zbliżała się do Winicjusza, lecz zamiast słów miłości miała w głowie Mikulę, etat, Konrada i rzeczywistość brała górę nad marzeniami. Jeszcze kilka takich rozmów, a zgłupieję totalnie, mówiła sobie.

– Przesyłka dla szanownej pani! – Leszek położył na biurku zaklejoną kopertę.

Zaciekawiona zajrzała do środka. Choćby nawet nie chciała, choćby nawet miała sto większych zmartwień, musiała się uśmiechnąć na widok kartki. Radosna dziewuszka, mały śmieszny bobas z wielką kokardą na głowie, siedziała tuż obok stareńkiej maszyny do pisania, bodaj jakiegoś continentala. Białe literki na górze zachęcały: *Nie zwlekaj, napisz.*

– Co mianowicie mam napisać? – spytała.

– Na twoim miejscu mianowicie obejrzałbym zadek tej małej. Na odwrocie jest wyjaśnienie.

Odwróciła kartkę. *Nie zwlekaj, Biedronko Siedmiokropko, i napisz, czy pójdziesz ze mną w sobotę potańczyć?*

– Muszę pisać? Nie mogę ci mianowicie powiedzieć, że z największą przyjemnością... chyba że wolisz towarzystwo pani Oli. – Dyskretnie wskazała głową gabinet dyrektora, gdzie szefowa wciąż rajcowała z Edytą.

– Załatwione. Mam zarezerwowany kawałek stolika w Teatralnej. Dlatego kawałek, że tam są potężne stoły, gdybyś nie wiedziała. Niestety, z Olą klapa – zaszeptał. – Dostałem kosza i mianowicie nie wiem dlaczego. Ciasto drożdżowe z ręki mi jadła, a potem fik mik i ble!

– To dla niej zarezerwowałeś ten stolik? – spytała domyślnie.

Skinął głową. Nie zauważyła, że zawahał się, jakby chciał coś wyjaśnić, odrobinę posmutniał i wyszedł, nie dodając już nic. Byli umówieni. Julia z radością pomyślała, że choć raz pobawi się w towarzystwie znacznie ciekawszym niż Serafin. Dotarło do niej, że bardzo dawno nie widziała anielskiego chłopaka, ale to był fakt bez znaczenia.

Podniesiona na duchu, wróciła do przeglądania poczty. Biurko zawalały głównie prospekty reklamowe, które konsekwentnie wrzucała do kosza. Że też ludziom nie szkoda lasów. Na jednej z kopert dojrzała nazwisko Karoliny Cierniak z adnotacją: *do rąk własnych*. Bez trudu poznała kopertę i charakter pisma. W środku namacała sztywne kartoniki, coś jakby zdjęcia. Pośpiesznie wepchnęła kopertę do swojej szuflady. Od tego momentu z biciem serca czekała na powrót przyjaciółki z sądu.

Karolina wpadła do firmy tuż przed piętnastą. Była zmęczona, ale radosna. Julia pomyślała ze smutkiem, że za moment całe zadowolenie z wygranej sprawy diabli wezmą. Taki to już widać był dzień, że gasił wszelką radość. Wyczekała na odpowiedni moment i bez słowa oddała kopertę.

– Czy to gówno przyszło z pocztą? – spytała Karolina, wynurzając się chwilę później ze swojego pokoju.

– Tak. To ja segregowałam korespondencję i nie musisz się bać.

– Skąd wiesz, że mogę się bać?

– Uff, jakby ci tu powiedzieć? Przed świętami identyczna koperta przyszła do Edyty. Zagapiłam się, otworzyłam i wiem. Potem jedliśmy drożdżówkę.

Karolina bez słowa rzuciła na biurko zmiętą kartkę i cztery zdjęcia, znacznie frywolniejsze niż te Edyty. Na jednym widać było także partnera. Nie mogło być żadnych wątpliwości, kim jest mężczyzna.

– Z Edytą też on był? – Karolina pstryknęła paznokciem w brzuch Mikuli.

– Nie wiem, zdjęcia były retro, oni też retro... zresztą możliwe, bo uszy jakby podobne. Reszta mogła się zmienić, ale uszy nie tak bardzo, jak myślisz?

– Do głowy by mi nie przyszło, żeby rozpoznawać gołych facetów po uszach – roześmiała się Karolina i natychmiast spoważniała. – Parszywy gnojek! Gdybym go tylko dorwała, to marne jego szanse wśród żywych. – Walnęła ręką w biurko. – Popatrz, co mi ten cham napisał!

Rozwinęła zmięty arkusik zapełniony wielkimi kulfonami. Widać, że nadawca się śpieszył, bo darował sobie interpunkcję, staranność i podpis. Właściwie na kartce były dwa zdania, które sprawiały wrażenie jednego: *O to ci chodziło no to masz co chciałaś.*

– Myślisz, że to Mikula?

– Nie, co ty! Chyba na starość nie został ekshibicjonistą? W innym wypadku po cholerę miałby mi przysyłać swój nagi portrecik? Wziął tyłek w garść, wyjechał, a Mikulowa być może ślęczy teraz nad identyczną przesyłką. To dopiero byłoby jajo!

– Jeżeli nie stary, to kto?

– Ten, kto ma bzika na punkcie fotografii i dodatkowo seksualne obsesje. Jeszcze nie wiesz kto? Nadworny pstrykacz i mentalny analfabeta, Chochla! Spójrz na ten list. Przecież nie wiadomo, czy to informacja, wyznanie czy szantaż! Oddam królestwo za wiadomość, gdzie ten pluskolec się zaszył!

– Schowaj sobie królestwo na potem. Za darmo ci powiem, że widziałam go dwukrotnie na Południu.

– I nic nie mówiłaś?

– Też mi rewelacja: Chochla snujący się po ulicy. Poza tym nie byłam pewna, czy to on.

– Na Południu, mówisz? Pamiętasz gdzie i kiedy?

– Pierwszy raz jakieś dwa, trzy dni po zaginięciu lazł w stronę Kujawskiej, a drugi raz... tuż przed świętami... też gdzieś w tej okolicy.

– W stronę Kujawskiej? – Karolina zastygła z ręką na czole. – Czekaj, czekaj, to całkiem możliwe! Dlatego Wacek nie umiał znaleźć... Juleczko, no to chyba mam karaczana! Złapię i usadzę na amen! Podwieziesz mnie?

W chwili kiedy Konrad dostał angaż do ręki, w zasadzie miał już naszkicowany plan komputeryzacji przedsiębiorstwa. Nie zamierzał wyważać otwartych drzwi, korzystał ze sprawdzonych wzorców, które dostosował do konkretnych warunków Budampolexu 2. Coś musiał robić przez te wszystkie dni, kiedy na próżno usiłował dostać się do dyrektora. A ponieważ wierzył, że swoją sprawę wygra i potrafi wymóc na Mikuli dotrzymanie obietnicy, wykorzystywał czas na zbieranie informacji o sprzęcie i o programach. Zadanie wcale nie było proste. Gdziekolwiek się zwrócił, napotykał mur obojętności i niewiedzy. Działu właściwie nie było; inżynier Kiciński po koleżeńsku, z czystej sympatii, sporo podpowiedział swojemu następcy, ale żył już nową pracą. Proponowane zmiany przede wszystkim wymagały nakładów oraz co najmniej dwóch dodatkowych etatów. Pieniądze dyrektor obiecał dopiero w maju. Konrad zamierzał jeszcze raz porozmawiać w tej sprawie i przyspieszyć zakup sprzętu. Przy okazji chciał też przedstawić konkretne propozycje obsadzenia etatów. Znał wielu dobrych informatyków, z kilkoma rozmawiał i był gotów operować nazwiskami. Obiecał też etat Julii. Idąc do starego, był pełen optymizmu.

Dyrektor słuchał niezbyt uważnie, szukał czegoś w otwartym biurku, kazał sobie powtarzać rzeczy oczywiste, najważniejsze zbywał machnięciem ręki. Zgodził się na wszystkie projekty inżyniera Orzechowicza, z wyjątkiem przyspieszenia zakupów i przeniesienia magister inżynier Blendy.

– Wie pan, panie kolego, ja tam, broń Boże, nie jestem antyfeministą, uważam jednak, że miejsce baby jest w łóżku i w domu. Można je wyuczyć tego i owego, szczególnie fajtając przed nosem marchewką, ale ich horyzonty zawsze będą tycie – na palcach pokazał zdumionemu Konradowi te damskie horyzonty, które nie były wyższe niż pół centymetra. – Nie wierzę, panie kolego, w umiejętności techniczne kobiet, chyba że chodzi o technikę rodzenia. To są oczywiście żarty... chociaż w każdym żarcie jest trochę prawdy.

– Rozmawiałem z panią inżynier Blendą i nie uważam, żeby była niedouczona. Jest chyba bardziej potrzebna w moim dziale niż w sekretariacie.

– Ocenę pracy sekretariatu, panie kolego, zostawmy Pałubskiej – powiedział z dobrotliwą przyganą Mikula. Uśmiechnął się nawet na znak, że nie przywiązuje wagi do drobnej niezręczności młodego inżyniera. – W tajemnicy panu powiem, że choć zdecydowanie wolę pracować z mężczyznami, a spać z babami, to nie upierałbym się przy tej Blendzie. Jest w końcu inżynierem, niechby sobie siedziała przy komputerze w pańskim dziale. Chodzi jednak o to, że ona jest potrzebna sekretarce. Zna języki, w przyszłości obsłuży komputer i tak dalej. To Pałubska się uparła, a ja dałem słowo, że nie będę ingerował w sprawy jej działu. Proszę więc, panie kolego, żeby nie stawiał mnie pan w kłopotliwej sytuacji. I niech pan to jakoś tej małej wytłumaczy, co?

Dyrektorska szczerość zaskoczyła Konrada. Nie chodziło o męskie przechwałki, te puścił mimo uszu, lecz o Julię. Nie podzielał opinii Mikuli, uznał jednak, że sprawa jest drażliwa i przy pierwszej rozmowie nie wolno przesadzić z uporem. Był zdecydowany poczekać na sprzyjającą okazję. Nagle zaczęło mu bardzo zależeć na tej dziewczynie jako na sile fachowej. Poza tym żal mu było biedaczki. Dusiła się w sekretariacie, gdzie nie miała okazji wykorzystać swojej wiedzy ani rozwinąć skrzydeł. Wychodząc z gabinetu, próbował podnieść ją na duchu i już do końca dnia prześladował go widok wielkich, smutnych oczu. Co sobie o nich przypomniał, zalewała go fala ciepłej sympatii. Podobnych uczuć nigdy wcześniej nie doświadczał. Lubił kobiety, niektóre mniej, inne więcej, ale żeby się nad nimi roztkliwiać?! Nawet kiedy myślał o Karolinie, czuł złość lub podniecenie, czasem tęsknotę i nic więcej. Czyżby ta mała jędza rzuciła na mnie urok? – pomyślał i zachciało mu się śmiać, że tak ściśle i po inżyniersku ujął tę kwestię. Mogłem jej chociaż powiedzieć na pocieszenie, że nie mam zwyczaju cofać raz danego słowa! Uznał jednak, że wrażliwa dziewczyna mogła potraktować takie zapewnienie jako przechwałkę, a tego nie chciał.

Włocławek z całą pewnością do metropolii nie należy, jednak w godzinach szczytu można odnieść wrażenie, że to nie przymierzając Łódź lub Warszawa. Błękitny matiz co chwila utykał w korkach. Początkowo Karolina milczała, zapatrzona w jakiś punkt przed sobą. Julia pilnowała kierownicy i zerkała od czasu do czasu na przyjaciółkę.

– Co właściwie zamierzasz? – spytała. – Nie chcę być wścibska, tak sobie jednak myślę, że do usadzenia Chochli potrzebny jest jakiś sensowny plan. Pokażesz zdjęcia i co? Rozwścieczysz faceta i dopiero wtedy gotów ci narobić brudu.

Wreszcie Karolina pękła. Jak najszybciej chciała się uwolnić od nagromadzonego żalu, więc wyrzucała słowa z prędkością karabinu maszynowego. Julia nie wszystko rozumiała, nie wszystko chwytała, jednak pytania odłożyła na później. Z dość nieskładnej wypowiedzi zdołała zrozumieć, że Mikula mieszkał z żoną na Zawiślu, w ładnym nawet domu, a drugie mieszkanie miał w pobliżu ulicy Kujawskiej bądź przy samej Kujawskiej. Małe, jednopokojowe, a nawet jednoosobowe, niczego nie potrafił znaleźć i wciąż się gubił między kuchnią i łazienką. Karolina odwiedziła go kilka razy, bynajmniej nie w celu podyskutowania o kłopotach firmy. Na dowód miała właśnie cztery zdjęcia. Pytanie najistotniejsze brzmiało: kto fotografował i na czyje życzenie? Zupełnie w tym galimatiasie zabrakło miejsca dla Chochli. Nie mógł sterczeć z aparatem fotograficznym w nogach tapczanu, bo Karolina, choćby najbardziej zajęta, musiałaby go zauważyć.

– Gdzie mam jechać? – spytała Julia, gdy już przebrnęły przez wiadukt na Wroniej.

– Adresu nie pamiętam, ale trafić na pewno trafię. Jestem więcej niż pewna, że ten skunks zaszył się właśnie tam.

– Dlaczego Chochla miałby się zaszywać w mieszkaniu Mikuli? – zdziwiła się Julia.

– Dowiemy się, jak trafimy. Oni mają jakieś ciemne interesy. Zauważyłaś, że stary cap wściekał się na brak dokumentów, lecz Chochli z roboty nie wywalił i specjalnie nie przejął się jego zniknięciem. Nawet policja była bardziej zainteresowana niż on, pracodawca niby.

– No, dobra, załóżmy, że masz rację: zaszył się u Mikuli i siedzi. A co my zrobimy?

– Postoimy na parkingu. Fachowo nazywa się to inwigilacją.

– Wiem. On nas zobaczy przez okno, pozna samochód i będzie obserwował. Tylko po co?

– Odwrotnie, to my... Julka, przestań! Nie mam teraz głowy do żartów! – jęknęła Karolina.

Błękitny matiz zgrabnie podjechał pod wskazaną klatkę. Julia, patrząc na rozdygotaną Karolinę, zdała sobie sprawę, że osobiste zaangażowanie bardzo przeszkadza w logicznym myśleniu. Chłodna, zwykle opanowana pani magister miała w oczach żądzę mordu. Ręce jej drżały, kiedy próbowała odpiąć pas. Dać tej biedaczce rewolwer do ręki, to gotowa wystrzelać wszystkich, nawet babinkę z parteru, pomyślała przytomnie. W tym momencie poczuła się odpowiedzialna za przyjaciółkę. Przytrzymała rękę, szarpiącą pas.

– Zostań! Pójdę sama, powiedz tylko, co mam sprawdzić?

– Do kogo należy mieszkanie na drugim piętrze... środkowe.

Julia wysiadła i spokojnym krokiem podeszła do drzwi. Na tabliczce przy domofonie ustaliła, że lokal musi mieć numer 23. Biały prostokącik tuż przy guziczku niezbicie dowodził, że właściciel skorzystał z przysługującego mu prawa do ochrony dóbr osobistych. On jeden w całej klatce. Nad nim było nazwisko W. Pasieczko, pod nim... Zaraz, zaraz! Pasieczko? – zastanowiła się Julia. Z całą pewnością słyszała już gdzieś to nazwisko. Błyskawicznie próbowała przypomnieć sobie wydarzenia z ostatnich dni. – Jasne – zaszeptała gorączkowo. – „O Duchu Święty, daj nam moc!". Coś mi się zdaje, że jednak będę musiała do niej zajrzeć!

Bez zbędnego pośpiechu wsiadła do samochodu i ruszyła powoli, jak ktoś, kto właśnie się pomylił. Szukał znajomego, nie znalazł, więc odjeżdża. Dopiero na Kaliskiej dodała gazu, a rozgadała się w domu. Za wiele nie umiała powtórzyć, bo niezbyt uważnie słuchała wynurzeń Wandeczki, ale zawsze coś tam jej w głowie zostało.

Pod nieobecność rodziców mieszkanie było oazą spokoju. Rozsiadły się w kuchni. Julia odgrzała swój obiad, który sprawiedliwie podzieliła na dwie porcje. Karolina, choć zasłaniała się brakiem apetytu, zjadła pierwsza i nerwowo krążyła po niewielkim pomieszczeniu.

– Usiądź, bo mnie szlag trafi – poprosiła Julia. – Pracuj głową, nie nogami.

– Kiedy ja muszę kompleksowo – wyznała przyjaciółka, ale oparła się o szafkę przy zlewie.

Co do jednego zgadzały się bez zastrzeżeń: przeciwnik był paranoikiem, a jeżeli nawet nie był, to zachowywał się jak rasowy paranoik – atakował z ukrycia i każdy następny ruch mógł być nieobliczalny w skutkach. Dopóki nie stawiał żądań, nie zdradzał intencji, wszystko było możliwe, zarówno chory żart, zemsta, w ostateczności nawet szantaż. Karolina chciała działać jak najszybciej.

– Opanuj się, jesteś prawnikiem, nie możesz tak na łapu-capu – tłumaczyła Julia.

– Ja się znam na kondycji firm, nie wariatów!

– Oprócz psychiatrów kto jeszcze zna się na wariatach? Nie adwokaci przypadkiem? – dopytywała się Julia. – Masz przyjaciół wśród prawników w Toruniu. Popytaj, podzwoń, jak będzie trzeba, chętnie z tobą pojadę. Poza tym wybiorę się do Wandzi Pasieczko. Jako najbliższa sąsiadka, nie wiem zresztą czyja, może być skarbnicą wiedzy.

Karolina uniosła wreszcie głowę znad pustej filiżanki. Patrzyła badawczo, z pionową zmarszczką między brwiami.

– Dlaczego angażujesz się w sprawę, która ciebie nie dotyczy?

– Nie angażuję się w sprawę, tylko w pomoc przyjaciółce. Gołym okiem widać, że nie da się pomóc bez wlezienia w bagienko. Trudno, wyższa konieczność!

Bodaj pierwszy raz Karolina przytuliła się do Julii i pocałowała ją w policzek. Normalnie nie uznawała babskich powitań, uścisków i buziaków rozdawanych w okolicy ucha. To był pocałunek na zasadzie wyjątku, dlatego cenny.

– Podzwonię. Popytam! – powiedziała już znacznie energiczniej. – A ciebie nie poznaję. Mam ochotę zanucić: gdzie się podziały lebiody z tamtych lat. Mówisz, że to Henia tak cię wyposażyła w moc?

– Spróbuj się z nią zaprzyjaźnić, ona podobno kocha wszystkich ludzi.

Droga od wielkiego smutku do wielkiej radości bywa czasem bardzo krótka. Wspomnienie Heni tak podziałało na dziewczyny, że nie mogły przestać się śmiać.

„Naiwność jest piękną cechą, dopóki gnieździ się w pokoju dziecięcym", lubił powtarzać Konrad. Sam bynajmniej nie uważał się za człowieka naiwnego, jednak w ostatnim czasie aż trzy razy zdziwił się mocno i po dziecinnemu. Raz na wiadomość, że Edyta Pałubska nie chce mu oddać pani inżynier. Z tego, co wiedział od Karoliny oraz od samej Julii, wynikało, że upierał się dyrektor, sekretarka zaś obiecywała dziewczynie pomoc. Ktoś namieszał, tylko nie bardzo było wiadomo kto.

Drugi raz zdziwił się, kiedy Karolina spytała, czy chciałby zostać jej mężem.

– Przecież sama mówiłaś, że nie będzie z nas pary.

– Ja? – Wlepiła w niego zielone oczy wypełnione bezbrzeżnym zdumieniem. – Przecież ja, ssaczku, z reguły mówię rozsądnie.

Wtuliła mu swoje loki między brodę a obojczyk i milczała. Siedzieli w jej mieszkaniu, na niewygodnej wersalce; zupełnie nie wiedział, co z tym wyznaniem zrobić. Mimo że krótko byli razem, zaszli bardzo daleko, bo do rozmów o wspólnej przyszłości. Drażniło go, że odbierała mu całą inicjatywę, chciała o wszystkim decydować i przesądzać. Na krótki dystans mógł jej pozwolić, lecz małżeństwo to już nawet nie długi dystans, to cały maraton. Konrad zbyt mocno cenił sobie samodzielność i niezależność, by zrezygnować z własnego zdania. Może gdyby był zakochany do szaleństwa... On jednak nie był zakochany. Tak przynajmniej uważał.

– Czemu zamilkłeś, ssaczku? Źle ci ze mną?

– Dobrze mi z tobą, tylko widzisz, przy mnie nieprędko dorobisz się luksusowego samochodu i willi z kucharką.

– Po co nam kucharka? Przecież mówiłeś, że umiesz gotować. – Roześmiała się psotnie jak dziecko, zawisła mu na szyi, by powoli zjechać niżej, potem jeszcze niżej. Jej długie, szczupłe palce mocowały się przez chwilę z paskiem u spodni, potem zajęły się zamkiem błyskawicznym. Ona znowu przejmuje inicjatywę, pomyślał, i nim Karolina zdążyła pisnąć, jednym silnym ruchem ramion zmienił całą konfigurację. Nie narzekała z tego powodu, a nawet wydawała się bardzo zadowolona.

Trzeci raz Konrad Orzechowicz zdziwił się za sprawą Henryki Luty. Rozmawiał właśnie w swoim gabinecie z Karoliną o prawnych aspektach komputeryzacji, gdy wydało mu się, że od strony korytarza ktoś majstruje przy zamku. Wstał i gwałtownie otworzył drzwi. Na wysokości pasa zobaczył pochyloną damską głowę. Żeby nie być posądzoną o podsłuchiwanie, pani Henia schyliła się jeszcze niżej i zaczęła poprawiać wycieraczkę.

– Magister Cierniak proszona do telefonu! Dyrektor dzwoni! – powiedziała bez cienia zmieszania.

Karolina wybiegła. Henryka Luty zajrzała do pokoju i zlustrowała kąty. Zdumionemu Konradowi wytłumaczyła, że sprawdza kurze. Szef informatyków nie miał dodatkowego zapotrzebowania na żadne usługi, z odkurzaniem włącznie, i nawet nie silił się na uprzejmość. Stał w otwartych drzwiach i czekał, aż pomoc gospodarcza opuści gabinet.

– Pojedzie za nim do Warszawy, zobaczy pan! – powiedziała poufale. – Wystarczy, że on zadzwoni albo palcem kiwnie. A przecież to człowiek żonaty. Co z żonatym za przyszłość dla wolnej kobiety? Tylko niech pan nic nie mówi, bo znowu na mnie wsiądzie. Prawda w oczy kole.

Wykręciła się na pięcie i wyszła. Konrad stał w progu jak pomnik zdziwienia. Własnym uszom nie wierzył i gotów był sam siebie posądzić o halucynacje. Jednak słyszał kobiecy głos i w mózg wwierciły mu się słowa o Warszawie, kiwnięciu palcem i romansie Karoliny z Mikulą.

Prywatne śledztwo aprilistów chwilowo utknęło w martwym punkcie. Wydawało się, że Leszek na próżno wychodzi ze skóry i zasypuje panią prezes komplementami. Śmiała się, napraszała o więcej, ale gawędzili wyłącznie przy świadkach. W języku Leszka nazywało się to urabianiem gruntu. Orał więc biedak bez żadnej pewności, czy kiedykolwiek wykiełkuje mu jakieś ziarno. Pani magister, choć dworowała sobie z kolegi, sukcesy miała jeszcze mniejsze. Mikula siedział gdzieś w Polsce i tylko co jakiś czas dzwonił. Wiadomo, że przez telefon nikt nie porusza delikatnych tematów. Poza tym Karolina miała na głowie Chochlę, który w każdej chwili mógł ją postawić w bardzo kłopotliwej sytuacji. Julia zaangażowała się w pomoc przyjaciółce i choć fizycznie była przygotowana do spotkania z Bujałą, odkładała wizytę z dnia na dzień.

Wybrała się natomiast do Wandzi Pasieczko i to wcześniej, niż zamierzała. Mówiąc prawdę, nie sądziła, że kiedykolwiek się wybierze, lecz w świetle ostatnich odkryć Wanda nabrała ceny worka złota. Julia obiecała sobie, że tym razem nie uroni ani słowa z opowieści, choćby nawet przyszło jej wysłuchiwać rzewnych wspomnień o dzieciństwie, mężu nieboszczyku i twórczości artystycznej.

Zadzwoniła delikatnie. Drzwi, chronione łańcuchem, uchyliły się, w ciemnej szparze błysnęło oko. Niemiły, burkliwy głos usiłował odpędzić intruza:

– Pomyłka. Środkowe drzwi.

– Wandziu, to ja, Julia!

– Kto? – Szpara nieco się powiększyła. – Ach, Julia! Trzeba było od razu tak mówić... tylko po głosie cię poznałam, tak się wysztafirowałaś!

Ani śladu nieufności, sama radość biła z twarzy Wandy Pasieczko. Nie wiedziała, biedna, gdzie posadzić gościa. Na krześle za twardo, na fotelu za nisko, wreszcie usadowiła speszoną dziewczynę na wielkiej otomanie, przysunęła mały stolik, który natychmiast zastawiła łakociami.

– Skosztuj ciasteczko... Ależ ty nic nie jesz... Częstuj się, kochana... – powtarzała w kółko, zaróżowiona i szczęśliwa.

Gotowa była nieba Julii przychylić, chwaliła jej kostium, chciała pokazywać swoje wiersze i książki z psychologii, zachęcała dziewczynę do jedzenia i skakała z tematu na temat. Wobec niespodziewanej wizyty wszystko zeszło na plan dalszy, nawet utarczki z sąsiadami. Julia odpowiadała na dziesiątki nieistotnych pytań, kiwała głową, wreszcie jakoś do tych sąsiadów nawiązała.

– O których sąsiadów pytasz, złotko? Bo ja mam samych diabła wartych. Ci z naprzeciwka na przykład... – Zerwała się nagle i wybiegła do przedpokoju. Julia bardziej się domyśliła, niż zobaczyła, że Wandzia dopadła wizjera. Na klatce schodowej dał się słyszeć jakiś hałas, trzasnęły drzwi i kobiecina wróciła.

– O czym to mówiłyśmy?

– Pytałam o sąsiadów. Skarżyłaś się ostatnio, że masz pod bokiem dom publiczny.

– A, to ci spod dwudziestego trzeciego. Ostatnio cicho tam, jak w akwarium. Nawet się zastanawiałam, czy gdzie nie wyjechali. Gorsi są ci z naprzeciwka, wciąż się kręcą, a jest ich...

– Kto mieszka pod dwudziestym trzecim? Rodzina czy jakiś samotnik?

– Kiedyś mieszkała Bronia Pałubska, świeć Panie nad jej duszą. Wcale jeszcze nie była taka stara, na nerki jej padło... Ale ty się w ogóle nie częstujesz! No, moja złota, skosztuj jeszcze delicji.

– Dzięki. Więc co z Bronią?

– Ano umarła. Takie jest życie. Naprawdę nie chcesz zobaczyć moich wierszy? Może ci przeczytam choć jeden. Piszę nie tylko hymny, mam kilka patriotycznych i uczuciowych.

– Piszesz erotyki? – zdziwiła się Julia.

– Jeszcze by tego brakowało! Czy ja wyglądam na taką, co świństwa wypisuje? – oburzyła się Wanda. – Uczuciowe wiersze mówią o miłości do ludzi, tak w ogólności. To co, przeczytać ci jakiś?

Zrezygnowana Julia kiwnęła głową. Nie było innego wyjścia. Wanda widać postanowiła bardzo drogo sprzedać swoje cenne informacje.

Podekscytowana, rozłożyła na stoliku gruby brulion, wsadziła okulary na nos i zabrała się do prezentacji poematu o urokach rodzinnego miasta. Czytała, ale uwagę miała podzielną. Co usłyszała jakieś podejrzane szmery, biegła do przedpokoju i przyklejała się do wizjera.

– Czekasz na kogoś? – spytała wreszcie Julia.

Była już tak znudzona poematem, że wolała bodaj posłuchać o sąsiadach z naprzeciwka niż o „strzelistym bulwarze nadwiślańskim, utkanym z domów i lamp".

– A na kogo ja bym miała czekać? – zdziwiła się Wanda. – Mało kto tu do mnie wpada. Bratanica Pałubskiej czasem albo sąsiadka z góry, i to całe moje towarzystwo. Teraz mam ciebie i bardzo się cieszę. Może herbatki ci jeszcze zrobię albo kawusi?

– Bratanica Pałubskiej tu mieszka? – zdziwiła się Julia.

Skojarzyła już wcześniej nazwisko pani Bronisławy z Edytą i przez skórę czuła, że najciekawsze wiadomości ma przed sobą. Była niemal pewna, czyje imię za moment padnie. Wanda, tuląc do piersi brulion z wierszami, niechętnie oderwała się od spraw wzniosłych. Rozumiała jednak, że gość ma swoje prawa i należy zaspokoić jego ciekawość. Wyjaśniła możliwie najkrócej jak się dało, że bratanica Pałubskiej ma własnościowe mieszkanie na Reja, a to, odziedziczone po ciotce, wynajmuje lokatorom za pieniądze. Dla sąsiadów byłoby lepiej, gdyby sprzedała porządnym ludziom o sprawdzonej moralności. Najemcy się zmieniają, trudno wyczuć, kto jest kim, różni się kręcą, różni nocują i czasem bywa nieprzyjemnie. Ściany cienkie, a oni wszyscy jurni są nad podziw. Konsumują kobiety i alkohol, stałych lokatorów mają w poważaniu.

– Jak chcesz, to sama posłuchaj! – zachęcała Wanda. Sięgnęła na półkę po pustą szklankę i podeszła do ściany. Przytknęła ucho do denka i przez moment nasłuchiwała. – Cichutko! Edyta to się nawet wystraszyła, czy morderstwa jakiego nie było, odpukać w niemalowane.

– Jaka Edyta? – spytała obojętnie Julia.

Wanda spojrzała uważnie. W łagodnych dotychczas oczach pojawił się błysk nieufności.

– Przecież ty musisz znać Pałubską?!

Jej okrzyk miał moc nagłego i niemiłego odkrycia. Julia wzruszyła ramionami na znak, że może zna, może nie, lecz przypomnieć sobie nie potrafi.

– Henię znasz z pracy, to i Pałubską musisz znać! – nacierała Wanda.

– Sto osób pracuje w tej firmie, albo i więcej, a ja dopiero od dwu miesięcy – wyjaśniła ze znudzoną miną.

Jej czas z całą pewnością dobiegł końca. Na więcej wiadomości o Edycie i sąsiadach nie miała co liczyć, poematy zaś pani Pasieczko nie zdołały jej zachwycić. Obiecała, że jeszcze kiedyś wpadnie, i znowu rozstawała się z Wandą w przekonaniu, że na pewno nie zajrzy do niej nigdy więcej.

Wracając do domu na skróty znajomymi uliczkami osiedla, próbowała wyciągnąć jakieś sensowne wnioski ze zdobytej wiedzy. Niestety, nic nie chciało się trzymać kupy. Najmniej kłopotów było z Mikulą. Najzwyczajniej okłamał Karolinę, kiedy mówił o własnej garsonierze. U facetów to normalne, lubią szpan. Ale jak pogodzić właścicielkę mieszkania numer 23, nobliwą i dystyngowaną Edytę, z burdelem? Wiedziała, co się dzieje pod jej dachem, czy nie wiedziała? Dlaczego Wanda dostała nagłej amnezji, gdy uświadomiła sobie, że Julia może znać Edytę? Co ja właściwie wiem o Edycie, zastanowiła się dziewczyna. Tyle co sama powie, trochę z plotek Heni, czyli prawie nic. Piękna samotnica z wyboru. Podobno w młodości jakaś wielka miłość, podobno zranione serce, ale kto, co? Nie wiadomo. A co wiadomo? Kobieta samodzielna, wyzwolona i zamożna. Mieszkanie po ciotce to pryszcz wobec spadku, jaki odziedziczyła po wuju, przemysłowcu z Anglii. Ciuchy w znakomitym gatunku, piękna biżuteria, zainteresowania wyższego rzędu: teatr, koncerty, wystawy. Pod tym względem Włocławek nie był pustynią: działo się sporo, choć może niezbyt często. Przyjaciele? Nie, przyjaciół chyba nie miała. W ogóle nie używała tego słowa. Czasem mówiła o koleżankach, częściej o znajomych, nigdy o życiu towarzyskim. Wyżywała się w pracy na trzech stanowiskach: swoim, Chochli i nierzadko Mikuli. Nikt w dziale nie potrafił zrozumieć, dlaczego tak bardzo chroniła Chochlę. Roztoczyła nad jełopem już nie tylko parasol, lecz całą cyrkową kopułę i nigdy z tego powodu nie narzekała.

Absolutnie dziwna kobieta, pomyślała Julia. Wydaje mi się, że coś o niej wiem, a nie wiem nic. Tak pewnie powiedziałby Leszek.

Na wspomnienie Leszka uśmiechnęła się ciepło. Była sobota. Wieczorem czekała ją dyskoteka i tańce w miłym towarzystwie, choć w niewygodnych butach. Starała się iść sprężyście, lecz prawa pięta coraz bardziej bolała. Pochyliła się, żeby poprawić wkładkę i wtedy zobaczyła wlepione w siebie oczy obcego mężczyzny. Stał obok trawnika i patrzył na Julię z takim zachwytem, że z miejsca poczuła się młoda, piękna i bardzo szczęśliwa. Czasem naprawdę niewiele trzeba, by wyzwolić w kobiecie energię. Wystarczy zachwycone spojrzenie starszego pana, pomyślała.

Ledwie jednak przekroczyła próg mieszkania, wyparowała z niej cała energia, a boląca pięta odezwała się ze zdwojoną siłą. Zabolała też dusza. Poprzedniego dnia matka z dziesięć razy przypominała o wizycie ajentki ubezpieczeniowej. Wyszukała polisę, spisała na kartce, co i jak należy załatwić, odliczyła pieniądze. Julia dała słowo, że odnowi ubezpieczenie, po czym kompletnie zapomniała o obietnicy i zniknęła na całe przedpołudnie. Nerwowo zaczęła szukać starej polisy, kartki i pieniędzy. Przetrząsnęła kuchnię, przedpokój, w końcu zajrzała do pokoju rodziców. Nic, tylko diabeł przykrył ogonem, pomyślała z rozpaczą. Nie tyle przejmowała się czekającym ją kazaniem, co czuła wyrzuty sumienia, że nigdy nie potrafi niczego do końca załatwić. Zajrzała do kilku szuflad. Z rozmachu ruszyła nawet jedną, opatrzoną patentowym zamkiem. Ku jej zdziwieniu była otwarta. Papiery, umowy, lokaty terminowe. Wzięła do ręki pierwszą z brzegu książeczkę, wystawioną akurat na nią. Na koncie miała trzydzieści tysięcy. Poczuła się jak ostatnia łachudra. Staruszkowie o niej myślą, odkładają pieniądze, a ona głupiego ubezpieczenia nie potrafi załatwić! Starannie zamknęła szufladę i wyszła do siebie. Polisa leżała na stoliku jak wół i kłuła w oczy. Jakieś pół godziny później przyszła również ajentka ubezpieczeniowa i Julia znowu poczuła się dobrze.

Całe sobotnie przedpołudnie Konrad spędził przy komputerze. Śpieszył się, żeby oddać pracę w terminie. Grzegorzowi bardzo na niej zależało, od kilku dni naciskał i nie było pomiłuj. Konrad z każdym mógł dyskutować o terminach, tylko nie z Grzegorzem. To był kontrahent, dzięki któremu zaczął wreszcie zarabiać prawdziwe pieniądze. Wystarczyły trzy lata współpracy, by Orzechowicz bez wstydu mógł patrzeć na wyciągi ze swojego konta bankowego. Na razie żył skromnie, niewiele wydawał, bo nie miał takiej potrzeby. Samotnemu facetowi wystarczyło mieszkanie po ciotce Ewelinie. Co innego, gdyby zdecydował się założyć rodzinę. Uśmiechnął się na myśl, że wymarzona willa Karoliny właściwie jest w zasięgu jego możliwości. Może nie przesadnie wielka, z basenem i oranżerią, jednak na pewno przyzwoita.

Karolina raz tylko napomknęła o wspólnej przyszłości i więcej do tematu nie wracała. On też nie i na pozór wszystko zostało po staremu. Ale tylko na pozór. W gruncie rzeczy nie darowała mu milczenia. Dziury w brzuchu nie wierciła, udawała zimną, obojętną lub rozkojarzoną. Śmiał się w duchu, że usiłuje go zmiękczyć.

– Czy w twoim życiu pojawił się nowy facet? – spytał, kiedy po raz któryś z rzędu nie zatrzymywała go na noc.

– Kto niby?

– Ktoś, komu powinienem zwolnić miejsce. Sama mówiłaś, że nigdy nie jesteś z dwoma jednocześnie.

– Tak mówiłam? No to siedź na tyłku i nie zawracaj głowy. Jak się pojawi, na pewno ci powiem.

To była cała Karolina. Słodka jak sama miłość, za moment zła jak szerszeń. Wciąż byli razem, lecz Konrad, choć jeszcze nie przyznawał się do tego nawet przed sobą, rozglądał się już za pretekstem do odejścia. Zaczynał się bać, że jeszcze miesiąc, dwa i uzależni się od Karoliny bardziej niż narkoman od marihuany. Wmawiał sobie, że nie kocha, jednocześnie był zazdrosny aż do zwariowania i za żadne skarby nie chciał się do tego przyznać.

– Co ciebie łączy z Mikulą? – spytał dzień wcześniej.

– Umowa o pracę, tak jak ciebie, plus wiedza o kilku niezbyt czystych interesach. Spowiednicy i prawnicy zwykle są najlepiej poinformowani. Czy o to ci chodziło?

– Naprawdę nigdy nie byłaś z nim bliżej?

– Raz byłam. Wiózł mnie na ramie roweru, no, ale to była damka. I nie mów mi, ssaczku, że to głupia odpowiedź. Na głupie pytanie innej nie dostaniesz. I jeszcze sobie zapamiętaj, że z facetami nigdy nie dyskutuję o innych facetach.

Patrzyła na niego ze złą, zaciętą miną. Kobiety z taką miną prędzej spalą za sobą mosty, niż zgodzą się odpowiedzieć na niewygodne pytania.

– Udajesz taką twardą czy rzeczywiście jesteś twarda? – spytał cicho. – Nigdy niczego się nie boisz?

– Potwornie boję się czterech żywiołów i wielkiej mocy plotki opluskwiającej. Z całą resztą, dzięki pomocy mojego aniołka stróża, jakoś sobie radzę.

Wczoraj też nie poprosiła, by został do rana. Obiecała zadzwonić w sobotę. Przedpołudnie minęło, a ona milczała.

Skończył pracę nad nowym programem, sprawdził całość i przegrał na dyskietkę. Telefon zadzwonił w momencie, gdy jedną nogą był już na klatce schodowej. Zamiast Karoliny usłyszał zachrypnięty głos Grzegorza i trochę się rozczarował. Odtajał dopiero pod wpływem pochwał.

– Masz jakieś plany na wieczór? – zainteresował się Grzegorz. – Jeśli nie, to może wyskoczysz z nami na tańce? Poderwałem niezłą lampucerę – zachichotał – ale towar chwilowo zastrzeżony. Mniejsza o dupę, mnie mianowicie chodzi o coś innego. Będzie też mój kuzyniak, z którym powinieneś pogadać.

Konrad nie przepadał za balangami w towarzystwie Grzegorza i jego paczki. Interesy interesami, jednak wieczory wolał mieć dla siebie.

– Hasło: piękna kobieta! – roześmiał się do słuchawki. Zaraz potem spoważniał. Piękna kobieta najwyraźniej machnęła na niego ręką.

Choć raz Julia wychodziła wieczorem z domu niezatrzymywana przez nikogo. Staruszkowie wyjątkowo dali się namówić znajomym na towarzyskie spotkanie. Wiele było z tego powodu zamieszania, sporów, marudzenia, na szczęście pojechali i mogła spokojnie zająć się sobą. Staranniejszy niż zwykle makijaż, trochę inne uczesanie i nowe ciuchy zrobiły z niej wyskokową dziewczynę. Z przyjemnością spojrzała w lustro. Nie miała wygórowanej opinii na temat własnej urody, uważała na przykład, że przy Karolinie jest zaledwie ładna, ale kompleksów też nie miała. Przynajmniej Leszek nie będzie miał powodów do narzekania, pomyślała ubawiona. Zawiesiła na szyi delikatny złoty łańcuszek ze swoim znakiem zodiaku i sięgnęła po buty. Pięta bolała jak nieszczęście. A jednak Leszek będzie miał powody do narzekania, stwierdziła zmartwiona. Przerzuciła błyskawicznie stertę starych butów. Nie pasowały wyglądem ani kolorem do całości, były to przeważnie ciężkie buciska na wysokich spodach, z jakich zrezygnowała raz na zawsze. Postanowiła zacisnąć usta i zapomnieć o pięcie. Niewielki opatrunek złagodził ból na tyle, że powitała kolegę promiennym uśmiechem.

– Ależ ty jesteś piękna! – westchnął zachwycony.

– Niedawno to samo powiedziałam Karolinie – zawołała ze śmiechem.

– Tak, ona jest piękna, ale ty piękniejsza.

– Czy wiesz, że całkiem niechcący kogoś zacytowałeś? – spytała, poważniejąc.

– Wiem. Leszka Wydronia.

Skłonił się elegancko i pomógł Julii włożyć żakiet. Zbiegając po schodach zastanawiała się, jak to jest: tyle razy marzyła, żeby ktoś chwalił jej urodę słowami Marka Winicjusza. Znalazł się Leszek, pochwalił – i nic. Może nie o tego mężczyznę chodziło, a może marzenia są przyjemniejsze od rzeczywistości?

Nigdy wcześniej nie była w kawiarni Teatralnej. Zwykle lokale wybierał Serafin, który gustował w ciemnych piwnicach i hałaśliwym otoczeniu. W Teatralnej Serafin nie miałby czego szukać. Towarzystwo było eleganckie i zróżnicowane: od ludzi bardzo młodych po wiek średni. Muzyka też była zróżnicowana, od dansingowej po dyskotekową. Julii wszystko się podobało: wielkie lustra w szatni, foyer ze zdjęciami znanych aktorów, lekkie schody prowadzące na piętro i sama kawiarnia. Może najmniej zachwycona była towarzystwem przy wspólnym stole. Oprócz nich siedziały dwie obce pary. Na pierwszy rzut oka uznała, że panowie są mężczyznami sukcesu, panie zaś pnączami. Lepiły się do swoich facetów, jeszcze zanim drinki wjechały na stół.

– Czemu zamilkłaś, biedronko?

Leszek pochylił się nad nią. Nigdy nie siedzieli tak blisko. Wyraźnie czuła ekscytujący zapach jego wody po goleniu. Pomyślała nawet, że tak blisko mogą siedzieć tylko zakochani, bo dla przyjaciół jest to trochę kłopotliwe. Ramię przy ramieniu, skroń przy skroni i nie bardzo wiadomo, co zrobić z oczami. Leszek jak zwykle był nienagannie elegancki. Przy ich stoliku on jeden nie ściągnął marynarki. Dwaj pozostali mężczyźni siedzieli w koszulach. Dumnie prezentowali rozpięte kołnierzyki i powywijane mankiety. Podobno był to nowy styl bycia w nowym włocławskim biznesie, jak to niedawno określiła Karolina. „I nie zdziw się – powiedziała – jak przy powitaniu ominą cię łukiem. Oni witają się tylko między sobą". Żadna z tych uwag nie dotyczyła na szczęście Leszka.

– Jak byś nazwał naszych współbiesiadników? – spytała szeptem, żeby nie przedłużać krępującego milczenia.

– Brunecik to kłopotek czarny, ten obok tutkarz bachusek, obie babki to osnuje – odszepnął natychmiast, wcale przy tym nie patrząc na sąsiadów.

– Ściemniasz! Nie ma mianowicie takich owadów.

– Widać, że w szkole nie lubiłaś biologii. Są. Masz moje zapewnienie.

Zanim poszli tańczyć, kłopotek parę razy zerknął w ich stronę. Oby tylko nie chciał się z nami bratać, pomyślała z przestrachem. Facet był nawet przystojny, gdyby włożył marynarkę i krawat, byłby też dobrze ubrany, lecz nie budził sympatii. Nie lubiła u mężczyzn modelowanych fryzur, wyłupiastych oczu i zębów równiutkich jak sztachety w płocie. Na wspomnienie twarzy kłopotka wzdrygnęła się i przytuliła do Leszka. W tangu było to naturalne, w stosunkach koleżeńskich jakby nieco mniej. Próbowała się wycofać, na co jej nie pozwolił. Dotańczyli do końca mocno wtuleni w siebie.

– Świetnie, że jesteście – powitał ich kłopotek. – Chciałem mianowicie wznieść toast za zdrowie naszego stołu!

– Czyżby mianowicie okulał? – spytała Julia.

Nie zdziwiło jej zdrowie stołu, lecz słówko „mianowicie”, którym lubiła przerzucać się z Leszkiem. Nie widziała powodów, by jakiś wyliniały kłopotek korzystał z ich szyfru.

– Dowcipna! Brawo! – Zaśmiał się hałaśliwie. – Lubię laski z ikrą.

Najlepsza byłaby flądra na kiju, pomyślała i nawet miała zamiar podzielić się tą cenną uwagą, poczuła jednak, że Leszek delikatnie ścisnął jej rękę, jakby dawał sygnał do zawieszenia broni. Uśmiechnęła się zdawkowo, co miało znaczyć, że dla świętego spokoju gotowa jest wypić zdrowie stołu, krzeseł, wszystkich gości i jeszcze flądry na dodatek. Kłopotek zamówił sześć drinków.

– Mam taki pomysł, żebyśmy mianowicie bawili się razem! – Wzniósł szklankę do góry i zatrzymał wzrok na Julii. – Mnie nazywają boss, panie to Arletka i Mila, albo odwrotnie, kolega też ma jakieś imię... Masz, stary, no nie? Mówimy na niego amant, bo kobitki za nim szaleją. Teraz wasza kolej.

Leszek chrząknął, lecz Julia nie dopuściła go do głosu.

– Ja nazywam kolegę patyczakiem, on mnie biedronką.

– Bez jaj, proszę państwa! – zaprotestował boss. – Na chrzcie dali wam chyba jakieś imiona, co?

– Nigdy nie słyszałam o świętym bossie – wyjaśniła spokojnie Julia. Minę przy tym zachowała bardzo niewinną.

Boss znowu zarechotał i pokiwał głową z uznaniem. Logika wywodu musiała trafić mu do przekonania, bo w nagrodę wyciągnął Julię na parkiet. Wyszła, przeklinając obolałą piętę i błogosławiąc jednocześnie didżeja za wiązankę szybkich, dyskotekowych melodii. Teoretycznie tańczyła z bossem, praktycznie trzymała go na dystans. Pląsał dość żwawo, pocił się przy tym, posapywał i aż strach było patrzeć, co się porobiło ze starannie wymodelowanych włosów.

– Chodź, miss paragraf, napijemy się czegoś. – Otarł czoło i pociągnął ją w kierunku bufetu. – Co ci postawić?

Była zła, że wyrywa ją z tanecznego kręgu jak bezwolną kukłę i wcale nie miała ochoty tkwić z nim przy barze.

– Sam sobie postaw! – mruknęła niezbyt uprzejmie. Dopiero kiedy parsknął śmiechem, zdała sobie sprawę z niestosowności propozycji.

– Nie muszę – rżał jak młody koń – sam mi staje na widok ładnej laski!

– Poproszę o tonik – powiedziała, puszczając mimo uszu głupawy żart.

– Nie wierzysz? Możesz się łatwo przekonać – odsłonił w szerokim uśmiechu swoje sztachetki. – Jesteś tak piękna, że mnie z wrażenia zatyka.

– Mnie też zatyka – przyznała Julia. Spojrzała na pewną siebie, mocno zadowoloną twarz bossa i nabrała ochoty na minutkę szczerości. Ciekawe, czy nadal by się tak cieszył, gdybym mu powiedziała, że przypomina mi kozła na rykowisku ze starej makatki? Przezornie jednak zachowała swoje myśli dla siebie. Mógłby się nie poznać na wyrafinowanym komplemencie. Wyglądał na faceta głupiego, lecz silnego. Co tam, okażę mu miłosierdzie, zdecydowała.

Lekki półuśmiech dziewczyny wprowadził bossa w błąd.

– Udałaś się rodzicom, Karolinko, słowo daję! – Spojrzał na nią rozbawiony.

Odpowiedziała mu równie rozbawionym spojrzeniem. Dla niego mogła być nawet Kunegundą, wolała jednak Karoliną. Zawsze miała słabość do tego imienia.

– Muszę iść, kolega czeka – powiedziała, odstawiając pustą szklankę.

– To poczeka jeszcze chwilę. – Przytrzymał jej ramię. – Jesteś bezbłędna i działasz na mnie jak afrodyzjak. Widzę wielkie okrągłe łoże, ciebie i siebie. Leżymy, mianowicie, rozumiesz?

– Siedzimy! Jeszcze siedzimy i przestań się roznamiętniać, bo spadniesz, a łoże daleko.

– Myślę po męsku. Przyszłościowo. Piękne kobiety są dla mnie wyzwaniem.

Już cię lubię, facet, fajny jesteś jak stado komarów, myślała nieprzychylnie. Skwitowała jego komplementy przelotnym uśmiechem. Od pewnego czasu, pod wpływem nauk Karoliny, oduczyła się dziękować za miłe słowa. Nie chciała się podobać bossowi, lecz nie miała na to wpływu. Podświadomie czuła, jak wyłupiaste ślepka przebijają materię sukienki, przenikają przez bieliznę i dotykają gołej skóry. Na szczęście siedział w bezpiecznej odległości i ręce trzymał na szklance z piwem.

– Masz jakieś plany na jutro? – spytał, odrywając wzrok od jej sukni. – Jeśli nie, to może wyskoczymy razem za miasto? Mam nad jeziorem szałową chatkę, naprawdę wartą obejrzenia. Podaj godzinę i adres. Podjadę po ciebie.

– Chcesz, żeby twoje Arletki obdarły mnie ze skóry?

– One? – Wykrzywił się pociesznie. – A co one mają do gadania? Pytam o twoje plany.

– Mam plany na jutro, na cały tydzień i na kilka następnych.

– A wiesz, mała, że boss dwa razy nie prosi?

– To dobrze, bo nie wiem, czy drugi raz umiałabym odmówić! – Obrzuciła go powłóczystym spojrzeniem, podpatrzonym u Karoliny, trzepnęła rzęsami i lekko zeskoczyła ze stołka. Pięta bolała coraz bardziej. Z ulgą opadła na krzesło obok Leszka.

– Nie chcę ci robić wyrzutów, drogi kolego, jeśli jednak porównam nasz stolik do kompotu, to my jesteśmy te dwie śliwki. – Westchnęła ciężko. – Boss jest łobrzydliwy!

– Tak? Goniłaś przez całą salę łobrzydliwego facia i jeszcze się skarżysz?

– Biegłam, bo mnie ciągnął. Nie widziałeś?

– Jakoś mi umknęło!

Zacisnął jej dłoń w swoich i bardzo leciutko pocałował. To była drobniutka, delikatna pieszczota, która mieściła się w granicach towarzyskiej i koleżeńskiej normy. Sam Leszek zachowywał się jednak zupełnie inaczej niż zwykle. I wcale nie chodziło o to, że tam firma, tu dyskoteka. Zniknęła gdzieś jego naturalna swoboda. Silił się na żartobliwy, lekki ton i czułe ucho Julii bezbłędnie wyłapało drobne fałsze. Sama też była rozczarowana. Cieszyła się na wspólny wieczór z dwu powodów: chciała potańczyć i chciała porozmawiać z Leszkiem. Obok Edyty był drugą chodzącą encyklopedią wiedzy o firmie. Przygotowała sobie litanię pytań, na które tylko on mógł odpowiedzieć. Niestety, pięta nie pozwalała na tańce, niechciane towarzystwo zaś na rozmowy. Boss jeszcze nie wrócił, ten drugi lał w siebie piwsko, jakby na potwierdzenie, że bardziej zasługuje na przezwisko tutkarza bachuska niż amanta. Był nieznośnie hałaśliwy i coraz bardziej chamski. Prężył pokaźny tors i demonstrował bicepsy. Gdyby doszło do jakiejś przepychanki, Leszek nie miał przy nim szans.

– Pij, mała! Jak nie ma bossa, ja jestem duszą tego...

– ...stołu – podpowiedziała Julia.

Podchwycił i na znak radości ucałował dekolt jednej z Arletek. Potem długo i zawile opowiadał o balandze na Wiśle bądź w Wiśle, tego już nie udało się ustalić. Julia spojrzała na Leszka.

– Pobladłeś coś, kolego! Źle się czujesz? – dotknęła czubkami palców bladego policzka.

– Nie najlepiej – przyznał.

Odczekała, aż bachusek porwał panny do tańca i zarządziła odwrót. Marzyła już tylko o prysznicu i domowych pantoflach bez pięt. O bossie nawet nie pomyślała, a właśnie na niego natknęli się w szatni.

– Co jest grane, Lechu! Chcesz się zmyć, brachu, jak ostatnia łachudra?

Przytrzymywał Leszka za klapę marynarki. Stał prosto jak struna i to właśnie wydało się Julii podejrzane. To była pozycja, jaką demonstrują kompletnie zalani faceci, którzy chcą uchodzić za trzeźwych. Leszek nie wydawał się zaskoczony, co ją znacznie uspokoiło. Powoli podeszła do lustra, wyjęła grzebień i stanęła tak, by widzieć odbicie obu mężczyzn. Coś jej nie pasowało, ale sama nie wiedziała co. Moment nie był najlepszy na sklejanie okruchów informacji. Uważnie patrzyła w lustro i z ruchu ust próbowała odgadnąć treść sprzeczki. Widziała złą twarz bossa i wściekłą minę Leszka. Z całą pewnością nie wymieniali komplementów. Leszek warknął, boss zaklął. W swoim zacietrzewieniu coraz bardziej przypominali dwa koguty. Efekt tragiczny zmieniał się w komiczny i dziewczyna zdecydowała się działać. Ściągnęła but i kulejąc weszła między nich. Bez słowa pokazała zakrwawioną piętę Leszkowi. Zrobiła to tak, żeby boss również mógł popatrzeć. Widok był znacznie paskudniejszy niż wielkość obrażenia i zadziałał piorunująco. Faceci są beznadziejni, zdążyła jeszcze pomyśleć Julia, zanim spadła na nią fala męskiej czułości. Boss usiłował ją podtrzymać ramieniem, jakby miała nagle paść, Leszek jedną ręką gładził ją po głowie, drugą rozpaczliwie szukał numerków do szatni.

– Odwiozę cię! – zdecydował boss. – Jestem tu autem.

– Ja też! – odpowiedziała pośpiesznie.

Dopiero kiedy wyszli przed teatr, pozwoliła Leszkowi zadzwonić na postój.

Chłopak całą drogę milczał. Julia próbowała powiązać w całość te elementy, które jej podpadły.

– Leszku, czy mi się zdawało, czy ten boss-kłopotek znał twoje imię? – spytała, gdy podjeżdżali już pod dom.

– Nie sądzę... Chyba że nas podsłuchał.

– W szatni powiedział: „Co jest grane, Lechu".

– Powiedział: brachu. Wiesz, jak jest ze sprawnością językową u nawalonego faceta!

– Skąd niby mam wiedzieć? Ale przyznasz, że to łobrzydliwy facet.

– Karaluch z nim tańcował! – mruknął Leszek.

I to mruknięcie też Julii podpadło. Przy drzwiach wejściowych uśmiechnęła się na dobranoc. Nie wymagała od zmęczonego kolegi, by ją odprowadzał na górę, choć miał taki zamiar. Wyraźnie próbował jej coś powiedzieć, przytrzymać rękę, nie zdążył, bo drzwi się zamknęły.

Transakcje z Grzegorzem miały tę dobrą stronę, że płacił za wykonaną pracę od razu, z ręki do ręki. Konrad nigdy nie pytał, czy to, co robi na zamówienie, jest w zgodzie z prawem. Od martwienia się o prawo i od pomysłów był Grzegorz, on natomiast był informatykiem artystą. Oprócz wiedzy miał w sobie tę iskrę, która niezbędna jest w każdym zawodzie. To ona odróżnia van Gogha od pospolitego pacykarza, a Carusa od wyjca. W technice wcale nie jest inaczej. Jeden inżynier zaprojektuje most wiszący, a drugiemu zawali się kładka nad strumykiem. Konradowi nic się nie zawalało. Bez większego wysiłku potrafił stworzyć program, nad którym gdzie indziej ślęczało kilku fachowców. A że w technice liczy się również szybkość, w zasadzie był bezcenny. Brakowało mu tylko znajomości i kontaktów, by rozpocząć działanie na własną rękę. Chwilowo nie zależało mu aż tak bardzo na samodzielności.

Późnym popołudniem podjechał do Michelina. Bez większych emocji patrzył na luksusowe wille i wielkie ogrody. Kiedyś też myślał, żeby właśnie tu postawić niewielki dom w lesie. Wtedy były to czyste mrzonki, teraz, gdy doszedł do jakich takich pieniędzy, Michelin przestał mu się podobać.

U Grzegorza nie zabawił długo. Cześć, cześć, dyskietka, kasa i po transakcji.

– Stary, oczywiście pamiętasz o naszej umowie? – upewnił się Grzegorz.

Przytaknął, że pamięta, wskoczył do samochodu i nie bardzo wiedział, jak zakończyć ten pracowity dzień. Miał do wyboru trzy domy: własny, Orskich i Karoliny. Wybrał ten ostatni. Po drodze rozważył trzy następne możliwości: pocałuje klamkę, przeszkodzi w praniu, zastanie dziewczynę z innym facetem. Tę ostatnią od razu wykluczył. Na dobrą sprawę człowiek nigdy nie wie, jak się zachowa w przykrej sytuacji, dopóki się w niej nie znajdzie. Nie życzył sobie zastawać Karoliny z obcym facetem i już. Na szczęście była w domu, sama. Nie wyglądała też na zdziwioną.

– Stało się coś, ssaczku? Masz taką śmieszną minę?

– Chyba pierwszy raz widzę cię w spodniach. Świetnie wyglądasz!

– Przejechałeś taki kawał drogi, żeby mi o tym powiedzieć?

– Jeżeli przeszkadzam... – Zrobił ruch, jakby chciał wyjść.

Roześmiała się i chwyciła go za rękaw.

– Ty mi nigdy nie przeszkadzasz. Wejdź, dostaniesz szklankę herbaty, ciepłe słowo, buziaka na dobranoc, ale na więcej dzisiaj nie licz.

Nie mam w domu nawet sucharka. Zapomniałam o zakupach, a teraz już mi się nie chce wychodzić.

Posadziła go na niewygodnej wersalce, zamiast stolika przyciągnęła kuchenny taboret, bo przy ławie nie dało się wypić herbaty. Na całej powierzchni leżały notatki, skoroszyty i książki. Górę piramidy zdobił kodeks karny. Karolina nie była wdzięczną rozmówczynią. Odpowiadała na pytania, nawet zdobyła się na żart, jednak oczy wciąż miała skierowane na ławę. Konrad dobrze znał to uczucie. Sam też nie znosił, gdy ktoś odrywał go od pracy. No, ale on nie był zwykłym ktosiem, on chciał być kimś ważnym, przynajmniej dla Karoliny.

– To ja już pójdę – powiedział z ociąganiem.

– Idź, ssaczku, bo czy chcę, czy nie chcę, muszę to skończyć. – Musnęła ustami jego policzek.

W drzwiach natknął się na kolejnego gościa.

– Panowie się znają, prawda? – spytała Karolina.

Skinęli głowami, uścisnęli sobie ręce. Zbiegając po schodach, Konrad rozmyślał nad złośliwością losu. Bał się, że zastanie Karolinę z mężczyzną. Do głowy mu nie przyszło, że może ją zostawić z Mikulą!

W poniedziałek dyrektor odwołał cotygodniową operatywkę i zarządził naradę ścisłego kierownictwa, z udziałem właścicielki Budampolexu 2. Zeszło się raptem pięć osób, z sekretarką włącznie, a krzyku narobiły za piętnaście. Julia zdążyła przyzwyczaić się do tembru głosu Mikuli i językowych umiejętności kadry, ale możliwości pani prezes jeszcze nie znała. Mikulowa, jeżeli nawet uczestniczyła w naradach, to na zasadzie wolnego słuchacza. Czasem wtrąciła swoje trzy grosze, częściej milczała, jak przystało na osobę, która niezbyt orientuje się w działalności firmy. Tego ranka było zupełnie inaczej. Wysoki, piskliwy głosik dominował nad pozostałymi, zagłuszał argumenty i uwagi innych. Pani prezes zwracała się do dyrektora per jełopie, durniu, kapuściana głowo i konsekwentnie usiłowała przekształcić naradę służbową w ostrą sprzeczkę małżeńską. Jeżeli chodzi o Mikulę, zachował daleko idącą powściągliwość, nie poruszał innych spraw poza merytorycznymi, nie odpowiadał na zaczepki prywatne, za to służbowo był wpieklony na żonę jak nieboskie stworzenie. Dwa tygodnie wcześniej zdecydował, że Budampolex 2 stanie do przetargu na budowę drogi przy hali sportowej, kazał zgromadzić i złożyć niezbędne dokumenty, ona zaś wycofała firmę z przetargu i jeszcze próbowała obciążyć winą dyrektora.

– Chodnik do hali sportowej ci się marzy? A gdzie sprzęt, gdzie fachowcy? Dywanu w domu nie potrafisz odkurzyć, jełopie, to chodnik wybudujesz? – wykrzykiwała histerycznie. Zacięła się przy tym w uporze i za nic nie chciała wytłumaczyć, jaki widzi związek między ulicznym chodnikiem a pokojowym dywanem.

– Edytki nie ma? – Henia zajrzała do sekretariatu, upewniła się, że drzwi gabinetu są zamknięte i z ulgą zajęła fotel dla gości. – Co oni tak hałasują, jakby ich kto ze skóry obdzierał? – spytała zdziwiona. – Wielka mi inteligencja, jeżeli wrzeszczy głośniej od prostaków! Mam rację? Mam. Jeszcze rok temu powiedziałabym: krzyczą, bo są zdenerwowani. Teraz w życiu tak nie powiem! Człowiek rozumny umie zapanować nad złością, nad bólem i wszystkim. Wiem, bo świeżo jestem po dwudniowym kursie psychologii i medytacji. Fantastyczna sprawa, Julciu. Tam dopiero człowiek rozumie, ile stracił, nie zmieniając własnej osobowości i nie pracując nad sobą! O tym, jaka jesteś, nie decydują żadne tam cechy wrodzone, tylko ty sama! Rozumiesz? Ale najpierw musisz pokochać siebie. Jak pokochasz siebie, to w drugim etapie musisz pokochać wszystkich ludzi, bo to jest sens najważniejszy naszego istnienia.

– Więc kiedy w końcu mam siebie pokochać: przed zmianą czy po zmianie osobowości?

– Siebie masz obowiązek kochać zawsze. Od siebie przechodzisz do innych ludzi i spełniasz się jako człowiek. Rozumiesz?

– Nie bardzo.

– To przez te ryki umysł ci się zlasował. Przyjdź jutro na medytacje, będę to wszystko wykładała jeszcze raz. Słyszysz starego, jaki kulturalny? Jego, to ja bym... no, może nie na hak, nie na suchą gałąź, ale w kosmos wysłała, żeby pomedytował i żebym nie musiała go oglądać.

– Nie wolno ci! Jak już kochasz wszystkich, to wszystkich, z Mikulą włącznie! – zaprotestowała Julia.

– Ma się rozumieć, tylko że miłość dotyczy... porządnych ludzi. A ty wiesz, co mi się dzisiaj śniło? Małpę dostałam w upominku.

– I co?

– Obudziłam się i nic. Luty chrapał obok. Paskudny to on jest... choć bardziej ratlerka niż małpę przypomina. Nie wiesz czasem, kto u nas zajmuje się snami?

– Pan Leszek – odpowiedziała Julia z przekonaniem i powagą, której nie zmąciły dziwne odgłosy chrząkania, docierające z pokoju magistrów.

– Jest u siebie?

– Oczywiście – przytaknęła zadowolona, że choć na chwile pozbędzie się Heni. Jednak najprostsze rozwiązania nie zawsze bywają najlepsze. Pomoc gospodarcza nie chciała iść do pokoju, gdzie siedziała magister Cierniak, więc poprosiła pana Leszka do sekretariatu. Nie wszedł, tylko stanął w progu; Julia była pewna, że za jego plecami czatuje Karolina.

– Paskudny sen! – Leszek zmarszczył czoło. – Paskudny. Wróży kolosalne nieprzyjemności spowodowane tymi... no... o właśnie, spowodowane plotkami. Aha i jeszcze jedno: możliwe, że ktoś czyha na pani cnotę. Proszę uważać!

– Na moją cnotę, mówi pan? E, niemożliwe. Sen można tłumaczyć na wiele sposobów, i tak wiadomo, że sprawdza się jeden. Mnie wyłącznie te plotki zmartwiły. Przecież pan wie i Julcia wie, że ja zawsze prawdę mówię. Chyba żeby nie daj Boże ktoś coś o mnie? Możliwe to, jak pan myśli?

– Możliwe!

Henia wyraźnie spochmurniała. Co o sobie mówiła, to mówiła, jednak do niej należała palma mistrzyni plotki opluskwiającej. Nie było złośliwszego języka w całej firmie, może z wyjątkiem kierownika Chochli, który od pewnego czasu „był na zaginięciu". Myśl, że ktoś mógłby ją pokonać jej własną bronią, tak zwarzyła kobietę, że bez słowa wyszła.

– Nieźle to wykombinowałeś – roześmiała się Julia. – Brawo!

– Byłem tylko tubą – przyznał uczciwie Leszek.

– Ale się przejęła, widzieliście? – cieszyła się Karolina. – Polowanie na czarownice to małe piwo w porównaniu z tym, co wyszykuje Henia.

– I jak to jest? – zastanowiła się Julia. – Komputery, rakiety, telefonia bezprzewodowa i senniki? Jedno do drugiego nie pasuje.

Leszek z czułością ucałował dziewczynę w czoło.

– Według mnie, biedroneczko, w każdym komputerze siedzi malutki diabełek i tak rączkami macha, tak macha, tak te wszystkie dane z szufladek wyciąga, że tylko dym leci. Nie inaczej w komórce i w telewizorze. Jak się czegoś nie rozumie, to się ma czarnego diabełka, kulę albo sny.

Jeszcze nawet nie zdążyli porządnie zabrać się do pracy, kiedy w drzwiach sekretariatu stanął olbrzymi bukiet kwiatów. Tak to właśnie wyglądało: olbrzymi bukiet, a dopiero za nim niewielki człowieczek.

– Dla pani Karoliny! – powiedział posłaniec i złożył swój ciężar na biurku Julii. Z wdzięcznością przyjął drobne za fatygę, jednak nic więcej nie umiał lub nie chciał powiedzieć: ani od kogo, ani z jakiej okazji.

– Kwiaciarnia – tłumaczył – dostała telefoniczne zlecenie, ja dostałem polecenie od kierowniczki, przyniosłem i rączki całuję.

Ze zdziwieniem oglądali potężne cudo sztuki kwiaciarskiej.

– Ty masz szczęście! – westchnęła Julia. – Domyślasz się, kto za tym stoi... oczywiście wyłączając posłańca?

– Ani w ząb! – przyznała Karolina. – To musi być romantyczny facet w rozmiarze maksi. Ja takiego nie znam.

– Całą trumnę by nakrył takim wiechciem – zadumał się Leszek. – Może w środku jest bomba?

– Oszalałeś? – wzdrygnęła się Julia.

Rozchyliła delikatnie wielkie liście. Do najokazalszego irysa przyczepiona była malutka karteczka. Bez słowa podała bilecik przyjaciółce.

– *Najpiękniejszej Miss Paragraf – zawiedziony wielbiciel* – przeczytała półgłosem Karolina. – Jeżeli myślicie, że rozjaśniło mi się w głowie, to jesteście w błędzie.

Za to Julia miała już pełną jasność. Była całkowicie pewna, że bukiet przeznaczony jest dla niej. Wiedziała również, kto go przysłał.

Karolina odszukała w kuchni spore wiaderko, wstawiła kwiaty do wody i natychmiast gdzieś wybiegła.

– Czemu się tak zamyśliłaś, biedroneczko? – Leszek pociągnął Julię czule za kosmyk włosów. – Kupię ci po południu jeszcze większy bukiecior od tego. Albo lepiej całą kwiaciarnię, chcesz?

– Nie chcę. Jeden bukiecior już mam – wskazała głową wiadro z kwiatami. – Posłuchaj i pomóż mi, bo oszaleję. Twój kłopotek...

– Co moje?

– No, ten facet, ten boss, czy jak mu tam, był...

– Nie mój!

– Zgoda, nie twój! Więc on był przekonany, że mam na imię Karolina. Początkowo myślałam, że to przypadek. Jak galopowaliśmy przez salę do bufetu, nazwał mnie miss paragraf. To też puściłam mimo uszu. Wreszcie w szatni raz powiedział do ciebie brachu, raz Lechu. Słuch mam dobry i na pamięć nie narzekam. Czy znajdujesz jakieś logiczne wytłumaczenie, dlaczego mnie pomylił, ciebie nie pomylił, a sam się nie przedstawił?

– Boss to boss. Każdy facet w miarę pękaty ma prawo nazwać się bossem i nawet w to uwierzyć. Może rzeczywiście to spotkanie było nieprzypadkowe? Może on śledzi mnie, a podrywa ciebie lub odwrotnie... No nie, odwrotność raczej odpada. Przejdę się do teatru, popytam. I co? Odbierzesz Karolinie bukiet?

– Co mi radzisz?

– Na twoim miejscu nic bym nie mówił.

Do południa Karolina była nieuchwytna, po południu wyszedł Leszek i właśnie wtedy do sekretariatu wbiegła rozżalona Henia. Ręce jej drżały, głos się łamał i dopiero napojona przez Edytę wodą sodową wstydliwie, choć głośno przyznała, że jest molestowana seksualnie przez magistra Wydronia. Edyta próbowała ją uspokoić, zażegnać burzę, jednak Henia nie pozwoliła się uspokoić. Coraz głośniej i głośniej mówiła o świństwach, jakie toleruje się w tej firmie, aż wywołała z gabinetu dyrektora Mikulę. Postał, popatrzył i zgrabnie, po męsku, umknął z sekretariatu. W biegu zlecił Edycie zbadanie sprawy. Sam obiecał zadowolić się wnioskami.

Henia była poszkodowaną i równocześnie jedynym świadkiem. Jej zeznania obciążały w równej mierze kierownictwo zakładu, jak i magistra Wydronia, a może nawet Wydronia nieco mniej. Pomoc gospodarcza, posługując się cytatami z książek psychologicznych, dowodziła, że w sprzyjających okolicznościach, gdy istnieje jawne przyzwolenie dla draństwa, mężczyzna – szczególnie samotny i porzucony przez żonę – może szukać rekompensaty gdzie indziej. Wydroń poszukał i trafił na nią. Jako kobieta świadoma swojej wartości, do tego mężatka, nigdy w życiu nie zgodzi się na proponowane jej bezeceństwa.

– Ale co on pani zrobił? – dopytywała się Edyta. – Uwiódł? Zgwałcił?

– No też coś, pani Edyto?! O gwałtach to ja mam swoje zdanie. Co druga zgwałcona kobieta sama prowokuje nieszczęście. Ja mówię o molestowaniu. Całowanie po rękach, jakieś przytulanki, zgrabne słówka. Dziećmi nie jesteśmy, wiemy, o co mężczyznom chodzi, prawda?

Posapała jeszcze chwilę, dorzuciła kilka nieistotnych szczegółów i wyszła. Jeżeli mogła sobie czegoś pogratulować, to na pewno zaszokowania Edyty. Mało komu udała się ta trudna sztuka. Sekretarka patrzyła bezradnie na Julię i Karolinę. Były świadkami nieudolnej mistyfikacji, to nie ulegało wątpliwości, tylko dlaczego oskarżenie padło na Leszka, człowieka powszechnie lubianego i bardzo grzecznego? Owszem, całował panie po rękach, lecz wyłącznie z czystej sympatii, bez podtekstów erotycznych. Komplementy prawił bezinteresownie i zachowywał się tak, jakby uwielbiał wszystkie kobiety, nie wyłączając pomocy gospodarczych.

Edyta była bezradna.

– Dziewczyny, spróbujcie odgadnąć, dlaczego ona zadziałała z takim opóźnieniem? Przez dwa lata cieszyła się jak żaba w deszcz i dopiero dzisiaj przypomniała sobie, że jest molestowana? Nie mówcie mi, że to przypadek. Nie uwierzę, zbyt długo pracuję z ludźmi.

– Może chodzi o sen? – zastanawiała się głośno Julia. – Leszek trochę z niej zażartował.

– Tylko tego brakuje, żebyśmy zaczęły analizować sny starej wariatki! – Karolina wzruszyła ramionami. – Według mnie, Edytko, to sprawka twojej przyjaciółki Mikulowej. Nie obraź się, takie mam wrażenie. Spróbujmy pójść tym tropem.

– Jeżeli mnie podpuszczasz, to rozumiem – powiedziała wolno Edyta – lecz jeśli mówisz poważnie, jesteś w błędzie. Henia nie cierpi Mikulowej i wszystko, co nam tu opowiada o pięknej pani prezes, jest czystą grą. Ona jest kuzynką i człowiekiem Wacka. Dziwię się, że na to wcześniej nie wpadłaś.

– Myślę – odpowiedziała Karolina – że niewłaściwie obsadziłaś tego tłuka. Ona nie zagrałaby nawet czaszki Yorika, a ty jej wpychasz rolę Hamleta. To jedna z najtrudniejszych kreacji i wymaga doskonałego aktora. O, ty byś się nadała z całą pewnością, lecz nie taki prymitywny naturszczyk jak Henia.

Przez chwilę mierzyły się oczami. Żadna nie chciała skapitulować. Karolina pierwsza odwróciła się i z gracją wyszła do swojego pokoju.

Główny winowajca wrócił przed piętnastą i trafił na wielkie milczenie. Mężczyzna wrażliwy, który pracuje wśród trzech, właściwie czterech kobiet, zna różne stany damskiego ducha i rzadko kiedy się dziwi.

– Przepraszam, czy ktoś nam wykopał topór wojenny? – spytał uprzejmie.

– Owszem! – przytaknęła Edyta. – Nie nam, tylko tobie i nie ktoś, tylko pani Henia. Oskarżenie jest najcięższego kalibru, chodzi o molestowanie seksualne.

– Kto niby mnie molestuje? – spytał.

– Ciebie nikt, to ty podobno robisz nieskromne propozycje pani Heni.

W miarę jak Edyta mówiła, przyjazny uśmiech Leszka zmienił się w grymas obrzydzenia. Samo molestowanie jako takie było mu wstrętne, a jeszcze pani Heni?! Westchnął ciężko i miał zamiar odejść do swojego pokoju. Gwałtowny sprzeciw Edyty zmusił go do powrotu. Sprawa była głupia, jednak głośna, należało ją wyjaśnić i zamknąć.

– Jak już musisz, to powiedz staremu, że to prawda – mruknął z rezygnacją. – Napadłem na gruboudkę, nie mogłem się pohamować. Tak ją dzisiaj obsobaczyłem, że rodzony chłop lepiej by nie potrafił!

– Ale za co?

– Za całokształt. I to ci jeszcze powiem, że należało jej się dawno.

– Pytam po raz drugi: za co konkretnie obsobaczyłeś panią Henię? – denerwowała się Edyta.

– Nie powiem, bo musiałbym powtórzyć to, czego nie chciałem słuchać.

Dalsze dociekania nie miały sensu. Leszek należał do nielicznego grona mężczyzn, którzy jakimś cudem nie zatracili jeszcze takich cech swojej płci, jak rycerskość wobec kobiet i wstręt do plotek. Można powiedzieć: ostatni Mohikanin.

Ani sprzeczka Edyty z Karoliną, ani wyjaśnienia Leszka nie dawały odpowiedzi na pytanie, dlaczego Henia poczuła się nagle molestowana. I nie było to jedyne pytanie, na które nie sposób było znaleźć odpowiedź.

Tuż po pracy Julia wyciągnęła Karolinę do miasta. Planowała drobny sprint po sklepach. W ostatniej chwili wspaniałomyślnie zrezygnowała z zakupów na rzecz obiadu w Zajeździe. Trudno rozmawiać o poważnych sprawach, biegając z wywieszonym językiem od lady do lady. W pustawym lokalu bez żadnych przeszkód zajęły ulubiony stolik Karoliny, w niszy, z widokiem na ulicę Brzeską i klasztor.

– Jak widzę tyle dań, to albo jadłabym wszystkie po kolei, albo żadnego – jęknęła Julia. – Wybierz coś dla mnie.

– Proszę uprzejmie! Zupka z cykuty, a na drugie pająk w śmietanie. Pasuje ci taki zestaw? Nie ma lekko, kochana! Płacz i ucz się wybierać. Na tym polega życie.

Julia zastanowiła się chwilę i zamówiła to samo co przyjaciółka, czyli w swoim mniemaniu dokonała najtrafniejszego wyboru. Bardziej niż na kołdunach w rosole zależało jej na wyjaśnieniach Karoliny. Co na przykład mówił Mikula o zdjęciach? Jakie plany mają Mikulowie wobec firmy i pracowników? Co z Chochlą? Co z Bujałą? Magister Cierniak tylko głową kręciła. Wiedziała niewiele więcej od Julii. Jednego była pewna: Mikulowie weszli w trwały konflikt. Ona z dnia na dzień zaczęła znać się na kierowaniu firmą i popełniła kilka kardynalnych błędów, narażając Budampolex 2 na poważne straty. Zmieniała decyzje męża, obcinała jego kompetencje, a Mikula robił wielkie oczy, bo nic innego zrobić nie mógł. Prosił nawet Karolinę, żeby znalazła jakieś paragrafy pozwalające ubezwłasnowolnić głupią babę. Sam osobiście pomagał wertować opasłe tomy, by dojść do wniosku, że paragrafy przemawiają na korzyść właścicielki, bez względu na stan jej umysłu. Pluł sobie w brodę, że tak bardzo zaufał żonie i poza jej plecami zaczął ratować, co się dało, czyli uciekać z majątkiem firmy. Jednak nawet przed Karoliną nie przyznał się do pożyczek zaciąganych tu i ówdzie, przede wszystkim u Bujały. Magister Cierniak miała związane ręce: nie mogła zapytać wprost bez zdradzenia źródła informacji.

– Stary truje! – zaprzeczyła gwałtownie Julia. – Edyta z Mikulową mają wszystkie dokumenty, w tym weksle... lub ich kserokopie! Wiedzą o zadłużeniu. On może działać wbrew żonie, lecz w żadnym wypadku za jej plecami.

– A skąd pewność, że Mikulowa zna zawartość zielonej teczki? – Karolina wzruszyła ramionami. – Równie dobrze stary mógł dogadać się z Edytą i razem zamierzają wykołować nadobną Olutkę!

Julia odsunęła talerz i głęboko się zamyśliła. Jej inżyniersko-artystyczna dusza buntowała się przeciwko zdradom, knowaniom i spiskom, chyba że spisek miał na względzie dobro przyjaciół i własne. Coraz bardziej zależało jej na powodzeniu grupy, której nadała nazwę aprilistów. Jeżeli Mikulowie rzeczywiście nie grali do jednej bramki, to z kim trzymała Edyta? Karolina uparcie twierdziła, że Edyta może trzymać wyłącznie ze sobą.

– Ta babka coraz bardziej mnie intryguje – mruknęła Julia.

– Dopiero teraz? – Przyjaciółka uśmiechnęła się złośliwie. – Myślałam, że wciąż jesteś pod jej urokiem. Zaczęłaś już nawet podobnie się szczerzyć i przybierać identyczne pozy.

– Lubię... to znaczy bardzo lubiłam Edytę, jednak dochodzę do wniosku, że ona coś za często występuje w duetach: to z Mikulową, to ze starym, teraz z Chochlą. Z kim ona trzyma, nie wiem, ale że trzyma Chochlę w mieszkaniu po ciotce, w tej niby garsonierze, tego jestem pewna. Powiedziałaś Mikuli, czyja jest chata?

Karolina westchnęła ciężko.

– A po co? On mi też wszystkiego nie mówi. Ten faun lubieżny jest głupszy niż ustawa przewiduje. Niestety, na jego tle wcale nie wypadłam mądrzej. Powinnam się domyślić, że facet, który nie wie, czy ma w łazience wannę, czy kabinę z natryskiem, nie może być u siebie. Rezerwację i klucze zawsze załatwiał Chochla, więc cap nie łamał sobie głowy prawami własności. Na widok zdjęć o mały włos nie dostał zawału i jestem pewna, że nie udawał. Nie mam pojęcia, kto fotografował i kiedy. W mieszkaniu wielkości przedziału kolejowego nie mógł się zmieścić nikt, kogo bym nie zauważyła. Aż tak bardzo nie byłam pochłonięta pieszczotami Wacka. Bez przesady.

– Człowiek by się nie zmieścił – powiedziała wolno Julia – ale... Pamiętasz, jak Leszek się dziwił, że stary kupił dla firmy kamerę przemysłową? Niewielka kamera da się schować nawet w małym mieszkaniu. Może stary kazał ją zainstalować w garsonierze nad tapczanem? Choć z drugiej strony, po licho miał to robić w cudzej chałupie? Jak myślisz?

– Stary cap odpada – powiedziała z przekonaniem Karolina. – Jeżeli nawet przypadkiem wie, do czego służy kamera, to nie miałby pojęcia, jak ją wykorzystać. To techniczne zero. On nawet wtyczki do kontaktu nie wsadzi właściwie.

– Więc zostaje Edyta, Chochla lub oboje razem. Pasują do siebie jak pies do jeża, jednak coś ich na pewno łączy. Muszą być jakieś powody, dla których Edyta bez protestów odwalała biurową robotę za Marcinka. Nie ulega wątpliwości, że on jest skończonym idiotą, ale coś mi się widzi, że swój rozum ma.

– Każdy idiota ma swój rozum, czego już nie da się powiedzieć o wielu ludziach rozumnych – mruknęła Karolina. Nie mogła sobie darować wpadki w garsonierze i tego, że uwierzyła Mikuli.

Twierdzenie o rozumie Chochli Julia oparła na dość wątłych przesłankach. Zastanowiły ją zdjęcia, które przed świętami otrzymała Edyta. Ten drobny na pozór fakt zdecydował, że skupiła podejrzenia na kierowniku. Od wielu lat uwieczniał na zdjęciach wszystkie oficjalne akademie i uroczystości w zakładzie. Całkiem prywatnie i jakby mimochodem mógł też fotografować część nieoficjalną, czyli tę radosną chwilę wieczoru, gdy znudzeni przemówieniami pracownicy organizowali sobie zajęcia w grupach. Trudno przypuszczać, by Chochla pstrykał dla czystej przyjemności, musiał mieć na uwadze jakiś cel. Kiedy liczba przyjęć gwałtownie zmalała, a jemu znudziło się polowanie na pojedyncze pary, zainstalował kamerę w miejscu, gdzie te pary same przychodziły. Bez kłopotów i zabiegów miał gotowy materiał, choćby do szantażu.

Julia sama zdziwiona była swoim odkryciem. Wcześniej jakoś nie wpadła ani na kamerę, ani na szantaż, dopiero po zjedzeniu łososia, czyli po sporej dawce fosforu, spłynęło na nią olśnienie. W oczach Karoliny dostrzegła szczery zachwyt.

– Rozumujesz logiczniej niż niejeden nadinspektor. Leszek miał genialne wyczucie, że zaprosił cię do analizy zielonej teczki – powiedziała.

– Leszek mi pod... – zaczęła Julia, lecz nie skończyła.

Karolina z wielką uwagą patrzyła w okno. Minę miała tak zaskoczoną, że Julia również się odwróciła. Po drugiej stronie jezdni, na tle klasztornego muru, stała pani prezes. Jej twarz promieniała, co dało się zauważyć nawet ze sporej odległości.

– Z czego ona tak się cieszy? – spytała zdziwiona Julia.

– Z życia się cieszy, poczekaj na ciąg dalszy! – szepnęła przyjaciółka. – Facet kłusem pobiegł w stronę kiosku z kwiatami, zaraz będzie się oświadczał.

Pomyliła się jednak w ocenie faceta. Obok kiosku, niewidocznego z okien restauracji, była smażalnia, reklamująca się wesołym napisem: *Nie bądź taki, jedz kurczaki.* Chwilę później do Mikulowej podszedł wyrośnięty men ze sporym pakunkiem w firmowej reklamówce. Pani Ola filuternie pogroziła mu palcem. Szła potem, a właściwie płynęła u jego boku, uwodzicielsko kołysząc biodrami.

– Ja go znam – wybąkała zaskoczona Julia. – Był w Teatralnej z bossem.

– Rozwijasz się jak rozmaryn. – Karolina pokręciła głową. – Nie wstyd ci hulać w takim towarzystwie?

– Co chcesz! On podobno jest przystojny.

Karolina wykrzywiła się z niechęcią.

– To tylko opakowanie zewnętrzne, ale ręczę ci, że cała maszyneria w środku jest do niczego. Sztuczny kulturysta, pędzony na sterydach. Zauważyłaś, jak daleko trzymał łapy od tułowia? Oni wszyscy tak chodzą, jakby pod pachami mieli kaktusy. Zresztą nie tylko pod pachami. Widziałaś, jak on szeroko stawia nogi. Fuj! Pożytku z takiego tyle, co kot nasikał.

– Chyba napłakał?

– Płakać to będzie ta idiotka. Na oko widać, że facio z dychę młodszy od niej i na subtelnego nie wygląda. Mam nadzieję, że zdążę prysnąć z Budampolexu, zanim Olutka mianuje go dyrektorem.

– Karaluch z nimi tańcował, jak mawia Leszek – mruknęła Julia i na wspomnienie magistra Wydronia wróciła jej ochota, by podzielić się z Karoliną swoimi wątpliwościami. Po sobotniej dyskotece wciąż miała nieodparte wrażenie, że serdeczny przyjaciel zaprosił ją do Teatralnej nieprzypadkowo, że zagrał nieczysto i coś próbował ukryć. Z detalami zrelacjonowała imprezę i swoje domysły.

– Podobno za nikogo nie wolno ręczyć głową – powiedziała Karolina – ale powiem ci, że gdybym miała dwie głowy, jedną bym za Wydronia oddała. On nie jest zdolny do świństw, a już na pewno nie wobec przyjaciół. Poza tym ten bukiet, którego w chałupie nawet nie miałabym gdzie wstawić, wcale nie jest twój – roześmiała się przekornie – facet myślał, że ty to ja, więc nawet gdyby coś, to spodziewał się mnie, nie ciebie. Jaśniej nie umiem tego wyłożyć. Podobnie jak Edyta nie wierzę w nadmiar zbiegów okoliczności, natomiast Leszkowi wierzę.

Przegadały w Zajeździe prawie trzy godziny, lecz z tego gadania wykluł się jedynie ogólny plan, właściwie zarys planu działania. Kłopoty w firmie, dociekania aprilistów i wizyta u Bujały, to był jeden biegun zainteresowań, na drugim zaś usadził się paranoik Chochla ze swoimi zdjęciami. Dla Karoliny Chochla był najważniejszy. Gdyby kompromitujące fotki dostały się w ręce Mikulowej, a także paru innych osób, mogły narobić sporo zamieszania. W małym mieście małe sensacje rozchodzą się dużo szybciej niż wielkie w dużym. Magister Cierniak nie życzyła sobie aż takiej popularności. Dlatego najpierw chciała zająć się Chochlą. Julia stanowczo odradzała rozmowy, wizyty w garsonierze i tym podobne zabiegi. Jej zdaniem tylko dobry i na dodatek znajomy adwokat mógł po przyjacielsku podpowiedzieć, jak unieszkodliwić głupiego Marcinka, odbierając mu zdjęcia i negatywy. Musiał być jakiś sposób, upierała się przy swoim. Dłużej niż do soboty nie mogły zwlekać z wizytą w Toruniu, bo po niedzieli Karolina jechała służbowo do Warszawy i miała tam zostać nieco dłużej. Obiecała, że jak tylko wróci, zastanowią się nad dotarciem do Bujały. Julia przytaknęła i nawet mrugnięciem oka nie zdradziła swoich zamiarów. Od trzech dni, odkąd w sklepie na osiedlu kupiła prześliczną bluzkę, rozsadzała ją chęć działania. Wyszukała numer sekretariatu Bujały i właśnie następnego dnia zamierzała umówić się na spotkanie. Bardzo starannie przygotowywała swoją nową rolę i nie mogła doczekać się premiery. Jakiś głos wewnętrzny podpowiadał jej, że odniesie detektywistyczny sukces, którym zaskoczy Karolinę i Leszka. Nawet gdyby pan prezes firmy ubezpieczeniowej Spokój okazał się równie cudny jak Mikula, gotowa była poświęcić się dla sztuki i dla przyjaciół.

Wyszły z Zajazdu dokarmione cieleśnie, lecz wciąż niedogadane.

Telefon oderwał Konrada od komputera. Próbował przeczekać, niestety, nie dało rady. Irytujące sygnały jeden po drugim wwiercały się w uszy. Wstał z ociąganiem.

– Nie stęskniłeś się za mną, ssaczku? Bo ja za tobą bardzo! – Cichy, zmysłowy głos Karoliny podziałał na niego całkiem niezgodnie z zamierzeniami rozmówczyni. Przypomniał sobie, z kim mijał się w drzwiach jej mieszkania, dobrze pamiętał też to, że ostatnio była wiecznie zajęta, rozkojarzona i nie miała dla niego czasu. Ale najbardziej był obrażony o Mikulę, rzecz jasna.

– Przepraszam, z kim rozmawiam, bo nie dosłyszałem? – spytał, siląc się na chłodny, uprzejmy ton.

Był przekonany, że dziewczyna zdenerwuje się, rzuci słuchawkę lub palnie jakieś głupstwo, i właśnie na to czekał. Karolina roześmiała się, jakby usłyszała najlepszy dowcip.

– Masz prawo dąsać się przez dwie minutki. Zaraz potem przyjeżdżaj do mnie, bo mi strasznie zimno. Chyba przestali palić albo co – powiedziała tym samym erotycznym głosem, przez który przebijał śmiech.

– Niestety, tym razem to ja jestem zajęty.

– No widzisz? Już sobie przypomniałeś z kim rozmawiasz, za moment sobie przypomnisz, jak ci ze mną dobrze i przyjedziesz, prawda?

Bardzo chciał odpowiedzieć, że nie ma mowy, niech sobie wybije z głowy i tak dalej, lecz kusiła tak pięknie, że w końcu ugiął się i pojechał. Przez całą drogę wyrzucał sobie brak konsekwencji. Ze dwa razy gotów był zawrócić, lecz na dwujezdniówce nie mógł, na przejeździe kolejowym też nie, a potem to już musiał nieźle się namęczyć, żeby znaleźć miejsce do zaparkowania samochodu. Jeszcze na schodach zastanawiał się, czy dobrze robi, lecąc jak ćma do ognia. Karolina otworzyła mu w staniczku i figach. W mieszkaniu było cieplutko.

– Jeżeli ci zimno, to czemu chodzisz prawie goła? – spytał.

– Mnie zimno? – zdziwiła się bardzo szczerze. – Przecież wiesz, że mnie nigdy nie jest zimno.

Mógł się tego domyślić, ale najwidoczniej nie chciał. Postanowił sobie, że nie będzie jej robił żadnych wyrzutów i nie spyta o Mikulę.

– Jak już koniecznie chciałaś mieć towarzystwo, mogłaś zadzwonić do Mikuli – powiedział zaraz potem.

– Do Mikuli? Po jakie licho miałabym dzwonić do Mikuli?

– Chcesz powiedzieć, że w sobotę to nie jego tu spotkałem?

Przysiadła na poręczy fotela i spojrzała na Konrada tak, jakby widziała go pierwszy raz w życiu. Ucieszyła się, że rozpoznał własnego dyrektora, i wyjaśniła spokojnie jak dziecku, że szefowie potrzebują czasem porady prawnej także po godzinach pracy. Ona jest tylko personelem i musi wykazać się dyspozycyjnością. Budampolex 2 ma poważne kłopoty, więc przesiedzieli z Mikulą do północy, żeby znaleźć rozwiązanie zgodne z prawem i korzystne dla firmy.

– Dlaczego nie w biurze, tylko u ciebie w domu? – spytał.

– Widziałeś, ile tu było książek? Miałam je wszystkie wieźć do firmy? – spytała mocno zdziwiona. – Coś mi się wydaje, ssaczku, że bredzisz.

Najgorsze, że Konradowi wydawało się całkiem podobnie. Miał nie robić wyrzutów, miał nie pytać i dwu minut nie wytrzymał. Teraz też korciło go, by dowiedzieć się czegoś więcej o kłopotach Mikuli. Tak do końca nie wierzył Karolinie, szczególnie po rozmowie z panią Henią. Sam pomysł, że jego rywalem mógłby być opasły dyrektor, wydał mu się okropny.

– Przy takim bałaganiarskim dyrektorze firma musi mieć kłopoty – powiedział niechętnie. – Facet, który pozwala sobie zwędzić listę dłużników, jest całkiem niepoważny. Zgodzisz się ze mną?

Patrzyła na niego uważnie.

– Skąd o tym wiesz? – spytała.

– Wiem! – odparł krótko i nawet nie zauważył, że jej piękne oczy zrobiły się czujne i chłodne.

Po pracy Karolina wracała z Konradem, Julia zaś po raz pierwszy od dość dawna miała jechać sama.

– Podwieziesz mnie, biedroneczko, do śródmieścia? – spytał Leszek i tytułem wyjaśnienia dodał, że jego zielona strzała rozkraczyła się rano przed domem.

Z parkingu wyjechali tuż za samochodem Orzechowicza. Karolina żywo gestykulowała, on chyba się śmiał i Julia poczuła drobniutkie ukłucie zazdrości. To nie była zazdrość o konkretnego mężczyznę, broń Boże, to była tęsknota za kimś własnym. Wiele by dała, żeby mieć obok siebie prawdziwego faceta z krwi i kości, poważnego, mądrego, który by przytulił, pocieszył i wyprowadził na spacer. Mógłby być podobny do inżyniera Orzechowicza, czemu nie? Mógłby też wyglądać jak ulubiony aktor i tylko charakter mieć inżyniera Orzechowicza. Na dobrą sprawę nie znała charakteru ani jednego, ani drugiego pana. Wymyślanie było jej pasją od bardzo dawna. Te wszystkie sceniczne obsesje nie były niczym innym, jak namiastką tego, co chciałaby przeżyć. Pożyczała sobie od znanych aktorów powierzchowność, tak jak się pożycza kostium teatralny, wypełniała ich głowy swoimi myślami, kazała im mówić niekoniecznie tekstem scenariusza i była w tym wszystkim naiwna jak pensjonarka. Gdybyż jeszcze wierzyła, że zagra w filmie lub na scenie, że pozna tuzów polskiego aktorstwa, to co innego, ale akurat w tym względzie była realistką. Utknęła w nudnym, prowincjonalnym mieście, pracę miała nudną i głupią, więc broniła się, jak umiała. Jedynym ratunkiem była radykalna zmiana, lecz nie fryzury, nie sukienki, tylko własnego życia. Miłość mogłaby ją zmienić, czemu nie. Kłopot był tylko jeden: nie miała w kim się zakochać!

Zajęta własnymi myślami, zapomniała, że ma w samochodzie pasażera. Leszek nie odzywał się, siedział cicho nawet wówczas, gdy całkiem odruchowo skręciła w kierunku swojego osiedla. Pomyłkę zauważyła w połowie wiaduktu na Wroniej.

– Ojejku, dlaczego nic nie mówisz! – wykrzyknęła przerażona.

– A to nie jest porwanie? – udał zmartwionego.

– Niestety, to tylko gapa ze mnie wylazła.

– Mogę być porwany na gapę byle... byle przez ciebie. Jeżeli uznasz, że bredzę, przerwij mi, ale w końcu muszę ci powiedzieć, że zwariowałem na twoim punkcie. Nie umiem sobie znaleźć miejsca... myślę o tobie w pracy i w domu... nawet po nocach mi się śnisz. Kocham cię, biedronko. Nie przerwałaś mi, więc... nie uważasz, że bredzę, prawda?

Początkowo sądziła, że to dalszy ciąg wygłupów, spojrzała na chłopaka i zrozumiała, że on nie żartuje. Wdarł się w jej myśli, jakby w nich czytał, niemal się oświadczył, a ona zamiast radości czuła skrępowanie. Chciała mieć obok siebie mężczyznę, lecz innego. Kochać też chciała innego

– Nie przerwałam ci – powiedziała, patrząc pilnie na drogę – ponieważ nie wiem, co mam odpowiedzieć. Bardzo cię lubię, dobrze się czuję w twoim towarzystwie... wszelkie inne zapewnienia byłyby już przesadą. Ty masz ułożone życie...

– Raczej zmarnowane – przerwał. – Nie liczyłem, że rzucisz mi się na szyję... Myślałem tylko, że jestem ci mniej obojętny.

– Ludzie, których lubię, nie są mi obojętni – zaprzeczyła gwałtownie.

– Nie uważasz, że słowo „lubię” jest wyjątkowo nijakie? Jak już nie można nic człowiekowi powiedzieć, ani że się go kocha, pożąda czy choćby nienawidzi, to się mu mówi, że jest lubiany. Henię też pewnie lubisz?

Milczała. Czuła się dotknięta, lecz niezbyt mocno. Rozumiała rozgoryczenie Leszka, nie chciała go jeszcze bardziej pogrążać i nic mądrzejszego ponad to, co powiedziała, nie przychodziło jej do głowy. Wysadziła go, tak jak sobie życzył, na placu Wolności i zawróciła w kierunku osiedla. Rozstali się właściwie bez słowa. Wysiadł ze spuszczoną głową, nawet nie zauważył, że pomachała mu ręką. O ileż łatwiej byłoby dać kosza takiemu Serafinowi, pomyślała. Zresztą Serafin zmył się bez dawania kosza, a ona prawie tego nie zauważyła. Telefonował co jakiś czas, opowiadał, że jest bardzo zajęty, i robił dziwne aluzje, których nie chwytała.

Ostatni raz spotkała go kilka dni wcześniej na parkingu przed domem. Wysiadała właśnie, kiedy podjechał z piskiem opon i o mały włos nie staranował matiza. Opel, granatowy i błyszczący nowością, nie zrobił na niej większego wrażenia, lecz kierowcę najchętniej posłałaby do wszystkich diabłów. Chronicznie nie znosiła kaskaderskich wygłupów, była na nie uczulona, więc z furią napadła na chłopaka.

– O co ci chodzi? Ty wiesz, jakie on ma hamulce? – bronił się, niezbyt przejęty jej krzykami.

– Co komu po hamulcach, jak kierowca wariat!

– Fajny mam wozik, co? Ty wiesz, ile on pali?

– A co mnie to obchodzi?

– Tyle, ile się wleje! Dobre, nie? Wybierzemy się w sobotę na dyskę? Poznasz moich kumpli.

– Wyjeżdżam w sobotę.

– Szkoda. Sporo byś się mogła dowiedzieć o interesach i w ogóle.

– Nie prowadzę żadnych interesów. Pracuję na etacie.

– Wiem. Twoi starzy prowadzą, no nie?

– Wobec tego rozmawiaj z nimi!

Odeszła, choć próbował ją zatrzymać, coś tam jeszcze opowiadał, coś obiecywał.

Głupi to on był zawsze, ale bodaj po raz pierwszy przemawiał do niej tonem pyszałkowatej wyższości. Nigdy wcześniej nie popisywał się forsą, wozem ani kumplami. To był znak, że wplątał się w nieczyste interesy. Wolała nie dochodzić w jakie i szczerze mówiąc, niewiele ją to obchodziło. Nawet nie mogła powiedzieć, że go lubi. Co innego Leszek. Uśmiechnęła się leciutko na wspomnienie oświadczyn. Bo to chyba były oświadczyny? W tej dziedzinie miała niewielką praktykę. Owszem, różni koledzy mówili jej miłe rzeczy, jednak żaden nie wariował z jej powodu ani nie cierpiał na bezsenność. Choćby z tego względu Leszek Wydroń zasłużył sobie na trwałe miejsce w sercu Julii. Poczuła się jak prawdziwa kobieta, niemal pożeraczka serc i było jej troszkę miło i troszkę smutno.

– Brak osobowości pokrywamy niewolniczym pryncypa... pializmem – dukała Henia. Uparła się, że zapozna członkinie klubu medytacyjnego ze swoimi notatkami z kursu. Widać jednak niezbyt starannie pisała lub oświetlenie suszarni było kiepskie, bo czytała z wyraźnym trudem. Julia nie miała zamiaru wchodzić, dyskretnie zajrzała do środka, a ponieważ nigdzie nie dostrzegła Wandy Pasieczko, ulotniła się cichutko. Szła raźnym, sprężystym krokiem w kierunku Kujawskiej i zastanawiała się, czy wizyta u Wandy w domu to dobry pomysł. Zarzekała się co prawda, że nigdy więcej, lecz potrzebowała jeszcze kilku informacji na temat lokalu nr 23. Po drodze wstąpiła do sklepu po jakąś bombonierkę, żeby przychylniej nastawić Wandę, i przy ladzie stanęła oko w oko z Marcinem Chochlą. Przez moment patrzyli na siebie w milczeniu.

– Pan tutaj? – spytała Julia.

– Tego... no tak, chleb i mannę kupuję – odpowiedział.

Poczekał na nią i wyszli ze sklepu razem. Zaczęła gwałtownie myśleć, jak go spławić, w którą przecznicę skręcić, żeby uwolnić się od niechcianego towarzystwa. Już miała powiedzieć, że bardzo się śpieszy, już zaczerpnęła powietrza i w tym samym momencie doznała gwałtownego olśnienia. Los sam wpychał jej w ręce największego wroga Karoliny, a ona, zamiast stawić mu czoła, zastanawiała się nad ucieczką! Przecież nie była już głupią lebiodą, tylko piękną Julią, której parę godzin wcześniej oświadczył się mężczyzna.

– Dawno pana nie widziałam, panie Marcinie. Zniknął pan tak nagle... smutno bez pana w firmie – zawiesiła głos i spojrzała powłóczyście w rybie ślepka Chochli.

– Przecież nie zniknąłem... tego, no... tylko nie pracuję już u Mikuli – wyjaśnił. – Nadojeło mi wszystko razem, tego, i mam inny pomysł na resztę życia. Bo to człowiek wie, ile mu jeszcze zostało? – zauważył filozoficznie.

– A wie pan, że mnie też nadojeło i zwalniam się z firmy? – zawołała uradowana. – Właśnie jutro idę sobie załatwiać nową pracę.

Chochla wyraźnie pożerał ją oczami, jednak znalazł w sobie tyle taktu, by spytać, gdzie niby Julia chce odejść. Nazwisko Bujały wzbudziło w nim prawdziwą wesołość.

– Jakby pani nie chciał przyjąć, niech się pani powoła na mnie!

– Mówi pan poważnie? Naprawdę chciałby mi pan pomóc?

– Tego, no... ja dużo mogę – stwierdził z jawną dumą. – Ale... pomoc... wie pani... nic za darmo.

Poczekaj, ty gzie przebrzydły, już ja ci zapłacę, pomyślała mściwie Julia, lecz wciąż uśmiechała się do Chochli najserdeczniej, jak umiała. Wyjaśnił jej po swojemu, że Bujała to najpierwszy w mieście krętacz, łajdak i złamany męski organ rozrodczy. Nie precyzował, na czym opiera swoje sądy, i niewiele więcej chciał zdradzić, choć czarowała go i zasypywała komplementami. Łykał chciwie miłe słówka, aż mu wielka grdyka na cienkiej szyjce skakała niczym piłka pingpongowa, jednak wolał mówić o Julii niż o Bujale. Zauważył, że się zmieniła i wypiękniała.

– Tego, no... jak ma pani trochę czasu, to może byśmy do mnie... na herbatkę? – spytał z nadzieją w głosie.

Julia bardzo ładnie weszła w rolę kobiety zaskoczonej, spłoszonej i jednocześnie zaintrygowanej propozycją. Szli cały czas w kierunku Kujawskiej. Już widać było blok, w którym mieszkała Wanda Pasieczko, a najprawdopodobniej także Chochla. Dziewczyna zatrzymała się na rogu. Wolała nie wchodzić w oczy znajomym i nieznajomym. Westchnęła i spróbowała zmienić temat.

– Wie pan, coraz częściej nachodzi mnie ochota, żeby rzucić to miasto i prysnąć gdzieś. Nie wiem, do Szczyrku, Łeby albo Kazimierza, wszystko jedno gdzie, byle jak najdalej stąd – palnęła bez większego zastanowienia.

– Tego... na zawsze, czy tak na tydzień albo dwa? – spytał. Wlepił w nią oczy i wyraźnie czekał na odpowiedź.

– Na tydzień albo dwa – przytaknęła. – Na zawsze byłoby trudno.

– Mogę załatwić nam taki wyjazd – powiedział. – Tylko tego, no, potrzebuję trochę czasu, żeby przygotować... no... wiadomo... Więc jak? Nie wycofasz się, nie zostawisz mnie na lodzie?

Takiej oferty nie przewidziała. Ona i Chochla na ryneczku w Kazimierzu? Opanowała wybuch wesołości i spojrzała na gzika. Przestępował z nogi na nogę, zaglądał jej w oczy i czekał na odpowiedź. Pomyślała, że „trochę czasu" wystarczy, by znaleźć sensowny powód do nieruszania się z Włocławka. Lekko spłoszona, lekko zawstydzona obiecała, że nie zawiedzie i nie zostawi na lodzie. W tym momencie liczyła głównie na numer telefonu Marcinka, lecz się zawiodła. Skwapliwie zapisał na bilecie autobusowym numer jej komórki, obiecał się odezwać. Na pożegnanie podała mu rękę.

– Słuchaj... tego... a Bujałę sobie odpuść. Szkoda cię dla takiego ścierwa! Jak zechcesz, tego, to załatwię ci każdą robotę w mieście... No, po powrocie z wczasów. – Zachichotał uwodzicielsko.

– Dobrze! – odparła, wyszarpując rękę z jego szponów. Odeszła pośpiesznie z wielkim zamętem w głowie. Dziwiło ją, że Chochla ani słowem nie wspomniał o firmie, nie interesował się, co o nim mówią i jak sobie bez niego radzą. Wytłumaczenie znalazła dwojakie: albo miał inne źródło informacji i widział wszystko, co chciał wiedzieć, albo ona zrobiła na nim tak oszałamiające wrażenie, że stracił głowę. To drugie wytłumaczenie, choć połechtało jej damską próżność, nie było specjalnie miłe. Kobiety oczywiście nie mają wpływu na to, komu się podobają, lecz zachwyt w oczach takiego Chochli do przyjemności nie należy. A jednak Julię rozsadzała duma. Czuła się niemal jak Mata Hari. Przed straceniem, ma się rozumieć.

Najgorsza chwila poranka to ta, kiedy rozgrzana snem noga, zamiast trafić w kapeć, dotknie zimnej podłogi. Julia gwałtownie skuliła się pod kołdrą w pozycji embriona. O szóstej rano nic jej nie cieszyło z wyjątkiem ciepłego łóżka. W kuchni matka programowała ojca na cały nadchodzący dzień. Musisz... powinieneś... pamiętaj... choć raz opanuj język... Dziwne, pomyślała Julia, jak ojciec może opanować język, jeśli prawie nigdy się nie odzywa?

– Julka, bój się kija! Czy ty wiesz, która godzina? – krzyknęła pani Blendowa. – Beze mnie oboje byście zginęli. Ani samodzielnie wstać, ani śniadania zrobić. Dobrze, że jeszcze każde za siebie sika!

Poganiana energicznymi okrzykami matki powlekła się niechętnie do łazienki. Zawiesiła zaspane oko na lustrze i zamiast rozczochranej dziewuszki zobaczyła kobietę, też wprawdzie rozczochraną, ale za to bardzo intrygującą. Zaledwie dzień wcześniej przeżyła oświadczyny jednego mężczyzny, z drugim nawiązała szpiegowski romans, wobec trzeciego zaś miała bardzo konkretne plany, które za kilka godzin zamierzała wprowadzić w życie. Myśl o Bujale natychmiast postawiła ją na nogi. Założyła sobie, że spotkają się właśnie tego dnia i nie brała pod uwagę takich drobiazgów jak delegacja czy chwilowa niechęć pana prezesa do oglądania kogokolwiek poza własną sekretarką.

– Nowa bluzka? – spytała matka, spoglądając krytycznie na Julię.

– Ładna, prawda?

– Zwariowałaś?! Żadnego umiaru, żadnego zastanowienia! Jak kupujesz płyty, to tylko płyty, jak teraz wzięło cię na ciuchy, to mi supermarket z domu robisz. Żeby to jeszcze było co ładnego! Mało to razy ci powtarzam, że nie szata zdobi człowieka!

Matka jak mało kto potrafiła podcinać Julii skrzydła, gasić radość w zarodku. Wyskakiwała z ostrą krytyką właśnie wtedy, kiedy córka oczekiwała drobnej choćby aprobaty. Pani Emilia nie chwaliła jej, bo w swoim rozumieniu nie miała za co. Należała do licznego grona zacnych i nieomylnych niewiast, które mają monopol na gust, takt i wiedzę. Julia nie była do niej podobna, z uporem podkreślała swoją inność, więc sama skazywała się na potępienie.

– Tato, prawda, że dobrze wyglądam?

– Mhm – przyznał pan Blenda i żeby z kretesem nie podpaść żonie, natychmiast dodał: – Ale matka ma rację!

– Biedny tatku, nie można zadowolić owcy i wilka jednocześnie – powiedziała Julia ze śmiechem. W ojcowskim „mhm" usłyszała męski podziw. Niczego więcej nie pragnęła tego ranka.

W drodze do pracy powtórzyła sobie punkt po punkcie cały scenariusz – nie przewidziała tylko jednego: że to będzie bardzo ciężki dzień. Dyrektor w gabinecie, Edyta za biurkiem, Leszek z Karoliną u siebie, a ona oczywiście zapomniała telefonu komórkowego. Jak na spiskowca, działającego w tajemnicy nawet przed przyjaciółmi, nie popisała się przebiegłością. Żeby zadzwonić do sekretariatu Bujały, musiała choć na moment zostać sama. Nieżyczliwie zerkała na Edytę, która nie wypuszczała słuchawki z rąk. Oho, udaje spokojną, ale jest wściekła, pomyślała. Co ona wyprawia?

Sekretarka nic specjalnego nie wyprawiała. Wystukiwała numer, odkładała słuchawkę, znowu wystukiwała i zaczynała bębnić palcami po biurku. Potem znowu to samo, jakby nie mogła się zdecydować, do kogo ma dzwonić i jak długo czekać na połączenie. Wreszcie chyba się udało, bo westchnęła z wyraźną ulgą.

– Gdzie łazisz, gamoniu? – spytała bez zbędnych wstępów. – Poczekaj chwilę! – Zasłoniła słuchawkę ręką i poprosiła Julię o herbatę. Odczekała moment, aż zaintrygowana dziewczyna wyszła do kuchenki i dopiero wówczas wróciła do rozmowy.

Podsłuchiwanie nie jest rzeczą prostą. Edyta mówiła cicho, siedziała daleko i tylko pojedyncze słowa docierały do uszu Julii. Zapominasz, kto ci... muszę natychmiast... Miała niejasne podejrzenie, właściwie tylko cień przeczucia, że sekretarka usiłowała postawić na baczność zaspanego Chochlę. Niestety, niczego więcej się nie dowiedziała. Do kuchenki wkroczyła Henia z naręczem ścierek i wymówkami. Chodziło oczywiście o spotkanie medytacyjne pań, na którym pomoc gospodarcza nie dostrzegła Julii. Dziewczyna aż się żachnęła na taką niesprawiedliwość.

– Ciekawie mówiłaś o braku osobowości – zauważyła. – Wyszłam przed końcem, bo byłam umówiona z mamą.

– Co tam osobowość! – wykrzyknęła z triumfem Henia. – Szkoda, że nie słyszałaś, jak dołożyłam tym wszystkim babkom za bezmyślność. Dla nich nic nie istnieje poza chłopem, dzieciakami i pieniędzmi. Żadnej do głowy nie przyjdzie, że są sprawy ważniejsze. Ale, ale, żebym nie zapomniała. Julciu, możesz mnie poratować skromną pożyczką? Potrzebuję trochę forsy – Henia zniżyła głos do szeptu.

– Ile to jest „trochę"? – spytała Julia.

– Potrzebuję osiemdziesiąt.

– Jasne. Mam wolną stówkę.

– Mówię o tysiącach – szepnęła konspiracyjnie Henia.

– Chcesz pożyczyć osiemdziesiąt tysięcy? Ładne mi trochę! – obruszyła się Julia. – W domu mam dwa, które odłożyłam na czarną godzinę. Jeżeli to cię urządza, to proszę.

– A od rodziców nie mogłabyś wziąć?

Julia tylko zamachała rękami. Dobrze znała podejście rodziców do pożyczek, poza tym kwota nawet jej wydała się nieskromna. Więcej nie zwracała uwagi na kwaśną minę Heni ani na jej mruczando, z którego wynikało, że pieniądze potroją się w ciągu dwóch miesięcy.

Bez słowa zaniosła herbatę Edycie, a chwilę później dorwała się wreszcie do upragnionego telefonu. Dociekliwa sekretarka Bujały chciała wiedzieć stanowczo za dużo. Nie wystarczyło jej, że magister inżynier Julia Blenda ma życzenie spotkać się z panem prezesem. Z pięć razy pytała w jakiej sprawie.

– Gdybym chciała pani powiedzieć w jakiej sprawie, nie musiałabym widzieć się z prezesem! – powiedziała wyniośle Julia. – Proszę mnie umówić. To wszystko, czego od pani oczekuję.

Poskutkowało. Audiencja została wyznaczona na poniedziałek, na godzinę piętnastą. Był dopiero piątek i Julia odrobinę się zdenerwowała. Nie lubiła czekać. Zajrzała na moment do pokoju magistrów. Leszek od rana zachowywał się tak, jakby dzień wcześniej nie było żadnej rozmowy, żadnych wyznań. Złapała tylko jego zachwycone spojrzenie, na które odpowiedziała uśmiechem. Karolina na jej widok jednym ruchem odsunęła papiery, zawalające biurko. Ze znawstwem oceniła bluzkę i zaczęła się głośno zastanawiać, czy przypadkiem Julia nie jest zakochana. Leszek cicho wymknął się z pokoju.

– Co on dzisiaj taki niedorobiony? – zastanowiła się Karolina i natychmiast zmieniła temat. – Juleczko, czy ty wiesz, że Marta wyszła za mąż za mecenasa?

– Nie wiem. Jaka Marta? Jaki mecenas?

– O Boże! – westchnęła Karolina. – Wciąż zapominam, z kim gadam. Politechnika warszawska pięć lat później, a ja mówię o kochanym toruńskim grajdole dziesięć lat wcześniej!

– A mogłabyś gadać logicznie, żeby politechnika też zrozumiała? – spytała Julia.

Spojrzały na siebie i jednocześnie wybuchnęły śmiechem. Jak na grajdoł i stolicę rozumiały się doskonale.

Karolina od kilku dni wydzwaniała popołudniami do dawnych przyjaciół, szukała kontaktów i odnawiała znajomości. Koledzy ze studiów, na których najbardziej liczyła, nie kwapili się z pomocą. Ich wymówki były dość czytelne. Głupio jest brać honorarium od koleżanki po fachu, ale jeszcze głupiej narobić się za darmo. Co do jednego byli zgodni: najlepszym ekspertem od ciemnych sprawek i szantażu był mecenas Wojciech Wąsik. Zadzwoniła do kancelarii, żeby się wstępnie umówić i padła z wrażenia. Sekretarka w kwietniu zaproponowała jej termin lipcowy. Niestety, tak długo czekać nie mogła, a słusznie podejrzewała, że i Chochla nie zechce. I właśnie wczoraj wieczorem jedna z koleżanek napomknęła, że mecenas ożenił się z Martą Wilani. To była najcudowniejsza wiadomość od kilkunastu dni.

– Jeżeli ją znasz, to jedziemy i nie ma sprawy! – wykrzyknęła Julia.

– O Boże, czy znam Martę? Słuchaj stara, ja dla niej i Kamili ukradłam kiedyś bułkę w sklepie. Ty czujesz? Ja, studentka prawa, ukradłam bułkę!

– I co?

– Nic. Zeżarłyśmy na kolację, bo to była wielka bagietka. Potem sumienie mnie ruszyło i po stypendium oddałam w sklepie pieniądze. Zabajerowałam, że przez pomyłkę, że coś tam... ale dziewczyny do dziś myślą, że ukradłam. Julka, co to było za życie! Marta z Kamilą mieszkały u właścicielki kamienicy na pierwszym piętrze, ja na drugim u takiej pani Krysi. Jedno stuknięcie w sufit lub podłogę znaczyło... Nieważne! Stukałyśmy stale. Nigdy wcześniej i nigdy potem nie byłam taka szczęśliwa jak wtedy, kiedy plastycy przyjęli mnie do swojej paczki. Oni wszędzie jeździli i chodzili całą grupą, a mnie zabierali w charakterze maskotki. Studenci piątego roku sztuk pięknych i taki smarkaty pierwszak z prawa! Ty wiesz, jaka byłam dumna? Przy nich poznawałam życie i uczyłam się rozumieć kolory. Do dzisiaj pamiętam szałowe stroje dziewczyn, kapelusze zdobione żywą jarzębiną, torby z makatek, jakieś spódnice z haftem. I swoją pierwszą miłość też pamiętam. Facet miał na imię Rafał i niestety kochał się w Marcie. Uparł się, że namaluje mój portret. To miała być „Dziewczynka z brzoskwiniami" czy jakoś tak. Nie wiem, bo jak zobaczyłam siebie z piersiami wielkości dyni, obraziłam się i nie chciałam więcej pozować. Może i szkoda, bo Rafał był podobno bardzo zdolnym malarzem. Wiesz, kto go bardzo przypomina? Orzechowicz. Pewnie dlatego tak długo z nim wytrzymuję.

Ledwie Karolina wspomniała Orzechowicza, zerknęła na zegarek i gwałtownie się poderwała.

Pożegnanie inżyniera Kicińskiego odbyło się w wąskim, nawet bardzo wąskim gronie. Nikomu z kierownictwa firmy do głowy nie przyszło, że można żegnać pracownika, który w pojęciu szefów niczego wielkiego nie dokonał, rozwalił dział i na koniec sam się wynosił. Była to ocena z gruntu niesprawiedliwa, ale o tym wiedział Kiciński, Konrad i ci pracownicy działu, którzy już wcześniej odeszli. Personalna oddała inżynierowi dokumenty i właściwie był wolny.

– To co, panie kolego, życzę sukcesów i zwijam żagle. Nic tu po mnie – powiedział, sięgając po płaszcz.

– O, nie, nie! – zaprotestował Konrad. – Jak się Polacy rozstawali, to wypijali po kawie. Tradycję trzeba szanować!

Postawił na biurku trzy filiżanki i talerzyk z francuskimi ciastkami. Nie zwracał uwagi na zdziwioną minę Kicińskiego.

– A to trzecie nakrycie, dla kogo?

– Zapowiedziała się pani prezes! – parsknął śmiechem Konrad.

Zagadka wyjaśniła się z chwilą wejścia Karoliny. Kiciński wydawał się wzruszony i szczerze zadowolony. Nie spodziewał się, że zostawiał w firmie aż dwie życzliwe dusze, to raz, a dwa, uwalniał się wreszcie od kompleksów prowincjonalnego przedsiębiorstwa. Miał na ten temat całą teorię. Nie wiązał prowincjonalizmu z prowincją, tylko z wąskim, głupim i ślepym sposobem myślenia. Wedle tej teorii ludzie pokroju Mikulów będą prowincjuszami bez względu na miejsce zamieszkania. Dla nich nie ma znaczenia, czy to Paryż, Tokio czy Lipno, obojętnie, gdzie się znajdą, szerzą swoją krzykliwość, brak manier i podstawowej ogłady. Myślenie ograniczają do interesów, pracują głównie łokciami, nie liczą się z nikim i z niczym.

– Chcę przez to powiedzieć – dowodził inżynier Kiciński – że dla prawdziwej inteligencji, tej z tradycjami, z kindersztubą, nadeszły ciężkie czasy. Mierzi mnie to, co się w tej chwili dzieje, ten radosny pochód ludzi ze slumsów, z melin, znikąd. Rozmawiałem niedawno, panie Konradzie, z pańskim wujem, inżynierem Orskim. Powiedział mi...

– Inżynier Orski nie jest moim wujem – przerwał mu Konrad i zmienił temat.

Wkrótce Kiciński zaczął się zbierać.

– Czy on powiedział coś niestosownego? – spytała Karolina po jego wyjściu. – Tak się zjeżyłeś, że niemal widziałam, jak ci kolce wyłażą.

Chciał spytać, czy na głowie i czy to przypadkiem nie rogi, jednak dał spokój. Wolał nie uchodzić za zazdrosnego typa. Wrócił do Kicińskiego.

– Faceta mierzi pochód ludzi ze slumsów, a mnie gadanie o rodzinnych tradycjach i kulturze. Zauważyłem pewną prawidłowość: jeżeli wykształcony facet do niczego nie dochodzi, to uzasadnienia szuka w inteligenckich korzeniach. Żebyś sobie przypadkiem nie pomyślała, że on gamoń, to ci wciska kit o naukach wyniesionych z domu: nie pchaj się łokciami, pracuj główką, szanuj starszych i nie czyń drugiemu, co tobie niemiłe. Znam jednego, który tak mówi i tak robi, ale co do reszty, mam poważne wątpliwości.

– A ty? Co ty o sobie mówisz?

– Zaszedłem wyżej, niż kiedykolwiek marzyłem.

Nie widział lub nie chciał widzieć niedowierzania w oczach dziewczyny. Sprzątnął ślady po uczcie, otworzył okno i zaczął porządkować dyskietki. Zewnętrznie zachowywał spokój, a w środku dręczyło go rozdygotanie, które brało się nie wiadomo z czego. Kiciński? Właściwie nie. Nic oryginalnego w tym, co mówił, nie było. Karolina? Chyba tak. Siedziała przy biurku Konrada, piękna i spokojna, bawiła się złożoną kartką papieru i mówiła o służbowym wyjeździe do Warszawy. Mikula załatwił duży kontrakt, jechali razem, żeby dopiąć i podpisać umowę. Nie słuchał, zajęty własnymi myślami. Usłużna wyobraźnia podsunęła mu obraz hotelowego pokoju i scenkę żywcem wyjętą z landrynkowej serii. Zamrugał oczami.

– Co o tym myślisz? – pytała Karolina.

Akurat to, o czym myślał, zupełnie nie nadawało się do powtórzenia.

– Nie chcę, żebyś z nim jechała do Warszawy! – powiedział stanowczym głosem.

Najwidoczniej mówiła o czymś zupełnie innym, bo spojrzała na Konrada z nieukrywaną kpiną.

– Pytałam, czy przyjmiesz moje zaproszenie na obiad?

– A, tak, oczywiście.

– Nie tak bardzo oczywiście, ssaczku. W ogóle mnie nie słuchałeś, prawda? Ale zaproszenie podtrzymuję.

Konrad nie chciał się nawet przed sobą przyznać, że ze wszystkich uczuć, które nim miotały, najautentyczniejsza była zazdrość. Nie wiedział, czy kocha Karolinę, nie wiedział, czy chce z nią zostać na resztę życia, i nie wiedział, że jest zazdrosny. Czuł tylko wewnętrzne rozdygotanie, które brało się nie wiadomo z czego.

Emilia Blendowa nie lubiła gości w domu. Zasłaniała się zmęczeniem, ciasnotą, ale tak naprawdę nie chciała, by ktokolwiek przeglądał jej kąty. Prawdę mówiąc, nie bardzo było co przeglądać, bo mieszkali zwyczajnie, bez antyków, bez obrazów na ścianach, otoczeni samą przeciętnością. Wnętrza miały nie mówić o fortunie właścicieli i nie mówiły, a mimo to Blendowie gości nie zapraszali. Spore więc było zdziwienie Julii, kiedy któregoś wieczora zastała w domu obcego mężczyznę. Matka szepnęła jej w przedpokoju, że to partner w interesach, że fatygował się specjalnie z Bydgoszczy, by na miejscu dograć pewne kwestie. Jakie? To już było tajemnicą rodziców. Siedzieli właśnie przy kolacji, kiedy Julia weszła.

– Kochanie, to jest pan Gustaw Rywal – matka z wdziękiem wskazała na łysawego młodzieńca w wieku średnim. Co do wieku można się było spierać, natomiast opakowanie na pewno było młodzieżowe, dobrej marki, podobnie jak złote precjoza.

– Witam! Mów mi Gutek. – Potrząsnął energicznie ręką oszołomionej Julii, po czym zasypał ją pytaniami o pracę i zarobki. – Emilka mówiła, że dostajesz osiemset na rękę. W weekendy pracujecie? – Wyciągnął z kieszeni kalkulator, postukał, popatrzył. – Pewnie, że siedemnaście tysięcy na miesiąc to żadna rewelacja, ale ty dopiero startujesz. Dobrze zrozumiałem?

– Startuję, ale te siedemnaście tysięcy to skąd pan wziął? – spytała oszołomiona.

– Mów mi Gutek. Tyle wychodzi ci na miesiąc. Uważam, że to niezła stawka.

– Z choinki spadłeś? Osiemset wychodzi mi na miesiąc, nie na dzień.

Jej zdziwienie niemal automatycznie spłynęło na niego. Sprawiał wrażenie człowieka, z którego zakpiono w sposób złośliwy, żeby nie powiedzieć perfidny. Wyjaśnił, że za taką stawkę on nie podniósłby tyłka z krzesła, i nie rozumiał, co ma do tego choinka.

– Uspokój się, Julio! Pan ma bardzo liczne znajomości we Włocławku, więc pytałam, czy nie mógłby znaleźć ci... to znaczy pomóc... podpowiedzieć... może wie o jakiejś pracy dla informatyka – plątała się zbita z tropu matka.

– Przecież pracuję – wyjaśniła chłodno Julia.

– Tylko za ile?! – wtrącił ojciec. – Nie dość, że trzeba się było Mikulowej podlizywać, to jeszcze dają ci takie grosze, że wstyd się komukolwiek przyznać! Bądź co bądź skończyłaś studia z wyróżnieniem. Informatyków wszędzie potrzebują.

Spojrzała na ojca z niedowierzaniem.

– Podlizywać Mikulowej?

– A co myślałaś, że przyjęli cię na piękne oczy?! Dzisiaj bez znajomości jesteś nikim.

Pozornie siedziała na krześle na wprost Gutka, ale tak naprawdę leciała głową w dół do samej piwnicy. Niżej już nie dało się upaść. Jedno zdanie rzucone mimochodem uświadomiło jej, że w rękach rodziców wciąż jest zwykłą marionetką. Oni pociągają za sznurki, ona posłusznie skacze i jeszcze jest szczęśliwa, że ma cokolwiek do powiedzenia w swoich sprawach. Nie chodziło nawet o Budampolex 2, lecz o zasadę. Po studiach wcale nie miała zamiaru wracać do Włocławka. Matka z ojcem uparli się, więc postawiła warunek: jeżeli w ciągu miesiąca sama nie znajdzie sobie odpowiedniej pracy, wyjeżdża. Odpowiedniej, to znaczy w wyuczonym zawodzie, niekoniecznie od razu na stanowisku dyrektora. Wydawało się to całkiem rozsądne, choć – jak podejrzewała – we Włocławku nierealne. Niby informatycy są potrzebni, niby ich brakuje, kiedy jednak człowiek szuka miejsca na własną rękę, wszędzie natyka się na nadmiar fachowców. Trafiła wreszcie do Budampolexu 2 i przez kilka miesięcy żyła złudzeniami, z których odarli ją jednym zdaniem, jedną uwagą. Nie dość, że niczego nie załatwiła sama, że zdecydowali za nią i poza jej plecami, to wciąż im było mało. Ze złością spojrzała na Gutka. Siedział i w zamyśleniu tarł czoło.

– Coś mi dzisiaj wpadło w ucho – powiedział – że tam u was nastąpiła zmiana właściciela. Firmę przejęła babka, tak?

– Właścicielką jest kobieta – mruknęła Julia.

– Wow! To długo nie pociągniecie. Tym bardziej trzeba pomyśleć o zmianie pracy. U mnie mogłabyś być akwizytorem. A właściwie nie, poczekaj: staż zrobiłaś, to dam cię na dyrektora marketingu. Słuchaj, co cię trzyma we Włocławku? Załatwiajmy od razu robotę w Bydgoszczy. Miasto wojewódzkie stwarza większe szanse ludziom prężnym. Będziesz miała do dyspozycji mieszkanie służbowe, samochód i dużą forsę. No co? Odpowiada ci?

Po raz drugi w ciągu kilkunastu minut uznała, że facet to zwykły palant, który urwał się z choinki. Zastanawiała się właśnie, co powiedzieć, żeby go skutecznie obrazić i niechcący spojrzała na matkę. Pani Emilia bladła i czerwieniała. Z wielkim niesmakiem słuchała wywodów gościa i widać było, że nie życzy sobie aż tak radykalnych zmian w karierze zawodowej córki. Zresztą natychmiast podzieliła się swoimi wątpliwościami.

– Julia, proszę pana, ma gdzie mieszkać, czym jeździć i z głodu nie umiera. Myślałam o pracy informatyka, a nie domokrążcy – powiedziała wyniośle.

Gustaw Rywal nie zdążył zasiedzieć się w domu Blendów. Po jego wyjściu Julia nie czmychnęła jak zwykle do swojego pokoju. Wszystko w niej dygotało od wewnętrznej irytacji. W matce zresztą też.

– Co za idiotyczna maniera tykania – denerwowała się pani Emilia. – Gdzie wy się tego uczycie? On to on, ale ty?

– Dostosowałam się tylko do manier waszego gościa. Możesz mi powiedzieć, kiedy wreszcie przestaniesz się wtrącać w moje sprawy?

– Wtrącać?

– Dlaczego nie powiedziałaś mi o Mikulowej?

Matka wydawała się zakłopotana. Po minie widać było, że najchętniej zapadłaby na amnezję i zapomniała, kim jest Mikulowa. Coś tam wybąkała o zbiegu przypadków, o starej znajomości i zajęła się sprzątaniem ze stołu. Kursując między kuchnią i pokojem, mniej była narażona na ostre pytania Julii. Tym razem jednak córka nie zamierzała niczego darować.

– Nie złość się, chciałam dobrze! – powiedziała wreszcie Emilia. – Głupio wyszło, bo facet palant. Takie jest życie, bez znajomości niczego nie załatwisz!

– Czasem mam wrażenie, że próbujecie za mnie przeżyć moje własne życie! – wybuchnęła Julia. – Kroku nie pozwalacie mi zrobić samodzielnie!

– Co ty mówisz? O kogo mamy się martwić, jak nie o jedyną córkę. Przecież my z ojcem dla ciebie tak... ani sobót wolnych, ani wieczorów...

– A ja nie chcę, rozumiesz?! – krzyczała. – Dlaczego raz nie powiesz prawdy, że pracujesz, bo się wyżywasz, bo to twoja pasja!

– No, cicho, cicho! – Matka objęła ją i cmoknęła w czoło. – Kiedyś to może była pasja, teraz trzeba pracować, żeby nie stracić tego, co mamy. Do grobu majątku nie weźmiemy... tobie zostawimy. – Zbystrzała nagle: – Zdzisiek, a te faktury wróciły? Sprawdziłeś? Bo wiesz, potem mogą nas szarpać.

Łagodnym ruchem odsunęła Julię i usiadła na krześle obok męża. Zaczęli dyskutować o rachunkach i należnościach. Julia nie miała już czego szukać w ich pokoju, zamienionym na firmowy kantor. Tak było zawsze, odkąd rodzice zaczęli pracować na własny rachunek. Matka potrafiła oderwać się od najważniejszej rozmowy, przerwać córce w pół zdania, żeby zajrzeć do kalendarza, zatelefonować do kontrahenta albo obrugać swojego Zdzisia. Potem jakby nigdy nic kazała sobie opowiadać dalej. Julii bardzo przeszkadzała taka podzielność uwagi, traciła wątek i chęć do zwierzeń. Z czasem w ogóle zaprzestała rozmów na swój temat. Ograniczała się do wysłuchiwania pouczeń, napomnień i dobrych rad. Tego pani Blendowa nie szczędziła ani jej, ani mężowi. Ale ogólnie była bardzo dobrą, kochającą matką i niewiele można jej było zarzucić. Może jedno: kochała zbyt mocno, dławiła swoją miłością i Julia z wielkim trudem łapała oddech. Coraz bardziej brakowało jej swobody. Chciała się poczuć dorosła, a matka na siłę wpychała ją w dziecięce ubranka.

Orzechowicz, przyjmując zlecenia, nie miał zwyczaju zadawania kłopotliwych pytań. Potrzebny był taki czy inny program, siadał i opracowywał. Tym razem jednak Grzegorzowi wykluło się w łepetynie straszne dziwactwo, z którego mogły wyniknąć jedynie kłopoty. Konrad wysłuchał propozycji z niesmakiem, pomyślał i odpowiedział krótko: Odwal się, stary, nie ten adres! Taka riposta zapowiadała czasowe ochłodzenie stosunków, czym akurat zbytnio się nie przejął. Ludzie, którzy znają swoją wartość, nie są strachliwi. Obiecał wykończyć na poniedziałek jeden drobiazg i zapowiedział, że zaraz potem zrobi sobie dłuższy oddech. Nie precyzował, co właściwie znaczy i jak długo trwa taki dłuższy oddech. W poniedziałek Karolina wyjeżdżała z Mikulą do Warszawy i to był powód do zmartwienia poważniejszy niż dąsy Grzegorza.

– Dlaczego ty się, ssaczku, tak głupio upierasz? – spytała ostatnio. – Muszę jechać. Szef dał mi polecenie i wyżej pępka nie podskoczę. Podpisujemy ważny dla firmy kontrakt, dzięki któremu i ty będziesz miał co robić.

– Podpisujecie w poniedziałek o dwunastej. Spokojnie zdążysz na Kujawiaka i wieczorem będziesz w domu.

– Ależ ty jesteś poinformowany! – Pokręciła głową z podziwem. – Skąd masz taką imponującą wiedzę: Reuter ci doniósł czy w radiu mówili?

Wzruszył ramionami. Co jej miał powiedzieć? Że wszystko, co wiedział, pochodziło od tej grubej sprzątaczki?! To nie było wiarygodne źródło informacji. Konrad nie znał jeszcze ludzi ani układów w firmie, ale Henia zdążyła mu podpaść. Krążyła niczym sęp wokół jego pokoju, czyhała, dreptała. Sam siebie zaczął posądzać o halucynacje, bo niby jaki interes mogła mieć do niego taka starszawa kobiecina? A jednak okazało się, że miała. Podeszła na korytarzu, kiedy rozmawiał z magistrem Wydroniem.

– Panie inżynierze, na jedną chwileczkę.

Gdyby nie mrugała przy tym, może by przeprosił Wydronia i odszedł na bok. Jej poufałość wydała mu się dziwna i niesmaczna.

– O co chodzi? – spytał bez większego zainteresowania.

– Chodzi o wyjazd pana... znajomej z dyrektorem – szepnęła poufale. – Delegacja jest na trzy dni, ale ja wiem, że umowę podpiszą w poniedziałek o dwunastej. To co będą robić do środy?

– Dyrektora niech pani spyta.

Kobieta tak była zaskoczona naiwnością Konrada, tak się przy tym rozzuchwaliła, że po raz drugi mrugnęła porozumiewawczo i zaczęła nadawać o grzesznym romansie, jawnej zdradzie i tak dalej. Najwyraźniej magister Wydroń również był uczulony na perskie oczka, bo pierwszy ochłonął ze zdumienia. Orzechowicz słabo znał człowieka, tyle co z działu organizacji, i nie posądzał go o znajomość tak jędrnej i dosadnej polszczyzny. Sprzątaczka przez chwilę łapała powietrze jak ryba, a dopiero potem oddaliła się truchtem do swoich zajęć.

– Rugnąć też bym potrafił, choć bez pańskiego polotu i tych wszystkich cytatów z zakresu obowiązków – powiedział Konrad z uśmiechem.

– Do czego te baby człowieka doprowadzą! – zdumiał się Wydroń. – Jeszcze rano uważałem, że pająkowi nóg z tyłka nie umiałbym wyrwać, a teraz Heni wyrwałbym obie razem z językiem.

Ani razu nie padło imię kobiety nazwanej tajemniczo „znajomą". Orzechowicz nie miał wątpliwości, że jego rozmówca doskonale wiedział, kogo broni przed wścibską babą. Poczuł do niego cichą sympatię i jednocześnie jakiś nieokreślony żal do Karoliny. Wyjeżdżała w poniedziałek. Jakby tego było mało, zapowiedziała, że w sobotę musi wyskoczyć do Torunia. Zdenerwował się, nie chciał słyszeć o żadnej delegacji, o noclegach w Warszawie i trzydniowej nieobecności.

– Dlaczego od razu nie powiesz, że masz mnie dosyć, że jestem wolny i kończymy naszą zabawę. Nie musisz uciekać w Polskę! – powiedział ze złością.

– Fiu, fiu! Aż taki jesteś zarozumiały?! Nie chwyciłam tylko tej wstawki o wolności. Nie czujesz się wolny? Zarozumiały niewolnik, ssaczku, to nie brzmi zbyt dumnie.

Próbował wytłumaczyć, co miał na myśli i w końcu zaczął się plątać pod jej poważnym spojrzeniem. Nie uśmiechała się, nie przekomarzała, tylko patrzyła.

– Zawsze się bałem kobiet zbyt ambitnych! – mruknął.

– Rozumiem. Nie szukasz partnerki, tylko gosposi. Przyjmij wyrazy współczucia i szukaj dalej.

– Mam sobie iść?

– Tak ci śpieszno do poszukiwań? Jakbyś nie zaczynał już dzisiaj, to możesz jeszcze chwilę posiedzieć.

Miał ochotę wyjść i nie miał. Dawno już sobie powiedział, że trwały związek z Karoliną nie wchodzi w rachubę, nie umiał się wycofać. A ona odpychała go i nie odpychała.

– Nie pamiętasz przypadkiem – spytała nieoczekiwanie – czy w czasie naszego burzliwego romansu dałeś mi choć jeden kwiatek?

Zasępił się i zdecydował, że jednak powinien wyjść. Nie dał jej nigdy ani kwiatka, ani najmniejszego drobiazgu. Jakoś nie wpadło mu to do głowy. Kiedy szli na obiad czy do kawiarni, oczywiście płacił rachunki i to było całkiem zrozumiałe. Karolinie chodziło jednak o coś innego: o miłe gesty, o pamięć, może odrobinę czułości. Rozumiał to, wyczuwał intencje, jednocześnie z przerażeniem odkrył, że jest w środku pusty. Gdyby było inaczej, nie musiałaby pytać o cholerny kwiatek, bo dostawałaby całe bukiety! Wstał.

– Lepiej będzie, jak sobie pójdę – powiedział.

Liczył na jej przekorę, na to, że zamieni swoje pytanie w żart, parsknie śmiechem lub zrobi jakiś inny czytelny gest, który pozwoli mu zostać. Bez słowa odprowadziła go do drzwi i odsunęła zasuwę.

– Powodzenia, ssaczku! – powiedziała.

Głucho trzasnęły drzwi. Był wolny czy nie? Chyba jednak znowu był.

W sobotę Julia wstała o normalnej porze, czyli około szóstej i to sama, bez pohukiwań matki. Wybierała się na podbój Torunia, chciała wyglądać atrakcyjnie, co wymagało staranniejszego niż na co dzień makijażu. Niby to nie filozofia, niby każda kobieta wie, jak się malować, lecz nie każda potrafi ustrzec się drobnych błędów, choćby głupiego kleksa na powiece. Trzeba zmywać, zaczynać od początku Aleź to wymaga wprawy, myślała, tuszując na brązowo rzęsy.

– Gdzie ty się wybierasz? Zapomniałaś, że dziś wolna sobota? – Zaspana matka zajrzała do łazienki.

Julia od trzech dni mówiła o służbowym wyjeździe, widać jednak pani Emilia zapomniała lub źle usłyszała, bo otrząsnęła się z resztek snu i zaczęła przemawiać normalnym, gderliwym głosem.

– I po co tam jedziesz?

– Służbowo.

– Ale po co? Nie mają już kogo wysyłać, tylko stażystów? Ty się Julka na takie wyjazdy nie zgadzaj. Powiedz szefowi, że...

– Mhm. Jak ty powiesz ojcu, że nie będziesz pracować w soboty, ja powiem to samo Mikule! – mruknęła Julia.

Dobrze wiedziała, kto w rodzinnej firmie rządzi. Oficjalnie mówiło się, że ojciec, lecz on na gruncie zawodowym miał tyle samo do powiedzenia, co w domu. Emilia Blendowa zaczęła fukać i coraz natarczywiej domagała się odpowiedzi na podstawowe pytanie: jakie interesy może mieć Julia w Toruniu?

– I ty mówisz, że się do mnie nie wtrącasz, że pozwalasz mi na własne życie! – wybuchnęła dziewczyna. – A gdybym jechała towarzysko, to co? Powinnam spytać o zgodę? Ty się, mamo, przestań ośmieszać, żyj sobie, jak uważasz, ale innym też daj żyć!

Wczesny ranek nie jest dobrą porą do szczerych wyznań. Julia całkiem niepotrzebnie rozpętała burzę. Sama się zdenerwowała, ręce jej drżały i nie mogła skończyć makijażu, pani Emilia zaś zrozumiała tylko jedno, że urodziła i wyhodowała potwora. Dziewczyna wybiegła z domu zła jak nieszczęście. Cała radość z wyjazdu wyparowała z niej niczym woda z kałuży w upalny dzień. Czy ona zawsze musi mi wszystko popsuć? – myślała rozżalona. Dopiero kiedy trzasnęła drzwiami matiza nieco silniej niż normalnie, trochę się uspokoiła. Ruszyła ostro i przez całą drogę na Zazamcze przeżuwała gorycz porannej awantury.

Karolina nerwowo przechadzała się przed blokiem.

– Nie zdzierżę, nie wyrobię, nie wytrzymam! – jęknęła Julia zamiast powitania.

Przyjaciółka wcale nie była w lepszym nastroju. Gdyby nie to, że osobiście rozmawiała z Kamilą, że namotała spotkanie w Toruniu, to najchętniej zostałaby w domu. Mruknęła coś o cholernym pampersowym życiu i lekko wskoczyła na przednie siedzenie.

– Zapnij pas – przypomniała Julia. – Masz taką minę, jakbyś chciała kogoś zarżnąć. Jeżeli ja mam taką samą, to już lepiej zjadę do Wisły i popłyniemy sobie z nurtem. Co za pożytek z takich jęczydudków?

Spojrzały na siebie i czy to za sprawą pięknej wiosennej pogody, czy młodości, która szybko znajduje pocieszenie, roześmiały się niemal jednocześnie. Był to krótki przerywnik, chichot odpoczynkowy, a nie zrodzony z nastroju. Obie miały głowy zajęte niewesołymi sprawami.

– Chyba zerwałam z Konradem – powiedziała Karolina, ocierając oczy.

– Jak można zerwać „chyba"? Albo się zrywa, albo nie.

– O, to jeszcze nie znasz Konrada! Wiesz, jak to jest: raz ustąpisz facetowi, a potem już będziesz musiała zawsze ustępować. Jego nie obchodzi, że masz swoje życie, swoje plany zawodowe. Zresztą, niech idzie do diabła. Nie cierpię facetów! Wszystkich bym powiesiła w rządku.

– No wiesz? Teraz to już chyba przesadziłaś! – żachnęła się Julia. – Wściekła jesteś na jednego, ale żeby zaraz całą resztę tak krzywdzić?! Powieś sobie Orzechowicza i full. Facet wydaje się trochę zarozumiały, jak podynda, to skruszeje.

– A znasz chłopa, który nie byłby zarozumiały? Wystarczy, że pacan nosi spodnie, jest jako tako wyposażony i od razu snuje sobie fantazje, że ma dwa razy większy mózg od kobiecego, pięć razy szybszy refleks i i nawet... jajniki też ma sprawniejsze. Wszystko wiedzą, wszystko potrafią. Dzieci nie rodzą tylko dlatego, że to boli. Ale jakby rodzili, to aborcja byłaby sakramentem nie przestępstwem. Już ja znam te przewrotne typy.

– Mówisz o Konradzie czy raczej ogólnie?

– Ogólnie, ale o nim też. Niestety, jest taki sam jak wszyscy.

– Taki sam, tylko trochę inny, bo to w nim się zakochałaś! – stwierdziła Julia. – Nieźle ci zalazł za skórę, jak widzę.

Karolina prychnęła jak rozzłoszczona kotka. Całą noc miała na przemyślenia i teraz mogła w miarę spokojnie mówić o tym, co się tak pięknie zaczęło i bardzo szybko skończyło. Jej długofalowy program, który realizowała punkt po punkcie, nie uwzględniał czegoś takiego jak zakochanie. Nie składała ślubów panieńskich, jeżeli już, to biznesowe, wykluczające łączenie wielkiej miłości ze spełnieniem zawodowym. Poznała Konrada i przez moment miała wrażenie, że dla niego warto zmienić zdanie, a częściowo także program. Co nie znaczy, by chciała rezygnować z własnej kariery zawodowej i potulnie podporządkować się mężczyźnie. On najwyraźniej nie był aż tak ambitny, nie myślał poważnie o awansach ani o pieniądzach. To mogła mu darować. Przeraziła się dopiero w momencie, kiedy prawem kaduka usiłował manipulować nią i wtrącać się do jej pracy.

– Nie wierzę – powiedziała stanowczo Julia. – Nie wierzę, żeby ludzie naprawdę zakochani nie dogadali się w takiej prostej sprawie.

– Naprawdę zakochani, mówisz? No tak, ale jest jeszcze coś takiego jak małpia zazdrość i wtedy nie ma pomiłuj! Zresztą, może to wcale nie miłość, tylko zmysły?

Na temat małpiej zazdrości oraz zmysłów Julia miała oczywiście własne zdanie, brakowało jej natomiast doświadczeń. O Leszku nie powiedziała przyjaciółce, bo jakoś nie umiała się przełamać, nie wiedziała, jak to zrobić, żeby nie wyglądało na zwykłe przechwałki. Zgłupiał, oszalał, powiedział... Nie, to stanowczo nie wchodziło w rachubę. Wyznanie Leszka było dziwnie dramatyczne, poważne i jakieś takie, że myślenie o nim odkładała na później, do czasu, aż zdobędzie się na dystans. Co innego zapały Chochli. O romantycznym spacerze ulicą Kaliską przekablowała następnego ranka, jednak temat nie był aż tak frapujący, żeby wałkować go przez całą drogę i jeszcze potem z mecenasem w Toruniu. Karolina siedziała poważna i zamyślona. Julia czuła, że jeżeli nie oderwie jej myśli od miłosnych rozważań, to zamiast energicznej dziewczyny dowiezie do Torunia żałosną kupkę nieszczęścia. Zaczęła więc opowiadać o facecie, którego dla swoich potrzeb ochrzciła „mów mi Gutek". Karolina powoli dochodziła do siebie.

– Bocian?! – krzyknęła zaskoczona. – Juleczko, zwolnij, chcę popatrzeć!

Kilka metrów od ruchliwej jezdni, w koronie rozłożystego drzewa tkwiło spore gniazdo. Jeden ptak siedział, drugi stał nad nim z rozłożonymi skrzydłami. Nic, tylko pan bocian, przed wyruszeniem na polowanie, uzgadniał z żoną menu.

– Najbardziej lubię patrzeć na bocianie gniazda, kiedy już wylęgną się młode – powiedziała Julia. – Są takie śmieszne, ni to szare, ni łyse, z dołu widzisz tylko ciekawskie łebki. Moje bociany mieszkają w Rakutowie. Znasz Rakutowo? Taka spora wieś za Kowalem, z drugiej strony Włocławka. W ubiegłym roku grad zabił w gnieździe dwa bocianie niemowlaki. Smutne bardzo, prawda? Ale powiem ci, że najsmutniejszy był widok starych bocianów. Przylatywały po kilka razy dziennie, kołowały nad gniazdem, siadały na skraju, znowu kołowały i mogę przysiąc, że w ich zachowaniu widziałam ludzki ból i strach. Tego nie da się opowiedzieć słowami. W końcu uznały, że gniazdo jest zajęte, założyły nowe po drugiej stronie ulicy i aż do odlotu kręciły się w pobliżu. W tym roku są już w Rakutowie dwa zamieszkane gniazda. Nie wiem, czy z tej historii można wysnuć jakiś logiczny wniosek, poza tym, że jest to pean na cześć rodzicielskich uczuć.

– Było jedno gniazdo, mówisz, są dwa, będzie więcej bocianiątek i życie toczy się dalej. Nie ma już miejsca na rozpacz, więc się nie roztkliwiaj.

– Ech, ty, zakuta realistko, zauważ, że mówisz do romantyczki!

– Też jestem romantyczką.

– Ty?

– A co myślałaś? Jestem. Tylko ten dziadowski świat jest taki parszywy, że nie ma w nim miejsca na romantyzm. Ja, Juleczko, jestem z innego gniazda, ja przeżyłam gradobicie i jeszcze trochę więcej. Kiedy miałam czternaście lat, moja matka zakochała się, co od biedy można uznać za historię romantyczną. Samotna kobieta z dzieckiem marzy o męskim ramieniu, które w końcu znajduje i w tym miejscu powinien być happy end. W posagu wniosła smutne doświadczenia z przeszłości, dziecko, trochę pieniędzy po rodzicach i wielką miłość. Mężczyzna nie miał dla niej nic, poza własną młodością. Od poświęceń i miłości wolał swobodę, więc uciekł. Matka zapadła na ciężką postać schizofrenii, a ja tułałam się po różnych ciotkach i przysięgam ci, że to nie były romantyczne wędrówki.

Mówiła spokojnie, cicho, jakby relacjonowała cudzą, nie swoją historię. Julia ścisnęła kierownicę aż do bólu palców. Nie ma co, urocza ze mnie towarzyszka podróży, pomyślała. Co zacznę temat, trafiam kulą w płot i jeszcze mam ochotę płakać.

– Nie wiem, nie rozumiem, jak matka mogła coś takiego zrobić córce – powiedziała cicho.

– Kiedyś też nie rozumiałam. Jako dorosła kobieta patrzę inaczej i nie potępiam nikogo. Człowiek oprócz instynktu ma jeszcze rozum i dlatego popełnia głupstwa, o jakich nie śni się bocianom ani żubrom.

Rozum, myślała Julia, rozum właśnie każe dbać o pisklaki i unikać głupstw. W tym samym gnieździe, ze dwa lata wcześniej, widziała bocianiątko zawieszone między gałęziami. Rodzice widać uznali, że trójki dzieci nie wykarmią i najsłabsze pisklę wyrzucili z gniazda. W bocianiej moralności taki czyn widać się mieści, ale przecież nie w ludzkiej. Człowiek nigdy by tak nie zrobił, bo rządzi się rozumem. Próbowała to jakoś wytłumaczyć Karolinie.

– Filozofujesz teraz czy bawisz się w ornitologa? Wiesz co, ty byś się nadała z Leszkiem. On lubi owady, ty ptaszki, mielibyście przynajmniej dwa tematy jak w banku.

Julia znowu ścisnęła silniej kierownicę i udawała, że bardzo pochłania ją prowadzenie auta.

– Czemu zamilkłaś, ptasia romantyczko? – roześmiała się Karolina.

– Straszny dzisiaj ruch – powiedziała cicho Julia. – Słuchaj, czy to prawda, co mówiła Henia o żonie Leszka?

– To akurat prawda. Ciekawe, skąd Henia wie?

– Też mi zagadka! Włocławek ma sto tysięcy mieszkańców i mniej więcej tylu znajomych ma Henia. Dlaczego ona go zostawiła?

– Henia? Kogo niby?

– Dobra, nie chcesz, to nie mów! – powiedziała ugodowo Julia.

Karolina po krótkiej chwili milczenia uznała, że nie ma co robić tajemnicy z historii, o której za sprawą jednej Heni może gadać całe miasto.

– Nie wiem, gdzie ją Leszek znalazł, z całą pewnością takie jak ona nie spadają z nieba. Mała heterka, napompowana pretensjami, to największe zło, jakie może się mądremu facetowi przytrafić. Zwiała, i pewnie teraz żałuje. Po Leszku każdy inny musi się wydać mało czuły i troskliwy.

– Nie ucieka się od czułego i troskliwego męża – powiedziała zamyślona Julia.

– Przecież ci tłumaczę, że to idiotka. – Karolina wzruszyła ramionami. – W każdym razie chłopak wystąpił o rozwód i jest prawie wolny. Dobrze ci radzę, ty się nim zainteresuj!

– A ty nie masz ochoty?

– Jakbym miała, to pewnie byłabym już panią Wydroniową. Na szczęście to inteligentny facet i szybko zrozumiał, że nie jesteśmy stworzeni dla siebie. Nam wystarczy przyjaźń.

Julia odetchnęła głęboko. Wyznanie Leszka wydało się jej o wiele mniej dramatyczne, niż gotowa była sądzić pół godziny wcześniej. Poczuła maleńkie ukłucie zazdrości, że to nie dla niej pierwszej oszalał, i pogratulowała sobie, że niczego nie wypaplała. Nie chciała być dla mężczyzny tą drugą, nawet gdyby miała ją wyprzedzić piękna Karolina. Żony w tym wyścigu nie uwzględniała, żona zresztą odeszła.

Na toruńskiej starówce Karolina wpadła w szał. Ciągnęła Julię od bramy do bramy, pokazywała schodki, kute kraty, detale architektoniczne. Tu malował Rafał, tu Marta biedziła się nad maszkaronem, tu to, a tam jeszcze coś innego. Dotarły wreszcie na miejsce. Narożna kamienica niewiele się zmieniła, tyle że kiedyś na parterze była jakaś rupieciarnia, teraz galeria U plastyczek, o czym informował szyld z kutego metalu. Karolina spojrzała roziskrzonymi oczami i pchnęła drzwi.

Na dźwięk gongu z zaplecza wyjrzała drobna, rudowłosa kobieta. Moment zdziwienia przemienił się w wielką radość, przetykaną okrzykami. Z rozmachu obie dziewczyny zostały uściskane i doprowadzone na zaplecze, gdzie z dumnie wypiętym brzuchem siedziała popielata blondynka. Julia musiała w duchu przyznać, że rzadko która kobieta w zaawansowanej ciąży potrafi wyglądać tak pięknie, jak pani mecenasowa Wilani-Wąsik. Seria uścisków i poklepywań została dokładnie powtórzona. Ruda Kamila i popielata Marta nie mogły nacieszyć się Karoliną. Wypiękniała im przez te lata, wydoroślała i nie było żadnych wątpliwości, że ściskały ją z wielką radością. Natychmiast zabrzęczały szklanki, zabulgotał elektryczny czajnik i aromatyczny zapach herbaty wypełnił niewielkie pomieszczenie. A pamiętacie tego?... a tę?... Kto umarł? Kto ożył?

Julia siedziała nieco z boku i wypełniało ją paskudne uczucie zazdrości. Brało się z samego patrzenia i słuchania. Też miała swoje koleżanki ze szkoły i ze studiów, też czasem spotykała jedną lub drugą, lecz takiej zażyłości, takiej serdeczności nie doświadczyła chyba nigdy. Właściwie Karolina była jej pierwszą przyjaciółką, taką, z którą można pogadać bez strachu, że wypaple, że ośmieszy. A te trzy szalały. Nie było końca chichotom i przekrzykiwaniom, jakby zaledwie wczoraj, najdalej przedwczoraj dzieliły się bułką, papierosami i ostatnią łyżeczką kawy. To nie do wiary, ile wspólnych tematów da się wygrzebać z pamięci, nawet jeżeli dotyczyły jednego, dawno minionego roku. Wreszcie przyszła pora na interesy i Karolina z ciężkim westchnieniem spytała o mecenasa.

– Wzdychasz, aż kotary falują – roześmiała się Marta. – Męża nie ma chwilowo w kraju, powiedz, o co chodzi, na pewno zrobię, co będę mogła. Znam ludzi w jego kancelarii i nie zostawię cię bez pomocy.

Zwięźle, najkrócej jak się dało, Karolina opowiedziała o garsonierze, Chochli i zdjęciach. Połączyła w zgrabną całość to, co wiedziała na pewno, z tym, czego się domyśliła wspólnie z Julią. Pewnik w zasadzie był jeden: w rękach Chochli pozostawały fotografie kompromitujące ją oraz dyrektora Mikulę. Cała reszta to już były domysły. W ślad za pierwszą przesyłką, zawierającą pogróżkę „masz co chciałaś", można się było spodziewać następnych listów z konkretnymi żądaniami, z próbą zastraszenia czy szantażu. Chochla nieprzypadkowo i na pewno nie w celach kontemplacyjnych usunął się w cień, zamknął samotnie w celi, czyli w garsonierze. Coś knuł, ale czy sam, czy ze wspólnikami, tego nie dało się ustalić. W każdym razie materiały dowodowe miał raczej bogate i mógł zagrażać wielu ludziom. Karolina nie zamierzała występować w imieniu wszystkich narażonych na szykany, chciała tylko odzyskać negatywy i odbitki swoich zdjęć. W miarę jak opowiadała, piękne oczy Marty zwęziły się niczym szparki.

– Coś ci powiem, Karolinko: żaden, nawet najlepszy mecenas nie załatwi tej sprawy jak należy! – powiedziała pewnym głosem.

– Wiem... Nie chcę, żeby załatwiał, chcę, żeby mi poradził, co mam robić i co mówią w tej materii przepisy prawa – tłumaczyła Karolina.

– Daruj sobie mecenasów i przepisy prawa. Z gnidami trzeba walczyć ich własną bronią, tylko inteligentniej. Mnie możesz wierzyć, uwolniłam Toruń od kilku kanalii.

– Martusiu! – Rudowłosa Kamila patrzyła na przyjaciółkę z jawną naganą. – Przestań się zachowywać jak kombatantka i pamiętaj, co obiecałaś Wojtkowi.

Marta pokręciła głową. Obiecać obiecała, ale w innej sytuacji. Nie wiedziała jeszcze wtedy, że jej przyjaciółka, która podzieliła się z nią ostatnią bułką, wpadnie w tarapaty. Musiała zająć się sprawą i pomóc, bo nikt nie miał tylu doświadczeń, co ona, a przede wszystkim takiej woli zwycięstwa. Zaczęła szczegółowo wypytywać o Chochlę, jego zwyczaje i zainteresowania. Potem kazała sobie narysować plan mieszkania z dokładnym usytuowaniem wersalki, drzwi, lampy i wielu innych szczegółów. Karolina odpowiadała precyzyjnie, lecz wierciła się przy tym, jakby siedziała na gwoździach, nie na wyściełanym krześle.

– Mogę walczyć z kanalią, czemu nie, byle w zgodzie z prawem – stwierdziła, spoglądając niepewnie na Martę.

Julia wychyliła się ze swojego kąta i przysunęła krzesło bliżej stolika. Była pod całkowitym urokiem pani mecenasowej i dosłownie piła z jej ust każde słowo.

– Karolinko, to twoje prawo jest do kitu! Małego człowieczka wsadzi za kraty, wielkiego złodzieja wypuści za kaucją – powiedziała stanowczo. – Najlepiej na jakiś czas zapomnij, kim jesteś z zawodu, albo pozwól mnie działać. Rozumiem intencje pani Marty, nie jestem zaangażowana emocjonalnie, poza tym nawiązałam kontakt z Chochlą i mogę się przydać.

Marta spojrzała na Julię z uznaniem.

– Brawo, kochana! Tak właśnie trzymaj! W pojedynkę trudno drania usadzić, ale dwie, trzy zgrane babeczki poradzą sobie z każdym, choćby za nim stał nie wiadomo kto. Jesteś informatykiem, prawda? Znasz się na podsłuchu, fotokomórkach i ukrytych kamerach?

– Średnio. Jeżeli uważa pani, że Chochla mógł się znać, to popytam, poczytam i też będę mądra – stwierdziła z przekonaniem.

– Fantastycznie! Tylko nie mów do mnie pani, bo przyjaciółki naszych przyjaciółek i tak dalej, sama wiesz!

– Ja wiem tylko, że przyjaciele naszych przyjaciółek są naszymi kochankami. O tym mówicie? – ożywiła się Karolina.

– A mężowie przyjaciółek? – Marta spojrzała z udaną surowością.

– Mężowie? – zastanowiła się Karolina. – Mężów przyjaciółek traktuję jak nieboszczyków, nie istnieją dla mnie. Co do innych nie jestem taka radykalna.

– Pocieszyłaś mnie, bo właśnie zamierzałam was zaprosić do siebie, kiedy już wróci Wojtek. Same wiecie, jak to jest: jedna piękna, druga piękna, a ja w ciąży. W każdym razie, jeżeli już się odważę, to ani słowa o naszej tajemnicy. On jest cudownie łagodny, tylko czasem wyłazi z niego męska małpa.

– Widzisz, Juleczko – zawołała Karolina – to samo ci tłumaczyłam, kiedy tu jechałyśmy. W każdym, nawet najwspanialszym, najprzystojniejszym facecie siedzi zazdrosna małpa. Marta to potwierdza.

Mecenasowa Wilani-Wąsik skinęła głową na znak, że oczywiście potwierdza, i zaczęła porządkować rozrzucone kartki. O czternastej, kiedy Kamila zamykała galerię, gotowy był plan unieszkodliwienia Chochli – i to w dwóch wariantach. Drugi, roboczo nazwany „ostatecznościowym", uwzględniał nawet włamanie do mieszkania, jednak wariant pierwszy był tak doskonały, że wykluczał wszelką przemoc. Zakładał wizytę w garsonierze dwu pań i to przy pełnej aprobacie lokatora. Jedna kobieta zajęłaby się mężczyzną, druga jego zbiorami. Nic prostszego.

– Chwileczkę! – zaprotestowała Karolina. – Nie znam nikogo, kto chciałby zająć się Chochlą!

– Ale ja znam – powiedziała spokojnie Julia. – Znam dziewczynę z agencji towarzyskiej. Zaaranżujemy jakąś randkę w ciemno lub coś równie miłego, ona nie da chłopu zipnąć, ty spenetrujesz archiwum. Ja będę czuwała na dole, w samochodzie...

– Szczegóły opracujecie na miejscu – wpadła jej w słowo Marta. – Plan musi być elastyczny, bo i tak będziecie musiały parę razy go zmienić, zależnie od potrzeb i okoliczności. Zastanawiam się właśnie, czy nie pojechać z wami, bo...

– Marta! – nie wytrzymała Kamila. – Chyba nie zamierzasz zajmować Chochli? Zresztą Julka już kogoś ma.

– Ależ ty się zrobiłaś rozsądna, aż przykro słuchać! – prychnęła Marta. – Na miejscu mogłabym podpowiedzieć to i owo.

– Jasne! Najlepiej, żebyś się władowała pod stół w pokoju! Pod fotel nawet nie próbuj, bo nie wleziesz – wyzłośliwiała się Kamila. – Trochę więcej wiary w ludzi, droga przyjaciółko!

Wychodziły z galerii późnym popołudniem, oderwane od teraźniejszości i znowu zanurzone we wspomnieniach. Przyjaciele się postarzeli, one wciąż czuły się młode. Pani mecenasowa nabrała apetytu na wielką kradzioną bagietkę. Życzyła sobie powtórkę z rozrywki.

– Nie dręcz jej. – Kamila objęła Karolinę ramieniem. – Jeśli chcesz wiedzieć, mała, to wcale tej buły nie ukradłaś. Marta na drugi dzień sprzedała obraz i oddała forsę w sklepie.

– Ja też oddałam po stypen... – Karolina spojrzała na dziewczyny i wybuchnęła szalonym śmiechem. Nie chciała powiedzieć, co ją tak rozbawiło, mamrotała coś o mitach i sentymentach.

Konrad położył na biurku Julii dyskietkę.

– Mogłaby pani zerknąć na ten program? – spytał.

Zgodziła się skwapliwie i zamierzała schować dyskietkę do torebki. Przytrzymał jej rękę. Zależało mu na czasie, więc głową wskazał komputer stojący na biurku Edyty.

– Panie inżynierze, monitor może i działa, ale pudło jest puste – szepnęła Julia. – Teraz wszędzie stoją komputery, nawet w pralni, więc szefowa chciała, żeby w Budampoleksie też stał.

Był pewien, że dziewczyna żartuje. Zamierzał osobiście obejrzeć to cudo techniki. Julia bez sprzeciwu podeszła do wielkiego biurka i uniosła monitor. Konrad w tym czasie pochylił się, żeby włączyć komputer, i kiedy gwałtownie uniósł głowę, monitor trzepnął go prosto w czoło.

– O Boże! – krzyknęła Julia i popędziła do kuchenki, gdzie Henia, bodaj pierwszy raz od miesiąca, zmywała szklanki.

Zakręciła się, złapała największy nóż i wróciła do sekretariatu. Konrad próbował udawać, że nic się nie stało. Nie słuchała. Usadziła go na fotelu dla gości, przytuliła jego głowę do piersi, a nóż przycisnęła do czoła.

– Podbił mi pan rękę... nie utrzymałam... to moja wina – szeptała i gładziła lekko chropowaty policzek. – Będzie siniak, bo skóra nie pękła.

– Ma pani ochotę poprawić? – spytał z udawanym przestrachem, choć głowy nie ruszył.

– Niech pan już lepiej nic nie mówi!

– Czemu? Przecież zębów mi pani nie wybiła.

Doceniała jego męstwo i to, że próbował bagatelizować incydent. Pochyliła się tak nisko, że brodą dotykała ciemnych włosów.

– Bardzo boli?

– Szczególnie pod okiem. Jak pani trzyma rękę na policzku, to jakby trochę mniej...

Nie uwierzyła, ale ręki z policzka nie zdjęła. Ostatecznie coś się cierpiącemu biedakowi należało. Pomyślała, że od wyjazdu Karoliny nie minęło nawet pół dnia, a ona już utula jej chłopaka. Nóż zrobił się ciepły, więc odjęła go od czoła Konrada.

– Proszę reanimować dalej, bo mogę umrzeć – zagroził.

Leczniczą sielankę przerwało wtargnięcie Heni. Rozsiadła się nieproszona w drugim fotelu i z ciekawością patrzyła na zabiegi Julii.

– Metal nie pomoże, masaż trzeba zrobić, oczyścić kanały energetyczne na karku – powiedziała pewnym tonem.

Uniosła się, gotowa nieść pomoc i własnymi rękami energię przekazywać, jednak Konrad był szybszy. Zanim Henia wstała, zerwał się i pociągnął Julię do biurka Edyty.

Nieszczęsny komputer rzecz jasna w całości okazał się atrapą. Zaczęli rozmawiać o potrzebach firmy i nowych zakupach. Pomoc gospodarcza, choć czuła się dotknięta zachowaniem inżyniera, nie obraziła się i nie wyszła. Wręcz przeciwnie, słuchała ze sporym zainteresowaniem i nawet wtrąciła do dyskusji swoje trzy grosze. Stanowczo odradzała pośpiech w zakupach aż do wyklarowania sytuacji.

Najwyraźniej miała ochotę podzielić się jakimiś nowinami, ale wrócił Leszek Wydroń. Od pamiętnej awantury Henia nigdy więcej nie wspominała o molestowaniu i bardzo starannie unikała specjalisty do spraw organizacji. Wyszła z sekretariatu tuż za Orzechowiczem. Julia najchętniej pobiegłaby za nimi. Jakoś niezręcznie jej było siedzieć w jednym pokoju z Leszkiem i żeby nie dać mu okazji do zwierzeń, sama zaczęła rozmowę na neutralny temat.

– Jak myślisz, po co twojej gruboudce...

– Tylko nie mojej! – obruszył się Leszek.

– Jak myślisz, po co Heni osiemdziesiąt tysięcy? Ja wiem, że pieniądze potrzebne są każdemu, ale zaskoczyła mnie kwota. Tyle miano... dokładnie tyle chciała ode mnie pożyczyć w piątek.

– I pożyczyłaś jej?

Julia zakręciła urocze kółko na czole. Leszek wzruszył ramionami na znak, że nic nie wie o interesach Heni. Patrzył przy tym na Julię coraz cieplej, aż poczuła ciarki na plecach.

– A dowiedziałeś się może czegoś o bossie?

– Niczego. Można powiedzieć: facet znikąd.

Tym razem Julia wzruszyła ramionami na znak, że nie wierzy. Ot, obiecał, nie poszedł i teraz zmyśla. Przesiadła się na fotel Edyty i skwapliwie sięgnęła po sporą paczkę, przewiązaną sznurkiem. Próbowała dać do zrozumienia, że czas przeznaczony na pogaduszki dobiegł końca i trzeba wziąć się do segregowania poczty.

– Ojej, całkiem bym zapomniała! Dzisiaj muszę wyjechać piętnaście minut wcześniej; gdyby Edyta nie wróciła, zastąpisz mnie?

Zgodził się, nie miał innego wyjścia. Złowiła jego zachwycone spojrzenie. Pomyślała, że chłopak, który znał się na kolorach, z całą pewnością docenił urodę nowej bluzki. Konrad też gapił się na nią jak sroka w gnat, więc nie miała wątpliwości, że i Bujałę oczaruje. Jeszcze za dobrze nie wiedziała, co zrobi z oczarowanym prezesem, lecz jak najprędzej chciała mieć za sobą to pierwsze spotkanie.

– Julio, muszę ci coś wyjaśnić! Wtedy...

Nie pozwoliła mu skończyć, przerwała gwałtownie i może nawet trochę niegrzecznie. Zapewniła, że żadne wyjaśnienia nie są potrzebne, że wszystko wie i rozumie, lecz nie widzi sensu, by o tym rozprawiać. Próbował jeszcze coś dodać, ona jednak wertowała korespondencję z takim zapałem, jakby nigdy w życiu nie widziała głupich prospektów reklamowych i ostemplowanych kopert. Na szczęście do Leszka przyszli interesanci. Ledwie zniknął z nimi w swoim pokoju, Julia straciła chęć do pracy. Bezmyślnie przerzucała koperty aż do momentu, gdy jedna przykuła jej wzrok. Przesyłka do rąk własnych dyrektora Mikuli. Bez trudu poznała charakter pisma, a w środku wyczuła zdjęcia. Szybkim ruchem wsunęła kopertę do swojej torebki. Po chwili wsunęła również drugą, zaadresowaną do Edyty. Z bijącym sercem przerzuciła resztę korespondencji. Dla Karoliny nie było nic.

Parking przed biurowcem firmy ubezpieczeniowej był zapchany i gdyby Julia miała większy samochód, to pewnie spóźniłaby się na spotkanie. Mały matiz dał się jakoś wcisnąć między dwa auta, ale z wysiadaniem miała spore kłopoty. Musiała bardzo uważać, żeby swoimi drzwiami nie zarysować czerwonego fiata punto.

– Niech się pani nie pcha, już wyjeżdżam!

Spojrzała na wielkoluda i usiadła – bardziej z wrażenia niż z potrzeby. Na upartego mogła wyjść, lecz po co się było upierać, jeżeli amant pani prezesowej, znany Julii jako tutkarz bachusek, i tak wyjeżdżał. Bez zbytniego pośpiechu manipulował przy zamku i nie rozglądał się na boki. Całkiem bezkarnie mogła nadrobić zaległości z Teatralnej i obejrzeć go sobie dokładniej. Jasna cera blondyna, upstrzona śladami po trądziku, grube rysy i mięsisty nos nie tworzyły zbyt porywającej całości. Mina bufona pasowała do potężnej postury. Ktoś, kto ma takie bicepsy, nie musi się przesadnie liczyć z otoczeniem, pomyślała.

– Panie Grzesiu! – dobiegło z góry i z okna na piętrze wychyliła się kobieca buźka z wiśniową kreską ust. – Panie Grzesiu, szef kazał, żeby pan coś odebrał od Konrada!

Nie odwrócił się, uniósł tylko rękę z kluczykami na znak, że dotarło do niego polecenie szefa i wreszcie władował się do samochodu.

W sekretariacie Julia ponownie natknęła się na wiśniowe usta – należały do ciekawskiej sekretarki. Spokojnie podała swoje nazwisko, spokojnie zniosła oględziny i całkiem spokojnie weszła do gabinetu. Nogi ugięły się pod nią dopiero na progu.

– Nabrałaś mnie! – ryknął radośnie boss. – Zastanawiałem się mianowicie, jaką sprawę może mieć do mnie informatyczka, a to ty! Siadaj, miss paragraf! Lubię konspirę, dodaje smaczku każdej transakcji. Następnym razem nie strasz mi sekretarki, to zaufana babka. Nie pogadamy dziś, bo już jestem spóźniony na ważną naradę. Żebym wiedział mianowicie, że to ty... no, ale...

Osunęła się na fotel i niechcący zaczepiła rękawem o papiery, niestarannie rozrzucone na brzegu biurka. Tuż obok jej nóg upadła broszura i jakaś koperta. Choć nie kazał jej niczego podnosić, wyciągnęła rękę. Wielkie kwadratowe kulfony i adnotacja „do rąk własnych" nie pozostawiały cienia wątpliwości, kim był nadawca. Odłożyła kopertę na biurko. Na szczęście boss nie zostawiał jej czasu na myślenie, cały czas gadał. Nie częstował kawą, bo się śpieszył, przepraszał, był zachwycony jej wyglądem, pytał, czy bukiet ładny, i sam sobie odpowiadał, że oczywiście piękny.

– Orzechowicza znasz, prawda? Musimy się spotkać w czwórkę...

– Zagramy w brydża? – spytała.

Odkąd znalazła się w gabinecie, było to pierwsze zdanie, jakie udało jej się wtrącić do monologu Bujały. Spojrzał na nią i zarechotał.

– Najpierw interesy, miss paragraf, a potem... potem to już moja głowa, żebyś tylko wzdychała... sam na sam i bez brydża. Dobrze mówię?

Lepiej niż katarynka, pomyślała, lecz patrzyła z zainteresowaniem w wyłupiaste oczka bossa. Dość szybko odzyskała równowagę i nawet przestała żałować, że nie dawał jej okazji do zademonstrowania talentów aktorskich. Jej własny scenariusz, tak starannie reżyserowany przez kilka wieczorów, okazał się niepotrzebny. To on gadał jak nakręcony i wszystko wiedział z góry. Nie rób sobie przesadnych nadziei, facet, myślała uspokojona, zostaw trochę pary na moment rozczarowania. Umówił się z nią na piętnastą trzydzieści następnego dnia i poprosił o numer telefonu. I to był ten drugi raz, kiedy w gabinecie Bujały zabrzmiał dźwięczny głos Julii. Wychodziła z uczuciem rozsadzającej ciekawości. Niczego już nie rozumiała, niczego nie wiedziała, wszystko ją zaskakiwało. Orzechowicz miał prawo znać Bujałę, ale kim był ten czwarty do brydża? Najpierw pomyślała o Chochli, potem o Leszku. Za Chochlą przemawiała koperta, za Leszkiem... Właściwie nic nie przemawiało za Leszkiem. Chyba tylko spotkanie w Teatralnej.

Ledwie wpadła do domu, zamknęła starannie drzwi wejściowe, potem te od swojego pokoju i dopiero tak odizolowana od świata, w pustym mieszkaniu, odważyła się wyciągnąć z torebki przesyłki, zaadresowane nie do niej. W kopercie Mikuli były dwa zdjęcia starego i Karoliny. Biedak na obydwu wyszedł nieszczególnie jako mężczyzna i o to chyba nadawcy chodziło. Do zdjęć dołączony był liścik: *1 szt – 1000 zł płatne do banku natychmiast po otrzymaniu nie później niż w ciągu dwu dni jeśli nie chcesz świecić przydatkami w gazecie i gdzie indziej.* Zamiast podpisu była nazwa banku i numer konta. Koperta Edyty zawierała cztery fotki z tej samej serii, z bardziej wyeksponowaną postacią Karoliny. Listu nie było.

Julia starannie schowała obydwie koperty i skuliła się na fotelu. Zakręciło jej się w głowie od faktów, nazwisk i twarzy. Ale się władowałam w towarzystwo, pomyślała z niechęcią. Jeżeli wciąż jestem Matą Hari, to całe podobieństwo sprowadza się do nieuchronnej egzekucji. Co ja właściwie wyprawiam? Uwodzę szantażystę, kradnę cudze listy i pcham się w jakąś szaloną aferę, o której nie mam zielonego pojęcia. Przez chwilę zapragnęła rzucić wszystko i umknąć samotnie do Szczyrku, gdzie nikogo nie znała, lub jeszcze chętniej na plan „Quo vadis", gdzie nikt jej nie chciał. Jednocześnie czuła, że nie potrafi się wycofać. Namąciła trochę i przynajmniej winna była pomoc Karolinie. Mogła sobie darować Mikulę, losy firmy, Bujałę, bo im niczego nie obiecywała

– Graj, Juleczko, dalej, nic innego ci nie zostało – powiedziała głośno dla dodania sobie odwagi. Właściwie wszystko było przed nią. Dlaczego niby miała zakładać przegraną, jeśli chciała wygrać! Próbowała zebrać myśli i wyciągnąć logiczne wnioski. Nadal niczego nie rozumiała, ale coś zaczynało jej świtać.

Chochla! Facet najwyraźniej połknął przynętę, którą niechcący zarzuciła, i zaczął gromadzić pieniądze na wspólny wyjazd. Prosił przecież, żeby mu dała trochę czasu. Skąd mogła wiedzieć, że jednym skinieniem głowy ugotuje Mikulę i paru innych ludzi, choćby Bujałę? A co z Karoliną? To, że zdjęcia Karoliny były w kopercie dla Edyty, mogło znaczyć bardzo dużo. Albo kompletnie nic. Marcin był nieobliczalnym durniem, więc w grę wchodziła zarówno zwykła pomyłka, jak i współdziałanie z sekretarką.

Boss! Zaskoczenie było obopólne. Nie jego spodziewała się zastać w fotelu prezesa Bujały. Prawdopodobnie był szantażowany przez Chochlę, na pewno znał amanta Mikulowej, a ją, Julię, brał za prawniczkę Karolinę Cierniak. Nie wyprowadziła go z błędu, po pierwsze dlatego, że nie dopuścił jej do głosu, po drugie, sama nie wiedziała, jak będzie lepiej dla sprawy. Przyjęła jednak wyzwanie i następnego dnia zamierzała jeszcze raz złożyć wizytę bossowi. Liczyła, że w razie czego Konrad stanie w jej obronie.

Leszek! Na wspomnienie Leszka poczuła przykry skurcz w piersiach. Kłamał cały czas, od momentu, gdy pokazał Karolinie zieloną teczkę. Wypierał się znajomości z Bujałą, wiedział znacznie więcej, niż mówił, i z jakichś powodów podpuszczał obie dziewczyny. Spotkanie w Teatralnej było ukartowane. Naszła ją ochota, by natychmiast porozmawiać z Leszkiem. Jeżeli oszukiwał, to nie dlatego, że miał taką fantazję, tylko krył się za tym jakiś cel. I właśnie o ten cel chciała zapytać.

Sięgnęła po książkę telefoniczną i całkiem przypadkowo otworzyła na literce P. Jak Pałubska. Nazwisko Edyty podkreślone było czerwonym pisakiem i wyraźnie odcinało się od innych. Zerknęła bez większego zainteresowania. Tuż nad Edytą była Bronisława, czyli świętej pamięci sąsiadka Wandy. Julia zastanowiła się moment i nowy szalony pomysł zaświtał jej w głowie. Od śmierci pani Bronisławy minęły dwa czy trzy lata, zmienił się charakter mieszkania, ale numer telefonu najprawdopodobniej pozostał ten sam. Wystarczyło zadzwonić, by przekonać się, czy rzeczywiście siedzi tam głupi Marcinek.

Długie sygnały jeden po drugim nieprzyjemnie dźwięczały w uchu. Próbowała jeszcze ze dwa razy i nic. Chochla mógł wyjść, mógł siedzieć i nie podnosić słuchawki lub – co też należało brać pod uwagę – trop był niewłaściwy. Co do tropu Julia miała jednak inne zdanie, uważała, że jest bardzo właściwy. Telefon sprawił, że znowu poczuła się w środku wydarzeń, które za namową Marty rozkręcały wspólnie z Karoliną. Zapomniała o Leszku, szykowała się do usadzenia Chochli.

W czasie gdy Karolina pertraktowała w Warszawie, Julia miała zebrać na miejscu jak najwięcej informacji. Przede wszystkim ustalić, czy Marcinek wychodzi z domu, w jakich godzinach i czy ktoś go odwiedza. Bardzo w tym względzie liczyła na znajomość z Wandą. Musiała też pozyskać trzecią wspólniczkę. Przed powrotem rodziców wyskoczyła na chwilę do Renaty. Rozumowała logicznie, że dla dziewczyny zatrudnionej w agencji towarzyskiej obce jest uczucie obrzydzenia. Idzie z partnerem, który płaci, i koniec. Tym razem płacić miał nie mężczyzna, tylko one z Karoliną. Powiedzmy, że miały swój dzień dobroci dla zwierząt i postanowiły zafundować miłemu Chochli godzinkę przyjemności. Julia szła do koleżanki w przekonaniu, że interes jest czysty, dyskusja zaś może dotyczyć jedynie ceny. A jednak.

– Julka, w co ty mnie chcesz wrobić? – spytała Renata. – To nie jest uczciwe, co mi proponujesz. Pracuję w agencji, wcale się tego nie wypieram, ale to nie znaczy, że biorę każdą robotę. Nie pomogę wam wynieść zdjęć ani niczego. Wy znikniecie, ja zostanę i po co mi taki szajs? Za dobrze zarabiam, żebym miała ochotę ryzykować.

– Reniu, chodzi tylko o jedną dziewczynę, o moją przyjaciółkę! – błagała Julia.

– Będę z tobą szczera! Te babki z garsonier, te co dają na czarno, robią nam konkurencję. Ja się nad takimi nie lituję. Takie czasy nastały, niestety!

Stanowcza i zdecydowana odmowa Renaty sprawiła, że najważniejsza część planu zawaliła się z hukiem. Ktoś musiał zabawić Chochlę, by ktoś inny wyniósł z mieszkania archiwum, czyli zdjęcia i filmy. Chciała oczywiście pomóc Karolinie, zgadzała się odwalić najczarniejszą robotę, byle tylko nie wystąpić w charakterze niańki lub... brr... nałożnicy. Na samo wspomnienie Marcinka dostawała zimnych dreszczy. I kiedy tak nieprzychylnie sobie o nim rozmyślała, w przedpokoju rozdzwonił się telefon. Podbiegła natychmiast, przekonana, że to Karolina lub Marta. Męski głos, który chciał rozmawiać z Julią Blendą, wpadał do ucha i – licho wie jakim cudem – niebezpiecznie wpływał na dygot nóg. Wywołała wilka z lasu i z wrażenia musiała oprzeć się o ścianę.

– Dlaczego twoja komórka nie działa? – spytał z wyrzutem Chochla. Potem długo jej tłumaczył, ile starań kosztowało go zdobycie numeru domowego.

Siedział w domu, pluskolec przebrzydły, tylko nie odbierał telefonów, pomyślała ze złością. Mruknęła coś uspokajająco o awarii komórki i z przerażeniem stwierdziła, że Marcin z wyrzutów skoczył prosto w sentymenty. Plótł jak prawdziwie zakochany i nawet nie świntuszył, co zupełnie do niego nie pasowało.

– Tego... no, ty lubisz jakąś biżuterię? – spytał nieoczekiwanie.

– Znasz kobietę, która nie lubi? – odpowiedziała wymijająco.

– Nie wiem... no... ale oprócz ciebie nie znam żadnej, której chciałbym coś dać.

Uczepiła się tej biżuterii, żeby mu wytłumaczyć, że bardziej ceni u mężczyzn szczerość niż hojność. Zachichotał ubawiony. Widać miał zupełnie inne doświadczenia w tej materii.

– Nie śmiej się, nie masz do mnie zaufania. Też chciałabym dzwonić do ciebie, kiedy przyjdzie mi ochota.

– Wiem, tego... ale ty też mi dałaś zły numer. A mój telefon – znowu zachichotał – jest przedpotopowy i on odbiera tylko... no... niektóre rozmowy.

– Zwłaszcza od Edyty, prawda! – powiedziała tonem rozkapryszonej zazdrośnicy.

– No, tego... ona wie, ale wiesz... ona to co innego. Ja ciebie kocham.

Wyznanie było czułe, można powiedzieć – wyczerpujące, lecz na Julii nie zrobiło dobrego wrażenia. Był daleko, mógł sobie gadać, co chciał, a ona nie miała zamiaru więcej go oglądać. Musiała natomiast – i to za wszelką cenę – zdobyć numer telefonu. Obiecała to Karolinie. Najprościej byłoby spytać Edytę, pomyślała ubawiona. Co takiego mogła wiedzieć Edyta, o czym Julia nie miała pojęcia? Uruchomiła wyobraźnię. Zobaczyła wielkie biurko i sekretarkę bębniącą palcami po blacie. To było tego ranka, gdy chciała dzwonić do Bujały. Coś ją wtedy uderzyło, ale co? Od dedukcji oderwał ją następny telefon.

– Mikula mi się oświadczył! Co ty na to? – spytała Karolina.

– A mnie Chochla. Co ty na to? – odpowiedziała Julia i już chichotały razem, jedna w Warszawie, druga we Włocławku. Karolinie widać nie miał kto przerwać, ale nad Julią czuwała matka i rozmowa z konieczności została skrócona do minimum.

Głupia jestem jak stołowa noga, wyrzucała sobie Julia, ścieląc tapczan. Przecież mam tę cholerną komórkę, która daje mi niezależność... tylko gdzie ją mam? Postanowiła zaraz po kąpieli odszukać telefon, podłączyć do ładowarki i więcej się z nim nie rozstawać.

W firmie zaczęły się dziać dziwne rzeczy. Przede wszystkim od ubiegłego tygodnia, od piątku lub nawet czwartku, nie pokazała się pani prezes. Ostatnio wpadała nawet za często, po trzy, cztery razy dziennie i nagle jak nożem uciął. Dyrektor wciąż był w Warszawie i normalnie dla sekretariatu powinny nastać złote czasy. Pod nieobecność szefa zawsze pracy ubywało. Tym razem jednak w Edytę wstąpił duch reformatora. Od poniedziałku twardą ręką chwyciła swój personel. Wyspowiadała Leszka z tego, co zrobił i czego nie zrobił, potem dobrała się do skóry Julii.

– Instrukcja obsługi kombajnu? – zdziwiła się, patrząc na biurko. – Przecież nawet nie mamy takiej maszyny. Kto ci to kazał tłumaczyć?

– Pani na polecenie szefa.

– Kiedy to było! Nie wyrywasz sobie rękawków, prawda? Wyrzuć te papierzyska do kosza! Od dzisiaj usiądziesz na moim miejscu i przejmiesz moje obowiązki. Nie rób takich oczu. Jak widzisz, Mikula jeszcze mnie nie zwolnił i nieprędko zwolni. – Roześmiała się krótko, ostro i niewesoło.

Julia posłusznie, choć z duszą na ramieniu, przeniosła się za biurko Edyty. Nie bardzo rozumiała, co się dzieje. Sekretarka urzędowała w gabinecie dyrektora, asystentka dyrektora zastępowała sekretarkę, jedynie Leszek został u siebie. Edyta zachowywała się zupełnie inaczej niż do tej pory. Przede wszystkim zmieniła ton i sposób rozmowy. Nie prosiła, lecz wydawała polecenia. Nawet pomoc gospodarcza odczuła na własnej skórze, że coś jest nie tak. Raz tylko spróbowała zrzucić na Julię mycie szklanek i to, co usłyszała, przejęło ją największą grozą.

– Albo pani pracuje, albo jutro proszę się nie fatygować. Na pani miejsce czeka kilkanaście kobiet – powiedziała Edyta.

Purpurowa ze złości Henia wycofała się bez słowa i co było zupełnie do niej niepodobne, starła podłogę w kuchence, potem siłą rozpędu jeszcze kurze w sekretariacie. Jedyną osobą, z którą Julia mogła porozmawiać, był Leszek. Ostatnio go unikała, lecz po rozmowie z Bujałą zmieniła zdanie.

– Napijesz się herbaty? – spytała, zaglądając do pokoju magistrów.

Podniósł głowę znad papierów. Twarz miał bledszą niż zwykle, oczy podkrążone.

– Zaraz sobie zrobię, nie fatyguj się, Julio! – odpowiedział poważnie i tak jakoś zasadniczo, że dziewczynę zamurowało.

– Mocną, z dwiema łyżeczkami cukru, o ile pamiętam! – Uśmiechnęła się leciutko i wyszła do kuchenki zagotować wodę. Niczym spod ziemi wyrosła obok Henia.

– Ty widzisz, jakie zmiany? – szepnęła konspiracyjnie. Zajrzała przy tym do sekretariatu, by upewnić się, że Edyty nie ma.

Julia wzruszyła ramionami.

– Albo szykuje się nowy przekręt, albo firma splajtowała, jedno z dwojga. Nie wiem, co bym wolała, bo zdaje się w obu przypadkach czeka nas to samo, czyli bezrobocie – odpowiedziała.

– E, nie jest tak źle. Mikulowa sprzedała firmę, wiesz? Powiem ci, że możemy na tym wyjść dużo lepiej. To na razie tajemnica. Ludzie reagują histerycznie na takie zmiany, nie trzeba ich straszyć. Każdy psycholog ci to powie. Jedynie pana Leszka możesz uprzedzić.

– Sama go uprzedź. Narobiłaś chłopakowi brudu...

– No i co ty opowiadasz? To były żarty. – Henia wydawała się zawstydzona. – Ja tam przesądna nie jestem, ale w sny wierzę. Pamiętasz, jak mi się śniła małpa? Wyszły plotki i dybanie na moją cnotę, pamiętasz przecież?! Plotek się boję, to trochę pomogłam losowi. Nagadałam, bo nagadałam, tylko mi nie mów, że dla chłopa jest to poważny zarzut. Oni wszyscy są jak te psiaki, za spódniczkami tylko ganiają, czy to Leszek, czy inny.

Na szczęście czajnik zabulgotał i Julia mogła zająć się parzeniem herbaty. Nie bardzo wiedziała, co odpowiedzieć i jak zareagować, jednak dzięki Heni znalazła pretekst do rozmowy z Leszkiem. Uspokoiła chłopaka, że nie będzie odpowiadał za molestowanie seksualne pomocy gospodarczej, i natychmiast, jako zwykłą ciekawostkę, przekazała wiadomość o sprzedaży firmy. Była przekonana, że w gadaniu Heni tyle prawdy, co w historii z cnotą.

Leszek widać był innego zdania, bo patrzył poważnie, bez uśmiechu.

– Wiesz coś więcej na ten temat? – spytała zaskoczona.

– Więcej, to znaczy komu sprzedała, tak? Nie mam pojęcia, komu by się opłacało kupować taki burdel na kółkach. Budampolex 2 to nie Nobiles ani Delekta, zagraniczni kontrahenci odpadają. Nie, Julio, nie wiem nic więcej.

Julia przypomniała sobie „mów mi Gutek". Facet plótł coś o sprzedaży i być może wcale nie wspominał starych dziejów, jak początkowo sądziła.

– A gdyby nową właścicielką była kobieta – powiedziała z namysłem – to kogo byś typował?

– Może Henię?! – Napił się gorącej herbaty i wykrzywił pociesznie.

Julia jednak nie miała ochoty na żarty. Była pewna, że wiedział dużo więcej, niż mówił. Delikatnie dotknął jej ramienia.

– Nie martw się, jakoś to będzie!

– Jakoś, to ja sobie radzę z matką w domu. W pracy chciałabym robić to, co umiem, i mieć pewność.

– Może jeszcze będziesz miała.

– Jak Bujała zostanie właścicielem? – rzuciła z zaczepką w głosie. – Nie znasz Bujały? Za to znasz kłopotka, inaczej bossa, prawda? To ten sam facet i nie mów mi, że nie wiedziałeś.

Wydroń pobladł jeszcze bardziej.

– Byłaś u niego? – spytał cicho.

Julię zastanowiła ta nagła bladość i ten dziwny, głuchy szept. Oho, pomyślała, niechcący nadepnęłam patyczakowi na odcisk.

– A po jaką cholerę miałabym odwiedzać twoich kumpli? – powiedziała gderliwym tonem własnej matki. – Umówiliśmy się, że gramy zespołowo. Lubię trzymać się zasad, takiego mam konika. Od początku nie chciałeś, żebym do niego poszła, teraz robisz minę kota na puszczy, zamiast po ludzku wyjaśnić, o co chodzi.

– Nie jest tak, Julio, jak myślisz.

– Skąd możesz wiedzieć, co ja myślę?

– Nie jest tak! – powtórzył z cichym uporem.

– Wiem. Jest dużo gorzej, bo jeden z partnerów gra znaczonymi kartami! Nie będę pokazywała palcem który.

Mógł zaprzeczyć, zaprotestować, mógł się bronić, ale wybrał milczenie. Julia zrezygnowana wróciła do sekretariatu.

Przed wyjściem z biurowca zajrzała do działu informatyki. Edyta nie zgodziła się, żeby w godzinach pracy pomagała inżynierowi Orzechowiczowi przeglądać programy komputerowe. Do czasu zmian organizacyjnych chciała ją mieć w sekretariacie. Julia wstąpiła więc do Konrada, by zaproponować popołudniową współpracę. Wyraźnie się ucieszył.

– To co, pojedziemy do mnie? – spytał.

– Nie, nie, ja też mam dobry sprzęt! – zaprotestowała gwałtownie.

– W porządku! – uśmiechnął się nieznacznie, kącikiem ust.

Poczuła, że się rumieni. Nie była z siebie zadowolona. Gwałtowny protest i rumieńce uznała za swoją wpadkę.

Śliczna mała i jeszcze potrafi się rumienić, pomyślał Konrad.

Uczciwie przepracowali u Julii całe popołudnie z dwiema niewielkimi przerwami na jedzenie. Od komputera oderwał ich dopiero powrót

Blendów z pracy. Matka za nic w świecie nie chciała sobie darować kolacji w towarzystwie pana inżyniera. Nie przyjmowała do wiadomości grzecznej, aczkolwiek stanowczej odmowy Konrada.

– A cóż to się panu stało w oko? – spytała, gdy próbował się pożegnać.

– Drobiazg. Upominek od pięknej kobiety – odpowiedział z uśmiechem.

– Coś ci kipi! – krzyknęła Julia. Za dobrze znała matkę, by po minie nie zorientować się, co zaraz powie. Dzięki fałszywemu alarmowi Konrad umknął w samą porę.

– Wypuściłaś gościa bez kolacji? – zirytowała się matka.

– Zje w domu.

– To ta baba go tak urządziła? Jak mówiłam, że awanturnica, nie chciałaś mi wierzyć. Miły chłopak, ale mógłby zdjąć buty w przedpokoju, jak wszyscy. Następnym razem podpowiedz mu... Możesz nawet powołać się na mnie.

– Wykluczone! To mój gość i najwyżej sama sprzątnę. Facet w skarpetkach wygląda komicznie.

– Niby czemu? Co w tym komicznego, że oszczędza moją pracę? I nie gadaj mi, że sprzątniesz! Twoje majtki leżą już drugi tydzień w łazience i zastanawiam się, co włożysz na tyłek, jak ci nie wypiorę?

Julia nie lubiła gadania matki nawet wtedy, gdy znajdowała w nim ziarno prawdy. Fakt, nie sprzątała, nie prała, nie robiła w domu właściwie niczego, ale to dlatego, że matka chciała czuć się potrzebna i niezastąpiona, żeby móc o tym rozprawiać przy każdej okazji.

Dobra, od dzisiaj piorę i sprzątam u siebie, postanowiła Julia, zamykając się w pokoju pod pretekstem dalszej pracy.

Wieczorem zadzwoniła Karolina. Nastąpiły nieprzewidziane trudności w negocjacjach i pobyt w Warszawie wydłużał się do czwartku. Pytała o Konrada i Chochlę, choć o każdego inaczej.

– Wracaj szybko. Tutaj zmiana goni zmianę, ale to nie jest rozmowa na telefon. Co w stolicy? Jak towarzystwo?

– Same mordochlejki! Rzygać mi się chce od tych pustych gadek.

O Mikuli i jego oświadczynach nawet nie wspomniała.

Przed snem Julia próbowała poczytać. Sięgnęła po „Quo vadis", ale jakoś zabrakło jej ochoty, by spotkać się z partnerem. Myślała Winicjusz, a widziała ostre rysy, głęboko osadzone oczy i sporego guza na czole.

Następnego dnia, kiedy Konrad zapytał, gdzie będą pracować po południu, zgodziła się pojechać do niego. Był odpowiedzialnym facetem, zachowywał się normalnie, poza tym mama Blendowa nie znała jego adresu, Julia zaś była ciekawa, jak żyje i mieszka samotny mężczyzna.

Konrad wciąż jeszcze miał kłopot z odpowiedzią na pytanie, kim jest dla niego Karolina. Nie kochał tej zakręconej dziewczyny, ale tęsknił za jej pieszczotami, za ciałem, wspominał miłe chwile i wtedy gotów był gryźć palce ze złości, że przegrał z kimś takim jak Mikula. Wystarczyło jednak, że trochę ochłonął i już zaczynał się zastanawiać, czy nie powinien dziękować losowi. Jeszcze nie zdążył podziękować, gdy przed oczami jawiły się ślicznie zaokrąglone piersi, a z nimi wracała ochota, by gryźć palce. Huśtał się od chłodnej logiki po gorącą zazdrość. Nie zwariował chyba tylko dlatego, że był przywalony pracą i niewiele miał czasu na myślenie.

Nie zwariował również dlatego, że inżynier Julia Blenda rozbiła mu głowę. Pozornie jedno z drugim nie miało żadnego związku. Oberwał solidnie i to było przykre; przykry był również późniejszy siniak. Natomiast wszystko, co się zdarzyło między oberwaniem i siniakiem, było wyjątkowo miłe, szczególnie dotyk delikatnej dłoni na policzku. Niestety, Julia opatrzyła ranę i koniec. Następnego dnia pracowali razem całe popołudnie i wychodziło na to, że bez drugiego guza nie ma mowy o żadnym gładzeniu policzka. Dziewczyna była miła, serdeczna, lecz skupiona wyłącznie na analizie programów. Podziwiał jej błyskotliwość, cieszył oczy śmiesznymi piegami na nosie i nie bardzo wiedział, jak zwekslować rozmowę na inne tory. Julia ucieleśniała typ, jaki go zawsze pociągał. Delikatna i krucha, budziła opiekuńcze instynkty. Spoglądał na nią coraz cieplej i dzięki niej przestawał myśleć o Karolinie. Oj, Raduś, Raduś, kiedy ty się ustatkujesz, przemawiał do siebie czule słowami ciotki Eweliny. Żyjesz na świecie trzydzieści trzy lata i albo uciekasz przed babkami, albo chwytasz dwie jednocześnie.

Zapraszając Julię do swojego mieszkania, wcale nie zakładał, by miało z tego wyniknąć coś złego. Czy to nie wszystko jedno, w czyim mieszkaniu siedzi się przy komputerze?

– Ojej! – wykrzyknęła zaskoczona Julia.

Z niedowierzaniem patrzyła na meble, które mimo ich wieku trudno byłoby nazwać antykami, na białe szydełkowe serwetki i doniczki z kwiatami. Brakowało tylko mruczącego kota na poduszce.

– Co panią tak zaskoczyło? – spytał. Wystraszył się, że zobaczyła pająka albo zwały kurzu. Poprzedniego wieczoru posprzątał trochę na wypadek, gdyby przyjęła jego zaproszenie.

– Pan mi pasuje do zupełnie innego wnętrza. Regały na książki, grafika na ścianie... Tylko biurko się zgadza. Ile razy wyobrażałam sobie pana... – zamilkła zawstydzona, zarumieniła się i dokończyła o wiele ciszej: – to zawsze w takim nowoczesnym pokoju.

Uśmiechnął się leciutko, po swojemu, jednym kącikiem ust. Szczera naiwność Julii przypadła mu do gustu. To było bardzo miłe, że myślała o nim, wyobrażała go sobie na tle surowego wnętrza. Czy tylko na tle wnętrza? Męska próżność kazała mu w to wątpić. Czemu kobiece myśli miałyby być skromniejsze od męskich? Rozejrzał się po pokoju, jakby widział go po raz pierwszy w życiu.

– Wszystko jest tak, jak ona urządziła – powiedział, wskazując fotografię starszej kobiety. Pomyślał, że takie dziewczyny lubią sentymentalne wyznania.

– To babcia? Bo chyba nie mama? – spytała Julia, wpatrując się w okrągłą, serdecznie uśmiechniętą twarz ciotki Eweliny.

– To moja największa miłość, pani Julio. Jak pani wiadomo, serce nie ma zmarszczek, więc proszę się nie dziwić.

– Dobrze, nie będę się dziwić – obiecała, choć ciekawość aż zapierała dech. Bardzo jej się podobało, że szanował rodzinną tradycję.

On zajął się parzeniem herbaty, ona oglądaniem pokoju. Trochę zagracony, lecz czysty. Podeszła do okna. W dole huczała ulica Toruńska, zapchana o tej porze samochodami, dalej widziała Wisłę i zielone skarpy zarośnięte lasem. Od okna wróciła do zdjęcia na serwantce. Kiedy zabrzęczały filiżanki, usiadła przy stole, na wprost Konrada.

– Czasem mi się wydaje, że jestem facetem ze spóźnionym zapłonem – powiedział. – W moim życiu nic nie dzieje się w porę, wszystko po czasie. Choćby i ona – oczami wskazał zdjęcie. – Bardzo chciałem się nią zająć, spłacić wielki dług, i jakoś nie wyszło. Najpierw była zbyt energiczna, zaraz potem umarła. Odziedziczyłem po niej mieszkanie i dbam, żeby wszystko było tak jak kiedyś. W tym domu spędziłem swoje najszczęśliwsze lata.

– Nie myślałam, że pan jest sentymentalny.

– Tego bym o sobie raczej nie powiedział. – Roześmiał się, patrząc na ożywioną twarz dziewczyny. – Doceniam siłę wszelkiej tradycji, tej złej również, lecz to już całkiem inna opowieść. Tak więc sentymentalny nie jestem, ale mam inne dobre cechy, na przykład silnie rozwinięty instynkt opiekuńczy. Nie żartuję! Jako dzieciak modliłem się, żeby ojciec zachorował i żebym mógł się nim zająć. Powiedziałem o tym księdzu na spowiedzi. On to potraktował jako poważny grzech, a ja tylko chciałem się komuś pochwalić, że tyle mam w sobie dobroci.

– Teraz też pan się chwali?

– Nie. Teraz zanudzam panią wspomnieniami.

– Proszę zanudzać dalej. Rozumiem, że modlitwy nie zostały wysłuchane i pański ojciec cieszy się zdrowiem?

– Tego nie wiem. Zresztą, tak naprawdę nigdy nie miałem ojca. Matki też nie miałem.

– Jak to: nie miał pan?

– Tak wyszło – uciął krótko.

Patrzyła na niego i zastanawiała się: dziwak czy pozer? W każdym razie na pewno nie mruk, jak początkowo sądziła. Kiedy już się rozkręcił, mówił dużo i chętnie. Ale choć przegadali całe popołudnie, właściwie niczego o sobie nie powiedział.

Ten facet nosi jakąś tajemnicę, pomyślała, gdy się żegnali w przedpokoju.

Wrażliwa, umie słuchać, kupiła wszystkie moje dyrdymałki, a do tego biust ma jak wyrzeźbiony, przyznał w duchu, podając Julii żakiet.

Podał jak należy, starannie i tak, żeby od razu mogła zapiąć pierwszy guzik. Nie zdjął rąk z jej ramion; przytrzymał przez moment w silnym uścisku, pocałował we włosy, w ucho, potem zdecydowanym ruchem odwrócił twarzą do siebie i pocałował w usta.

– Panie Konradzie, przyjaciele naszych przyjaciółek nie muszą być naszymi... kochankami – szepnęła Julia.

– Umówmy się tak, kochanie – powiedział, dotykając czołem jej czoła. – Najpierw zostanę dla ciebie Konradem, potem porozmawiamy o przyjaciółkach przyjaciół, czy tam odwrotnie, jak sobie zechcesz. Zgoda?

– Nie wiem... muszę się z tą propozycją przespać.

Chciał zażartować, że nie musi spać akurat z propozycją, ale nim otworzył usta, uznał żart za trywialny i nie powiedział nic.

Odprowadził dziewczynę do samochodu, poczekał, aż odjechała, i wrócił do mieszkania. Wydało mu się podwójnie puste. Na stole wciąż stały dwie filiżanki. Potarł ręką zmęczone oczy. Miła dziewczyna, pomyślał, sentymentalna, naiwna, takiej można raz dwa zawrócić w głowie, tylko co potem? A może... może właśnie taką warto by mieć?

W nocy odezwały się dawne koszmary. Miał bardzo plastyczny sen: widział czarne ściany z sieciami pajęczyn i wielkiego, przygarbionego mężczyznę przy stole. Gdzieś w tym pomieszczeniu był jeszcze mały chłopiec. I kobieta. Wiedział, czuł to, że za chwilę wielkolud podejdzie do chłopca, złapie go za koszulkę na karku i uniesie do góry jak psiaka. Tym razem było jednak inaczej. Zniknęły czarne ściany, pojawiła się wąska ulica. Usłyszał ostry zgrzyt hamulców i poczuł ból w nodze. Na wpół przytomny usiadł na łóżku. Hałasowały auta jadące Toruńską. Sam już nie wiedział, czy obudził go hałas, czy ból. Pewnie szykuje się zmiana pogody, pomyślał.

Julia wracała od Konrada z mętlikiem w głowie i wyrzutami sumienia. Głupio się czuła wobec Karoliny. Wyrzucała sobie, że posunęła się stanowczo za daleko. Rozwalenie głowy to był wypadek, ale już całowanie powinna sobie darować. Miała zamiar wszystko starannie przemyśleć, dopóki rodzice nie wrócą z pracy. Zwykle zjawiali się w domu koło dwudziestej. Zanim jednak wyjęła klucz, matka otworzyła drzwi na całą szerokość i porwała Julię w objęcia.

– Gdzie ty jeździsz wieczorami, gdzie jeździsz? Nie wiesz, nie słyszałaś, że na Noakowskiego wysadzili garaż?! W południe dwie ulice dalej była strzelanina. Żyjemy w bandyckim mieście i w bandyckich czasach. Już tylko w domu można się czuć bezpiecznie.

– Myślisz, że w innych miastach jest inaczej? – zdziwiła się Julia.

– Mnie obchodzi moje miasto i moja rodzina. Mam się o kogo martwić. Obiecaj, że po pracy będziesz siedziała w domu!

– Czy nam coś grozi?

– To samo co wszystkim.

– Zachowujesz się tak, jakby co najmniej wybuchła wojna. Nie mam żadnych porachunków z gangami i to wszystko guzik mnie obchodzi. Chcę żyć normalnie, wychodzić z domu, kiedy mam potrzebę, i tak samo wracać.

– Głupia jesteś i życia nie znasz! Czy ja ci kiedy źle radziłam? Zresztą, o czym tu gadać: tak ma być i koniec!

Julia zamknęła się w pokoju i włączyła komputer, żeby przynajmniej udawać zapracowanie. Myślenie o Konradzie i uczuciowe remanenty odłożyła na późny wieczór. Co sobie przypomniała zdarzenie w jego przedpokoju, czuła przyśpieszone bicie serca. Nie, nie, porozklejam się potem, teraz muszę myśleć logicznie, powtarzała z uporem. Pomogło. Skupiła się na Chochli. Najbardziej martwił ją wybuch matki, która co jakiś czas miewała obsesyjne napady strachu. Jeśli teraz mnie uziemi, pomyślała przerażona, diabli wezmą cały plan. Potrzebuję jednego, najlepiej dwu wolnych wieczorów. Trudno, pod pretekstem delegacji – albo jeszcze lepiej kursu – zamelinuję się u Karoliny.

Było to jedyne wyjście i kiedy je znalazła, z miejsca się uspokoiła. Przejrzała jeszcze raz wiadomości na temat fotokomórek, ukrytych kamer i innych cudów techniki. Znajomy, którego prosiła o pomoc, patrzył podejrzliwie, jakby szykowała się co najmniej do obrobienia banku. A ona zamiast planu banku miała przed sobą rozkład kawalerki, naszkicowany przez Karolinę. Z wąskiego przedpokoju pierwsze drzwi po prawej prowadziły do łazienki, drugie do kuchni. Na wprost był pokój, ten z tapczanem, nad którym ktoś zamontował kamerę. Reszta urządzeń do monitorowania znajdowała się prawdopodobnie w kuchni, niedostępnej dla gości. Tam właśnie Julia musiała się dostać. Zakładała, ba, przyjęła jako pewnik, że Chochla przeniósł swoje archiwum do garsoniery. Pamiętała, jak po zniknięciu kierownika jego żona płakała, że zabrał tylko skarpetki, majtki i kartonowe teczki. Teraz miała już pewność, co było w tych pilnie strzeżonych teczkach. Im głębiej wnikała w szczegóły, tym większe czuła podniecenie.

W porze wiadomości, kiedy rodzice zajęci byli telewizorem i mniej podsłuchiwali, zadzwoniła do Torunia. Konspiracyjnym szeptem poinformowała Martę, że zaczynają akcję w piątek wieczorem.

– Wspaniale! – zawołała Marta. – Słuchaj, będziesz się bała, będziesz się dziadowsko bała, ale pamiętaj o jednym: to ty masz być górą, nie twój strach. On ma na ciebie działać mobilizująco. Trzymam za was kciuki i zapraszam do siebie na opijanie sukcesu!

Po takim zastrzyku optymizmu Julii nie pozostawało nic innego, jak zająć się czymś naprawdę pożytecznym. Spakowała drobiazgi niezbędne każdemu człowiekowi w delegacji: szczotkę do zębów, ręcznik i piżamę. Rodzicom zamierzała powiedzieć o wyjeździe dopiero przy śniadaniu, żeby krócej słuchać gadania mamy. Zanim wyłączyła komputer, przejrzała jeszcze pocztę elektroniczną.

Nie wiem, jak na jednym malutkim nosie zmieściło się 138 prześlicznych piegów. Policzyłem i tyle jest. Każdy wygląda jak małe słoneczko i nie pozwala o sobie zapomnieć. Życzę Ci miłych snów. K.

Masz szczęście, drogi K., że wyrosłam z kompleksów na punkcie swoich piegów. Pięć lat temu taka czuła wiadomość pogrzebałaby wszystkie twoje szanse, pomyślała. I zaraz sobie uświadomiła, że przecież on nie ma żadnych szans. Gdyby nie był chłopakiem Karoliny, to tak, owszem, na pewno i z wielką radością, lecz on był chłopakiem Karoliny i *fine*! Posmutniała.

Wieczorem rozmawiała jeszcze raz z Toruniem. Tym razem to Marta zadzwoniła z przypomnieniem, że po udanej akcji Karolina obowiązkowo powinna zniknąć na jakiś czas.

– Poradź jej, żeby wzięła tydzień urlopu i przyjechała do mnie – mówiła z przejęciem.

– Tak, oczywiście – odpowiedziała Julia.

Dłużej nie mogła rozmawiać, bo matka stała w przedpokoju i kręciła głową z wyraźną naganą. Jej zdaniem córka niepotrzebnie blokowała telefon, który służył do załatwiania poważnych spraw.

– Ja nie rozumiem, żeby tak gadać i gadać! To już chyba twoja ósma rozmowa. I zgaś wreszcie światło, to wszystko kosztuje!

Rodzice byli ludźmi zamożnymi, nawet bardzo zamożnymi, jednak nie potrafili wyzbyć się nawyków przesadnego oszczędzania prądu, gazu i wszystkiego, co się dało. Nie żałowali pieniędzy na jedzenie i na zachcianki córki: samochód, komputer, stroje – proszę bardzo. Jeśli jednak nie gasiła światła lub przy kąpieli lała zbyt dużo wody, obrywała, aż furczało.

– Nie wiem, po co kupiłam ci komórkę. Domowy aparat tańszy, co?

Prawda była taka, że Julia znowu zapomniała o podłączeniu telefonu do prostownika. Pamięć miała krótką, wystarczyło, że nie zrobiła czegoś od ręki, natychmiast zapominała. Sprawny telefon był jednym z nieodzownych elementów planu, który przygotowywały z Karoliną. Odszukała aparat, włączyła do sieci i dopiero wtedy przypomniała sobie o Wandzie Pasieczko. Gdy tylko matka zniknęła w łazience, po cichu, niemal konspiracyjnie, skorzystała jeszcze raz z domowego telefonu. Wanda ucieszyła się jak małe dziecko. Niemal chlipała do słuchawki. Nie było w niej ani cienia chłodnej rezerwy, jaką zademonstrowała pod koniec ostatniego spotkania.

– Masz gości? – spytała domyślnie Julia. Daleko w tle słyszała męski głos i urywany śmieszek.

– Nie, to tylko... kuzynka nocuje, bo rano wyjeżdża – wyjaśniła pośpiesznie.

– Nie widziałam cię na medytacjach i zaczęłam się obawiać, czy nie zachorowałaś – powiedziała dziewczyna.

– Ścięłam się z naszą główną. – Wanda przeszła na szept. – Wiesz, kogo mam na myśli. Odrzuciła mój najnowszy hymn, przepiękny zresztą. Odkąd stała się właścicielką zakładu, strasznie zadziera nosa.

Julia odłożyła słuchawkę uspokojona, że niczego nie zaniechała.

Bujała zadzwonił przed południem i wyznaczył Konradowi spotkanie o piętnastej trzydzieści u siebie w biurze.

– I nie mów do mnie, żebym się odwalił, bo mianowicie mogę tego nie ścierpieć! – powiedział niby żartem, lecz poważnie. Natomiast całkiem już żartobliwie określił prawniczkę Karolinę Cierpik jako fest dupę, czym zaskoczył Konrada.

– Cierniak chyba – poprawił odruchowo. – Dawno ją znasz?

– Znam wszystkie dupy warte grzechu! – pochwalił się Grzegorz i zaraz dodał, że ta Cierniak również będzie o piętnastej trzydzieści.

To był wystarczający powód, by Konrad przyjął zaproszenie. Przecież nie mógł sobie podarować spotkania z Karoliną w gabinecie Bujały! Za dobrze pamiętał obiad w Zajeździe i te wszystkie pytania, którymi go zasypała. Nieźle musiała się bawić, kiedy on złościł się i zmieniał temat. Poza tym był rozczarowany, że wróciła i nie dała znaku życia. Niby się rozstali, ale przecież obowiązywały jakieś formy towarzyskie; tak przynajmniej myślał.

Zjawił się w Spokoju kilkanaście minut przed czasem. Oprócz Bujały w gabinecie siedział Grzesiek Majdziak, prawa ręka szefa, chłopak do specjalnych poruczeń, nie zawsze czystych. Konrad nigdy za facetem nie przepadał i nawet dziwił się, że Bujała, inteligentny przecież i obrotny, dobrał sobie takiego kumpla, z którym można było pogadać jedynie o samochodach i babach. Chociaż z drugiej strony przy Bujale nie trzeba było gadać, wystarczyło słuchać, a do słuchania Majdziak nadawał się jak mało kto. Gorzej było z myśleniem.

– To co, panowie, po koniaczku?

Bujała wyciągnął napoleona i z wielką uwagą lał na dno kieliszków złoty płyn. Lał do przepisowej wysokości, czyli tyle, co nic.

– Samochodem jestem – bąknął Majdziak.

– Człowiekiem jesteś, Grzesiu, nie samochodem – pocieszył go szef. – Przy twojej masie i pół butelki nie zaszkodzi. Zresztą, jak cię smerfy capną, powołasz się na mnie.

– O co innego się rozchodzi. Do pięknej jadę, a ona uczulona na procenty.

– Wacek jej nie przyzwyczaił? To co z niego za chłop? – zarżał Bujała.

Konrad nie wzbraniał się przed jedną lampką. Wolał inne trunki, koniak traktował jak lekarstwo i właśnie tego mu było trzeba przed spotkaniem z Karoliną. Zerknął na zegarek. Lada moment powinna wejść. Bujała z przyjemnością i znawstwem mówił o interesach, o stałej konieczności inwestowania, obracania pieniędzmi. Upomniał Konrada, że teraz nie pora na branie oddechu. Wysapie się później, kiedy pomyślnie zakończą całe przedsięwzięcie. Uparcie wracał do propozycji, która już raz rozsierdziła Orzechowicza. Konrad nie słuchał. Cudze pieniądze go nie obchodziły, na swoje od dawna miał pomysł. Przede wszystkim chciał zdobyć niezależność, a to gwarantowała jedynie praca na własny rachunek. Do Budampolexu 2 poszedł na prośbę Bujały i nie zamierzał siedzieć długo.

– No, panowie, coś nam się mianowicie dupa spóźnia – powiedział z niezadowoleniem Bujała. Patrzył na zegarek i chyba tylko dlatego nie zauważył otwartych drzwi.

– Wolne żarty, boss, jest co do minuty piętnasta trzydzieści – odezwał się od progu dźwięczny głos.

Poderwali się gwałtownie – Bujała w przepraszających uśmiechach i podskokach, Majdziak z miną obojętną. Konrad obejrzał się i oczom nie uwierzył. Odruchowo chwycił ze stołu butelkę i opróżnił ją do dna.

– Panowie, czapki z głów! – zakrzyknął Bujała. Wybiegł zza biurka z rozłożonymi ramionami, jakby miał zamiar przycisnąć Julię do serca.

Dziewczyna wciąż stała w progu. Jeszcze dwie minuty wcześniej, poprawiając w sekretariacie urodę, przeżywała iście hamletowską rozterkę: wejść czy też uciec. Jedno słowo sprawiło, że wstąpił w nią duch wielkiej, dramatycznej aktorki. Wkroczyła na scenę wyprostowana, z dumnie podniesioną głową.

– Niepokoiliśmy się mianowicie, czy...

– Słyszałam pański niepokój – powiedziała.

– Och, mężczyźni to straszni barbarzyńcy! – zawołał Bujała z udanym zawstydzeniem. – Cywilizują się mianowicie dopiero pod wpływem pięknych kobiet, droga pani magister!

– Magister inżynier, jeżeli już upierasz się przy tytułach. Magister inżynier Julia Blenda.

– Oj, żartownisia, żartownisia! – pogroził palcem Bujała. Ponieważ dziewczyna nie kwapiła się z podaniem mu ręki, pocałował ją po ojcowsku w głowę i wskazał fotel. – Znasz moich przyjaciół? Jasne, że znasz. Mój imiennik Grześ Majdziak, ten drugi przystojniak to oczywiście inżynier Konrad Orzechowicz. Tylko nie zakochaj się, dziewczyno, bo jestem okrutnie zazdrosny i na ucho ci powiem, że żaden z nich nie może się ze mną równać. No, nie stój, Karolinko, siadaj. Mamy kupę spraw do omówienia.

On jest jeszcze głupszy niż Chochla, pomyślała z podziwem Julia.

Bujała uznał widocznie, że w kwestii powitań załatwił wszystko, co do niego należało. Zagadał niezręczność, pośmiał się i rozruszał towarzystwo. Siadając za biurkiem, ani na moment nie przestawał gadać.

– Więc jak już mówiłem, mamy wielką kupę spraw. Interesy wymagają, żebyśmy się naradzili...

– Z facetem, który nie potrafi słuchać, nie będę się naradzała nad żadną kupą. Ani wielką, ani małą! – powiedziała głośno i wyraźnie Julia. – Mam w nosie twoje interesy, na których, podobnie jak ty, wcale się nie znam.

Chciała go leciutko drasnąć, a ukłuła, i to boleśnie. Uniósł się w fotelu i nie ryknął tylko dlatego, że wielkie zdziwienie zaparło mu dech i nie był pewien, czy dobrze usłyszał. Dziewczyna przygryzła język. W uszach zadźwięczały jej słowa Karoliny: „Facetowi możesz powiedzieć wszystko, czego nie zniosłaby normalna kobieta – że kłamie, że jest bezwzględny i pozbawiony serca. On ci to daruje, a nawet będzie dumny, że widzisz w nim twardziela. Jednak nie mów nigdy, że jest kiepski w łóżku i w interesach". Ojejku, chyba przegięłam, pomyślała spłoszona. Zwilżyła językiem suche usta.

– Jestem tu gościem i należą mi się jakieś względy – powiedziała ugodowo. Na osłodę posłała Bujale jeden z ładniejszych uśmiechów, lecz głosu nie pozwoliła sobie odebrać. – Daj mi skończyć, zanim powiesz za dużo i zdradzisz sekrety, o których nie chcę słuchać. Nie jestem prawnikiem i nie jestem Karoliną Cierniak. Trzeci raz próbuję ci to wytłumaczyć, a ty i tak wiesz lepiej. Mam ci pokazać metrykę, dowód osobisty i prawo jazdy?

Boss ochłonął i patrzył po obecnych z miną, która wykluczała jakąkolwiek pomyłkę. Majdziak dusił się ze śmiechu, Konrad siedział ze smętnie opuszczoną głową, ale to on w końcu poparł Julię.

– To nie jest żadna Karolina... to jest... Julia – powiedział i zwiesił głowę jeszcze niżej.

– Nie rozumiem, jak to w ogóle mogło... jak... – plątał się zbity z tropu Bujała.

– Chętnie wyjaśnię. Gadatliwa babka to nieszczęście, jednak gadatliwy boss to już cała tragedia. Ty słuchasz wyłącznie własnego słowotoku i na nieszczęście wszystko wiesz najlepiej.

Majdziak zaczął rechotać całkiem głośno i przymknął się dopiero pod ostrym spojrzeniem szefa.

– Ktoś mi za to zdrowo beknie! – mruknął Bujała ze złą miną. – Zdrowo beknie – powtórzył.

– A sam nie możesz zapanować nad własnym językiem? – zdziwiła się Julia. Była przekonana, że boss ma pretensje do Majdziaka. Uznała, że wizyta dobiegła końca i dotknęła ramienia Konrada.

Orzechowicz wsiadł do matiza o własnych siłach; dopiero w drodze padł jak zwiędły tulipan. Abstynentem nie był, lecz pijał mało, rzadko i nigdy na pusty żołądek. Pół butelki koniaku rozebrało go szybciej i dokładniej niż niejedna nocna libacja w męskim gronie. Z libacji zawsze wychodził z podniesioną głową, a tu, ledwie wsiadł do auta, własna szyja odmówiła mu posłuszeństwa. Nie poddawał się, walczył z niemocą.

– Wiesz, co ci powiem? No wiesz? – powtarzał uparcie.

Początkowo Julia sądziła, że chce jej przekazać coś bardzo ważnego, że dusi w sobie jakąś wielką tajemnicę, której nie potrafi wyartykułować. Ujechali spory kawałek, a on nie mógł wyjść poza te dwa powtarzane w kółko pytania. Zegar na tablicy rozdzielczej przypominał nieubłaganie, że czas mija. Musiała jeszcze skoczyć do Wandy Pasieczko, przygotować grunt do jutrzejszej akcji.

– Oszukałaś mnie... Wysiadam! – zdecydował Orzechowicz na rondzie. – Słyszysz? Nie przyszłaś się przywitać.

– Dzień dobry, Konradzie! – powiedziała uspokajająco.

– Myślisz, że ja nie wiem, że ty to nie Karolina? – spytał. – Masz mnie za pijanego?

– Ależ skąd – zaprzeczyła. – Nie majstruj przy zamku, bo wypadniesz.

– Ja wpadnę? Ja? Nigdydzie... ni... nie wpadnę!

Westchnęła ciężko. Co temu wielkoludowi strzeliło do łepetyny, żeby za jednym pociągnięciem wchłonąć pół butelki koniaku? A co jej z kolei strzeliło do głowy, że uparła się odwieźć do domu ten ludzki stan nieważkości? Boss protestował i pewnie dlatego postawiła na swoim. Na wspomnienie Bujały ogarnęło ją miłe ciepło. W całym swoim dorosłym życiu wobec nikogo nie była tak szczera, jak wobec tego bubka. Zwykle litowała się nad ludźmi, nie chciała ich ranić i częściej mówiła to, co chcieliby usłyszeć niż to, co rzeczywiście myślała. No, ale też żaden facet do tej pory nie odważył się publicznie nazwać jej dupą. Bez scenariusza, bez wstępnych przygotowań, z samej tylko wściekłości tak pięknie odegrała swoją rolę, że natapirowany boss nawet nie miauknął. Z Bujałą poszło o wiele łatwiej, niż myślała, za to z Konradem nie umiała się uporać. Nie chciała go zostawiać na pastwę tamtych dwu typów i teraz miała za swoje. Marudził, denerwował się, plótł coś bez ładu i składu o zdradzie i porachunkach. Jak każdy ululany facet miał swoją koncepcję, której uparcie się trzymał. Chciał wysiąść w trakcie jazdy i powstrzymywanie go było zajęciem bardzo skomplikowanym. Machał rękami, wiercił się, parę razy zdzielił ją w głowę, raz w ucho i nawet tego nie zauważył. A matiz jak wiadomo jest wozikiem zgrabniutkim, lecz ciasnym.

Z wielką ulgą podjechała wreszcie pod dom i nawet zaparkowała blisko drzwi.

– Jesteśmy na miejscu. Dasz sobie radę?

– Wyrzy... wyrza... wyrzucasz człowieka?

Był wyraźnie oburzony. Całą drogę chciał wyskakiwać, lecz na własnym parkingu zmienił zdanie i zaczął się mościć do snu. Julia okrążyła auto i otworzyła drzwi od strony pasażera. Co ta wódka robi z człowieka, pomyślała słowami matki. Pani Blendowa zwykle tak wzdychała na widok każdego człapiącego lub leżącego pijaczka. W domu nie musiała wzdychać, bo mąż, podobnie jak ona, nie pił. Miało to same dobre strony i tylko jedną złą: Julia nie wyniosła z domu doświadczeń w postępowaniu z ludźmi, delikatnie mówiąc, nietrzeźwymi. Prośby i tłumaczenia trafiały w próżnię. Stała przy otwartych drzwiach i z rosnącym przerażeniem patrzyła na Konrada. On nie miał zamiaru wysiadać, ona zaś nie miała tyle siły, by wywlec go z samochodu. Zaczynała poważnie się obawiać, że spędzą tę noc razem w ciasnym aucie.

– Wyłaź, bo zacznę krzyczeć i zawołam sąsiadów – powiedziała ostro.

Łypnął okiem, ale się nie ruszył. Powtórzyła po raz drugi nieco głośniej. Poskutkowało dopiero za czwartym razem i to tylko dlatego, że bardzo się obraził. Mruczał coś o babskim uporze i męskim nieszczęściu. Najpierw wystawił jedną nogę, potem drugą, podumał chwilę i wreszcie z wielkim trudem stanął. Miał poważny kłopot z utrzymaniem pionu i gdyby go nie podtrzymała, pewnie runąłby na asfalt. Rozejrzała się bezradnie. Potrzebowała pomocy silnego mężczyzny, wokół bloku biegały tylko nieletnie dzieci. Od dłuższej chwili jej zmaganiom przyglądała się szczupła kobieta w ciemnej męskiej marynarce. Patrzyła tak, jakby chciała pomóc, ale nie miała śmiałości. W końcu się zdecydowała. Razem jakoś dotaszczyły Konrada do drzwi, potem do windy.

– W ojca się wdał – powiedziała kobieta.

– Pani go zna?

– Brat przecież.

Po wyjściu z windy Julia stanowczo podziękowała za pomoc. Kobieta nie budziła zaufania. Drobna i zapyziała, nie wyglądała na siostrę inżyniera Orzechowicza. Oszustka jak nic, myślała Julia. Szuka pretekstu, by wejść i okraść. Długo trwało, zanim przy niezdarnej pomocy Konrada trafiła na właściwy klucz.

– Zamknij dobrze drzwi, rozumiesz mnie?

– Nie jesteś Karoliną! To kłamstwo!

– Nie jestem. Zamkniesz drzwi?

– Same się zamkną, ja nie mam... nie mam... ja żyję przy otwartej kurrrtynie!

To długie przemówienie nadwątliło jego siły. Drzwi oczywiście za sobą nie zamknął, tylko ułożył się na tapczanie i więcej sobie Julią głowy nie zawracał.

Stała niezdecydowana, nie wiedząc, czy go rozbierać, okrywać, poić wodą z cytryną, czy po prostu zostawić własnemu losowi. Spojrzała na zegarek. Dochodziła osiemnasta, za parę minut powinna być u Wandy. Złapała pierwszą z brzegu kartkę i wielkimi literami napisała: *Musiałam Cię zamknąć. Skorzystaj z zapasowych kluczy, a jak nie masz, zadzwoń wieczorem. Julia.* Jeszcze większymi wołami wymalowała numer swojej komórki i wybiegła.

Przy matizie stała ta kobieta. Czy była krewną, czy zwykłą oszustką, nie miało już żadnego znaczenia. Orzechowicz spał bezpiecznie we własnym mieszkaniu dzięki pomocy chudej mizerotki. Julia podeszła, żeby jeszcze raz podziękować i natychmiast pożałowała swojej decyzji. Tamta patrzyła dziwnym, psim wzrokiem.

– Pani jest narzeczoną Radka? – spytała. Głos miała ochrypły i nieprzyjemny.

– Pracujemy razem.

– Szkoda, bo myślałam, że pożyczy mi pani na bilet. Zimno się zrobiło, a do domu daleko.

Julia otworzyła drzwi i wskazała miejsce w samochodzie. Kobieta zawahała się.

– Podwiozę panią. Niech pani wskakuje, bo się śpieszę.

Jechały w milczeniu. Julia rozważała, jak najprościej dostać się na Cygankę, żeby niepotrzebnie nie krążyć po wąskich, jednokierunkowych uliczkach śródmieścia.

– Radkowi dobrze, nie to co nam! – powiedziała kobieta.

Wyraźnie czekała na zachętę, na jakieś pytanie, a ponieważ nie padło, rozgadała się na dobre z własnej woli. Beznamiętnym głosem chrypiała opowieść o domowej nędzy. Rodzice mieli kiedyś warsztat stolarski. Krótko, ledwie przez rok, bo tyle im zajęło uporanie się ze schedą po dziadku. Przepili, przetracili, nie zostało nic. Nawet najstarszy, Olaf, już nie pamiętał dostatnich czasów. Czworo ich było w domu, właśnie ten Olaf, który zaginął gdzieś w świecie, Milena, Żaneta – czyli ona – i najmłodszy Radek, ten, któremu się powiodło, bo miał wypadek i trafił do zamożnych ludzi. Wykształcił się i nie chce znać rodziny. Tylko ona wie, gdzie go znaleźć. Ze dwa razy ją poratował, ale zeźlił się i więcej pieniędzy dawać nie chce. Wyczekuje więc pod jego domem, liczy, że może któregoś dnia zmieni zdanie.

– Tu mieszkamy! – wskazała palcem kamienicę ani gorszą, ani lepszą od innych. Julia zatrzymała samochód. – Wejdzie pani na chwilę?

Sama nie wiedziała, czemu zgodziła się wejść, co – oprócz niezdrowej ciekawości – ciągnęło ją na obskurne podwórko, do zaniedbanego pokoju z brudną szmatą w oknie. W życiu nie podejrzewała, że ludzie mogą tak mieszkać. Kilka osób kręciło się po zawalonym rupieciami wnętrzu. Na łóżku pod ścianą chrapał odrażający staruch, spocony i blady jak nieboszczyk. W mrocznej sieni wcisnęła Żanecie sto złotych i pośpiesznie wybiegła. Gdyby nie przykry zapach, który ciągnął się za nią, gotowa była pomyśleć, że to sen. „Nigdy nie miałem ojca ani matki" – powiedział kiedyś Konrad, a ona w duchu nazwała go pozerem. Zmieniła zdanie. Ktoś, kto odbił się od takiego dna, musi być pioruńskim twardzielem. Niemożliwe, żeby poszedł w ślady ojca! To czemu ta babka tak powiedziała?

Wanda musiała czatować z okiem przy wizjerze, nim bowiem Julia zdążyła podnieść rękę do dzwonka, drzwi otworzyły się gościnnie. Łzy szczęścia spłynęły na pudełko czekoladek.

– Ależ nie trzeba było! Po co taki wydatek! – wzbraniała się Wanda ze staroświecką elegancją.

Julia weszła do pokoju i omal nie zawróciła na pięcie. Za plecami miała jednak korpulentną postać gospodyni, która skutecznie odcinała odwrót. Sądziła, że będzie jedynym gościem, uwierzyła zapewnieniom Wandy, że kuzynka wyjeżdża, tymczasem owa kuzynka kwitła na kanapie i rozświetlała pokój włosami w kolorze jajecznicy. Obok niej siedział atletyczny Grześ Majdziak, którego Julia ostatni raz oglądała w gabinecie Bujały. Przy powitaniu oboje zapadli na zanik pamięci. Wymienili uściski dłoni jak ludzie, którzy widzą się pierwszy raz w życiu. Ola Mikulowa cmoknęła Julię w policzek.

– Co tam w firmie, kochana, co o mnie mówią? – spytała.

Julia miała dobry zwyczaj przechodzenia na ty z każdym, kto ją bezceremonialnie tykał. Jedyny wyjątek czyniła dla zwierzchników. Ale Mikulowa już nie była jej szefową.

– Podobno sprzedałaś firmę – powiedziała swobodnie.

– A co, miałam czekać, aż ta kapuściana głowa wszystko utopi w długach? No powiedz sama, miałam czekać? Mnie potrzebne są pieniądze. – Uśmiechnęła się i pogłaskała kark amanta, jakby tym samym dawała Julii do zrozumienia na co, lub raczej na kogo, zamierza wydawać swoje pieniądze.

– Najśmieszniejsze jest to, że nie wiadomo, kto został nowym właścicielem.

– Żartujesz?! – wykrzyknęła zdumiona Mikulowa. – No nie, ja się zastrzelę! Nikt nie wie, mówisz? No przecież Pałubska!

– Pani Edyta? – Julia nie musiała udawać zdziwienia, tym razem było autentyczne. Spodziewała się raczej usłyszeć nazwisko Bujały, może nawet Mikuli, ale nie Edyty.

– To dlaczego Henia Luty przechwala się, że ona kupiła zakład? – spytała Wanda.

Mikulowa wzruszyła ramionami. Ona najlepiej wiedziała, z kim była u notariusza. Zaczęła opowiadać, ile to miała kłopotów z formalnym podpisaniem umowy kupna-sprzedaży, ile się nabiegała z Edytą po bankach i urzędach.

– Co tam! – zakończyła. – Było, minęło, najważniejsze, że cel został osiągnięty. – Zaśmiała się znacząco i przytuliła policzek do ramienia Majdziaka.

Mikulowa wyglądała jak kobieta szczęśliwa, choć niezbyt gustownie ubrana. Kiedy przechadzała się po pokoju, wąska, obcisła spódnica z długim rozporkiem z tyłu brzydko odsłaniała pełne uda w kształcie baniaczków. Od kolan w dół nogi miała niezłe, za to uda fatalne. Nawet Majdziak patrzył bez zachwytu. Obcałowywał wprawdzie Olę po rękach, nazywał swoją królową, brał obecne panie na świadków, że słodszej kobietki nie ma w całym Włocławku, jednak to całe jego zaangażowanie wydawało się Julii mało zaangażowane. Sama też lubiła udawać coś, czego nie było, więc w Majdziaku odkryła bratnią, choć znacznie mniej zdolną duszę. Jego czułości były machinalne i zdawkowe, jakby rzucane na pociechę, nie zaś z potrzeby serca. Tak to przynajmniej wyglądało z boku. Od strony Mikulowej musiało wyglądać całkiem inaczej. Każde słowo Grzegorza oprawiała w ramki zachwytu i cieszyła się jak pensjonarka. Jej okrzyki – Ach, jakiż on cudowny, nieprawdaż! – brzmiały czysto i szczerze. Julia za nic nie mogła zrozumieć, co pięknego mogła widzieć Ola w pryszczatej cerze i wielkim nochalu Majdziaka. Widać jednak coś tam dostrzegła, bo kręcąc się po pokoju, nie opuściła żadnej okazji, żeby choć dotknąć ukochanego. A Wanda Pasieczko w tym czasie nasłuchiwała. Przy lada szmerze dochodzącym z korytarza biegła natychmiast do przedpokoju. Za czwartym czy piątym razem Julia podniosła się i zaczęła żegnać.

– Jeszcze moment – błagała Wanda.

Dziewczyna stanęła obok Mikulowej, tuż przy ścianie, za którą z całą pewnością siedział samotny Chochla. Usłyszała stłumiony dźwięk telefonu. Dwa sygnały i cisza. Po chwili telefon odezwał się ponownie i w tym momencie na Julię spłynęło olśnienie. Zobaczyła Edytę za wielkim biurkiem, jak nerwowo bębni palcami po blacie. Odkłada słuchawkę i znowu podnosi. Dwa sygnały, myślała gorączkowo dziewczyna, brakowało mi tych dwu sygnałów tylko dla wtajemniczonych! Telefon przestał dzwonić, widać Chochla był w domu. Julia wróciła do pożegnań.

– Państwo zostajecie we Włocławku? – spytała, podając rękę Mikulowej.

– No, nie! Tu, w tej dziurze, gdzie wszyscy się znają? Wyjeżdżamy jutro rano.

Uściskały się szczerze, od serca. Życzyła młodej parze szczęścia i wcale nie przemawiała przez nią perfidia. Jak każda kobieta lubiła romantyczne historie. Majdziakowi przykazała, żeby opiekował się Olą.

– Jasne! – odpowiedział.

Przed samym wyjściem wciągnęła na moment Wandę do kuchni, pod pretekstem, że chce pogadać o kolejnym zebraniu kobiet. Rozszeptały się gorąco, choć krótko.

– To naprawdę twoja kuzynka? – spytała Julia.

Wanda zatrzepotała rękami. Pośpiesznie wyjaśniła, że to nieszczęsna ofiara mężowskiej tyranii oraz serdeczna przyjaciółka Edytki Pałubskiej. To Edytka zapoznała panią Olę z panem Grzesiem i patronowała ich miłości. Dwa dni temu prosiła, żeby Ola mogła zostać u Wandy aż do wyjazdu z miasta. Przy obcych kazała ją nazywać kuzynką i to wszystko.

To była wyjątkowo owocna wizyta. Julia obawiała się tylko jednego: by miły Chochla nie sterczał przypadkiem w oknie za żaluzjami. Lekkim sprintem pobiegła na sąsiedni parking, gdzie przezornie zostawiła samochód. Przez moment wahała się, czy nie pojechać do Konrada, ale ostatecznie uznała, że to niezbyt mądry pomysł.

Z produktów nadających się do jedzenia Karolina miała w lodówce dwa jajka i odrobinę dżemu. Wróciła do domu tuż przed Julią i właśnie zastanawiała się, jak wyczarować smaczny obiad z tego, co było w lodówce. Wymyśliła omlet, który nie udał się z braku tłuszczu. Julia machnęła ręką na wątpliwy efekt kulinarnych eksperymentów przyjaciółki i jako ochotnik pobiegła do sklepu. Wróciła obładowana niczym mały dżip. Pomyślała nie tylko o obiedzie, ale także o kolacji i śniadaniu. Karolina z niedowierzaniem oglądała płaty wędzonego łososia, wędliny w kilku gatunkach, sery i zimne sosy. Wszystko było apetyczne, pięknie opakowane i drogie. Właśnie ze względu na cenę rzadko pozwalała sobie na takie delikatesy, chyba że znalazła sponsora. Julia nie zapomniała też o białym winie i słodyczach.

– Fiu, fiu! Nie przesadziłaś z tą ucztą?

– Co tam! – parsknęła śmiechem Julia. – Dzielimy się po połowie: ja daję wsad do kotła, ty robociznę, łącznie ze zmywaniem naczyń.

Uspokojona Karolina sięgnęła po talerzyk i odłożyła po kawałku tego, co dało się odłożyć. To była żelazna porcja dla mojej Gajewskiej, dowód wdzięczności za pyszne domowe pierogi i naleśniki, którymi staruszka od czasu do czasu ją podkarmiała. Żeby było szybciej, Julia chwyciła talerzyk i zaniosła sąsiadce dary serca.

Dziesięć minut później zasiadły do wielkiego jedzenia i wielkiego gadania. Białym winem popijały wiadomości strawne, herbatą niestrawne. Można było inaczej, ale one wolały właśnie tak. Za wiadomość niestrawną Julia uznała wizytę u Bujały. Od tego zaczęła swoją opowieść, żeby uzyskać rozgrzeszenie Karoliny i zamknąć niewygodny temat. Przeleciała po nim szybciutko.

– Wiesz – kończyła – wczoraj to wczoraj, ale najgorsze jest to, że nie mogę sobie przypomnieć, po jakie licho polazłam tam dzisiaj! Miałam faceta poderwać, rozgryźć, a zaczęłam wychowywać. Nie wyglądał na zadowolonego i co gorsza wcale nie jestem pewna, czy mi uwierzył, że ja to nie ty. Nie wiem, jak on sobie radzi z tym całym zbójowaniem? Gangster powinien być elastyczny.

– Nie roztkliwiaj się, Juleczko, każde miasto ma takich gangsterów, na jakich zasługuje. Bujały nie mamy się co wstydzić. Słynie z dobrych pomysłów i nieco gorszej realizacji. Tak przynajmniej twierdzi Wacek Mikula, do niedawna jeszcze właściciel Budampolexu, gdybyś zapomniała.

– Ojej, przecież pamiętam. Nie rozumiem tylko, co jest grane teraz? – Julia upiła łyk wina, zadowolona, że przyjaciółka uznała sprawę Bujały za zamkniętą.

– Co jest grane? Marsz Mendelssohna, kochana! Jeśli nie widać jawnej przyczyny, trzeba szukać kobiety. Francuzi to wymyślili, a im można wierzyć.

– Przypadkowo też czytałam Dumasa. Tylko gdzie tu miejsce dla kobiety?

Wiedza Karoliny pochodziła od Mikuli i w związku z tym była jednostronna. Biedny cap jako jeden z największych uwodzicieli w mieście padł ofiarą babskiego spisku i swojej naiwności. Chciał zostać malowanym bankrutem, został prawdziwym, bo nie docenił kobiecej stałości oraz kobiecej niestałości. Wcieleniem stałości była Edyta, pierwsza narzeczona i prawie żona. Trzydzieści lat temu, kiedy przygotowania do ślubu były już w toku, suknia zamówiona, menu ustalone, pojawiła się ta trzecia, Ola, czyli symbol niestałości. Wbiła się klinem między narzeczonych i po miesiącu zabrała Mikulę jak swojego. Wyprawili bardzo skromne wesele, bo nie przebrzmiały jeszcze echa poprzedniego skandalu, i rozpoczęli życie pełne niespodzianek z obu stron. Matka potrzebowała dwudziestu lat, żeby zrobić z Mikuli człowieka, Ola zrobiła z niego idiotę w ciągu roku. Sam tak twierdził. Jego niewierność nie brała się z wybujałego temperamentu, była jedynie odwetem za jej niewierność. To również jego opinia. Ich związek był wieczną wojną nerwów. Żarli się, ale mimo wszystko zaufał żonie i na nią przepisał cały swój majątek po bankructwie Budampolexu 1. I to był błąd, perfidnie wykorzystany przez Edytę. Postanowiła odkupić firmę od Mikulowej. Przez te wszystkie lata nie wyszła za mąż, cierpliwie przeczekała burze i zawirowania, wciąż była w pobliżu ukochanego i co najważniejsze, potrafiła uśpić czujność żony.

– Matko święta, nie gadaj! – jęknęła Julia. – Chcesz powiedzieć, że wygrała wojnę trzydziestoletnią i teraz zgarnie wszystkie łupy?

– Jest przekonana, że wygrała, chociaż wątpię, czy Wacek da się wziąć w jasyr. Ostatnio zrobił się nad podziw rozważny. On boi się Edyty i tu go rozumiem. To mądra baba. Ja też jestem mądra, lecz mnie się nie boi, kocha mnie i zaraz po rozwodzie z Olą będzie się żenił.

– A ty? – przeraziła się Julia.

– Palić się nie palę, choć przyznam, że rozważałam i taką możliwość – odparła ze śmiechem Karolina. – Chciałabym zobaczyć minę Edyty, to raz, a dwa, przy Wacku, nawet zbankrutowanym, biedy nie zaznam. Nie płacz, ostatecznej odpowiedzi jeszcze nie dałam.

– Bój się Edyty! Jeśli przez te wszystkie lata rzeczywiście go kochała, to marny twój los.

– Wiem. Jest perfekcjonistką, a z takimi nigdy nic nie wiadomo. Wyznaczyła sobie cel i choćby o lasce, na wózku inwalidzkim, swego dopnie. Ale ja też uważam się za perfekcjonistkę.

– To nie powód, żeby przez następne trzydzieści lat walczyć z Edytą o Wacka! On wam tego nie przeżyje – jęknęła Julia.

Nie do końca wierzyła w wersję Mikuli. Gotowa była wzruszyć się i zadumać nad siłą ludzkich namiętności, jednak nie mogła dojść do ładu z finansami. Skąd niby średnio zamożna Edyta wzięła tyle pieniędzy, by kupić dużą firmę? Niechby nawet zadłużoną, niechby po promocyjnej cenie. W grę wchodziły wielkie pieniądze, zbyt wielkie, nawet po uwzględnieniu spadku po wuju.

Karolina zajęła się sprzątaniem ze stołu i zmianą dekoracji. Smakowity aromat kawy rozszedł się po mieszkaniu. Zabrzęczały łyżeczki. Julia zadzwoniła do Konrada. Mimo że nie podniósł słuchawki, miała wrażenie, że słyszy głośne chrapanie.

Przy kawie i ciastkach zaczęły wreszcie rozmawiać o szczegółach planu antychochlowego. Sytuacja była patowa: kiedy Renata kategorycznie odmówiła współpracy, zabrakło chętnych do uszczęśliwiania Chochli. A przecież ktoś musiał go zająć, by ktoś inny mógł wejść do archiwum. Tu nie można było zdać się na przypadek, liczyć, że jakoś się samo ułoży. Wszystko powinno być zaplanowane do ostatniego szczegółu: czas akcji, system porozumiewania się, moment wejścia i wyjścia. Karolina tak naprawdę wcale nie miała wyboru. Gra toczyła się o jej godność i jej skórę, nie mogła więc zwalać najpaskudniejszego zadania na Julię. Z odrazą sięgnęła po telefon. Wystukała numer, odczekała, aż przebrzmiały dwa sygnały i odłożyła słuchawkę. Ponownie wystukała ten sam numer. Julia wisiała na plecach przyjaciółki i nerwowo przygryzała usta. Po dłuższej chwili usłyszały piskliwy głos Chochli.

– Witaj, Marcinku! A jednak serce dobrze mi podpowiedziało, gdzie cię szukać. Karolina mówi, nie poznałeś?

– Cierniak? – upewnił się Marcinek.

– A znasz jakąś inną, mój piękny?

Julia gwałtownie zasłoniła dłonią usta i niebezpiecznie poczerwieniała.

– Chyba tego, no... nie znam.

– Dostałam od ciebie miły liścik, trochę dawno, to prawda, jednak pamiętam każde słowo.

– Niemożliwe, tego... Ja do ciebie nie pisałem.

– Nie mów! Najpierw dostała swoje zdjęcia Edyta, ja zaraz potem. Powiem ci na ucho, że ona nie była zadowolona.

– Wiem. – Zachichotał. – To był... no... żart, żeby nie zapomniał wół, tego... jak cielęciem był. Stale tylko daj i daj... to tego, to dostała. Do ciebie nic nie wysyłałem.

Karolina spojrzała znacząco na Julię. Nie wyglądało na to, by wypierał się z czystej przekory. Jednak przesyłka przyszła. Magister Cierniak dostała zdjęcia, dostała liścik. Westchnęła do słuchawki z udawaną namiętnością.

– Jeśli tak mówisz, to najwidoczniej mi się śniłeś. Stęskniłam się za tobą, wiesz? Nie mam z kim pogadać, pożartować.

Chochla mądry nie był, lecz nie był też doszczętnie głupi. Miękł, słuchając komplementów, co wcale nie odebrało mu zadziwiająco dobrej pamięci. Drobiazgowo wyliczył dziewczynie wszystkie złośliwości, wszystkie sytuacje, w których zrobiła go na szaro. Tłumaczyła, że to z nadmiaru uczuć, z zazdrości o Edytę, potem o Julię. Na wspomnienie Julii natychmiast się zjeżył. Nie pomogły żadne podpytywania, nie chciał rozmawiać o pani inżynier i Karolina musiała szybko zmienić temat.

– Zaszyłeś się w swojej norce jak borsuczek. Nie nudno ci? Może spotkamy się jutro? Powiedz, o której mam przyjechać.

– Spotkać się... tego... mówisz? E, nie! Ja mam już kogoś fajniejszego – wyznał z rozbrajającą i niepozbawioną dumy szczerością.

Karolina wykonała w powietrzu gest niezbyt pasujący do damy, lecz głos zachowała zmysłowy, ciepły, kiedy przekonywała Marcinka, że nie musi wszystkiego opowiadać żonie.

– Iii, tego... ja nie o żonie. Mam fest babkę, oczy by ci wyszły z orbit, a cysie ze stanika. – Zaśmiał się obleśnie, bardzo czymś rozbawiony.

Paplanie zaczęło zbaczać na niebezpieczne tory. Karolina próbowała jeszcze namówić go na spotkanie, skusić, skołować. Próżny trud. On wolał żarciki męsko-damskie i pikantne aluzyjki. Obiecała, że zadzwoni następnego dnia i kompletnie skołowana odłożyła słuchawkę.

– Julio! – zawołała ze zgrozą. – To największa porażka w moim życiu. Nie dostałam jeszcze kosza od żadnego mężczyzny, a tu nawet nie mężczyzna, tylko zwykła Chochla zrobiła mi taki afront!

– Tego... no... ale pomyśl, dla kogo on stracił głowę – zauważyła skromnie Julia.

Wariacki śmiech rozładował napięcie, jednak nie posunął sprawy do przodu. Kto mógł przypuszczać, że amory Chochli rozłożą cały plan?! I jeszcze na domiar wszystkiego Julia wcale nie czuła się dumna z wierności swojego adoratora.

Wieczorem zadzwoniła do domu, żeby uspokoić matkę, że żyje i ma się dobrze. Wysłuchała rad i wątpliwości, ale tak naprawdę interesowało ją tylko jedno: czy ktoś do niej dzwonił. Dowiedziała się, że nikt, z wyjątkiem jakiejś wydry z jej pracy. W języku matki wydra była synonimem niemiłej kobiety – tyle że niemiłe jej były wszystkie kobiety z otoczenia córki. Julia już miała się żegnać, kiedy nieoczekiwanie usłyszała, że on, znaczy ten Wydra, nic nie wiedział o kursie Julii. Z wielkim trudem skończyła rozmowę i popadła w przykry stan niepewności. Po jakie licho Wydroń miałby do niej dzwonić, i to teraz, kiedy byli poróżnieni? Na pewno nie chciał jej wsypać z kursem komputerowym, o którym nawet nie wiedział, czyli musiało się coś nieoczekiwanego wydarzyć. Jak na złość jego telefon milczał. Natomiast późnym wieczorem odezwała się komórka. Dziewczyny, gotowe do snu, leżały na niewygodnej wersalce i rozprawiały o wydarzeniach ostatnich dni. Julia, przykładając słuchawkę do ucha, pomyślała, że Karolina całkiem niepotrzebnie wysłucha przeprosin Orzechowicza. A jednak to nie był Konrad. W miarę jak słuchała rozdziamdzianego głosu, jej rysy tężały.

– Cieszę się – powiedziała. – Będę jutro wieczorem. Pa!

– Wykluczone! Nigdy się na to nie zgodzę! – krzyknęła Karolina, wysłuchawszy skróconej relacji przyjaciółki.

– Innego wyjścia nie mamy! – wyjaśniła spokojnie Julia.

Nie myślała o konsekwencjach, szykowała się do nowej roli. Nawet najznakomitszy aktor nie zawsze gra to, co sobie wymarzył, pomyślała. Chciałam być Ligią, a wcielę się w postać Poppei Sabiny, najniegodziwszej z kobiet. No, bez przesady: Chochla to nie Neron.

Konrad obudził się nad ranem z przepotężnym bólem głowy. Najpierw zdziwił się, że leży na tapczanie w ubraniu. Potem doszedł do wniosku, że zupełnie nie pamięta, jak do domu trafił. Zagłębiając się z trudem w nieodległą przecież przeszłość, przypomniał sobie spotkanie u Bujały. Uniósł głowę i jeszcze szybciej opuścił. Nigdy nie lubił karuzeli, to zaś, co czuł pod czaszką, do złudzenia przypominało diabelski młyn. Chciało mu się pić, było mu niedobrze i sam nie wiedział, co robić.

Po raz drugi obudził się o zwykłej porze, czyli piętnaście po szóstej. W normalnych warunkach był to czas wystarczający na mycie, golenie i zjedzenie śniadania. O jedzeniu w ogóle nie mógł myśleć, umyć się musiał. Spojrzał w lustro i natychmiast zamknął oczy. Jedno w granatowej otoczce, drugie w żółtej; ostry kontrast sprawiał, że nie dało się patrzeć na własną gębę. Powoli wykonywał wszystkie podstawowe czynności. Kiedy znowu spojrzał na zegarek, wpadł w popłoch. Właściwie powinien już siedzieć w samochodzie. Samochód? Samochodu nie było przed domem. Oparł się ciężko o stół, potem usiadł. Co z tym samochodem? Film mu się urywał w momencie, gdy do gabinetu Bujały wkroczyła Julia, a on poczuł silne pragnienie. Wzdrygnął się na wspomnienie tamtego momentu. Wypił pół butelki koniaku. Normalnie wystarczyłoby mu na rok. Machinalnie zaczął bawić się kartką, leżącą na stole. Zgniótł, rozprostował, obejrzał literki i zanim zgniótł drugi raz, zobaczył słowo *Julia*. Poczuł nową falę gorąca. Czyżby ona go tu... do domu...?

Kluczy zapasowych nie miał, to znaczy miał, lecz nie w domu, tylko u Orskich. Co za sens trzymać zapasowe klucze w domu? Jedno, co mógł zrobić, to zatelefonować do firmy. Sam się zdziwił, że jego głos przypomina dudnienie pustej beczki. Julia natomiast niczemu się nie dziwiła. Poradziła, żeby wziął dzień wolny i odpoczął. Nie była obrażona, nie łapała figur, zupełnie jakby ostatnim razem widzieli się przy komputerze, nie zaś w okolicznościach co najmniej niestosownych.

– Julio, czy bardzo się wygłupiłem? – spytał zgnębionym głosem.

– W każdym razie na rękach nie chciałabym cię więcej nosić! – odpowiedziała rozbawiona.

Fantastyczna dziewczyna, pomyślał, siadając ciężko na tapczanie. Czuł się wyjątkowo podle. Do tego stopnia, że zaczęły mu się przypominać czasy odległe i bardzo odległe.

Gdyby w odpowiednim momencie, najlepiej jeszcze przed poczęciem, ktoś spytał Konrada, do jakiej rodziny chce trafić, na pewno nie wybrałby Orzechowiczów. Niestety, los nie stawia takich pytań i próżno się zastanawiać, czemu jedni mają wszystko, a drudzy nic, nawet nadziei. Rodzice Konrada dali swoim dzieciom życie i oryginalne imiona, resztę zostawili opatrzności. Dom? Cóż, nie był przytulny, pachnący czystością i dobrym jedzeniem. Konrad nawet nie wiedział, że takie domy istnieją. To była nora, dokładniej mówiąc melina, bo wieczorami schodzili się okoliczni pijacy, lała się wódka, a jak zabrakło wódki, to denaturat, pieszczotliwie zwany panienką. Czasem przyjeżdżała milicja. Radiowóz na Cygance nikogo nie dziwił.

Ledwie trochę podrósł i zmądrzał, urywał się z domu na całe dnie. Ulica była jego prawdziwym życiem i jednocześnie szkołą przetrwania.

Z prawdziwą szkołą poszło nieco gorzej. Udało mu się tylko zlekceważyć zerówkę. Od września, wbrew własnej woli, trafił do szkoły; na wiosnę następnego roku miał wypadek.

Wśród dzieciaków panowała wtedy moda na przebiegankę. Reguły były proste: należało przebiec na drugą stronę ulicy tuż przed maską nadjeżdżającego samochodu – im bliżej, tym lepiej. Konrad był niekwestionowanym mistrzem, miał refleks i sprężyny w nogach. Wyskakiwał zawsze w ostatniej chwili, jak diabełek z pudełka, co było punktowane bardzo wysoko. Przez kumpli oczywiście, nie przez kierowców. Tak się rozzuchwalił, że gdy któregoś dnia usłyszał znajomy pisk hamulców i nie mógł biec dalej, to ze zdziwienia zemdlał. Ocknął się w szpitalu. Przy jego łóżku siedziała młoda piękna kobieta. Po chwili dołączył do niej mężczyzna. Tak poznał Grażynę i Lucjana Orskich. Miał bardzo dużo szczęścia, że wpadł właśnie pod ich samochód.

Niech sobie ludzie wybrzydzają, ile chcą, ale mały Orzechowicz nie mógł się nachwalić szpitala. Każde dziecko leżało w oddzielnym łóżku z białą pościelą. U niego na szafce zawsze były owoce i słodycze. Grażyna przychodziła codziennie, Lucjan – kiedy tylko mógł. Wszystkie dzieci na sali myślały, że to są jego rodzice. Prawdziwi nie przyszli ani razu i Konrad bardzo się z tego cieszył. Potem było jeszcze sanatorium rehabilitacyjne w Ciechocinku. Pierwszy raz w życiu jechał wtedy samochodem osobowym. A po powrocie odbyła się pamiętna rozmowa.

– Chcemy – powiedział Lucjan – żebyś został z nami.

– Dobrze! – zgodził się bez chwili wahania.

Wtedy jeszcze nie wiedział, ile zdrowia stracili Orscy, by przekonać sąd rodzinny, że lepiej będzie dla dziecka, gdy zamieszka z nimi. I pewnie wróciłby Konrad do swojej meliny, gdyby nie stary Orzechowicz. Owszem, początkowo chciał oskubać Lucjana, wyciągnąć ile się da za straty moralne, kiedy jednak zaczęły go nachodzić przedstawicielki różnych instytucji opiekuńczych, nawracać i zachęcać do pracy, podpisał zrzeczenie się praw do syna. Spojrzał potem na chłopca z niechęcią i powiedział:

– Jedna gęba mniej!

Matka przytaknęła. Zawsze przytakiwała mężowi. Była biblijnym wręcz przykładem posłuszeństwa i bez zastrzeżeń uznawała dominację mężczyzny. Rodzice wyrwali Konrada z korzeniami ze swojej pamięci – jeżeli kiedykolwiek czuł do nich wdzięczność, to tylko za to jedno, jedyne ojcowskie zdanie. Więcej nigdy ich nie widział.

Orscy wzięli na siebie wszelkie koszty związane z utrzymaniem i wykształceniem chłopca. Jedynym problemem było mieszkanie. Sami gnieździli się w kawalerce, byli młodym małżeństwem, więc Konrad sypiał u ich przyjaciółki, pani Eweliny Zagrodzkiej, dwa piętra niżej. Z tego sypiania zrodziła się wielka przyjaźń dwojga samotników. Ciotka Ewelina była mu mamą, nianią, powiernicą i wszystkim. Obmywała podrapane kolana, utulała do snu, ukrywała przed Lucjanem i Grażyną chłopięce przewinienia, często wcale nie takie drobne. Konrad był wychowankiem meliny i ulicy, przyzwyczaił się do swobody i decydowania o sobie. W nowych warunkach opiekunowie wymagali od niego posłuszeństwa, czystych paznokci, codziennego dreptania do szkoły, i to wcale nie było takie miłe. Buntował się, wpadał w tarapaty, uciekał do dawnych kumpli. Tylko do rodzinnego domu nigdy nie zachodził. Dom chciał mieć nowy, swobodę starą. Ciotka Ewelina była jedyną osobą, która to rozumiała. Na górę chodził odrabiać lekcje, uczyć się manier, tam obrywał bury za złe stopnie, na dół wracał, żeby się pławić w cieple i miłości. I w końcu wyrósł na człowieka. Ilekroć ktoś go pytał o rodziców, odpowiadał, że nigdy nie miał ojca ani matki. Więcej nie tłumaczył. To więcej to była właśnie jego tajemnica. A poza tym uważał się za wielkiego szczęściarza.

W firmie rozpruł się worek z plotkami. Ludzie przekazywali sobie różne dziwne informacje, wśród których jedna powtarzała się najczęściej: Mikulowa sprzedała Budampolex i uciekła z pieniędzmi i młodym kochankiem. Niektórzy podejrzewali, że uciekła z Chochlą, inni prostowali, że Chochla jest nowym właścicielem i nigdzie nie będzie uciekał, tylko właśnie wróci. Na pracowników padł blady strach. Jaki Budampolex był, taki był, jednak pensje płacił regularnie, co na włocławskim rynku pracy nie było praktyką częstą. I to nie płacił w ratach, nie w naturze, lecz w prawdziwych złotówkach, tyle, ile się należało.

Co chwila ktoś wpadał do sekretariatu, próbował wypytywać Julię o szczegóły.

– Nic nie wiem – powtarzała do znudzenia.

Edyta zapowiedziała, że przyjdzie około czternastej. Mikula w ogóle się nie pojawił, co nikogo nie zdziwiło, zastanawiająca natomiast była nieobecność magistra Wydronia. Leszek zawsze zjawiał się bardzo punktualnie. Jeżeli ktoś chciał zastać go w biurze, to ranek był najlepszą porą. Potem wybiegał, wracał, ginął na dłużej i znowu wracał. Jeżeli nie przyszedł, to znaczyło, że miał powód. W domu też go nie było, bo Karolina dzwoniła od rana.

– Co to, pana Leszka nie ma? – spytała Henia. – Matko święta, chyba nic mu się nie stało? – zawołała ze zgrozą.

Zaraz potem przypomniała sobie, że musi pędzić do lekarza. Julia zwolniła ją na dwie godziny.

Koło jedenastej do sekretariatu wkroczył Grzegorz Bujała. Niósł przed sobą potężny bukiet kwiatów, nie tak wielki jak ten dla miss paragraf, ale wystarczająco okazały. Julia na wszelki wypadek uśmiechnęła się pogodnie.

– Szefowej nie ma!

– A po co mi twoja szefowa? – zdziwił się Bujała.

– Myślałam, że ten ogród to dodatek do gratulacji, że...

– Mogą być gratulacje, czemu nie, ale dla ciebie. Żadna du... dama nie odważyła się na mnie krzyczeć. Daruję ci ze zrozumiałych względów i przy okazji dam ci radę na przyszłość: nie dawaj się ponosić gadulstwu.

– Ty mnie?

– Jako mężczyzna i przyjaciel! – przytaknął Bujała. – Wielka szkoda, że ty nigdy nie rozumiesz moich intencji. – Westchnął, całując dłoń Julii. – To są mianowicie kwiaty dla ciebie.

– A intencje?

– Co intencje?

– Za kwiaty dziękuję, pytam o intencje, których podobno nie rozumiem.

– Zawróciłaś mi w głowie i nie rozumiesz? Oj, ty czarodziejko, czarodziejko! – pogroził jej palcem.

Zgodził się wypić kawę, pod warunkiem, że Julia dotrzyma mu towarzystwa. Niestety, dzień był wyjątkowo nerwowy i dziewczyna pomyślała nawet, że spokojniej pogadaliby na dworcu autobusowym. Stale ktoś wpadał, telefony dzwoniły i trudno się było skupić. Prezes budził w niej niechęć, pomieszaną ze strachem. Do sekretariatu zajrzała Karolina.

– Dzwonię i nic. Chyba gdzieś polazł – powiedziała zniechęcona.

Julia odetchnęła z ulgą. To był wymarzony moment, by przedstawić Karolinie człowieka, który w każdej dziewczynie chciał widzieć panią magister Cierniak. Tak to właśnie zgrabnie określiła.

– Dlaczego dowiaduję się o tym dopiero dzisiaj? – zdziwiła się Karolina, posyłając Bujale przeciągłe spojrzenie spod rzęs. – Chociaż nie... chyba zaczynam rozumieć. Na twoim miejscu, Julio, też byłabym zazdrosna o takiego mężczyznę – powiedziała i posłała mu drugie spojrzenie.

Gadatliwy zwykle Bujała stał jak trusia. Z cichutkim zachwytem wpatrywał się w biust Karoliny. Julia posadziła przyjaciółkę przy stoliku dla gości, na wprost bossa, i wzięła się do pracy. Od czasu do czasu wciągali i ją do rozmowy. Obrzucała ich wtedy roztargnionym wzrokiem, jednak swoje widziała. Na nią obleśny tapirek patrzył łakomie – Karolinę dosłownie pożerał oczami. Życzyła mu w duchu, żeby się udławił. Poszedł wreszcie z wielkim ociąganiem. W drzwiach ze trzy razy się odwracał, żeby choć popatrzeć.

– No co? Prawda, że fajniutki?

– Wygląda na niezłego cwaniaka – odparła Karolina. – Ma o sobie doskonałe zdanie, ale nie wiem, czy nie ukręcę z nim jakiegoś interesu.

– Z nim czy jemu? – spytała niewinnie Julia.

– Widzisz, jak się przy mnie wyrobiłaś! – zawołała uradowana magister Cierniak. – Świntuszysz nie gorzej niż Chochla, a rumieńców na buźce nie widzę! Byle tak dalej, a wyjdziesz na prawdziwego wampa. Po pracy skoczę na obiad z panem prezesem.

– Myślałam, że pojedziesz ze mną otworzyć Konrada.

– Nie! Zjem obiad z Bujałą, ty sobie otwieraj Konrada sama. O osiemnastej spotkamy się w domu. Zrozum: Orzechowicz to przeszłość. Jeszcze dzień, dwa i całkiem się z niego wyleczę. Obejdzie się bez szpitala.

– A skąd! Właśnie ze szpitala wracam! – Zziajana Henia, z ulgą padła na fotel. Była blada i wystraszona.

– Chorujesz? – spytała Julia. Wobec ludzi chorych zawsze odczuwała dziwny lęk. Sama była nad podziw zdrowa, przerażało ją takie piętno nieszczęścia zawieszone nad cudzą głową.

Dopiero kiedy Karolina wyszła, Henia szepnęła Julii na ucho, że w szpitalu, na ortopedii, widziała Leszka Wydronia.

Konrad zwlókł się z tapczanu około drugiej. Od rana wypił chyba z osiem filiżanek herbaty i powoli dochodził do siebie. Język nie przypominał już kołka, szare komórki zaczynały pracować. Zrobił sobie niewielką kanapkę i był to pierwszy posiłek od dwudziestu kilku godzin.

Julia przyszła dopiero wpół do czwartej. Ledwie ją było widać spoza wielkiej reklamówki, którą oburącz tuliła do piersi.

– Przyniosłam trochę jedzenia. Poprosiłam w sklepie coś na kaca i babka dała mi kefir, jogurt i cytryny. Lubisz kefir?

– Julio, ta cała torba to kefiry dla mnie?

– Chciałbyś?! Ta cała torba to jedzonko dla ciebie, dla chorego w szpitalu i dla nas na kolację.

– Zostaniesz u mnie na kolacji?

– Mówiłam o sobie i Karolinie.

Wypakowała torbę, położyła na stole klucz i szykowała się do wyjścia.

– Nie drażnij chorego człowieka – poprosił cicho Konrad. – Usiądź, wypij kawę i pogadaj ze mną, bo oszaleję. Co ty mówiłaś przez telefon? Nosiłaś mnie na rękach?

– Nie chciałeś przebierać nogami, więc cię niosłam. Bardzo wierzgałeś i to nie była lekka praca – wyjaśniła ze śmiechem.

– Jak nosiłaś? Tak? – Nim zdążyła zaprotestować, chwycił ją na ręce jak małe dziecko. – Tak mnie nosiłaś? – spytał.

Jego twarz była tuż nad jej twarzą. Obejmował ją mocno, pewnie, i to było szalenie miłe. Czuła jego ciepło, widziała tuż nad sobą gęste zrośnięte brwi i oczy, każde inne. Jedno ciemne, głęboko osadzone, drugie otoczone granatową łatką. Zachciało jej się nagle pogładzić tę łatkę. Mówiła: – Puść – a myślała: – Pocałuj. On też myślał. Myślał tak: Nie pocałuję cię, dziewczyno, bo jestem skacowany i gdyby coś, to ja dętka. Ale pożerał ją wzrokiem, tulił w ramionach i wcale nie miał zamiaru stawiać na podłodze. Objęła go za szyję, zręcznie wyślizgnęła się z objęć, bo zdjął ją lęk, że to nie on, lecz ona może się dać ponieść o jeden krok za daleko.

– Będziesz jeszcze silniejszy, jak coś zjesz! – powiedziała lekko speszona.

– Usiądź, zrobię ci herbaty.

Przycupnęła na krześle i poprosiła o pół szklanki wody mineralnej. Godzina była późna, chciała jeszcze pojechać do szpitala, a jednocześnie wcale nie miała ochoty wychodzić. Konrad przyniósł dwa jogurty i dwie bułki. Wmówił Julii, że jest głodna, że podobnie jak on nie jadła obiadu.

– Wiesz, co mnie męczy? – spytał.

Żeby wiedzieć takie rzeczy, wcale nie trzeba politechniki kończyć. Uśmiechnęła się i opowiedziała mu o dyskotece, na której wystąpiła incognito, potem o poszukiwaniu pracy i dziwnym zbiegu okoliczności, gdy dyskotekowy boss okazał się prezesem Bujałą.

– Uparł się, że jestem Karoliną, sam wszystko przesądził i jeszcze miał do mnie pretensje o swoją pomyłkę – powiedziała, dopijając jogurt. – Widzisz, do czego prowadzi nadmierne gadulstwo mężczyzn?

– To nie tak, Julio! – Patrzył na nią w napięciu. Głęboka bruzda między brwiami wyglądała jak kreska. – Znam Bujałę parę lat i mogę ci zagwarantować, że jest wyjątkowo ostrożny w kontaktach z ludźmi. On nie nazwał cię Karoliną przez pomyłkę, on wiedział, że ty jesteś Karoliną. Ktoś go celowo wprowadził w błąd. Współczuję człowiekowi.

Julia patrzyła przerażona. Czuła, że blednie i że wszystkie siły z niej uchodzą.

– Leszek – wyszeptała – Leszek jest w szpitalu.

Nagle zaczęła się bardzo śpieszyć i gdyby nie przytomność Konrada, zapomniałaby o reklamówce z darami dla chorego.

O tym, że ortopedia jest na drugim piętrze, wiedziała od czasu, gdy ojciec złamał nogę. Leszka odnalazła bodaj na tej samej sali. A może jednak obok? Leżał z przymkniętymi oczami. Podeszła na palcach i delikatnie położyła mu dłoń na policzku. Uśmiechnął się, lecz oczu nie otworzył.

– Mój złoty plaster miodu... zgadłem?

– Otwórz patrzałki i sprawdź.

– Moja pszczółka, moja biedronka, moje szczęście. Zgadłem!

– Za to ty wyglądasz jak nieszczęście – pokiwała głową Julia. Wolała nie przeciągać romantycznego powitania. Uprzątnęła szafkę, ustawiła soki, cytrusy i nadziewane cukierki, za którymi Leszek przepadał. Bardzo się zmartwiła na wspomnienie kwiatów, które zostawiła w aucie. Był to wielki bukiet od bossa, o czym już nie wspomniała.

– Daj spokój, kochanie! Kwiatom trzeba zmieniać wodę. Kto miałby to robić, jak wszyscy na sali leżymy?

Usiadła na szpitalnym taborecie, najbliżej jak się dało, nakryła dłonią jego dłoń i chwilę patrzyła na otarty policzek i zadrapania na brodzie.

– Widzę, że urwałeś się z huździawki głową we wdół na azwald – uśmiechnęła się lekko. Zdankiem tym, zasłyszanym w radiu, zabawiali się kiedyś tak, jak potem słówkiem mianowicie. Nawet nie przypuszczała, że nadarzy się okazja, by zacytować je całkiem poważnie. – Powiedz, co się stało? Strasznie dużo tajemnic narosło między nami.

– Tajemnic? Dawno już chciałem powiedzieć ci prawdę, tylko ty nie dopuszczałaś mnie do głosu.

– No wiesz?!

Julia już szykowała się do wielkiego wybuchu, już nabrała powietrza w płuca i... szybko wypuściła. Uczciwość kazała jej przyznać Leszkowi rację. Rzeczywiście, parę razy zaczynał jakieś dziwne rozmowy, ale przerywała mu wtedy lub zmieniała temat. Nie chciała znać jego prawdy, bo miała swoją. Zupełnie jak Bujała, pomyślała z niechęcią.

– Co się stało? – spytała cicho.

– Dlaczego pytasz?

– Staram się uprzedzić świętego Piotra. I w ogóle, co to znaczy „dlaczego”? Jesteś moim przyjacielem czy nie jesteś? Nie złość mnie, mów po kolei. Telefonowałeś do mnie, prawda?

– Najpierw Bujała zatelefonował do mnie. Zdaje się, że coś mu zazgrzytało w twoim imieniu czy nazwisku. Trochę wrzeszczał, więc dokładnie nie zrozumiałem i zadzwoniłem do ciebie, żeby uściślić, o co chodzi. Jeszcze niedawno przekonywałaś mnie, że to ja gram znaczonymi kartami, że... Zresztą mniejsza o szczegóły. Twoja mama upierała się, że wyjechałaś w delegację, więc zamiast wyprowadzać ją z błędu, połączyłem obie informacje i wyszło mi, że jesteś u tego drania. Nie wiedziałem tylko, czy jest to wizyta dobrowolna, czy raczej przymusowa. Wściekłem się i pojechałem do Michelina. Bujała też się wściekł i oddał mnie pod opiekę swoim gorylom. To wszystko.

Julia szybko zamrugała oczami. Kręcisz, patyczaku, pomyślała. Kręcisz, próbujesz coś ukryć, całkiem jak ja. Mam ci powiedzieć prawdę, czy lepiej cię nie martwić?

Nie chciała płakać, łzy same spływały po policzkach i miękko padały na kołdrę. Leszek delikatnie dotknął jej twarzy, próbował zetrzeć wilgotne ślady. Patrzył przy tym z taką miną, takimi oczami, jak ta babka, siostra Orzechowicza. Wyraźnie nie miał ochoty opowiadać więcej o Bujale, Julia z kolei nie miała ochoty ustąpić.

– Znałeś go wcześniej, jeszcze przed Teatralną, prawda?

– Poznałem go, kiedy jeszcze ciebie nie było na świecie, biedroneczko. Grzegorz Bujała to najwcześniejsze wspomnienie mojego dzieciństwa. Podobno intelektualnie przewyższałem go już w kolebce, on natomiast bił mnie swoją siłą fizyczną... w przenośni i dosłownie. Siostra mamy, ciocia Uta, była prekursorką wychowania bezstresowego. Malutki Grześ rozwijał się zgodnie z prawami natury, aż się całkiem rozwinął i wyrósł na bossa. Jedno ci mogę powiedzieć: jestem o rok młodszy i do rodziny go nie zapraszałem. Sam się zaprosił... kłopotek czarny. Udaję, że go nie znam, bo co innego mogę zrobić?! Do jego interesów też się nie mieszam.

Julia nawet nie usiłowała ukryć zaskoczenia. Patrzyła i nie wierzyła własnym oczom: Leszek miałby być kuzynem Bujały? W głowie zaszumiało jej od pytań i wątpliwości. W pokrewieństwo uwierzyła, nie mogła jednak uwierzyć, że obydwaj dżentelmeni unikają spotkań.

– Nie kręć, Lesiu – poprosiła. – Spotykasz się z nim i wiesz więcej, niż mówisz.

Przemógł się i przyznał, że specjalnością firmy ubezpieczeniowej Spokój były całkiem niespokojne działania. Jakie? O to by trzeba spytać samego bossa. W każdym razie były to interesy ciemne, żeby nie powiedzieć czarne. Czy jest największą szychą w mieście? Trudno powiedzieć, bo na wysokich gangsterskich szczeblach ostatnio zrobiło się bardzo tłoczno. Niedługo trudniej będzie o dobrego goryla niż o bossa. Sam Bujała utrzymywał, że należy do krajowej czołówki i zna wszystkich, których powinien znać.

– To czemu chciałeś mu jeszcze przedstawić mnie czy raczej Karolinę? Nas nie musiał znać. Próbowałeś się podlizać czy co? – spytała Julia.

Ścisnął jej rękę, aż zabolało. Leżał chwilę z przymkniętymi oczami. Nie chciał się podlizywać. Po prostu nieopatrznie kiedyś wspomniał, że zna wyjątkowo piękną i obrotną prawniczkę. Padło nazwisko i Bujała się napalił. Wymyślił neutralny grunt, zaaranżował spotkanie, bo on uwielbia pozory. Leszek miał przyprowadzić Karolinę. Ale bał się o nią. Za dobrze znał jej pazerność na władzę i pieniądze i za dobrze znał Bujałę. Julię uważał za psychicznie odporniejszą, zresztą był przekonany, że przy prezentacji wszystko się wyda. Julia zabawiła się w biedronkę i patyczaka, zamknęła mu usta i gra się rozpoczęła.

– Mogłeś mi powiedzieć prawdę!

– Żebyś zaczęła go uwodzić i załatwiać pracę? Znałem przecież te plany i musiałem jakoś wybić ci z głowy niemądry pomysł.

– I dlatego powiedziałeś, że mnie kochasz?

Drgnął, podniósł się na tyle, na ile pozwalały mu obrażenia.

– Jeżeli nie widzisz, że cię kocham, to te twoje śliczne oczy są chyba szklane!

– Mnie kochasz, Karolinę kochasz, ty kochasz wszystkich, Leszku, no, może oprócz Bujały i Ileni. Gdybyś nam powiedział wszystko, co wiesz, nie byłoby spisku i całego zamieszania. Nie wierzyłeś chyba, że komukolwiek pokrzyżujemy plany?

– Nie wierzyłem – przytaknął. – To był jedyny sposób, żebyś wreszcie odwiedziła mnie w domu. Wciąż mi umykałaś... Bardzo się bałem, że nie zdążę cię przekonać, ile dla mnie znaczysz. Nie, nie mów nic, posłuchaj choć raz do końca. – Przytulił jej dłoń do szorstkiego policzka. – Bujała od czasu do czasu prosił mnie o pomoc prawną. To haracz, jaki mu płaciłem za pewną przysługę. Stare dzieje, nie ma o czym mówić. Pokazał mi dokumenty zebrane przez Edytę. Nawet się nie zorientował, że mu zwinąłem zieloną teczkę. On i tak wiedział już wszystko, co chciał wiedzieć, poza tym miał oryginały. Ja za to miałem swój wielki dzień. Bardzo trudno jest zrobić krok od przyjaźni do miłości... nie wiedziałem, że aż tak trudno. Obiecaj mi, że pomyślisz poważnie nad tym, co powiedziałem... zastanowisz się, czy naprawdę nie możesz mnie pokochać...

Zmęczyło go to wyznanie. Leżał przez chwilę z zamkniętymi oczami. Julia przysunęła taboret jeszcze bliżej i oparła głowę o ramię Leszka. Cichutko przyrzekła, że się zastanowi. Nie było to kłamstwo ani wybieg. W tamtym momencie, z policzkiem na jego ramieniu poczuła, że tuli się do kogoś naprawdę bliskiego. Gdyby jeszcze miał czarne oczy pod czarnymi brwiami, był nieco muskularniejszy i... Uniosła głowę i spojrzała na bladą, ale szczęśliwą twarz Leszka.

– No widzisz! Mikulowa sprzedała, Edyta kupiła, czy to nie wszystko jedno, która baba nami rządzi? – powiedziała bez większego związku z jego wyznaniem i swoimi wątpliwościami.

– Bujała by cię sprostował. On twierdzi, że firma należy do niego – mruknął cicho, gładząc delikatnie jej włosy.

To był najbardziej romansowy dzień w życiu Julii. Jeden mężczyzna dał jej kwiaty, drugi nosił ją na rękach, trzeci zasypał najczulszymi wyznaniami, a w perspektywie miała jeszcze spotkanie z czwartym. Aż bała się myśleć o niespodziance, jaką zgotował jej Chochla. Miała przyjść o zmroku, nie świecić światła na klatce, nie rzucać się sąsiadom w oczy, dwa razy przycisnąć guzik domofonu, potem dwa razy zapukać do drzwi mieszkania. Widać Chochla był zwolennikiem systemu dwójkowego.

Karolina już była w domu.

– Załatwiłaś urlop? – spytała Julia.

– Hm, jak by ci tu powiedzieć – zastanowiła się głośno. – Załatwiłam zaległy urlop, po którym mogę już nie wracać. Nowa właścicielka nie ukrywała, że na stanowisku prawnika firmy widzi wyłącznie mężczyznę.

– Zgłupiała? Przecież załatwiałaś rzeczy niemożliwe, paragrafy tańczyły, jak im zagrałaś, i co?

– Chcesz do rymu czy rzeczowo? Jak do rymu, to gówno, jak rzeczowo, to też. Chłopa antyfeministę jeszcze przekonasz, ale baby za chińskiego luda. Baby antyfeministki są stokroć gorsze niż filmy pornograficzne emitowane w polskiej telewizji. Oglądasz czasem?

– Nie lubię. I co teraz zrobisz?

Ku zdziwieniu Julii przyjaciółka nie wydawała się szczególnie zmartwiona. Tak długo drżała przed utratą pracy, że w końcu zżyła się z myślą, że ten moment nadejdzie. Mikula jaki był, taki był, ale bronił jej interesów przed swoimi harpiami. W innych sprawach dawał się przekonać, kapitulował dla świętego spokoju, lecz w tej jednej był niezłomny. Mikuli zabrakło i realistka Karolina nie mogła liczyć na żadne względy.

– Co zrobisz? Jak sobie poradzisz? – dopytywała się Julia.

– Na razie jadę do Torunia, do Marty. Popytam przyjaciół, poszukam, coś wymyślę. Jeśli się nie uda, zawsze mogę skorzystać z propozycji Bujały... chociaż wolałabym nie. Przez skórę czuję, że to śmierdzące jajeczko. Aż się wierzyć nie chce, że to kuzyn Leszka. Z jednym możesz konie kraść, a drugi kradnie ci kieckę. Co tak patrzysz? – parsknęła śmiechem. – Nie miałaś wrażenia, że te jego wyłupiaste oczka obierają cię z ubrań? Głowę daję, że dzisiaj w czasie obiadu siedziałam w restauracji nagusieńka.

– To pewnie wcale nie siedziałaś! – mruknęła Julia, czym wprawiła przyjaciółkę w jeszcze lepszy humor.

Julia chciała coś jeszcze dodać, ale spojrzała na zegarek i przypomniała sobie o Chochli. Ogarnęło ją twórcze podniecenie, pomieszane ze zdenerwowaniem. W takim dniu jak ten, była tego pewna, żaden mężczyzna nie oprze się jej urokowi. Należało się śpieszyć, by Marcinek zbyt długo nie czekał. Upięła włosy, poprawiła makijaż i obciągnęła króciutką spódniczkę.

– Tak idziesz? – spytała Karolina.

Pakując w domu ciuchy, Julia przygotowała się do roli agenta pomocniczego. Miała działać sprawnie i nie wchodzić w oczy: ciemna bluza, ciemne dresowe spodnie i wygodne buty, to było to, co zapewniało jej niewidzialność. Jeden kaprys Chochli wywrócił do góry nogami cały plan, łącznie ze strojem. Zamierzała iść w tym, w czym była w pracy.

– Włóż to! – Karolina wyciągnęła z szafy nowe dżinsy, sztywne jak drewno. – Zaręczam ci, że facet, który spróbuje to z ciebie ściągnąć, najpierw sam padnie. Uważaj na paznokcie przy zapinaniu guzików.

Julia aż tak naiwna nie była, by lekceważyć cudze dobre doświadczenia. Wyszła z domu w ciemnej bluzie z kapturem i w ciasnych spodniach Karoliny. Przez całą drogę omawiały szczegóły planu. Julia wchodziła pierwsza. Jej głowa w tym, żeby zostawić otwarte drzwi wejściowe i zamknięte od pokoju. Miała piętnaście minut na przygotowanie drogi dla przyjaciółki. Dwa krótkie sygnały komórki znaczyły, że wszystko gotowe.

– Jak przez piętnaście minut nie będzie sygnału, dzwonię i wywabiam cię z chałupy, pamiętaj – denerwowała się Karolina. – I siadaj jak najdalej od tapczanu.

Julia prowadziła samochód, więc nie mogła pozwolić sobie na rozdygotanie. Karolina natomiast szalała. Po pięć razy sprawdzała zawartość torby małego włamywacza, liczyła gumowe rękawiczki, raptem dwie, i wciąż gadała, jakby chciała zagłuszyć własny strach.

– Trzymaj się, będzie dobrze! – powiedziała Julia, gdy wreszcie dojechały.

– Przytul mnie – poprosiła nieoczekiwanie Karolina. – Jesteś twardsza ode mnie. Sama bym się nie zdobyła na ten krok.

Julia objęła przyjaciółkę i uniosła kciuk do góry na znak zwycięstwa.

Z domofonem poszło łatwo. Schody pokonała błyskawicznie. Z bijącym sercem zapukała dwa razy do drzwi. Coś się ruszyło, coś zachrobotało i nic. Zapukała znowu. Niemal słyszała skrzypienie podłogi kilka kroków dalej, u Wandy Pasieczko. Rusz się, ty plujko burczało, ty podrzucie myszaty, ty śmietko cholerna, ty... ty ogonie wołowy, zaklinała w duchu Chochlę. No rusz się, gamoniu!

Ten ślimaczy pośpiech wart był najsroższej kary.

– Juliaa?

I ten rozdziamdziany głos też wart był kary. Warknęła, że tak, i już nie wiedziała, czy to Wanda sapie za swoimi drzwiami, czy dureń Marcinek za swoimi. W jasnej szczelinie, ograniczonej łańcuchem, dostrzegła wreszcie rybie oko. Upłynęła następna długa chwila, nim stanęła w przedpokoju.

– Już bardziej nie mogłeś się guzdrać!

Nie bardzo rozumiał, o co Julii chodzi. Przecież śpieszył się, ale musiał otworzyć drzwi. Spojrzała na te drzwi i nogi się pod nią ugięły. Dwa solidne zamki wzmacniała zapora złożona ze stolika, szafki i długiego drąga. Marcin właśnie usiłował dosunąć do drzwi tę barykadę, przez którą karaluch może by się bezszelestnie przecisnął, lecz nie Karolina.

– Zostaw to! – tupnęła gniewnie. – Ustawisz sobie, jak wyjdę. Nie chcę się tu czuć jak małpa w klatce.

Potulnie odstawił drąg do kąta i wskazał wejście do pokoju. Zatrzymała się w progu z jękiem obrzydzenia. Nie dość, że zaduch zatykał dech w piersiach, to jeszcze wszędzie walały się ciuchy, stare gazety, opakowania od chipsów.

– Zaprosiłeś mnie i nawet nie posprzątałeś? Mam siedzieć z tobą w tym chlewie? – powiedziała z zimną wściekłością. Nie spodziewała się takiego przyjęcia.

– Tego, no... nie miałem kiedy, za to mam dla ciebie niespodziankę. Wyciągnął z kieszeni klucz i cofnął się do przedpokoju. Widziała, że wchodzi do kuchni. Nie zapalał światła, przymknął drzwi. Z konieczności obejrzała sobie jeszcze raz pokój. Porządny był tam tylko telewizor i magnetowid, reszta to same graty, każdy z innego kompletu. Tapczan, stolik, szafa, chyba z dziesięć krzeseł i pusty regalik na kasety.

Chochla zamknął starannie drzwi, schował klucz i dopiero wtedy podał Julii małe pudełeczko. Pierścionek był nawet niebrzydki, cały ze złota, bez kamienia. Do obrączki przyczepiona była karteczka: *Dla Blendy od Marcina.*

– Ładny – pochwaliła – ale za wcześnie na biżuterię. Wezmę go kiedy indziej... dopiero jak wyjedziemy.

Nie nalegał. Odłożyła etui na stół i spojrzała na zegarek. Dziewięć minut zmitrężyła i niczego nie przygotowała. Najważniejszy był klucz, który Chochla nosił przy tyłku. Nie miała pojęcia, jak mu go odebrać w ciągu sześciu minut, zdecydowała się więc odwołać akcję. Podała Marcinowi rękę na pożegnanie.

– Chyba jeszcze nie wychodzisz? – spytał.

– Daję ci szansę, żebyś tu posprzątał. Jutro wpadnę, to pogadamy. I pamiętaj, nie chcę widzieć żadnych barykad. Nie będę sterczała na korytarzu ani minuty. Masz otwierać natychmiast, rozumiesz?

– Ten... tego... myślałem, że dziś... no... pociupciamy. – Przełknął głośno ślinę i niezdarnie usiłował ją objąć.

– Jutro, Marcinku, wszystko jutro! – powiedziała, zrzucając jego rękę ze swojego ramienia.

Na parterze ktoś śmiał się identycznie jak Konrad. Jakie to szczęście, pomyślała, że nie wszyscy mężczyźni są podobni do Chochli. Dobiegła do samochodu w momencie, gdy Karolina szykowała się z odsieczą. W garści trzymała komórkę Julii.

– Zadzwoniłam, a ta małpa odezwała się z tylnego siedzenia. O mało zawału nie dostałam – jęknęła.

– Chyba ją sobie na szyi uwiążę – westchnęła Julia.

Program, tak starannie opracowany, wymagał zmian, i to radykalnych. Dyskutowały nad nimi do północy.

– Co to znaczy: ciupcianie? – spytała Julia, gdy już szykowały się do snu.

Karolina patrzyła na nią oczami wielkimi jak spodeczki.

– Właśnie to? – Julia załapała i zaczęła chichotać. – Ale jajo! Obiecałam Marcinowi, że jutro pogadamy i pociupciamy. Myślałam o żarciu. Nie patrz tak! Znam parę innych określeń, tego akurat nie.

– Jutro ja pójdę do Marcina – zdecydowała Karolina i nie dała już sobie tego pomysłu wybić z głowy. Przez następną godzinę dostosowywały plan do zmienionych warunków.

– Bez bab bieda, a z babami żyć się nie da! – podśpiewywał Lucjan Orski. Ustawił na stole talerzyki, pokroił chleb i wędlinę. – Bez bab, bez bab... O, jeszcze serwetki.

– Co to za aria? – zagadnął z uśmiechem Konrad.

– Moja własna. Jak sobie chcę coś porządnego pośpiewać, to wymyślam.

Zasiedli do kolacji. Konrad zastanawiał się nad pewnym fenomenem: mógł nie widzieć Lucjana i Grażyny przez miesiąc, dwa, pięć, przychodził i było tak, jakby w ogóle się nie rozstawali. Ostatnio czuł się wobec nich winny. O tym, że zmienił pracę, powinni dowiedzieć się od niego, nie od obcych ludzi. W święta też ich zawiódł. Zatelefonował z życzeniami, ale przez dwa dni nie znalazł okazji, żeby wpaść choć na dziesięć minut. Wreszcie zebrał się, przyszedł i zastał tylko Lucjana.

– Co właściwie jest Grażynce?

– Jakieś torbiele tam, gdzie ich nie powinno być. Na szczęście dzisiaj się wszystko wyjaśniło. Wyniki histopatologiczne są dobre, więc śpiewam sobie.

– Śpiewasz, że z babami żyć się nie da! Coś chyba nie tak? – uśmiechnął się Konrad.

– Mówisz, że głupio śpiewam? To zaraz zmienię... Wiesz – głos mu niebezpiecznie zadrgał – jak się z kimś przeżyje pół życia i nagle w oczy zagląda tragedia, to z człowieka ulatuje cała siła. Gdyby z nią coś... to ja nie mam już czego szukać na tym świecie. Dzieci nie mamy, ty już jesteś samodzielny, czasem aż za bardzo... Nie krzyw się, Radek, nie trzeba. Nie robię ci z tego powodu wyrzutów, wiem, że masz duszę rogatą, ale w gruncie rzeczy świetny z ciebie facet. Udałeś nam się, chłopcze, lepiej niż niejeden syn.

Wcale nie krzywił się dlatego, że ubodły go słowa starego przyjaciela. Próbował zapanować nad wzruszeniem i tamten dobrze o tym wiedział.

– Są jakieś dni odwiedzin w tym szpitalu? – spytał cicho Orzechowicz.

– Dni otwarte, jak kiedyś na uczelniach. Wchodzi, kto chce i kiedy chce. Tylko jakbyś przypadkiem oglądał szpitalny serial w telewizji, to nie zdziw się, że on tak ma się do życia, jak krowa do chomika. Niby jedno zwierzę i drugie, ale spróbuj chomika wydoić.

– Krowy też bym nie wydoił.

Rozmawiali do późnej nocy. Właściwie mówił głównie Lucjan. Przeskakiwał z tematu na temat, wspominał całe swoje życie i obojętnie, o czym opowiadał, zawsze kończył na Grażynie. To było silniejsze od niego. Schudł, oczy mu się zapadły i Konrad, patrząc na niego, czuł się jak ostatni drań. W najtrudniejszej chwili, zamiast warować obok przyjaciela, marnotrawił czas na amorach. Fruwał sobie, gdy Lucjan do niego telefonował. A gdyby to była sprawa poważna, bardzo poważna? Wzdrygnął się na samą myśl.

Odkąd pamiętał, Grażyna i Lucjan byli zawsze razem. Jako mały chłopak współczuł Orskiemu, że nie ma kolegów, że nigdy nie wychodzi z domu sam, tylko zawsze z żoną. Konrad nie wyobrażał sobie życia bez kumpli, dziewczyny go nudziły, więc czasem, powodowany męską solidarnością, wyciągał Lucjana na mecz. Ale to było dawno! Teraz siedział na wprost tego samego Lucjana i doskonale go rozumiał: nie można nudzić się z kobietą, którą się kocha. Nuda jest zawsze wynikiem obojętności. Gdyby nie chodziło o przyjaciół, gotów był im zazdrościć, że tak bezbłędnie odnaleźli się wśród masy ludzi.

Do domu dotarł przed dwunastą. Kac już mu przeszedł, ale duszę miał chorą. Umówił się z Orskim na następny wieczór. Mieszkanie bez Grażyny to już inne mieszkanie. On to czuł, a co dopiero mąż. Wróciła stara tęsknota za własnym domem. Przypomniał sobie wielkie oczy, śmieszne piegi i zrobiło mu się jeszcze smutniej. Trzymał Julię na rękach, tu, w tym pokoju, i nie miałby nic przeciwko temu, żeby ją znowu potrzymać, ponosić od drzwi do tapczanu i z powrotem, lub lepiej bez powrotu. Szczególnie tapczan bardzo rozbudził jego wyobraźnię. Julia sprawiała wrażenie obojętnej, jednak gdyby się postarał, to kto wie?

Zanim położył się do łóżka, nabrał przekonania, że chciałby mieć właśnie taką dziewczynę. Ale czy taka dziewczyna chciałaby mieć faceta, który za jednym zamachem wypija pół butli koniaku? Żeby jeszcze wypił i był trzeźwy, to co innego.

Zmodyfikowany plan antychochlowy zakładał, że to Karolina wchodzi do mieszkania pierwsza. Czyli nie był to wcale plan zmodyfikowany, tylko powrót do pierwszej wersji, jak słusznie zauważyła Julia. Obeszło się bez dodatkowych przygotowań. Musiała jedynie zadzwonić do domu i uprzedzić, że przyjedzie w niedzielę. Na poczekaniu wymyśliła wiarygodną historyjką o koleżance ze studiów, wspólnym weekendzie, a w odpowiedzi usłyszała, że ma natychmiast wracać. Dosyć, wracaj, wracaj, dosyć, masz swój dom i od początku to samo. Dom miała, ale żyć chciała po swojemu. Powtórzyła, że wróci w niedzielę wieczorem i poirytowana skończyła rozmowę.

– Nie słyszałaś o jakimś małym mieszkaniu do wynajęcia? – spytała.

– Wyrobisz bez ich pomocy?

Julia wątpiła, czy wyrobi, i właśnie dlatego zwlekała z ostatecznym odcięciem pępowiny.

Pod blok na Kujawskiej podjechały o zmroku. Julia zaparkowała z dala od okien garsoniery.

– W życiu nie czułam się tak podle – mruknęła Karolina.

– Nie pękaj. Pas cnoty masz, idziesz na wysprzątane i wywietrzone pokoje, nie tak, jak ja wczoraj – powiedziała Julia. Panowała nad nerwami, wydawała się spokojna i wyluzowana. No, ale ona szła do konkretnej pracy włamywacza, a co mogło czekać Karolinę?

Tak naprawdę Julia zaczęła się denerwować godzinę po tym, jak Karolina zniknęła za drzwiami drugiej klatki. Rozdygotana i przerażona czekała na sygnał, że droga otwarta. Czas wlókł się wolniej niż sparaliżowana żmija. Nie mogła myśleć ani o wielkich rolach, ani o niczym innym. Przed oczami miała wąski korytarz, wejście do łazienki, do kuchni i do pokoju. Obojętnym wzrokiem obserwowała pustą uliczkę przed domem. Tylko jakiś mężczyzna nieśpiesznie wędrował chodnikiem. Mikula? – niemal wykrzyknęła. Przysunęła się do szyby – rzeczywiście, to był dyrektor. Podszedł do drzwi drugiej klatki i wcisnął guzik przy domofonie. Julię przebiegł dreszcz. Stary stanowił przeszkodę nie do pokonania. Tam gdzie dzwonił, najwidoczniej go nie oczekiwali, bo dał za wygraną. Odprowadziła go wzrokiem aż do rogu budynku. Ledwie za nim zniknął, odezwał się upragniony sygnał, na który czekała – zerknęła na zegarek – godzinę i pięćdziesiąt minut! Przewiesiła przez ramię maleńki plecak z latarką, śrubokrętem i uniwersalnym wytrychem, którym nie umiała się posługiwać, zamknęła samochód, włożyła cienkie gumowe rękawiczki i pewnym krokiem podeszła do drzwi. Domofon! Nie pomyślały wcześniej o cholernym domofonie! Wcisnęła pierwszy lepszy guzik. Kobieta po tamtej stronie nie bardzo rozumiała, jaka sąsiadka, ale sygnał zabrzęczał i droga była wolna. Julia, przeskakując po kilka stopni, pobiegła na drugie piętro. Bezszelestnie wsunęła się do oświetlonego przedpokoju. Zniknęła gdzieś zapora antywłamaniowa, za to na podłodze walały się powiększalniki, lampy, kuwety, jednym słowem, cały sprzęt, który zwykle stoi w ciemni fotograficznej. Z łazienki, poprzez chlupot wody, dochodziły głosy Karoliny i Chochli.

– Gdzie z tą łapą! – śmiała się Karolina. Na szczęście odzyskała już wigor i nie traciła głowy. – Szczupły jesteś, ale bardzo harmonijnie zbudowany – łgała, a on pomrukiwał z zadowolenia i łykał komplementy, niczym pies muchy. – Wydajesz się silny, borsuczku, jak niedźwiedź!

Julia tylko głową pokiwała. Znała teorię Karoliny o wpływie pochlebstw na naturę męską, teraz miała okazję przekonać się o jej słuszności. Podobno nie ma mężczyzny, którego nie można zbałamucić miłymi słowami, dawkowanymi umiejętnie i dostosowanymi do oczekiwań. Jedni reagują na pochwałę intelektu, inni bicepsów. Chochla należał do tej drugiej grupy.

– No, tego... właściwie dlaczego przyszłaś zamiast Julii? Nie powiesz, ten... no, że mnie kochasz?

– Tego jeszcze żaden mężczyzna ode mnie nie usłyszał! Pociągasz mnie do szaleństwa. Kiedy dowiedziałam się, że ty i ta mała, to myślałam, że zwariuję. Od dawna już miałam na ciebie ochotę.

– Ona też – powiedział z dumą.

– Widać ma gust. Postaram się, żebyś nie żałował, że musiała wyjechać. To mówisz, że ona naprawdę jest taka dobra?

Karolina znacząco zawiesiła głos, a on tajemniczo zachichotał.

Kamera i archiwum, kamera i archiwum, powtarzała w duchu Julia, ale zatrzymała się tuż za drzwiami łazienki. Takiej rozmowy nie mogła sobie darować. Niestety, Chochla zaczął opowiadać dyrdymały i tak ją zbrzydził swoją chorą fantazją, że natychmiast wzięła się do pracy.

Włączyła światło w pokoju. Zaduch wciąż wisiał w powietrzu, jednak widać było ślady sprzątania. W tapczanie znalazła tylko pościel, w szafie wszystkie śmieci, które wcześniej walały się po pokoju. Odnalezienie oka kamery okazało się dziecinnie proste, jednak najważniejsze było dotarcie na zaplecze, czyli do kuchni. Gasiła właśnie światło, kiedy z hukiem otworzyły się drzwi łazienki. Na szczęście wyszła Karolina. Była w spodniach i w bluzce. Podwinęła tylko rękawy i rozpięła guzik pod szyją.

– Kończ, zanim się porzygam – szepnęła. – I natychmiast dzwoń.

Wcisnęła Julii klucz i zaczęła krążyć po przedpokoju.

– Mocz się, borsuczku, mocz – wołała. – Nie myłeś się chyba z rok. Dolej sobie gorącej wody. Nie pamiętasz, gdzie położyłam torebkę? Ależ ty masz tu syf, świntuszku!

– No przecież sprzątałem. To mówisz, że Julka opowiadała o mnie?

– Podpytałam ją i pękła. Chyba się zabujała. To jeszcze smarkula, jej nie można wierzyć.

– Pieniądze tego... no... ją przekonają. Dziś obdzwoniłem wszystkich, którzy są mi winni. Najdalej... tego... we wtorek będę bogaty.

Julia przekręciła klucz i weszła do kuchni. Na moment zatrzymała się w drzwiach, zaskoczona panującym tu wzorowym porządkiem. Czas jednak naglił. Dobrze wiedziała, co robić, żeby odzyskać najświeższą taśmę. W pudełkach po butach znalazła ze dwadzieścia innych oraz filmy i całą stertę kopert. Pozostawały jeszcze kartonowe teczki. Nie było ich nigdzie w zasięgu wzroku. Przeszukała szafki, zajrzała do piekarnika i kiedy unosiła się z klęczek, dostrzegła nad drzwiami niewielki pawlacz. Chwiejąc się niebezpiecznie na taborecie, sięgnęła ręką i o mały włos nie runęła na ziemię. Chochla rozprawiał właśnie z Karoliną o swoich wdziękach.

– Bo ja tego... no... zawsze myślałem, że jestem za chudy.

– Mówiłam ci już, że nie – uspokajała go Karolina. – Zresztą wiesz, tusza nie ma znaczenia. Mężczyzna może nie mieć ręki lub nogi, byle nie był kaleką. Słyszałeś to powiedzenie?

– Tego... no... jak nie ma ręki, to chyba jest kaleką – sprostował rzeczowo i właśnie w tym momencie Julia zgrabnie zeskoczyła na podłogę, błogosławiąc w duchu swoje mięciutkie adidasy. Wpakowała wszystkie skarby do ortalionowej torby. Czas był najwyższy, bo Marcinek dość już miał kąpieli i szykował się do opuszczenia wanny.

– A pazury u nóg? – zaprotestowała Karolina. – Siedź, zaraz przyniosę cążki!

Spotkały się w przedpokoju, gdy Julia zamykała drzwi kuchenne. Uniosła kciuk na znak zwycięstwa i cichusieńko opuściła mieszkanie. Torba nie była zbyt ciężka, ale przerzuciła ją przez ramię, żeby nie wyglądać na obładowaną. Przed blokiem, na wprost okien garsoniery, stał Mikula z jakimś potężnie zbudowanym facetem. Na widok wychodzącej dziewczyny facet rzucił się, żeby przytrzymać drzwi. Na szczęście nie zdążył. Julia nasunęła kaptur na oczy i choć czuła w nogach strach, pobiegła przed siebie leciutko jak sprinterka. Zanim wsiadła do samochodu, zadzwoniła do Karoliny.

– Pędź piętro wyżej, właśnie do klatki włazi Mikula!

Mogła już tylko się modlić, nic więcej. Z daleka widziała, że klatka schodowa rozbłysła światłem. Ci dwaj nie mieli powodów, żeby się kryć. Zmitrężyli w środku z dziesięć, może piętnaście minut, wyszli, rozprawiając o czymś zawzięcie, i skręcili tuż za blokiem. Karoliny wciąż nie było, a jej telefon nie odpowiadał.

Cicho, Julka, cicho, myśl logicznie! – mówiła sobie. Karolina mogła zostać u Chochli, ale równie dobrze mogła złamać nogę, kiedy uciekała po ciemku. I to jest najbardziej prawdopodobne. Trzeba wejść i przeszukać klatkę do czwartego piętra.

Dochodziła ósma. Julia schowała torbę do bagażnika, zamknęła samochód i postanowiła złożyć wizytę Wandzi Pasieczko. Ledwie wcisnęła dzwonek domofonu, odezwał się radosny głos:

– Czekamy, czekamy!

Czekamy? Kto mógł z nią czekać, chyba tylko Mikulowa? Gdy doszła na drugie piętro, drzwi już były gościnnie uchylone i Julia nie mogła pójść wyżej, musiała przekroczyć próg Wandy i zostawić przyjaciółkę na pastwę losu.

– Straciłaś tylko wstęp – zawołała wesoło Karolina. Stała w drzwiach pokoju i wydawała się całkiem zadomowiona. – „Oda do Włocławka" jest rewelacyjna!

Od Wandy Pasieczko wyszły przed dziesiątą, w samą porę, by nie spotkać się z kolejnymi gośćmi. Siedziały już w samochodzie, gdy Karolina zobaczyła Henię z Edytą. Zmierzały prosto do drugiej klatki.

– Wygląda na to, że cały Budampolex przenosi się na noc na Kujawską! – stwierdziła zaskoczona Julia. – Ciekawe, do kogo idą te dwie?

– Najbardziej potrzebuje pociechy Chochla. W ciągu minuty został sam, rozpalony do białości. Biedny Marcinek. I rozumek też ma taki malutki!

– Opanuj się! Chcesz, żebym nas rozkwaczyła na drzewie? Zapomnij już o Marcinku i jego wdziękach.

– Niemożliwe! Nie widziałam i chyba już nie zobaczę równie porażającej męskiej urody. A ten samochód, który stał na końcu parkingu, to nie...

– Owszem! – wpadła jej w słowo Julia. – Orzechowicz też tu jest.

Bałaganiarz i brudas Chochla w pracy lubił porządek i precyzję. Na kopertach były daty, imiona, nazwiska, nawet godziny, a w kopertach przegląd towarzyskiej śmietanki miasta. Ukryta kamera nakręciła kilometry taśm, z których potem mistrz Chochla przenosił na fotografie co celniejsze ujęcia. Można było obejrzeć nawet pary małżeńskie, tyle że nigdy nie kładły się na tapczanie razem. Jak choćby Mikulowie: on z Karoliną, ona z Majdziakiem.

– Niezła kolekcja – przyznała z podziwem Julia. – Teledyski, a raczej erotodyski, i fotki, czyli pełne wyposażenie rasowego szantażysty. Jak myślisz, ile mógł na tym zarobić?

– Jedź z nim do Szczyrku, to ci powie – zaśmiała się Karolina. – Zdaje się, że ruszył z szantażem dopiero za twoją sprawą. Słyszałaś, co mówił o telefonach do dłużników?

Julia słyszała, lecz nie przejęła się zbyt mocno. Była bardzo zadowolona, że nie stchórzyła, wygrała z własnym strachem i nie okazała się gorsza, niż kiedyś Marta Wilani. Zresztą zaraz po akcji zadzwoniła do Torunia, żeby przyjąć gratulacje i zaproszenie na babską pogaduchę. Natomiast Karolina nie mogła oderwać się od skarbów Chochli. Dokopała się do zdjęć i klisz bardzo starych, jak choćby te z Edytą i Mikulą w rolach głównych. Kartonowe teczki zawierały dokumenty, notatki, kalendarze z adnotacjami, kto, co i gdzie. Jednak nurt historyczny był znacznie uboższy od współczesnego i przedstawiał mniejszą wartość przetargową. Kogo mogły przerażać zdjęcia sprzed dwudziestu kilku lat? Zresztą może i mogły, nigdy nie wiadomo, czego ludzie się wstydzą ze swojej przeszłości, a co jest dla nich powodem do dumy.

– Nie chcę nic mówić: mamy pół miasta u stóp – stwierdziła Karolina.

– Żartujesz? – wystraszyła się Julia.

– Ja tak, ale Chochla chyba nie żartował. Zobacz, kogo my tu mamy!

Julia nie była aż tak bardzo otrzaskana towarzysko. Kobiety, z wyjątkiem przyjaciółki oraz Oli Mikulowej i Edyty były jej obce, wśród mężczyzn rozpoznała Bujałę, Majdziaka, Mikulę i ze trzech innych, których widywała w sekretariacie, lecz nie kojarzyła z konkretnymi nazwiskami.

– Ten łysawy – powiedziała, wpatrując się w potężny tors – był chyba dzisiaj z Mikulą pod domem. Może mi się wydaje, bo widziałam go przez moment, kiedy usiłował przytrzymać drzwi.

Karolina nie widziała ani Mikuli, ani jego towarzysza. Krzyknęła Marcinkowi, że idą goście i ma zamknąć drzwi, a sama w pośpiechu wybiegła. Tamci dwaj dochodzili do pierwszego piętra. Nie uciekała, tylko nasunęła kaptur na głowę, stanęła przy drzwiach Wandy Pasieczko i zadzwoniła. Minęli ją i konspiracyjnie weszli piętro wyżej. To wystarczyło. Wanda na dźwięk słowa „Julia" gościnnie uchyliła drzwi. Karolina z wrodzonym sobie wdziękiem zabajerowała starszą damę.

– A ja czekałam na sygnał od ciebie! – mruknęła Julia.

– Cały wieczór ci tłumaczę, że moja komórka została u Chochli. Skafander i torebkę chwyciłam w biegu, telefon bezmyślnie odłożyłam. Jutro zadzwonię do Nokii... nie, raczej do operatora sieci... w każdym razie jutro zgłoszę zaginięcie aparatu. Wolę to, niż jeszcze jedną wizytę u Marcinka.

Grażyna zajmowała łóżko przy samych drzwiach. Była blada, choć nie wyglądała źle. Konrad przysunął taboret. Nie miał sumienia jej budzić. Ona jednak nie spała, leżała tylko z zamkniętymi oczami i kiedy już usiadł, poszukała jego ręki i dopiero wtedy z przestrachem otworzyła oczy.

– Myślałam, że to Lucek, ale ręka nie ta! – Uśmiechnęła się, jakby przepraszając za ten gwałtowny strach.

– Patrz, co ci przyniosłem!

– „Pan Samochodzik i templariusze" – szepnęła. – Chcesz mi poczytać?

– Mnie kiedyś pomogło. Jak się czujesz?

– Dobrze... chyba dobrze... Mam za dużo czasu i obsiadają mnie różne głupie myśli. Boję się o Lucjana.

Byłem wczoraj u niego i gadaliśmy do późnej nocy. Dzisiaj znowu pójdę, bo twój Lucek robi pyszne kolacje. On wcale nie jest taki niezaradny, jak sądzisz.

– Wiem, że nie jest, ale z nas dwojga to kto powinien spodnie nosić, on czy ja? Raduś – uniosła się z trudem na łokciu – obiecaj mi, że gdyby coś... ja nie mówię, że będzie źle, ale gdyby coś, to nie zostawisz go samego!

– Nie. Natychmiast go ożenię i mam już nawet kandydatkę: grubą, brzydką, rozplotkowaną babę, która Lucka natychmiast weźmie pod pantofel. Dlaczego mówisz takie rzeczy? Jest dobrze i będzie dobrze. Musi być! – Pochylił się, objął ją i ucałował w czoło.

Powoli uspokoiła się i nawet uśmiechnęła. Konrad nie uważał się za specjalistę od kobiecej psychiki, jednak skłonny był przypuszczać, że choroba Grażyny jest natury bardziej duchowej niż cielesnej. Nie wytrzymywała atmosfery szpitala, bezruchu i tęsknoty za swoim Luckiem. Znalazł więc odpowiednie lekarstwo: zaczął jej opowiadać o swoich kobietach, tak jakby miał dwie. Prawdę mówiąc, nie miał żadnej, ale zaczął trochę zmyślać. Wahał się między piękną i przedsiębiorczą prawniczką a cichutką, skromniutką panią inżynier, między Karoliną i Julią. Bez intymnych szczegółów, bez zbytnich drobiazgów przyznał, że obie mu się podobają. Trafił w dziesiątkę. Musiał dokładnie opisać urodę jednej, potem drugiej i dodatkowo odpowiedzieć na wiele pytań. Jakie żarty lubią? Czy oglądają seriale? Jak się ubierają? Czy mają poczucie humoru? Czy potrafią gotować?

Wychodząc przed kolacją, zostawił Grażynę ożywioną, z cieniem rumieńców na policzkach. Była przejęta rozmową i nie ukrywała, że bardziej przypadła jej do serca Julia. Nie zaskoczyła tym Konrada. Tak dobierał informacje, żeby przychylnie nastawić Grażynę właśnie do pani inżynier. Czy miał w tym jakiś własny cel? Tego jeszcze na sto procent nie wiedział. Prosto ze szpitala pojechał do Lucjana, żeby go pocieszyć.

Julia zapowiedziała powrót na niedzielę, lecz postanowiła wykorzystać wolność do ostatniej minuty. Dobre choć kilka godzin bez gadania, pretensji i odpytywania z każdej chwili spędzonej poza domem, myślała. Zamierzała wrócić wieczorem, po odwiezieniu Karoliny na dworzec. Do południa siedziały nad notatkami Chochli.

– Ty mi powiedz, jakim cudem analfabeta został magistrem? – chciała wiedzieć Julia.

– Normalnie. Myślisz, że on jeden na swoim roku był skończonym tumanem? Popatrz sobie na innych wykształconych i przestań się łudzić. Poza tym, jak widać gołym okiem, Chochla nie miał zamiaru żyć wyłącznie z pisania.

Notatki z lat wcześniejszych mieściły się w wielkim, grubym brulionie. Z braku czasu odłożyły je na bok. Kogo jeszcze mogło interesować, że pod koniec lat osiemdziesiątych jakiś P. wymigał się od pochodu pierwszomajowego? Marcin skrupulatnie zapisywał potknięcia kolegów, wpadki, spóźnienia. Może nawet niektóre z tych informacji zdążył wykorzystać już wcześniej. Julia ani Karolina nie znały ludzi, nie wiedziały, czy fakt, że „Marek W. ma braki w magazynie" był w swoim czasie ważny, bardzo ważny czy zupełnie bez znaczenia. Skupiły się więc na kalendarzach z ostatnich lat. Lektura okazała się ciekawa, choć niezbyt łatwa. Marcin zupełnie ignorował znaki przestankowe i niejednokrotnie trudno było uchwycić nie tylko niuanse, ale sam sens wypowiedzi. *Wszedłem na naradę na stół E podała kawę którą M wylał na raport długów i na MO która się wściekła.*

– Pamiętam! – wykrzyknęła Karolina. – Pod nieobecność prezesicy stary chciał pogadać o zadłużeniu firmy. Dyskutowaliśmy w najlepsze, kiedy wszedł spóźniony Chochla z Mikulową. Stary, niewiele myśląc, wylał kawę razem z fusami na dokument i widocznie kapnęło na żonę. Ola zachwycona nie była, ale chyba się nie wściekła?!

– Marcin pisze wyraźnie, że się wściekła!

– Sama mówiłaś, że facio niczego nie pisze wyraźnie, że wpadł we wtórny analfabetyzm, o ile nie siedzi w nim od dziecka. To co się teraz czepiasz? Choć raz spójrz na niego wybaczającym wzrokiem zakochanej kobiety!

W odpowiedzi Julia przyłożyła Karolinie jaśkiem, aż zafurczało. Karolina zamierzyła się swetrem i w ten sposób odsunęły od siebie nadmiar przygnębienia. Pokotłowały się trochę na tapczanie, pochichotały i odprężone wróciły do lektury. Kronikarz Marcin Chochla wyłapywał tylko złe i bardzo złe wiadomości, przynajmniej jeżeli chodziło o innych ludzi. Pozytywnie zaczął pisać w momencie, gdy rozkręcił swój podejrzany biznes. Dwa ostatnie kalendarze rzucały nieco światła na duet Marcin–Edyta. Ona od dwóch lat była właścicielką mieszkania przy Kujawskiej. On wpadł na pomysł urządzenia i wyposażenia garsoniery. *Dzisiaj znowu nalegałem na E żeby przekonała starego do zakupu kamery dla firmy.* Nieco dalej: *Jutro osobiście jadę do Chojnic po zakup kamery. I jeszcze dalej. Kamera kosztowała 500 zł wybrałem najmniejszą za resztę urządzeń do monitorowania dałem 32 tys złotych. Jutro będę montował w mieszkaniu zwróci się szybciej niż E myśli. Kamera na fotokomórkę pójdzie nad tapczan w ozdobną lampę. W kuchni postawię resztę urządzeń i dam patent w drzwi Ciemnia pójdzie do łazienki.* Był więc Chochla skończonym durniem, jak wszyscy sądzili, czy nie był? Sam, własnymi rękami i siłą swoich szarych komórek uruchomił i doprowadził do rozkwitu interes, który przynosił pokaźne zyski, niestety, nie jemu. Za swoją ciężką pracę, za dbanie o taśmy, czyste prześcieradła i ręczniki otrzymywał zaledwie piętnaście procent wpływów. Tak przynajmniej brzmiała oficjalna umowa. Jednak w rubryce „dochody" sporo było skreśleń i dziwnych przeksięgowań, z których wynikało, że nie o wszystkim wspólniczkę informował. Pieniądze wpływały z wypożyczania pokoju parom oraz działaczom klubu męskiego. Chochla pisał, jak umiał, ale nie dawał odpowiedzi na najważniejsze pytanie: czym się zajmowali członkowie klubu męskiego?

– Parki wiadomo, tylko co z tym klubem? – zamyśliła się Julia. – Może chodzi o odmienną orientację seksualną?

– No co ty! Bujała jest prezesem!

Nic nie chciało się ułożyć w logiczną całość. Bujała pewnie by wiedział, autor notatek też, lecz wolały nie pytać.

– Jestem ciekawa, czy Edyta wiedziała o szantażu? – zainteresowała się dla odmiany Karolina.

– Diabli wiedzą, może nawet nie, bo przecież wcześniej nikogo nie szantażowali. Edyta inkasowała pieniądze i reszta jej nie obchodziła. Marcinek próbował na własną rękę dorobić sobie do nędznych piętnastu procent. Ile lat grozi za szantaż?

– Teoretycznie, nie pamiętam, a praktycznie nic. Wyobrażasz sobie Mikulę występującego do sądu w takiej sprawie? Wyobrażasz sobie wysoki sąd debatujący nad zdjęciami starego capa? Już prędzej Bujała mógłby wystąpić, bo wnioskując po obrazkach, nie ma się czego wstydzić.

Julia nie życzyła sobie rozmów na temat męskich wdzięków. Jak najszybciej chciała spalić wszystkie dowody przeciwko Karolinie. Bała się, by nie wpadły w ręce następnego zboczeńca. W wielkiej metalowej popielniczce urządziły ognisko. Obrzydliwy smród wypełnił całe mieszkanie i trzeba było szeroko otwierać okna.

Po obiedzie pojechały do szpitala. Chciały odwiedzić Leszka Wydronia, ale zastały puste łóżko. Julia próbowała zasięgnąć języka w pokoju pielęgniarek.

– Wydroń? – zastanowiła się młoda dziewczyna. – Ach, ta ofiara bijatyki w pubie?

– W Michelinie – uściśliła Julia.

– Nie, gdzieś w centrum. Wyszedł wczoraj, na własne żądanie. Ma tylko lekki gips na nodze, może siedzieć w domu.

Ktoś jednak musiał wypić trzy soki owocowe i zjeść kilogram mandarynek, więc prosto ze szpitala pojechały na Świętego Antoniego.

Leszek w domu wyraźnie odżył. Po oczach widać było, że ma się lepiej. Poruszał się o dwu szwedkach, jednak najchętniej siedział na plażowym leżaku z wygodnym podnóżkiem. Obecność koleżanek dodatkowo poprawiła mu humor. Wciąż powtarzał, że czuje się jak ranny powstaniec, przy którym czuwają dziewice.

– Szczególnie te dziewice cię rajcują, co? Zaszyłeś się w norce jak borsuczek i obrażasz ludzi – Karolina pokręciła głową z dezaprobatą.

– Obrażam? – zdumiał się Leszek.

– Wybacz, stary, ale gdybym w moim wieku miała być jeszcze dziewicą, to chybabym się ludziom na oczy nie pokazała. Już ty lepiej zrezygnuj z patriotycznych uniesień.

– Słyszałeś, żeby powstańcy nawalali się kuflami w barze? – zażartowała Julia. – Wyglądasz, kochany, jak członek klubu męskiego.

Z zagadkowym uśmiechem czekała na złośliwą ripostę, ale w pokoju zapadła cisza. Leszek odezwał się dopiero po chwili.

– Czy ty aby wiesz, co mówisz? – spytał. Patrzył na dziewczynę uważnie, jakby domagał się dodatkowych wyjaśnień.

– Nigdy nie kojarzę mordobicia z kobietami – broniła się Julia.

– Chwileczkę, z niczego się nie tłumacz, bo nic złego nie powiedziałaś. Gadaj, Lesiu, co to za klub, że podskoczyłeś jak przy zastrzyku – natarła Karolina.

Próbował się wymigać, ale była nieubłagana. We dwie osaczyły chłopaka i dosłownie wydarły z niego wiedzę na temat, o którym nie wypadało mówić w przyzwoitym towarzystwie.

Działacze klubu odznaczali się orientacją jak najbardziej właściwą, ba! byli zagorzałymi wielbicielami kobiet. Kandydatki typowali spośród babek pięknych, ogólnie znanych i najchętniej na stanowiskach. Ciągnęli losy bądź robili zakłady i raz w tygodniu, czasem rzadziej, jeden z nich przyprowadzał do mieszkania upatrzoną zdobycz. Ukryta kamera filmowała całe spotkanie. Raz w miesiącu urządzali festiwal filmów erotycznych, połączony z dyskusją o wdziękach i umiejętnościach partnerek. Typowali następne panie i robili zakłady, komu uda się babkę poderwać.

– Swoje kwalifikacje też oceniali? – spytała zaskoczona Karolina.

Magister Wydroń nie należał do klubu i nie potrafił do końca zaspokoić ciekawości koleżanek.

Żeby zmienić nie tak znów wdzięczny temat, Karolina napomknęła o archiwum Chochli, nie wspominając jednak jego nazwiska. Leszek niespodziewanie bardzo się ożywił.

– Nie uwierzę, dopóki nie zobaczę! – zawołał podekscytowany.

– Nie zobaczysz, bo prosto od ciebie jedziemy za miasto palić cały ten szajs. W domu za dużo dymu – wyjaśniła spokojnie Julia.

Leszek jednak tak się zapalił, że nie przyjmował do wiadomości żadnych tłumaczeń. Jeżeli mu na czymś zależało, potrafił być uprzykrzony. Pierwsza skapitulowała Karolina. Mrugnęła na Julię, żeby przyniosła z samochodu ortalionową torbę. Gdyby w tym momencie ktoś spytał Julię, co to jest zaufanie, miałaby kłopot z odpowiedzią. Obdarzała ludzi zaufaniem szybko i chętnie, potem najczęściej dostawała po nosie. Tak było choćby z Edytą. Leszkowi wciąż jeszcze ufała, lecz jego gwałtowne zainteresowanie skarbami Chochli trochę ją zmroziło. Wiedział o męskim klubie, mógł wiedzieć również o hobby Marcinka, ale skąd ten nagły i niezdrowy apetyt na cudzą goliznę? Jego zdjęć tam nie było, więc czego się spodziewał? Karolina mrugała i mrugała, a Julia uparcie popijała kawę, szukała odpowiedzi na nurtujące ją pytania i dla niepoznaki z wielkim zainteresowaniem oglądała stare pianino. Podeszła nawet, uchyliła wieko i próbowała wystukać jakąś dawno zapomnianą melodię.

– Umiesz grać? – spytała, zerkając na Leszka.

– Na pewno nie tak świetnie jak ty na nerwach! – roześmiała się Karolina. – Daj kluczyk od bagażnika, sama przyniosę. Niech sobie chłopak poogląda. Przecież widzisz, że na nic więcej nie ma szans!

W zasadzie te wszystkie paskudztwa nie należą do mnie, pomyślała Julia i sięgnęła do torebki. Karolina wybiegła, a ona została z Leszkiem sama.

– Wpadniesz jutro? – spytał.

Nie przerwała zmagań z upartymi klawiszami, nawet się nie odwróciła, tylko mruknęła coś o areszcie domowym. Spojrzała na niego dopiero wówczas, gdy poprosił, żeby podeszła. Spojrzała, lecz nie ruszyła się z miejsca.

– Boisz się mnie?

Odpowiedziała zgodnie z jego oczekiwaniami, że nie, skądże i wcale.

– Więc podejdź!

– Za chwilę – odpowiedziała i wróciła do wystukiwania melodii.

– Jednak się boisz lub... lub zdarzyło się coś, o czym nie wiem, a ty nie chcesz powiedzieć. Mam rację?

– Nigdy nie mówiłeś, że umiesz grać – stwierdziła z wyrzutem.

– Po prostu nie lubię się chwalić! O innych talentach też ci nie zdążyłem powiedzieć. Wolałbym, żebyś sama się o nich przekonała. I co? Nie podejdziesz?

– Masz te talenty przy sobie, gdzieś na wierzchu? – Uśmiechnęła się przelotnie i dalej katowała biedne klawisze. Przerwała dopiero, gdy wróciła Karolina.

Wyjeżdżała od Leszka w przekonaniu, że jej przyjaciółka popełnia błąd. Archiwum Chochli to była bomba z odbezpieczonym zapłonem, należało ją rozbroić, unieszkodliwić, a na pewno schować przed oczami ludzi postronnych, choćby nawet tak bliskich jak Leszek.

– Zaufanie za zaufanie. Zapomniałaś o zielonej teczce? – zdziwiła się Karolina.

– On nam wtedy nie powiedział, skąd miał teczkę.

– My też nie powiedziałyśmy, skąd mamy zdjęcia. I zauważ, że nawet nie pytał. Obiecał spalić u siebie i wierzę, że spali.

Po wyjeździe Karoliny Julia poczuła się bardzo samotna. Ani z kim pogadać od serca, ani powygłupiać się czy choćby pomilczeć. Konrad jakby jej unikał, Leszek i Bujała milczeli i Julii groziło spędzanie wieczorów zgodnie z życzeniem matki: w domu. Po wyjątkowo ostrej awanturze pani Blendowa doszła do wniosku, że córkę trzeba wydać za mąż. Kandydata wprawdzie nie było pod ręką, ale była zapięta na ostatni guzik wizja rodzinnej przyszłości: wyda się Julię, kupi wreszcie dom i młodzi otoczą opieką staruszków. Ojciec nie przekroczył co prawda jeszcze pięćdziesiątki, matka była młodsza od niego, a werwy w nich było tyle, co w trzydziestolatkach, jednak przy każdej okazji kokietowali swoją starością. Julia obserwowała ich teraz oczami dorosłej kobiety i zaczęła dostrzegać nie tylko drobne śmiesznostki. Nie tak dawno spotkała na ulicy Stasia Borkowskiego, niegdyś serdecznego przyjaciela ojca. Przy kolacji opowiedziała o spotkaniu, przekonana, że się ucieszą. „E, głupi piździorek! Tyle ma, co w kiblu zostawi!" – powiedział z niechęcią ojciec. Stwierdziła wtedy z przerażeniem, że to chyba pieniądze i powodzenie w interesach tak bardzo zmieniają ludzi. Rodzice osiągnęli niemało. Zaczynali od pośrednictwa w handlu nieruchomościami, od ogłoszeń wieszanych na płotach, skończyli na własnej agencji reklamowej, dwóch kantorach wymiany walut, sklepie jubilerskim i czymś tam jeszcze. Wykorzystywali każdą okazję, nie gardzili żadnym zarobkiem. Mogli być z siebie dumni. Julia też była z nich dumna, bo utwierdzali ją w przekonaniu, że uczciwą pracą można się dorobić. Wciąż jeszcze wierzyła w ich uczciwość, mniej w nieomylność, choć od dziecka wpajali jej taką ładną zasadę, że starsi zwykle mają rację, natomiast rodzice zawsze. Po niedzielnej awanturze zdecydowała się jak najprędzej wynająć mieszkanie w mieście. Liczyła się z kłopotami i była na nie przygotowana.

W Budampoleksie rozpoczęły się rządy Edyty. Wacław Mikula wyjechał do Szczawnicy na krótki urlop zdrowotny i nowa właścicielka urzędowała w jego gabinecie. Do powrotu dyrektora nie przewidywała zmian w funkcjonowaniu firmy, z wyjątkiem reorganizacji w najbliższym sobie dziale. Leszek Wydroń został kierownikiem dwuosobowej komórki organizacyjno-prawnej, Julia awansowała na kierowniczkę sekretariatu. Pomoc gospodarcza, Henryka Luty, z końcem miesiąca miała podzielić los Karoliny.

Koło dziesiątej Julia weszła do gabinetu z kawą.

– Usiądź na sekundę – powiedziała szefowa, zajęta telefonem. Wcisnęła pamięć, odczekała dwa piknięcia i spróbowała jeszcze raz. Julia bardzo musiała się starać, żeby się złośliwie nie wykrzywić.

– Może ja spróbuję panią połączyć – zaproponowała.

– Och, nie, to nic ważnego. – Edyta uśmiechnęła się prawie przyjaźnie. – Od rana patrzysz na mnie tak, jakbyś zamierzała o coś spytać. Słucham?

Pod uważnym spojrzeniem szefowej zawahała się, ale nie straciła głowy.

– Dlaczego Karolina odchodzi? Przecież jest bardzo dobra.

– Nie kwestionuję umiejętności magister Cierniak – odparła spokojnie Edyta. – Jednak zaszły pewne okoliczności, które uniemożliwiają dalszą współpracę. Proszę, żebyś to, co powiem, zachowała dla siebie. Magister Cierniak musi odejść, ponieważ zostaje dyrektor Mikula, który nie życzy sobie jej obecności. To dość rzadki wypadek, by personel molestował seksualnie dyrektora. Nam się właśnie coś takiego przytrafiło. Wiem, co mówię, i mam konkretne dowody, które przekonają każdy sąd.

Skinęła głową na znak, że rozmowa skończona, i wróciła do wystukiwania numeru. Julia usiadła w sekretariacie przy wielkim biurku z uczuciem, że coś wie, coś ma na końcu języka, że wystarczy jeszcze odrobina wysiłku, żeby dało się złapać i wyartykułować. Nie chodziło o molestowanie. Ten numer, ściągnięty z Heni, nawet nie był zabawny. Chodziło o coś całkiem innego: o dowody! Edyta powiedziała, że ma, lecz uparcie próbowała dodzwonić się do Chochli, czyli wyglądało na to, że dopiero czekała na przesyłkę. Podekscytowana Julia zrobiła szybki przegląd wydarzeń ostatnich tygodni. Przesyłki od Chochli zaczęły przychodzić przed świętami. Pierwsza na nazwisko Edyty i wbiła się w pamięć dzięki drożdżówce. Po świętach przyszła adresowana do Karoliny, z pamiętnym liścikiem – *O to ci chodziło no to masz co chciałaś* – potem dwie jednocześnie, do Edyty i do Mikuli. Te dwie nigdy nie trafiły do rąk adresatów i dawno zakończyły żywot w popielniczce. Chochla twierdził, że do Karoliny nie pisał, więc? Usiadł do adresowania koperty, obok leżały zdjęcia, zaczął się ślinić jak mały buldog i zamiast Pałubska napisał Cierniak? To wydawało się całkiem prawdopodobne, zatem wszystkie zdjęcia Karoliny wysyłał do Edyty, na jej wyraźne życzenie. Na razie przyszły dwie koperty, jedną odebrała Karolina, drugą podebrała Julia, zatem Edyta wciąż nie miała swoich dowodów. Jeżeli Marcin uwinął się z ostatnią przesyłką przed sobotą, to bardzo prawdopodobne, że jeszcze jakieś odbitki mogą być w drodze. Julia z wrażenia przygryzła usta i do czasu przyjścia listonosza nie umiała się na niczym skupić. Bez trudu poznała kulfony Marcinka i dosłownie w ostatniej chwili wepchnęła kopertę do torebki. Tuż po niej pani prezes nerwowo przerzuciła pocztę, nie znalazła niczego dla siebie i ze złością zatrzasnęła drzwi gabinetu. Źródełko wyschło, pomyślała z radością Julia. *Fine*, klops, kropka!

Przez cały dzień Julia miała sporo pracy i jeszcze więcej emocji. Edyta zrobiła z niej kierowniczkę sekretariatu i podniosła pensję nie po to, by przenosić do działu informatyki. Spokojnie, bez histerii przyjęła te zmiany. Zaświtał jej niegłupi pomysł, by wrócić do Warszawy. W wolnej chwili napisała krótki list do Małgorzaty. Razem studiowały, razem miały pracować w jednej z warszawskich firm. Julia wróciła do Włocławka, tamta została i wydawała się bardzo zadowolona. *Popytaj, poszukaj i jeżeli będziesz coś wiedziała o etacie dla informatyka, natychmiast daj mi znać* – prosiła w liście i podała adres Budampolexu. W domu list z Warszawy nie byłby bezpieczny nawet przez minutę.

Powrót do stolicy wydawał się najlepszym rozwiązaniem. Jeżeli czuła smutek, to tylko dlatego, że wyjazd oznaczał rozstanie z Karoliną i inżynierem Orzechowiczem. Ciekawe, czy on zauważy, że wyjechałam? – pomyślała.

Z biurowca wyszła sporo po piętnastej. Na parkingu stało zaledwie kilka samochodów. Podeszła do swego matiza, wyjęła kluczki i w tym samym momencie poczuła, że z tyłu chwyta ją żelazna obręcz. Uścisk był bardzo silny, napastnik stał tak blisko, że mogła tylko dreptać, popychana jego ciałem. Krzyknęła głośno, a kiedy próbował zatkać jej usta i zwolnił nieco chwyt, z całej siły wbiła mu kluczyki w bok. Zatoczyli się razem i ten moment dostrzegli dwaj młodzi mężczyźni, którzy nieopodal wsiadali do samochodu. Kiedy ruszyli w ich stronę, napastnik puścił Julię i rzucił się do ucieczki. Jeden z mężczyzn pobiegł za uciekającym, drugi dopadł Julii prawie równocześnie z Konradem. Chwila upłynęła, zanim oprzytomniała na tyle, by wyjaśnić, co się stało. Tylko właściwie co się stało? Sama nie wiedziała. Rozcierała obolałe przedramię, rozglądając się z przerażeniem. Teraz dopiero przyszła pora na strach. Czuła, że drżą jej kolana, że ledwie stoi.

– Już dobrze, niech się pani nie boi – mówił ten pierwszy mężczyzna, ten, który z nią został. Chciał ją podtrzymać, ale uprzedził go Konrad.

Drugi, zmęczony i zziajany, wrócił po chwili.

– Uciekł drań! – wysapał. – Wysoki, rudawy, zna go pani?

– Nie wiem... nie widziałam – powiedziała cicho Julia. – Otwierałam samochód... Naprawdę nie wiem, co i kto... ani dlaczego...

– Namnożyło się cholernego złodziejstwa! – mruknął pierwszy ze złością.

Miał jasne, kręcone włosy i okrągłą twarz z perkatym nosem. Julia wciąż tuliła się do Konrada. Nawet dziękując chłopakom za pomoc, tuliła się do Konrada.

– Nie chcesz zawiadomić policji? – spytał.

Żachnęła się i z miejsca poczuła przypływ sił. Złodziej uciekł, życzyła mu połamania nóg, lecz nie zamierzała nadawać sprawie rozgłosu. Policja, rodzice i areszt domowy do końca życia?! O nie! Tego sobie nie życzyła. Ochłonęła już na tyle, że mogła spokojnie wsiąść do samochodu. Konrad usadowił się obok niej. Tego dnia był akurat bez auta.

– Gdzie cię podwieźć? – spytała.

– Przepraszam, kto się kim opiekuje? – próbował uściślić.

– Załóżmy, że ty mną, więc gdzie mam jechać?

– Jeżeli masz apetyt na omlet z pieczarkami, to do mnie – powiedział.

Na wspomnienie omletu Julia poczuła ucisk w żołądku. To danie kojarzyło się jej z Karoliną. Uśmiechnęła się, co on odczytał jako przyjęcie zaproszenia.

Wciąż jeszcze miał podbite oko. Nie straszył już ciemnym granatem, tylko kokietował jasną zielenią, przemieszaną z lekkim fioletem.

– Wiesz, że Karolina dostała w piątek wypowiedzenie? – zagadnęła Julia.

Wydawał się niemile zaskoczony. No tak, pomyślała, niedawno stłukłam lusterko, więc czego tu oczekiwać! On wciąż myśli o Karolinie. Poczuła w piersiach chłód i straciła apetyt na wspólny obiad. Podwiozę go i zawrócę, postanowiła.

– To jak z zaproszeniem? Przyjęte? – spytał, gdy zatrzymała się przed blokiem. – Uwierz mi, robię naprawdę wyśmienite omlety.

Zawahała się, spojrzała w zielono-fioletowe oko i postanowiła zaryzykować. Kiedy z kuchni zaczęły dochodzić smakowite zapachy, wmawiała sobie, że to wizyta głodomora, nie kobiety. Zje, czemu nie, i pojedzie do domu. Konrad rozłożył na stole serwetki, wniósł dwa talerze pachnące pieczarkami i Julia poczuła, że kobieta bierze górę nad głodomorem. Danie było pyszne, lecz ona myślała wyłącznie o mężczyźnie, który przez żołądek pakował się jej do serca.

– Czemu jesteś taka milcząca? – spytał.

– Nie jestem – zaprotestowała.

Są różne rodzaje milczenia. Na przykład porozumiewawcze łączy ludzi. Kiedy zakochani siedzą obok siebie, trzymają się za ręce, wcale nie są potrzebne słowa. Milczą sobie razem, najczęściej na wspólny temat, i jest im dobrze. Na przeciwnym biegunie jest milczenie obrażone, strawne tylko w krótkich dawkach. Ma ukarać winnego, wymusić na nim konkretne działania. Podpadł, niech przeprasza. Bywa też milczenie znudzone, bardzo łatwe do przełamania, bo wymaga jedynie zmiany partnera. Najtrudniejsze do zniesienia jest milczenie sondujące. Milczą, bo nie chcą się wychylić, bo jedno czeka, aż drugie zacznie, cisza przedłuża się, dzwoni w uszach i sprawia, że nie wiadomo co zrobić z rękami, gdzie uciec z oczami i w ogóle jak się zachować. Takie milczenie wisiało nad stołem Konrada i unosiło się nad omletami: Julia pochwaliła, on się ucieszył i temat został wyczerpany.

– Kogo ty masz na Kujawskiej? – spytał, żeby spytać, żeby nie przedłużać kłopotliwej ciszy.

– Znajomą! – odpowiedziała szybko i zdecydowanie. – Dlaczego pytasz?

– Tak sobie. W piątek i w sobotę byłem wieczorem u przyjaciela i widziałem twojego matiza.

– Mnie też widziałeś?

– Nie – uśmiechnął się lekko – tylko samochód.

Tak ją zmieszał i przeraził, że zamilkła na dobre, a on znowu pytał, czemu nic nie mówi.

– Przecież cały czas chwalę twoje talenty kulinarne, nie słyszysz? Przeraził mnie ten głupi napad. Miałam szczęście, że akurat byłeś w pobliżu.

– Po prostu czekałem na ciebie – powiedział. – Odnoszę wrażenie, że boczysz się na mnie i masz o coś żal.

Zdziwił ją nieco ten żal, bo na parkingu tak się do niego tuliła, że mógł ją raczej posądzać o uczucia całkiem odmienne. Zastanowiła się przez chwilę, spojrzała w zielono-fioletowe oko i nie znalazła odpowiedzi.

– Julio!

– Nie mam żalu, to wcale nie chodzi o żal! Jeżeli nawet chodzi, to nie chodzi!

– Ujęłaś to z inżynierską precyzją – zauważył z podziwem. – Wobec tego wytłumacz mi jeszcze, dlaczego ja nic nie rozumiem.

Zaczęła się śmiać. Siedzieli na wprost siebie, rozdzieleni stołem i pustymi talerzami, patrzyli sobie w oczy i bredzili jak pokręceni.

– Ma być szczerze? – spytała, ocierając delikatnie oczy.

– Ma być.

– Dopóki jesteś chłopakiem mojej przyjaciółki, wstrzymaj się od wyznań, bo stawiasz mnie w głupiej sytuacji. Lubię cię, nie chcę obrazić, lecz nie odpowiada mi rola tej trzeciej. Jeżeli powiesz, że wciąż nie rozumiesz, wyjdę, bo nie lubię nierozgarniętych facetów.

Teraz on zbierał myśli, ważył słowa, żeby nie wyjść na nierozgarniętego, nie zrzucić winy na Karolinę, nie zrazić Julii, a jakoś jej wytłumaczyć, że nie jest trzecią ani drugą, tylko pierwszą. Pozbierał talerze, odstawił je na bok i wyciągnął rękę przez stół. Czekał moment, zanim z wahaniem podała mu swoją.

– Karolina to zamknięty rozdział – powiedział. – Nawet gdyby nie wysłała mnie do wszystkich diabłów, to i tak nie byłoby między nami tanga. Mamy różne oczekiwania wobec partnerów i wobec życia. Tyle o przelotnej fascynacji twoją przyjaciółką. Ani się zapieram, ani zaprzeczam, tak było. A teraz o nas. Całkiem niedawno sobie pomyślałem, że gdybym kiedyś wreszcie chciał skończyć z kawalerskim stanem, to pod jednym warunkiem: dziewczyna musiałaby mieć takie oczy jak ty, takie włosy, identyczne piegi i całą resztę, łącznie z anielskim charakterem. Nie chcę szukać sobowtóra, skoro mam oryginał obok.

Mówił tak ładnie, z takim żarem, że zapomniała o przyjaciółce i stłuczonym lusterku. Nie protestowała, kiedy obchodził stół, obejmował ją, całował włosy, czoło, piegi i usta. Jego niespokojne ręce błądziły po jej bluzce i pod bluzką. Z trudem złapała oddech, odsunęła się nieco.

– Napiłabym się herbaty – powiedziała.

Jeżeli go zaskoczyła, zachował zimną krew. Skinął głową i wyszedł do kuchni. Bardzo chciała zostać, naprawdę bardzo i dlatego cichutko, żeby nie robić hałasu, wzięła z wieszaka żakiet, torebkę i zamknęła za sobą drzwi. Uciekła.

Potem przez całą drogę robiła sobie wyrzuty, że zachowała się głupio i nieodpowiedzialnie. Żal jej było Konrada, siebie, tego, co mogło nastąpić później. W domu zamknęła się w pokoju i postanowiła nie odbierać telefonów. Ledwie postanowiła, zaraz przypomniała sobie Karolinę i Martę. Przecież specjalnie wróciła do domu wcześniej, by czekać na telefon od nich.

Zadzwonił jakąś godzinę później. Wanda Pasieczko przypomniała sobie, że nie doczytały do końca ody i serdecznie zapraszała Julię i Karolinę do siebie. Wymówiła się nawałem pracy i wizytą znajomych. Ledwie usiadła przy biurku, znowu odezwał się telefon.

– A jednak boisz się mnie, Julio?

Zaprotestowała stanowczo i bardzo energicznie. Nikogo się nie bała i w ogóle wypraszała sobie takie insynuacje.

– To świetnie. Wobec tego wsiądź w samochód i przyjedź.

– Właśnie odprowadziłam go do mechanika.

– Są jeszcze taksówki.

– Czy coś się stało? – spytała zaskoczona.

– Potrzebuję twojej pomocy, to mało?

Pomocy choremu przyjacielowi nie wypadało odmawiać.

Konrad nalewał właśnie wrzątku do filiżanek, kiedy usłyszał szmer w przedpokoju i ciche stuknięcie drzwi. Odstawił czajnik i wybiegł na korytarz. Gdzieś niżej, coraz niżej, stukały obcasy Julii. Szalona dziewczyna, nie poczekała na windę, bała się, że ją zawróci i pędziła na złamanie karku po schodach. Mógłby spróbować pogoni, przez moment myślał o tym, w końcu jednak dał spokój. I co powiem? – pomyślał. Wniosę ją na górę i rzucę na tapczan? Ogarnęła go złość. W myślach nazywał smarkulę swoją Julią, wiązał z nią poważne plany, a ona bez słowa uciekała, jakby był pospolitym gwałcicielem. Dziewczyny owszem, miewają różne fanaberie, wolno im, ale Julia przekroczyła granicę przyzwoitości. Nie bardzo wiedział, jak powinien się zachować następnego dnia. Udawać obrażonego? Przecież był obrażony i jeżeli już miałby udawać, to raczej nieobrażonego. Pomyślał o Karolinie.

O ileż prostsze było życie u jej boku. Nie toczyła świętej wojny o majtki, potrafiła być najczulszą, najwspanialszą kochanką i... czemu u diabła nie próbował jej zatrzymać? Dyktował swoje warunki bez wnikania w jej racje, dyktował po to, żeby nie mogła ich przyjąć. To on odszedł, bo chciał odejść. Nagły, niespodziewany przypływ żalu zdziwił go i zastanowił. Był przekonany, że Karolina to już przeszłość, nie okłamywał Julii, mówiąc o zamkniętym rozdziale, więc skąd wzięła się ta głupia, spóźniona tęsknota?

Pozmywał talerze, wylał herbatę zaparzoną specjalnie dla Julii, lecz te proste czynności nie zdołały oderwać go od niewesołych myśli. Kiedy zadzwonił telefon, był pewien, że to pani magister Blenda. Postanowił udawać, że nie zauważył jej wyjścia. To powinno jej dać do myślenia.

Zachrypnięty głos Bujały błyskawicznie sprowadził go na ziemię.

– Znasz Wydronia? – spytał bez zbędnych wstępów.

– Z widzenia.

– Podjedź do niego, jest sprawa do obgadania. Majdziak wyjechał, nie mam kogo posłać. Chodzi mianowicie o...

– Co ty, do dziwki nędzy, myślisz, że jestem twoim chłopcem na posyłki?! – wściekł się Orzechowicz. – Zagalopowałeś się, stary, to misja dla twoich goryli, nie dla mnie!

Odłożył słuchawkę, aż echo poszło. Telefon dzwonił jeszcze dwa razy, ale Konrad nawet do niego nie podszedł.

Julia zaparkowała tuż przed domem Leszka. Wbiegała po schodach lekko, choć na duszy było jej wyjątkowo ciężko. Nie rozumiała sama siebie. Nie umiała powiedzieć, dlaczego uciekła od Konrada, tak jak nie umiała powiedzieć, dlaczego szła do Leszka. Prosił ją, lecz to chyba za mało, żeby się ubierać i pędzić przez pół miasta. Zwłaszcza że ta wizyta była jej bardzo nie na rękę. Ledwie jednak spojrzała na wspartego na dwu szwedkach Leszka, poczuła się głupio.

– Gapa jestem, nie zrobiłam ci po drodze zakupów – powiedziała na powitanie.

– Zakupy zrobione, woda na herbatę wstawiona, jesteś tu wyłącznie w charakterze gościa, Julio.

– Mówiłeś, że potrzebna ci moja pomoc. Chyba sam niczego nie kupujesz?

– Nie mam szans. Najwyraźniej jestem w typie kobiet: same zabiegają, żeby mi niczego nie brakowało. – Uśmiechnął się dawnym, ciepłym uśmiechem. Stali na wprost siebie, na tyle blisko, że poczuła znajomy zapach wody po goleniu, ten sam co wtedy w tangu, gdy przytulił ją mocno.

Coś mi się ci mężczyźni zaczynają sypać jak złoty deszcz, pomyślała. Zwiałam jednemu, żeby wąchać drugiego, to chyba paranoja.

Ostry gwizd czajnika sprawił, że wróciła do rzeczywistości i zajęła miejsce w kuchni.

– Dlaczego nie powiedziałeś przez telefon, że chodzi ci o herbatę? – krzyknęła w stronę pokoju.

– Uważaj, bo niedomyślne biedronki giną w ptasich dziobkach! – odkrzyknął wesoło i głośno.

– A te domyślne zostają pożarte przez patyczaki – zażartowała, wchodząc z tacą w rękach do salonu.

– Dlaczego nie może być tak na co dzień? – spytał Leszek, wpatrując się z zachwytem w twarz dziewczyny. – Ja sobie kwitnę na leżaku, ty wnosisz herbatę, potem znikamy w sypialni. Sama powiedz, czy to nie sielanka?

– Zapomniałeś o kąpieli – powiedziała Julia z poważną miną. – Przed spaniem zawsze biorę prysznic. Nie truj, Lesiu, dobrze? Dlaczego do mnie dzwoniłeś?

– Bo się stęskniłem, bo muszę nacieszyć oczy twoim widokiem, bo bez ciebie odechciewa mi się żyć. Czy to nie są ważne powody?

– Muszą być ważne, jeżeli przeciągnąłeś mnie przez całe miasto.

– Przepraszam, biedroneczko, ale wiesz co? Wcale nie musisz wracać przez całe miasto. Możesz przenocować u mnie. Mam nawet dla ciebie nowiutką szczotkę do zębów.

Leszek był nastawiony na rozmowę lekką, miłą i przyjemną. Wszystkie poważniejsze kwestie zbywał żartami. Na pytanie o archiwum Chochli kiwnął głową, że oczywiście spalił, o swoim awansie w firmie wiedział, o Edycie nie chciał mówić, uparł się natomiast, żeby Julia podpięła wysoko włosy. Rozumiała, że mężczyzna ruchliwy, wiecznie czymś zajęty, kiedy zostanie przygwożdżony do leżaka i dwu szwedek, ma prawo się nudzić. Przyjaciele w takiej sytuacji powinni go zabawiać, ale ona nie czuła się na siłach. Miała swoje kłopoty i głowę zajętą Konradem.

– Usiądź bliżej i daj mi rękę – poprosił Leszek.

Ile czasu można udawać głuchą? Tylko do następnej prośby. Z wahaniem podeszła. Leżak był niski, więc przyklękła i spojrzała prosto w niebieskie, szczere oczy. Objął ją delikatnie jedną ręką i przytulił do ramienia.

– Wciąż mi gdzieś uciekasz, pędzisz przed siebie szybciej niż twój matiz. Wystarczy, że życie ucieka, my powinniśmy łapać takie chwile jak ta.

Poprawiła się i przytuliła mocniej do jego ramienia. Pachniał tak ładnie, był ciepły, życzliwy i mówił chyba szczerze. Spłynął na nią miły spokój. Nie drżała, jak w objęciach Konrada, nie czekała na nic, słuchała tego, co mówił o przyjaźni, o swojej miłości, i było jej dobrze.

– Usnęłaś, biedronko? – spytał.

Nie widziała jego twarzy, ale czuła, że się uśmiechnął.

– Zastanawiam się, czy to, co mi teraz mówisz, można nazwać molestowaniem? – Uniosła głowę i napotkała jego zdziwione spojrzenie. – Wszyscy ostatnio pogłupieli na punkcie molestowania. Najpierw Henia. Wiesz, pamiętasz. Dzisiaj z kolei Edyta tłumaczyła mi, że Karolina molestowała Mikulę. Teraz ty mnie tulisz, a zważ, że jesteś moim szefem.

Pocałował ją leciutko w nos.

– Możesz się tulić spokojnie, nie jestem twoim szefem, biedronko. Nie wrócę już do Budampolexu, chyba że w całkiem innym charakterze. Ja będę prezesem, a ciebie zrobię dyrektorem.

– Więc znowu będziesz moim szefem! – prychnęła rozbawiona. – Naprawdę nie wracasz?

– Naprawdę. Jestem już facetem po trzydziestce, najwyższy czas, żeby się usamodzielnić, pomyśleć o przyszłości i pieniądzach.

– Co będziesz robił?

– Zostań ze mną, to się przekonasz. Po nocach będę cię tulił i kochał, w dzień zasypywał prezentami i grał Mozarta, nie będę cię zmuszał do pracy; co ty na to?

– Bujasz!

– Bujam tylko z Mozartem. Dawno nie ćwiczyłem i mógłbym cię rozczarować. Zamiast Mozarta będę ci grał pieśni patriotyczne, chcesz?

– Nie chcę. Mnie w ogóle nie odpowiada strona bierna: tulona, zasłuchana, rozleniuchowana. Chcesz mnie zmienić w rozlazłą kluchę?

– Nie chcę cię zmieniać, tylko kochać taką, jaka jesteś – zaprotestował gwałtownie.

– Akurat! Jak nazwałeś te dwie od Bujały? Osnuje, tak? Ty chcesz ze mnie zrobić osnuję.

– No widzisz, nie uważałaś na lekcjach biologii i teraz opowiadasz herezje. Chociaż... wiesz co? Gdybyś czasem poczuła w sobie żarłoczność larwy, to ja mogę być twoim świerkiem. Ja dla ciebie wszystko!

– Mam cię zeżreć? – zgorszyła się Julia.

– Mhm! – mruknął rozmarzony.

Dziewczyna zaczęła się śmiać. Wierzyła i nie wierzyła w uczuciowe deklaracje, jednak skłaniała się ku tematom bezpieczniejszym. Musnęła ustami jego policzek i wstała, nim zdążył zaprotestować. Coś jeszcze mówił, chciał ją przekonywać i zatrzymać choćby na chwilę.

– „W drogę! Żegnajcie, chłopcy. W drogę! Już na mnie czas" – zanuciła Julia.

– Jacy chłopcy? Sam tu jestem jak palec – jęknął Leszek.

Nastrój jednak zmienił się radykalnie. Julia pozbierała filiżanki ze stołu i wyszła do kuchni. Przez szum wody usłyszała dźwięk dzwonka u drzwi.

– Mam otworzyć? – spytała, wsuwając głowę do pokoju.

Dał znak ręką, że sam otworzy. Trochę to trwało, zanim wstał z leżaka i o kulach wyszedł do przedpokoju. Julia w tym czasie wycierała filiżanki.

– Czy ty, Lechu, nie zagalopowałeś się trochę? – Bujała od drzwi załatwiał jakieś swoje interesy. – Wiesz, co robię z ludźmi, którzy wchodzą mi w drogę?

– Przetrącasz im nogi?

Julia wyszła do przedpokoju, przekonana, że bez niej Leszek nie da sobie rady.

Bujałę na moment zamurowało, ale tylko na moment. Z domyślnym uśmieszkiem, który Julii wydał się idiotyczny, zapewnił, że nigdy nie tyka słabszych. Nie był to dla Leszka komplement. Uznała, że powiedział tak specjalnie, że toczy jakąś swoją grę, której ona nie rozumie. Nie miała kiedy się nad tym zastanowić. Powinna już jechać do domu, jednak bała się zostawiać przyjaciela na pastwę nieoczekiwanego gościa.

– Dobra, przy pięknej kobiecie nie będziemy gadać o interesach. Kobiece główki stworzone są do całkiem innych celów – oświadczył Bujała, całując dłoń dziewczyny.

– Do jakich niby? – zainteresowała się Julia.

– To ty powinnaś wiedzieć! Ja mam typowo męską głowę.

Jasne, pomyślała. Tylko po co ci, facet, głowa, jak masz pięści i adidasy? Natomiast głośno zgodziła się z nim i bardzo żałowała, że musi się pożegnać.

– Poczekaj moment, ja też już biegnę! – zawołał Bujała.

Leszek natychmiast zbystrzał.

– To biegnij! Julia jeszcze zostaje.

Ustawił się w progu kuchni tak, że własnym ciałem, wspartym na dwu kulach, odgrodził bossa od Julii. Z przedpokoju docierały jedynie strzępy słów i soczyste przekleństwa rozsierdzonego Bujały. Chodziło o przekręt czy szantaż. Z miejsca pomyślała o Chochli i ogarnął ją pusty śmiech. Boss, jak niegdyś Henia, nie mógł pewnie przeżyć, że ktoś próbuje go pokonać jego własną bronią. I to kto? Chudziutki Marcinek.

– A mówiłem Orzechowiczowi, żeby do ciebie przylazł i dograł szczegóły, to mu się muchy w nosie zalęgły – powiedział już w drzwiach Bujała. – On też zapomina, z kogo żyje!

Julia z wrażenia odkręciła kran do oporu, choć miała go zakręcić. Wycierając podłogę, pomyślała, że tylko Konrada brakowało w tym towarzystwie. Pośpiesznie zaczęła się ubierać.

– Naprawdę tak ci zależało, żeby wyjść razem z nim? – spytał Leszek.

– Z kim?

– Z Bujałą.

– Kicham na twojego Bujałę. Jak mama mnie dorwie, to po raz drugi dzisiaj już nie ocalę głowy.

– A kiedy ocaliłaś po raz pierwszy? – spytał, wpatrując się w twarz Julii.

– Kiedy? Nie wychodząc z Bujałą, oczywiście – odpowiedziała wesoło.

Julia była dobrym kierowcą, uważnym i myślącym, lecz czasem zapominała, że samochód potrzebuje paliwa. Wieczorem wracała od Leszka podekscytowana i nie zwróciła uwagi na czerwoną kontrolkę. Rano najzwyczajniej w świecie autko nie zapaliło. Nie zastanawiając się, pobiegła na przystanek autobusowy. Do sekretariatu wpadła punkt siódma. W biegu ściągnęła żakiet, poprawiła włosy i dopiero wtedy zobaczyła na swoim biurku gałązkę białego bzu. Leszka w pracy nie było, więc pomyślała od razu, że może Konrad, że nie wszystko stracone. Kto inny mógłby ofiarować jej kwiatki? Niewiele myśląc, pobiegła do działu informatyki. Z gałązką bzu w garści stanęła w progu. Chyba byłby ślepy, gdyby nie wyczytał wszystkiego w jej oczach.

– Jeżeli myślisz, że wiem, dlaczego to zrobiłam, to jesteś w błędzie – powiedziała. – I jeżeli myślisz, że nie żałuję, to też jesteś w błędzie.

Obiecywał sobie, że więcej nie da się nabrać na słodkie minki i czułe słówka. Miał przygotowaną ostrą odpowiedź, lecz zobaczywszy Julię, zapomniał, co zamierzał jej powiedzieć.

– Przybiegłaś z samego rana, żeby wytknąć mi moje błędy?

W jego charakterystycznym, krzywym uśmiechu dostrzegła obok ironii także przebaczenie. Odpowiedziała ciepłym uśmiechem. Chciała jeszcze coś dodać, dopowiedzieć, ale wystraszyła się, że będzie to niepotrzebne gadulstwo.

Wróciła do siebie uspokojona i radosna. Edyta miała przyjść dopiero koło dziewiątej. Julia zajrzała do kuchenki.

– Ładny bez położyłam ci na biurku? – zapytała Henia.

– Ty?

– A kto? Jak sobie babki same kwiatów nie zorganizują, to wiesz, co mają? No wiesz? Nie będę się wyrażała. Następne medytacje poświęcam dowartościowywaniu się kobiet. Przyjdź koniecznie.

Julię ogarnął pusty śmiech. Gdyby dostała do ręki gałązkę od Heni, w życiu by jej nie całowała, nie tuliła do policzka i na pewno nie pobiegłaby z nią do Konrada. Mało tego. Gdyby nie ta gałązka, nie byłoby pojednania. Henia mnie dowartościowała, pomyślała, a ja dowartościowałam Konrada. Te medytacje widać nie są takie głupie.

– Z czego się, Julciu, śmiejesz?

– Z radości.

– Jakbym ci coś powiedziała, byłabyś jeszcze bardziej uradowana. – Henia zniżyła głos do szeptu. – Co tam, powiem ci, ty jesteś dyskretna. Wiesz, że Budampolex ma nowego właściciela?

– Edytę. O tym akurat wszyscy już wiedzą.

– A wcale że nie! – zawołała triumfalnie Henia. – Edyta kupiła sobie wyłącznie Mikulę, bo na firmie wyjdzie jak Zabłocki na mydle. Wspomnisz moje słowa. Z długami może by się uporała, nie wygra jednak z właścicielami gruntów. Znaleźli się i zamierzają podyktować twarde warunki. Za pół roku nic tu nie zostanie.

– To niby z czego mam się cieszyć? Dlaczego powiedziałaś, że będę uradowana?

– Bo ciebie to nie dotyczy, a ja mam coś innego na oku. Stara myśli, że będę ją błagała o etat, bo nie wie, że to zwolnienie jest mi na rękę. Posłannictwo muszę spełnić, misję wielką, rozumiesz? Nic więcej zdradzić nie mogę. Sza! Milczę jak kamień.

Julia wzruszyła ramionami. Nieraz już miała okazję przekonać się, ile warte są rewelacje Heni. Kobieta lubiła uchodzić za najlepiej poinformowaną i czasem dla kilku minut chwały najzwyczajniej wymyślała różne historie, które tak się miały do rzeczywistości jak koń do koniaku.

O piętnastej do sekretariatu zajrzał Konrad. Wyszli razem. To było zupełnie zrozumiałe, że wsiadła z nim do forda, bo przecież do pracy przyjechała autobusem. Również i to było zrozumiałe, że on spytał, dokąd jadą. Natomiast odpowiedź Julii nie była już taka oczywista. Podała swój domowy adres. Tego Konrad najwyraźniej się nie spodziewał. Obojętnie skinął głową. Przez całą drogę nie zamienili słowa. W milczeniu zatrzymał samochód i czekał, aż wysiądzie.

– Potrzebuję ośmiu minut. Poczekasz? – spytała cichutko. Patrzyła mu prosto w oczy.

Zacisnął zęby, przekonany, że kpi.

– Poczekasz? Zaraz wracam! – powtórzyła.

Wróciła po siedmiu minutach. Tyle czasu zajęło jej napisanie kartki, że wyjeżdża i wróci następnego dnia. Szczotkę do zębów wetknęła do kosmetyczki i mogła zacząć sprint w dół. Lekko zdyszana usiadła obok Konrada.

– A teraz gdzie? – spytał.

– To zależy wyłącznie od ciebie.

Na rondzie, zamiast skręcić w Toruńską, pojechał w stronę miasta. Szczęście mu sprzyjało, bo na ciasnym parkingu przy placu Wolności akurat zwolniło się miejsce.

– Zajazd czy Notina? – Patrzył wyczekująco. – Innego wyboru nie mamy.

Chciała powiedzieć, że mają, że wolałaby omlet z pieczarkami albo nawet surowe jajko, byle tylko zostali sami. Odłożyła jednak tę szczerość na później i wybrała Zajazd. Przed przejściem dla pieszych objął ją gwałtownie i przytrzymał, bo szła pewnym krokiem prosto pod nadjeżdżający samochód. Nie zdjął ręki z jej ramion do samych drzwi restauracji.

– Wejdziesz sama czy poczekasz chwilkę? – zagadnął, gdy chwytała za klamkę.

Po przeciwnej stronie ulicy kusił napis *Nie bądź taki, jedz kurczaki.* Majdziak też kupował żarcie przed randką, pomyślała niechętnie. Już miała na końcu języka drobną złośliwostkę, lecz w samą porę przypomniała sobie o swoim anielskim charakterze. Kiwnęła głową, że oczywiście postoi, czemu nie.

Konrad wrócił z piękną czerwoną różą i Julia poczuła się jak niedowiarek. Zapomniała, że obok punktu gastronomicznego był też kiosk z kwiatami, a Konrad to na szczęście nie Majdziak.

Prosto z restauracji pojechali na Toruńską. To już był wybór Julii. Konrad proponował najpierw kino, potem spacer i kawiarnię – wyraźnie się z nią droczył, jednak przy deserze przestał udawać, że nie zależy mu na szybkim powrocie do domu. Po drodze zrobili jeszcze drobne zakupy. Obiecała, że zostanie u niego na kolacji. O śniadaniu chwilowo nie wspominała. Miało być niespodzianką.

Późnym popołudniem dobili do przystani. Konrad zakrzątnął się, uchylił okno i spojrzał na Julię. Ślicznie wyglądała z nagłym onieśmieleniem na buzi, z różą przy policzku.

– Napijesz się herbaty? – spytał.

Wstawiła różę do pustego wazonu i odwróciła się, stając z nim twarzą w twarz.

– Może nie zawsze zachowuję się racjonalnie – powiedziała poważnie. – Jednak dwa razy tych samych błędów nie popełniam.

Porwał ją na ręce i zaniósł na tapczan tak, jak to sobie wcześniej wymarzył.

Pani Ewelina patrzyła na nich z serwantki z przyjaznym uśmiechem. Wcale się nie dziwiła, gdy Raduś zachłannie całował dziewczynę i nie gorszyła się, gdy z tapczanu zaczęły spadać na parkiet łaszki damskie i męskie. Przecież to ona mawiała: „Rób Raduś tak, żeby było dobrze, po twojemu i żebyś drugiego człowieka nie skrzywdził!”. To Konrad się zawahał. Julia była pierwszą dziewczyną w jego życiu, dla której miał być pierwszym mężczyzną. Szepnęła, że to nic, że właśnie tego chce. Potem leżała obok, wyciszona, i chciało jej się płakać. Wmawiała sobie, że to z nadmiaru szczęścia. Szczęście jest ciałem lotnym, lubi się skraplać i wtedy spływa powolutku po policzku, aż do kącika przy ustach.

– Co, kochanie? – spytał, tuląc ją mocno.

Uśmiechnęła się do niego poprzez to swoje szczęście, ale milczała. Nie mogła przecież powiedzieć, że spodziewała się czegoś niesamowitego, olśnienia, szału, zapamiętania, a było boleśnie i niezbyt przyjemnie.

– Czemu płaczesz?

– To ze szczęścia – odpowiedziała, a on delikatnie zaczął całować jej oczy i wilgotne policzki.

Czym jest miłość? Julia próbowała wytłumaczyć ten fenomen Konradowi.

– Wyobraź sobie kamerę, która pokazuje rozwój kwiatu magnolii. Najpierw jest maciupeńki pączek, rośnie, pęcznieje, rozchyla delikatne płatki, by wreszcie wystrzelić, dosłownie wystrzelić pełnią urody. Ale żeby to pokazać na jednym, króciutkim filmie, trzeba zrobić setki pojedynczych ujęć, w różnych fazach rozwoju. Tak samo jest z miłością. Najpierw są setki drobnych zdarzeń, gesty, spojrzenia, niedomówienia, drobne czułości i z nich wybucha miłość.

– Pięknie. Teraz mi opowiedz o motylkach i bocianach – poprosił ze śmiechem.

Lubił jej się sprzeciwiać, lubił, kiedy z zapałem broniła swoich racji, a jeszcze bardziej, gdy kapitulowała, przybita jego argumentami. Nie przypuszczał, że miłość tak bardzo go odmieni. Czym jest miłość? Konrad próbował rozwiązać ten fenomen po swojemu, inaczej niż Julia. Kochał jej ciało, a nade wszystko jej uległość. Niczego nie próbowała mu udowodnić, była dziecinnie nieporadna i od niego uczyła się, że miłość może być rozkoszą. Gestem, spojrzeniem, słowami podkreślała, że należy wyłącznie do niego, że tylko z nim jest szczęśliwa. I on jej wierzył. Wiara to też cząstka miłości. Podobnie jak odpowiedzialność i staranie, żeby nie była głodna, zmarznięta, żeby miała powody do radości. Kiedy ona się cieszyła, część tej uciechy spadała na niego. Z radością patrzył, jak pięknieje i rozkwita. To miłość ją zmieniła, bo Pan Bóg stwarza dziewczynę, a mężczyzna kobietę.

Wkrótce cały Budampolex wiedział, że Julia i Konrad to zakochani. Nie afiszowali się ze swoim uczuciem, ale też się nie kryli.

Karolina dzwoniła niemal codziennie i po samym brzmieniu głosu odgadła, że coś się wydarzyło. Po swojemu zaczęła dociekać.

– Serafin puścił cię kantem, Chochla raczej odpada, Lesio przetrącony, zostaje chyba tylko Bujała?

– Bujałę zostawiam tobie – odparła ze śmiechem Julia. – Jest niepocieszony i co drugi dzień pyta, kiedy wracasz.

– Widzisz, jaki słodki, a mówiłaś, że to gnojarek! Czekaj, czekaj, Bujała odpada, to zostaje tylko Orzechowicz. Zgadłam, sto punktów dla mnie. Dobry jest w łóżku, prawda?

– On w ogóle wszystko robi znakomicie: od omletu z pieczarkami po... po całą resztę – wyjaśniła spokojnie Julia i bodaj po raz pierwszy zaszokowała Karolinę, nie odwrotnie. Takiej odpowiedzi magister Cierniak się nie spodziewała. Też miała w zanadrzu kilka ciekawostek, lecz nie mówiła o nich tak spontanicznie jak przyjaciółka. Mikula zamienił urlop zdrowotny w Szczawnicy na szarpiący nerwy pobyt w Toruniu. Wystąpił o rozwód z żoną i coraz natarczywiej nalegał na małżeństwo z Karoliną.

– Potrafisz go pokochać? – spytała przerażona Julia.

Karolina miała własną teorię na temat uczuć. Miłość jest grą hormonów, dowodziła; hormony pójdą spać i zaczynają się kieszonkowe tragedie z powodu krzywego spojrzenia, małego skoku w bok lub przypalonej zupy. Dla kobiety w życiu najważniejsza jest pewność, że partner nie zawiedzie, otoczy opieką, pomoże w każdej sytuacji. Dla niej, Karoliny, liczy się też zaradność i zamożność. Mikula obdarzony jest wszystkimi zaletami idealnego faceta, z wyjątkiem jednej, niestety, też ważnej, która chwilowo zeszła na plan drugi. Plan pierwszy zdominował bezsensowny pomysł, by przepisać na Karolinę większość uratowanego majątku i przy sprawie rozwodowej wyjść na bankruta. Karolina nie znosiła bankrutów, czy to prawdziwych, czy fałszywych, wyśmiała więc Mikulę i wysłała do diabła. Mecenas Wąsik załatwiał jej świetną pracę w Toruniu i nie miała zamiaru wracać do Włocławka, do starych, niezdrowych układów. Mieszkanie przy Budowlanych przekazała pod opiekę Julii z życzeniami, żeby zrealizowała swój plan odcięcia pępowiny.

– Chochla nie dzwoni? – spytała na koniec.

Julia codziennie przesłuchiwała automatyczną sekretarkę w mieszkaniu Karoliny i oprócz stęsknionego pisku Bujały niczego tam nie znajdowała. Do niej Marcin też nie zadzwonił ani razu; wiedziałaby, bo nauczyła się już nosić komórkę przy sobie. Przesadą byłoby twierdzić, że tęskniła za nim, zastanowił ją jedynie fakt, że odkochał się tak nagle.

W cichości ducha Julia wciąż rozmyślała, jak przenieść się na Budowlanych bez wywoływania w domu kosmicznej awantury. Wszystkie wolne chwile spędzała z Konradem, wieczorami jednak wracała do domu. Matka, choć zapracowana i zagoniona, jeżeli chodziło o jedynaczkę, oczy miała otwarte. Szybko zauważyła zmianę w zachowaniu i wyglądzie córki. Wiedziała, że spotyka się z Konradem, że razem wychodzą do kawiarni i na spacer. To był sygnał do wzmożenia czujności. Inżynier Orzechowicz sprawiał wrażenie człowieka kulturalnego, był wykształcony i poważny, tego nie kwestionowała, jednak to wystarczało zaledwie na przepustkę, nie na bilet stały upoważniający do bywania w ich domu. Skąd mogła mieć pewność, że to nie oszust matrymonialny, łowca posagu, podrzutek lub zboczeniec? Julii to nie interesowało, bo młoda i głupia, lecz matkę bardzo. Zasypywała córkę pytaniami, które wciąż pozostawały bez odpowiedzi, i Julia drżała na samą myśl o pierwszej oficjalnej wizycie. Wejdzie biedny Konrad, usiądzie, a matka rzuci się na niego ze swoją dyplomacją i przemagluje gruntowniej niż prokurator.

– Dlaczego nigdy nie opowiadasz o swojej rodzinie? – spytała kiedyś, gdy wspominał, jak pani Ewelina broniła go przed gniewem Lucjana Orskiego.

– Właśnie ci opowiadam o mojej rodzinie. Chcesz posłuchać o rodzicach biologicznych, tak? Nie uważam, żeby biologia była ważniejsza od serca i uczuć. Szanujesz i kochasz rodziców tak, jak oni cię tego nauczyli, mam rację?

– Nie wiem... nigdy w ten sposób nie myślałam – broniła się przerażona, że całkiem niepotrzebnie wywołała bolesny temat. On już się rozgadał, widać chciał wyrzucić z siebie to, o czym normalnie starał się nie pamiętać. Nie przerywała, gdy opowiadał o nędznym dzieciństwie i pijackiej melinie. Na własne oczy widziała przecież to rodzinne gniazdo.

– Błogosławię przypadek, właściwie wypadek, który wyrwał mnie z bagna – powiedział. – Nie mam żadnych uczuć wobec moich biologicznych rodziców, poza najgorszą formą litości. W końcu to ludzie, prawda?

– O Boże! – jęknęła Julia. Patrzyła na kochaną twarz, na mądre oczy i widziała nie jego, tylko swoją matkę. Dobrą matkę, kochającą, która z miłości do córki zrobi wszystko, żeby Konrad nigdy nie przekroczył progu ich domu. To było tak oczywiste, że nawet nie mogła liczyć na cud. Konrad siedział ponury, ze zmarszczonymi brwiami i z niechęcią myślał o swoim garbie, który zawsze wyłaził spod marynarki w najmniej oczekiwanym momencie. Gdyby wyjechał z miasta, zaszył się na Śląsku albo na Kurpiach, pewnie byłoby inaczej. Ale tu, gdzie spotykał kumpli z Żabiej, Cyganki, Zapiecka, tu nie chciał kłamać. Zresztą nie widział potrzeby. Lucjan zawsze mu powtarzał, że liczy się to, jakim jest człowiekiem, jak daleko zaszedł i odbił się od środowiska, a to, z jakiej wywodzi się rodziny, nie ma znaczenia. Julia myślała tak samo. Przed oczami miała bocianie gniazdo i pisklaka zawieszonego między gałęziami. Przytuliła się do swojego Konrada.

– Kocham cię bardzo.

Poczuł na swoich dłoniach wilgotne plamki. Delikatnie uniósł jej zapłakaną twarz.

– Jeżeli płaczesz nade mną, to całkiem niepotrzebnie. Uważam się za cholernego szczęściarza, szczególnie teraz, kiedy mam ciebie.

Wcale nie płakała nad nim, tylko nad nimi. Miłość każe ludziom używać liczby mnogiej. Przeczuwała, że obojgu im może być jeszcze bardzo gorzko.

– Cokolwiek się stanie, będę przy tobie – powiedziała cichym, spokojnym głosem.

Nie precyzowała, co niby ma się stać, a on nie wypytywał.

W Toruniu Karolina zatrzymała się w dawnym mieszkaniu Marty, którego pani mecenasowa sprzedawać nie chciała, wynajmować zaś nie musiała. Zabrała obrazy i osobiste drobiazgi, resztę zostawiła. Przydawało się takie małe mieszkanko w mieście, gdy na przykład zabalowali z mężem nieco dłużej i nie chciało im się wracać do domu. Przeważnie jednak stało puste.

– No, no! To cały apartament. – Julia rozglądała się po wnętrzu. – Nawet nie ma porównania z twoją włocławską kawalerką.

– W kawalerce też przeżyłam kilka ładnych chwil – powiedziała Karolina.

Wyglądała ślicznie, była pogodna i jak zawsze elegancka. Pracowała dorywczo, nie narzekała; od lipca miała zaklepane stałe zajęcie.

– Powiedz coś o Wąsiku – poprosiła Julia.

– Kurczę, Juleczko, że też on nie ma swojego klona! Właśnie taki chłop by mi się przydał! Mój aniołek stróż chyba gdzieś się zawieruszył i zamiast dbać o moje interesy, podsyła mi jak nie Mikulę, to Bujałę. Czy ja mam w ogóle jakiś wybór? – westchnęła ciężko.

– Oczywiście, że masz. Obydwu każ przerobić na karmę dla kotów.

– No widzisz! Już drugiego oblubieńca wybijasz mi z głowy – zmartwiła się Karolina. – Bujała jest cholernie atrakcyjny po przeliczeniu na te dwa domy, jacht, samochód, teraz jeszcze Budampolex. Niestety, swoimi ciemnymi interesami mógłby mi popsuć karierę zawodową i dlatego co tydzień dostaje kosza. Ja muszę stać mocno na ziemi. A oni niech się żrą beze mnie.

– Bujała z Mikulą?

– Cała banda czworga, nowi i starzy władcy Budampolexu. Wiesz, co to jest polska ruletka? Tak grać, żeby zniszczyć wszystkich sojuszników i samemu też nie wygrać. Oni właśnie to robią.

Julia jechała do Torunia z nastawieniem, że pogada od serca z Karoliną, a po południu wspólnie odwiedzą Wąsików. Marta wciąż ponawiała zaproszenie. Julia paliła się do wizyty, była ogromnie ciekawa, jak też wygląda ten piękny dom w ogrodzie, o którym tyle słyszała od przyjaciółki. Koło południa zaczęła wiercić się niespokojnie. Spacer po mieście i obiad jeszcze przeżyła, ale tęskniła coraz bardziej za Konradem. Każdy dzień bez niego był dniem straconym. Wyjeżdżając, zostawiła go w nie najlepszym nastroju. Wcale nie krył, że miał jej za złe wypad do Torunia. Nie chciał siedzieć w domu sam, jechać z nią też nie chciał, uważał, że miejsce Julii jest przy nim. Nie zakazywał, nie zabraniał, dawał do zrozumienia jedynie, że zbyt serdeczne kontakty z Karoliną są nie na miejscu. To było wyjątkowo bolesne odkrycie. Nie pojmowała, co on ma przeciwko Karolinie. Wzruszał ramionami i mówił, że nic. Czuła jednak, że coś ma.

– Nie obraź się, ale ja chyba powinnam już wracać – powiedziała, kiedy wyszły z chińskiej restauracji.

– Masz rację, pilnuj go, jeżeli jest taki rewelacyjny, jak mówisz. – Karolina uśmiechnęła się domyślnie. – Tylko uważaj... coś mi się zdaje, że on wciąż jest zamieszany w interesy Bujały.

– W te brudne? Niemożliwe! – zaprzeczyła gwałtownie Julia.

– Bujała innych nie prowadzi.

– Skąd wiesz, że Konrad...

– Nie wiem. Parę razy coś mi podpadło, raz Bujała powiedział o jedno słowo za dużo i wyszedł mi taki jakiś pokraczny obrazek, z którego trudno coś wyczytać. Nie wariuj, nie rób afery, mówię ci tylko po to, żebyś miała oczy otwarte.

Kiedy wreszcie Julia wybrała się do Leszka, był już bez gipsu i poruszał się o jednej szwedce.

– Biedronko, aleś ty wypiękniała! – zawołał uradowany.

– Ty też wyglądasz całkiem, całkiem!

– Co dobrego się wydarzyło, że tak promieniejesz? – spytał. – Powiedz, że to miłość do mnie tak cię odmieniła... no powiedz!

Roześmiała się, bo świetnie wyglądał ze złożonymi rękami i prośbą w oczach. Przez chwilę, przez jedną maleńką chwileczkę pomyślała, że w samą porę zakochała się w innym, bo kto wie, czy nie uległaby w końcu Leszkowi. Nie chciała sprawiać mu przykrości, więc powiedziała tylko o przymiarce do samodzielności. Karolina odstąpiła jej mieszkanie, a ona zamierza żyć na własny rachunek. Rodzice są wspaniali i kochani, jednak przy nich nigdy nie wydorośleje. Pieniądze to nie wszystko.

Teraz on roześmiał się głośno i szczerze.

– Jak myślisz, co lepsze: dostatnie dzieciństwo czy uboga dorosłość? – zapytał.

– Jeżeli czyhasz na mój posag, to się rozczarujesz!

– Ciebie, biedroneczko, wziąłbym tak, jak stoisz. Nawet gdybyś nie miała tej pięknej bluzki i spódniczki, też bym cię wziął – zapewnił.

– Uważaj, bo skończysz jak Mikula – powiedziała i zrobiło jej się głupio, że całkiem niepotrzebnie ostrzy sobie język na chorym biedaku. Aluzja do ucieczki żony była całkiem nie na miejscu. Na szczęście Leszek nie wyglądał na zranionego. Patrzył na Julię, uśmiechał się i całkiem nieoczekiwanie zaczął opowiadać o Mikulowej. Naiwna, bo naiwna, mówił, ale czy to jej wina, że pan Bozia zapomniał o rozumie? Powiesz takiej, że ładna, ona zaraz uważa się i za inteligentną i skacze z jednej głupoty w drugą. Zakochała się w dyżurnym amancie ze stajni Bujały. Ukochany oskubie ją z pieniędzy, mąż będzie miał powód do rozwodu i klops.

– Obrzydlistwo! – wzdrygnęła się Julia.

– Co obrzydliwego widzisz, biedronko, w trudnej walce o byt?

– Majdziaka widzę. Nochal wielkości buta, pryszcze i sterydy.

– A skąd ty wiesz o sterydach?

Pokazała mu, jak chodzą faceci nafaszerowani sterydami, jak trzymają ręce. Wiedzę czerpała wyłącznie z opowieści Karoliny, a naśladować potrafiła od zawsze. Leszek śmiał się głośno i szczerze.

– Mam dla ciebie prezent – powiedział. – Obiecaj, że otworzysz dopiero w domu i zastanowisz się poważnie, zanim odeślesz mnie do czorta lub... nie odeślesz. Zgoda?

Trzymał w ręku małą, pękatą kopertę, taką, w jakiej wysyła się dyskietki. W środku namacała twarde, płaskie pudełeczko.

– Dajesz słowo, że tam nie siedzi czarna wdowa ani inne żarte paskudztwo?

– Ostrożna jesteś i podejrzliwa – zaśmiał się wesoło. – Daję ci również słowo, że nie jest to puszka Pandory. To wyłącznie malutki przyczynek do poważniejszej refleksji.

Przytulił ją i pocałował we włosy. Wywinęła się delikatnie, lecz stanowczo. Kopertę schowała do torebki.

Orscy znowu byli razem. Grażyna wróciła ze szpitala i z dnia na dzień odzyskiwała chęć do życia. Konrad, pomny na swoje obietnice, nie zwlekał długo z pierwszą wizytą. Wybrał popołudnie, gdy Julia umówiona była z Leszkiem Wydroniem. Kupił kwiaty, butelkę bordeaux i pojechał na Kujawską.

– Sam? – zdziwiła się Grażyna. – Myślałam, że przyjdziesz z Julią.

– Przyjdę, przyjadę – obiecał, całując ją w policzek. – Skąd mogłem wiedzieć, że będziesz w tak doskonałej formie.

– Byłaby w jeszcze lepszej, gdyby mogła wziąć pod lupę twoją dziewczynę – żartował Lucjan. – Nie wiesz, jak to jest z kobietami? Uprzedź tę małą, że jeśli ma coś do ukrycia, to niech starannie chowa. Moja żoneczka ma sokole oko.

Grażyna nie przejmowała się ich gadaniem. Siedziała w fotelu, patrzyła, jak mąż się krząta, a Radek mu pomaga, czyli jak chłopcy szykują popołudniową herbatę, i wydawała się bardzo zadowolona.

– Jak się czujesz? – spytał Konrad.

– Właściwie dobrze, trochę jeszcze pobolewają szwy, ale idzie żyć. Wiesz, co jest najgorsze? Zapachy. Jestem chyba wyjątkowo uczulona, bo prześladuje mnie paskudny smrodek. Lucjan mówi, że nic nie czuje, a ja czasami aż się duszę.

– Może znowu jakaś myszka straciła życie.

Myszka wywołała lawinę wspomnień. Orscy zatrzasnęli biedaczkę w tapczanie tuż przed wyjazdem na wczasy. Pościel wyjęli, żeby się wietrzyła, myszkę zostawili. Po powrocie musieli pozbyć się jedynego mebla do spania. Żaden środek nie chciał wywabić ohydnego zapachu, którym przesiąkły drewno i materiał.

– Gdzie myśmy wtedy byli? – spytał Konrad.

Zaczęli sobie przypominać i wyszło im, że albo w Bułgarii, albo na Węgrzech, albo w czeskich Tatrach. Zjeździł z nimi całą Polskę i dodatkowo ładny kawałek Europy, ten dostępny w tamtych latach.

Wychodził już, kiedy Grażyna przypomniała mu, że chce wreszcie poznać Julię.

– Jak ona się nazywa? – spytała.

– Julia Blenda – powiedział.

Orscy spojrzeli na siebie i choć był to ułamek sekundy, błysk ledwie, Konrad w lot pojął, że coś jest nie tak. Za szybko Grażyna spoważniała, za szybko Lucek zmarszczył czoło, by chodziło jedynie o błahostkę.

– Znacie ją?

– Nie, nie! – zaprzeczyli zgodnie.

– Więc o co chodzi?

– Och, o nic! – Grażyna starała się mówić swobodnie, wyszło aż za swobodnie, czyli podpadająco. – Znałam kiedyś jednego Blendę. Nie był to miły człowiek, tyle ci mogę powiedzieć. Dawne dzieje i nie ma dowodów na to, że jest spokrewniony z twoją Julią.

– Moment. – Konrad wycelował palec w pierś Lucjana. – Ojciec Julii pośredniczył w handlu nieruchomościami. Czy to jemu zawdzięczacie dom w Michelinie, a raczej brak domu?

– Radek, ja cię proszę, tylko bez głupstw! – powiedział kategorycznym tonem Lucjan.

Konrad już był na klatce schodowej. Nagle zrobiło mu się bardzo duszno i gotów był zgodzić się z Grażyną, że coś fatalnie śmierdziało.

Zapomniał o samochodzie i ruszył piechotą, na skróty. Sam nie wiedział, kiedy pokonał drogę z Kujawskiej na drugi koniec osiedla. Nie wiedział również, co chce i co powinien zrobić, czuł, że od środka rozsadza go wściekłość, a w takich chwilach stawał się niepoczytalny. Ostry marsz uspokoił go na tyle, że pukając do Blendów wyglądał jak człowiek zmęczony, nie jak furiat. Drzwi otworzyła pani Emilia – wyjątkowo w tym dniu zrobiła sobie wolne popołudnie – i zgarnęła Konrada z przedpokoju prosto do salonu. Julii jeszcze nie było, ona zaś zostawiła pracę specjalnie po to, żeby poważnie porozmawiać z panem Konradem.

Trafiła w dziesiątkę. Orzechowicz przypominał wulkan tuż przed wybuchem i do pełnego szczęścia brakowało mu tylko śledztwa pani Blendowej. Usiadł przy stole i wsłuchał się w czar kobiecej dyplomacji. Matka Julii zaczęła od stwierdzenia, że mają z mężem jedną córkę i że jej los bardzo głęboko ich obchodzi. Jeżeli pan inżynier Orzechowicz myśli poważnie o Julii, to ona prosi o szczerą odpowiedź na kilka pytań. Z kilku zrobiło się kilkanaście. Konrad nie kwapił się z odpowiadaniem. Ostrym, zimnym głosem, bez cienia dyplomacji, spytał o Orskich. Użył mocnych słów, takich jak: oszustwo, drańska, czyste złodziejstwo. Nie owijał w bawełnę swoich żądań. Do godziny dwunastej pojutrze pieniądze miały znaleźć się w rękach Orskich. Emilia Blendowa histeryzowała, on cedził słowa i tak się zapamiętali w swojej sprzeczce, że nie usłyszeli skrzypienia drzwi. Konrad dostrzegł Julię, gdy już wychodził. Wielkie przerażone oczy, a w nich nieme pytanie. Dotknął tylko jej ramienia i bez słowa wybiegł. Julia za nim. Ogłuchła na krzyk matki, nie słuchała, że ma natychmiast wracać, próbowała dogonić Konrada.

– Czemu tak pędzisz? Co się stało? Porozmawiaj ze mną!

Zwolnił kroku, wreszcie stanął.

– Wracaj! Wracaj, póki czas! – powiedział ostro.

– Przepraszam cię za moją mamę. Czasem jest niemożliwa, wiem. Chce jak najlepiej, tylko nie zawsze nasze chęci zbiegają się w tym samym punkcie.

– Wracaj, Julio! – powtórzył. Chciał jeszcze coś dodać, ale głos uwiązł mu w gardle. Żal mu było jej i siebie.

– Spójrz na mnie – powiedziała – i powtórz to samo po raz trzeci. I jeszcze powiedz dlaczego? Przekonaj mnie, to... wrócę.

Uniosła głowę. Nad sobą miała chmurną, obcą twarz.

– Julio, ja chcę dobrze dla ciebie.

– Mama też chce dla mnie dobrze i zobacz, co z tego wychodzi. A ja chcę decydować sama o sobie, rozumiesz?

Nie pojechała z nim na Toruńską. Siedzieli z godzinę w jego samochodzie i rozmawiali. Julia początkowo gotowa była oddawać głowę za uczciwość rodziców, w porę jednak przypomniała sobie nocny napad i zamilkła. Wtedy też chodziło o zwrot pieniędzy. W interesach jest różnie, myślała, nie znam się na tym, dlaczego więc mam pewność, że to Konrad mówi prawdę?

– Jak można załatwić taką transakcję, żeby nabywca wpłacił trzydzieści tysięcy zaliczki i nie wnikał w takie drobiazgi jak prawo własności? – spytała.

Konrad nie wiedział, nie załatwiał nigdy tego typu transakcji. Sam był zły na Lucjana za dziecinną naiwność, z jaką traktował ludzi. Julia zamyśliła się głęboko. Przejęta opowiadaniem Konrada nawet nie zauważyła, że stoją pod dobrze znanym blokiem na Kujawskiej.

– W drugiej klatce na drugim piętrze mieszka moja znajoma – powiedziała.

– A na parterze Orscy – wyjaśnił Konrad.

Przypomniała sobie ostry sprint po ciemnych schodach i śmiech Konrada na parterze. Wtedy sądziła, że to halucynacje. Przytuliła policzek do jego ramienia i spojrzała w okna Chochli. Kuchenne było lekko uchylone.

– Coś takiego! Wietrzy swój chlewik – powiedziała zaskoczona.

– Jaki chlewik? Kto?

Chyba się zarumieniła, jak dzieciak przyłapany na gorącym uczynku. Zapomniała, że nie o wszystkich wydarzeniach z przeszłości opowiadała Konradowi. Wykręciła się zręcznie znajomą znajomej i szybko zmieniła temat.

Podwiózł ją pod dom. Wysiadała uspokojona i przekonana, że dobrze wie, co ma robić. W ostatniej chwili cofnęła się i uchyliła drzwi od strony kierowcy.

– Proszę cię, żebyś nigdy więcej nie odpędzał mnie tak jak dzisiaj – powiedziała poważnie.

Przytulił usta do jej dłoni.

– A co będzie, jeżeli zostaniesz zmuszona do wyboru: rodzice albo ja?

– To mój wybór i nie chcę, żebyś mnie wyręczał. Zresztą już wybrałam. Pojutrze przenoszę się do mieszkania po Karolinie. Rodzice mają prawo trochę ode mnie odpocząć.

Julia wróciła do pustego mieszkania i bardzo się ucieszyła z chwilowej samotności. Nie chodziło o awanturę, na gadanie była uodporniona, chciała załatwić sprawę o wiele bardziej poważną. Pamiętała, że kiedyś natknęła się w szufladzie rodziców na książeczkę oszczędnościową, którą w tajemnicy założyli dla niej. Zamierzała swoimi – choć tak naprawdę jeszcze nie swoimi – pieniędzmi zlikwidować plamę na rodzicielskim honorze. Bez problemów odnalazła kluczyk w schowku i otworzyła szufladę. Nie grzebała wśród papierów, nie przewracała, wyjęła tylko tę jedną książeczkę. Ona była właścicielką, rodzice pełnomocnikami. Czuła się trochę jak w kuchence Chochli. Zabierała coś, co nie było jej własnością, i nie miała przy tym wyrzutów sumienia.

Wieczorem czekała na solidną awanturę. Matka wróciła jednak bardzo zaaferowana i przez cały wieczór siedziała z ojcem w pokoju. Wydzwaniali gdzieś, załatwiali interesy. Dopiero przy kolacji napomknęła, że nie chce więcej widzieć Orzechowicza w domu.

– W porządku – powiedziała Julia. – Będzie, jak sobie życzysz. To twój dom.

Wróciła do siebie z postanowieniem, że pojutrze wyprowadza się, choćby nie wiem co. Następnego dnia chciała jeszcze załatwić sprawę z Orskimi i przy okazji wpaść do Wandy. Wyciągnęła torbę i spakowała najpotrzebniejsze rzeczy. Nie miała ich tak wiele. Trochę książek, ulubione płyty, kosmetyki. I ciuchy. Starych nie zamierzała zabierać, a w nowe jeszcze tak bardzo nie obrosła. Ustawiła torbę w kącie pod oknem i naszły ją wątpliwości. Przypomniała sobie różne miłe chwile z dzieciństwa, domek dziadka, wczasy nad morzem. Sama nie wiedziała, czy dobrze robi, idąc za mężczyzną. Nie powinni mnie zmuszać do takich wyborów, nie powinni, myślała zgnębiona. Miała żal do rodziców i jakby odrobinę do Konrada. Po raz pierwszy od bardzo dawna próbowała wrócić do swoich filmowych fascynacji. Zobaczyła zapomniane już trochę twarze aktorów, którzy kiedyś tak bardzo jej się podobali. I po co mi to, mruknęła zniechęcona. Gdyby jakiś aktor poprosił o moją rękę, to dopiero byłaby piękna awantura!

Po południu Julia nie znalazła czasu dla Konrada. Nie chciała mu za dużo tłumaczyć, więc sam sobie wytłumaczył nieco opacznie, że go unika. Pomyślał, że to sprawka mamy Blendowej i ogarnął go bezsilny żal. Julia prosto z pracy pojechała do banku i zaraz potem do Orskich. Choć trzymana z dala od biznesu, nasłuchała się rozmów o ostrożności w interesach.

Orscy sprawiali wrażenie ludzi miłych, kulturalnych, miała dla nich swoją prywatną wdzięczność za Konrada, lecz z pierwszego spotkania nie wyniosła zbyt dobrych wrażeń. Zwątpiła w sprawność umysłową Lucjana Orskiego w chwili, gdy zobaczyła pokwitowanie, jakim się zadowolił, dając do ręki obcemu facetowi trzydzieści tysięcy złotych. Obracała w ręku najdroższy chyba skrawek papieru, jaki kiedykolwiek trzymała: *Kwituję 30 tys. zł, które dostałem od L. Orskiego*. Data, podpis ojca i nic więcej. Co to było? Pożyczka? Darowizna? Zwrot długu? Powstrzymała się od wszelkich uwag. Cokolwiek by powiedziała, godziło również w ojca. Swój dokument przygotowała sama. Postarała się, żeby odpowiadał na wszystkie najważniejsze pytania: kto, komu, kiedy, z jakiego tytułu i ile pieniędzy oddaje. Niewiele wiedziała na temat pożyczek, zaliczek i zwrotu długów, kierowała się wyłącznie zdrowym rozsądkiem i dobrą wolą.

Grażyna Orska chciała ją poczęstować pomarańczowym musem swojej roboty. Usiłowała być miła. Julii nie smakował mus, tak jakoś nieszczęśliwie machnęła ręką, że połowa zawartości znalazła się na żakiecie. Już my się chyba nigdy nie polubimy, pomyślała, wychodząc. Na wizytę u Wandy zabrakło jej ochoty. W całej klatce roznosił się paskudny fetor. Z ulgą wyszła na świeże powietrze.

Książeczkę z pokwitowaniem Orskich włożyła do szuflady i uznała, że jest wolna i mogłaby od razu przenieść się do mieszkania po Karolinie. Zgrzyt klucza w zamku ostudził jej zapał. Na koniec musiała jeszcze przeżyć dużą dawkę wyrzutów.

Mama Blendowa nie należała do kobiet, które łatwo się poddają. Takie kobiety nigdy nie dochodzą do majątku, a ona doszła i z tego powodu czuła uzasadnioną dumę.

Jak i dzięki komu zdołała się dowiedzieć niemal wszystkiego o rodzinie Orzechowiczów, pozostało jej tajemnicą. Trzęsła się z oburzenia i wściekłości, kiedy opisywała córce mieszkanie przyszłych teściów, do którego osobiście się pofatygowała, żeby niczego nie zaniedbać.

– To sobie teraz porównaj tę norę i jego! – krzyknęła Julia.

– Porównałam. Masz rację, ja nawet czuję szacunek dla tego Orzechowicza. Jednak i ty musisz mi przyznać rację, że istnieje coś takiego jak geny. Dziedziczy się po rodzicach, nie po opiekunach. Poza tym, co zrobisz, jak oni wszyscy zwalą ci się na gwiazdkę? Tam mieszka dwanaście osób, sami najbliżsi krewni. Skrzynka denaturatu nie wystarczy, żeby ich zadowolić. Nie masz wyboru, Julka! Tu jest twoja rodzina i twój dom. Męża jeszcze sobie znajdziesz.

– Już znalazłam. Nie chcę wybierać między Konradem a wami. Jeśli mnie zmusicie, zostanę przy nim.

Powiedziała to ostrym, pewnym głosem. Zaciśnięte usta matki nie wróżyły nic dobrego. Jeżeli teraz powiem, że się wyprowadzam, pomyślała Julia, to gotowa zamknąć mnie w piwnicy albo ubezwłasnowolnić. Wycofała się do swojego pokoju.

Rano wstała przygnębiona. To był dzień przeprowadzki. Po torbę zamierzała wpaść po południu, gdy rodzice będą w pracy. Snuła się po domu jak wyrzut sumienia i wszystko leciało jej z rąk. Matka, pogrążona we własnych myślach, nawet nie wspomniała o Konradzie. Ojciec jeszcze spał, gdy wychodziła.

– Włóż żakiet, bardzo się ochłodziło – powiedziała matka.

Sięgnęła po ciuszek i ze złością powiesiła go z powrotem na wieszaku. Resztki musu pomarańczowego ułożyły się w malowniczą skorupę i żakiet nie nadawał się do użytku.

– Zaradna jesteś, aż żal patrzeć! – zauważyła zjadliwie matka. – I ty mi mówisz, że dasz sobie radę sama? Nie grzeb w tych ciuchach, nie rób bałaganu. Weź moją brązową marynarkę i idź już, bo późno.

Była tak skołowana, że pozwoliła się matce ubrać i zbiegła na parking. Tego dnia, kiedy od samego rana wszystko się układało inaczej, niż powinno, samochód znów nie ruszył. Pobiegła na przystanek, co miała robić. Nerwowo zerknęła na zegarek. Przez dziesięć minut nie miała szans dojechać do firmy.

– Podrzucić? Jadę dokładnie tam, gdzie pani chce się dostać.

Tuż obok niej przy krawężniku zatrzymał się polonez. Kierowca uśmiechał się przyjaźnie i potrząsał jasnymi loczkami. Odetchnęła z ulgą. Miała przed sobą jednego z dzielnych młodzieńców, którzy śpieszyli jej z pomocą na parkingu przed Budampolexem. Wskoczyła zwinnie i zatrzasnęła drzwi.

– Góra z górą, no nie, a człowiek człowieka wytropi – cieszył się chłopak.

– Mieszka pan tu gdzieś na osiedlu?

– Dziewczyna tu mieszka niedaleko – mrugnął porozumiewawczo. – Co z pani samochodkiem? Pewnie się rozkwaczył przed domem?

Chłopak prowadził stanowczo zbyt brawurowo jak na wymagania Julii. Przymykała oczy, kiedy z piskiem hamulców wjeżdżał na kolejne skrzyżowania. Milczała. Siedział za kierownicą, więc pewnie miał prawo jazdy i z grubsza wiedział, co robi.

– Którędy pan jedzie? – spytała zaskoczona, gdy na rondzie skręcił w kierunku przeciwnym, niż należało.

– Bez popeliny! Muszę podrzucić kumplowi przesyłkę, dlatego przycinam trochę ostrzej.

Po prawej stronie pojawiły się opuszczone budynki starej Celulozy. Powybijane szyby w oknach, wywalone fragmenty murów, jakieś plątaniny rur górą i dołem, wszystko to sprawiało przygnębiające wrażenie. Wjechał boczną bramą i zatrzymał się ni to przed magazynem, ni bunkrem.

– Wysiadaj, stokrotko! – poradził przyjacielskim tonem. – No, nie patrz tak, bo mnie wzruszysz. Mówiłem ci, że mam dostarczyć przesyłkę kumplowi. Dostarczyłem właśnie, więc wyskakuj! Szybko, bo muszę jeszcze odstawić wozik facetowi, zanim się skapnie, że pożyczałem.

Dwóch mężczyzn wyszło po Julię. Nie miała żadnych szans, żeby się bronić czy uciekać. Krzyczeć też nie było po co. Wokół same ruiny, pustka i beznadzieja.

– Mogę wiedzieć, o co chodzi? – spytała cicho.

– Jak będziesz miała trochę szczęścia, to się dowiesz – powiedział wyższy z osiłków, młody i lekko rudawy. – Żarty się skończyły.

– Więc o co chodzi?

– Bo ja wiem?! My się nie mieszamy do cudzych interesów! – mruknął.

Niższy w ogóle się nie odzywał. Bez zbędnych ceregieli wyszarpnął Julii torebkę i starannie przejrzał zawartość. Portmonetka go nie zainteresowała, wyciągnął telefon komórkowy, wieczne pióro, notesik z adresami i grubą kopertę z upominkiem od Leszka. Ostatnio tak była zagoniona, że w kamień zapomniała zajrzeć do środka.

Wepchnęli ją do jakiegoś pomieszczenia. Głucho szczęknęły ciężkie, metalowe drzwi. Przez chwilę stała jak wmurowana w betonową posadzkę. Stwierdziła, że głowa przestała ją boleć, że na pewno nie zdąży do pracy i Edyta się wścieknie. Potem rozejrzała się po wnętrzu. Pomieszczenie było wysokie, z oknami pod samym sufitem. W jednym kącie leżała sterta jakichś śmieci, obok nich drewniana paleta i to było właściwie całe umeblowanie. No to *fine*, klops, kropka, pomyślała Julia. Podniosła torebkę i zrezygnowana oparła się o ścianę. Sama była zdziwiona, że wcale się nie boi. Powinna się bać, krzyczeć, walić w drzwi, a ona stała sobie spokojnie, powtarzała, że *fine*, klops, kropka i nic. Ani przez moment nie wierzyła, że to jest porwanie na serio. Czekała, że lada moment otworzą się drzwi, wejdzie ten rudzielec lub ten z loczkami, przeproszą, powiedzą, że pomyłka i odwiozą ją do Budampolexu. Dopiero gdzieś tak po czterech godzinach sterczenia pod ścianą, gdy nogi jej ścierpły, gdy poczuła głód i pragnienie, zaczęła powoli dopuszczać do siebie myśl, że to nie pomyłka i że to dzieje się naprawdę. Czego mogli od niej chcieć? Oczywiście, archiwum Chochli! Jakoś dotąd nie wpadła na pomysł, że Marcin nie działał sam. W grę wchodziły duże pieniądze, więc wokół niego musiało się roić od pazernych facetów, pośredników i prymitywnych ochroniarzy. Oni też chcieli dobrze żyć. W momencie, gdy Marcinek zorientował się, że został okradziony, dał cynk swoim i wcale nie musiał dzwonić do Karoliny lub Julii, żeby się dowiedzieć, kto go okradł. Karoliny nie było we Włocławku, więc porwali Julię. Prostota wyjaśnienia aż biła po oczach.

Nie miała zamiaru kapitulować. Nie zabiją mnie, póki nie odzyskają swojego skarbu, rozumowała logicznie. Nie muszę mówić, że Leszek wszystko spalił. Każę się zawieźć w ruchliwe miejsce, narobię wrzasku i spróbuję uciec. Plan wydawał się dziecinnie prosty.

Ciężkie drzwi zazgrzytały. Julia nawet nie drgnęła. Niech oni się podlizują, ona nie będzie.

– Cześć, Julka!

Gdyby nie stała tuż przy ścianie, kto wie, czy z wrażenia by nie upadła.

W sekretariacie zawsze rano było najwięcej pracy. Edyta zgrzytała zębami na widok pustego biurka Julii. Posadziła Henię przy telefonach i osobiście pofatygowała się do działu informatyki, żeby zasięgnąć języka u źródła. Zaskoczona mina Orzechowicza wystarczyła za całą odpowiedź.

– Czuję się, jakbym miała dziś osiemdziesiąt lat – westchnęła Edyta.

– To widać – przytaknął Konrad.

Pani prezes przełknęła antykomplement, bo nie chciała być drobiazgowa w momencie, gdy waliła się praca nie tylko sekretariatu, ale całego działu.

– Co ona mogła wykombinować? – zastanowiła się głośno. – Matka szaleje z niepokoju, przysięga, że mała wyszła rano o normalnej porze. Chyba nie miała po drodze jakiegoś wypadku? Samochód został przed domem... Może ją porwali, jak pan myśli?

Nie miał zamiaru zdradzać się ze swoimi myślami. Był więcej niż pewien, że Julia nie wytrzymała szalonego parcia z dwu stron, nacisków matki i jego oczekiwań, zostawiła ich swojemu losowi i wyjechała. Myśl ta była mu wyjątkowo przykra. On też myślał o wyjeździe, ale wspólnym. Jeszcze nie zdecydował dokąd, w każdym razie jak najdalej od paraliżującej miłości jej rodziców i złej pamięci swoich. Ucieczkę Julii odbierał jak zdradę, jak wotum nieufności. Gdyby choć powiedziała słowo, gdyby nie zaczęła go unikać, może coś by wspólnie zaradzili. Obiecywała przy nim trwać i – kobieca konsekwencja – wyjechała.

Koło południa zadzwoniła Emilia Blendowa. Spodziewał się ataku histerii, gróźb i płaczu, a usłyszał głos kompletnie załamany. Błagała, godziła się na wszystko, byle pomógł jej odnaleźć córkę. Na słowo „policja" wybuchnęła płaczem. Nie chciała mieszać policji, nie chciała nikogo, tylko jego. Nie bardzo rozumiał, więc mu wytłumaczyła.

– Niech się pan zorientuje, czy przypadkiem Orscy czegoś nie wiedzą? – wyjęczała przez łzy.

– Pudło – warknął. – Musi się pani rozejrzeć wśród innych oszukanych, bo za Orskich ręczę.

Odkładając słuchawkę, drżał z hamowanej wściekłości. Rozglądał się po pokoju, co by roztrzaskać, rozbić, wyrzucić przez okno. Miewał czasem, bardzo rzadko, takie napady szewskiej pasji, nad którą z wielkim trudem panował. Otworzył okno na całą szerokość i pozwolił, żeby chłodny wiatr owiał rozgorączkowane czoło. Powoli sam zaczął wierzyć w porwanie, oczywiście nie przez Orskich. Blendowie mogli mieć sporo nieczystych interesów, wątpił jednak, by zechcieli rozmawiać z nim na ten temat. Czuł się kompletnie bezradny. Jedno, co mu przychodziło do głowy, to zawiadomienie policji o porwaniu. Koło południa ubrał się i pojechał na komisariat. Znał trochę metody pracy policji i wiedział, że nikt nie zacznie szukać młodej dziewczyny po pięciu godzinach nieobecności. Przez telefon go wyśmieją, a tak chociaż ich uczuli.

– Cześć! – powiedziała cicho i niemal w tym samym momencie odezwał się w niej refren ślicznej piosenki. „A on był piękny jak młody bóg, żebyż on jeszcze...". Widać ten refren raz na zawsze złączył się z Serafinem i na to nie było rady.

– Chcesz czegoś? – spytał.

– Chcę stąd wyjść.

Zaśmiał się głośno.

– Jasne! To nie ode mnie zależy, tylko od twoich starych. Pacjenci nie płacą długów, a my mamy pełne ręce roboty.

Była pewna, że albo żartuje, albo jest niedoinformowany. Nie zamierzała kolaborować z głupotą, czyli zniżać się do jego poziomu, i czekała, co sam wymyśli. Stał w otwartych drzwiach. Za jego plecami widziała następne pomieszczenie, po którym plątał się wielki pies.

– Żal mi ciebie, Julka, bo cię lubiłem... Może nawet więcej niż lubiłem, dzisiaj to już nie ma nic do rzeczy. Robię teraz w rewindykacji długów i niestety jesteś zakładniczką mojego szefa.

– Pomyliłeś, palancie, kidnaping z rewindykacją. Nie reprezentujesz sądu, nie możesz ściągać należności w zgodzie z prawem.

– Sama jesteś głupia palancica. To my stanowimy prawo. Twój stary też nie chciał w to uwierzyć. Dostał dwa ostrzeżenia i teraz albo rybka, albo akwarium. – Zachichotał. – Co sobie przypomnę gadki twojej mamuni o uczciwości, to mi się chce rżeć jak ogierowi. Szkoda, że tak mało wiesz o interesach, z których żyjesz.

– Wystarczy, że ty wiesz, co to jest rewindykacja. Jak długo mam tu siedzieć? Dzisiaj jeszcze mnie wypuścicie?

Nie przypuszczała, że Serafin potrafi się tak szczerze śmiać. Aż się zanosił tą swoją wielką radością. Głupia Julia ma nadzieję wyjść tak wcześnie! Przysiadła na palecie, patrzyła na chłopaka i wreszcie dotarło do niej, że została porwana nie za własne winy, lecz za jakieś rodzicielskie machlojki, z którymi nie miała nic wspólnego. Co oni mogą mi zrobić? Wypuszczą chyba, no bo co? Zastanowiło ją jedno: dlaczego mężczyźni, z którymi się do tej pory stykała, od kędzierzawego amorka, poprzez rudzielca, jego kumpla i teraz Serafina, wszyscy mieli odkryte twarze, jakby zupełnie nie obawiali się, że w przyszłości Julia ich rozpozna. O Boże! Nie będzie żadnej przyszłości, pomyślała przerażona. Trzymają mnie, dopóki mogę im być potrzebna do telefonicznych pertraktacji i zaraz potem zamordują. Mam być postrachem dla innych niepokornych. Dopiero teraz naprawdę zaczęła się bać. Serafin wciąż stał w otwartych drzwiach i jak nigdy dotąd próbował zabawić Julię rozmową. Opowiadał o swojej oszałamiającej karierze. Zaczynał od prostego ochroniarza, ale miał odwagę, trochę fartu i wsławił się wielką strzelaniną. Pod letni dom szefa, taki śliczny, na podmurówce, jasny, kryty prawdziwym gontem, więc pod ten dom nad jeziorem podeszli pacjenci z kałaszkami. Od frontu trzech. Siedzieli ukryci w krzakach, nie było siły, żeby ich wypłoszyć. W chałupie szef z babką, a wiadomo, życie szefa jest najważniejsze, bo to on trzyma kasę. Serafin, niewiele myśląc, gwizdnął na psa, wyciągnął dwie spluwy i ruszył na trzy kałaszki. Walił jak taran, prosto przed siebie, prosto na nich. Potracili głowy i uciekli. Nawet karabiny zostawili. Szef w tym czasie zdążył umknąć. Nic mu się nie stało, podrapał się trochę i tyle. A mógł zginąć, gdyby nie Serafin. Za ten czyn awansował bardzo wysoko, został prawą rękę szefa.

Julia łowiła przechwałki jednym uchem. Bardzo chciało jej się siusiu, poza tym była głodna. Powiedziała o tym Serafinowi.

– Hm! – zasępił się chłopak. – Wyjdziemy, tylko pamiętaj, żadnych sztuczek, bo mój pies nie zna się na żartach.

Z wielką ulgą skryła się w wysokich chwastach na tyłach bunkra. Porządkując garderobę, poczuła, że wewnętrzna kieszeń marynarki jest czymś obciążona. Sprawdziła i z wrażenia o mały włos nie zemdlała. Miała przy sobie komórkę matki, całkiem malutkie cudeńko, które dla niej stało się przepustką do świata żywych. Bardzo musiała nad sobą panować, żeby Serafin nie zauważył jej radości. Szła nieśpiesznie, udając wahanie, aż musiał huknąć, że to nie spacer po parku. Najwyraźniej zamierzał dotrzymywać jej towarzystwa, bo nawet przyniósł sobie z sąsiedniego pomieszczenia taboret.

– Jestem głodna. Nie mógłbyś mi czegoś kupić? – poprosiła cicho. – Mam pieniądze.

– Też mam – machnął ręką – tylko może przyjechać szef i się wścieknie, jak zobaczy, że zostawiłem zakładniczkę samą. Ty uważaj na niego, Julka, bo to ostry facet. Grzeczny, ale ostry.

– A co on mi może zrobić? Najwyżej mnie zastrzeli, prawda?

– To mało? – zdziwił się Serafin.

– Słuchaj, w mojej torebce była taka gruba koperta. Zaklejona, niepodpisana. Dostałam ją rano od mamy, jestem ciekawa, co jest w środku.

– Gówno – burknął, spojrzał na dziewczynę i może nawet zrobiło mu się jej żal.

Cofnął się dwa kroki i sięgnął ręką gdzieś w bok, gdzie widocznie stał jakiś stolik. Wymacał kopertę i przez chwilę oglądał ją nieufnie. Nie spuszczając oczu z Julii, rozerwał brzeg. W środku było pudełeczko, w pudełeczku malutki pierścionek, cały ze złota, bez kamienia. Serafin z głupawym śmieszkiem wsunął drobiazg na mały palec i z daleka pokazał dziewczynie. Poczuła, że krew spływa jej do nóg. Pamiętała ten pierścionek aż nazbyt dobrze.

– Przeczytaj, co jest na kartce? – poprosiła cicho.

Oderwał karteczkę i rzucił w jej stronę. Zmięła ją i włożyła do kieszeni. Ta sama kartka, ten sam pierścionek, tylko inny ofiarodawca, pomyślała zgnębiona. Niczego nie rozumiała. Serafin z głupawego chichotu dostał czkawki.

Konrad po powrocie z pracy nie mógł sobie znaleźć miejsca. Źle mu było w domu, ale bał się wychodzić, bo czekał na jakiś znak od Julii. Ucieczka nie wchodziła w rachubę. Emilia Blendowa wprawdzie przyznała, że córka miała chyba zamiar wyjeżdżać, nawet spakowała rzeczy, jednak torbę zostawiła w domu. Samochód stał na ulicy.

– I nikt się nie odzywał, nie było jakichś żądań? – spytał Konrad.

Zaprzeczyła po krótkiej chwili wahania i dość niepewnie. Zrozumiał, że żądania były i że Julia została porwana. Nie pozostawało mu nic innego, jak wierzyć, że Blendowie nie pozwolą skrzywdzić ukochanej jedynaczki i dogadają się z porywaczami.

Zadzwonił również do Orskich. Grażyna miała dla niego trzy ważne wiadomości: Blendowie oddali pieniądze, poznała Julię i mają w bloku morderstwo. Najbardziej interesowała go Julia, lecz Grażyna nie lubiła niczego robić połowicznie. Konrad, słuchając obszernej relacji, zastanawiał się, dlaczego Blendowie wysłali córkę do Orskich, i właśnie to najmocniej go zaniepokoiło.

– Może głupio im lub próbują nawiązać z nami bliższe kontakty? – zastanowiła się Orska. Nie znała Blendów tak dobrze jak on, więc mogła nawet uwierzyć w ich dobre intencje. Konrad nie uwierzył, domyślił się, że to wyłącznie dzięki Julii Orscy odzyskali swoje pieniądze. Zaczął wypytywać o dziewczynę.

– Jak ci się podobała? Jest śliczna, prawda?

– Tak – odpowiedziała Grażyna z ociąganiem. I znowu musiał się domyślać, co to „tak" znaczyło i dlaczego zabrakło w nim entuzjazmu. Zrozumiał, że Julia nie zachwyciła.

Jak to śpiewał Lucek: bez bab bieda, a z babami żyć się nie da! Konrad posmutniał. Dziwne, dwie tak wspaniałe kobiety nie przypadły sobie do gustu? Niczego więcej o wizycie już się nie dowiedział, bo Grażyna przeszła do opowieści o morderstwie.

– Śmierdziało u nas na klatce, śmierdziało, aż sąsiedzi kogoś tam zawołali i odkryli nieboszczyka na drugim piętrze. Musiał leżeć ze trzy tygodnie, bo podobno całkiem się rozłożył.

Po takim zastrzyku horroru Konrad już w ogóle nie mógł sobie miejsca znaleźć. Co godzinę dzwonił na policję, miotał się od ściany do drzwi jak lew w klatce i wcale nie czuł się przez to spokojniejszy. Ochłonął dopiero, kiedy dał w gębę Bujale. I to solidnie, bez taryfy ulgowej.

Grzegorz wpadł przed wieczorem. Miał jakieś problemy z ostatnim programem.

– Porwali dla okupu Julię – powiedział Konrad, kiedy już wyjaśnił mu co i jak.

– Porwali? – Bujała zaniósł się śmiechem. – Poszukaj lepiej swojej Julii u Wydronia.

Konrad natychmiast się zjeżył, zacisnął dłonie w pięści.

– To nie wiesz, że sypiała z nim, jeszcze zanim ciebie poznała?

Wiedział, że nie sypiała, i dlatego dał w gębę Bujale.

Serafin wyraźnie się nudził.

– Słuchaj, rozumiem, że jesteś fantastycznym ochroniarzem, bądź jeszcze człowiekiem! Kup mi coś do picia i do jedzenia. Inaczej poskarżę twojemu szefowi, że mnie źle traktowałeś!

– No dobra! Za pięć minut jestem z powrotem.

Podniósł się niechętnie. Siedzieć mu się nie chciało, iść też nie, wolał jednak, żeby niczego nie kablowała. Szef był porządnym facetem i Serafin czuł przed nim respekt.

Starannie zamknął drzwi za sobą. Julia nabrała powietrza w płuca i ręce jej opadły. Za dużo miała wrażeń jak na jeden dzień. W głowie czuła tak kompletną pustkę, że nawet nie pamiętała swojego domowego numeru. Czas płynął, a ona stała na środku celi, bezradna jak pisklę. To było coś najgorszego, co mogło jej się przytrafić. – Mamo – szeptała – wpakowałaś mnie w tarapaty, to teraz mi pomóż, oświeć mnie. Trzymam telefon w garści i co mam z nim robić?

Wreszcie jak przez mgłę dotarło do niej, że powinna wystukać trzy dziewiątki. Dodzwoniła się na pogotowie. Musiała mieć bardzo przerażony głos, bo babka nie dyskutowała, tylko od razu podrzuciła właściwy numer. Trzy razy wystukiwała dziewięć, dziewięć, siedem, bo za każdym razem palec trafiał na inne cyferki. Szybciej, szybciej, powtarzała, dygocąc jak galareta. Głos dyżurnego policjanta brzmiał spokojnie i Julia nie rozumiała, jak w takiej sytuacji można zachować spokój. Na szczęście przypomniała sobie, że on o niczym nie wie, że to ona musi go przekonać, że nie żartuje, że znalazła się w śmiertelnym niebezpieczeństwie i bardzo liczy na jego dobrą wolę i sprawność policji. Przedstawiła się, opowiedziała o porwaniu, opisała drogę, bramę od strony ulicy Łęgskiej i budynek, w którym ją trzymają. Nie mogła zapanować nad szczękającymi zębami, gdy wyjaśniała, że pilnuje jej jeden człowiek z psem, że ma przyjechać szef i że potwornie się boi. Wysłuchał i od początku zaczął wypytywać o to, co już mu powiedziała. Nazwisko, adres, skąd dzwoni, spokojnie, metodycznie, jakby to była towarzyska pogawędka. Zaczęła krzyczeć ze strachu i z bezsilności. Krzyczała, że nie żartuje, że za moment wróci ten, co tu czuwa, i niech się śpieszą. Miała wielką ochotę zadzwonić jeszcze do Konrada, ale nie zdążyła. Wystukała połowę numeru, gdy zgrzytnęła zasuwa. Kiedy wszedł Serafin, siedziała na palecie i dygotała.

– W sklepie nic nie ma. Kupiłem rybki w puszce i bułkę.

– A sok?

– Zapomniałem.

– To chociaż otwórz mi puszkę.

– Nie mam czym.

– I ty mówisz, że jesteś prawą ręką szefa? – wściekła się Julia i rzuciła w niego rybkami w sosie pomidorowym. To ją odrobinę uspokoiło, rozładowało napięcie.

– No, no! – powiedział ostro Serafin. – Ty się nie ciskaj i nie zapominaj, w czyich jesteś rękach. Jakbym chciał, mógłbym cię zgwałcić, i co?

Nie rwał się jednak do gwałtu. Na wszelki wypadek, żeby za dużo sobie nie myślała, wyciągnął pistolet i zaczął się nim bawić. Może chciał popisać się przed szefem swoją gotowością, może postraszyć podopieczną, tak czy owak siedział na wprost niej na stołku i bawił się bronią. Julia pochłonęła bułkę i poczuła się nieco lepiej. Rano w domu prawie nic nie zjadła, a zbliżała się siedemnasta.

– Musisz tu siedzieć? – spytała niezbyt przychylnie. – Zamknij mnie i idź, bo jak na ciebie patrzę, to mi się myśli rozsypują.

– Ty mi nie wchodź na antenę! Mam cię pilnować i koniec – stwierdził wyniośle i nagle zbystrzał.

Pies przed bunkrem zaszczekał, a potem zaczął gwałtownie ujadać. Wypadki potoczyły się tak gwałtownie, że Julia zrozumiała, co się dzieje, dopiero w momencie, gdy Serafin rzucił się do przodu, jakby powtarzał szarżę sprzed letniego domu szefa. Przed sobą zamiast trzech facetów z kałaszkami, miał jedną bezbronną dziewczynę i ci, co nadbiegli z tyłu, uniemożliwili strzał. Runął tuż u jej nóg.

Dzielnie zapanowała nad sobą, chyba nawet nie krzyknęła, tylko podniosła obie ręce do ust. Zdążyła pochylić się nad nim, kiedy miał jeszcze otwarte oczy.

– Wy... wyd... nie uciek... – szepnął.

– Mówił coś? – zapytał policjant, podtrzymując Julię.

– Nie dosłyszałam... nie wiem.

Wyprowadzili ją z bunkra. Jeden z policjantów pytał o coś, co miało związek z porwaniem. Kwinęła głową, że rozumie, a zaraz potem poprosiła po angielsku, żeby zechciał mówić jaśniej, bo jednak nie rozumie.

– Jak się pani nazywa?

Wysoki policjant ujął ją delikatnie za ramiona. Drugi przyniósł taboret, na którym przed chwilą siedział Serafin.

– Co oni pani zrobili? Boli panią coś?

Nic ją nie bolało, ale poczuła, że musi im koniecznie opowiedzieć o rybkach w puszce. Zaczęła i nie miała siły skończyć. Chciała jechać do domu. Padło słowo szpital, badania i jeszcze jakieś. Zebrała się w sobie, oprzytomniała i normalnym już głosem powtórzyła, że fizycznie nic jej nie dolega, nikt jej nie bił, nie gwałcił, a w domu na pewno dojdzie do siebie.

– Jak się pani nazywa?

– Julia... Julia Orzechowicz. Ulica Toruńska. Numeru nie pamiętam, pokażę palcem.

– Ma pani jakieś dokumenty przy sobie?

Energicznie zaprzeczyła. W dokumentach była Julią Blendą i nie mieszkała na Toruńskiej. Za nic na świecie nie chciała znaleźć się w domu rodziców. Chciała jechać do siebie, czyli do Konrada.

– Orzechowicz? – Młody policjant zajrzał do notesu. – Faktycznie, jakiś Orzechowicz zgłaszał zaginięcie dziewczyny.

– To właśnie ten! – stwierdziła z przekonaniem Julia.

Podjechały jeszcze dwa samochody policyjne i karetka pogotowia. Wokół bunkra kręciło się sporo ludzi. Wynieśli Serafina na noszach. Chyba żył, bo odjechał karetką. Ktoś obok spytał, czy Julia może składać zeznania, ktoś inny proponował, żeby przełożyć to na dzień następny, bo dziewczyna jest w szoku. Julia chciała zabrać swoje drobiazgi, komórkę, notesik, ale jej nie pozwolili.

Odwiózł ją młody, wysoki policjant. Siedziała skulona na przednim siedzeniu i nie bardzo kontaktowała, którędy jadą. Ocknęła się na Świętego Antoniego. Przed domem Leszka zobaczyła samochód Bujały. Przypomniała sobie Serafina i jego szept, żeby uciekała do Leszka, a może od Leszka? Bzdura, przecież od przyjaciół nie powinno się uciekać. Tylko zupełnie nie mogła sobie przypomnieć, kto był jej przyjacielem: Leszek czy Bujała?

Policjant odprowadził Julię aż pod drzwi mieszkania. Na szczęście nie był ułomkiem, tym bardziej skórką od śledzia. Kiedy opadła z sił, nie pozwolił jej upaść, tylko wziął na ręce. Konrad stanął wystraszony w progu i zrobił trzy kroki w ich kierunku. Julia delikatnie przeszła z rąk do rąk. I to Konrad przeniósł ją przez próg mieszkania tak, jak mąż powinien przenieść żonę.

Tulił ją potem przez cały wieczór jak dziecko, uspokajał, gładził i znowu tulił. Nie mogła zapomnieć niczego, a przede wszystkim widoku Serafina leżącego na posadzce. Nie rozumiała, że aż tyle zbiegów okoliczności zdarzyło się w ciągu jednego dnia. Musiał jej tłumaczyć, że jedynym zbiegiem okoliczności była komórka pozostawiona w kieszeni matczynej marynarki i to, że właśnie tę marynarkę włożyła rano. Wszystko, co się zdarzyło potem, było już starannie zaplanowaną akcją: od niby-napadu na parkingu Budampolexu poczynając, poprzez celowe uszkodzenie autka, aż po łagodne porwanie z przystanku pełnego ludzi.

– Zadzwoń do domu – powiedział. – Matka przez cały dzień szalała.

Skinęła głową i zadzwoniła, żeby powiedzieć, że jest wolna i dlatego do domu nie wróci.

Leżała przytulona mocno do ciepłego ciała mężczyzny i zastanawiała się, jak to możliwe, że dla niego gotowa jest zerwać z całym dotychczasowym życiem. Przypomniała sobie matkę Karoliny i swoją. Ilu ludzi, tyle odcieni miłości, pomyślała. Nie było to odkrywcze stwierdzenie, lecz jej się wydawało, że jest. Wydawało jej się również, że żadna kobieta przed nią nie kochała aż tak bardzo swojego mężczyzny. Przytuliła się jeszcze mocniej.

– Nie możesz zasnąć? – zapytał cicho, z ustami przy jej uchu.

– Chyba mogę, ale nie wiem, czy chcę – odpowiedziała.

Ile wspólnych nocy, tyle odcieni miłości, myślała, poddając się jego pieszczotom.

– Kocham twoje włosy – szeptał – i sto trzydzieści osiem twoich piegów, usta i szyję, twoje piersi i twój brzuch...

Przesuwał delikatnie rękę od głowy coraz niżej i niżej, a ona topniała z zachwytu i oczekiwania na ciąg dalszy.

Usypiali już, kiedy Julię poderwało bicie dzwonów w mieście. Podskoczyła gwałtownie i usiadła na łóżku. To tylko telefon, pomyślała z ulgą. Konrad trzymał słuchawkę przy uchu i odpowiadał monosylabami: – Tak, nie, mhm.

– Śpij, to tylko znajomy w interesach – powiedział, tuląc ją mocno.

– O tej porze? Konradzie, czy ty prowadzisz jakieś interesy z Bujałą?

– Tak – odpowiedział całkiem spokojnie. – Daje mi różne zlecenia, za które nieźle płaci.

– Ale jakie? Po co? Co on z nimi robi?

– Juleczko, jeżeli zlecisz architektowi projekt domu, to on cię nie spyta, kogo będziesz podejmowała, w jakich godzinach i dlaczego. Zrobi projekt i weźmie pieniądze, prawda?

– Prawda – odpowiedziała uspokojona.

Obudziła się wpół do szóstej w całkiem nowej rzeczywistości. Inny pokój, inne łóżko, inne życie. Wydarzenia minionego dnia siedziały w niej jak zadra. Noc przespała dobrze, bez zwidów i majaków, ale poranek przyniósł nową porcję strachu. Przymknęła oczy i zobaczyła bladą twarz Serafina. Poruszał ustami, coś szeptał, coś próbował jej przekazać, niestety, nie potrafiła sobie przypomnieć, co to było. Pewnie nic ważnego, myślała. On nigdy nie mówił nic mądrego, więc trudno przypuszczać, by w ciągu kilku tygodni doznał nagłego olśnienia tylko dlatego, że z dobiegacza zmienił się w porywacza. Chciał mnie zamordować, powtarzała sobie i nie mogła uwierzyć, że to nie był sen ani wymysł chorej fantazji. Ciężko ranny Serafin, dopóki tkwił w szpitalu, nie był dla niej groźny. Wciąż jednak biegał po mieście facet z loczkami i ci dwaj, którzy zamknęli ją w bunkrze. Nawet jeżeli rodzice uregulowali swoje długi, też nie mogła czuć się bezpieczna, bo sytuacja się odwróciła i teraz porywacze mieli prawo bać się, że Julia poda ich rysopisy policji. Próbowała nie myśleć o tych strasznych rzeczach, ale wtedy z kolei przypominała sobie ucieczkę z domu i zaczynały się całkiem inne wątpliwości. Powinnam wstać i zrobić śniadanie, pomyślała i w tym samym momencie chyba przysnęła, bo kiedy znowu otworzyła oczy, usłyszała, że Konrad krząta się po kuchni. Wyskoczyła spod kołdry.

Wspaniale było tak siedzieć przy jednym stole i jeść śniadanie, niczym stare, dobre małżeństwo. Julia, wbrew namowom Konrada, zdecydowała się jechać do pracy.

– Muszę się czymś zająć, uciec od własnych myśli – tłumaczyła.

Wielkie biurko w sekretariacie wydawało się najlepszym lekarstwem na lęki. Nie licząc Heni, była jedynym pracownikiem działu i nie musiała obawiać się nudy ani nadmiaru wolnego czasu.

– Nic ci się nie stało? – Edyta przytuliła ją i pocałowała w policzek. – Wiesz, że Chochla nie żyje?

– Nic mi się nie stało, jak to nie żyje? – odpowiedziała Julia jednym tchem.

Edyta wyglądała na bardzo zmęczoną. Śmierć Marcina Chochli wyraźnie rozstroiła jej nerwy. Niczego więcej nie zdołała wykrztusić, zniknęła w gabinecie i starannie zamknęła drzwi.

– Co za tragedia! – Henia z ciężkim westchnieniem wynurzyła się z kuchenki. – Żeby jeszcze chorował, wpadł pod samochód, dostał zawału, to powiedziałabym: normalna sprawa, każdemu może się zdarzyć. Morderstwo na tle rabunkowym nie jest normalną sprawą. Zwłoki ukryli w tapczanie, całe mieszkanie ogołocili kompletnie ze wszystkiego.

– Tapczan też ukradli? – przeraziła się Julia.

– A po co komu taki tapczan?! Mebli nie tykali.

– Mówiłaś, że ogołocili ze wszystkiego.

Henia spojrzała na Julię spod oka.

– Już złodziej wie najlepiej, po co przychodzi. Mebli nie ruszył. Chochla leżał bardzo długo w ogołoconym mieszkaniu i dopiero jak zaczął brzydko pachnieć, sąsiedzi ściągnęli policję.

– Brzydko pachnieć, mówisz? A żona nie poczuła? – Julia uważnie wpatrywała się w pomoc gospodarczą.

Kobieta tylko głową pokręciła na taką niedomyślność. Wyjaśniła już innym tonem, że zwłoki Chochli zostały odnalezione w cudzym mieszkaniu przy ulicy Kujawskiej.

– Bywałaś przecież u Wandy Pasieczko, tej poetki od siedmiu boleści? Sąsiadowała z nim przez ścianę. Tak się zaczadziła, że leży w szpitalu.

W południe, kiedy w sekretariacie panował względny spokój, Julię odwiedził policjant. Wystraszyła się, że przyszedł w sprawie Chochli, już chciała gwałtownie zaprotestować, że o śmierci kierownika wie tylko tyle, ile usłyszała od Henryki Luty, lecz przystojny stróż prawa spytał o Serafina. Spojrzała na mężczyznę uważnie. Jak przez mgłę przypomniała sobie, że to chyba z nim usiłowała poprzedniego dnia dogadać się po angielsku. O porwaniu mogła mówić, czemu nie. Zaczęła od niby-napadu na parkingu. Wysłuchał, pokiwał głową, spytał o samopoczucie Julii, a zaraz potem zarzucił ją pytaniami, jak długo spotykała się z Serafinem, kiedy ostatni raz go widziała, dlaczego nie są razem, czy kiedykolwiek jej groził. Odpowiadała zgodnie z prawdą, że była to znajomość przelotna, spotykali się krótko, nie tęsknili za sobą, a w samym porwaniu ważniejszy był ten facet z loczkami. Policjant nie chciał słuchać o kręconych włosach jednego ani rudych drugiego mężczyzny i z uporem maniaka krążył wokół Serafina: jak długo, czy zazdrosny, czy groził. W końcu zgłupiała od tych pytań i już tylko patrzyła szeroko otwartymi oczami. Wtedy położył przed nią na biurku foliowy woreczek z pierścionkiem. Wrażenie było piorunujące. Przymknęła oczy. Zobaczyła najpierw Chochlę, potem Leszka, na końcu rękę Serafina.

– Czy to jest pierścionek zaręczynowy? – spytał policjant.

– Nie. To jest pierścionek wyjęty z mojej torebki. Serafin pilnował mnie, bawił się pistoletem i twierdził, że czekamy na szefa. O uczuciach nie rozmawialiśmy.

– Całkiem niepotrzebnie gmatwa pani taką prostą sprawę wyjaśnił dobrotliwie policjant. – Zakochani popełniają różne głupstwa. Samo porwanie jest czynem nagannym, chłopak twierdzi, że był zdeterminowany. Oczywiście odpowie za swój czyn, bo prawo...

– Pan też chodzi na randki ze spluwą? – spytała.

– Niestety, nie chodzę na randki – wyjaśnił z nutką żalu. – Od pięciu lat jestem żonaty.

– Ale pierścionek zaręczynowy sam pan kupił czy wyciągnął narzeczonej z torebki?

– Zaraz, zaraz, czy ja w ogóle kupowałem pierścionek zaręczynowy? – zastanowił się głęboko. – Chyba jednak nie.

– Straszny z pana sknera! – mruknęła Julia. – Skąd wiadomo, jaki był motyw porwania?

– Z zeznań pani chłopaka.

– To nie jest mój chłopak!

– Potwierdzają to zeznania pani rodziców.

Dalsze dociekania mijały się z celem. Jak mogła przekonać człowieka przekonanego?

Ledwie jeden stróż prawa wyszedł, przyszli dwaj następni. Ci chcieli rozmawiać wyłącznie z Edytą. Wpuściła ich do gabinetu i natychmiast zadzwoniła do Leszka. Ucieszył się po swojemu i obsypał dziewczynę miłymi słówkami. W tej materii nie miał sobie równych.

– Dobra – przerwała niezbyt uprzejmie. – Co to za idiotyczny pomysł z pierścionkiem?! Skąd go masz?

– Wiedziałem, biedronko, że taka skromna błyskotka cię nie ucieszy – powiedział. – Dla mnie jesteś warta brylantów i gotów jestem...

Przerwała mu po raz drugi.

– Wiesz co?! To jest pieprzenie kotka za pomocą młotka! Jak tylko policja odda mi ten parszywy pierścionek, natychmiast będziesz go miał z powrotem. I nie pytaj, dlaczego policja i co się stało, bo wiesz lepiej ode mnie! – krzyknęła.

Musiała być bardzo zdenerwowana, jeśli nie zapanowała nad językiem, stylem i treścią wypowiedzi. Odłożyła słuchawkę i dopiero wtedy zaczęła poważnie się zastanawiać, jakim sposobem prezent Marcina trafił do rąk Wydronia. Jeżeli Leszek chciał ją nastraszyć, to mu się udało. Ale nawet on nie mógł przewidzieć, że Julia zapomni zajrzeć do koperty i zrobi to za nią dopiero Serafin. Czyli nie powinna łączyć Leszka z Serafinem, z Chochlą natomiast jak najbardziej. Wszystko niby było logiczne i jednocześnie bezsensowne. Zadzwonił telefon.

– Co się stało, biedronko? – Głos Leszka nie był już żartobliwy. – Nie chciałem cię obrazić, tylko...

– Przepraszam, szefowa mnie wzywa!

Znowu nie dałam mu dojść do słowa, pomyślała zgnębiona, odkładając słuchawkę. Ale czy usłyszałaby z jego ust jakieś sensowne wyjaśnienie? Jeżeli ktoś mógł jej pomóc i rzucić choć trochę światła na ostatnie wydarzenia, to tylko Serafin. Zdecydowała, że po pracy pojedzie do szpitala. Nie przewidziała tylko jednego: nie była już sama. Konrad miał swoje poglądy na temat tego, co powinna i czego nie powinna. Wizytę w szpitalu uznał za niepotrzebne szarpanie nerwów.

– Muszę jechać – tłumaczyła – bo dzieje się coś absolutnie złego. Bodaj po raz pierwszy mama zgadza się z Serafinem i oboje kłamią.

Z porwania dla okupu robią romansową farsę. Przecież sama wiem najlepiej, jak było!

Nie chciała, żeby ją podwoził, lecz on widać uznał to za swój obowiązek. Milczał przez całą drogę z miną tak naburmuszoną, że Julia sto razy wolałaby jechać autobusem. Boże, myślała rozżalona, czy już do końca życia będę musiała spowiadać się z każdego swojego kroku?

Serafin był nieprzytomny.

– Pani jest jego dziewczyną? – spytała pielęgniarka.

Julia na wszelki wypadek skinęła głową. Bała się, że z koleżanką nikt nie zechce rozmawiać, natomiast jako dziewczyna dowiedziała się, że chory z rana był przytomny, rozmawiał z policjantami, potem popadł w śpiączkę. Od czasu do czasu wzywał ją, Julię, ale nic więcej nie mówił. Postała chwilę za szybą. „A on był piękny jak młody bóg...". Dwie łzy powoli spłynęły po policzkach. Nie rozumiała, dlaczego płacze. Może z żalu nad kruchością ludzkiego życia? Pielęgniarka patrzyła na nią ze szczerym współczuciem i najwyraźniej była pod wrażeniem romantycznej historii. Julia zostawiła jej swój numer telefonu i wybiegła pośpiesznie.

Pod opieką Konrada trudno było nie dojść do siebie. Robił śniadania i kolacje, gotował obiady. Zjawiła się u niego tak jak stała, czyli w jednej spódnicy, w jednej bluzce i w matczynej marynarce. Pani Emilia Blendowa kategorycznie zaprotestowała przeciwko oddaniu córce samochodu, nie chciała też słyszeć o zwrocie torby z ubraniami. To były dobra nabyte za pieniądze rodziców, mogła z nich korzystać, mieszkając we własnym domu, nie kątem u obcego mężczyzny. Leszek kiedyś żartował, że wziąłby ją i bez ubrania, Konrad był bardziej praktyczny i sam kupił Julii czarną bluzkę. Zdecydowanie wolałaby sama wybierać sobie bluzki, on jednak był tak zadowolony z zakupu, że musiała się ucieszyć.

– Kochany jesteś – powiedziała, cmokając wygolony policzek. Po raz pierwszy uświadomiła sobie wtedy, że broniąc się przed uzależnieniem od rodziców, wpadła w uzależnienie od Konrada. Nie była przyzwyczajona do życia bez pieniędzy. Matka hojnie ją wspierała i właściwie nigdy nie rozliczała z wydatków. Marudziła oczywiście, że córka jest rozrzutna, że trwoni, wydaje bezmyślnie i tak dalej, jednak w ślad za słowami nie szły żadne ograniczenia. Po prostu musiała narzekać, więc narzekała. Konrad natomiast milczał, lecz poza bluzką nie dostrzegał innych potrzeb Julii. W portfelu zostało jej ledwie parę groszy, a nie miała dosłownie niczego: szczotki do zębów, kremu do rąk, głupich majtek na zmianę. Kosmetyki na szczęście nosiła w torebce przy sobie. Wiedziała, że wystarczy poprosić, że on nie ze skąpstwa, tylko z niewiedzy tak sobie milczy. Nigdy nie miał żony, więc skąd miał znać damskie potrzeby? Poprosić czy nie prosić, zastanawiała się Julia. Wolała nie prosić i wytrzymać jakoś do wypłaty. I może wszystko byłoby dobrze, gdyby Konrad nie zaczął rozmowy o zaręczynowym pierścionku. Julia zaparła się jak oślica. Nie i nie, powtarzała. On mówił pierścionek, a ona widziała Chochlę, Leszka i rękę Serafina.

– Najpierw zaręczyny, później ślub – dowodził. – Innej kolejności sobie nie wyobrażam.

– Sami zmieniliśmy kolejność i to już na początku – powiedziała zdecydowanym tonem. – Nie chcę, żebyś skończył na dworcowych schodkach z kapeluszem na datki i z tabliczką: „Jestem ofiarą kobiecej zachłanności".

– Ofiarą w żadnym wypadku! – obruszył się Konrad. – Ten napis trzeba staranniej przemyśleć. Poza tym na dworcu wieje, nie mówiąc już o tym, że wolę siedzieć przed bankiem, bo wcale nie czuję się biedakiem.

Żartował, choć jego nieufna natura podpowiadała mu, że Julia boi się zobowiązań i dlatego umyka przed zaręczynami. Patrzył ze zmarszczonymi brwiami i nie rozumiał, że dziewczyna może nie chcieć pierścionka. Ona z kolei też patrzyła na niego ze zmarszczonymi brwiami i w duchu przeliczała, ile za taki pierścionej mogłaby sobie kupić majtek i bluzek. Tego wieczoru bodaj pierwszy raz kładli się spać z uczuciem wzajemnego niezrozumienia i pretensji.

Konrad powoli zaczynał dojrzewać do remontu mieszkania. Narzekał na ciasnotę i głowił się, jak na tych niewielu metrach kwadratowych po ciotce Ewelinie urządzić pokój dzienny, sypialnię i pokój do pracy. W kuchni od biedy można by wykroić kawałek miejsca na jadalnię, w przedpokoju na szafy z suwanymi drzwiami.

– Jeżeli teraz się mieścimy, to po remoncie tym bardziej, prawda? – powiedział któregoś dnia, patrząc na Julię bezradnie.

– Teraz mieścisz się tu sam – sprostowała. – Zauważ, że w całym domu nie ma ani jednej mojej rzeczy.

Pokiwał głową, bo nie mógł odmówić dziewczynie racji. Chciał tego remontu, ale bał się bałaganu i najchętniej zostawiłby wszystko po staremu. Coraz częściej zastanawiał się, czy Grażyna Orska nie miała racji, mówiąc o jego starokawalerskich nawykach.

– Na czas remontu możemy się przenieść do kawalerki Karoliny – powiedziała Julia. – Mam klucze i wolną rękę.

– Nie, nie! – zaprotestował energicznie. – Damy sobie radę bez zastępczego lokalu.

– Boisz się wspomnień? – spytała.

– Życie to nie powieść. Do pewnych zamkniętych rozdziałów nie wolno, a nawet nie należy wracać. Tamto mieszkanie jest dla mnie takim właśnie rozdziałem. I wcale nie chodzi o sentymenty, Julio. Gdyby to była wielka miłość, potrafiłbym o nią walczyć. Ja nie poddaję się łatwo, możesz mi wierzyć.

Uwierzyła z wielką chęcią. Podjeżdżali właśnie na parking przed domem. Julia wysiadła pierwsza, on otworzył bagażnik i też wysiadł. Nie zamknął jeszcze drzwi, kiedy obok wyrosło trzech drabów. Obstąpili Konrada i próbowali docisnąć do samochodu. Julia zawahała się, czy ma krzyczeć, czy od razu walić w łeb tego, co stał do niej tyłem.

– O co chodzi, panowie? – spytał spokojnie Konrad.

– Nie szanujesz przyjaciół, facet! – warknął najwyższy z mężczyzn i podniósł łapsko do góry, najwyraźniej w celu udzielenia lekcji szacunku. Nie opuścił jednak ręki, tylko zawył jak bity pies.

– Kurwa, chłopy, toż to mały Orzech! – krzyknął głośno ten, co stał tyłem do Julii.

Zbystrzeli wszyscy czterej, łącznie z poszkodowanym, który rozcierał sobie rękę.

– To wy na kumpla gałęzie podnosicie? – zdziwił się Konrad.

– Sorry, stary, zlecenie było. Podobno ty pierwszy obtłukłeś komuś facjatkę – tłumaczył najniższy.

Wiem nawet komu! – przyznał Konrad. – Należało się draniowi.

– Bez obrazy, Radek, ale robotę trza szanować. Zleceniodawca stały, zaliczkę dał... To jakby co, powiedz, że napad był. Możesz mu nawet podziękować po swojemu. A jeszcze jakby co, jakbyś ty miał potrzebę dać komuś w mordę, to my dla kumpli po promocyjnej cenie. Wiesz, gdzie nas znaleźć.

Rozstali się elegancko. Jedynie skowyt tego pierwszego psuł ogólny obraz koleżeńskiej pogawędki. Julia patrzyła za nimi przerażona.

– Co to było?

– Jak by ci tu powiedzieć... To był gest solidarności prostaczków przeciw nowobogackim inteligentom.

– Siebie do której grupy zaliczasz?

Konrad się roześmiał.

– A jak myślisz? Moi starzy kumple chyba na nowobogackich inteligentów nie wyglądali?!

Mimo drobnych niedomówień pierwsze dni wspólnego życia były wspaniałe. Szczęście zakochanych mąciły jedynie zmasowane telefony Emilii Blendowej. Dzwoniła do pracy i do nowego domu córki. Wróć i wróć, powtarzała, coraz bardziej stanowczo i ostro. Przeżycia ostatnich tygodni sprawiły, że Julia okrzepła i nie poddawała się rozkazom. Jej „nie" było zdecydowane i twarde.

– Mów sobie, co chcesz – denerwowała się matka – ale Serafina rozgryzłam pierwsza. I wyszło na moje. Patrzyłaś w niego jak w obrazek.

– Jeśli go rozgryzłaś, to pewnie wiesz, dla kogo pracował? Ostatnio ścigał opornych dłużników.

Pani Emilia dawała się zbić z tropu na krótko. Broniąc się, atakowała córkę za złe prowadzenie, za nieodpowiednie znajomości. Julia zazwyczaj po prostu przerywała rozmowę.

– Dopóki nie wrócisz, twoje rzeczy i auto należą do nas – powtarzała w nieskończoność matka.

– Jakoś to przeżyję – odpowiadała spokojnie Julia.

Wreszcie Emilia skapitulowała. Obiecała dać swoje błogosławieństwo i zgodę na poślubienie Konrada, pod warunkiem jednak, że do czasu wesela Julia zamieszka u rodziców, jak przystało narzeczonej. Była to więc kapitulacja bardzo pozorna.

– Nie! – odpowiedziała Julia. – Pobierzemy się najszybciej, jak to będzie możliwe, ale do czasu ślubu zostanę u Konrada.

Emilia Blendowa wymyśliła więc wspólny dom. Upatrzyła bardzo ładną willę w Michelinie. Na dole pomieszczenia wspólne, salon, pokój telewizyjny, kuchnia, jadalnia, na górze sypialnie. Konrad dostał szczękościsku. Nie potrafił wykrztusić słowa. Julia okazała się odporniejsza i to ona kategorycznie zaprotestowała w imieniu ich dwojga.

– Niestety, mamy inne plany. Wyjeżdżamy z Włocławka.

Powiedziała tak, żeby zniechęcić matkę i trafiła kulą w płot. Na wiadomość o wyjeździe córki rodzice wpadli w szał wybijania młodym z głowy niedorzecznego pomysłu. Wybijali głównie telefonicznie i po paru dniach Julia bliska była znienawidzenia telefonu.

– Chyba rzeczywiście trzeba będzie wyjechać, zanim nas uduszą nadmiarem swoich uczuć – powiedziała zgnębiona.

– A właściwie co nas tu trzyma? – zastanowił się Konrad.

– Mieszkanie i praca. Ciebie jeszcze Orscy, mnie w jakimś sensie oni. Ale nie bój się, jeżeli zdecydujemy się wyjechać, to wyjedziemy. Zawsze pociągały mnie duże miasta. Tęsknię za Warszawą. Inne życie, inne możliwości.

– Mnie – Konrad się uśmiechnął – zawsze pociągały małe miasteczka. Spokojniejsze życie, możliwości dużo większe, byle mieć pomysł i łeb na karku.

Śledztwo w sprawie porwania Julii nie posunęło się ani o krok. Blondyn z loczkami, rudzielec i osiłek rozpłynęli się we mgle, Serafin albo milczał, albo był nieprzytomny, Blendowie wyparli się szantażu i tylko Julia została policji na osłodę. Powoli zaczynała mieć wszystkiego dosyć i zastanawiała się nad zmianą zeznań. Dla świętego spokoju gotowa była nawet przyznać, że Serafin o niczym innym z nią nie rozmawiał, jak tylko o swoich zawiedzionych uczuciach. Jednocześnie z małym śledztwem ciągnęło się wielkie w sprawie śmierci Marcina Chochli. Policja bez trudu ustaliła, do kogo należało mieszkanie przy Kujawskiej. Edyta szybko się pozbierała, zresztą naprawdę nie miała czym się niepokoić. Chochla wynajmował od niej mieszkanie oficjalnie. Umowę miała, o reszcie nie musiała wiedzieć. Kierowała firmą, wyjeżdżała w interesach, podejmowała decyzje i w Budampoleksie ludzie poczuli się pewniej. Stanowisko dyrektora wciąż czekało na Mikulę. Leszek był na zwolnieniu lekarskim, sekretariatem kierowała Julia. Przestała bać się telefonów, interesantów i spraw. Uczyła się szybko i radziła sobie lepiej niż dobrze. Tak przynajmniej twierdziła Edyta.

– Jesteś bardzo podobna do ojca – powiedziała kiedyś, gdy Julia ustawiała na biurku filiżankę z herbatą.

Dziewczyna przysiadła na moment w fotelu i spojrzała wyczekująco. Nie miała pojęcia, że Edyta znała jej ojca. Matkę zresztą też. Należeli kiedyś do jednej paczki, tytułowali się włocławską inteligencją i wieczory spędzali w starym, poczciwym klubie NOT-u. Tamten klub, choć mały, miał klimat i niepowtarzalną atmosferę. Można było wypić koniak, zjeść coś, zagrać w brydża. Do stałych bywalców należeli rodzice Julii, którzy wtedy nie byli jej rodzicami ani nawet małżeństwem, Mikula, Edyta i paru innych ludzi, obecnie uznawanych za rekinów lub płotki miejscowego biznesu. Jednym się powiodło, innym nie, jak to w życiu. Kontakty się urwały, przyjaźnie również i nic, poza wspomnieniami, nie zostało z tamtych lat. Czasem jeszcze zdarzało się, że ktoś kogoś poparł bezinteresownie, bo zagrały sentymenty.

– Twój ojciec był wyjątkowo przystojnym chłopakiem. – Edyta uśmiechnęła się ciepło do Julii. – Oczytany, rzutki i energiczny, miał powodzenie.

– Nie myli go pani z kimś innym?

– Nie mylę! Dłużej znam Zdzisia Blendę niż ty, moje dziecko. Wiesz, jak mówiliśmy kiedyś o twoich rodzicach? „Ćma opętała pazia królowej". Ale jak widać oboje nieźle na swoim małżeństwie wyszli.

– Chyba tak... choć paź całkowicie poddał się rządom ćmy.

Przelotny uśmiech Edyty był przytaknięciem. Domyślała się lub wiedziała, że tak właśnie musiało być. Julia bardzo chciała dowiedzieć się czegoś więcej o ludziach i czasach, których nie mogła pamiętać.

– Mikulowa też należała do grupy?

– Ola to był desant. Przyprowadził ją kiedyś twój ojciec. Emilia miała jednak oczy otwarte, więc Ola zakręciła się koło Wacka Mikuli. Popatrz, jak niewiele brakowało, żebyś miała inną mamusię!

– A Chochla?

– O, bywali jeszcze Wydroniowie.

– Leszek z żoną? – zdziwiła się Julia.

– No nie, przedszkolaków nie zrzeszaliśmy – zaprotestowała Edyta. – Rodzice Leszka. Doktor Wydroń i jego utalentowana żona, pianistka czy flecistka, nie pamiętam. Pytałaś o Chochlę? Też bywał. Głupi, biedny Marcin. Przeżył swoje ostatnie babie lato. Ty wiesz, że on podobno na starość się zakochał! Szantażem chciał zdobyć pieniądze i uciec z jakąś dziewczyną. Pół miasta postawił na nogi swoimi żądaniami.

– Chochla i szantaż? – Julia wydęła usta. Bez problemu zapanowała nad twarzą: przecież nie po to wywołała temat, żeby drżeć jak osika pod sondującym spojrzeniem Edyty.

– Chochla nie pasuje ci do szantażu?

– Nie pasuje mi do miłości, do szantażu owszem. Nie pasuje mi też do inteligencji włocławskiej.

– A Mikulowa ci pasuje?

Julia pokręciła głową, przy czym wcale nie myślała już o Chochli ani o Mikulowej.

Policja nie kwapiła się z oddaniem Julii pierścionka; jak na razie był najważniejszym dowodem w sprawie o porwanie. Bez pierścionka nie chciała pokazywać się Leszkowi, choć miała z nim sporo do omówienia. Magister Wydroń dzwonił często, wypytywał o zdrowie, troszczył się też o Konrada. Skąd wiedział, gdzie Julia mieszka? On zawsze dużo wiedział i zwolnienie lekarskie niczego nie zmieniło.

– Co tam słychać, biedronko? Podobno wygraliście przetarg na budowę pawilonu handlowego?

– No widzisz! Bez ciebie też jakoś sobie radzimy – odpowiadała ostrożnie.

Może to za sprawą pierścionka, może jakichś niedomówień, a może zwykłej babskiej intuicji czuła, że zaczyna się bać. Ważyła każde słowo i starała się mówić jak najmniej. Leszek koniecznie chciał się z nią spotkać. Właściwie dzwonił tylko w tej sprawie, o innych wspominał mimochodem. Ostatnio coraz bardziej był zainteresowany postępem śledztwa.

– Daj mi święty spokój! – zdenerwowała się wreszcie Julia. – Zadzwoń sobie na policję albo do prokuratora. Co mnie obchodzi Chochla?!

– Nie pytam o Chochlę, pytam o porwanie. Dlaczego mi nie powiedziałaś?

– Początkowo myślałam, że to twoja sprawka – odpaliła, żeby zaskoczyć go choć na moment i spokojnie pomyśleć. Nikt w Budampoleksie, z wyjątkiem Edyty i Konrada, nie wiedział o porwaniu. Tę wiadomość udało się utrzymać w tajemnicy. Skąd mógł wiedzieć Leszek?

– Przecież ja dopiero mam zamiar cię porwać! – wykrzyknął i roześmiał się swobodnie, jakby wcale jej nie uwierzył.

A może właśnie uwierzył i tak ładnie zagrał? – pomyślała nagle. Przeraził ją ton głosu Leszka i ten beztroski śmiech. Możliwe, że to było złudzenie, jednak strach w niej siedział. Nie posądzała go o porwanie, tylko o kontakty z Chochlą. Bardzo bliskie – i dalekie od serdeczności.

Tuż przed piętnastą zadzwonił telefon. Edyty już nie było, Julia właśnie porządkowała papiery i bardzo niechętnie pomyślała o spóźnionym interesancie. Na dźwięk głosu Karoliny ucieszyła się i chciała krzyknąć, że ściągnęła ją myślami. Nie krzyknęła. Zasłoniła usta ręką, żeby nawet nie pisnąć. Na plecach czuła miliony ciarek.

– ...się w swojej norce jak borsuczek. Nie nudno ci? A może spotkamy się jutro? Powiedz, o której mam przyjechać.

– Spotkać się... tego... mówisz? E, nie! Ja mam już kogoś fajniejsze...

Połączenie zostało przerwane. No tak, zapomniałyśmy o automatycznej sekretarce, pomyślała Julia. Myśleć mogła całkiem logicznie, tylko nie miała siły wstać ani nawet ruszyć ręką. Jednak telefon odezwał się ponownie i należało podnieść słuchawkę. W krzyku matki nie było już nic tajemniczego. Odkryła właśnie pokwitowanie Orskich i pustą książeczkę.

– Co ci do głowy... rodziców okradłaś... co ci do głowy!!! Co ty wiesz!!!

– Na pewno to, że nie chcę więcej wstydzić się za was! – powiedziała zimno Julia i tym razem to ona przerwała połączenie. Zaraz potem wybiegła z sekretariatu, żeby już nie odbierać żadnych telefonów. Jak na jeden dzień miała stanowczo dosyć. Była przerażona i musiała natychmiast skontaktować się z Karoliną. Ale Konrad nie chciał sam jechać do domu i czekać, aż Julia przesłucha automatyczną sekretarkę w mieszkaniu przyjaciółki i podleje kwiaty.

– Nie żartuj! Tam nie ma żadnych kwiatów.

Julia była u kresu wytrzymałości i tylko dlatego zrezygnowała z dalszych wyjaśnień. Po prostu odwróciła się na pięcie i poszła w kierunku przystanku autobusowego. Dogonił ją, złapał za rękaw i zażądał wyjaśnień. Nie mogła mu powiedzieć, bo jak? Bo co? Że musi koniecznie zatelefonować do Torunia, że teraz jeszcze nie ma Karoliny w domu, a potem, przy nim, nie będą mogły rozmawiać? Taka była prawda, lecz wydawała się zbyt brutalna dla uszu ukochanego.

– Wrócę za godzinę – powtórzyła. – Poczekaj w domu. Czy ty nie rozumiesz, że mogę mieć jakieś własne sprawy, które ciebie nie dotyczą? Jakieś... rozdziały, które chcę zamknąć, żeby więcej do nich nie wracać. Nie rozumiesz?

– Nie.

– A jednak mam! – powiedziała chłodno, patrząc mu prosto w oczy.

Wsiadł do samochodu i odjechał. Została na przystanku w tłumie ludzi i drażniło ją kompletnie wszystko: to, że się śmieją, że ktoś żuje gumę, a inny obrzydliwie klnie.

W mieszkaniu Karoliny natychmiast otworzyła okna. Meble pokrywała gruba warstwa kurzu. Starła tylko stolik przy telefonie, żeby się nie pobrudzić. Konrad miał rację. W pokoju nie było ani jednego żywego kwiatka. Włączyła automatyczną sekretarkę. Ostatnio najwyraźniej nikt nic nie chciał od Karoliny lub wszyscy, którzy chcieli, dzwonili do Torunia. Julia też zadzwoniła z wiadomością, że Leszek wie dużo więcej, niż powinien, i zaczyna z tego robić użytek.

– Julio, on nie próbuje cię zastraszyć, tylko zdobyć – uspokajała ją Karolina. – Biedak podkochuje się w tobie, od kiedy do nas przyszłaś, i stara się zwrócić na siebie twoją uwagę. Sama jestem zaskoczona, że wali czasem jak łysy o beton, ale widać miłość ogłupia nawet najmądrzejszych. Nie drażnij go, nie wmawiaj, że wiesz więcej, niż wiesz. Postaraj się traktować go jak kiedyś, normalnie i po koleżeńsku.

– Nie umiem. Puścił mi zapis rozmowy telefonicznej. Ten fragment o borsuczku.

– Cholera! Skąd wiesz, że to on?

– A kto?

– Julio, posłuchaj! Chochla zginął w sobotę, dokładnie tego dnia, kiedy wyniosłyśmy archiwum. Wiem od Mikuli, że policja już to ustaliła... znaczy datę ustaliła, nie archiwum... Oj, wszystko mi się plącze! W każdym razie Leszek miał wtedy nogę w gipsie i nie biegał jak chart po naszych śladach. Dokładnie obgadamy wszystko, jak przyjadę pojutrze. Mam wezwanie do prokuratury w charakterze świadka. Fajnie, co?

– Ty? Dlaczego ty?

– Pewnie znaleźli moją komórkę.

– Zbyt dużo dzieje się jednocześnie, nie ogarniam tego i zaczynam się gubić. Porwanie, Leszek, umierający Serafin, rodzice, Chochla i na dodatek dzisiaj pokłóciłam się z Konradem.

– To wracaj do domu, pogódź się z chłopakiem i weź coś na uspokojenie... chyba że on cię uspokoi. Jeden kłopot będziesz miała z głowy. – Karolina mówiła spokojnym, pewnym głosem i Julia z miejsca poczuła się lepiej.

Zamykała właśnie starannie drzwi, kiedy odezwała się komórka. Dzwoniła pielęgniarka ze szpitala. Stan Serafina był bardzo ciężki. Chłopak właśnie odzyskał przytomność i chciał rozmawiać z Julią. Niby to tylko jeden przystanek autobusowy, ale jeżeli człowiekowi pilno, to droga dziwnie się wydłuża. Wpadła zziajana i nie mogła tchu złapać. Zatrzymała się dopiero przy łóżku. Kredowa twarz Serafina, naznaczona cierpieniem, nabrała szlachetności, choć z nosa sterczały jakieś wężyki, podłączone dalej do nieznanej Julii aparatury.

– Cześć! – powiedziała, pochylając się nad łóżkiem. – Możesz mówić?

– Dobrze, że przyszłaś... – Próbował uśmiechnąć się do niej, ale tylko wykrzywił lekko usta. – Nie chciałem cię zabić... chciałem wziąć jako zakładniczkę – wyszeptał. – Przecież... nie strzelałem.

Pokiwała głową, że rozumie.

– Wiem, że to nie ty wymyśliłeś, wszystko wiem – mówiła, gładząc wychudłą rękę.

– Wyd... Wydroń... mój przyjaciel... Ten pierścionek, to ja jemu... Orzechowicz, to... to... szef jest...

Z najwyższym trudem zapanowała nad mimiką, żeby nie zdradzić zaskoczenia, nie przerazić chorego. Ale nie miała już siły pokiwać głową, czuła, że łzy same nabiegają do oczu.

– Konrad? – wyszeptała. – O czym jeszcze powinnam wiedzieć?

– Śledziliśmy jednego faceta na Południu... znałaś go... bywałaś... W tym dniu, kiedy go załatwili, też byłaś... dużo ludzi tam wtedy było...

– Miałeś tego faceta zabić?

– Śledzić. Zabił... ten... Siostrę... sios...

Wybiegła po pomoc. Wokół Serafina zrobiło się błękitno od pielęgniarskich uniformów. Potem pozwolili jej usiąść przy chorym. Zmarł po godzinie, z dłonią w jej dłoni. Był pierwszym człowiekiem, któremu towarzyszyła w przejściu na drugi brzeg. Wyszła ze szpitala zapłakana i chora od smutku. Najgorsze, że nie miała dokąd iść. Nagle zawróciła, biegiem wpadła na oddział. Nie znała imienia pielęgniarki, wiedziała tylko, że młoda, z ciemnymi włosami. Znalazła ją przed gabinetem lekarskim.

– Siostro, czy tego chłopaka, tego Serafina, ktoś odwiedzał?

– Kobiety?

– Nie! Pytam o mężczyzn.

Zamyśliła się, spojrzała niepewnie na zapłakaną Julię.

– Ze dwa razy widziałam rudawego faceta, a wczoraj szczupłego blondyna.

– Włosy miał takie jak... żółty mop?

– No, może... Chyba tak.

Wyszła jak najprędzej na świeże powietrze, żeby zdążyć przed własną słabością. Wiatr chłodził gorące od łez policzki i po chwili intensywnego marszu mogła wreszcie skupić uwagę. Serafin mówił mało i z trudem, lecz skutecznie zamącił jej w głowie. Wydronia nazwał przyjacielem, o Orzechowiczu wspomniał dość niejasno. Nie była pewna, czy nazwał Konrada szefem, czy próbował jeszcze coś dodać. Męczyła ją wizyta Leszka w szpitalu. Co do rudzielca nie miała wątpliwości. W dniu porwania kręcił się koło bunkra, więc musiał być kumplem Serafina. Ale Leszek? Nagle zobaczyła Leszka i Serafina pod blokiem na Kujawskiej. Pierwszy wsparty na dwu kulach, drugi z lornetką i karabinem w garści. Serafin powiedział wyraźnie: śledziliśmy, czyli nie był sam. Obraz był tak plastyczny, że z wrażenia aż poklepała się po policzku, żeby wrócić do rzeczywistości. Skręciła w Budowlanych i jeszcze raz tego dnia zatelefonowała do Karoliny.

– Julka, nie świruj – poradziła dobrotliwie Karolina. – Leszek tego dnia był w szpitalu. A jeżeli chodzi o Konrada, to wiesz co? Jemu zwyczajnie nie chciałoby się bawić w szefa gangu. Dzwoń do Edyty, bierz dwa dni urlopu i przyjeżdżaj. Pojutrze wrócisz ze mną.

Pomysł był znakomity, lecz trudny do wykonania. Cały majątek Julii wynosił raptem pięć złotych, a to nie wystarczało na bilet. Zdecydowała się wrócić do Konrada.

To dziwne, jak szybko dom przesiąka drugą osobą. Konrad od lat wracał do pustego mieszkania. Ledwie jednak zamieszkał z Julią i przyszło mu wrócić samemu, odczuł to jak kataklizm. Gdyby jeszcze wyszła do fryzjera, na zakupy, nawet na plotki z koleżanką, uznałby, że wszystko jest w porządku. Jednak rozstanie przed Budampolexem nie było w porządku.

Próbował zająć się obiadem. Pokrywki leciały mu z rąk i właściwie wcale nie czuł głodu. Usiadł przy kuchennym stole i czekał. W spadku po Julii zostały mu tylko telefony pani Blendowej. Uparła się, dzwoniła co piętnaście minut, bo nie wierzyła, że Julii nie ma, i próbowała go zmęczyć. Konrad był u kresu wytrzymałości. Pokochać Julię to nie sztuka, pomyślał, ale co z mamuśką? I całkiem niechcący doszedł do wniosku, że związek z kobietą samodzielną ma mnóstwo dobrych stron. Nikt się nie wtrąca, nie radzi, nie wychowuje i nie stawia żądań. Zatęsknił za Karoliną. Kiedy ponownie zadzwonił telefon, wyciągnął przewód z gniazdka, ale cisza też go drażniła.

Julia przyszła w porze wieczornych wiadomości. Była blada i zapłakana.

– Co się stało? – spytał przerażony.

– Serafin nie żyje – odpowiedziała cicho.

– Ten porywacz?

Kiwnęła głową, a on poczuł wzrastającą wściekłość. Nie zwykłą złość, nie rozdrażnienie, tylko właśnie wściekłość. Kim był do licha Serafin, żeby tak rzewnie go opłakiwać? Żeby uciekać z domu na całe popołudnie bez słowa wyjaśnienia? Chciał ją o to spytać, lecz bał się, że nie opanuje nerwów i wybuchnie. Wyszedł do kuchni i zamknął drzwi. Nie zdążył zauważyć wystraszonych oczu Julii.

Przez cały wieczór nie zamienili ani słowa. Siedzieli oddzielnie, pogrążeni we własnych, złych myślach. Julia przemówiła dopiero rano.

– Co złego zrobiłam, że patrzysz na mnie wilkiem? Czemu nic nie mówisz?

– Nie chcę tobie przerywać.

– To wszystko?

– Z mojej strony tak, z twojej nie wiem – powiedział i zrobiło mu się głupio. W końcu ona pierwsza wyciągała rękę do zgody i nie wypadało odtrącać tej drobnej łapiny. Przemógł się i objął dziewczynę. – Darujmy sobie dzisiaj obiad w domu. Pójdziemy do Zajazdu i spokojnie pogadamy. Dobrze?

Przytuliła się do niego gwałtownie, żeby nie zobaczył łez.

Był czas, że Julia całkowicie uległa czarowi Edyty. Potem to się zmieniło i wielkie zauroczenie przerodziło się nie tyle we wrogość, to za duże słowo, ile w zwykłą niechęć. Kiedy zostały we dwie, wróciła dawna sympatia.

– Pani Edyto, co się stało? – spytała, kiedy rano jak zwykle weszła do gabinetu i zastała szefową bladą i wyraźnie zmęczoną.

– O to samo mogłabym ciebie spytać – odpowiedziała Edyta i nagle obie zaczęły się śmiać. Julia dobrze wiedziała, że po wczorajszym dniu i nieprzespanej nocy nie wygląda świeżutko i ślicznie.

– Wie pani, jak to jest, kłopoty zawsze łażą parami!

– Żeby tylko łaziły! Spadają na nas jak grad, jak odłamki kamieni. Znasz prawo Priestleya? Na pewno słyszałaś: gdy tylko ktoś urządzi coś dobrze, to na pewno to się wkrótce skończy z tej lub owej przyczyny. Uporałam się z tym całym bagnem, powoli wychodzę na prostą i nagle pojawiają się ludzie, którzy próbują mi wmówić, że Budampolex wcale do mnie nie należy.

– A do kogo? Do Mikuli?

– Pół biedy, gdyby do Mikuli. On przynajmniej dał część pieniędzy. Wyobraź sobie, że wielkiego apetytu na firmę nabrał Wydroń. Podobno jest właścicielem ziemi, na której Budimex stoi.

– Leszek?! – wykrzyknęła Julia. – On to pani powiedział?

– Henia Luty widziała dokument.

Patrzyły na siebie ze zgrozą w oczach. Julia od dawna miała wyrobione zdanie na temat wieści rozpowszechnianych przez Henię, tym razem jednak dała się ponieść emocjom. Próbowała rozumować logicznie: Henia widziała, czyli dokument istnieje, czyli Leszek kręci, czyli... siedzi w bagnie po uszy, jest gorszy od Bujały i to on ją porwał. Wnioski nawet jej wydały się zbyt śmiałe, innych jednak chwilowo nie potrafiła wyciągnąć. Wybiegła z gabinetu i po chwili wróciła z dwiema mocnymi kawami. Bez zaproszenia usiadła w fotelu. Wszystko, co dotyczyło Leszka Wydronia, bardzo ją interesowało. Zastanawiała się właśnie, jak zachęcić szefową do mówienia, kiedy nieoczekiwanie Edyta rozgadała się sama. Nawet najbardziej skryci ludzie od czasu do czasu potrzebują kogoś, kto ich wysłucha. Monolog nie był może idealnie szczery, bo wiadomo, że te same wydarzenia oglądane z różnych punktów wyglądają całkiem inaczej, ale i tak Julia dostała spory zastrzyk informacji. Edyta formalnie była właścicielką, nieformalnie zaś wspólniczką. Można powiedzieć, że firma została kupiona ze składkowych pieniędzy: część dał Mikula, część ona z własnych oszczędności. Pewne plany wiązał też z Budampolexem Bujała, ale jego roszczenia okazały się bezpodstawne, dotyczyły rozliczeń z byłym dyrektorem, nie z firmą. I teraz, kiedy wreszcie prawa własności zostały uregulowane, Mikula wierzga i nie chce dyrektorować, Wydroń natomiast chce stawiać warunki.

– Co panią bardziej martwi: wierzganie Mikuli czy roszczenia Wydronia? – spytała Julia.

– Mikula nie jest mi do niczego potrzebny. Dogadaliśmy się; chce tylko zachować swoje udziały i nie zamierza mi bruździć. Jak widzisz, radzę sobie bez niego i to o wiele lepiej – powiedziała odrobinę za szybko i odrobinę za pewnie, jakby chciała za wszelką cenę przekonać Julię, że Mikula nic dla niej nie znaczy. Było chyba trochę inaczej. To wierzganie godziło w nią jako w kobietę i wyraźnie bolało. Przynajmniej takie wrażenie odniosła Julia. Edyta nie bała się Mikuli, Wydronia natomiast zaczynała się bać.

Leszek nigdy nie mówił, że jest właścicielem jakiejkolwiek działki. To musiała być sprawa nowa lub nawet bardzo nowa. Błysk, moment i Julia zobaczyła gabinet Leszka, siebie i Karolinę. Na biurku leżała zielona teczka, a oni zakładali spisek aprilistów. To ona wspomniała o gruntach, zacytowała im bodaj własną matkę. Leszek wyskoczył jak z procy i zaczął biegać po pokoju. Czyżbym go natchnęła? – pomyślała zgnębiona.

Doradzić nic Edycie nie mogła, wysłuchała więc tylko, pocieszyła i w duchu darowała wszystkie wcześniejsze krzywdy. Powoli zaczynała rozumieć, dlaczego szefowa nie chciała jej wypuścić spod skrzydeł. W dziale, który na początku wydawał się Julii oazą życzliwości, nikt nikomu nie dowierzał. Pozbierała filiżanki i ruszyła do wyjścia.

– Julio, czy ty wierzysz w duchy? – spytała nagle Edyta.

Taca niebezpiecznie zachybotała w rękach dziewczyny. Zrozumiała pytanie, ale nie wiedziała, co powiedzieć. Patrzyła zaskoczona i czekała na ciąg dalszy. Edyta uśmiechnęła się z przymusem.

– Po nocach budzą mnie telefony Chochli – podjęła po chwili cicho. – Albo to początek demencji starczej, albo duchy są wśród nas.

– Nie wierzę w duchy! – powiedziała twardo Julia i wyszła.

Koło południa zadzwoniła Karolina ze swojego włocławskiego mieszkania. Przyjechała specjalnie wcześniej, żeby spokojnie pogadać z przyjaciółką. Umówiły się zaraz po pracy i Julia, ledwie odłożyła słuchawkę, czuła, że tego numeru ukochany mężczyzna już jej nie daruje. Mogła mu powiedzieć tylko prawdę, że z dwu ważnych rozmów wybrała tę z Karoliną.

– Rozumiem – powiedział. – To jest twój wybór.

– Niczego nie rozumiesz – zaprotestowała. – Nie rozumiesz, a przesądzasz. Ja nie chcę być na siłę do nikogo przywiązywana, muszę mieć choć odrobinę swobody.

– Czy ja cię przywiązuję, Julio? Jesteś wolna, w każdej chwili możesz odejść.

– Prosiłam kiedyś, żebyś nigdy więcej mnie nie wyrzucał – powiedziała powoli. Chciała jeszcze coś dodać, ale przygryzła usta i zamilkła.

Po pracy nie czekała na niego. Miała jeszcze pięć złotych w kieszeni, kupiła bilet autobusowy i pojechała, by wpaść w stęsknione ramiona przyjaciółki.

– I jak? Love kwitnie?

– Chyba właśnie przekwitła. – Julia westchnęła. – Nie planuj żadnej randki nocnej, śpisz dziś ze mną. I, niestety, chyba już tu zostanę, bo nie mam gdzie iść.

Prywatne kłopoty, choć poważne, z konieczności zeszły na drugi plan. Nie widziały się dość dawno, tematów do obgadania zebrało się tyle, że i noc wydawała się za krótka. Przede wszystkim Leszek Wydroń. Argumenty Julii były rzeczowe i w końcu przekonały nawet Karolinę. Trzęsła się ze złości, nie umiała mówić normalnie.

– To cholerny patyczak, mafioso od siedmiu boleści – irytowała się coraz bardziej. – I ja temu spuszczelowi, tej ścierwicy, zajadkowi przebrzydłemu osobiście wręczyłam archiwum Marcinka. W życiu sobie tego nie daruję. Czy u niego w kuchni jest chociaż kuchnia?

– Gazowa, jak wszędzie – mruknęła Julia.

– Obiecywał spalić w kuchni węglowej! Gówno prawda! Ty wiesz, do czego taki widłogonek może wykorzystać archiwum Marcinka?

– Do tego samego co Marcinek, tylko mądrzej – zgodziła się Julia.

– I o to mądrzej chodzi. Rekinom daruje, poleci po babkach. On mnie kopnął w ambicję i w kobiecą solidarność. Idę tam!

Karolina gotowa była wykradać po raz drugi dokumenty raz już wykradzione. Czuła się oszukana, wystawiona do wiatru przez najlepszego przyjaciela i łaknęła zemsty. Nie żeby zaraz dusić i zatrzaskiwać w tapczanie, ale żeby pozbawić jadu, wyrwać żądło. Zaczęły sobie przypominać czasy wspólnej pracy. Magister Wydroń zawsze miał mnóstwo telefonów, zawsze był zabiegany i załatwiał tysiące różnych spraw. Budampolex nie wymagał aż tak wielkiego wysiłku. Po prostu facet pracował na swoje konto. Lub cudze.

– Dla Bujały? – zastanawiała się Karolina. – Ten podrzut myszaty też jest dobry. Oficjalnie ubezpieczenia, nieoficjalnie prawie bank lub raczej lichwa. Pożyczki, szybki obrót gotówką, ale przede wszystkim trudno ściągalne wierzytelności. W jego języku nazywa się to mobilizowaniem dłużnika do uregulowania zobowiązań. Metody poznałaś na własnej skórze. Nie wykluczam, że Leszek pracował dla niego, a teraz zamierza się usamodzielnić. Stąd te dziwne ruchy. Przy okazji podpytam Bujałę, lecz teraz trzeba mi Wydronia rozbroić, bo zwariuję.

– Myślisz, że to nie Leszek mnie porwał. – Julia patrzyła z niedowierzaniem na przyjaciółkę.

– Chciałabyś, co? On może by cię i porwał, ale w innym celu. Kilka dni temu podsłuchałam, jak Bujała gruchał przez komórkę z Konradem. Powiedział mniej więcej tak: „Czy ty się, kurwa, nigdy nie pomyliłeś? Gdybym skojarzył nazwisko tej... bum, bum, zadziałałbym inaczej. Nie przeprosiłem cię od ręki? Przeprosiłem, kurwa, więc się nie czepiaj jak pijany płotu”. Mówię ci, on jest naprawdę milutki jak słodyszek rzepakowy. A Leszek? Sama nie wiem. Nie po to odwiedzał Serafina w szpitalu, by pytać o zdrowie, lecz by coś tam wymusić. Już ja się wszystkiego dowiem, już on mnie nie wpuści w kanał po raz drugi.

Karolina rozmawiała z Julią, ale już stała przed lustrem w nowej szarej spódnicy i próbowała dobrać do niej bluzkę. Julia podeszła i wyjęła z rąk przyjaciółki eleganckie ciuszki.

– Nigdzie nie pójdziesz – powiedziała spokojnie. – To jest mój ruch. Przy okazji rozejrzę się i dopiero wtedy zdecydujemy, co dalej. Leszek to nie prymityw Chochla. Na niego pochlebstwa nie działają, a kąpie się sam.

– Myślisz, że ja sobie radzę wyłącznie z facetami w typie Chochli? – zaperzyła się Karolina.

Julii nie było specjalnie wesoło, lecz mina przyjaciółki serdecznie ją rozbawiła.

– W życiu! – wykrzyknęła ze śmiechem. – Ja chcę tylko, żeby patyczak na własnej skórze przekonał się, co miał na myśli poeta, kiedy mówił: „Słowicze trele w dziewczyny głosie, a w sercu lisie zamiary".

– Poeta mówił o facetach! – sprostowała Karolina.

– Rewolucja Październikowa ujęła się za kobietami i wyrównała szanse – zapewniła Julia, przyczesując włosy. – A może nie Październikowa tylko inna? Zresztą, kogo to teraz obchodzi?!

Zawróciła od drzwi z lekkim ociąganiem.

– Możesz mi pożyczyć parę groszy? Nie nauczyłam się jeszcze podróżować na gapę.

– Fiu, fiu! Juleczko, nie spodziewałam się, że dożyję takich czasów! Ja tobie parę groszy? Bierz całą stówę. Zawsze miałam gest, tylko nigdy nie miałam forsy!

Świat Konrada runął. Siedział przy stole z opuszczoną głową i nie miał z kim walczyć. Jeszcze dwa, trzy dni wcześniej gotów był przysięgać, że Julia jest największym dobrem, jakie w ciągu trzydziestu kilku lat dostał od życia. Kapryśne dobro odeszło, a on nigdzie w zasięgu ręki nie widział rywala. Nie bruździł mu żaden mężczyzna, nie miał komu dać w zęby. Sięgnął ręką do kuchennej szafki i wyjął chopina. Kiedyś, dawno temu, miała być jakaś kolacja, coś przeszkodziło i butelka została. Odkorkował, powąchał i odstawił. Smutek leczony wódką jest znacznie trudniejszy do wywabienia niż ten nieleczony. Ale wytrzymać z takim smutkiem jest potwornie trudno. Pytania, przypuszczenia, wspomnienia cudownych chwil, to wszystko kłębi się w człowieku, dusi za gardło i nie wiadomo, co ze sobą zrobić. Zapragnął usłyszeć czyjś głos, obojętnie czyj, byle nie mamy Blendowej. Słuchawka milczała głucho. Sporo czasu upłynęło, zanim przypomniał sobie, że to jego robota z poprzedniego dnia. Podłączył telefon i całkiem bezwiednie wybrał numer Karoliny. Co u ciebie? Jak żyjesz? Pytania w zasadzie retoryczne.

– W moim karneciku tłok – powiedziała – ale wybór do kitu. Tylko nie zrozum, że jest to zaproszenie do tanga. A co u ciebie?

– Daj mi na chwilę Julię – poprosił cicho.

– Julia wyszła, za to ja mam dla ciebie propozycję nie do odrzucenia. Usiądź wygodnie w fotelu i zrób listę spraw czy wydarzeń, o których nigdy nie powiesz swojej dziewczynie. Jeżeli postarasz się o szczerość, sam zobaczysz, jaki to będzie długi rejestr. I nie kop się z koniem, bo nie warto. Pozwól małej rozliczyć się z przeszłością, zanim zaczniesz cenzurować jej myśli, słowa i uczynki. Mówię tak, bo naprawdę dobrze wam życzę.

Pocieszyła mnie czy zdołowała? – zastanawiał się, odkładając słuchawkę. Nie chciał być niczyim cenzorem, chciał mieć obok siebie swoją dawną Julię, tę czułą i uległą, chciał czuwać nad nią, chronić przed złem. Był od niej starszy, bardziej doświadczony, więc co w tym dziwnego, że interesowało go wszystko, co jej dotyczyło? Gdzie tu miejsce na cenzurę? Ale tamtej Julii już nie było. Nawet do telefonu nie chciała podejść. Nie, nie można wciąż tylko przebaczać, bo gotowa pomyśleć, że na niej świat się kończy. Zapragnął jeszcze raz usłyszeć głos Karoliny. Nie ten oficjalny, lecz tamten zapamiętany z przeszłości, drżący namiętnością. Wybrał numer, ale odwiesił słuchawkę, nim ona zdążyła swoją podnieść.

Leszek zachowywał się trochę tak, jak kiedyś Wanda Pasieczko. Nie wiedział, gdzie posadzić Julię, gdzie jej będzie najwygodniej. Wybrała fotel, lecz on zaproponował stylową, piękną kanapę. Sam usiadł obok, zachowując dystans na wyciągnięcie ręki, by dziewczyna nie czuła się skrępowana.

– Co ci podać? Koniak, whisky z lodem, dżin z tonikiem? Wybieraj, biedronko! Gotów jestem rzucić ci do stóp cały barek.

– Aż tak lubisz pijane kobiety? – zdziwiła się Julia.

– Zero trafienia! Prawdziwy dżentelmen lubi sączyć dobry alkohol w towarzystwie pięknej kobiety.

– A ja w towarzystwie dżentelmenów wolę sączyć herbatę – powiedziała.

Nie wypadało mu zrobić nic innego, jak tylko przynieść dwie herbaty – na to właśnie Julia liczyła. Wciąż siedział w pewnym oddaleniu. Wyciągniętą rękę położył na oparciu i gdyby chciała wygodnie usiąść, musiałaby dotknąć głową jego dłoni. Przycupnęła więc na brzegu.

– Naprawdę stęskniłaś się za mną?

– Nie wpadaj w megalomanię. Mam teraz tyle pracy, że na uczucia nie wystarcza mi czasu. Cały sekretariat na mojej głowie, Edyta ma kłopoty, wciąż ktoś nas szarpie, jednym słowem młyn.

– Nie jesteś chyba stworzona do siedzenia w młynie?

– Nie. Do mieszkania kątem u Karoliny też nie. Właśnie dzisiaj przyjechała na dwa dni i gnieciemy się razem. Dlatego, Leszku, wyjeżdżam. Dostałam z Warszawy odpowiedź. Praca w zawodzie, warunki niezłe, koleżanka wynajęła mi pokój, właściwie wszystko już załatwione. Przyszłam, żeby się z tobą pożegnać.

Leszek gwałtownie posmutniał. Coś ważył, nad czymś się zastanawiał i w milczeniu popijał herbatę. Żeby go ostatecznie przekonać o słuszności swojej decyzji, opowiedziała historię porwania. Od tamtej chwili bała się miasta, ludzi, rodzicielskich długów. Mówiła spokojnie, cicho, bez zbędnej emfazy.

– Najgorsze jest to, że z porwania dla okupu nawet policja usiłuje zrobić farsę. Nie dziwię się, prościej jest zwalić winę na nieboszczyka i zamknąć sprawę niż zawracać sobie głowę prawdziwymi sprawcami. Serafin, umierając, powiedział mi, że pracował dla Orzechowicza. Myślisz, że to możliwe, że Konrad kieruje jakąś mafią?

– Orzechowicz?

Leszek wspaniale zagrał zdumienie. Przyjemniaczek z ciebie, Lesiu, zachwyciła się w duchu. Masz talent, chłopie! A utalentowany chłop tłumaczył jej z błyskiem w oku, że nigdy nie uwierzy, by komputerowy jednokomórkowiec, świetny, prawda, ale tylko w swoim fachu, mógł kierować jakąkolwiek mafią. Mówił długo i wyczerpująco. Broniąc tak pięknie Konrada, sam sobie wystawiał świadectwo człowieka wiarygodnego, co Julia z zadowoleniem odnotowała. Wszystko do tej pory szło po jej myśli.

– Twój Orzechowicz, Julio...

– Skąd wiesz, że mój?

– Twój Orzechowicz – zignorował jej pytanie – od początku pracuje dla Bujały. Przyszedł do Budampolexu z określonym zadaniem. Miał zdobyć wiadomości o zadłużeniu firmy, wewnętrznych układach, organizacji i tak dalej. Jako informatyk miał dostęp do wszystkich dokumentów.

– W Budampoleksie? – zdziwiła się całkiem szczerze Julia. – Teraz to już przesadziłeś jak chłop sosnę. Przecież Budampolex dopiero ma mieć system komputerowy.

Roześmiał się, jak z dobrego żartu, i całkiem niechcący przysunął się o kilka centymetrów.

– Kiedyś nie było systemów komputerowych, a firmy jakoś funkcjonowały. Są różne sposoby gromadzenia informacji, Julio. Bujała wiedział, co robi, wybierając Orzechowicza.

– Popatrz, jak pozory mylą! Nie dałabym złotówki za intelekt Bujały, a ty mówisz, że on taki przezorny i cwany?!

Leszek znowu poprawił się na kanapie i jeszcze bardziej zmniejszył dystans dzielący go od Julii. Siedział już całkiem blisko.

– Popatrz, jak pozory mylą! Wyglądasz na taką bystrą dziewczynę, ale nie zauważyłaś, że Orzechowicz najpierw flirtował z Karoliną, potem przerzucił się na ciebie? Wykorzystał swój męski czar, wy zaś w dziobkach donosiłyście mu informacje. Nigdy o tym nie pomyślałaś, prawda?

Nie pomyślała. Wierzyła Konradowi bez zastrzeżeń, tym bardziej że nigdy o nic jej nie wypytywał. Czemu więc, słuchając Leszka, posmutniała nagle?

– Biedna, malutka biedroneczka – powiedział i objął ją po przyjacielsku.

Jego usta błądziły gdzieś w okolicach jej ucha, czuła, że robi się dziwnie bezwolna. Nie chciała szarpać się z nim ani krzyczeć, chciała rozegrać tę partię elegancko, jak dama. Coraz natarczywsze pocałunki sprawiły, że zakręciło jej się w głowie. Leszek delikatnie ujął rękę dziewczyny i próbował skierować w te rejony własnego ciała, o których wolała nie pamiętać. To ją otrzeźwiło. Zdecydowanym ruchem gwałtownie wyswobodziła się z jego objęć, odsunęła na tyle, na ile pozwalał rzeźbiony bok kanapy. Poprawiła bluzkę i sięgnęła po torebkę.

– Nie wychodź, porozmawiajmy – poprosił. – Boisz się, żebym nie okazał się lepszy od niego? Wolisz nie próbować?

– Chwalisz się, nie przymierzając, jak Chochla albo Bujała.

– Nie obrażaj mnie, Julio!

– Nie obrażam! Próbuję ci tylko powiedzieć, że nie jesteś oryginalny.

Odłożyła torebkę na fotel, na znak, że zamierza pozostać jeszcze chwilę i podyskutować. Leszek niespodziewanie się uśmiechnął.

– Wiesz, co mi się w tobie najbardziej podoba? Wyglądasz jak uosobienie niewinności, choć w gruncie rzeczy jesteś kuta na cztery łapki. Taki mały, cudny ścichapęk.

– Ścichapęk to taki odpowiednik pasikonika czy raczej świerszcza?

Roześmiał się cicho. Co jak co, ale poczucie humoru miał rozwinięte, kto wie, czy nie bardziej niż zmysł intrygi. Tak właśnie pomyślała Julia, patrząc w szczere, błękitne oczy Leszka.

– Nie wyjeżdżaj, dziewczyno! Bez ciebie życie straci cały sens – powiedział.

Oględnie, po przyjacielsku, próbował wyperswadować jej ten pomysł i robił to o niebo lepiej niż pani Blendowa. Tłumaczył, że dobra praca, zgodna z kwalifikacjami, jest w zasięgu jej ręki.

– U twojego kuzynka?

– Oj, biedronko, biedronko! Mało wiesz, bo rośniesz. Mówię teraz całkiem serio o moim Budampoleksie.

– Twoim? Ilu właścicieli może mieć jedna nędzna firma? Uważaj, bo jak się pozagryzacie tam na czubku, to władzę przejmie Henia.

– Wyraziłem się nieprecyzyjnie. Mój jest tylko plac, na którym firma stoi. Wymawiam dzierżawę obecnym właścicielom i zakładam własny interes. Proponuję ci stanowisko głównego informatyka i wielkie pieniądze. Mieszkać możesz u mnie, choćby od zaraz.

– Jako wieczna narzeczona, prawda? Pierścionek już mi dałeś.

– Daj spokój, Julio! Gdybyś zajrzała do koperty zaraz po wyjściu ode mnie, wszystko potoczyłoby się inaczej. Żart nie był w najlepszym stylu, przyznaję, ale chciałem cię jakoś ostrzec. Ten dureń Chochla narobił sporo bigosu i wystraszył telefonami pół miasta. Wyprzedziłyście co najmniej tuzin facetów, którzy chcieli z nim pogadać albo go uciszyć. Bujała też posłał tam swoich goryli. Serafin znalazł pierścionek i przyniósł do mnie. Oto cała historia.

– Chcesz powiedzieć, że Serafin pomylił pracodawców?

– Nikogo nie pomylił. Do nauki ten facet głowy nie miał, lecz wdzięczność potrafił okazywać. Tak się złożyło, że całkiem niechcący pomogłem mu wystartować w ciemnej strefie. Tu, w tym mieszkaniu, poznał Grześka Bujałę. Mam ci tłumaczyć dalej? Mnie traktował jak dobrego kumpla, co w jego wydaniu nie było groźne, w tobie się podkochiwał, co też nie było groźne. Geniuszem trudno go nazwać, jednak czasem myślał. Nie chciał, żebyś miała kłopoty przez ten pierścionek, więc odrobinę sprzeniewierzył się bossowi.

Julia patrzyła i słuchała uważnie. Słowa Leszka nie rozwiewały jej wątpliwości. Co to znaczyło, że Serafin nie chciał jej narażać na kłopoty? Kilka dni później uczestniczył w porwaniu i już nie miał żadnych oporów? Kręcisz, Lesiu, myślała, kręcisz jak nic.

– Wierzysz mi, biedronko? – Zaglądał jej w oczy, jednak nie ruszał się, żeby znowu dziewczyny nie spłoszyć.

– Wierzę ci, oczywiście.

– To powiedz mi, po jakie licho polazłyście do Chochli tamtego wieczoru?

– Nie do Chochli, tylko do jego sąsiadki, do takiej poetki, Wandy Pasieczko. Znasz może? Jak nie, to nie gadaj. Archiwum Chochli trafiło w nasze ręce przez żywy cud – powiedziała obojętnie Julia. – Spaliłeś ten cały szajs, tak jak obiecałeś?

– Mam ci dać na dowód urnę z popiołem?

– Poproszę. I moją torbę też poproszę.

– Za moment. Nie powiedziałaś jeszcze, co sądzisz o propozycji pracy.

– Nic, Leszku. Po prostu nie wierzę, że taki dokument istnieje.

– Dobrze. Mów, co dostanę, jak ci go pokażę?

– Hm! – Uśmiechnęła się tajemniczo. – Najpierw pokaż, potem będziemy pertraktować.

Spojrzał na nią przeciągle i wyszedł do gabinetu. W wielkim lustrze w przedpokoju dostrzegła, że zdjął ze ściany środkowy obraz.

– Leszku, czy mogę skorzystać z łazienki? – krzyknęła.

– Jasne, wcale nie pytaj!

Sięgnęła po torebkę. Z wieszaka po cichutku zdjęła marynarkę i bezszelestnie otworzyła drzwi wejściowe. Zobaczyła, co chciała zobaczyć. Zostać nie chciała, więc uciekła. Do placu Wolności biegła jak szalona, przeklinając swoją słabą kondycję. Wskoczyła do taksówki i kazała się wieźć na Budowlanych. Tak się wyspecjalizuję w uciekaniu facetom spod ręki, pomyślała, że do księgi Guinnessa trafię.

Pierwsza część planu została zrealizowana idealnie. Drugi krok należał do Karoliny. Julia pucowała się w łazience, kiedy zadzwonił Leszek.

– Nie ma Julii – tłumaczyła Karolina. – Nie wiem, kiedy wróci, ale wróci na pewno, bo teraz tu mieszka.

Pogadali po przyjacielsku i Wydroń przyjął zaproszenie na następne popołudnie. Upewnił się tylko, czy dzisiejsza uciekinierka będzie.

– A gdzie ja będę, jak mnie nie będzie? – zapytała Julia, wychodząc roześmiana z łazienki, w ręczniku na głowie, rozgrzana kapielą i wyjątkowo ponętna.

– Wcale się nie dziwię tym facetom, że wydzwaniają tu do ciebie, aż żal mi serce ściska – powiedziała Karolina.

– Nie gadaj! Obydwu odziedziczyłam po tobie. Teraz jeszcze mieszkanie doszło i można powiedzieć, że jestem twoim cieniem.

– To weź jeszcze Mikulę. Zamożny, chwilowo samotny i wewnętrznie rozdarty. Biedny taki, malutki, kłopotu nie sprawi.

– Nie chcę. Bujały też nie chcę.

– O, Bujała nigdy nie był mój. Zresztą, prawdę mówiąc, Leszek też nie. Mam na myśli sens zaimka „mój".

Konrad powoli oswajał się z myślą, że znowu jest sam. Miał za sobą niejedno rozstanie z kobietą, nigdy jednak nie odczuwał aż takiego żalu. „Dziewczyny są po to, żeby je zmieniać”, mawiał jeden ze starych przyjaciół. Cytowali sobie tę maksymę w miarę potrzeb i nie cierpieli przesadnie, gdy kolejne panny znikały z horyzontu. Konrad uważał się za człowieka stałego, natomiast niestałość przypisywał wyłącznie kobietom. Babki same zmieniały się u jego boku, chociaż prawdę mówiąc, nie było ich aż tak znów wiele. Nie zatrzymywał żadnej, bo wciąż szukał tej najwłaściwszej. Przez parę chwil miał wrażenie, że to będzie Karolina. Szalony romans skończył się jednak szybciej, niż zaczął, i wtedy pojawiła się Julia. Julię chciał zatrzymać, gotów był nawet o nią walczyć, tylko nie miał z kim. Odrzuciła miłość, uciekła, przedkładając własne sprawy nad ich wspólne. W niej siedział diabełek, który uniemożliwiał porozumienie. Konrad całkiem serio podejrzewał, że to Karolina mąci Julii w głowie. Przez całe popołudnie bił się z myślami, wzdychał, narzekał na baby i nie umiał znaleźć sobie sensownego zajęcia. Mam pecha, myślał, od dzieciaka miałem pecha. Przypomniał sobie pierwszy i jedyny pobyt w sanatorium, gdzie po wypadku zawieźli go Orscy. Był wtedy jak mały dzikus: czarny, krnąbrny i źle wychowany. Dziewczynami gardził i uważał, że są całkiem niepotrzebne na tym świecie. Zmienił zdanie, kiedy poznał Joasię. Samo imię było piękne i pachniało fiołkami albo perfumerią z ulicy 3 Maja. Joasia nie przypominała jego sióstr i dziewczyn z okolicznych podwórek. Włosy prawie białe, oczy błękitne i głos jak dzwoneczek. Wydawała się najpiękniejsza wśród dziewczynek. Nie wiadomo czemu polubiła Konrada i obiecała, że nauczy go grać w szachy. Konrad nigdy w życiu do żadnej nauki tak się nie rwał jak do tych szachów. Był śmiertelnie zakochany i pewnie dlatego. Mieli zacząć uczyć się w sobotę, a w piątek po Joasię przyjechali rodzice. Zabierali ją w połowie turnusu i Konrad wpadł w czarną rozpacz. „Napiszesz do mnie? Tu jest mój adres. Napisz, Raduś, dobrze?” – prosiła i wtykała mu do ręki karteczkę. Miał powiedzieć, że w ogóle nie umie pisać? Że nie wie, jak wygląda list i jak się go wysyła? Zacisnął oczy, żeby nie płakać, i kiwnął głową. Ledwie Joasia wyszła z pokoju, zjadł kartkę z adresem. Zjadł z rozpaczy i żalu za uciekającym szczęściem. Raz w życiu dostał coś najpiękniejszego i odebrano mu to, zanim zdążył się ucieszyć. Długo wspominał Joasię. Nawet jako dorosły mężczyzna też czasem o niej myślał. Nie zmieniała się wcale. Miała białe włosy i błękitne oczy, może tylko była ciut wyższa. Pomyślał, że historia się powtarza. I zaraz potem, że może warto porozmawiać z Julią, jednak, zniechęcony, machnął ręką.

Rano poszedł na rozmowę z szefową. W sekretariacie było kilka osób, więc nic nie mówiąc, wskazał ręką na drzwi gabinetu. Julia skinęła głową, co znaczyło, że szefowa jest wolna. Wszedł. Zamknął drzwi. Żal mu się zrobiło smutnych oczu i wesołych piegów, tak bardzo żal, że zdecydował się złożyć wymówienie.

Karolina wróciła z przesłuchania niezadowolona z siebie. Była pewna, że będą ją pytać o telefon komórkowy, który w pośpiechu zostawiła w mieszkaniu Chochli. Tymczasem albo telefon zwinął ktoś inny, albo policja nie ustaliła jeszcze właściciela, w każdym razie wszystkie pytania krążyły wokół wizyty u Wandy Pasieczko. Czy znała wcześniej? Nie znała. Po co poszła? Bo się umówiła. Z kim? Karolina z zawodu była prawnikiem i z paru rzeczy zdawała sobie sprawę. Telefon, jeżeli nawet do tej pory nie wpadł w ręce policji, mógł wpaść w każdej chwili, a był dowodem obciążającym, podobnie jak rozmowa z Chochlą, zarejestrowana na automatycznej sekretarce. Nagrania prawdopodobnie miał Leszek, kto jednak mógł przewidzieć, jaki z nich zrobi użytek? Zeznania magister Cierniak rzuciły całkiem nowe światło na śledztwo w sprawie zamordowania Marcina Chochli. Była pierwszym i bodaj jedynym świadkiem, który przyznał, że w tragicznym dniu odwiedził denata. Sprostowała oczywiście, że denat w chwili odwiedzin był jak najbardziej żywy. W jakim celu odwiedziła? Żeby pogadać, zobaczyć, jak mieszka i co robi facet, który dobrowolnie usunął się w cień. Byli umówieni telefonicznie. I co zobaczyła? Nic specjalnego. Bałagan. Jak się zachowywał denat? Nie przypuszczał, że za parę godzin będzie denatem, więc zachowywał się raczej normalnie. Pogadali chwilę i zaraz potem wstąpiła do Wandy Pasieczko, gdzie miała na nią czekać pani Julia Blenda. Przyjaciółki jeszcze nie było, więc posłuchała wierszy. „Jaśnieją dachy i ulice, lśnią w słońcu kamienice Maślanej, Tumskiej"... ble, ble, ble. Tego ble, ble już im nie dopowiedziała.

– Przykro mi, Juleczko! Bądź przygotowana, że i ciebie wezwą.

– Ależ jestem przygotowana – zapewniła Julia. – Pierwszego dnia niczego nie dotykałam, żeby się nie przylepić. Jedynie pierścionek miałam w ręku. Ten sam, który teraz leży na policji, dopięty do innej sprawy. Drugiego dnia operowałam w gumowych rękawiczkach. Przyznam się do spotkania z Chochlą w sklepie i do znajomości z Wandą. Weź na logikę: dlaczego mają posądzać nas o morderstwo, jeżeli wokół kręciło się tylu facetów? Mikula z jakimś typem, Serafin z gorylami Bujały, Orzechowicz i inni. Oprócz nich Edyta z Henią.

– Na logikę lepiej niczego nie brać, to raz, a dwa, kto o tych ludziach wie?

Julia wzruszyła ramionami. Nie lubiła martwić się na zapas. Kłopoty to mają do siebie, że czy się człowiek martwi czy nie, i tak spadają na łeb, kiedy same chcą. I wtedy trzeba myśleć, jak się z nich wykaraskać. A one właśnie, wspólnie z Karoliną, pakowały się w kolejne tarapaty, z których miały zamiar wyjść obronną ręką. Plan był dziecinnie prosty i wcale nie taki nowy. Zmieniły się tylko założenia. Teoretycznie Julia jechała do Warszawy, natomiast fizycznie miała sterczeć na klatce schodowej piętro wyżej i czekać, aż Karolina uwolni kieszeń Leszka od kluczy.

– A jeżeli on okaże się wierny i nie ulegnie twoim namowom? – spytała z niepokojem Julia.

Karolina wyglądała na zdegustowaną. Po pierwsze, żaden mężczyzna nie miał prawa oprzeć się jej wdziękom, po drugie, nie można mierzyć wierności mężczyzny kobiecą miarką. Mężczyzna nie zdradza, on tylko ulega grze hormonów. Poprawi krawat, przyczesze włosy i dalej uważa się za wiernego. Dla Julii była to całkiem nowa lekcja.

Leszek przyszedł punktualnie o osiemnastej. Niecałe dwadzieścia minut później klucze leżały pod wycieraczką. Julia złapała taksówkę i dotarła na Świętego Antoniego w rekordowym tempie. Bez przeszkód sforsowała drzwi. Lęk ogarnął ją dopiero wówczas, gdy znalazła się sama w pustym mieszkaniu. Mniej bała się u Chochli, bo tam czuła wsparcie Karoliny, tu była zdana wyłącznie na siebie. Pierwsze rozczarowanie spotkało ją w gabinecie. Za środkowym obrazem była niewielka skrytka z maleńkim pokrętłem zamiast klamki. Stanęła zrezygnowana i patrzyła jak sroka w gnat. Nie znała szyfru, więc inaczej patrzeć nie mogła. Ugryźć nie ugryzę, pilnikiem do paznokci nie podważę, myślała zgnębiona. Nie odchodziła jednak. Zastanowiły ją małe rozmiary skrytki. Jakieś pieniądze, jakieś najważniejsze dokumenty mogły się tam zmieścić, ale nie archiwum Chochli. Same koperty po wywaleniu pudełek od butów też by nie wlazły.

– On to musi trzymać w innym miejscu – powiedziała i wystraszyła się własnego głosu.

Powiesiła obraz na miejsce i zaczęła się rozglądać. Na brzegu biurka, w foliowej koszulce, leżał dokument, a na nim małe etui. Spojrzała i jęknęła. To był akt darowizny gruntów przy ulicy... i tak dalej. Wyjął to wczoraj, żeby jej pokazać, i potem nie schował. Zanim zdążyła pomyśleć, dokument już siedział w torbie. Z czystej ciekawości zerknęła do pudełeczka i z wrażenia cichutko gwizdnęła. Gamoń z tego Leszka, żeby tak rozrzucać rodzinne klejnoty, pomyślała. Niewielki brylant cudownie zaiskrzył w promieniach zachodzącego słońca. Doceniła starą robotę i niepowtarzalną urodę pierścionka. Delikatnie zamknęła pudełeczko i odstawiła na biurko.

Wychodziła właśnie z gabinetu, kiedy zadzwonił telefon. Nie przypuszczała, że dźwięk zwykłego telefonu może być tak denerwujący. Serce jej waliło jeszcze długo potem.

Szafa w przedpokoju, pomyślała. Wielka szafa z suwanymi drzwiami. Odsunęła właśnie ostatnie drzwi, zobaczyła na podłodze swoją torbę i wyciągnęła po nią rękę, kiedy zazgrzytał klucz w drzwiach wejściowych. Niewiele myśląc, wsunęła się między garnitury Leszka. Przez szparkę obserwowała przedpokój. Jeśli to on, myślała ze strachem, to wybiła moja ostatnia godzina.

W szparce pojawiła się okrągła postać Heni Luty. Henia w domu Leszka?! Pomoc gospodarcza najwyraźniej czuła się jak u siebie. Ściągnęła sweter i po chwili wahania położyła na krześle. Widać nie miała zamiaru dłużej zabawić, więc nie chowała okrycia do szafy. Julia prawie odetchnęła.

Henia kręciła się po mieszkaniu.

– Co tu sprzątać? – pytała samą siebie. – On nawet nabałaganić nie potrafi. E, dzisiaj sobie...

Zadzwonił telefon, więc przeszła do gabinetu.

– Pan Grzegorz? Okna przecierałam Lesiowi, tak na koniec, żeby na dłużej starczyło. Nie wiem. Jak wróci, to będzie. Napiszę mu na kartce. Mam pisać, że pan zadzwoni?... To po co pisać?!... No dobra. Co?... Niech pan tak nie mówi, mało pomogłam? Zrobiłam więcej, niż do mnie należało.

Rozmowa zaczynała być na tyle interesująca, że Julia powiększyła szparkę w drzwiach i z trudem się powstrzymała, by nie wystawić całej głowy. Bujała był gadatliwy, lecz Henia go przewyższała. Wyglądało na to, że nie jest to pierwsza rozmowa tych dwojga o nowym zakładzie bioenergoterapii. Wyremontowany lokal czekał na materace, kozetkę, jakieś biurko, jednym słowem na wyposażenie, Henia zaś czekała na pieniądze od Bujały. Przed oficjalnym otwarciem zamierzała uroczyście poświęcić gabinet i zorganizować prawdziwe medytacje. Bez mebli nie dało się tego zrobić. Ze trzy razy kończyli rozmowę, a Henia jeszcze wracała do pieniędzy i do swoich umiejętności.

– Energii mam pod dostatkiem, skończyłam kilka kursów, najwyższa pora, żeby pomyśleć o innych. Z moimi umiejętnościami szkoda mnie do mycia szklanek, nie uważa pan? Bioenergoterapia to teraz rzemiosło. Co pan nie wierzy? To niech pan sprawdzi, tak nas zaliczyli. Na rzemiosło musi pan znaleźć pieniądze. Może nawet ubezpieczę się u was.

Wreszcie odłożyła słuchawkę. Wydawała się mocno niezadowolona, tak mocno, że pozwoliła sobie na głośny monolog.

– Głupi ten Bujała czy co? – spytała i odpowiedziała sama sobie, że głupi, pazerny i Leszkowi do pięt nie dorasta.

Stała i stała w przedpokoju, miotana wewnętrzną walką: sprzątać czy wyjść. Julia błagała ją w myślach, żeby sobie odpuściła myślenie i poszła, bo ona nie zdąży wrócić z Warszawy. Nie powinna za bardzo się spóźniać, żeby Leszek nie nabrał podejrzeń. W końcu Henia zaczęła się zbierać. Powoli włożyła sweter, pozapinała wszystkie guziki i dopiero wtedy trzasnęła drzwiami.

Julia miała mokre od potu plecy. Z wrażenia nawet nie zajrzała do torby. Ortalionową włożyła do dżinsowej, z którą przyszła, i opuściła mieszkanie cichutko niczym duch.

Karolina otworzyła drzwi cała w uśmiechach. Kazała Julii zgadywać, kto je odwiedził. Zgrabnym ruchem wsunęła klucze do kieszeni Leszkowego płaszcza i dalej chciała się bawić w zagadki.

– Oj Boże, jaka jestem zlatana! – jęknęła Julia. – Kocham Warszawę, ale moje nogi nie wytrzymują tamtejszych odległości. Królestwo za kapcie i szklankę herbaty. Załatwiłam wszystko, nawet z nawiązką. – Puściła oko do Karoliny. – Mój wyjazd przesuwa się o dwa tygodnie.

Wsunęła torbę do ciasnej szafy i dopiero wtedy zajrzała do pokoju.

– Leszek nas mianowicie odwiedził, zgadłam? – krzyknęła bardzo radośnie.

Witając się z nim, uciekła z oczami w bok. Chciał buzi, więc nadstawiła policzek. Odwrócił jej głowę i pocałował w usta. W czasie, kiedy Karolina robiła herbatę, szeptał do ucha, że jest nieznośna, kochana i że porywa ją ze sobą do domu.

– Oszalałeś mianowicie czy na rozum ci padło? – spytała.

– Daj mi odetchnąć od kłopotka, dobrze?

– Dlaczego nie lubisz Bujały?

– Powiedz, że pojedziesz ze mną, no powiedz! Jeżeli się wahasz, coś ci poradzę...

– Daj spokój! Najlepsze rady daję sobie sama, tylko nigdy z nich nie korzystam – rzuciła lekko, roześmiała się psotnie i umknęła do kuchni.

– Pachniesz Leszkiem – szepnęła Karolina.

– Wisiałam u niego w szafie – odszepnęła Julia. – Co on taki namiętny? Oparł ci się czy co?

Karolina spojrzała na nią z wielkim politowaniem. Nie mogły chichotać w kuchni, kiedy on siedział w pokoju. Wniosły herbatę i zaczęła się miła pogawędka o niczym, po której Leszek pojechał na Świętego Antoniego sam.

Grzegorz Bujała innymi przejmował się tylko wówczas, gdy byli mu potrzebni. Konrada uważał za bezcenny skarb, dlatego wybaczał mu wiele. Kiedy więc ten po długim ignorowaniu telefonów bossa wreszcie przyjechał do Michelina, usłyszał w progu krótkie:

– Nie świruj, jesteśmy mianowicie kwita!

– Nie jesteśmy. Dostałeś, bo ci się należało za obrazę kobiety! – zdenerwował się Konrad. – I nie powinieneś nasyłać na mnie płatnych kozaków.

– Musiałem. Nikt bezkarnie nie wali bossa w mordę. Mogłem ci sam oddać, ale bałem się o swoje ręce.

– Pianista, cholera, się znalazł – warknął Orzechowicz. Po pierwszym wybuchu zdążył już ochłonąć i nie zamierzał przeciągać sporu. Dobrze wiedział, że Bujała jest podszyty tchórzem i siłę czerpie z mięśni ochroniarzy. Mit bossa tworzą jego ludzie, boss musi tylko wiedzieć, jak ich utrzymać przy sobie. Konrad nie dawał się trzymać i nie chciał uchodzić za człowieka Bujały.

– Pianista? A żebyś wiedział! Pochodzę mianowicie z muzykalnej rodziny. Moja ciotka była...

– To ty sobie powspominaj, a do mnie zadzwoń, jak przyjdzie czas na interesy – przerwał mu Konrad i podniósł się z fotela.

Bujała przytrzymał go za rękę.

– Siad na zad! Aleś ty we wrzątku kąpany, słowo daję. Trzymaj łapy przy sobie, to ci mianowicie coś powiem. Nie mam coś szczęścia do tej twojej Julki, jednak to małe piwo w porównaniu z twoim nieszczęściem. Jakbyś poszedł do Wydronia, kiedy cię prosiłem, sam byś się przekonał.

– Ty prosiłeś?

– Dobra, za długo się znamy, żeby łapać się mianowicie za słowa. Ja swoje zobaczyłem. Co do łóżka się nie wypowiadam. Jestem pewien, że mój kuzynek nasłał mi tę małą na przeszpiegi. Po co innego przyszłaby wtedy do mojego biura?

– A po co przyszła?
– Tego mianowicie, kurwa, nie wiem. Lesiu zhardział ostatnio, więc może im się wydaje, że coś wiedzą? Pożyjemy, zobaczymy i utniemy łeb wężowi, jak to się mówi. Mnie tam nie interesuje, kto z kim śpi, tylko jakie ma długi.
– Chyba jakiego ma długiego! – nie wytrzymał Konrad.
Bujała hałaśliwym śmiechem pokrył rozdrażnienie. Był uczulony na wchodzenie mu w słowa, bo gubił wątek i się rozpraszał.
– To akurat nie moja broszka. Jak sobie chcę pooglądać, to mianowicie mam co – wyjaśnił nie bez dumy.
Konrad zlekceważył przechwałki.
– O jakich dłużnikach mówisz, swoich?
– Ogłupłeś czy co? Swoich znam co do jednego. Ja chcę mieć rejestr długów na miasto, potem województwo, a jak się da, to i na kraj. Czujesz, co można osiągnąć, mając takie informacje w garści? Jakie to daje możliwości?
– Czuję, tylko skąd niby mam wziąć dane?
– To już zmartwienie twojej głowy. Stwórz odpowiedni program... zresztą, fachowca nie będę uczył. Otwierasz firmę, a ja ci daję zamówienie. O czym więcej gadać? Chyba tylko o cenie. Zależy mi i skąpy nie będę.
Orzechowicz wyjeżdżał od Bujały przekonany, że jeszcze moment, a głowa pęknie mu na tysiąc kawałków. Ochłonął nieco, kiedy minął tereny zabudowane. Po obu stronach drogi pojawił się las.
– O czym on chrzanił? – zastanawiał się głośno. Próbował przypomnieć sobie wszystko, co Bujała mówił o Julii. Ona i Wydroń? Bzdura! Zaraz... W gębę dałem Bujale tego wieczoru, kiedy mała uciekła. Czyli co? Prosto ode mnie pojechała do Wydronia, żeby się wyżalić? A może po instrukcje pojechała?
Wielkie rozżalenie jest wrogiem chłodnej logiki. Konrad zapomniał o tym, pogrążając się w niewesołych wspomnieniach. Nim minął las i wjechał w ulicę Kaliską, zadręczał się już tylko jednym pytaniem: Julia i Wydroń? Cholera, kto by pomyślał!

– Nie mogłaś gwizdnąć czegoś cenniejszego, musiałaś gumowce brać na pamiątkę? – zgorszyła się Karolina.
– Phi! Rozumna to ja będę dopiero na starość – obiecała Julia.
Stały obie nad otwartą torbą i patrzyły na zielone, solidnie zabłocone buty gumowe, dobre na ryby lub do pracy w ogrodzie. Takie buty

można bez problemu kupić na rynku, nie trzeba ich kraść w zaprzyjaźnionym domu. Poza tymi gumowcami w torbach było tylko kilka torfowych doniczek, które w dotyku przypominały karton.

– Macałam, naprawdę macałam – zapewniała Julia. – Te doniczki mnie zmyliły.

Gdyby nie akt darowizny gruntów, zabrany z biurka, wielki plan skończyłby się wielkim fiaskiem. Archiwum Marcina Chochli pozostało w rękach magistra Leszka Wydronia. Podobnie jak kaseta z automatycznej sekretarki i zapewne sporo jeszcze materiałów, o których ani Julia, ani Karolina nawet nie miały pojęcia.

– I pomyśleć, że oddawałam za tego faceta głowę – powiedziała zamyślona Karolina. – Drugą, co prawda, której nie mam, zawsze to jednak przykrość i wpadka.

– Zapakuję jutro buciska i poproszę kogoś, żeby zaniósł na pocztę – powiedziała Julia.

– Najlepiej Henię – mruknęła Karolina.

Henia stanowiła dla obu dziewczyn wielkie zaskoczenie. Kiedy teraz przypominały sobie pewne drobiazgi z przeszłości, utwierdzały się w przekonaniu, że pomoc gospodarcza od początku pracowała dla Leszka. Mogło go nie być w pracy trzy tygodnie, a wiedział doskonale o wszystkim, co działo się w firmie.

– I co? – spytała Julia. – Mogłaby Henia zagrać Hamleta?

– Ofelię, wiedźmę, Bonda, wszystko, co chcesz – przyznała Karolina. – Ale informowała też Mikulę... choć może nie zawsze prawidłowo. Pracowała dla dwóch wywiadów równocześnie, kto wie nawet, czy nie dla czterech, po wliczeniu Edyty i Bujały.

Akt darowizny Karolina uznała za dziwny. Wszystko w zasadzie było, co powinno być, ale były też pytania. Dlaczego niby dziewięćdziesięcioletnia pani Honorata Zajączkowska, zamieszkała ostatnio w Barcinie, przekazała swoją ziemię Leszkowi Wydroniowi z Włocławka, co potwierdził notariusz z Płocka? Pan Wydroń nie był powinowatym pani Zajączkowskiej, co również zostało w akcie ujęte.

– Mnie to pachnie grubym świństwem. Albo tylko świństewkiem, jeżeli grzecznie kobietę namówił – powiedziała Karolina.

Położyły się spać po północy. Stratę archiwum przebolały, bo innego wyjścia nie było. O wiele boleśniejsza wydawała się strata przyjaciela. Stuknięty entomolog, dowcipny i uroczy w każdym calu Leszek Wydroń objawił się nagle jako demon zła, facet pokroju Bujały, czyli z gruntu paskudny, choć na oko wciąż bardzo sympatyczny.

– Jaki on jest... – Julia zawiesiła głos, spojrzała na Karolinę i obie zaczęły chichotać.

– Fiu, fiu! Jedno ci powiem: na miejscu żony nie uciekłabym od niego, chyba że... że ze strachu.

Karolina wyjeżdżała rano. W pośpiechu usiadły do wspólnego śniadania. Zadzwonisz, zadzwonię, odwiedzisz, odwiedzę, patrzyły na siebie i każda już była w swoim świecie. Karolina w Toruniu, Julia zawieszona między niebem i ziemią.

– Oj, Juleczko, świetnie było, niestety przeszło, minęło jak grypa. Zostały powikłania. Teraz będziemy się spotykać na przesłuchaniach, co? I pamiętaj, gdyby coś, oddam za ciebie głowę, tę jedną jedyną, i wszystko, co będzie trzeba.

Obie były wzruszone. Ich przyjaźń zaczęła się od usadzenia Chochli, lecz wcale nie musiała skończyć się wraz z jego zejściem. Zadzwonisz? Zadzwonię. Odwiedzisz? Jasne, jak tylko się wyrwę.

Karolina zadzwoniła w południe, o wiele wcześniej, niż Julia mogła się spodziewać. Miała do zakomunikowania rewelację: w biurze ewidencji ludności w Barcinie dowiedziała się, że Honorata Zajączkowska zmarła przed rokiem, czyli musiała podarować ziemię Leszkowi Wydroniowi już po swojej śmierci.

Przed piętnastą Julia weszła do szefowej, żeby spisać ustalenia na dzień następny. Chciała też porozmawiać o swoich prywatnych sprawach. Z pocztą przyszedł list z Warszawy od Małgorzaty. Uśmiechnęła się przelotnie, bo wychodziło na to, że kłamiąc Leszkowi o swoim wyjeździe, wcale tak bardzo nie nałgała. *Jeżeli jesteś zainteresowana pracą, składaj ofertę natychmiast. Rozmawiałam z Golakiem, poczeka trzy dni. Mały pokój, klitkę właściwie, też możesz mieć. Samotnym jest dużo łatwiej* – pisała.

– Samotnym wcale nie jest łatwiej. – Edyta pokręciła głową. Nie precyzowała, co ma na myśli: mieszkanie czy życie. Patrzyła na Julię smutnymi, zmęczonymi oczami.

– Gdyby nie ta cholerna niepewność, co się z nami stanie, też miałabym dla ciebie propozycję: dział informatyki.

– U Orzechowicza?

Edyta znowu pokręciła głową i spojrzała na dziewczynę bardzo uważnie. Wyjęła z szuflady wypowiedzenie, które Konrad złożył dzień wcześniej. Julia mruknęła, że tak, że coś jej się o uszy obiło, że prywatna firma, i speszona zamilkła. To nie była dobra wiadomość. Sprawa musiała się wykluć w ostatnich godzinach i kto wie, czy nie miała związku właśnie z nią.

– Zdecydowałam się na wyjazd – powiedziała spokojnie. – A pani nie musi już bać się Wydronia. Miałam w ręku ten dokument, to nic poważnego, zwykła podróba dla hecy. Henia mogła się nabrać i o to pewnie chodziło.

Julia za bardzo bała się Wydronia, by dawać Edycie do ręki dokument, który osobiście ukradła. Niewiele mogła powiedzieć poza tym, że darczyńca zmarł przed spisaniem aktu darowizny. Tonący chwyta się brzytwy i Edyta również uchwyciła się słów Julii. Ożyła w oczach.

– Jeżeli jest, jak mówisz, to usilnie cię namawiam do zostania w Budampoleksie – powiedziała. – Orzechowicz zaproponował swojego następcę, bardzo dobrego informatyka, myślę, że się dogadacie.

– Pani Edyto, gdybym miała zostać, to interesuje mnie wyłącznie stanowisko kierownika działu – powiedziała Julia.

– Przecież ty nawet nie masz stażu?!

– Przepraszam, a dlaczego nie mam stażu? Pani wie i ja wiem, jak było. Jestem ambitna, szybko się uczę, a poza tym to ja popołudniami opracowywałam z inżynierem Orzechowiczem plan komputeryzacji firmy. Mam go w jednym palcu. Proszę spytać.

Wyszła z gabinetu szefowej z podniesioną głową i z obietnicą, że od nowego miesiąca obejmie dział informatyki. Edyta, w przeciwieństwie do Mikuli, bardzo dbała o wiarygodność i dotrzymywała słowa, więc Julia czuła się tak, jakby etat i i tysiąc osiemset złotych na początek miała już w kieszeni. Była bardzo dumna, choć wciąż jeszcze niezdecydowana: zostać czy wyjechać. Całą noc miała na myślenie.

Warszawa ciągnęła ją od dawna, bo gwarantowała pełną samodzielność z dala od rodziców. Wiedziała jednak, że i na awans, i na znośne mieszkanie będzie musiała poczekać. Duże miasto, duża konkurencja – nawet gdyby się bardzo starała, wcześniej niż za kilka lat nie stanie na nogi, chyba że poślubi worek z pieniędzmi, do którego będzie uwiązany jakiś pokurcz. Uśmiechnęła się na wspomnienie Karoliny i jej planów.

Budampolex to już było coś. Praca na kierowniczym stanowisku, więc siłą rzeczy pieniądze większe niż te w Warszawie, do tego Włocławek gwarantował tańsze życie i kawalerkę po przyjaciółce. Sporo względów przemawiało za pozostaniem. Konrad. Od dwóch dni, od chwili, gdy powiedział, że jest wolna, traktował ją jak powietrze. Nie chciał słuchać, nie chciał rozmawiać, nie miał jej nic do powiedzenia. Z każdą godziną czuła się coraz bardziej winna. Decydując się na pozostanie, myślała również o tym, że z ulicy Budowlanych na Toruńską jest bliżej niż z Warszawy do Włocławka. Jeszcze się łudziła, że on przemówi.

W firmie zaszły wielkie zmiany. Mikula ostatecznie zrezygnował ze stanowiska dyrektora i wyjechał z miasta. Edyta wreszcie zrobiła to, na co Mikulowie nie potrafili się zdobyć: ograniczyła administrację. Stanowisko dyrektora powierzyła młodemu inżynierowi po praktyce w Anglii. Dział informatyki objęła Julia, dwuosobową komórkę organizacyjno-prawną Grażyna Orska. Miejsce pięknej Karoliny zajął chudziutki prawnik bez cienia poczucia humoru.

– I jak ci się podoba? – spytała Edyta, gdy Julia po raz ostatni podała kawę do gabinetu.

– Wygląda jak zasuszony kleszcz.

– Pytam o reorganizację, nie o magistra Portulaka.

– Za naszych czasów było weselej.

– Od rozrywki jest teatr i kino, tu trzeba pracować!

– I pomyśleć, że Mikula nie uznawał kobiet na stanowiskach kierowniczych – zauważyła Julia z filozoficzną zadumą.

– Mylił się i dlatego musiał odejść.

Na parkingu przed blokiem sterczała Żaneta. Nie miała już na sobie męskiej marynarki, tylko odblaskową żółtą bluzkę. Konrad próbował przemknąć się niepostrzeżenie. Doskoczyła do niego, ledwie wysiadł z samochodu.

– Nie przychodziłam, jak kazałeś, teraz mam interes – powiedziała bez zbędnych wstępów. – Mały choruje, nie mam na lekarstwa. Musisz mi pomóc.

Zwykle jęczała, zawodziła, tym razem mówiła twardo, z determinacją.

– Pieniędzy nie dam. Przynieś recepty, to wykupię lekarstwa.

Skinęła głową i sięgnęła do zniszczonej torebki. Podała mu cztery druczki.

– Siadaj! – Otworzył drzwi samochodu.

– Masz większy wóz niż ta twoja panna, dobrze mówię? – zagadnęła, kiedy ruszyli. W jej głosie usłyszał coś, co przypominało dumę.

– Która panna?

– A ile ich masz?

Puścił żart mimo uszu. Jak najprędzej chciał mieć z głowy zakupy. W aptece zapłacił prawie sto pięćdziesiąt złotych. To rzeczywiście była kwota nie na kieszeń Żanety. Podał siostrze reklamówkę z lekarstwami.

– Ty, Radek, nie pij tyle – powiedziała nieoczekiwanie. – Jak już się wybiłeś na wielki świat, to nie pij. My z nią ledwie cię do domu wtaszczyłyśmy. Ona mała, ale silna. Nawet fajna babka.

Zaczął wypytywać, kto, co i kiedy, bo dawno już zapomniał o koniakowym wyczynie. Żaneta, chcąc odwdzięczyć się za leki, opowiedziała obrazowo, jak wspólnie z Julią transportowały go pijanego na górę.

– Odwiozła mnie potem i nawet weszła na chwilę do chałupy. Wiesz, tam się nic nie zmieniło.

Znowu nie rozumiał, kto wszedł i po co. Czuł tylko pulsowanie w skroniach i narastającą złość. Nie wiedział, czy bardziej zdenerwowała go Julia swoim wścibstwem, czy Żaneta swoją głupotą.

– Wcale jej nie ciągłam, sama chciała – powiedziała, żeby nie drażnić Konrada. – A potem była jeszcze u nas jej matka. Cyrulik myślał, że to jakaś pinda z opieki albo z pomocy i nagadał tyle, że łeb mały.

Bez słowa zostawił Żanetę na parkingu przed apteką i odjechał.

Kawalerka po Karolinie stała się nowym mieszkaniem Julii. Dawniej w domu cieszyła się z chwil spędzanych samotnie, u Konrada cieszyła się z jego obecności, w pustej kawalerce dostawała nerwicy. Znowu nie miała nic z wyjątkiem szczotki do zębów i bielizny na zmianę. Karolina zostawiła jej parę groszy na początek. Przy oszczędnym wydawaniu wystarczyłoby do wypłaty, ale Julia nie umiała żyć oszczędnie. W sklepie jak zwykle upchała w koszyku mnóstwo pyszności i potem musiała roznosić na dawne miejsca sardynki, serki pleśniowe, luksusową kawę. Wyszła z trzema bułkami i słoiczkiem pasztetu. To były te złe strony samodzielności. A dobre? Miała dużo wolnego czasu, z którym jednak nie było co robić w obcym mieszkaniu bez jednej książki. Z konieczności więc rozpamiętywała dzieje swojej miłości, pięknej, krótkiej i tak głupio przerwanej. Cierpiała. Początkowo szukała winy w sobie, z czasem zaczęła się skłaniać ku myśli, że uczucie było jedynie wytworem jej wyobraźni. Wyreżyserowała sobie spektakl, zagrała główną rolę, lecz nie przewidziała jednego: żywy partner tym się różni od wymyślonego, że w każdej chwili może się zmyć. I tak się właśnie stało. Sztuka zeszła z afisza, aktorzy poszli do domów. Inżynier Orzechowicz podjął pracę na własny rachunek, ona zajęła jego miejsce w dziale informatyki; urwały się nawet przelotne spotkania na korytarzu. Raz wpadła na niego na placu Wolności. Biegła do przystanku, a on wychodził z Bujałą z biura.

Chłodna wymiana ukłonów i błysk jego oczu, zachłanny jakiś, zrozpaczony; wtedy sobie pomyślała... Głupio pomyślała, bo oni wyminęli ją i wsiedli do samochodu.

Tego samego dnia późnym popołudniem zadzwonił telefon. Serce podpowiadało, że to Konrad. Ciepły, męski głos Leszka przeciął wszelkie złudzenia. Leszek wydzwaniał regularnie co dwa, trzy dni, wypytywał o pracę i zapraszał do siebie. Lubiła nawet te telefoniczne pogawędki, lecz tym razem nie umiała ukryć rozczarowania. Wysyłała w eter zaledwie monosylaby. Poruszyła ją dopiero wiadomość o napadzie na Henię Luty. Leszek niewiele wiedział poza tym, że szykowała do otwarcia jakiś gabinet odnowy moralnej i tam właśnie znaleziono ją pobitą.

– Chciała przekazywać moc i rozum innym, a widocznie miała tych dóbr za mało nawet dla siebie – skomentował mało oryginalnie i nieoczekiwanie zmienił temat. – Co z tobą, Julio? Siedzisz w swojej norce jak borsuczek, milczysz, nie masz ochoty na spotkanie?

Norka? Borsuczek? No to wpadłam, pomyślała Julia. On wie dużo więcej, niż powinien, i powoli przechodzi do ataku. Henię już usadził. Zostawiła przy telefonie jakieś bazgroły i na nią padło podejrzenie o kradzież aktu darowizny. Teraz kolej na mnie.

– Żal mi Heni – powiedziała cicho.

Nie nawiązała ani jednym słowem do borsuczka, potraktowała cytat z Karoliny jako normalną, przyjacielską odzywkę, a nie groźbę, którą już wcześniej sączył jej w ucho. Z bijącym sercem czekała na kolejne słowa.

– Heni nic nie będzie. Ma kilka siniaków i na trochę odjęło jej mowę. Wiedziałem, że cię nie wyciągnę, więc jadę do ciebie. Właśnie podjeżdżam pod dom, możesz nastawić wodę na herbatę.

Człowiek śmiertelnie przerażony albo głupieje totalnie, albo myśli z chłodną precyzją. Julia sprawdziła, czy ma w torebce akt darowizny – miała – i starannie zamknęła drzwi. Kiedy przekręcała klucz w zamku, w mieszkaniu odezwał się domofon, a po chwili szczęknęły drzwi na dole. Energicznie zapukała do mojej Gajewskiej i nim pies zdążył się rozszczekać, była bezpieczna.

Leszek zachowywał się bardzo kulturalnie – pukał, prosił; tylko szczekanie jamnika mojej Gajewskiej wskazywało na obecność obcego w klatce. Wyjrzał najpierw jeden sąsiad, potem drugi. Wydroń poddał się, bo nie miał innego wyjścia. Wyszedł przed blok i usiadł na ławce tak, by mieć na widoku drzwi wejściowe.

Moja Gajewska patrzyła na Julię z zainteresowaniem. W jej nieciekawym życiu takie wydarzenie jak ucieczka dziewczyny przed mężczyzną było szalenie ekscytujące.

– Prześladuje mnie ten facet... boję się – powiedziała Julia. – On chyba ma coś z głową. Muszę stąd wyjść, zanim mnie dopadnie.

– Oj, musisz, Juleczko, musisz. Ja też kiedyś miałam adoratora, którego nie lubiłam. Nachodził, napraszał się, więc raz uciekłam mu w przebraniu własnego taty. Do dziś to pamiętam!

Dwa krótkie dzwonki. Konradowi nie chciało się ruszyć, żeby otworzyć. Znowu dwa dzwonki.

Na progu stała biednie ubrana kobiecina w chustce na głowie. Do wytartego paltocika tuliła psa. W pierwszej chwili wkurzył się i pomyślał o Żanecie. Coś mu jednak nie pasowało. Tamta ubierała się bardziej kolorowo. Nie nosiła w lecie botków, grubych pończoch ani chuściny w kratkę.

– Mogę? – spytała kobieta. Podniosła głowę i spod chustki spojrzały na Konrada wielkie oczy Julii. – Przyszłam z żywym przybytkiem... pożyczonym.

Nie było dnia, żeby nie myślał o niej. Rano i wieczorem zastanawiał się, za co spotkała go taka krzywda. Był człowiekiem drażliwym, zaciął się w uporze i nie potrafił zrobić pierwszego kroku. Czekał, aż ona się przełamie, może jeszcze raz spróbuje, a wtedy oboje zapomną o urazach i zaczną wszystko od początku. Patrzył teraz na swoją dziewczynę, nie tyle ubraną, ile przebraną, i wszystko się w nim gotowało. Nie powiedział, że może wejść. Odsunął się tylko na bok, więc weszła. Głupia Figa rzuciła się z ujadaniem do jego nóg i Julia znowu musiała wziąć jamnika na ręce.

– Co to ma znaczyć? – spytał złym, ostrym głosem.

– Musiałam uciekać. Grozi mi niebezpieczeństwo – powiedziała cicho.

– Pobiłaś się z kumplami o resztki na śmietniku? Jak ty wyglądasz?

– Mówię ci, że uciekłam... Wydroń chce mnie zabić. On pracuje dla Bujały.

Stali w mrocznym przedpokoju i mierzyli się wzrokiem. Oboje gotowi do pojednania i oboje dziwnie nieprzejednani.

Przyszła tu, żeby mnie upokorzyć i ośmieszyć, myślał Konrad. Łże o Wydroniu i oczy mydli. U Grześka udawała Karolinę i nie wyglądała na przestraszoną. Nie znosił demonizowania ludzi tylko dlatego, że doszli do majątku. Sam pracował dla Bujały i nie widział w tym nic zdrożnego. Zwykle pracuje się dla tych, którzy mają dość pieniędzy, żeby płacić. Powiedział to Julii ostrym, kategorycznym tonem.

Ależ jestem głupia, przeraziła się Julia. Szukam schronienia u człowieka, który sam jest bossem.

– Pójdę już – powiedziała. – Pies się wyrywa.

– To go wyrzuć za drzwi, ściągnij te łachy i porozmawiajmy.

Sam się zdziwił swojej propozycji – przecież był rozżalony i zły.

Julia położyła rękę na klamce.

– Gdzie ty się znowu wybierasz? – spytał.

– Muszę oddać psa właścicielce, przebrać się i zastanowić.

– Ale wracaj szybko – powiedział nieco łagodniej.

– Szybko się nie da.

Chciała dodać, że szybko i bez zastanowienia to ona się zakochała, a teraz potrzebuje trochę czasu na refleksję. Spojrzała w jego chmurne oczy i tylko zagryzła usta.

– Julio, tak nie możemy żyć. Rządzić i decydować może tylko jedno z nas.

– Ty, prawda?

– Solidnie dostałem od życia po głowie i wiem, jak się bronić i jak ochraniać swoich najbliższych. Kocham cię, Julio, ale na samowolę, na pętanie się po Toruniu i ucieczki z domu nigdy się nie zgodzę. Dom nie jest hotelem.

– Wiem.

Odwróciła się i wyszła. Z Toruńskiej żaden autobus nie jechał w kierunku Budowlanych, musiała dreptać piechotą. Buciki mojej Gajewskiej uwierały ją w palce. Nie czuła bólu. Całą żałość niosła w duszy. Szła ze spuszczoną głową. Nie myślała o miłosnych porywach, tylko zastanawiała się, jaki sens ma przechodzenie z jednego więzienia do drugiego. Matka, Konrad. Oboje chcieli decydować za nią, ona zaś chciała robić to sama. Niestety, z tych wszystkich chciejstw nie dało się stworzyć jednego szczęścia. Zapomniała o swoim przebraniu, o Leszku i całym świecie – przecież nic gorszego już jej nie mogło spotkać. Zatrzymała się przed drzwiami, żeby odszukać klucze.

– Cudownie wyglądasz, kochanie! Tobie nawet w papierowym worku byłoby do twarzy!

Nie musiała się odwracać, żeby wiedzieć, kto tak pięknie do niej przemawia.

– To na moją cześć ten strój? Jak wychodziłaś, nie poznałem cię, ale teraz patrzę, patrzę i oczom nie wierzę: toż to moja Julia!

– Czego ty chcesz ode mnie? Prześladujesz mnie, straszysz... Przecież ja ci nic nie zrobiłam.

Czy to możliwe, żeby tak wspaniale zagrał zdumienie? Raczej nie. On naprawdę był zdumiony. Złapał Julię za ramiona i odwrócił twarzą do siebie.

– No, no! Panie! Staruszkę będziesz pan szarpał?

Sąsiad z pierwszego piętra chwycił Leszka za ramię. Chciał jak najlepiej, ale w efekcie sytuacja z tragicznej stała się nagle komiczna, i Julia, choć smutek zżerał jej duszę, musiała parsknąć śmiechem. Przeprosiła sąsiada, a Leszka chwyciła za rękę. Chyba mnie nie zje ani nie zabije, pomyślała, biegnąc po schodach na górę.

– To ten sam pan? – spytała szeptem moja Gajewska.

– Czekał do tej pory – odszepnęła Julia. – Muszę z nim porozmawiać.

– Wiedziałam, że tak będzie. Ten mój też na mnie czekał wtedy przez całą noc, a potem przeżyliśmy razem czterdzieści pięć lat.

Leszek dał się posadzić za stołem, dał się napoić gotowaną wodą, bo herbaty zabrakło, ale nie dał się zbyć byle czym. Zażądał spowiedzi ze wszystkiego, co Julia wiedziała, czego się domyślała, co jej wpadło w ucho i czego kompletnie nie wiedziała. Miało być szczerze, po kolei i bez taryfy ulgowej. Jak źle o nim czy o sobie, to źle, jak dobrze, to dobrze. Julia kiwnęła głową. Chciał Leszek szczerze, to mu opowiedziała szczerze od dyskoteki w Teatralnej, po swoją wizytę w jego szafie. W tym momencie uśmiechnął się lekko.

– To cię bawi? – spytała zaskoczona.

– Rozumiem, że dostanę swoje buty z powrotem?

– Akt darowizny też.

Sięgnęła do torebki i podała mu starannie złożony papier.

– Akt to całkiem inna zabawka. – Machnął ręką z rezygnacją. – Sam jest tylko nędznym falsyfikatem, wymaga dodatkowych rekwizytów. Potrzebny mi był do pewnej scenki, którą tak ładnie sobie wyreżyserowałem.

Nieoczekiwane odkrycie w Leszku bratniej duszy wcale nie ucieszyło Julii.

– Kogo chciałeś zagrać?

– Kogo ja mogę zagrać, jak nie Leszka Wydronia?! Powiedzmy:

Wydronia w ulepszonej formie. Zagram ci, obiecuję, ale nie dzisiaj. A co do butów, to... zależy mi na nich. Gdybym wiedział, że tobie też, tobym je wcześniej umył. – Spojrzał na nią rozbawiony. – Ostatni raz miałem je na nogach, kiedy paliłem w ogrodzie archiwum Chochli.

– Spaliłeś?

– I jeszcze polałem wodą. Masz na to moje słowo.

– Dlaczego tak... dlaczego wtedy... – plątała się Julia.

– ...tak mi zależało na zanurzeniu się w tym bagienku Chochli? – skończył za nią. – Podejrzewałem, słusznie zresztą, że znajdę tam zdjęcia mojej byłej żony. Przez jakiś czas była dziewczyną Bujały.

– Ojej! – westchnęła Julia. – Nie wiedziałam. A co zrobiłeś z taśmą z automatycznej sekretarki?

– Nie wiem, o czym mówisz.

– Jadąc tu do mnie, zacytowałeś słowo w słowo Karolinę o borsuczku i norce. Ten sam fragment puściłeś mi wcześniej przez telefon!

– Być może bezwiednie zacytowałem Karolinę, jednak o żadnej taśmie nie wiem. Każesz mi cierpieć za cudze wygłupy.

I znowu biedna Julia była w kropce: mógł mówić najszczerszą prawdę, lecz nie musiał. Przyznał się do paru grzechów. Wszystkie miały to samo źródło: chęć wzbudzenia zainteresowania Julii. Nic nie mógł poradzić na to, że zakochał się jak sztubak i to od dnia, w którym pierwszy raz ją zobaczył. Nosił w sobie tę miłość i nosił, nim wreszcie zaczął działać. Nie najmądrzej, co przyznał, za to konsekwentnie. Zaprzyjaźnił się z Serafinem, gotów był przyjaźnić się z Konradem. Ale nie z Bujałą.

– A Henia? – spytała Julia.

– Henia była dochodzącą gosposią u moich rodziców. Kiedy zostałem sam, zaofiarowała się, że poprowadzi mi dom. Zgodziłem się, niestety. Choć o sprzątaniu i gotowaniu mam niewielkie pojęcie, lepiej sobie radzę niż Henia. Natomiast w dostarczaniu informacji nie ma sobie równych. Co jeszcze chcesz wiedzieć, biedronko? Co będę robił w najbliższej przyszłości? Kursy, szkolenia, doradztwo. Zajmuję się tym od roku i nie narzekam.

– Powiedz o pobiciu. Ty mówiłeś Michelin, pielęgniarka, że pub w centrum miasta.

– Kochanie, nikt nie chce robić sobie kłopotu pod własną rezydencją! Gorylątka mojego kuzyna przywiozły mnie do Włocławka na lekcję pokory. Nawet nie mogę ich skarżyć o pobicie, bo sam sprowokowałem awanturę. Pytaj dalej. Możesz nawet świecić mi lampą prosto w oczy. Aha, żona! Dzisiaj właśnie dostałem rozwód i chciałem to jakoś uczcić. Widzę jednak, że coś cię gnębi, że nie masz humoru, więc odłożymy to na inny dzień. Zgoda? Poczekam. Poczekam, aż ci przejdzie i znowu zechcesz mnie oglądać.

Objął Julię, przytulił i delikatnie pocałował we włosy. Spuściła głowę i nie wiedziała, co powiedzieć. Myślała o tym, że w ciągu jednego popołudnia świat przewrócił się do góry nogami. Najbliższy człowiek zawiódł ją i niemal wyprosił z domu, a największy wróg okazał się wcale nie być wrogiem. Tulił, gładził po policzku i pocieszał.

– Nie masz do mnie żalu? – spytała cicho.

Delikatnie uniósł jej twarz ku górze. Nie uciekała z oczami, wytrzymała jego wzrok, przekonana, że usłyszy kilka gorzkich słów. Posądzała przyjaciela o porwanie, szantaż, nieczyste interesy. Teraz sama nie wiedziała, jakim cudem te wszystkie brednie zalęgły się w jej głowie. Przypadek, cudze gadanie, naiwność.

– Zawsze chciałem być strasznym twardzielem – podjął Leszek z uśmiechem – takim, co to z trzech pistoletów wali równocześnie. Myślałem, że to niemożliwe. Ty jedna uwierzyłaś we mnie.

– I Karolina – dorzuciła.

– Ona też?

Zamiast gorzkich wyrzutów na twarz Julii spadły gorące pocałunki. Trochę się broniła, lecz tylko trochę. Coś mu była winna za te głupie posądzenia. Z trudem uwolniła się z jego objęć. Pogłaskał ją po policzku i westchnąwszy teatralnie, ruszył do drzwi. Nagle stanął.

– Kompletna skleroza! Biedronko, jak będziesz się widziała z Karoliną, oddaj jej pieniądze.

Odliczył tysiąc złotych, jeszcze raz przytulił Julię i poszedł na dobre.

Nie ma chyba takiego żalu, którego nie da się rozpuścić pocałunkami, myślała Julia. Myliła się: w niej samej tkwił żal, którego nie mogła rozpuścić niczym. Musiał się w niej wypalić. Nie wiedziała, ile to potrwa: miesiąc, rok, całe życie? Zadzwoniła do Karoliny, żeby podzielić się swoim smutkiem i swoją radością.

– Wyszło na moje! – ucieszyła się Karolina.

– Akurat. Tak samo zwątpiłaś jak i ja. Aha, oddał ci dług, okrągły tysiąc.

– Ja niby pożyczyłam Leszkowi tysiąc złotych? Nie wiesz kiedy? I z czego? To pożyczka dla ciebie. Spokojnie wydaj, ile musisz, a po wypłacie mu oddasz.

Pierwsza prawdziwa pensja przyniosła Julii tyleż radości, co niepokoju. Z najwyższym trudem powstrzymała się, by nie wyskoczyć do miasta i za jednym zamachem nie stracić wszystkich pieniędzy. Potrzeb miała mnóstwo. Głupiej zupy nie umiem wybrać w restauracji, bluzki w sklepie, nie wiem nawet, co kupować, a czego nie – myślała. To jak ja będę żyć? Musi być jakiś sposób. W końcu Karolina miała mniej pieniędzy i nie zginęła.

Julia usiadła przy stole i bodaj pierwszy raz w życiu zrobiła listę najpotrzebniejszych zakupów. Metodą eliminacji z czterdziestu dwóch pozycji zeszła do ośmiu, zaskoczona i uradowana swoim racjonalizmem. Cóż, zdana wyłącznie na siebie, musiała jeszcze oddać dług Leszkowi. Matka dzwoniła wprawdzie dwa razy dziennie, ale tylko po to, by przekonywać córkę, że jej miejsce jest w domu, przy rodzicach. Nie wiedziała o zerwaniu z Konradem i fakt, że Julia zamieszkała oddzielnie, potraktowała jako swój sukces wychowawczy. Połowiczny co prawda, jednak sukces.

– Dosyć już tego! Pokazałaś nam, jaka jesteś mądra i samodzielna, na co cię stać, możesz już wracać. Matczyne serce wszystko daruje.

– Wydaje ci się, mamo. To byłby twój ulubiony temat przez najbliższe dziesięciolecie – odpowiedziała pogodnie. Telefony bywały czasem bardzo irytujące, lecz Julia przyjmowała je już bez zdenerwowania. Matka po prostu taka była i nie mogła się zmienić. By dojść do tego odkrywczego wniosku, trzeba było opuścić dom rodzinny i samej poboksować się z życiem.

Konrad, co było do przewidzenia, nie zadzwonił. Ostatni raz Julia rozmawiała z nim przebrana za moją Gajewską. Nie wróciła wtedy, a on więcej się nie odezwał. Grażyna Orska parę razy wspominała z dumą, że inżynier Orzechowicz założył we Włocławku studio komputerowe czy coś w tym rodzaju, świetnie zarabia i ma się dobrze. Julia przyjmowała te informacje ze spokojem, nie rozwijała tematu i o nic nie pytała. Wciąż jeszcze musiała bronić się przed tęsknotą, lecz coraz częściej i z coraz głębszym przekonaniem powtarzała sobie, że samotność jest lepsza od życia z facetem, który zamiast dialogu wybiera monolog albo milczenie. Z całą pewnością nie zaliczał się do takich Leszek. Dzwonił już teraz codziennie, złaknięty dialogu z Julią. Wyciągał ją na spektakle, koncerty i wystawy.

– Biedronko, dzisiaj wielki koncert, nie możesz go opuścić. Stroje wieczorowe nie obowiązują.

– Gdzie, co, kto? – dopytywała się Julia. Zdążyła już rozsmakować się w tych wypadach z Leszkiem i nawet była zdziwiona, że w nudnym Włocławku wcale nie jest tak nudno.

– To będzie kameralny koncert u mnie – wyjaśnił poważnie.

– Rozumiem. W miasteczku Chandra Unyńska, gdzieś tam w kujawskim powiecie, ekonomista Lech Wydroń, nie umiał grać na klarnecie – wyrecytowała Julia.

– Lubisz „Płaksina"? – spytał z ożywieniem.

– Próbuję zaimponować ci znajomością poezji. „Płaksina" też lubię.

Przyjęła zaproszenie na kameralną imprezę i spędziła jeden z najmilszych wieczorów. Leszek kupił kilka płyt i to one właśnie złożyły się na bardzo urozmaicony program. Szperając w bogatej płytotece, Julia natknęła się na kasetę magnetofonową ze starymi tangami. Dla Leszka nie było rzeczy niemożliwych. Natychmiast uruchomił magnetofon.

– Zatańczymy? – zapytał, pochylając się nisko i wyciągając rękę, żeby wyłuskać Julię z fotela.

Miała wielką ochotę, jednak przestraszyła się, że nastrojowe tango może za szybko przenieść ich z parkietu na ozdobną kanapę. Tego wolała uniknąć, wyszła więc, unosząc w torebce pożyczoną kasetę.

Śledztwo w sprawie porwania Julii Blendy zostało umorzone z powodu śmierci głównego oskarżonego. Dziewczyna zyskała moralne prawo, by jeszcze wnukom opowiadać o swoim fenomenalnym powodzeniu lub o gapiostwie wielkiego bossa, który przez niedopatrzenie porwał ukochaną swojego przyjaciela.

Znacznie poważniej wyglądała sprawa zamordowania Marcina Chochli. Denat podobno trudnił się szantażem, o czym mogła świadczyć zamontowana w mieszkaniu kamera. Sama nie była jednak wystarczającym dowodem, a innych policja nie znalazła. Opoką śledztwa i głównym świadkiem była Wanda Pasieczko. Dzięki jej informacjom na liście podejrzanych, obok Mikuli, Karoliny, Julii, Edyty i Heni znalazło się kilkanaście różnych rysopisów. Wanda żyła z okiem przy wizjerze i znała ludzi głównie z wyglądu. Jej zeznania za każdym razem wprowadzały sporo zamieszania.

Julia kategorycznie wyparła się jakichkolwiek związków z Chochlą. Wspomniała tylko o przypadkowym spotkaniu na ulicy. Nie była widać interesującym świadkiem, bo dość szybko wykluczono ją z przesłuchań, ona z kolei nie upierała się, że chce cokolwiek dodawać. Przyszedł jednak moment, że dochodzenie skupiło się wyłącznie na niej.

Jeden z rysopisów podanych przez Wandę pasował idealnie do niejakiego Serafina, tego samego, który kilka dni później porwał Julię. Znów musiała odpowiadać na setki pytań: od kiedy znała, czym się zajmował, czy groził, czy się chwalił, jakie aspiracje, jakie zainteresowania. Przebrnęła zwycięsko i przez ten etap. Nie chciała myśleć o Chochli ani obarczać się winą za zniszczenie archiwum. Trochę męczyła ją myśl, że prawdziwy morderca mógł ujść bezkarnie. Kimkolwiek był, życzyła mu, by wpadł przy innej okazji. Przecież Serafin też jej nie porwał dla siebie, choć pośmiertnie odpowiadał tak, jakby porwał.

Pomysł, by założyć studio programów komputerowych, okazał się strzałem w dziesiątkę. Konrad prawie nie wychodził ze swojego biura w centrum miasta. Bujała nie był już jego jedynym klientem, ale nadal jednym z najważniejszych. Orzechowicz opracowywał dla niego internetową giełdę wierzytelności.

– I co ty masz z życia, kochany? – spytała kiedyś Grażyna. – Pracujesz od rana do nocy i nawet nie masz jak wydać tych swoich pieniędzy.

Nie odpowiedział. Domyślał się, że chciała go podpytać o sprawy sercowe, może nawet o Julię. Z drobnych uwag i napomknień mógł się zorientować, że Grażyna nie lubi Julii. Matkowała Konradowi, traktowała go jak syna, chciała ożenić, jednak żadna dziewczyna nie wydawała jej się dość dobra.

Zbyt dużo nadziei wiązał z Julią, by rozstanie nie zburzyło jego spokoju. Na szczęście miał jeszcze pracę, która pozwalała zapomnieć o uczuciach. Powoli odzyskiwał równowagę. Czasem nachodziły go wspomnienia; nie mógł uwierzyć, że rozstali się z winy Julii, a nie pod presją jej rodziny. Swojej nie brał pod uwagę, jedynie w przypływach szczególnie podłego nastroju gotów był sądzić, że Julię wystraszyła wizyta na Cygance. To bolało bardziej niż zadra pod paznokciem. Pobiegła tam z babskiej ciekawości, z czystej głupoty i nawet nie miała odwagi się przyznać. Tego nie umiał jej darować, nie mógł i chyba nie chciał.

Na początku września Julia zadzwoniła z pytaniem o jeden z programów, nad którym pracowali wspólnie, a który zaginął.

– Te wszystkie programy były autorskie. Nie jestem pewien, czy macie do nich prawo – powiedział.

– Wobec tego za co brałeś pensję? – spytała.

Czuł, że zagrał głupio. I wcale nie chciał tak powiedzieć. Tylko że kiedy usłyszał jej głos, najzwyczajniej w świecie zbaraniał. Obiecał, że poszuka i poprosił, żeby wpadła do niego do biura. Dwa dni później odwiedził go drobny człowieczek, który się przedstawił jako magister Portulak, prawnik Budampolexu. Przyszedł między innymi na prośbę Julii, by rozwiać wątpliwości inżyniera Orzechowicza. Konrad rzucił na stół dyskietkę. Nie miał już żadnych wątpliwości.

Julia weszła do gabinetu Edyty, żeby zwolnić się nieco wcześniej. Przed piętnastą musiała być w prokuraturze. Ponarzekały trochę na ślimacze tempo śledztwa i na sklerozę Wandy Pasieczko. Jako jedyny świadek ze słuchu, z widzenia i z pamięci znosiła swoje informacje jak kura jaja.

– Chochla w grobie się przewraca – mruknęła Julia.

– Chyba tak, bo ostatnio dzwoni do mnie co noc. Powiem ci, że już się nawet nie denerwuję.

– E tam, jakiś bałwan puszcza pani taśmę z automatycznej sekretarki.

– Ba! Tyle to ja też wiem. Niestety, nie wiem najważniejszego: kto i po jaką cholerę próbuje mnie nastraszyć.

Julia też się zastanawiała, w czyich rękach może być nieszczęsna kaseta. Leszka raz na zawsze skreśliła z listy podejrzanych. Pozostawał Bujała, któryś z jego osiłków lub morderca. Na temat zamordowania Chochli miała swoje zdanie wyłącznie na własny użytek. Serafin niewiele zdążył jej powiedzieć poza tym, że z kimś jeszcze śledził Marcina i że nie oni zabili. Owszem, po wyjściu mordercy spenetrowali mieszkanie. Kasetę i komórkę Karoliny zabrali więc albo oni, albo ten, kto uwolnił Chochlę od doczesnych zmartwień.

W prokuraturze nie zabawiła długo. W malutkim gabinecie wielki i całkiem przystojny prokurator wręczył jej pierścionek. Zerknęła na złote oczko, uspokoiła się, że nie chodzi o oświadczyny i odruchowo cofnęła ręce. Dostawała ten sam pierścionek od czwartego faceta, jeśli wliczać do obłędnego korowodu także Serafina. Czuła dziwny lęk przed dotknięciem błyskotki.

– Jest pani chwilowo wolna – powiedział obojętnym tonem mężczyzna.

– Chwilowo? Myśli pan, że mogę przejść na własność prokuratury?

– Nie ma takiej potrzeby – stwierdził krótko.

Nie dała Bozia poczucia humoru, oj, nie dała! – westchnęła w duchu Julia. I zaraz pomyślała, że wesoły prokurator byłby takim samym dziwem natury jak pięcionoga żyrafa. Z odrazą wrzuciła pierścionek do torebki, podpisała, co trzeba, i wybiegła. Na wąskich schodach musiała nieco zwolnić, bo przed nią majestatycznie staczała się w dół barwna kopka siana, przyobleczona w indyjskie szaty. Natapirowane i wysoko upięte włosy odsłaniały szyję, owiniętą grubo ozdobami z łańcuchów i koralików. Fantastyczny cudaczek, zdążyła pomyśleć Julia i zaraz potem wpadła w objęcia Heni Luty.

– To taka z ciebie przyjaciółka! – darła się Henia. – Ja mało nie umarłam, a ty mnie nawet nie odwiedziłaś!

Julia czym prędzej wyciągnęła ją na świeże powietrze. Korytarz prokuratury nie wydawał się jej odpowiednim miejscem do serdecznych i głośnych pogawędek. W jasnym świetle dnia mogła wreszcie dokładnie obejrzeć nowe wcielenie pani Luty. To już nie była dawna pomoc gospodarcza w wytartym fartuchu ani nawet guru w błękitnej garsonce. Nadmiar kolorów i ozdób doprowadził Julię do oczopląsu.

– Cudownie wyglądasz! – wykrzyknęła z zachwytem, który zabrzmiał całkiem naturalnie.

– Dziękuję, dziękuję! Staram się, widzisz, jak mogę – przyznała skromnie Henia. Zaraz potem zasypała Julię pytaniami o firmę, ludzi i porządki. – Jak mnie zabrakło, to pewnie w sekretariacie smoki się lęgną, co?

Julia zbyła pytanie milczeniem. Zaprzeczać nie chciała, przytaknąć nie mogła. Prawda była taka, że z odejściem Heni sekretariat wiele zyskał. Edyta zmieniła cały jego wystrój i zatrudniła nową sprzątaczkę.

– Ja dopiero teraz wiem, że żyję! – oświadczyła Henia. Z wielkiej radości, że znalazła słuchacza, zaprosiła Julię do Café Blue. Musiała przecież opowiedzieć komuś o swoich terapeutycznych sukcesach. Obracała się teraz w eleganckim świecie, wśród kobiet z klasą. Przychodziły radzić się w trudnych sytuacjach życiowych, opowiadały o swoich lękach i porażkach. Henia słuchała, podnosiła je na duchu i wyposażała w dodatkową moc. – Bo widzisz, Julciu, babki, ogólnie biorąc, są głupsze od mężczyzn.

– Zawsze twierdziłaś, że jest odwrotnie – zdziwiła się Julia.

– Z psychofizycznych uwarunkowań mózgu kobiecego wynika, że jest on wyposażony w mniejszą liczbę komórek i jako taki nie jest w stanie pomieścić wszystkich percepcji zachodzących w otaczającej rzeczywistości – wyjaśniła Henia. – To oczywiście duży skrót myślowy. Dokładnie chodzi o to, że babki myślą uczuciami, znaczy sercem, faceci tylko intelektem. Rozumiesz?

Julia nie rozumiała, ale wolała nie narażać się na wysłuchiwanie kolejnego wykładu, więc skwapliwie zgodziła się z Henią.

– Jeżeli masz, Julciu, kłopoty uczuciowe lub inne, zapraszam na moją kozetkę. Współczesne czasy nie sprzyjają rozwojowi kobiecej wrażliwości. Bez przerwy trzeba pielęgnować własne ego. Ty pielęgnujesz? No, powiedz, jak często mówisz sobie miłe rzeczy? Patrzysz rano w lustro, widzisz zmarszczki, podpuchnięte oczy i zwiotczałe policzki, a mimo wszystko powtarzasz sobie, że jesteś piękna, warta gorącej miłości i wszystkiego, co najlepsze. No, powiedz, jak często?

– Nie mam zwyczaju rozmawiać sama ze sobą – przyznała Julia i machinalnie dotknęła twarzy, by sprawdzić, czy w trakcie pouczającej rozmowy nie dostała zmarszczek i obwisłych policzków.

– Błąd! – wykrzyknęła Henia. – Mężczyźni rodzą się przekonani o swojej wspaniałości, kobiety dopiero muszą się przekonać. Wpadnij do mnie koniecznie. Widzę, że masz problemy z ego.

– Raczej z finansami – westchnęła smętnie Julia.

– Finanse to nie moja specjalność. – Henia wzruszyła ramionami. – A ty wiesz, że jeden facet próbował mnie wyrolować i zastraszyć? Gad był mi winien pieniądze za pomoc i takie tam usługi, zobowiązał się wyposażyć gabinet, a zamiast tego nasłał na mnie zbója!

– I co? – Julia wydawała się bardzo poruszona.

– Więcej tego nie zrobi – roześmiała się Henia. – Z gardła wydarłam wszystko, co mi się należało.

– Własną mocą?

– E, niekoniecznie. – Mrugnęła figlarnie. – Ja lubię dużo wiedzieć o świecie i świat mi to wynagradza.

Julia nie wątpiła już w wielką moc terapeutki, zwątpiła natomiast w wielkość Bujały. W drodze do domu zastanawiała się, jak i gdzie Henia ugryzła bossa.

– Biedronko, ratuj! Nie żartuję. Łap taksówkę i przyjeżdżaj!

– Skąd dzwonisz?

– Z łazienki.

I cisza. Wyłączył widać komórkę. Julia przestraszyła się nie na żarty. Potknął się pewnie, biedak, połamał na swoich kafelkach, może stracił przytomność? Pobiegła na postój taksówek po drugiej stronie ulicy i kazała wieźć się na Świętego Antoniego.

Dzwonić czy łomotać? Na wszelki wypadek nacisnęła klamkę. Drzwi były otwarte. Leszek, cały i zdrowy, pojawił się w przedpokoju. W oczach panika, palec na ustach, a za moment czysta radość.

– Jesteś nareszcie, kochanie! To cudownie!

Popchnął ją, oszołomioną, w stronę salonu. Na pięknej stylowej kanapie siedziała piękna żółtowłosa Ola Mikulowa. Na widok Julii wyraźnie się speszyła.

– Mamy gościa, Julio! Pani Ola dowiedziała się o naszych zaręczynach... dobrze mówię? Majdziak powiedział pani, że się zaręczyliśmy?

– Niech mi pan nawet nie wspomina o tym skurwielu! – wykrzyknęła Mikulowa. Nabrała powietrza i potoczyście, bez cienia wdzięku puściła klasyczną wiązankę przekleństw, po czym, uspokojona, zgodziła się wypić herbatę.

Julia, jak na narzeczoną przystało, zniknęła w kuchni. Z salonu docierały odgłosy normalnej rozmowy. O firmie, o pracy.

– Patrz pan, panie Leszku, wszystko dla niego poświęciłam i co teraz mam robić? – Ściszyła głos. – Ja myślałam, że u pana będę mogła na dzień, dwa... może na dłużej? Pan mnie tak dobrze rozumiał... jak żaden mężczyzna. Mikula domy sprzedał, wziął dupę w troki... Nawet adresu nie zostawił, impotent jeden.

– Możesz przecież zatrzymać się u kuzynki, u Wandy Pasieczko – podpowiedziała Julia. Stała w drzwiach z tacą w rękach i patrzyła na Olę bez specjalnej życzliwości.

– Jaka tam z niej kuzynka! – prychnęła Mikulowa. – No cóż... Przejdę się do Edyty. Coś mi jest chyba winna, że tak na krzywy ryj firmę dostała.

Nie przytaknęli, nie zaprzeczyli, nie próbowali wyprowadzać pani Oli z błędu. Jeżeli chciała złożyć wizytę Edycie, miała do tego pełne prawo. Do firmy już nie.

– Panie Lesiu, a nie ma pan kapki koniaku albo whisky? – spytała Ola.

Leszek poderwał się z fotela.

– Mam jedno i drugie, proszę wybierać.

– Jak ja mam do wyboru whisky i koniak, to biorę to i to! – zaśmiała się Ola. – Tylko nie myślcie, że się rozpiłam albo co! Majdziak, ten to dopiero smolił wódę. Czystą wódę, dacie wiarę? Ja przy nim byłam taka abstynentka, aż żal tyłek ściska.

Wychyliła jednym haustem koniak i poprosiła „na drugą nóżkę". Julia dyskretnie trąciła Leszka pod stołem. Z trzeźwą Olą były kłopoty, co dopiero z pijaną. Mikulowa delikatnie otarła usta rękawem bluzki.

Nie zatrzymywali jej, kiedy zaczęła zbierać się do wyjścia, a kiedy już wyszła, nie próbowali nawet zachować powagi. Tak się rozbawili, rozdokazywali, że kiedy Leszek niby niechcący przytulił Julię, ona nie zaprotestowała, a nawet sama przylgnęła do jego boku. Opowiedziała o spotkaniu z Henią.

– A jak z twoją mocą duchową? – spytała na koniec ze śmiechem.

– Dziękuję. Też dobrze.

– Też? Niech ci będzie, chwalipięto! A jesteś przekonany o własnej wspaniałości?

– O, do licha! Sam nie wiem... ale chyba tak.

– Nie ma chyba! – zaprotestowała. – To powinna być twoja cecha wrodzona. Jak nie jest, maszeruj do Heni na kozetkę reperować swoje ego.

Julia była tego dnia wyjątkowo pogodna. Myślała o Heni, o Oli i kompletnie zapomniała o wizycie w prokuraturze. Dopiero kiedy przed wyjściem przyczesywała włosy, dostrzegła w torebce kasetę z tangami i pierścionek Chochli. Kasetę upchnęła głębiej, pierścionek podała Leszkowi. Jak ona w prokuraturze, tak on teraz gwałtownie schował ręce za siebie. Nie rościł sobie najmniejszych praw do błyskotki.

– W życiu nie zamierzałam przyjmować prezentów od Chochli – powiedziała Julia zmartwiona. – To jawna złośliwość losu, że po tylu perypetiach dar Marcina znowu trafił do mnie. Co ja mam zrobić?

– Potraktuj to jako dar losu i schowaj na czarną godzinę – poradził Leszek.

Majdziak od dwudziestu minut siedział u inżyniera Orzechowicza w biurze i cały czas gadał. Nie o samochodach, lecz o życiu i innych poważnych sprawach. Zaskoczony Konrad odsunął się od komputera i słuchał. Nie ze wszystkim się zgadzał. Raziły go zwłaszcza uogólnienia. Majdziak upierał się, choć był zupełnie trzeźwy, że życie to majaczenie wariata, a wszystkie baby są dziećmi jednej maci.

– Podpadłeś szefowi, że tak wszystko widzisz w czarnych kolorach? – spytał wreszcie Konrad.

– Ty, jakby boss był taki bystry, za jakiego się uważa, to grałby w mieście pierwsze skrzypce. A co on robi? Pojękuje w kącie i duma go rozpiera, że tak wysoko ciągnie. Zobacz, ilu go już wyprzedziło? Dorobić się na przemycie fajek i spirtu nie było trudno, problem tylko, jak utrzymać pozycję! Strzelaninki, wysadzanie autek to dobre dla amatorów. Ja lubię pracować z fachowcami, dlatego przyszłem do Bujały. Fachowiec, kurde! Głupiej babie pozwolił zrobić z siebie wała.

Konrad zaproponował gościowi herbatę, rozsiadł się wygodnie i dopiero teraz nastawił uszu. Majdziak dużo wiedział i jak już zaczął mówić o Bujale, warto było posłuchać. Pod wpływem rozgoryczenia mógł powiedzieć coś naprawdę ciekawego. Historyjka wydawała się banalna, dopóki nie padło nazwisko Luty. Henryka Luty. Konrad pamiętał oczywiście wścibską sprzątaczkę z Budampolexu, nie przypuszczał jednak, by kobiecina trudniła się szantażem. Za trzy zdjęcia zażądała piętnastu tysięcy i Bujała zapłacił. Trochę się targował, napuścił na babę rudzielca, jednak poszła w zaparte, postraszyła adwokatem i w końcu pieniądze dostała.

– Co takiego mogło być na tych zdjęciach? zdziwił się Orzechowicz.

– Bujała z obcą kobietą w pościeli bez przykrycia – prychnął Majdziak. – Jak mówiłem wałowi, że z babami prominentów nie warto się fotografować, to mnie wyśmiał. Teraz portkami trzęsie. Ten facet jednym palcem przewali Bujałę i wszystkie jego interesy. A kto wie, co ta Luty może jeszcze trzymać pod poduszką? Tych zdjęć było więcej. Pół miasta za nimi gania, nie wyłączając policji. Ja tam nie wierzę, że babsko znalazło je na śmietniku.

Zamyślił się, posmutniał i wyraźnie szukał u Konrada wsparcia. Zwykłe słowa pociechy nie bardzo na niego działały. Zwątpił w bossa i wyraźnie cierpiał. Jedyny ratunek widział w giełdzie wierzytelności, między innymi dlatego tak szczerze rozmawiał z Konradem.

– Nie wierzę w pomysły Bujały, ale w ciebie wierzę! – powiedział z powagą. – Ty, Konrad, ja maturę prawie skończyłem, Bujałę z zawodówki wylali, to który z nas bardziej wykształcony? Czego on traktuje mnie jak przygłupa?

Orzechowicz miał szczerą ochotę parsknąć śmiechem. W porę powstrzymał nietaktowną wesołość i próbował podtrzymać Majdziaka na duchu. Nie musiał się specjalnie wysilać, jego gość miał wysokie mniemanie o własnym intelekcie, pragnął tylko potwierdzenia, że prawdziwym przygłupem jest Bujała. Na taką szczerość Konrad nie chciał się jednak zdobyć i zmienił temat na mniej wybuchowy. Zaczęli rozmawiać o kobietach.

– A wiesz, że ta twoja mała Blenda z Wydroniem teraz kręci? – ożywił się Majdziak. – Wydroń to ten nieślubny braciszek Bujały.

– Jak z Wydroniem, to najlepszy dowód, że już nie moja – powiedział głucho Konrad.

– A ja bym takiej babki od siebie nie puścił – rozmarzył się Grześ. – Są, rozumiesz, baby, które się rzuca, bo głupie i nudne, a są i takie, od których się nie odchodzi. Nigdy nie zapomnę, jak dała popalić Bujale! Kurrrwa, jak ona mi wtedy zaimponowała. – Potraktował milczenie

Konrada jako zachętę do dalszych zwierzeń i zaczął opowiadać o najnowszej flamie bossa: – Ładna, no, muszę powiedzieć, że ładna, ale żeby aż tak świrować, to przesada. On teraz częściej w Toruniu siedzi niż w domu. Ledwie wróci, wydzwania, meile śle... Mówię ci, czysty wariat. Dzisiaj babka przyjechała, to ją na kawkę do Blue zabrał, a mnie kazał czekać z autem. Cierniak się nazywa... Ty to ją powinieneś znać?

Konrad niedbale kiwnął głową, że zna, spojrzał na zegarek i zerwał się gwałtownie. Przypomniał sobie o bardzo ważnym spotkaniu, przeprosił Majdziaka i już w biegu zbierał jakieś papiery. Z biura do kawiarni było bliziutko.

Karolina zapowiedziała przyjazd na piątek i Julia już od czwartku nie umiała sobie miejsca znaleźć. Telefonicznie gawędziły prawie codziennie, lecz nie widziały się ponad miesiąc. Przez ten czas Julia ucywilizowała trochę kawalerkę odziedziczoną po przyjaciółce. W końcu pracowała w Budampoleksie i znała kilku majstrów, którzy za niewielkie pieniądze zgodzili się pomalować ściany i okna. Najbrzydsze meble wyniosła do piwnicy. W ich miejsce postawiła nowe biurko, niewielki regał i wygodną kanapę. Matka nie pogodziła się wprawdzie z samodzielnością córki, jednak oddała komputer, książki, torbę z rzeczami osobistymi. Po tych zmianach Julia wreszcie poczuła, że ma własny kąt. Z zakupów czy z pracy wracała do siebie. W czwartek wieczorem zdjął ją strach, czy Karolina nie poczuje się obco. Właściwie nie ma powodów, pomyślała. Tu jest teraz tak milutko.

Jako pani domu też nie była już zieloną lebiodą. Pierwszą szkołę gotowania przeszła u boku Konrada, potem z oszczędności sama sobie przyrządzała skromne posiłki, korzystając z porad w kobiecych pismach. Kolację postanowiła w całości zrobić sama: panierowane piersi kurczaka, leczo i pieczony schab. Na deser zaplanowała drożdżówkę. Zdecydowała się skorzystać z niezawodnego przepisu Edyty i wszystko wskazywało na to, że ciasto będzie doskonale wyrobione. Od kilku dni siedziała w niej złość, której musiała dać ujście, by raz na zawsze zamknąć wszelkie porachunki z Konradem. Zadzwoniła do niego w sprawie czysto służbowej. Poznał ją, nie mógł nie poznać, i chyba tylko dlatego zachował się niezbyt elegancko. Z wielkim trudem zapanowała nad sobą, by nie powiedzieć jednego zdania za dużo. Przemilczała, lecz teraz musiała gdzieś tę powściągliwość wyładować. Rozczyniła ciasto, a potem tyle serca włożyła w wyrabianie, że odchodziło od rąk, od stolnicy i niemal fruwało w górze. Nie zostawiła na Konradzie suchej nitki.

Przypięła mu wszystkie epitety, którymi tak obficie szafował Leszek. A masz pluskolcu, wołała, masz pędrusiu, śmietko i wołku... ty nastroszu i koziorogu! Całkiem już spokojnie przykryła miskę czystą ściereczką i znowu poczuła, że ma dwadzieścia pięć lat i piękną przyszłość przed sobą.

Dochodziła czternasta; pora bardziej obiadowa niż kawiarniana. W Café Blue zajęty był tylko jeden stolik, pod oknem. Bujała siedział tyłem, za to Karolina dostrzegła go natychmiast.

– Jesteś wreszcie! – krzyknęła radośnie.

Przez moment sądził, że ktoś jeszcze stoi za jego plecami i omal się nie odwrócił. Takiego powitania nie oczekiwał. Karolina zerwała się od stolika i zaczęła zbierać swoje drobiazgi. Odwrócił się wreszcie i Bujała.

– To ty się umawiasz z moim kumplem? No, no, już ja się temu Orzechowiczowi przyjrzę! – Niby żartował, lecz zbyt mocno ściskał zęby i minę miał całkiem niewesołą.

– Przecież uprzedzałam cię, że będę zajęta.

Podała mu rękę, zostawiła na stole niedopity sok i wyprowadziła z kawiarni lekko otumanionego Konrada.

– Samo niebo cię zesłało – szepnęła konspiracyjnie, gdy już znaleźli się na ulicy, z dala od ciekawskich uszu Bujały. – Żałuję, że nie mogłeś wypić swojej kawy. Chętnie ci to wynagrodzę w innym lokalu.

Patrzyła po swojemu spod wywiniętych rzęs. Była bodaj jeszcze piękniejsza niż przed wyjazdem. Ujął ją mocno pod ramię.

– Chcesz powiedzieć, że się za mną stęskniłeś? – spytała.

– A ty za mną?

– Julia ci nie mówiła? Codziennie o ciebie pytam!

Tylko ona potrafiła prawić złośliwości bez złośliwego uśmiechu, z miną tak niewinną, jakby mówiła o urodzie wszechświata.

– Nie mówiła. – Przez moment mierzyli się wzrokiem. – Zjesz ze mną obiad?

– Najpierw wolałabym odwiedzić twoje biuro. Powiedziałam Bujale, że mam do załatwienia sprawę służbową i niech sobie kłopotek myśli, że to prawda. – Roześmiała się wesoło. Fakt, że uciekła bossowi, wprawiał ją w znakomity nastrój. Wypytywała Konrada o pracę, opowiadała o swojej, lecz już ani słowem nie wspominała o Julii. Wie więcej niż ja, myślał Konrad, i nie musi o nic pytać. Przed wejściem do NOT-u puścił wreszcie ramię dziewczyny, by otworzyć drzwi.

– Wykupiłeś cały budynek? – spytała.

– I wszystkie okoliczne, żeby mi nikt do komputera nie zaglądał – odpowiedział równie poważnie i oboje parsknęli śmiechem. Konrad z zadowoleniem stwierdził, że rozmawia z Karoliną całkiem inaczej niż dawniej, że stać go na swobodę i dowcip. Kiedy przekroczyła próg jego biura i cichutko gwizdnęła, przyjął to jako najszczerszy komplement. Po godzinie przenieśli się do restauracji na parterze budynku. Tu mogli siedzieć bezkarnie. Notina nie budziła żadnych wspomnień.

W końcu sami do nich nawiązali, bo nie dało się inaczej.

– Masz kogoś? – spytał Konrad.

– Nie widziałeś Bujały? – zdziwiła się niewinnie. – Sam powiedz, czy warto mieć kogoś takiego? Chwilami mam wrażenie, że jak włączam radio, to też słyszę jego głos. Mam alergię na tego faceta.

– Na Bujale nie kończy się świat.

– Jak mnie ustrzeli, to się skończy. Chętnie sama bym go skróciła o głowę, gdyby za gangsterów dawali mniejsze wyroki.

– Dlaczego nam się nie udało? – spytał cicho. Przytrzymał jej rękę, czuł, że wali mu serce i czekał na żart, kpinę, na wszystko, tylko nie na łzy. Piękne oczy zaszkliły się niebezpiecznie, Karolina nakryła je powiekami, zamrugała i nie powiedziała nic. – To moja wina, prawda?

– Nie ma twojej, nie ma mojej, jeżeli jest, to nasza – odpowiedziała.

– Spróbujemy jeszcze raz? Ja jestem gotów.

– Gotów to ty jesteś od trzydziestu trzech lat, ssaczku. Ale powiedz, od ilu lat potrafisz wyciągać wnioski z porażek. Właściwe wnioski, nie te wygodne.

– Ty potrafisz?

– Nie! Nie potrafię! – przyznała ze złością. – Dostaję po łbie, ale uparłam się, ze nie po to studiowałam, żeby teraz siedzieć w kącie i potakiwać mężowi. Mam swoje ambicje, mam swoje plany i pomysł na własne życie.

– Wiem i chyba zaczynam to rozumieć. Proszę, spróbujmy!

– W Julii siedzi aniołek, we mnie diabełek, dlaczego nie po drodze było ci z aniołkiem?

– Widać diabełki są bliższe mojej naturze. Kochałem Julię, chciałem... Wszystko się rozpadło i nie zostało nic... z wyjątkiem żalu. Nie wiem dlaczego... wiem jedynie, że nigdy żadnej kobiety tak nie pragnąłem jak ciebie.

Karolina dotarła na Budowlanych dopiero wieczorem. Wszystkie zmiany przyjęła wybuchami wielkiej radości. Nie mogła tylko odżałować starej, poczciwej wersalki i za nic nie chciała powiedzieć, z jakich powodów. Przy drożdżówce o mało nie rozpłynęła się z zachwytu.

– Rozumiem, że upiekłaś na moją cześć, ale na czyją intencję wyrabiałaś? Wyrosło cudownie. Sam puch.

– Bardzo się starałam – przyznała Julia. – Waliłam z sercem i chyba mam z głowy rozliczenie z przeszłością. Zamknęłam rozdział, dopisałam słówko koniec, a to znaczy... koniec. Tylko trochę się zapamiętałam i to jest niestety wytrawna drożdżówka. Zapomniałam o cukrze.

Nie bardzo wiadomo, co zabawnego może być w wytrawnym cieście, w każdym razie smarowały drożdżówkę dżemem i pękały ze śmiechu. Przegadały cały wieczór i pół nocy. Tematy mnożyły się i wyskakiwały jeden z drugiego. Mikula? Zniknął z horyzontu. Dzwonił do Karoliny parę razy, zapraszał do siebie. Ma uraz na punkcie Edyty. Podobno odnalazła go i namawia do powrotu.

– Myślisz, że to możliwe? – spytała Julia.

– Trudno posądzać Wacka o fantazję. Jeżeli tak mówi, to raczej nie zmyśla.

– Swoją drogą, biedna ona. Do tej pory leczy firmę z ciężkiego przypadku choroby, którą na własny użytek nazywamy mikulozą, a nie ma dosyć samego Mikuli! Myślisz, że to miłość?

Karolina nie zareagowała; siedziała zamyślona i Julia musiała ją delikatnie pociągnąć za włosy, żeby wróciła do rzeczywistości.

– Hej, Karolinko, to ja, Julia, poznajesz mnie?

Karolina objęła ją gwałtownie i przytuliła.

– Strasznie głupio jest ten świat urządzony – westchnęła.

– Jakieś nowe komplikacje w życiu uczuciowym? Tylko nie mów o Bujale! On mianowicie jest mężczyzną, jednak...

– E! Daj spokój! – wykrzywiła się Karolina. – Prawdziwego chłopa poznasz w akcji, kiepski wyżywa się w gadaniu. To stara prawda, której wcale nie trzeba sprawdzać.

– Miałaś nie mówić o Bujale – śmiała się Julia – tylko o życiu uczuciowym. Jesteś zadurzona?

– A ty?

– Odkochana.

– Rozmawiałaś z Konradem?

Julia przestała się śmiać.

– Nie było o czym.

– Zawsze jest o czym. Jeżeli liczysz na domyślność facetów, to się przeliczysz. Im trzeba wszystko wykładać jasno i klarownie, a i tak po-

łowy nie zrozumieją. Są niedoskonałym prototypem człowieka. Ile razy mam ci to powtarzać?

– Zapamiętam sobie na przyszłość, bo rozdział pod tytułem Konrad opatrzony jest słówkiem koniec.

– Na pewno?

Julia tak energicznie pokiwała głową, że Karolina nie mogła mieć żadnych wątpliwości. Jak koniec to koniec.

Bolący ząb można wyrwać, bolący żołądek skazać na dietę, na nogę przyłożyć kompres, lecz co zrobić z bolącą duszą? Julia patrzyła na Wandę Pasieczko i nie wiedziała, co kobiecinie poradzić.

– Duszę mam chorą, Juleczko, duszę – wzdychała poetka.

Spotkały się na targowisku przy Kaliskiej i Julia w żaden sposób nie mogła zgubić roztrzęsionej Wandy i tym samym wymigać się od odwiedzin. Ludzie przesadnie gościnni i przesadnie uprzejmi zwykle sprawiają otoczeniu same kłopoty. Trudno za serce płacić czarną niewdzięcznością, niestety zwykłe podziękowania nie odnoszą skutku. Wreszcie Julii zrobiło się żal obładowanej torbami kobieciny, wzięła od niej połowę bagażu i poszła na kawusię z ciastuchnem. Wanda rozgadała się na dobre dopiero w domu. Narzekała na rozstrój żołądka, bała się policji, bała się sądu, najbardziej zaś bała się nowej sąsiadki, pani Oli.

– Jak ta Edyta mogła mi coś takiego zrobić za tyle serca? Gdybym ja powiedziała na policji wszystko, co wiem... no, no.

– To Mikulowa teraz tu mieszka? – zdziwiła się Julia.

– Zastraszyć mnie chciała, dasz wiarę? Mówiła: ty, Wandziu, lepiej milcz i udawaj, że cię tu nie było. Tak mówiła... Jak ja mogłam nie pomóc policji? Musiałam.

– Mikulowa cię straszyła?

– E tam, jaka Mikulowa?! Chyba że niedoszła. – Zaśmiała się złośliwie. – O Edycie mówię. Nie dałam się zastraszyć, to nasłała mi Olę. Jak można wynająć mieszkanie takiej bezmoralnej kobiecie?! Sodomka z gomorką, mówię ci... sodomka... i to pod moim bokiem. Ona jeszcze nie wie, że ja głosy ujarzmiłam. Same mi pod drzwi przyszły, na wycieraczce się położyły.

Julia wzdrygnęła się i skrzyżowała ręce na piersi. Dosyć miała obłędnego bredzenia Wandy. Z grzeczności udawała, że słucha i bezmyślnie rozglądała się po pokoju. Na parapecie przybył piękny kroton, na stoliku przy telefonie dostrzegła całkiem przyzwoity radiomagnetofon, którego wcześniej nie widziała. W skrytce tkwiła kaseta.

– Słuchasz sobie muzyki? – spytała, żeby choć na moment zmienić temat.

– Nie, nie, tylko wiadomości. Muzyka się popsuła... Ojej, ale mnie w brzuchu kręci! Myślisz, że ona mogła mi zatruć wodę?

Dziewczyna poczuła na plecach niemiłe ciarki. Wanda wyglądała dobrotliwie jak zawsze, zachowywała się jak zawsze, czyli biegała od wizjera do stołu, dbała, żeby ciasto było na talerzykach, a jednocześnie plotła jakieś niesamowite brednie. Złorzeczyła Oli, przeklinała Edytę i chwaliła sukienkę gościa. Wszystko tym samym tonem, na jednej nucie. Co jakiś czas chwytała się za brzuch, wreszcie zatrzepotała gwałtownie rękami i popędziła do łazienki. Julia podeszła do stolika z magnetofonem i machinalnie wcisnęła przycisk.

– Edytaa? Tego... no... to ja. Nie myśl sobie...

Wrażenie było piorunujące. Z łazienki dobiegały odgłosy spuszczanej wody i nie było czasu na logikę. Julia o mały włos nie wyrzuciła zawartości torebki na dywan. Ręce jej drżały z emocji, kiedy dogrzebała się wreszcie do kasety ze starymi tangami. Parę sekund później Wanda zastała ją w fotelu, pogrążoną w myślach.

– A wiesz, Julciu, to ja go zabiłam – powiedziała prawie dobrotliwie.

Julia nie potrafiła wykrztusić słowa. Wpatywała się w Wandę, jakby pierwszy raz w życiu widziała małe oczka w siatce drobnych zmarszczek i zadarty nos.

– Ja! – przytaknęła z dumą. – Aż sama jestem zdziwiona, że zgromadziłam w sobie tyle mocy. Medytowałam, myślałam, wreszcie zebrałam w sobie całą tę moc w jedną kulę i wysłałam człowieka w kosmos. Skąd mogłam wiedzieć, komu Edyta wynajmie mieszkanie po nim?!

Leszek zadzwonił po południu, spragniony wieści o Karolinie. Opowiedziała mu w wielkim skrócie, że ich wspólna przyjaciółka zgłupiała na punkcie małej Zuzanny Wąsik i nie ukrywa, że zachorowała na własne dziecko.

– Próbuje to sama załatwić? – spytał zdziwiony.

– No coś ty? – roześmiała się Julia. – Teraz wyjeżdża na tydzień do Wisły na jakieś szkolenie, a potem zobaczymy... Myślałam, że wpadniesz do mnie – dokończyła zawiedzionym głosem.

– Właśnie za moment będę się ustawiał na twoim zapchanym parkingu. Jeżeli chcesz, możesz zacząć się przebierać w jakieś stare ciuchy.

Rozbawił ją do łez. Sprawdziła, czy ma kawę i herbatę, wstawiła wodę i w biegu poprawiła uczesanie. Kiedy otworzyła drzwi, najpierw

zobaczyła wielki bukiet pąsowych róż, dopiero potem Leszka. Był pachnący, uroczysty i jeszcze bardziej elegancki niż zwykle. Kobieca intuicja podpowiedziała jej, że nadeszła chwila wielkich decyzji. Od pewnego czasu, dokładnie od pamiętnej wizyty w gabinecie Bujały, niczego w swoim życiu nie reżyserowała. Szła na żywioł i była to o wiele wygodniejsza droga. Nie zastanawiała się wcześniej, jak i kiedy Leszek poprosi ją o rękę, wiedziała jednak, że ta chwila nadejdzie i wiedziała, jaką da odpowiedź. Uparty chłopak wygrał z jej lękiem i z obojętnością. Chociaż nie, obojętności w niej nigdy nie było. Przyjaźń, wielka sympatia, przez jakiś czas strach, ale nie obojętność.

– Biedroneczko! – Był wzruszony i głos mu leciutko drżał. – Moja śliczna biedroneczko, czy chcesz tego oto mężczyznę, Leszka Wydronia, za męża? Znam faceta od trzydziestu pięciu lat. O wadach nieskładnie teraz mówić, więc powiem o jego trzech największych zaletach: po pierwsze kocha cię, po drugie kocha cię bardzo, po trzecie kocha cię jak wariat. – Spoważniał nagle i podszedł do Julii całkiem blisko. Nie broniła się, kiedy zaczął ją całować. – Nie masz pojęcia, jak ja cię kocham – powtórzył.

– Wiem – powiedziała. – I dlatego wezmę za męża Leszka Wydronia, bo też go kocham.

Ostry gwizdek czajnika sprowadził ich na ziemię. Julia musiała zająć się parzeniem herbaty. Kiedy wróciła z filiżankami, przyciągnął ją do siebie.

– To jeszcze nie koniec, Julio! – powiedział.

Poczuła i zaraz potem zobaczyła, że wsuwa jej na palec pierścionek, ten sam, który oglądała u niego na biurku: brylancik w platynie, ze złotą obrączką.

– A to miał być dodatek do prezentu. – Podał jej kopertę z aktem darowizny ziemi i chichotał już całkiem radośnie. – Miałem ci to wręczyć, gdybyś uznała mnie za partię niepoważną. Kiedyś tak ładnie mówiłaś o gruntach, pamiętasz, to sobie pomyślałem, że dam ci te grunty choćby na papierku. Kto się dał powiesić dla dobrego żartu? Cygan czy kowal?

– Powiesić dla żartu? Nie głuptak czasem?

– A, wszystko jedno. Jestem szczęśliwy i tak zakochany... tak zakochany od tylu miesięcy...

– Nie zrozum mnie źle... ale co z twoją wiernością? – Spojrzała spod rzęs. – Myślę o...

– Wiem, o czym myślisz. Zastanawiam się tylko, czy masz rację? Moja absolutna wierność, kochanie, zaczyna się od momentu, kiedy usłyszałem od ciebie „tak”.

– Dobrze. Wobec tego i ja mam dla ciebie prezent – uśmiechnęła się Julia i położyła przed Leszkiem na stole kolorową paczuszkę. Znalazł w niej nowiutką szczotkę do zębów, jednorazową maszynkę do golenia i krem. Niczego więcej nie potrzebował.

Julia bardzo lubiła jesienne kolory – wszystkie te złocistości, beże i czerwienie dzikiego wina – jednak za samą porą roku nie przepadała. Dni były coraz krótsze, zamglone i nostalgiczne. Nie spała od piątej, żeby tylko nie spóźnić się do pracy. Ledwie nauczyła się żyć i mieszkać samotnie, Leszek zaczął namawiać ją do przeprowadzki. Nie śpieszyła się. Serce ciągnęło ją na Świętego Antoniego, rozsądek kazał zostać na Budowlanych i to co najmniej przez najbliższy miesiąc. Skończyły się czasy, gdy inżynier Blenda z niechęcią siadała za biurkiem. Teraz nie miała czasu na zjedzenie drugiego śniadania. Kupowała i instalowała sprzęt, szkoliła pracowników, wprowadzała nowe programy. Uczyła się przy tym przez cały czas. W domu zasypiała obłożona fachową literaturą. Parę razy, kiedy nachodziły ją poważniejsze wątpliwości, skorzystała z rad inżyniera Kicińskiego. Edyta nie kryła zadowolenia.

– Wiesz co? Niczego już nie rozumiem – powiedziała któregoś dnia, kiedy Julia zajrzała do jej gabinetu. – Dzisiaj w nocy Chochla zagrał mi tango!

– Może to było ostatnie tango? – zapytała Julia z tajemniczym uśmiechem. Nie dodała nic więcej. Ktoś zgubił, ktoś znalazł, jeszcze inny ktoś wykradł, ale to już nie miało znaczenia. Własnoręcznie pocięła taśmę nożyczkami na makaron i w ten sposób uwolniła od lęków nie tylko Edytę. Sama też się uspokoiła i uznała za oczywistą interpretację Leszka. Pierwszy telefon, ten do niej, kiedy Karolina podrywała Chochlę na borsuczka, był, jego zdaniem, ewidentną pomyłką. Wanda Pasieczko zadzwoniła do sekretariatu do Edyty, nie do Julii. A to, że puściła ten akurat fragment nagrania, to już sprawa przypadku bądź nieumiejętności w obsługiwaniu magnetofonu.

– Słyszałaś o nowej rewelacji w śledztwie? – spytała Edyta. – Głównym oskarżonym jest teraz świętej pamięci Serafin. Ciekawe, czy wlepią mu dożywocie? Straszny złoczyńca był z tego chłopaka, nie uważasz?

Julia wyszła z gabinetu przygnębiona. Jemu teraz jest wszystko jedno, myślała, a mnie i tak nikt nie uwierzy.

– Pani Julio! – Grażyna Orska wybiegła zza biurka. – Była pani kiedyś w Wiśle?

– Byłam, i to kilka razy.

– Radek mi właśnie przysłał widokówkę. – Podsunęła Julii kolorowe zdjęcie.

Konrad w Wiśle? No, no, a raczej fiu, fiu, pomyślała Julia.

W skrytce na listy była kartka od Karoliny. Parę godzin wcześniej oglądała identyczną u Orskiej. Uśmiechnęła się. Właściwie całkiem dobre rozwiązanie, pomyślała, pod warunkiem, że zmądrzał i nie zabroni Karolinie spotykać się ze mną.

Przyjaciółka odezwała się dopiero następnego dnia. Była w skowronkowym nastroju i opowiadała o wszystkim naraz.

– Zgadnij, z kim byłam?

– Wiem, z kim byłaś, nie muszę zgadywać – odpowiedziała Julia spokojnie.

– Czy to ciebie zabolało?

– Nie zabolało.

Karolina odetchnęła z ulgą. Wydawała się odmieniona i szczęśliwa. Nie myślała o stałym związku, przypieczętowanym w urzędzie, śmiała się, że jeżeli będzie tak, jak prorokuje Konrad i tak jak ona myśli, to za jakieś trzydzieści lat powinni się dotrzeć.

– A co w firmie? Co porabia mój następca, magister Portulak? – spytała. – Wciąż robi maślane oczy na twój widok?

– Och, Portulak... naczelny dziwak firmy. Ostatnio przekonuje mnie, że w samej pracy nie ma nic ciekawego. Po prostu rano wypada gdzieś iść i człowiek z rozpędu idzie właśnie do pracy. Zabawny jest i już go nie mylę z zasuszonym kleszczem. Jednak pustki po tobie i po Leszku nie jest w stanie zapełnić.

– A co u Leszka? – spytała ostrożnie Karolina.

– Niedługo będzie się żenił.

Głuche milczenie z drugiej strony słuchawki świadczyło, że Karolina doznała chwilowego szoku.

– Z kim? – spytała w końcu.

– Ze mną – odpowiedziała pogodnie Julia.

– Ach ty wredoto! – wykrzyknęła Karolina. – Nie mogłaś od tego zacząć?

Rozchichotały się, rozgadały. Na szczęście ani w Toruniu, ani we Włocławku nie było nikogo, kto chciałby im przerwać to świergotanie. Karolina cieszyła się szczerze, autentycznie i podwójnie.

Ostatni telefon tego wieczoru należał do pani Blendowej. Zadzwoniła jak zwykle z bogatymi przemyśleniami na temat mezaliansu córki.

– Ten Orzechowicz, Julio, to nie dla ciebie partia.

– Tak, mamo. Teraz przeszłam do partii Leszka Wydronia. Niedługo się pobieramy.

– Wydroń... Wydroń? Kto to taki? Wykształcony? Co robi? Czym zajmują się jego rodzice?

– Ojciec był lekarzem, matka muzykiem, a on...

– Zaraz, zaraz, dziecko. Akurat to wiem: ten Wydroń jest żonaty z młodszą...

– Już rozwiedziony, mamo.

Pani Blendowa wpadła w histerię – już lepszy ten Orzechowicz niż rozwodnik! – i Julia musiała przerwać połączenie. Na samą myśl o codziennych telefonach matki dostawała białej gorączki. Całkiem niepotrzebnie. Pani Emilia zadzwoniła następnego dnia, by się upewnić, że córka nie żartowała, i zamilkła. Julia mogła czuć się wyklęta.

*

– Ja ciebie kocham, Kallino... boska moja!

Julia oderwała oczy od ekranu i spojrzała na mężczyznę obok. Poszukała jego ciepłej ręki. Uśmiechnęła się do wspomnień. On pomyślał, że do niego, i odpowiedział ciepłym uśmiechem. Nie umiał patrzeć na nią inaczej jak tylko z zachwytem. I pewnie dlatego nie chciała już grać Ligii, Poppei ani nikogo – tylko Julię Wydroniową. Zanim ekipa nakręciła film, ona zbudowała sobie nowe życie. Miała kochającego męża, piękne mieszkanie, niezależność finansową i ambitną pracę. Była naprawdę szczęśliwa.

Patrzyła przejęta na ekran. Wciąż trwała uczta w pałacu Nerona. Znała na pamięć większość dialogów, powtarzała je w myślach za aktorami. Pochłonięta filmem nie przegapiła jednak malutkiego drgnięcia, ledwie uchwytnego poruszenia gdzieś w głębi siebie. Ścisnęła z całej siły rękę Winicjusza... to znaczy Leszka i położyła tę rękę na swoim brzuchu, w miejscu, gdzie przed chwilą po raz pierwszy poruszyło się nowe życie. Zrozumiał i do końca filmu częściej patrzył na żonę niż na ekran.